BRITAIN BETWEEN THE WARS

BRITAIN BETWEEN THE WARS

WARS

1918–1940

by

CHARLES LOCH MOWAT

THE UNIVERSITY OF CHICAGO PRESS

Library of Congress Catalog Card Number: 55-5139

THE UNIVERSITY OF CHICAGO PRESS, CHICAGO 60637
Methuen & Co., Ltd., London, W.C. 2, England

Preface

THE student of recent history ignores at his peril the warning of Gibbon: 'I should shrink with horror from the modern history of England, where every character is a problem, and every reader a friend or an enemy; where a writer is supposed to hoist a flag of party, and is devoted to damnation by the adverse faction.' To the dangers of partiality are now added the dangers of obliteration—obliteration by the mass of materials from which recent history must be written. Some may complain of a lack of materials. The proper complaint is of their abundance: the writings of the times in books and periodicals, the contemporary and later studies of politics, economic conditions, social progress; the biographies and memoirs which tell a good deal, already, about the ideas and motives of the makers of policy. There will always be much more for the historian to read about these years than any one man can hope to master; so that he will need, as I do, more than the usual indulgence for his sins of omission. He will also find that he must be stern in using his pruning-hook, lest length and price keep readers at a distance.

The dangers of partiality are perhaps more difficult to avoid because less easily perceived by one's self. Since any work of this kind is bound to be, in some sort and however unwittingly, auto-biographical, I must explain that the first twenty-three years of my life have been spent in England, and mainly in Oxford, and most of the remainder, since 1934, in the United States. I have tried to discover the truth, by reading and by conversation—particularly on two lengthy visits to England in 1947–48 and 1952. I have tried throughout to exercise judgment and to profit from the perspective afforded by some lapse of time and the interposition of the Second World War.

For help in my task I owe many debts of gratitude. The first is to the John Simon Guggenheim Memorial Foundation, which honoured me with one of its fellowships in 1947–48, enabling me to spend over a year in Great Britain, reading and travelling. I am grateful for this help; but even more for the magnanimous way in which it was given, as characteristic of the foundation as it is inspiring to those who share its bounty. By this means I was able, among other things, to pay a series of visits to factories, mills, steelworks and coal-mines in the Midlands and the north of England, in South Wales and in Scotland, and to learn something, by watching and talking, of the processes of modern British industry. The hospitality and friendliness of the directors, managers and foremen whom I met in this way are a vivid and refreshing memory.

My second debt of gratitude is to the University of Chicago, where most of this book has been written. To the university I am indebted for grants-in-aid and the resources of a great library, and much more for those most precious of all commodities, freedom and time for writing. To my colleagues I am indebted for welcome encouragement and advice, to my students for many fruitful ideas, to my typists for their cheerful industry and care. I also owe a debt to the University of California (Los Angeles), where this work was begun, and particularly to its friendly librarians. Librarians everywhere are, indeed, the allies we too often take for granted. I am especially indebted to the London School of Economics, which permitted me the use of its library, the British Library of Political and Economic Science, for several months on end; also to the British Museum and the library of Bristol University.

I have been greatly helped by the comments of many people, whom I forbear to name only from the fear that the use I have made of their advice may seem unequal to their kindness in giving it. I must, however, make mention of those who have read parts of my manuscript or given particular help in other ways: Professor Herbert Heaton, Mr. Colin Clark, Professor E. A. Shils, the late Professor H. J. Laski, Mr. Jules Menken, my old friends H. B. Wells and A. V. S. Lochhead, and my brother John.

C.L.M.

Chicago

Contents

Chapter   *Page*

1. BACKWARDS OR FORWARDS? 1918–1920   1

   1. 'Not perhaps the golden age.' 2. The 'Coupon' Election. 3. The Coalition Leaders. 4. The new Leviathan. 5. The passion of Labour. 6. The winter of our discontent. 7. Boom and inflation. 8. Decontrol. 9. The foiling of Labour. 10. The placating of Labour. 11. Strikes and the threat of strikes. 12. Socialism by the back door. 13. The Paris Peace Conference. 14. The aftermath: diplomatic and military. 15. Ireland: the war of the I.R.A. and the Black and Tans. 16. The partition of Ireland.

2. RETRENCHMENT, 1920–1922   79

   1. The war in Ireland: the last phase. 2. Prelude to a truce. 3. Truce and pause. 4. Negotiating a treaty. 5. The debate over the treaty. 6. The rift widens. 7. Civil war. 8. The Irish Free State and the boundary. 9. The changing empire. 10. Eclipse of Lloyd George's policies in Europe. 11. Chanak. 12. Another coal crisis: Black Friday. 13. The slump and unemployment: the dole is born. 14. The economy drive. 15. The crisis in party politics. 16. The fall of the Coalition.

3. COMING TO REST: 1922–1925   143

   1. The return of the Conservatives. 2. The tramp of Labour. 3. The patchwork of peace in Europe. 4. Baldwin becomes Prime Minister. 5. Baldwin's strategy: the election of 1923. 6. A Labour government in being. 7. The Labour government's record. 8. MacDonald, the peacemaker. 9. The government's sudden fall. 10. The 1924 election and the Red scare. 11. Post mortem on the Zinoviev letter. 12. Baldwin and the return to normalcy; Locarno and the gold standard.

4. STABILITY AND CHANGE: THE CONDITION OF BRITAIN IN THE TWENTIES   201

   1. The ringing grooves of change. 2. The old order changeth. 3. The distribution of the national income. 4. Education: the cautious approach. 5. Eat, drink and be merry. 6. New styles, new themes. 7. The advancement and dispersal of knowledge. 8. The Church and the

vii

Chapter   *Page*

churches. 9. All sorts and conditions of men. 10. The changing city: suburbs and housing estates. 11. The neotechnic age: buses and motor cars. 12. The railways. 13. Airways. 14. The new Behemoth. 15. The uses of leisure: sport, betting, greyhounds, pubs. 16. Ill fares the land. 17. Country towns and villages.

5. THE WORLD'S WORKSHOP ON SHORT TIME   259

1. Diagnosis. 2. The changing character of British trade. 3. Handicaps to British trade, principally monetary. 4. New industries for old? 5. The ailing giants.

6. DEAD CENTRE : THE GENERAL STRIKE AND AFTER, 1925–1929   284

1. Cross-currents in the Labour movement. 2. Red Friday. 3. Six months' delay. 4. Negotiations at half-speed. 5. Last-minute efforts. 6. The nine days. 7. Calling off the strike. 8. To the bitter end: the coal strike. 9. The government blunders. 10. Tory socialism. 11. Foreign and imperial affairs: a halting-place. 12. The Conservatives' decline, the Liberals' renaissance, Labour's quandary. 13. The general election of 1929.

7. THE TURNING POINT : 1929–1931   353

1. Labour accepts the call. 2. The challenge of unemployment: an opportunity missed. 3. The Coal Mines Act and other hazards. 4. Protection or Free Trade: Tory troubles and the 1930 Budget. 5. Affairs foreign and imperial. 6. The financial crisis. 7. The government peters out. 8. The National government: whose child? 9. The consequences. 10. Off gold anyway. 11. Cashing in.

8. SITTING IT OUT : ECONOMIC RECOVERY AND POLITICAL APATHY, 1931–1935   413

1. The National government. 2. The triumph of the tariff: the end of the honeymoon. 3. The paralysis of foreign policy. 4. Imperial interlude. 5. Cold war with Ireland. 6. Conditions of recovery. 7. Tariffs, quotas, currencies. 8. The old industries: restriction and expansion. 9. Air services and London's transport: two cases of nationalisation. 10. The sources of recovery: increasing consumption. 11. Deflation or cheap money? 12. The housing boom. 13. The new economics, and the idea of 'planning'. 14. The distressed areas. 15. Scots wha hae. 16. Unemployment relief: the government's pride and fall. 17. Fascism for Britain? 18. The beginning of rearmament: the resignation of MacDonald.

Chapter   *Page*
9. THE SECRET PEOPLE AND THE SOCIAL CONSCIENCE :
    THE CONDITION OF BRITAIN IN THE THIRTIES   480
    1. Introspection. 2. Out of work. 3. Class and income.
    4. The welfare state in scaffolding. 5. 'That's the way the
    money goes.' 6. Ill fed. 7. Ill housed. 8. The chances of
    survival. 9. '. . . and men decay.' 10. Ultra-modern.
    11. Faith and works. 12. Writers in arms.

10. GREAT REVERSALS: 1935–1937   532
    1. Jubilate. 2. The choices in foreign policy. 3. Midsummer
    nights' dreams. 4. Peace by wishing: the Abyssinian
    crisis. 5. Stocktaking in the Labour party. 6. The last
    general election of the peace. 7. The retreat from collec-
    tive security: the Hoare-Laval deal. 8. Mailed fist and
    velvet glove: Rhineland crisis and rearmament. 9. The
    mobilisation of the Left: the Spanish civil war. 10. A
    message from His Majesty.

11. SAY NOT THE STRUGGLE NAUGHT AVAILETH : 1937–1940   589
    1. The logic of appeasement. 2. Exit Eden: exit Austria.
    3. Ireland appeased? 4. The fatal quadrilateral: Czecho-
    slovakia, Germany, France, Great Britain. 5. War
    averted: Berchtesgaden, Godesberg, Munich. 6. Winter,
    1938–39: is it peace? 7. Rearmament: argument and
    achievement. 8. Politics gone sour. 9. The great swing
    in foreign policy. 10. The summer's dalliance. 11. Shall I,
    shall I not? 12. The fall of Chamberlain. 13. Alone.

    BIBLIOGRAPHICAL NOTE   659

    LIST OF CABINETS   665

INDEX   675

CHAPTER ONE

Backwards or Forwards ? 1918—1920

1. 'NOT PERHAPS THE GOLDEN AGE'

WHEN the war ended in November 1918, there were few who did not hope that the losses and sufferings it had brought might be redeemed in a better world—a happier society at home, the nations of the earth living in peace and unity. Woodrow Wilson expressed these hopes in Manchester in December 1918:

> I believe that . . . men are beginning to see, not perhaps the golden age, but an age which at any rate is brightening from decade to decade, and will lead us some time to an elevation from which we can see the things for which the heart of mankind is longing.

The history of the twenty years between the two world wars is the history of the disappointment of these hopes.

In Britain, more than in most countries, the effort was made to find a better society by returning to the prewar order purged of its grosser inequalities. By 1931 it was clear that the effort had failed, just as the noble experiment of collective security under the League of Nations was failing to maintain the peace. Thereafter, depression and the fear of another war drove the British people inwards, to tariffs, quotas and restrictionist policies with which to chase economic recovery, to treaties and personal diplomacy outside the League to appease the dictators without war. In the twenty years there were a few quiet spells, particularly in the late twenties. A hopeful generation grew up which remembered little of the first war and had not yet come to accept the inevitability of the second. It was not for long. Postwar shaded into prewar; war remembered or war prefigured was seldom absent.

Yet it was no barren time. There were advances towards the better life. When war came again in 1939 it did not close an era, it continued it. All the lines and markings on the face of Britain after the Second World War were traced there by the First and by the twenty years which separated them.

Not what was ahead but what was behind gave a sombre cast to the celebrations of the Armistice. In London, where maroons, fired at 11 a.m. on November 11, announced the Armistice, there was some dancing in the streets, some joy-riding in taxis and buses and vans, the over-eager finding precarious places on hood or roof. People crowded the streets, waving flags, ringing handbells, blowing whistles. In other towns the factories closed, church bells were rung, flags flown, and services held in the churches. At the front the automatism of endless days of fighting made it difficult for the men to realise that cessation had come: 'motionless in the silence the soldiers looked at each other with vacant eyes'.[1]

2. THE 'COUPON' ELECTION

The first thing which compromised the hopes of a better world was the general election which followed close on the heels of the Armistice and prolonged into the peace the wartime Coalition government of David Lloyd George.[2] An election was long over-due: the House of Commons elected in December 1910, had pro-longed its own life during the war. Now the emergency was over; and in addition to the normal increment of men reaching voting age each year there were for the first time large numbers of women recently added to the registers by the extension of the franchise. A new parliament to deal with the problems of peace was certainly to be desired.

The idea of a postwar Coalition was chiefly Lloyd George's. It had been under discussion for months, receiving much support in Lord Northcliffe's[3] newspapers, which had played no small part in Lloyd George's elevation to power. It was natural that Lloyd George should want to apply to the peace the genius which he had shown in war. By becoming Prime Minister in 1916 he had split the Liberal party; and though he might have sought a new mandate as a Liberal the prospects for a united party were at the time poor, whereas his Conservative allies were willing to campaign under

[1] Winston S. Churchill, *The Aftermath* (New York, 1922), p. 4.
[2] David Lloyd George (1863–1945), brought up by his uncle, Richard Lloyd, a shoe-maker, in Llanystumdwy, near Criccieth, North Wales; trained as a lawyer: elected to parliament in 1890 as a Liberal. President of the Board of Trade, 1905–1908; chancellor of the Exchequer, 1908–15; minister of munitions, 1915–16; secretary of state for war, 1916; prime minister, 1916–22; created Earl Lloyd-George of Dwyfor, 1945.
[3] Alfred Harmsworth, Lord Northcliffe (1865–1922), born at Chapelizod, near Dublin, son of a barrister; elder brother of Lord Rothermere. Largely self-educated in London. Journalist. Founded *Answers*, 1888; acquired *Evening News*, 1894; founded *Daily Mail*, 1896, *Daily Mirror*, 1903. Acquired control of *The Times*, 1908. Baronet, 1903, Baron Northcliffe, 1905 (viscount, 1917). Director of British war mission to U.S., 1917; director of propaganda in enemy countries, 1918.

his leadership. The friendship at the time between Lloyd George and Andrew Bonar Law,[1] the leader of the Conservative party and Chancellor of the Exchequer, made this co-operation easy. Labour members of the Coalition were not so complaisant: the Labour party, at a meeting of delegates on November 14, decided to withdraw from the Coalition and contest the election on its own— an important decision, not reached without opposition.

The complexion of the new Coalition, if it won the election, could be foreseen from the distribution of its candidates. Lloyd George, having broken with the official Liberal party, had no machine of his own, but the Conservatives, thanks to the efforts of the chairman of the party organisation, Sir George Younger (later Lord Younger of Leckie), had kept theirs in good trim. In the negotiations over candidates it was decided that the Conservatives should provide the majority of the Coalition candidates—some 400, to 140 of the Lloyd George Liberals;[2] sitting members who supported the Coalition were endorsed whether Conservatives or Liberals, but the majority of new candidates were Conservatives. The test to decide which candidates should receive the endorsement signified by a letter signed by Lloyd George and Bonar Law—the 'coupon', as Asquith[3] contemptuously called it, thus giving the election its historic name—was the vote in the 'Maurice debate' in the Commons on May 9, 1918. Major-General Sir Frederick Maurice had charged the government with having dangerously weakened Sir Douglas Haig's forces on the Western Front before the start of Germany's spring offensive in March 1918. Asquith moved for a select committee of inquiry; the 106 Liberals who had supported him were denied the coupon.[4]

With these arrangements agreed upon, it was announced on November 14 that parliament would be dissolved on November 25 and the election take place on December 14.

[1] Andrew Bonar Law (1858–1923), born in New Brunswick, Canada, the son of a Presbyterian minister; brought up in Glasgow by his mother's family, well-to-do bankers and iron merchants, and subsequently inherited a comfortable fortune. Entered parliament as a Conservative in 1900, elected leader of the Conservative party in 1911; chancellor of the Exchequer, 1916–18; lord privy seal, 1918–21; prime minister, 1922–23.

[2] *The Times*, Dec. 6, 1918.

[3] Herbert Henry Asquith (1852–1928), born Morley, Yorks., son of a wool-spinner. Scholar of Balliol College, Oxford, president of the Oxford Union. Barrister. M.P., 1886–1918, 1920–24. Home secretary, 1892–95. Chancellor of the Exchequer, 1905–8; prime minister, 1908–16. Created Earl of Oxford and Asquith, 1925. His second wife was Margot Tennant, a gifted writer and leader of society, author of a valuable autobiography. .

[4] J. A. Spender and Cyril Asquith, *Life of Lord Oxford and Asquith* (London, 1932) II, 303–8, 314–16.

The actual campaign was short—little over two weeks—and has been characterised as one of violent emotion and rowdy demonstrations. Its picture was painted soon afterwards by J. M. Keynes[1] in his classic work, *The Economic Consequences of the Peace*, whose biting wit and vivid portraiture, phrased in an exciting and quotable style, ensured for it much greater acceptance than the facts warranted. The campaign started quietly, with Lloyd George's pledge of a 'fit country for heroes to live in'. Audiences seemed, however, to want something more, and Lloyd George let himself be carried along by the tide. On November 29 he stated that the government had taken legal counsel and was informed that the Kaiser was guilty of an indictable offence. Next day's *Times* took up the cry that the Kaiser and other wrongdoers should be brought to trial. G. N. Barnes,[2] on November 30, answered a questioner by saying, 'Well, I am for hanging the Kaiser'. The reparations issue also appeared. On November 29 Lloyd George, at Newcastle-on-Tyne, declared that Germany must pay up to the limit of her capacity. In an angry editorial on December 7, *The Times* denied that it was Britain's business to inquire how much Germany could pay: 'Our sole business [is] to present our bill.' Finally came Sir Eric Geddes'[3] historic utterance at Cambridge on December 9: 'If I am returned, Germany is going to pay restitution, reparation, and indemnity, and I have personally no doubt that we will get everything out of her that you can squeeze out of a lemon and a bit more. . . .' To which Lloyd George added, on December 11, at Bristol: 'We propose to demand the whole cost of the war' from Germany. Meanwhile the *Daily Mail* published, in a box on the front page, each day, the totals of British casualties,

[1] John Maynard Keynes (1883–1946), the economist, son of registrary of Cambridge University. Eton and King's College, Cambridge. Civil servant (India Office), 1906–8. Fellow (1908) and bursar of King's College, Cambridge. Served in the Treasury, 1915–19 (representative of Treasury at Paris peace conference), and 1940–46. Created baron, 1942.
[2] G. N. Barnes (1859–1940), machinist, assistant (later general) secretary of Amalgamated Society of Engineers, 1892–1908; leader in the great engineering strike, 1897–98; Labour M.P., 1906–18; succeeded Arthur Henderson in war cabinet, 1917 and remained in the government (having resigned from the Labour party) until 1920 and in parliament until 1922.
[3] E. C. Geddes (1875–1937), son of a Scots civil engineer, gained experience in railway operation in India and on the North Eastern Railway in England; director (later inspector) general of transportation, with honorary military and naval rank, 1916–17; first lord of the Admiralty, 1917–18; knighted, 1916; in Coalition government, 1919–22; subsequently chairman of Dunlop Rubber Company and Imperial Airways. His brother, Sir Auckland Geddes (1879–1954), professor of anatomy at McGill University (Principal of the University, 1919–20), was minister of national service in Lloyd George's government, 1917–19, president of the Board of Trade, 1919, British ambassador to the United States, 1920–24, and was made a baron in 1942.

and thus endeavoured to keep the demand for vengeance at fever heat.[1]

In certain constituencies, the campaign was especially acrimonious. In East Leicester, a determined effort was made to unseat Ramsay MacDonald,[2] the Labour party's former leader, whose ambiguous attitude to the war was wrongly ascribed to pacifist convictions. After the results, as level-headed a magazine as the *Fortnightly Review* published an article which said: 'Leicester and Blackburn did their duty nobly, and rid themselves of their Red Flag representatives [MacDonald and Philip Snowden[3]] . . . the Red Flag is the only flag which stirs his emotions, and the European Revolution will not, if he can help it, be confined to the Continent'[4] a grotesque misunderstanding of MacDonald's real views. 'Bolshevism' might, in fact, be called one of the major themes of the campaign: even Lloyd George, in his closing speech at Camberwell on December 13, declared: 'The Labour party is being run by the extreme pacifist, Bolshevist group' and attacked it as a class party, a bad thing—'Look at what has happened in Russia.'[5]

Yet the chief impression left on observers by the campaign was not one of violent feeling, but of a quiet, sober contest. Rival candidates frequently spoke from a common platform; rowdyism was not common; voters not demonstrative. It is probable that the temper of the campaign has been exaggerated.

The greatly enlarged electorate made predictions difficult. The Representation of the People Act, passed in 1918, was the outgrowth of a bill introduced in 1916 to provide for the registration

[1] *The Times, passim*; D. C. Somervell, *Reign of King George the Fifth* (New York, 1935), pp. 203–6; J. M. Keynes, *Economic Consequences of the Peace* (London, 1919), pp. 125–33 (published also in New York, 1920); Thomas Jones, *Lloyd George* (Cambridge, Mass., 1951), pp. 161–3 (also published in Oxford, 1951). On the election see also R. B. McCallum, *Public Opinion and the Last Peace* (Oxford, 1944), pp. 30–42.

[2] James Ramsay MacDonald (1866–1937), born out of wedlock and brought up by his mother in Lossiemouth, Morayshire; came to London in 1886 and supported himself by clerical and secretarial jobs and journalism; joined Fabian Society in 1886 and the Independent Labour Party (I.L.P.) in 1894; married Margaret Gladstone, grand-niece of Lord Kelvin, 1896 (she died in 1911); secretary of Labour Representation Committee (subsequently the Labour party), 1900–11, treasurer of the party, 1912–24, entered parliament 1906; prime minister, 1924, 1929–31, 1931–35, lord president of the Council, 1935–37.

[3] Philip Snowden (1864–1937), born in the hamlet of Ickornshaw, near Keighley, the son of a weaver; entered the civil service and served as exciseman, 1886–93; crippled as a result of a bicycle accident in 1891; joined I.L.P. and was one of its greatest speakers from 1895 onwards (chairman, 1903–6); entered parliament, 1906; chancellor of the Exchequer, 1924, 1929–31, and in the National government, 1931; lord privy seal, 1931–32; created viscount, 1931.

[4] J. B. Firth in *Fortnightly Review*, 111, 197 (January, 1919).

[5] *The Times*, Dec. 14, 1918.

of voters who had changed their residence because of war work. This had led to a proposal to enfranchise all soldiers, and this inevitably led others to ask for the enfranchisement of women. The 1918 Act was the result. It revised the boundaries of constituencies, and attempted, though not without leaving several exceptions, to divide the country into uniform single-member constituencies representing 70,000 people each. Plural voting was limited to the right to vote in not more than two constituencies. Elections were to be held on one day, and that the same for the whole country. Candidates were to be required to put up a deposit of £150, which would be forfeited by those failing to receive one-eighth of the votes cast in the division. Most important of all, manhood suffrage was at last conceded: all men over twenty-one, except peers, lunatics and felons under imprisonment,[1] received the right to vote after six months' residence in a constituency. The female of the species was treated less generously. She received the vote only if she was thirty or over, and then only if she or her husband were qualified on the local government franchise by owning or occupying land or premises of an annual value of £5. None the less, what Mrs. Pankhurst and the suffragettes had battled for in vain was conceded in wartime with hardly a flutter by the same Parliament which had so sternly refused it in peace.[2] With two million men added to the register, and six million women, no one could tell what the results would be. The new voters had no party affiliations. Many of the constituencies were new sub-divisions of the electoral map; old divisions had new boundaries; everything was uncertain. It was observed, however, on December 14, that the women went to the polls in unexpectedly large numbers.

The votes were not counted till December 28, to give time for the receipt of soldiers' ballots though, in the event, only one man in four in the forces cast a vote. About half of the electorate went to the polls (57·6 per cent). The Coalition polled 5,091,528 votes and elected 484 members, of whom 338 were Conservatives, 136 were Liberals and 10 were Labour and other supporters of the Coalition. Labour polled 2,374,385 votes, and was the largest of

---

[1] Conscientious objectors were disfranchised for five years after the war; and certain other persons are legally incapacitated from voting.

[2] *Annual Register, 1918*, pp. 51–2; D. E. Butler, *Electoral System in Britain, 1918–1951* (Oxford, 1953), pp. 7–12. The 'emancipation' of women was further advanced by the Sex Disqualification Removal Act, 1919. The first woman to take a seat in the House of Commons was Lady Astor, the Virginia-born wife of the second Viscount Astor, who was elected in 1919 for the Sutton division of Plymouth, vacated by her husband on his succession to the peerage.

the Opposition parties, with 59 members. The Asquith Liberals polled 1,298,803 votes, but elected only 26 members. There were also 48 Conservatives returned who did not have the Coalition coupon; independents elected numbered 9, Irish Nationalists 7, and Sinn Feiners, who did not take their seats, 73.[1]

It was a decisive victory for the Coalition, and even more so for the Conservatives. For them the result was recompense for almost twice seven lean years, ever since the disaster of 1906. They were back in their battalions. Many of their members were newcomers, including those who qualified as the 'hard faced men who looked as if they had done well out of the war', in Stanley Baldwin's phrase, given such wide and unfortunate currency in the pages of J. M. Keynes. The new House contained more company directors than did later parliaments (179 as compared with an average of 139 in the parliaments between the wars) and more members associated with commerce and finance (86 compared with an average of 69).[2] Most though not all of these were Conservatives. Almost twenty years of undistinguished Tory rule began with this adventitious victory.

For Labour the results distorted the truth. Many of the party's principal figures were defeated: not only MacDonald and Snowden, but also Arthur Henderson,[3] who had been a member of the Coalition Cabinet until 1917. In the Coalition's triumph, Labour's gains were neglected; yet its popular vote had increased from 400,000 to 2,374,000, partly because it had more candidates running, and its representation in parliament increased from 42 to 59. This gave it the claim to be the official Opposition, though the independent Liberals disputed it. Its leader in the Commons was William Adamson, a Scottish miner;[4] in 1921 he was replaced by J. R. Clynes.[5]

It was, however, for the Liberal party that the results were decisive and tragic. The party's strength in parliament was nearly

[1] *Annual Register, 1919*, pp. 164–5; D. E. Butler, *Electoral System*, p. 172.
[2] J. F. S. Ross, *Parliamentary Representation* (London, 1943), pp. 61, 76.
[3] Arthur Henderson (1863–1935), born in Glasgow, the son of a cotton-spinner, and brought up in Newcastle-on-Tyne; worked as an iron moulder, and became active in the Ironfounders' Union and as a Wesleyan Methodist lay preacher; entered parliament in 1903; secretary of the Labour party, 1911–34; member of the cabinet (subsequently of the War cabinet), 1915–17; home secretary, 1924; foreign secretary, 1929–31; president of the world disarmament conference at Geneva, 1932–35.
[4] A sketch of Adamson (1863–1936) is in M. I. Cole (ed.), *Beatrice Webb's Diaries, 1912–24* (London, 1952), pp. 142–5; see also Thomas Johnston, *Memories* (London, 1952), pp. 100–3.
[5] J. R. Clynes (1869–1949), one-time 'piecer' in a cotton mill; official of National Union of General and Municipal Workers; entered parliament, 1906; food controller, 1918; lord privy seal, 1924; home secretary, 1929–31.

halved, and to make matters worse it was divided. The greater part, which had followed Lloyd George into the Coalition, had become prisoners of the Conservative majority. The non-Coalition Liberals, with almost all their leaders defeated from Asquith downwards, were a mere rump, and considered disbanding altogether, but held together under the leadership of Sir Donald Maclean.[1] Subsequently, the party recovered a good deal of its strength, and for a time also its unity; but never again was it anywhere near to obtaining a parliamentary majority. Not that the coupon election was more than a milestone on the road of its decline. The split between Asquith and Lloyd George, dating from 1916, was fatal, and it was never healed, in spite of several attempts, particularly in 1918.[2] Even further back, the party had showed mortal weakness, when its formula of discussion and compromise had failed to meet the prewar tests of the Tory revolt over Ulster, the suffragettes' campaigns, and the great strikes of 1910–13. The rise of the Labour party had ended its claims to Radicalism; and the middle ground which was all that remained to it proved no more than a sand spit.

Another result of the election was its influence on the character of postwar politics. The new House of Commons had more new members (260) than any other of the inter-war parliaments, but the average age both of the new members ($48\frac{1}{2}$) and of all members ($51\frac{1}{2}$) was also somewhat higher. If we consider those under 41 as representing the war generation in 1918, the new parliament contained 100 of the war generation; the number under 41 elected in 1922 was 116, and the average number of persons under 41 elected to the inter-war parliaments was 126.[3] Here was the rather slender origin of postwar disillusion, of the idea that only the old and the stale could gain office.

The return to the world of 1914, with the illusion of time standing still, was symbolised in many ways.

> The Brigade of Guards got back into Scarlet, and the Treasury set about restoring Treasury control. After the march of armies, the wriggling of martinets . . . Mr. Austen Chamberlain returned to the Treasury to which he had first been appointed in 1903; Lord Curzon

[1] See *Dictionary of National Biography* (*D.N.B.*), 1931–40, s.v. Sir Donald Maclean. Donald Maclean (1864–1932), solicitor, entered parliament as Liberal in 1906, deputy speaker, 1911–18, knighted 1917, president of the Board of Education, 1931–32.
[2] For attempts to reunite the Liberals, see A. C. Murray, *Master and Brother* (London, 1945), pp. 172–7 (the author's brother was Lord Murray of Elibank who, as the Master of Elibank, was Liberal chief whip from 1910–12); J. A. Spender and C. Asquith, *Life of Asquith*, II, 312–13.
[3] J. F. S. Ross, *Parliamentary Representation*, pp. 20, 27, 32, 39.

presided over the Foreign Office, and Mr. Arthur Balfour, fresh from the Congress of Berlin, exchanged reminiscences with M. Clemenceau, whose memories stopped short at 1870. No wonder that no one knew . . . whether we were going on or going back.[1]

Most things, and most people in politics, were all too familiar. Mark Abrams has well pointed out that anyone who knew the England of 1914 would find little superficial change by 1939: the same names on the fronts of chain stores, the same newspapers owned by the same press lords, the same popular brands of cigarettes and chocolate, the same popular novelists, the same football teams, and the same express trains (sometimes a little slower, sometimes a little faster by 1939). The traveller who journeyed back to 1914 would meet then, in the prime of life, half the members of parliament of 1939.[2]

One reason was always advanced for this: the lost generation. Of course, a whole generation had not perished in the war, but many of its leaders had, particularly through the heavy losses among infantry officers. The remainder felt themselves to be a small generation, and the many gaps broke 'the cohesion, the subtle cumulative power of the survivors'.[3] This gave them less than their proper influence, and made them unable to mediate between the prewar and the postwar generations behind and before them. The older men hung on to the positions of power without being challenged until the thirties; then the challengers were the young men who had not been in the war, between whom and the old generation the gap was unusually wide, with no influential members of the middle-aged in between. Partly this was because of the coupon election. Shut out then, and rebelling against the tone of the campaign, the wartime generation acquired a distaste for politics which never left it.[4] There was a lost generation in this sense: lost to politics. 'The men who came back from the war have counted for less, perhaps, in the political life of their country than any generation during the last two or three centuries.'[5] An ageing second team remained on the field.

[1] Douglas Jerrold, *Georgian Adventure* (New York, 1938), pp. 209–10.
[2] Mark Abrams, *Condition of the British People, 1911–45* (London, 1945), pp. 11–12.
[3] E. L. Woodward, *Short Journey* (London, 1942), p. 116.
[4] M. A. Hamilton, *Remembering My Good Friends* (London, 1944), pp. 92–5. Mrs. Hamilton, a Labour M.P. in 1929–31, has written several biographies of Labour leaders, and as a writer had a wide circle of friends inside and outside the party.
[5] E. L. Woodward, *Short Journey*, pp. 114–15, 117–21. Cf. L. B. Namier, *Conflicts* (London, 1942), 'The missing generation'; and the lament for the lost generation in Richard Aldington, *Death of a Hero* (American edition: New York, 1929), especially pp. 15, 28, 301.

B*

3. THE COALITION LEADERS

The new Cabinet, whose composition Lloyd George announced on January 10, 1919, reflected the character of the election. It was little changed from the previous Coalition Cabinet. Like a basket of strawberries, the quality was excellent at the top, less so underneath. For a time, however, the abilities of the leaders obscured the imperfections of the rest.

Lloyd George himself was then at the height of his powers and prestige, the 'man who won the war'. His appearance was striking: the fine head, piercing blue eyes, a great mane of hair, already nearly white, more than offset his small stature. 'L.G.' was the sort of man people admired or loathed; there were no half measures either in him or in people's opinion of him. He was above all things clever, with a mind extraordinarily quick and versatile. With this went a buoyancy and courage that were almost brazen, a tendency to ruthlessness and tyrannical behaviour, and a readiness of decision and action which terrified some, but carried others to heights they would never have scaled alone. With him, the end was more important than the means: his methods were personal, improvised, and on occasion unscrupulous; he liked to cut through the rules. There was also a sort of sixth sense, a 'medium-like sensibility' to persons around him, a personal charm and intuition which anticipated thoughts and saw the quickest way to persuade an adversary or tackle a problem. He was a genius with a double dose of everything, good and bad; he could do as well with his left hand as his right. Yet it was wrong to deduce from all this, as Keynes did, that he was 'rooted in nothing' and without principles. A deep patriotism was his, and a hatred of oppression. 'The volatility of his methods', observed Harold Nicolson, 'concealed the rock-like immobility of his aims.' John Buchan said of him as a war minister, 'I put him in the class of Cromwell and Chatham.' And Winston Churchill who admitted him alone as master—in itself a tremendous tribute—summed him up when he wrote: 'He was the greatest master of the art of getting things done and of putting things through that I ever knew; in fact no British politician in my day has possessed half his competence as a mover of men and affairs. When the English history of the first quarter of the twentieth century is written, it will be seen that the greater part of our fortunes in peace and in war were shaped by this one man.'[1]

[1] Perhaps the best impressions of him are those in Robert Boothby, *I Fight to Live* (London, 1947), pp. 26–33, 45. This is a semi-autobiographical work by a Con-

Next to Lloyd George in the government was Bonar Law, Lord Privy Seal and leader of the House of Commons; and indeed the government's strength rested largely on the close co-operation and confidence of these two men, at opposite poles in temperament though they were, just as its weakness really dates from Bonar Law's temporary retirement in 1921. Bonar Law was not a natural Conservative, since he lacked any great respect for tradition. He had an extremely clear mind and an unusually retentive memory; his speeches, including long series of figures, were made without using a single note. He was a great debater and a very able leader of the Commons. His prevailing mood was one of melancholy and scepticism. Though normally diffident, he could be a very stubborn fighter on occasion. His private character was simple and kind, and his manner gentle and charming; selfishness was not in him. His caution and moderation were the ideal complement to Lloyd George's volatile nature, making what has been called 'the most perfect partnership in political history'.[1] Lloyd George relied heavily on his advice. A communicating door between their houses, Numbers 10 and 11 Downing Street, made consultation possible at all hours; and on countless occasions a quiet word from Bonar Law led the Prime Minister at once to abandon an impetuous idea. Bonar Law on his part had a tremendous admiration for Lloyd George. He told Sir Archibald Salvidge at the time of the Armistice: 'Salvidge, I tell you we must never let the little man go. His way and ours lie side by side in the future. I want you to remember what I am saying now and act upon it, not only in this election but afterwards, when all the shouting has died away.'[2]

Next to these two, the principal members of the Coalition were

servative M.P. (1924 onwards) of very wide contacts and great acumen. J. M. Keynes' sketch in *Essays in Biography* (London, 1933), pp. 16, 32–40 is brilliant but unfair, and should be compared with Sir J. Arthur Salter's picture in *Personality in Politics* (London, 1947), pp. 38–53, and *Recovery* (New York, 1932), p. 157; and with Harold Nicolson, *Curzon, the last phase, 1919–25* (London, 1934), p. 223. See also A. J. Sylvester, *The real Lloyd George* (London, [1948]). The passage quoted from Winston Churchill is from his *Thoughts and Adventures* (New York, 1932), p. 60. I have also had the benefit of a conversation with Thomas Jones, C.H., deputy secretary of the cabinet under Lloyd George, Bonar Law, Baldwin and MacDonald. Thomas Jones' *Lloyd George*, cited previously, supersedes all earlier studies of his character and his career. For a more critical picture see *Beatrice Webb's Diaries, 1912–24*, pp. 111–12 ('the little Welsh conjurer').

[1] See the article on him in the Dictionary of *National Biography, Supplement for 1922–30*; also J. M. Keynes, *Essays in Biography*, pp. 42–7; Nourah Waterhouse, *Private and Official* (London, 1942), by the wife of Sir Ronald Waterhouse, private secretary to Bonar Law, Baldwin, and MacDonald as prime ministers.

[2] Stanley Salvidge, *Salvidge of Liverpool* (London, 1934), pp. 166–7; Sir Archibald Salvidge (1863–1928), was for long the head of the Conservative and Unionist organisation in Liverpool and high in national Conservative circles.

the Lord Chancellor, Lord Birkenhead, Austen Chamberlain, the Chancellor of the Exchequer, Arthur James Balfour, the Foreign Secretary (all Conservatives), and Winston Churchill, the War Secretary, Lloyd George's strongest Liberal adjutant. Lord Birkenhead,[1] who was raised to the peerage on becoming Lord Chancellor in 1919 at the early age of forty-six, was, until then, F. E. Smith ('F.E.' or 'Galloper Smith' to admiring friends and enemies). He had had a meteoric rise in parliament since his entry in 1906; his brilliant mind and eloquent tongue, at times ruthless and arrogant, had ensured him a place in the government in 1915. Chamberlain,[2] very much his father's son in looks and manner (even to the monocle), had a certain stiffness in public; actually he was shrewd, sociable, unselfish and a supremely loyal colleague. Balfour,[3] the aristocratic and urbane ex-Prime Minister, apparently more interested in philosophic speculation and in conversation than in practical affairs, had sagacity and charm, good judgment and, for Lloyd George, warm enthusiasm. Churchill,[4] still in his forties, had already filled many offices of state in Asquith's and Lloyd George's administrations, and as the courageous man of action and eloquent speaker was at the time perhaps second only to his chief, for whom he had and retained tremendous admiration and loyalty: he was one of the very few men who addressed Lloyd George as David.

Other ministers included Lord Curzon,[5] Lord President of the

---

[1] F. E. Smith, first Earl of Birkenhead (1872–1930), solicitor-general, 1915; attorney-general, 1915–18; lord chancellor, 1919–22; secretary of state for India, 1924–28.

[2] Austen Chamberlain (1863–1937), entered parliament in 1892, chancellor of the Exchequer, 1903–5, secretary of state for India, 1915–17, member of war cabinet, 1918, chancellor of the Exchequer, 1919–21, leader of the Conservative party and of the House of Commons, 1921–22, foreign secretary, 1924–29, first lord of the Admiralty, 1931.

[3] Arthur James Balfour (1848–1930), nephew of third Marquess of Salisbury, born at Whittinghame, East Lothian, the family estate. M.P., 1874–1922. Chief secretary for Ireland, 1887–91; leader of the House of Commons, 1891–92, 1895–1902; prime minister, 1902–5; first lord of the Admiralty, 1915–16; foreign secretary, 1916–19; lord president of the council, 1919–22, 1925–29. Created Earl of Balfour, 1922.

[4] Winston Churchill, born 1874, son of Lord Randolph Churchill. Entered parliament, 1900, as Conservative. Served at Board of Trade, Home Office, Admiralty, in Asquith's cabinet, 1908–16; minister of munitions, 1917; war secretary, 1918–21 (also air secretary); colonial secretary, 1921–22; chancellor of the Exchequer, 1924–29; first lord of the Admiralty, 1939–40; prime minister, 1940–45 and 1951–5. Knight of the Garter, 1953.

[5] George Nathaniel Curzon (1859–1925), son of Rev. N. H. Curzon, fourth Baron Scarsdale, rector of Kedleston, Derbyshire. Eton and Balliol College, Oxford, president of the Oxford Union, fellow of All Souls. A great traveller in early life. M.P., 1886–1898; under secretary for foreign affairs, 1895–98. Viceroy of India (Baron Curzon of Kedleston, earl, 1911, marquess, 1921), 1898–1905. Lord privy seal, 1915. Member of Lloyd George's war cabinet, 1916–18, foreign secretary (at first as deputy for Balfour) 1919–24, lord privy seal, 1924–25. Restorer of Tattershall Castle, Lincs.

Council; Walter Long,[1] First Lord of the Admiralty; Lord Milner,[2] Secretary of State for the Colonies, E. S. Montagu,[3] Secretary of State for India; H. A. L. Fisher,[4] President of the Board of Education; Dr. Addison,[5] President of the Local Government Board; Sir Eric Geddes, Minister of Transport, and G. N. Barnes, Minister without Portfolio.

4. THE NEW LEVIATHAN

At its hands the new Cabinet had the controls of a machine of government much larger than any previous one. Here, as in so much else, the war moulded the succeeding years. There had been nothing like it before, in its calls for man-power, its absorption of women into heavy industry, in the tremendous increase of industrial production, the demands for more and more materials, in the shortages which only rationing could alleviate. In such times, the power of the state must increase enormously; and Lloyd George, as Prime Minister after 1916, with his passion for getting things done quickly, had accelerated the process. Departments, bureaux, committees, controllers were created and piled on top of each other; business leaders were brought into government; Orders in Council and ministers' orders and regulations side-stepped much of the legislative power of parliament. Though the flood subsided,

and Bodiam Castle, Sussex; tenant of Hackwood Park, Basingstoke. His first wife, Mary Leiter, was daughter of a Chicago millionaire; his second wife, Grace, widow of Alfred Duggan of Buenos Aires, was also American.

[1] Walter Long (1854–1924), M.P., 1880–1921, created viscount, 1921. President of the Board of Agriculture, 1895–1900, of Local Government Board, 1900–5, chief secretary for Ireland, 1905; President of Local Government Board, 1915; colonial secretary, 1916–18, first lord of the Admiralty, 1918–21. An excellent example of the country squire in politics.

[2] Alfred Milner (1854–1925), high commissioner in South Africa, 1897–1905. Baron, 1901, viscount, 1902. Member of war cabinet, 1916–18; war secretary, 1918; colonial secretary, 1919–21.

[3] E. S. Montagu (1879–1924), second son of first Baron Swaythling, a banker. M.P., 1906–22. Private secretary to Asquith as chancellor of the Exchequer; held minor office, 1910–15; chancellor of the Duchy of Lancaster, 1915; minister of munitions, 1916; secretary of state for India, 1917–22.

[4] H. A. L. Fisher (1865–1940), son of the tutor and private secretary of Edward VII as Prince of Wales; his mother was niece of Mrs. Leslie Stephen. Winchester and New College, Oxford. Fellow of New College, 1888. Author of a study of Napoleon and many other historical works. Vice-chancellor of Sheffield University, 1914. President of the Board of Education, 1916–22. Warden of New College, 1926. O.M., 1937.

[5] Christopher Addison (1869–1951), M.D., one-time professor of anatomy, entered parliament as a Liberal, 1910; minister of munitions, 1916–17; minister in charge of reconstruction, 1917; president of the Local Government Board and first minister of health, 1919–21; joined Labour party and was minister of agriculture, 1930–31; created baron, 1937; viscount, 1945; leader of the House of Lords in the Labour government, 1945–51; secretary of state for Commonwealth relations, 1945–47; lord privy seal, 1947–51.

government never returned to its old channel. *Étatisme*, as Halévy observed, became the hallmark of the times.[1]

One effect was to exalt the power of the Prime Minister. At the time this was ascribed to Lloyd George's personality, and to his perpetuation of the habits of personal government and of improvisation which had served the country well in the war. He continued, in effect, the War Cabinet: meetings of a small number of his principal colleagues. The full Cabinet of twenty did not meet until late in October 1919, and only infrequently after that. And the Prime Minister's private and much-enlarged secretariat, the 'garden suburb' (so named from the temporary quarters in the garden of Number 10 Downing Street where it was housed), continued in being.[2] It became, with other examples of his personal methods, one of the causes of Lloyd George's unpopularity and downfall, despite the ability of such members as Philip Kerr[3] (later Lord Lothian), and Lionel Curtis.[4] Yet without it, all Lloyd George's successors enjoyed an ascendancy in the Cabinet and in parliament such as earlier prime ministers had never had.

The Cabinet itself gained from one of Lloyd George's innovations which became permanent. In 1917 the small secretariat of the Committee of Imperial Defence under Colonel Maurice Hankey[5] had been used as the secretariat of the War Cabinet. In 1919 the Committee of Imperial Defence was revived with its own secretariat, but the Cabinet secretariat continued in being, with Hankey as secretary of both bodies until his retirement in 1938.[6]

Larger plans for the reconstruction of the machinery of govern-

[1] E. Halévy, *L'ère des tyrannies* (Paris, 1938), p. 153 (in his essay 'État present de la question sociale en Angleterre' [1922]). Cf., C. C. Gillispie, 'The work of Élie Halévy: a critical appreciation', *Journal of Modern History*, 22 (1950), 245–8.

[2] See Joseph Davies, *The Prime Minister's Secretariat*, 1916–20 (Newport, Mon., 1951).

[3] Philip Henry Kerr (1882–1940); member of Milner's 'kindergarten' in South Africa, 1904–8. First editor of *Round Table*, 1910. Private secretary to Lloyd George, 1916–21. Secretary to Rhodes trustees, 1925. Succeeded cousin as Lord Lothian, 1930. Held minor office in National government, 1931–32. Ambassador to the United States, 1939–40.

[4] Lionel Curtis (1872–1955); Town Clerk of Johannesburg and one of Milner's 'kindergarten' in South Africa after the Boer War; influential in bringing about the Union of South Africa; second secretary to the British delegation in the Irish Treaty negotiations, 1921; Fellow of All Souls, Oxford; C. H., 1949; author of several books on the British Commonwealth and world government.

[5] Maurice Hankey, born 1877; served in Marines and Naval Intelligence; assistant secretary, Committee on Imperial Defence, 1908, secretary 1912–38; secretary, war cabinet, 1916–18, secretary of cabinet, 1919–38; created baron, 1939; served in Chamberlain and Churchill governments, 1939–42.

[6] W. Ivor Jennings, *Cabinet Government* (Cambridge, 1937), pp. 186–8, 232–40; D. N. Chester, 'Development of the Cabinet, 1914–49', *British Government since 1918* (by Sir Gilbert Campion *et al.*; London, 1950), pp. 32, 37–40; K. B. Smellie, *A Hundred Years of English Government* (London, 1937), pp. 373–8.

ment came to very little. Among the many reports issued by the Ministry of Reconstruction (created in July 1917 as successor to a committee) one of the most important was that of the committee headed by Lord Haldane[1] on the machinery of government, which has been called the most thorough examination of the functions of government since Bentham. It proposed that the government be organised in departments corresponding to services to be performed: Finance, Defence, External Affairs, Research, Production, Employment, Supplies, Education, Health, Justice. Of the new departments it proposed only one came into being: the Ministry of Health, created by act of parliament in 1919; it replaced the National Health Insurance Commission and the Local Government Board and applied, in the relations between central and local government, and particularly in matters of housing and health, something more than the old 'poor law' spirit of the Board. The Ministry of Transport was also born in 1919, though without the large powers originally proposed for it. The Ministry of Labour, created in 1916, was a wartime ministry which survived. So were the Ministry of Pensions and the Air Ministry. In 1919 a curious relic of old constitutional practice disappeared when the Re-election of Ministers Act relieved persons appointed ministers from the necessity of submitting themselves to their constituents for re-election unless they received office later than nine months from the previous election (a limitation removed in 1926).

The civil service was not much changed, except in size, after the war. In scientific research the government showed new interest through the activities of the Department of Scientific and Industrial Research, created in 1916, and the Medical Research Council, established in 1920. The Forestry Commission was another child of 1919, inheriting the forestry powers of the Board of Agriculture and carrying out afforestation on crown lands (after 1923) and on other lands acquired by it.[2] The numbers in the civil service increased with the state's new functions. In 1914 all grades of the civil service (administrative, technical, executive, clerical) numbered 57,706; in 1923 116,241, in 1930 120,418. The number of higher civil servants (the administrative class) within these totals rose from 1077 in 1914 to 1596 in 1923 and 1708 in 1930.

[1] R. B. Haldane (1856–1928), born in Edinburgh; the Haldanes were an old Perthshire family, owners of the estate of Cloan, near Auchterarder. Educated at Edinburgh and Göttingen universities. Barrister and philosopher. M.P., 1885–1911. Secretary of state for war, 1905–12; lord chancellor, 1912–15, 1924. Created viscount, 1911. O.M., 1915.

[2] K. B. Smellie, *Hundred Years of English Government*, pp. 379–420; W. A. Robson (ed.), *Public Enterprise* (London, 1937), pp. 59–72 (the Forestry Commission).

The numbers in the executive and clerical grades increased from 33,329 to 82,900 between 1914 and 1930; typists and writing assistants increased from 3034 to 14,046.[1]

The exaltation of the state was, of course, the result not only of the war but of the attitude towards it which the war encouraged. Collectivism had grown apace, and dominated the interwar years in ways not always apparent at the time. Dicey had placed the beginning of the period of collectivism in Great Britain in 1865, defining collectivism as 'faith in the benefit to be derived by the mass of the people from the action or intervention of the state'.[2] He was writing before the war; before his death its growth had far exceeded his wildest fears. The state had intervened, more pryingly than before, in such matters as conditions of employment, industrial hygiene, housing, the daily bread. The individual looked to the state to help satisfy his needs, to promote social equality as a means of completing his political liberty.[3] The former transition from status to contract was reversed, as E. L. Woodward has observed;[4] for example, the unemployed man's status, as unemployed, became his most important asset for survival. And the idea of equality had been promoted by rationing; for meat and margarine, palace and cottage had been treated alike.

Nationalisation of the industries of greatest public concern—one aspect of collectivism—also seemed to be imminent. During the war the state had taken over the operation of some of the largest industries: the railways, coal-mining, shipping. Other industries were under controls hardly less exacting. In such concerns as the railways and the production and distribution of electricity there was a general assumption that the old order should not return or continue unchanged. During his election campaign at Dundee in December 1918, Winston Churchill had advocated the nationalisation of the railways.[5] The *Spectator* early in 1919 accepted it as inevitable, but later changed its mind.[6] J. L. Garvin,[7] editor of the *Observer*, bell-wether for independent conservatism, declared that

---

[1] Figures in K. B. Smellie, *Hundred Years of English Government*, p. 455, derived from May Report, 1931.

[2] A. V. Dicey, *Lectures on the Relation between Law and Public Opinion* (second edition, London, 1914), p. 259.

[3] Cf. Keith Feiling, *History of England* (London, 1950), p. 1078 (the concluding chapters give a good summary of the years 1918–38). See also chapter 8, 'The State and Society since 1918' in K. B. Smellie, *Hundred Years of English Government*.

[4] E. L. Woodward, *Short Journey*, p. 142.

[5] *The Times*, Dec. 11, 1918.

[6] *Spectator*, March 22, July 26, 1919.

[7] J. L. Garvin (1868–1947), editor of the *Observer*, 1908–42.

the nationalisation of the 'inseparable Triad', transport, electricity, coal, was inevitable.[1]

In the event, there was no nationalisation of industries immediately, and little in the next twenty years. Other parts of collectivism (or socialism) fared better: the advance of equality, the enlargement of public concern for social welfare. In both matters, the pressure of Labour played some part, the force of circumstances more. The agents of collectivist measures between the wars were chiefly the Conservatives—sometimes unwillingly, often unconsciously. Why this should be, why collectivism, scorned at the front door, was admitted by the back door, is partly to be explained by the teachings of the war, partly by the compulsions of economic depression.

Immediately, however, the aftermath of the war was an apparent setback for collectivist measures and socialist ideas. This is the more surprising when the growth of the Labour movement by the time of the war's end is considered.

5. THE PASSION OF LABOUR

The war brought new strength to the Labour movement. Before the war the Labour party had made a small but respectable showing in the House of Commons. Outside, the syndicalist movement and current discontents had produced the great strikes of 1910–12 and the Triple Alliance of the miners, railwaymen and dockers in 1914. The war had increased the working men's belief in their own power, encouraged by the shop stewards' movement and, around Glasgow, the revolutionary temper of the Clyde Workers' Committee. The Russian Revolution in 1917 came as a tremendous inspiration, which in spite of later disillusionments never quite left the Labour movement; in 1917, while the revolution was still in its moderate phase, enthusiasm for it was strong enough to sweep even MacDonald and Snowden into support of the large meeting at Leeds to hail the Russian Revolution and to discuss the formation of workers' and soldiers' councils in Great Britain. The Labour party itself, in spite of appearances to the contrary, was greatly strengthened by the war. It was divided into two parts, that which opposed the war (led by MacDonald and Snowden) and that part under Henderson and Clynes which supported it and whose leaders took part in the Coalition governments. Both parts gained experience from the war, the one from opposition, the other from office.

[1] A. H. Gleason, *What the Workers Want: a Study of British Labor* (New York, 1920), p. 162.

The division was never complete and was never personal. It was healed when Henderson was forced out of Lloyd George's cabinet in 1917 and was free to devote his powers of organisation and mediation to the rebuilding of the party.

In 1918 the Labour party acquired a new constitution and a new programme in keeping with the times. Previously, the party was an association of trade unions and of socialist organisations (the Independent Labour Party (I.L.P.) and the Fabian Society). It had no individual members, and, except through the I.L.P. and the Fabians, little or no support from the middle class. The new constitution converted it into the national party with local branches and individual members. It also committed it, but in a gingerly fashion which would alarm none but the most timid, to the objectives of socialism:

> to secure for the producers by hand and by brain the full fruits of their industry, and the most equitable distribution thereof that may be possible, upon the basis of the common ownership of the means of production and the best obtainable system of popular administration and control of each industry and service.

This constitution was discussed at the party's annual conference in Nottingham in January, 1918, and adopted at a special conference in February.

The new programme, 'Labour and the New Social Order', written by Sidney Webb,[1] elaborated the cautious commitment to socialism. It called for a new social order, based not on competitive struggle but on 'the socialisation of industry' and the 'deliberately planned co-operation in production and distribution for the benefit of all who participate by hand or by brain'. 'The Four Pillars of the House that we propose to erect' were:

(a) The Universal Enforcement of the National Minimum;
(b) The Democratic Control of Industry;
(c) The Revolution in National Finance; and
(d) The Surplus Wealth for the Common Good.

Under the first point were included several proposals for social security and the maintenance of full employment through public

---

[1] Sidney Webb (1859–1947), civil servant, 1878–91; married Beatrice Potter, 1892; member of London County Council, 1892–1910 and active in the development of London's system of public education; founder of the London School of Economics; the leading Fabian socialist, and author, with his wife, of numerous historical and political works; Labour M.P., 1922–29; president of the Board of Trade, 1924; created Baron Passfield, 1929; secretary of state for the colonies, 1929–31; O.M., 1944.

works—things which were commonplaces by the 1940's, but were new, or largely so, in 1918. The second point referred to the nationalisation of industries, mentioning the railways, the coal mines, electrical power, industrial life insurance, 'the manufacture and retailing of alcoholic drink'; it also called for the 'common ownership of the nation's land'. Democratic control and socialism were not explained; workers' control was only mentioned once, parenthetically, in connection with the 'united national service of Communication and Transport'. The revolution in national finance aimed to secure both the national minimum and equality of sacrifice in taxation, and included a capital levy to reduce the national debt, with exemption for capital sums below £1,000.[1]

In the trade-union world similar changes could be seen, but the pace was characteristically measured and deliberate. The war, with the great expansion of industry, had brought opportunity, shown by the doubling of membership, from 4,189,000 in 1913, to 8,081,000 in 1919; but it had brought also the challenge of the militant shop stewards' movement. The tendency, well-marked before the war, for smaller unions to merge into larger amalgamations and federations, continued: outstanding examples were the Amalgamated Engineering Union (1920), the massive Transport and General Workers' Union (1921), Ernest Bevin's creation,[2] and the General and Municipal Workers' Union (1924), a merging of Will Thorne's Gasworkers with the National Amalgamated Union of Labour and the Municipal Workers. These large trade-union organisations were, of course, only the counterpart of the many employers' organisations of long standing, which were also consolidating themselves at this time.[3]

Confronting the employers was the old-established 'parliament' of the trade-union movement, the Trades Union Congress (T.U.C.) Its weakness had been that between its annual congresses it had no existence save through several committees with little individual and no collective strength. To remedy this the T.U.C. accepted, in 1920, a plan of reorganisation which created a General Council, representative of the principal unions and occupations, in place of the old Parliamentary Committee. The General Council was to exercise executive powers between the congresses, and consti-

[1] *Labour and the New Social Order* (1918). For the reorganisation of the Labour party in 1918, as for much else in the history of the Labour movement since 1914, G. D. H. Cole's *History of the Labour Party since 1914* (London, 1948) replaces all earlier works as the indispensable authority. See pp. 39–40, 44–61. The new constitution is given on pp. 71–81.
[2] Francis Williams, *Ernest Bevin* (London, 1952), pp. 102–11.
[3] G. D. H. Cole, *Organised Labour* (London, 1924), pp. 19, 85–6, 155.

tuted a sort of 'general staff' for organised labour. At the same time the T.U.C. became more closely linked with the Labour party by the creation of the National Joint Council (later called the National Council of Labour), which replaced the old Joint Board, and contained representatives of the General Council, the national executive of the Labour party, and the Parliamentary Labour Party. The T.U.C. and the Labour party shared the same buildings as their physical headquarters, first in Eccleston Square, near Victoria, in London, from 1928 the fine office block known as Transport House, built by (and also serving) the Transport and General Workers' Union, in Smith Square, almost under the shadow of the Houses of Parliament in the old and lovely quarter of Westminster behind the school. The T.U.C. and the party also became partners in maintaining the solvency of the *Daily Herald* in 1922. The paper had been founded in 1912 and been edited for most of its existence by George Lansbury.[1] During the war it had become a weekly, but it resumed daily publication in 1919, and was soon in difficulties in spite of a circulation of 330,000, because of an advertisers' boycott.[2]

One other sign of the ferment in the Labour movement was the founding of the Communist party of Great Britain. It was a fusion—and one not easily achieved—of several small Marxist groups such as the British Socialist party, aided by some of the shop stewards and by Russian inspiration. Its birthplace was an unlikely one, the Cannon Street Hotel in London (a railway hotel much used for the annual meetings of business companies) where a conference was held on July 31, 1920; but complete unification was only achieved at a later meeting, in Leeds, on January 29, 1921. The new party at once sought affiliation with the Labour party, and received the first of many refusals in a letter from Arthur Henderson on September 11, 1920.[3]

Such events were signs of a new spirit which it was easy to misinterpret as revolutionary. A temperate statement of it was the 'Memorandum on the Causes and Remedies for Labour Unrest', signed by Arthur Henderson and G. D. H. Cole[4] on behalf of the

---

[1] George Lansbury (1859–1940), elected to Poplar Board of Guardians, 1892; M.P., 1910–12, 1922–40; first commissioner of Works, 1929–31.

[2] Raymond Postgate, *Life of George Lansbury* (London, 1951), pp. 183–215, 221; G. D. H. Cole, *History of the Labour Party*, pp. 127, 151.

[3] T. Bell, *The British Communist Party: a short history* (London, 1937), pp. 47–67; G. D. H. Cole, *History of the Labour Party*, pp. 96, 102–3, 112–13.

[4] G. D. H. Cole (1889–), fellow of Magdalen College, Oxford, 1925–44; Chichele professor of social and political theory, Oxford, 1944; honorary secretary of the Labour Research Department until 1925; prominent guild socialist, Fabian, and Labour party supporter; prolific writer on history, economics, socialism, and author, with his wife, of detective stories.

trade-union representatives of the joint committee of the National Industrial Conference in March 1919, which declared:

> The extent to which workers are challenging the whole system of industrial organisation is very much greater today than ever before, and unrest proceeds not only from more immediate and special grievances but also, to an increasing extent, from a desire to substitute a democratic system of public ownership and production for use with an increasing element of control by the organised workers themselves for the existing capitalist organisation of industry.[1]

More important, however, was the evidence that the 'passion of labour . . . to make the world a better place for the people who inhabit it' was reciprocated by many outside the movement. They found their justification in R. H. Tawney's[2] *Acquisitive Society*, published in 1920. This was a persuasive indictment, blandly self-confident and witty, of the system in which industry was not directed to the service of the community and in which the rights of property existed quite apart from any contemporary justification. The system was not merely unjust but morally wrong and socially absurd. An economic weekly of unimpeachable orthodoxy, the *Statist*, was saying much the same thing; the present order was condemned by the pauperism it produced, the waste of man-power, unemployment, and the shameful standard of life of the working classes; only 5 per cent of the community earned sufficient to be subject to income tax.[3]

On the other side there were expressions of the same mood, but in tones of pessimism or alarm. The *Fortnightly Review* in 1919 published several articles on labour unrest, the very titles of which are suggestive of the current mood: 'The Policy of Industrial Suicide', 'Labour and the State', 'On the Road to Ruin', 'The Permanent Settlement of the Labour Trouble'. The first of these declared that labour was determined to challenge the whole existing structure of capitalist industry.

[1] A. H. Gleason, *What the Workers Want: a Study of British Labor* (New York, 1920), pp. 373; abstract in *The Times*, March 27, 1919. Cf. A. Hutt, *Post-War History of the British Working Class* (London, 1937), pp. 9–16.

[2] R. H. Tawney, born in Calcutta, 1880. Rugby and Balliol College, Oxford. Teacher in extra-mural classes, Oxford University, 1908–14; member of executive of Workers' Educational Association, 1908–47 (president, 1928–44); professor of economic history (previously reader), University of London, 1931–49; member of consultative committee of Board of Education, 1912–31; University Grants Committee, 1943–48. Married sister of W. H. Beveridge (Lord Beveridge).

[3] Robert Lynd, *The Passion of Labour* (London, 1920), p. 1; 'When the War Ends', *Statist*, Jan. 4, Feb. 15, 1919; 'The Revolt of Labour', *New Statesman*, Jan. 25, 1919.

6. THE WINTER OF OUR DISCONTENT

The first winter of peace brought little comfort. There was a serious shortage of coal. 'We sat shivering round very small fires —in our overcoats . . .' is the recollection of one writer.[1] And the shadow of the great influenza epidemic darkened many a doorstep. The plague had first reached England in June 1918, and gradually increased in severity, until in the worst week, early in November, 7560 persons died of influenza in London and 95 other large towns. The epidemic then declined, but a new outbreak began late in January 1919, and reached its peak at the beginning of March, when 3889 deaths from influenza were recorded in a week in London and the other '96 great towns'. A survey made in Manchester in December showed that about half the people contracted the disease, and 7·9 per cent succumbed to it. The 'flu respected neither youth nor age, but was most deadly to children under one, of whom 2·2 per cent died of it. London's total deaths from influenza in 1918–19 were 15,054; in the 96 great towns (including London) the toll was 62,815. In England and Wales as a whole 150,000 persons died of influenza, gleaner of the war's harvest.[2]

Plans for demobilisation also went awry at first. The plans had been drawn up by the Ministry of Reconstruction some time before the end of the war; they were based on the belief that the ending of the war would cause large-scale unemployment, and they therefore provided for the release first from the armed forces of key men in industry, whose return to work would open up jobs for others. In the event, this favoured men who had entered military service most recently and who had fresh contacts with employers; last in, first out, seemed to be the resulting rule. Trouble followed speedily. On January 3, 12,000 soldiers in the rest camps at Folkestone and Dover demonstrated against embarking to return to France. There were other incidents elsewhere, the most alarming being that at the Army Service Corps depot at Kempton Park, where the men formed a 'soldiers' council' and declared their intention to fraternise with the workmen of the neighbourhood. On January 6 and 7 there were three separate demonstrations near Whitehall: soldiers in lorries carried signs such as 'We won the war. Give us our tickets'; 'We want civvie suits'; 'Promises are not pie crust'. Faced by these events, Winston Churchill, as Secretary of State

---

[1] D. C. Somervell, *Reign of George V*, p. 199, cf. *Annual Register, 1918*, pp. 139–40.
[2] Local Government Board, *48th Annual Report, Supplement: Report of the Medical Department for 1918–19* (Cmd. 462; 1919), pp. 7–32; Ministry of Health, *Annual Report of the Chief Medical Officer, 1919–20* (Cmd. 978; 1920), p. 46.

for War, acted swiftly. The whole basis of demobilisation was changed. Releases were to be dependent on length of service— first in, first out—and of the 3,500,000 men in the army, all but 900,000 needed for the armies of occupation in Germany would be discharged. These orders, published on January 29, ended most of the trouble, though unrest continued here and there, notably among the troops at Calais and, in March, in the Canadian camp at Kinmel Park, near Rhyl, where five men were killed and twenty-three injured in a two-day riot over delays in repatriation. Demobilisation proceeded at the rate of 10,000 men a day for nearly six months. Within a year over four million men had been released from the services, and the task was almost completed.[1]

The absorption of men from the forces into civil employment, and the contraction in the number of men and women at work in the war factories, were carried out more smoothly than had been expected, though many ex-officers found it difficult, for a time, to obtain civilian berths. In the postwar boom of 1919, industry was able to take into employment all who offered. The number of persons receiving the 'out-of-work donation', both ex-servicemen and civilians, never exceeded 1,100,000, and by October 1919 was below half a million.[2]

The departure of women from employment, whether voluntarily or by discharge, was equally rapid. During the war the number of women in employment in Great Britain and Ireland rose from just under 6 millions to 7·3 millions, chiefly through the increased numbers employed in industrial occupations (especially in the munitions industry). One of the rosy hopes for the postwar world was that there would be an increase in the opportunities for women in industry and in the higher positions in business. Little came of it. Within a year after the Armistice three-quarters of a million women had been dismissed. Those who remained in employment were absorbed by the occupations formerly dependent on them, especially domestic service, in which the number engaged had fallen by 400,000 during the war.[3] The 1921 census for England and Wales showed a decrease since 1911 in the proportion of women in occupations, from 34·1 per cent to 32·3 per cent; and the greater number of occupied women were, as before the war, in a

[1] W. S. Churchill, *Aftermath*, pp. 40–55; S. R. Graubard, 'Military demobilization in Great Britain following the first world war', *Journal of Modern History*, XIX (1947), 297–311. *Annual Register, 1919*, pp. 5–6, 11, 41.
[2] A. S. J. Baster, *The Little Less* (London, 1947), p. 4; Humbert Wolfe, *Labour Supply and Regulation* (Carnegie series: Oxford, 1923), pp. 298–307. *The Ministry of Labour Gazette* gives unemployment figures month by month.
[3] Vera Brittain, *Women's Work in Modern England* (London, 1928), pp. 9–11.

very few occupations: 33 per cent in domestic service, 12 per cent in the textile industries, 11 per cent in clothing; 9 per cent were shop assistants, 8 per cent clerks, 4 per cent teachers.[1]

As if the difficulties of demobilisation were not enough to try the nation, the new year had opened with the threat of a general strike. It began in Glasgow, in January 1919, and seemed at first to herald the beginning of revolution. In reality it was the last flare-up of the agitations which had kept the Clydeside region in turmoil throughout the war. The Clyde Workers' Committee—in effect, the shop stewards—was joined by the trade-union leaders in calling a general strike for January 27, to enforce the demand for a forty-hour week as a means of absorbing the unemployed expected to result from demobilisation. William Gallacher,[2] Emanuel Shinwell,[3] and David Kirkwood[4] were among the leaders, as they had been during the war. On Monday, the 27th, all the principal factories were 'struck to a man'. A mass meeting was held in and outside St. Andrew's Hall, with about 30,000 present. From the hall, the crowd made its way to George Square, where more speeches were made, and a red flag hoisted on the municipal flag-pole. Another demonstration in the Square occurred on Wednesday, when a delegation was received by the Lord Provost, who promised to transmit the strikers' demands to the government and asked the delegation to return on Friday for an answer.

The answer, on Friday, January 31, was the 'battle of George Square'. The government had taken alarm: the raising of the red flag, the huge demonstrations, perhaps gave colour to the idea that this *was* the start of the revolution. The strike might spread, though it actually did not do so except to Edinburgh and Belfast. Counter-action in Glasgow was decided on. Troops were concentrated, with tanks and machine guns, to surround the city, though those in Maryhill Barracks, on the outskirts of Glasgow, were kept within grounds—perhaps for fear of their sympathies with the strikers. When, on the fateful Friday, another large crowd gathered in George Square, in front of the City Chambers, the police suddenly began a baton attack on the rear, felling

[1] *Census of England and Wales, 1921; General Report*, pp. 89, 117.

[2] William Gallacher, born 1881; chairman of the Clyde Workers' Committee, 1914–18; leading member of Communist Party since 1920; M.P. for West Fife (Communist), 1935–50.

[3] Emanuel Shinwell, born in London, 1884; M.P., 1922–24, 1928–31, and since 1935; mines secretary, 1924, 1930–31; minister of fuel and power, 1945–47; war secretary, 1947–50, minister of defence, 1950–51.

[4] David Kirkwood (1872–1955); engineer at Beardmores' works, Parkhead; deported from Clyde munitions area in 1916 as one of the leaders of the Clyde workers. M.P., 1922–51. Created baron, 1951.

men and women. The crowd began to counter-attack, and a free fight was in process by the time the Sheriff came out of the City Chambers and read the Riot Act. After this the police did not have it all their own way, particularly in North Frederick Street, where a barricade of cases of aerated water bottles from a passing van was put up and the police assailed with the bottles. Next day the troops marched in in full panoply and 'occupied' the city. By February 11 the Clyde strike was over. In April twelve of the leaders were tried in Edinburgh: the majority were acquitted; Shinwell and Gallacher received brief prison sentences for 'inciting to riot'.[1]

By the end of the year, though there had been several more strikes, some of them of a very serious character, the cutting edge of revolution and of reconstruction alike had been blunted.[2] Instead of the expected depression in business from the ending of war orders there was an immediate though short-lived boom. This knocked into a cocked hat all the plans for the new society, whether of government or labour.

7. BOOM AND INFLATION

The hope that the high profits of wartime would continue, and the war's legacy of large sums seeking investment, stimulated speculation. The war had also left the habits of large, careless planning, and of thinking that more and bigger amalgamations and absorptions were part of the order of nature. The government added to the fun by an inflationary policy, increasing the floating debt to meet continued heavy expenditures, and using sales of surplus war material for the same purpose. Domestic capital issues in 1919 totalled £187·7 millions, in 1920 £331 millions, as compared with the figure of £44 millions in 1913.[3] The number of new companies registered in Great Britain also increased, reaching 11,000 in 1920, compared with 7425 in 1913. In addition, it was estimated that in 1920 235 companies issued bonus shares totalling £65 millions on capital of only £97 millions; thus profits were distributed without liability for supertax, while the capital on which dividends must be paid in future was greatly

[1] W. Gallacher, *Revolt on the Clyde* (London, 1936), pp. 217–42; David Kirkwood, *My Life of Revolt* (London, 1935), pp. 171–4; *Annual Register, 1919*, pp. 9–10.
[2] W. H. Crook, *The General Strike* (Chapel Hill, 1931), pp. 240–5. There were large-scale strikes, more political than economic in character, in several parts of the world in 1919: in Germany, Paris, Seattle, Winnipeg; see Crook, p. 288.
[3] E. V. Morgan, *Studies in British Financial Policy, 1914–25* (London, 1952), p. 264.

inflated; on the average, the 235 companies distributed two fully paid-up shares for every three shares held.[1]

The 'craze for speculation', as the *Economist* called it in December 1919, was to be seen at its worst in the buying-up of Lancashire cotton mills. Huge combines were floated on a number of small firms, whose success in the past had depended on the initiative and skill of individual owners.[2] In 1919 and 1920 238 mills, comprising 42 per cent of the capacity of the cotton spinning industry, changed hands. Their capital had totalled £10,815,000, yet the money paid for them was £71,875,000.[3] Much of the financing of this speculation was done by the banks—a new and dubious development. Speculation was equally rife in the shipping, shipbuilding,[4] and engineering industries. There were several amalgamations in the steel industry, and increased integration of collieries and steel companies.[5] In banking, the consolidation of ownership in the Big Five was completed: the Midland and the National Provincial took shape in 1918; the Westminster absorbed Parr's Bank. In December 1920 the *Economist* recorded the passing of the last of the old country banks, Beckett's, of Leeds, bought by the Westminster after being in the hands of a single family for six generations.[6]

The collapse of the boom began in April 1920. The government, uneasy at the course of events, raised the bank rate from 6 to 7 per cent; but by then the 'once-for-all work' of postwar replacement and reconstruction was completed,[7] and the raising of the rate not merely slowed down investment, but stopped it altogether. The new Budget, which showed a surplus of anticipated revenue over expenditure for the first time since the war, and which actually increased the excess profits duty it was expected to repeal, had a similarly deflationary effect. Prices at once began to fall and unemployment to rise. 'In April 1920 all was right with the world. In April 1921 all was wrong.'[8]

The results of the boom were almost wholly disastrous to in-

[1] Labour Research Department (L.R.D.), *Wages, Prices and Profits* (London, 1922), p. 92; J. M. Rees, *Trusts in British Industry, 1914–21* (London, 1922), p. 238.
[2] *Economist*, Dec. 6, 1919.   [3] L.R.D., *Wages, Prices and Profits*, pp. 96–7.
[4] E.g., the expansion and the exuberant financial policies of Palmers' of Jarrow: Ellen Wilkinson, *Town that was Murdered: the life-story of Jarrow* (London, 1939), pp. 120–37.
[5] D. L. Burn, *Economic History of Steelmaking, 1867–1939* (Cambridge, 1940), pp. 370–4.
[6] *Economist*, Dec. 18, 1920.
[7] A. C. Pigou, *Aspects of British Economic History, 1918–25* (London, 1947), p. 188; cf. pp. 5–7; E. V. Morgan, *British Financial Policy*, pp. 81–6.
[8] R. H. Tawney, 'Abolition of Economic Controls, 1918–21', *Economic History Review*, XIII (1943), 15.

dustry. Large-scale concerns increased in size and number, becoming top-heavy and threatening the economy with dangerous rigidities. The problem of trusts, which had caused disquiet during the war, was intensified, though nothing was done to carry out the mild suggestions of the Report of the Committee on Trusts (Cd. 9236; 1919), which was the product of this alarm.[1] Many companies, through watering their capital or through unwise expansion of plant, ill-judged investments, and unsound absorptions, had crippled their earning capacity. The power of finance-capital had shown itself in England.[2] Beyond all this, the speculation and the false hopes of easy prosperity induced by the boom handicapped Britain's economic recovery during the next twenty years.

Among the people at large the immediate effect was an inflation of prices. This affected all classes, and perhaps the middle class more than the working class. Prices had roughly doubled during the war, and wage rates had increased, though more slowly. With the further rapid increase in prices in 1919 and 1920 wages did not generally keep pace. By the end of 1920 the peak had been passed. If the index-number for July 1914 is 100, wholesale prices stood at 226 in January 1919, 249 in July, and 300 in January 1920; the peak was 323 in March 1920, after which the index-number declined to 229 in December. Retail food prices stood at 230 in January 1919, declined later in the year, but rose again the following winter, reaching 258 in July 1920, and a peak of 291 in November. As to wages, the rough average of increase in the time rates and the piece rates of the principal industries from the prewar index-number of 100 was to 175–180 by July 1918, 210–215 in July 1919, and 260 in July 1920.[3] One study claimed that a specimen family budget for a week's food, costing £1 5s. 9d. in 1914, would cost, for the same items, £4 6s. 10½d. in June 1920, an increase of 237 per cent;[4] but an official committee estimated that actual expenditures on food, allowing for substitutions, had increased only 97 per cent by July 1919 and 115 per cent by January 1920.[5] One pound was worth only 8s. 8d. in its purchasing power for food in January 1919 as compared with 1914, 7s. 9d. in July 1920, 9s. 2d. a year later. It was claimed that real wages, taking

[1] J. M. Rees, *Trusts in British Industries*, is based upon this report.
[2] H. A. Marquand, *Dynamics of Industrial Combination* (London, 1931), pp. 121, 190–2.
[3] A. L. Bowley, *Prices and Wages in the United Kingdom, 1914–20* (Carnegie series: Oxford, 1921), pp. 10, 35, 70–1, 106. More detailed indices of wholesale prices are given in E. V. Morgan, *British Financial Policy*, pp. 267–82.
[4] L.R.D., *Wages, Prices and Profits*, p. 25.
[5] A. L. Bowley, *Prices and Wages in the United Kingdom, 1914–20*, p. 39.

July 1914 as 100, stood at anywhere from 66·7 to 117·8 by the end of 1919, with the workers in the greater number of industries being on a lower standard of living than before the war, but those in the steel and textile industries and on the railways being better off. By the end of 1920 the figures were much the same; the railway-men still showed the most improvement (117·1), and the dockers had by then bettered their prewar standard.[1]

One result was that the trade unions turned from long-range schemes of nationalisation to short-range demands for wage increases. These the business community could for the time being satisfy in part, thus weakening the campaign for large reforms in industry. The hopes for Labour's 'new social order', and particularly for nationalisation, were quenched before they had really caught fire, as the unions returned to their traditional objectives. At the same time the boom provided the leaders of business with irresistible arguments for the scrapping of the government's plans for reconstruction. Decontrol became the order of the day.

8. DECONTROL

In the latter part of the war 'reconstruction' had been a magic word. In July 1917 an earlier committee was replaced by a Ministry of Reconstruction under Christopher Addison. Under it were committees innumerable, and from them came reports on many matters: health, housing, education, local government, agriculture, electricity, transport, re-employment, women in industry, afforestation, the future of various industries. Implicit in them was the continuation into the peace of the wartime controls exercised by government over industry. Nationalisation was not involved directly; but if controls were prolonged they might well lead industries into nationalisation rather than back to their former patterns. At the end of the war the times seemed ripe for nationalisation; the rapid crescendo of demands for decontrol banished it.[2]

The government took the cue. During the war, ten new ministries and 160 new boards and commissions had come into existence. Controls under the Board of Trade and the War Office were allowed to run out in 1919, and the controls on shipping at the same time. Rationing of food was ended in 1919 and 1920, and price controls mostly in 1920. The official date of the end of the

---

[1] L.R.D., *Wages, Prices and Profits*, pp. 87, 89, 106–10.
[2] E.g., 'Official muddlers and capitalist slackers', *Economist*, July 26, 1919.

war was January 10, 1920. The ministries of Munitions, Shipping, and Food came to an end on March 31, 1921. The Liquor Control Board was abolished by the Licensing Act of August 17, 1921, though not the profitable experiments in the state monopoly of public houses in the Carlisle, Gretna, and Cromarty Firth areas, which still continue. The control of the railways and the coalmines continued until 1921. Meanwhile, by a tremendous effort, the government divested itself of the hoards of 'war surplus' goods and of many of the national factories constructed under the Ministry of Munitions' ægis during the war. Of 245 such factories at the Armistice, 105 were sold, though not at fire-sale prices, since Lord Inverforth,[1] the Minister of Munitions, who directed this operation, insisted that his fellow-industrialists should pay more than a song for the properties. The press made the motor-vehicle repair depot at Cippenham, near Slough, the test of the government's sincerity in getting out of business. The depot had been started in June 1918, but its construction was not complete until the middle of 1919, and the papers complained loudly and often about it, till it was sold, supposedly at a profit to the government of £850,000, in April 1920.[2] A shipyard at Chepstow aroused equal ire.

In this bonfire of controls, the plans for the reorganisation of industries were also consumed. The principal industries affected were two of public concern which might otherwise have been nationalised: electricity and the railways. The original plan for the Ministry of Transport, embodied in the Ways and Communications Bill of 1919, would have given the Ministry the power to nationalise any transport undertaking (concerned with roads, railways, canals, docks), simply by order in council, and to control the supply of electricity. Little was left of these powers in the final act, as a result of the opposition to the bill in parliament, product of distrust at the vagueness of the government's proposals and suspicion of the somewhat domineering personality of Sir Eric Geddes, the minister-designate. In the event, a new public body, the Electricity Commissioners, was created in 1919 to exercise the regulatory powers previously belonging to various government departments; but the ambitious plans for the generation and dis-

[1] Andrew Weir (Lord Inverforth), a Scottish shipowner; surveyor general of Supplies, 1917.
[2] R. H. Tawney, 'Abolition of Economic Controls, 1918–21', *Economic History Review*, XIII (1943), 7–17; *Economist*, July 12, 1919; *Annual Register, 1919*, pp. 39, 89; *1920*, p. 39; A. C. Pigou, *Aspects of British Economic History*, pp. 114–38; A. Shadwell, *Drink in 1914–22: a Lesson in Control* (London, 1923), pp. 135–38.

tribution of electricity by public boards were all defeated in parliament.[1]

The decontrol of the railways was accomplished in a peculiar way. The Ministry of Transport, foiled in its own plans of nationalisation, proposed in June 1920 that the 120 operating companies should be combined into seven groups, each under a private company. In parliament the groups were reduced to four by leaving out the proposed grouping of London's passenger services and by eliminating the North Eastern group, and dividing the Scottish railways between the two northern groups. The resulting measure, the Railways Act, 1921, brought into being the four systems of the interwar years: the Great Western (the original company retaining its name and character and merely absorbing the other lines, mainly Welsh, within its area), the London, Midland and Scottish, the London and North Eastern, and the Southern. The Act also created the Railway Rates Tribunal, to take over existing powers over rates, and to adjust rates so that the companies should earn as 'standard revenue', the revenues of 1913. The government control of the railways ended on August 15, 1921: and the new 'groups' began active life on January 1, 1923, when the historic old companies ceased to operate their lines and, shortly afterwards, passed out of existence.[2]

9. THE FOILING OF LABOUR

Inflation and decontrol, while arresting the postwar tendencies towards collectivism, could not in themselves have prevented the advancement of Labour's schemes for nationalisation had they been pressed immediately after the war, while their inevitability was still believed in. To explain how Labour missed the opportunity—to the weakening of Labour's interest in socialism, despite all protestations, for the next twenty years—we must notice the intervention of Lloyd George and the Coalition government. It was Lloyd George, according to Halévy, who 'foiled' Labour's manœuvres;[3] and by the simple device of gaining time. The San-

---

[1] H. H. Ballin, *Organization of Electricity Supply in Great Britain* (London, 1946), pp. 98–155; W. H. Wickwar, *Public Services* (London, 1938), pp. 174–80.

[2] W. E. Simnett, *Railway Amalgamation in Great Britain* (London, 1923); C. E. R. Sherrington, *A Hundred Years of Inland Transport, 1830–1933* (London, 1934), pp. 307–17; *Economist*, July 3, 1920, May 14, July 2, 1921, and *passim*; *Railway Gazette*, Oct. 31, 1947. The six groups first proposed (the London group being the seventh) were similar to the six regions into which the British railways were divided upon nationalisation in 1948; i.e., the North Eastern Railway would have formed a separate group.

[3] É. Halévy, *L'ère des tyrannies*, pp. 169–70, 202: 'Le très habile homme d'État qui avait su déjouer les manœuvres du Parti Travailliste et du Parti Trade-Unioniste en Angleterre, c'était Lloyd George; et le Parti Travailliste ne le lui a jamais pardonné' (p. 202).

key Coal Commission and the National Industrial Conference were the principal means. Nothing was settled by them, but that did not matter. They had served their purpose, to get the leaders of the trade unions to talk rather than act, to restore to prominence the moderate leaders of the movement. Things settled back into their old grooves; 1919, the critical year of transition, was safely passed.

Once an immediate and direct clash between labour and capital was averted, secondary outbreaks of trouble could be limited or prevented. The extension of social insurance helped in this process; discontent seldom reached the flash point, for state aid, even if grudgingly given and ungratefully accepted, damped it down. The last and most potent sedative was the depression. Chronic unemployment ended serious talk of revolution; apathy settled on the mass of the people.

Lloyd George's genius for improvisation showed itself clearly in the means by which he postponed the strike which threatened in the coal-mines in 1919. In January, at a special conference at Southport, the Miners' Federation put forward its postwar programme: a 6-hour day, a 30 per cent increase in total earnings, and the nationalisation of all mines and minerals. The reply of the government, which was still controlling the mines, was unsatisfactory, and the miners then balloted for or against a national strike. The result was six to one in favour of a strike (615,164 votes to 105,082). Meanwhile Lloyd George had asked the miners' executive to postpone the strike and take part in a commission to investigate the coal industry, studying both the question of wages and hours, on which an interim report would be called for by March 20, and the larger question of nationalisation. To this the miners agreed.

The Coal Industry Commission was a peculiar, indeed, a unique body. It was created by act of parliament rather than by the government as a royal commission; this was in order that it might have power to compel the production of documents and the attendance of witnesses. Its membership was unusual.[1] Almost half of it represented the side of Labour; it included three coal-owners, three industrialists (Sir Arthur Balfour, Sir Thomas Royden, Sir Arthur Duckham), the three leading men among the coal-miners, Robert Smillie, and Frank Hodges, president and secretary of the Miners' Federation, and Herbert Smith, president

[1] For light on the manner of its appointment, see *Beatrice Webb's Diaries, 1912–24*, pp. 146–50.

of the Yorkshire Miners' Federation, and three economists nominated, in effect, by the miners, Sidney Webb, R. H. Tawney, and Sir Leo Chiozza Money.[1] The chairman was Sir John Sankey,[2] one of the judges of the King's Bench, and the commission has always been known as the Sankey Commission. From the start it was not as other commissions are. Its sessions were held amid the gold, blue and red glories of the King's Robing Room in the House of Lords, and here it arraigned and interrogated witnesses both high and lowly, probing into all the secrets of the industry: profits, royalties, miners' housing. The miners made it into a grand jury, investigating the industry, cross-examining the royalty-owners and questioning their contribution to society, and in general building up the case for nationalisation. 'They successfully kept "private enterprise" on its trial before the Commission, and compelled the mine-owners to remain throughout on the defensive.'[3] Such publicity, such documentation from government experts had been unknown before. No wonder it was the big show, the preoccupation of the press for several weeks.

The lion's share of the questioning of witnesses was done by the miners' representatives; most of all by Smillie, but with Sir Leo Money and Sidney Webb frequently intervening, Tawney, Hodges, and Smith somewhat less so. All could be disconcerting, even devastating, in the way in which a series of questions led the hapless witness up to the damaging admission. The owners' side of the Commission intervened on occasion to lend a helping hand to their friends. Smillie became for the time a national figure; the official minutes of evidence give little hint of the determination behind his soft Scots speech, nor do they picture him, a solid man in his sixties, in an old grey suit, drawing on an aged pipe.[4]

The Commission rendered an interim report on March 20—or rather, three reports. The six representatives of the miners' side recommended that the miners' claims be met in full. The three coal-owners' representatives recommended an increase of 1s. 6d. per day in the wages of adult workers, and a 7-hour working day. Sir John Sankey and the three industrialists made a report which

[1] Leo Chiozza Money (1870–1944); M.P., 1906–18 as Liberal; defeated as Labour candidate, 1918; Knighted, 1915. Author of *Riches and Poverty* (1905).

[2] John Sankey (1866–1948); Judge of the King's Bench Division, 1914–28; a Lord Justice of Appeal, 1928–29; Lord chancellor, 1929–35; created viscount, 1932. Life member of the Governing Body of the Church of Wales.

[3] G. D. H. Cole, *Labour in the Coal-Mining Industry* (Carnegie series: Oxford, 1923), p. 78.

[4] A. H. Gleason, *What the Workers Want*, pp. 33–8, 58–69. Gleason gives several extracts from the hearings.

steered between these two positions: a 7-hour day, to be reduced to 6 hours in July 1921, if the economic condition of the industry justified it; a wage increase of 2s. per day for adults (totalling £30 millions); and a levy of 1d. per ton (producing £1 million a year) to improve the housing and amenities of the mining districts, many houses being, it said, 'a reproach to our civilisation' for which 'no judicial language is sufficiently strong or sufficiently severe to apply to their condemnation'. On the matter of nationalisation it declared, in heavy type:

> Even upon the evidence already given, the present system of ownership and working in the coal industry stands condemned, and some other system must be substituted for it, either nationalisation or a method of unification by national purchase and/or joint control. (Recommendation IX.)

It further stated:

> . . . it is in the interests of the country that the colliery workers shall in the future have an effective voice in the direction of the mine. For a generation the colliery worker has been educated socially and technically. The result is a great national asset. Why not use it? (Recommendation XV.)[1]

The government accepted Sir John Sankey's report, and subsequently the miners did so also, in a national ballot.

The second report of the Commission, dealing with nationalisation, appeared on June 20; this time there were four reports. All recommended the nationalisation of royalties, improvements in the distribution of coal, and the creation of a minister of mines. Sir John Sankey's report went further: 'I recommend on the evidence before me that the principle of State ownership of the coalmines be accepted.' He justified this on the grounds both of the inefficiency of the system of divided ownership (3,000 pits owned by 1,500 concerns) and of the 'present atmosphere of distrust and recrimination' between owners and men. His recommendations

---

[1] The reports are given in Coal Industry Commission, *Reports*, I (Cmd. 359, 1919), pp. vii–xxiii; the minutes of evidence in the first stage of the enquiry in the remainder of the volume, pp. 1–414; the documents submitted are in vol. III (Cmd. 361, 1919). The best account of the work of the Sankey Commission, and of the history of the mining industry just after the war, is G. D. H. Cole's *Labour in the Coal Mining Industry* (1914–21). See also A. H. Gleason, *What the Workers Want*, for a valuable contemporary account of the Commission, and of this period in the history of the British working class, by a shrewd and sympathetic American observer; *Beatrice Webb's Diaries, 1912–24*, pp. 153–7, 161; R. A. S. Redmayne, *Men, Mines, and Memories* (London, 1942), p. 208 ff.; R. P. Arnot, *The Miners: Years of Struggle: A History of the Miners' Federation of Great Britain (from 1910 onwards)* (London, 1953), p. 189 ff.

C

were endorsed by the second report, that of the six miners' representatives, but they went further in providing for workers' control. The report of the three coal-owners and two of the industrialists condemned nationalisation as 'detrimental to the development of the industry and to the economic life of the country', and recommended no change in the system of private ownership; its only proposals to meet the miners' claims were for pit committees and district councils and a national council representing the owners and the men, to discuss questions relating to the industry (but not, apparently, to conditions of employment in it). The fourth report, that of Sir Arthur Duckham, an industrial engineer, was an interesting compromise between nationalisation and unreconstructed private ownership, and reflected the suggestions made to the commission by Sir Richard Redmayne, the chief inspector of mines. He proposed that in each area all collieries should be acquired by a single company (to be called the District Coal Board), and operated by it, subject to a limit on its profits.

There was thus no clear majority report, though Sir John Sankey's and the miners' representatives' reports together, which both recommended nationalisation of the mines, commanded seven votes out of the thirteen on the Commission. This was the government's excuse for not carrying out the recommendation. The bitterness and the troubles in the coal-mines for the next seven—or for that matter twenty-seven—years derived in great part from the feeling of both miners and owners that they had been betrayed. The miners, who had hoped for too much from the Commission, felt tricked when they got nothing from it. The owners were furious that the government had come so near to conceding nationalisation, and having had a narrow escape were more determined than ever to stand firm in future. From then on, what they had they held—until, in the nature of human affairs, they lost it all.

How did the government conduct the strategic retreat from the commitments it seemed to have undertaken in appointing the Sankey Commission? Public interest had already waned, through the prolongation of the hearings long after the original strike threat had disappeared. Other matters held the stage—the conclusion of the peace negotiations at Paris, for one. Before ever the recommendations of the final reports were taken up, a strike broke out in the Yorkshire mines over the means of carrying out the recommendation of the interim report concerning higher wages and the 7-hour day. It lasted from July 17 to August

14, and a week longer in west Yorkshire. The strike confused the public, and Lloyd George used it, and the fact that it was against the Coal Controller and the government, as his reason for rejecting the majority recommendations for nationalisation, in his statement in the Commons on August 18. He accepted the nationalisation of royalties, and for the miners proposed the essence of Sir Arthur Duckham's plan—amalgamations of collieries within the mining areas. Vernon Hartshorn, the Welsh miners' leader, replied that the Commission had apparently been nothing but a large game of bluff, and that the miners had been 'deceived, betrayed, duped'. The Miners' Federation, in conference, rejected the Duckham plan—with the result that the government had a perfect excuse for abandoning even this moderate reform, which neither owners nor miners accepted, and so was relieved from having to do anything at all.

All that came of the high hopes of the Sankey Commission was the Coal Mines Act of 1919, which enacted the 7-hour day; an emergency act in 1920, which limited profits temporarily and extended the duration of the government's control; and the Mining Industry Act of 1920. Here the mountain laboured and brought forth a mouse: an enfeebled Mines Department inside the Board of Trade, inheriting the Board's powers concerning safety and statistics; the Miners' Welfare Fund, the product of a levy of one penny a ton on coal-owners, to provide amenities for the miners—baths, clubs, scholarships; and an abortive scheme of pit committees, district committees, and area boards, in which representatives of the owners and of the miners would discuss questions concerning the industry, including wages. As for the nationalisation of royalties, though the government declared in February 1920 that it intended to introduce a bill for the purpose and repeated this in November, the matter was allowed to die, and received very little public attention.

The truth was that the miners and the Labour movement generally never caught up with the government and the public after Lloyd George had taken a running start by rejecting nationalisation on August 18, 1919, The miners appealed to the T.U.C., meeting in Glasgow in September 1919. The congress voted support, and decided on the means—a deputation to the Prime Minister. Later, the 'Mines for the Nation' campaign was started on December 9, with the support of the T.U.C., the Labour party, and the Co-operative Union. It was a total failure The issues were cold and could not be fanned back into flame. The more humdrum matters of wages and hours kept Labour occupied for the next few years.[1]

10. THE PLACATING OF LABOUR

The same tactics of delay and masterly inactivity were used on other occasions, along with some constructive measures, to placate the working class. One instance was the holding of the National Industrial Conference. This was summoned by the government, and high hopes were held of it, as a parliament of employers and workers, when it met on February 27, 1919, in Central Hall, Westminster. Five hundred workers were present, representing all the principal unions, including the miners and transport workers, and trades in which Whitley Councils had been organised; the three hundred employers present represented the Federation of British Industries and employers in all the principal industries. Sir Robert Horne,[2] the Minister of Labour, opened the conference, declaring that the government was anxious to get its advice for meeting the unrest and difficulties accompanying the change-over from war to peace. The conference appointed a joint committee to consider means of improving the relations of employers, workpeople and the state, especially as concerned wages and hours, and the avoidance of unemployment. The report of this committee, signed by Arthur Henderson and Sir Allan Smith, representing the employers, was unanimously adopted at a second session of the conference on April 4. It proposed that the maximum working week be fixed by law at 48 hours. To prevent unemployment it recommended organised short time, housing schemes, state development works (afforestation, reclamation, waterways, light railways, roads), and the stabilisation of employment by a government policy of postponing works in good times and pushing them forward in periods of falling trade. More generous unemployment and sickness benefits and old age pensions were recommended. Finally, there should be a permanent National Industrial Conference of 400 members, half elected by trade unions and half by the employers. A noble scheme; but the

[1] G. D. H. Cole, *Labour in the Coal-Mining Industry*, pp. 101–36; W. A. Orton, *Labour in Transition* (London, 1921), pp. 217–22; A. Hutt, *Postwar History of the British Working Class*, pp. 18–24.

[2] R. S. Horne (1871–1940), born at Slamannan, Stirlingshire, son of a minister. George Watson's College, Edinburgh; Glasgow University. Barrister. Served in several government departments during the war. M.P., 1918–37. Minister of Labour, 1919–20; president of the Board of Trade, 1920; chancellor of the Exchequer, 1921–22. Director of Lloyds Bank and several other companies; chairman of Great Western Railway Company, 1934. Created Viscount Horne, 1937.

government did little to carry it out. The Conference came to an end in July 1921, when the trade-union members resigned in disgust. The lion and the lamb were not yet to lie down at the cockatrice's den.[1]

Another scheme to improve relations in industry—the Whitley Councils—had a little more success, though far less than had been hoped for. In 1916 the government had appointed a committee under the chairmanship of J. H. Whitley,[2] on the 'relations between employers and employed', partly to head off the advance of the shop stewards' movement. Its reports in 1917 (when it became one of the committees under the Ministry of Reconstruction) proposed the creation of national industrial councils for each industry, with district councils and works' committees operating under them. All were to include both employers' and trade-union representatives, and were to discuss industrial problems—training, welfare, production methods—as well as wages and hours. The idea of the 'Whitley Councils' was enthusiastically accepted by the government, and by 1920 there were fifty-six 'joint industrial councils' in existence, embracing some three and a quarter million workpeople. The industries affected were, however, mostly small, though pottery, building, chemicals, flour-milling, road transport, boot and shoe manufacturing, printing, wire-working, wool textiles, hosiery, were among the larger ones included. Government employees, in the post office and the royal dockyards, and, after the government's reluctance had been overcome, the civil service, received the benefits of the government's prescription. The workers in the big industries held aloof—the miners, railwaymen, engineering and shipbuilding workers, and the cotton operatives. Even in the industries with national 'Whitley Councils' the district and local machinery was seldom created, and many of the councils perished after a few years.[3]

Not more successful was the Industrial Courts Act of 1919. This created a permanent court of arbitration, successor to a wartime body, and extended the Ministry of Labour's powers of conciliation to threatened, as well as actual, disputes by providing for the

[1] A. H. Gleason, *What the Workers Want*, pp. 70–4, 317–38; *Annual Register, 1919*, pp. 41–2; *The Times*, February 28, March 27, April 5, 1919.
[2] J. H. Whitley (1866–1935), cotton spinner, Liberal M.P., 1900–28; Speaker of the House of Commons, 1921–28; chairman of board of governors of the B.B.C., 1930–35.
[3] A. H. Gleason, *What the Workers Want*, pp. 70–1, 358–70; G. D. H. Cole, *Workshop Organization* (Carnegie series: Oxford, 1923), pp. 115–23; L. D. White, *Whitley Councils in the British Civil Service* (Chicago, 1933), pp. 3–9; J. B. Seymour, *The Whitley Councils Scheme* (London, 1932).

appointment of courts of inquiry. But the Act did not include pro-vision for compulsory arbitration or the enforcement of awards made under it. It had, however, one large achievement to its credit in 1920, the settlement of the dockers' claim for higher wages, which first brought Ernest Bevin[1] before the general public. The men had demanded higher wages in November 1919; the employers had offered to submit the claim to arbitration, and the union agreed. The hearing was presided over by Lord Shaw of Dunfermline, a distinguished judge, and the court included both employers and trade-union men. The hearings began in the Law Courts, in the Strand, on February 3, 1920, and attracted attention for several days. Bevin presented the dockers' case in person, and not only argued it with great force and skill, supported by ample figures on wages, profits and living costs, but was able to pour ridicule on the food budget submitted by the employers' advocate, by bringing into court packages of food which demonstrated how much (or rather how little) the existing wages compelled a docker and his family to support life on. The court awarded the men most of what they were asking for, though not the scheme for the decasualisation of dock labour, which Bevin proposed. For a while, Bevin was known as the 'dockers' K.C.' after this success.[2]

11. STRIKES AND THE THREAT OF STRIKES

In spite of the government's gestures of reconciliation, there were several strikes, and the threat of more, during 1919, 1920, and 1921; many of them with the menace of a general strike in their shadow. None the less, a distinct change could be seen in the trade unions after the middle of 1919. There was a return to old ways. Improvements in wages, rather than political influence, were the objectives for which most strikes occurred. On the sur-face, however, the strikes were not the less alarming for that.

The fear of a police strike was a disquieting if intermittent reminder of the insecurity of the times. The National Union of Police and Prison Officers, started before the war, had called a strike of the Metropolitan and City of London police on August

---

[1] Ernest Bevin, born at Winsford, Somerset, 1881, son of a farm worker; orphaned at six; held various odd jobs in Bristol, principally as a van driver; secretary, carmen's branch, Dockers' Union, Bristol, 1904; organiser for the union, 1910; member of government's Port and Transit Executive Committee, 1915; organised and became general secretary of the Transport and General Workers' Union, 1921; chairman of T.U.C., 1937; minister of labour and national service in Churchill government, 1940; foreign secretary in Labour government, 1945, died 1951.
[2] F. Williams, *Bevin*, pp. 74–81.

30, 1918, in protest at the delay in raising the wages of the force, always low, and made even more so by the wartime increases in the cost of living. Six thousand of the Metropolitan Police and almost all of the City of London force came out on strike. Lloyd George had granted swift redress of the grievance over wages, and had hurriedly installed a new commissioner, Sir Nevil Macready, the adjutant-general of the army, a soldier who had seen service of a political character against Welsh miners and Ulster rebels before the war, and was to see more against the Irish Republican Army in 1920–21. The second strike, on August 1, 1919, was in protest against Macready's policy (backed up by a bill in parliament) forbidding policemen to belong to the union. In London, 1083 men came out on strike, out of some 19,000; the strike fizzled out in a few days, and all the strikers were dismissed. Elsewhere, the strike was more serious: 932 men came out at Liverpool in a force of 2100; the military were called in to quell a riot, and much damage was done. Never again, however, in the years to follow, did the police threaten to make common cause with labour, or refuse to carry out orders.[1]

Hardly was the police strike over when another threat to the community appeared, a strike on the railways. The railways were still under government control, and the railwaymen had been negotiating with Sir Auckland Geddes since February for an increase in wages. The government's view, however, tended rather towards reductions, euphemistically referred to as 'standardisation' of wages; and it was Geddes' high-handed bearing which really brought on the strike, when he produced the definite terms (which he then altered to 'definitive') which would mean for many grades an actual reduction in wages—a minimum wage of 40s. a week as compared with the current wage of 51s., and the prewar minimum of 18s. In the Labour movemeut it was believed that the government courted the strike as a means of attacking the power of the working class and forcing down the level of wages.[2] The strike began suddenly, on September 26, and brought almost all the railways of the country to a standstill (though in later days a skeleton train service was operated by volunteers). The government's press releases charged the railwaymen with an anarchist conspiracy, a wanton attempt to hold up the community. A railway strike was not a general strike

---

[1] *Annual Register, 1919*; Sir Nevil Macready, *Annals of an Active Life* (London, [1924]), I, 301–36, II, 345–413; Sir Basil Thomson, *Story of Scotland Yard* (London, 1935), pp. 231 ff.; G. Dilnot, *Story of Scotland Yard* (London, 1926), pp. 130–48.

[2] *Beatrice Webb's Diaries, 1912–24*, pp. 167–9.

but might easily become one. Troops were called out in large numbers; a beginning was made of enrolling 'Citizen Guards'; everything seemed set for the 'fight to a finish' for which *The Times* called (September 29). A scheme of emergency road transport, previously worked out by the government, was put into operation; drivers were registered, 25,000 lorries were requisitioned, and food distribution arranged by the Food Controller (in the wartime Ministry of Food) in the sixteen areas into which the country had been divided. With the wartime Defence of the Realm Acts still in force the government had no lack of powers at its disposal; requisitioning of vehicles was done on the Food Controller's declaration of an emergency. The machinery for these arrangements was kept in being, and was part of the government's preparations against the general strike of 1926.

The government's actions may have been intended to dramatise the national danger inherent in the strike, and so stampede the railwaymen into a settlement. For once, however, it had met its match in the arts of publicity. The National Union of Railwaymen inserted full-page advertisements in the papers, and was well supplied with ammunition by the *Daily Herald* and the Labour Research Department;[1] J. H. Thomas,[2] the secretary of the Union, had a film made of himself, with appropriate captions, explaining the railwaymen's case, which was flashed on the screen in hundreds of cinemas throughout the country. There was also heavy support from the trade-union movement. Within a week the strike was over; the settlement of October 5, announced to a great throng at the Albert Hall, provided for the maintenance of wages at the existing level for a year.[3] The government's self-induced alarm remained, however, and led to the provision of emergency powers a year later. Other strikes at this time included that of the Lancashire cotton operatives in June 1919, and the ironmoulders' strike from September 20, 1919 to January 26, 1920, which involved 50,000 men and a further 100,000 made idle through lack of castings.

[1] An independent organisation (an offshoot of the Fabian Society) associated with the Labour party until the latter created its own research department in 1921.

[2] James Henry Thomas (1874–1949) born in Newport, Mon.; cleaner, fireman, engine-driver on G.W.R.; general secretary, National Union of Railwaymen, 1918–31; M.P., 1910–36; colonial secretary, 1924, 1931, 1936; lord privy seal, 1929–30; dominion secretary, 1930–35.

[3] *The Times*, Sept. 27–Oct. 7, 1919; *Annual Register, 1919*, pp. 117–19; *Economist*, Oct. 4, 1919; A. Hutt, *Post-War History of the British Working Class*, pp. 25–30; G. W. Alcock, *Fifty Years of Railway Trade Unionism* (London, 1922), pp. 550–5; G. Glasgow, *General Strikes and Road Transport* (London [1926?],) pp. 11–14 (introduction by Lloyd George); W. H. Crook, *General Strike*, pp. 247–63; F. Williams, *Bevin*, pp. 69–72.

In 1920 came an extraordinary demonstration of labour solidarity against the government's policy towards Russia. The action was potentially revolutionary, and marked a swing back towards the use of the power of the trade unions for political purposes. The policy of intervention against Soviet Russia had long been obnoxious to Labour, so much so that the Labour party's annual conference, at Southport, in June 1919, had gone on record in favour of 'direct action' to end it; the debate over the question, involving the resort to a general strike as a political weapon, had been keen and the vote decisive, over two to one. Nothing happened; except that in November a national 'Hands Off Russia' committee had been formed, with general Labour support. In May 1920, the Polish offensive against Soviet Russia in the Ukraine brought matters to boiling point; on the 10th dockers at the East India Docks, London, suspecting that munitions they were loading on the *Jolly George* were destined for Poland, stopped work and prevented the ship from sailing by refusing to coal it. By early August, the Russian counter-offensive was, in turn, threatening Warsaw, and Lloyd George and the Cabinet seemed set on intervention, even though the Poles and Russians resumed negotiations. On August 4 Henderson, as secretary of the Labour party, sent telegrams to all local organisations, urging demonstrations, against war on Russia, next Sunday. There was an immediate response, and great demonstrations took place. On the 9th a meeting representative of the T.U.C., the Labour party executive and the Parliamentary Labour party, passed a resolution against a war as a 'crime against humanity', warning the government that 'the whole industrial power of the organised workers' would be used to prevent this, and urging trade unions to instruct their members to down tools as soon as called on to do so. A Council of Action—a significant name—was appointed to carry out the decisions. It sent a delegation to see Lloyd George next day; he remained obdurate. On the 13th, after less than four days' notice, a special national conference of trade unions and the Labour party was held at the Central Hall, Westminster. It endorsed the action taken, to the tune of fiery speeches, even from such peaceable and constitutionally-minded leaders as J. H. Thomas, Ernest Bevin, and Clynes; Thomas said the resolution to down tools would be a 'challenge to the whole Constitution of the country'. The threat was enough. The government, without admitting it, had backed down, and the Poles' victory in the battle of the Vistula on August 14 ended the threat of a general war. Intervention was over, and

c*

with it this brief essay in direct political action by the Labour movement.[1]

Before 1920 ended, there was one further crisis, once again in the coal-mining industry, which threatened at one point to lead to a general strike. Having shelved the demand for nationalisation, the miners, faced by the rising cost of living, sought an increase in wages, and after complicated negotiations, many of them directly with Lloyd George, obtained it on March 29, 1920. In June, however, a further increase in wages was demanded. The government and the owners were prepared to concede it in return for an increase in total output, but dispute remained as to the tonnages (the 'datum line') at which the wage increase, rising in relation to increased output, would operate. In mid-September matters became serious, for it seemed as if at last the Triple Alliance would be involved. A full delegate conference of the unions of the Triple Alliance (miners, railwaymen, transport workers) was held on September 22, but J. H. Thomas, in his normal quest for compromise, insisted on further negotiations before any general strike was decided on. Twice the strike was postponed, as the differences in the figures of the miners' demands and the owners' offers were reduced. Finally, the 'datum line' strike began on October 16, and a complete stoppage occurred—perhaps not so much over a small wage demand as from the pent-up dissatisfaction of the last five years. At once the Triple Alliance came to life again; on October 20 the National Union of Railwaymen, at a special delegate meeting, decided on a strike on October 24 in support of the miners; and the road-transport workers seemed likely to follow suit.

Two things followed: the passage of the Emergency Powers Act, and negotiations which rapidly ended the coal strike. Following the meeting of the N.U.R., the government introduced on October 22 a bill which was enacted into law by the 27th, the Emergency Powers Act. This empowered the government, whenever action was threatened which might deprive the community of the essentials of life, to declare that a state of emergency existed, and thereafter to make emergency regulations by Order in Council and to set up courts of summary jurisdiction.[2] This was, of course,

---

[1] G. D. H. Cole, *History of the Labour Party*, pp. 103–7; A. Hutt, *Post-War History of the British Working Class*, pp. 33–40; W. H. Crook, *General Strike*, pp. 263–9; F. Williams, *Bevin*, pp. 82–7. See also below, p. 56. A similar recommendation of a general strike to compel the government to end the fighting in Ireland was passed by a special trade-union conference in July, 1920.

[2] All regulations must be approved by parliament within seven days; the state of emergency ends after a month unless it is renewed with the consent of parliament.

the restoration of the sort of emergency powers which the government had possessed during the war under the Defence of the Realm Acts. The immediate effect was considerable. Negotiations were resumed, aided by the conciliatory J. H. Thomas. The railway strike was postponed, and terms for ending the coal strike were agreed to on October 28. The miners won their 2s. per shift increase immediately, to run, with temporary provision for further increases proportionate to total output pending a permanent settlement, until March 31, 1921, when the next crisis in the coal-mines punctually arrived.[1]

12. SOCIALISM BY THE BACK DOOR

Thus harmlessly did the acute industrial unrest which followed the war die away, without bringing about either the reconstruction of society or the nationalisation of industry. Yet two measures were enacted in 1919 and 1920 by parliament—the parliament in which the Conservatives were by far the largest party—whose effect, apparently quite unobserved by their authors and the public, was tremendously to enlarge the functions of the state in promoting the welfare of the people. The two measures were the Housing and Town Planning Act of 1919 and the Unemployment Insurance Act of 1920. Both aroused little or no opposition on points of principle in parliament. Both provoked no comment in Conservative periodicals such as the *Spectator* and the *Round Table*, or in the Fabian *New Statesman*, which revealed any understanding of their implications. The reasons are clear enough. There were ancient and modest precedents for both bills. The experiences of the war had prepared the country for them. And the immediate need for action which only the state seemed capable of swept aside all discussion of principle.

In housing, the government was committed to action by its campaign promises of 'homes fit for heroes', by the housing studies of the Ministry of Reconstruction, and by immediate needs. It was estimated that at least 800,000 houses were needed after the war, to provide for wartime arrears of new construction, the increase of population, the deterioration of more and more houses into the condition of those in the slums. How to provide them? Private builders could do little, it was argued, to provide houses for working people at rents which their tenants could afford while the costs of materials and labour were as high as they had become.

[1] G. D. H. Cole, *Labour in the Coal-Mining Industry*, pp. 122–9, 140–61; W. A. Orton, *Labour in Transition*, pp. 223–8; R. P. Arnot, *The Miners*, pp. 236–75.

The state could not itself go into the business of building houses. Therefore, let the local authorities be entrusted with the task, spurred on by carrot and stick: the carrot of government subsidies, the stick of the government's reserve powers of compulsion.

This was the essence of the government's Housing Bill of 1919, usually known as the Addison Act after Dr. Christopher Addison, its author and the first Minister of Health. It had two novel features. It required the local authorities to survey the housing needs of their districts and to prepare and carry out schemes accordingly. And it offered national subsidies to aid the local authorities in the building of houses called for by their schemes. Under the Addison Act the subsidy took the form of a guarantee of payment for the annual loss incurred on municipal schemes beyond that covered by a penny rate, the houses being let at uneconomic rents fixed by the local authority and the Ministry of Health. A second act of 1919 provided a capital subsidy of £260 for any house within certain dimensions built by private enterprise, whether for rent or sale. Both types of subsidy proved very costly, as building costs rose sharply in the period of inflation. In March 1921 tenders for building parlour-type houses averaged £838; by January 1923, this had fallen to £371. As a result of the economy campaign of 1921, the number of grants under the Addison Acts was limited, and Dr. Addison left the ministry; in 1922 new grants under the acts ceased, and subsequent government subsidies took different forms. Some 213,800 houses were built in England and Wales under the acts.[1]

From the Addison Act flowed three consequences. It carried the government into the business of housing. Later acts carried it further. The building of houses with the aid of government subsidies was one of the largest enterprises—certainly the largest collective enterprise—of the years between the wars. It meant that the new Ministry of Health was in large part a ministry of housing, and as such one of the most important departments of state. It helped to cover the outskirts of towns with municipal housing

[1] Marian Bowley, *Housing and the State, 1919–44* (London, 1945), pp. 15–33, 271; R. L. Reiss, *Municipal and Private Enterprise Housing* (London, 1945), pp. 14, 32–3, 61; A. C. Pigou, *Aspects of British Economic History, 1918–25*, pp. 88–94; G. D. H. and M. Cole, *Rents Rings and Houses* (London, 1923), pp. 47–55, 91. From March, 1919 to March, 1923, 171,003 houses were built in Great Britain by local authorities with state assistance; 45,857 were built by private enterprise with state assistance; and some 53,800 working-class houses were built by private enterprise alone. In 1921, the peak year, the corresponding figures in the first two categories were 86,579 and 21,577. *Statistical Abstract of U.K., 1930*, p. 43.
Dr. Addison left the Ministry of Health in April, 1921, and was minister without portfolio until July, when he resigned from the government.

estates and to embellish the villages with the ubiquitous 'council houses' of the interwar years, much criticised on aesthetic grounds, and insufficient in numbers for the need, but in general far better planned and equipped than the older houses for working-class families which they supplemented or replaced.

The Unemployment Insurance Act of 1920 had an equally easy passage. There was, however, one difference: it was taken for granted in the debates in parliament over the bill that men and women ought to be protected against the effects of involuntary unemployment; but the argument of need was less strong since at the moment, while the boom lasted, there was no serious problem of unemployment. There was, however, a sufficiency of precedents. The National Insurance Act of 1911 had provided unemployment insurance for workers in three industries in which employment fluctuated seasonally, engineering, building, shipbuilding. During the war this protection had been extended to munitions workers at large. When the war ended, the 'out-of-work' donation had been provided by the government for ex-servicemen and civilian workers alike who were displaced from employment by demobilisation and the end of war production. This was a non-contributory payment, pointing two fingers to the future: one, the inclusion of nearly all wage-earners; second, the provision of additional payments for dependants—the principle of family allowances. Ex-service men were entitled to benefits for 39 (ultimately 50) weeks, civilians for 26 weeks. When the scheme ended (for civilians on November 24, 1919), no substitute was provided. Hence the demand, now backed by respectable precedent, for a permanent scheme; for example, the National Industrial Conference recommended that unemployment insurance be made universal.

The bill introduced by Sir Robert Horne, Minister of Labour, was for these reasons accepted with little demur. It provided, in return for weekly contributions from employers and employed, weekly benefit payments of 15s. for a man, 12s. for a woman (but with no allowances for dependants), for fifteen weeks in any one year after twelve contributions had been made, provided the unemployed person registered at a labour exchange and was capable of work. It brought the number of insured persons to over eleven millions—nearly everyone, in fact, earning below £250 a year with the exception of domestic servants, agricultural labourers, and civil servants. The criticism of Labour members was confined to the contributory features of the scheme, and the low rates of benefit.

The Act had large consequences hardly to be foreseen. By providing aid for the unemployed from the state in the form of
something like 'outdoor relief', it carried further the process of
breaking-up and ending the Poor Law recommended (though with
variations of emphasis) by the majority and minority reports of
the great Royal Commission on the Poor Laws of 1905–9 and
begun by the health and unemployment provisions of the National
Insurance Act of 1911. It did not itself provide for family allowances, but they followed soon afterwards. It did not provide for
non-contributory benefits; indeed, one reason why the bill was
accepted so easily was that it was based on the beguiling principle
of insurance. Yet the modest insurance scheme of 1911 was
extended by it into a vast, uncharted area at a time when there
had been no recent experience of large-scale unemployment and
when the conditions of the boom seemed to promise that no such
event would occur. Thus the Act owed as much to an accident of
timing as to prewar precedent and war-born ideas of a new society.
The onset of heavy and continuous unemployment in 1921
swamped the new scheme, and wrecked its solvency, piling an
'ever-changing mass of doles' on top of the system of insurance.[1]
For once the principle of state aid to protect the unemployed
workers from the consequences of industrial fluctuations was
accepted, the state's aid could not be withdrawn just because it was
irreconcilable with a system of insurance; payments which were
not covered by previous contributions would be expected and
would be granted.

13. THE PARIS PEACE CONFERENCE

All this while, the attention of Lloyd George and the government, and that of the public, was taken up with matters of war and
peace: the peace conference at Paris and the sequels to it, and the
troubles in Ireland. In foreign policy as in domestic there was
hesitation between old policies and new, between going backwards or forwards. There was, however, little choice. The war
had changed the map of Europe. The old empires, the Ottoman,
the Austrian, the Russian, were gone. New nation-states had
appeared. During the coupon election campaign the talk might
be about hanging the Kaiser and making Germany pay. The real
issues were different: how to rebuild a peaceful world, substituting

[1] R. C. Davison, *Unemployed: old policies and new* (London, 1929), pp. 80–107;
W. H. Wickwar, *Social Services* (London, 1936), pp. 182 ff.; H. F. Hohman, *Development of Social Insurance and Minimum Wage Legislation in Great Britain* (Boston,
1933), pp. 227–34.

the security of a collective will to peace for the security of arms and military alliances. There was the opportunity for a new beginning, not least because of the intervention of the United States in the affairs of Europe. The experiment failed, and in the thirties the divisions between the major powers in Europe were sadly reminiscent of the old order of 1913. The failure began in Paris in 1919.

The peace conference assembled at Paris by January 12, 1919, and was formally opened on January 18. It thus took place much sooner after hostilities had ended than was the case after the Second World War, though part of the work of the conference in 1919, the creation of the League of Nations, was repeated in the San Francisco conference in 1945, while war was still continuing. The conference in 1919 was a conference of victors, at which the main treaty of peace with Germany, the Treaty of Versailles, was worked out and presented to the German delegates for their signature; the treaty contained the covenant of the League, and the territorial and other arrangements demanded of Germany. Subsidiary treaties with the other defeated powers finished the work. In these treaties the map of Europe was re-drawn with regard to national groupings, strategic frontiers, and economic factors; the 'succession states' the heirs of the old empires, were accepted; the principle of 'self-determination' was expressed in practice.

Never was a conference so carefully prepared for—the large and able staffs of experts, the British at the Hotel Majestic, the American, with its large contingent of professors, at the Crillon. All that was lacking in either of these delegations was a single, clear, complete plan-of-action—only the French had that. The work of the conference was largely done in commissions and committees, many of which overlapped in functions and worked in ignorance of each others' decisions. Things moved slowly at first; after the beginning of April, when it was decided to bring the conference to an early conclusion, the work was speeded up until the pace became hectic: 'appalling dispersal of energy', inconsequence, and finally sheer exhaustion succeeded one another, and the conference ended as a 'study in fog'. Paris at the time was not a city to correct this: a city of jangled nerves, still frayed from the anguish and anxieties of war, drugging itself with the brittle entertainments of the dance bands and the ballrooms: all 'shrank to the glitter of a limousine flashing reflected in the gyrations of a hotel doorway.'[1] The Paris press, with its cynicism and its malicious ridicule of personalities, only made things worse.

[1] Harold Nicolson, *Peacemaking, 1919* (New York, 1933: also London, 1933), p. 77 and *passim*.

The effect of these conditions was, however, reduced by the fact that the main decisions of the conference were made by a few men. A council of ten, consisting of two representatives each from Great Britain, France, the United States, Italy and Japan, was created, but latterly most of the work was done by the council of four and, even more, by the Big Three (Wilson, Clemenceau, Lloyd George) after the withdrawal of the Italian premier, Orlando. The British Empire delegation consisted of Lloyd George, Balfour, Bonar Law, G. N. Barnes, and one or other of the members of the panel of Dominion prime ministers. The Dominions also had small delegations of their own at the conference.

The influence of the British delegation at the conference was brought to bear on many issues. Wilson had made the idea of the League of Nations peculiarly his own, and his was the resolve to incorporate it as an integral part of the treaty. But the idea owed much to British opinion—from the Left, as expressed in the Union for Democratic Control, in the *New Statesman*, and in the Labour party's statement of 'War Aims' (1917), from the Right in the ideas of Lord Robert Cecil[1] and General Smuts: the latter's pamphlet, *The League of Nations, a practical suggestion* (1918) had much weight with Wilson.[2] In the conference's League of Nations Commission, it was an Anglo-American draft (Hurst-Miller) that was followed rather than the French proposals of Emile Bourgeois, and it was Cecil who was in the forefront of the struggle for the League as a free association of nations respecting the rule of law rather than as a military alliance of the victorious powers against Germany.

In the application of the mandates principle to the former German colonies, the British delegates won a partial victory, Wilson a greater one. The mandates idea was developed by various Labour writers and by the *Round Table*, and accepted by Wilson; that the well-being of the peoples of the colonies was a 'sacred trust of civilisation' which the League should assume, giving a mandate for the actual administration of particular colonies to certain countries (the mandatory powers), for which they would have to furnish annual reports to the League. Wilson had hoped that the mandatory powers would be small nations. Much of Germany's former colonial empire had, however, already

[1] Lord Robert Cecil, born 1864, third son of third Marquess of Salisbury. M.P., 1906–23; created Viscount Cecil of Chelwood, 1923; lord privy seal, 1923; chancellor of the Duchy of Lancaster, 1924–7; president of League of Nations Union, 1923–45.
[2] H. R. Winkler, *The League of Nations Movement in Great Britain, 1914–1919* (New Brunswick, N.J., 1952).

been appropriated by its liberators—the South Africans in German South-west Africa, the Australians in New Guinea, the New Zealanders in Samoa; and Lloyd George, the father of the Imperial War Cabinet, had perforce to listen to the wishes of the Dominion prime ministers, and particularly the redoubtable 'Billy' Hughes, of Australia. At Paris, where the question was thrashed out very early, between January 23 and 30, the Dominions concerned eventually agreed to hold the territories they coveted— for reasons of security, so they said—as mandates, after Smuts had devised, and Wilson accepted, the category of the 'Class C Mandate' which might be administered as an integral part of the mandatory state. Even then, however, Hughes insisted on an immediate, official award of the mandate over New Guinea to Australia, and when Wilson asked him if Australia was prepared to 'defy the appeal of the whole civilised world' in the matter, Hughes replied, 'That's about it, Mr. President.'[1] The decision entailed giving the Japanese a Class C Mandate over the German islands in the Pacific north of the equator. However, the mandates principle was applied much more faithfully in the Class B mandates given to Great Britain over East Africa and part of the Cameroons, to France over the Cameroons and Togoland; the Class A mandate, a much looser one, was applied to parts of the former Turkish empire, Palestine, Syria, and, at first, Iraq.

At the centre of the conference's work was the question of maintaining the peace of Europe; disarmament, reparations, Germany's boundaries, the character of the League were all determined by the answers given. The French, obsessed by their suspicion of Germany, were even unwilling to see her heavily disarmed, because of the difficulties of inspection, and because of the danger of internal revolts; they proposed she be allowed a conscript army of 200,000, safeguarded by the continued military occupation of the Rhineland by the Allies, and by detaching the left bank of the Rhine from Germany. While Wilson was absent on his visit to the United States in February, Foch tried to get a preliminary treaty of peace prepared, covering the military provisions, including armaments, boundaries, reparations. On Wilson's return the plan was dropped; it would have involved the ratification of two treaties by the United States Senate, and would have weakened the force of the final treaty. In the end, Germany's army was limited to a volunteer force of 100,000, and the proposals for

---

[1] W. S. Churchill, *The Aftermath*, p. 153; Paul Birdsall, *Versailles Twenty Years After* (New York, 1941), p. 72.

general disarmament survived only as a preamble to the clauses of the treaty providing for Germany's disarmament.[1]

France's plans for security really turned not on the disarmament but on the dismemberment of Germany; a strong Poland, strong at Germany's expense, in the east; the detaching of the Rhineland in the west. It was Lloyd George who resisted the extreme claims advanced for Poland, which resulted, *inter alia*, in giving Danzig the status of a free city, neither German nor Polish, under the supervision of the League. When news of his stand was deliberately 'leaked' by the French to the press, he insisted that the Council of Ten be replaced by the Council of Four, and then withdrew for a day with a few of his advisers to Fontainebleau, where he drafted his memorandum, 'Some Considerations for the Peace Conference before they finally draft their Terms' (March 25),[2] urging a policy of moderation towards Germany, lest Bolshevism should gain strength and she be thrown into the arms of Russia. The crisis of the conference followed, in the first week of April, when Wilson (confined to bed by an attack of influenza) cabled for the *George Washington* to come from Brooklyn to Brest, ready to take him home should the imminent breakdown of the conference occur. The Rhineland, the Saar, and reparations were all involved; and in the background was the deterioration of the situation in central Europe: the Communist revolution of Bela Kun in Hungary, the Spartacist (Communist) revolts in Germany, the Bolshevist occupation of Odessa. Clemenceau's objectives regarding the Rhineland were two: that the left bank be detached from Germany as an autonomous republic; and that the occupation of the left bank and the four bridgeheads (as provided for under the Armistice terms) be continued indefinitely. It was Lloyd George, as much as Wilson, who defeated these ideas. France was offered and accepted three safeguards: the demilitarisation of the Rhineland, including the entire left bank, and a zone on the right bank extending fifty kilometres (thirty-one miles) eastward; the occupation of the left bank by the forces of the Allies for fifteen years; and a guarantee treaty of security entered into by the United States, Great Britain and France—in other words, a military alliance. By April 14 the crisis was over.

Meanwhile, the crucial question of reparations had also been

---

[1] 'In order to render possible the initiation of general limitation of the armaments of all nations Germany undertakes strictly to observe the military, naval, and air clauses which follow' (Preamble to Part V of Treaty of Versailles).

[2] Text in David Lloyd George, *Memoirs of the Peace Conference* (New Haven, 1939), I, 266–73. The British edition is *The Truth about the Peace Treaties* (London, 1938).

settled after a fashion. Both Lloyd George and Clemenceau were committed to extracting as much out of Germany as possible, the former by his election promises to make Germany pay the whole cost of the war, the latter by the desire not only to recover France's war costs, but to weaken Germany. Wilson had agreed, as a rider to the Allies' acceptance of his Fourteen Points of January 8, 1918, in the negotiation of the Armistice, that Germany was liable for compensation for damages inflicted on civilian property during the war. But how to compute the sum this would amount to, and what would be its relation, not only to the cost of the war, but to Germany's capacity to pay? The conference's expert commission on the subject grappled with these problems from the end of January. By April 1, the Big Three had agreed to two things: to set no figure for reparations in the treaty, but leave it to be decided by a Reparations Commission subsequently; and to include the cost of military pensions in the bill to be presented to Germany.

In spite of this Lloyd George was criticised at home and especially in Lord Northcliffe's newspapers *The Times* and the *Daily Mail* for excessive leniency. On April 8 he received a telegram, signed by 233 Conservative members of parliament marshalled by Kennedy Jones, M.P., Lord Northcliffe's principal associate, expressing anxiety over reports that the delegation, instead of presenting the country's bill for reparations in full, was discussing what amount could be exacted from Germany. Lloyd George returned to London and defended himself in the Commons on April 16. His speech included an attack on Lord Northcliffe, without naming him, as suffering from a 'disease of vanity', intensified by his being omitted from the delegation to the conference; and *The Times* was contemptuously dismissed as a 'threepenny edition of the *Daily Mail*.'[1]

The treaty was presented to the German delegates at a meeting of the entire conference on May 7. The strong German protest at the severity of the terms led Lloyd George to last-minute efforts to modify it, lest the German government should refuse to sign and chaos ensue. Over the disposition of Upper Silesia, which instead of being allotted to Poland was made the subject of a plebiscite (which ultimately left most of it to Germany), he was successful. After a change of government in Germany the final act was staged. In the Hall of Mirrors in the Palace of Versailles, on June 28, the German delegates, cowed and pale, signed the

[1] For Northcliffe's quarrel with Lloyd George, see *The History of The Times*, vol. IV, part i (London, 1952), pp. 385 ff.

Treaty of Versailles, followed by the Allied representatives. In the gardens outside the fountains played for the first time since the war.[1]

The peace, however, was still far from complete. The conference remained in being in Paris, until January 21, 1920, while treaties with the other defeated powers were negotiated. Meanwhile, in the United States, in spite of President Wilson's heroic campaign, and perhaps because of his subsequent illness, the Senate had failed to ratify the Treaty of Versailles. With reservations, particularly over the obligation of members of the League of Nations to preserve the territorial integrity of its members (Article X), the Republican majority in the Senate was willing to ratify the treaty; but for Wilson it was all or nothing, and he was able to prevent a two-thirds majority being obtained for ratification on these terms (the vote was 49 for and 35 against).

14. THE AFTERMATH: DIPLOMATIC AND MILITARY

What had the treaties accomplished? A new Europe had arisen from the old. Germany was disarmed and had lost some territory, but remained a solid and potentially powerful state at the very heart of Europe. Momentarily, France and Great Britain could dominate the scene, and on their unity the future peace depended. The League of Nations came into being: the Council first met in January 1920, the Assembly in November. It was without the United States—and Russia, and Germany. For the moment the powers did not use it to settle the unfinished business arising from the treaties; instead they continued the wartime practice of dip-

---

[1] *Note on the Paris Peace Conference and the Treaty of Versailles.* This account is based mainly on P. Birdsall, *Versailles twenty years after*; H. Nicolson, *Peacemaking, 1919*; R. B. Mowat, *History of European Diplomacy, 1914–1925* (London, 1927), pp. 136–88; David Lloyd George, *Memoirs of the Peace Conference*; Blanche E. C. Dugdale, *Arthur James Balfour* (New York, 1937), II, 193–215; R. B. McCallum, *Public Opinion and the Last Peace*, pp. 61–85; W. M. Jordan, *Great Britain, France, and the German Problem, 1919–1939* (London, 1943), pp. 13–44 and *passim*. A full-length account of the conference is H. W. V. Temperley (ed.), *History of the Peace Conference of Paris* (6 volumes: London, 1920–4).

The Treaty of Versailles. The main provisions were: (1) Covenant of the League of Nations; (2) Germany surrendered her colonies, Alsace-Lorraine, part of Posen (the Polish Corridor), Danzig, Memel, the Saar Basin and the Saar mines, Schleswig (subject to a plebiscite); (3) the left bank of the Rhine was demilitarised, and was to be occupied with the bridgeheads by the Allies for fifteen years, and a zone 50 kilometres (31 miles) deep on the right bank was demilitarised; (4) Germany was prohibited from having an air force, her naval forces were limited and her army limited to a volunteer force of 100,000; (5) Germany was made liable to reparations; her war-guilt was admitted (Article 231); her war criminals were to be tried; (6) Austria, Czechoslovakia and Poland were recognised.

Part of the German fleet was surrendered to the British, and was scuttled by the Germans near Scapa Flow on June 21, 1919.

lomacy by conference between the heads of governments—the old
'concert of Europe', but with prime ministers, not foreign secretaries and ambassadors in the principal roles.

This sort of diplomacy was peculiarly suited to Lloyd George's
genius; and he made full use of the tremendous prestige he then
enjoyed in Europe to give it scope in a series of conferences
(twenty-three in the three years 1920–22) which he initiated at the
pleasure-resorts of Europe and in which he attempted to advance
his policies and maintain the unity of the Allies. As the only
war leader of the great powers surviving in public life, and the
only representative of the 'Big Four' of the Paris conference
at the later conferences, he had a unique position, to which
were added the qualities and defects of his extraordinary personality.

The foundation of Lloyd George's foreign policy was conciliation, as advocated in his Fontainebleau memorandum. The war
was over, and a lasting peace would follow not from the dominance
of the victors, but from bringing back the defeated and the outcast into the comity of nations, in full friendship and in economic
well-being. To satisfy Germany of the justice of the peace, to win
back Russia by fair dealing—these were the ends; the means
(which themselves failed) tragically involved the estrangement of
France, for whom security preceded conciliation. This difference,
which fractured the victorious wartime coalition, is the fundamental fact of postwar international relations in Europe. It
clouded the discussion of almost every question of policy toward
Poland, of joint action regarding Turkey, of the problem of
Germany.

For both, the heart of Europe's problem was Germany, and
remained so until the Second World War took it from the hands
of politicians. Britain and France were at cross-purposes as to
means and ends: how strong might Germany become without
menacing them? The French had abandoned their hopes for the
Rhine frontier in return for the provisions in the peace treaty for
the occupation and demilitarisation of the Rhineland, and had
accepted the offer of treaties guaranteeing assistance against
German aggression from Great Britain and the United States. The
last, however, had broken in the hand; parliament ratified the
Anglo-French treaty, but the Senate rejected its twin, and both
treaties therefore lapsed. No Anglo-French treaty replaced this
until 1936. France was, therefore, left to grapple with the problem of security against Germany in other ways. One result was

the Little Entente with Czechoslovakia, Jugoslavia and Rumania, formed in 1921.[1]

The downfall of the Turkish empire had left the Allies with a host of problems. One group concerned the disposition of sundry parts of it in Asia Minor; Armenia, Syria, Palestine, Mesopotamia. Much of this had been partitioned by secret agreements during the war: Mesopotamia to Britain, Syria and Cilicia to France, under the Sykes-Picot agreement of May 16, 1916; a large area extending inland from the Aegean and Mediterranean coasts, including Adalia and Smyrna, to Italy under the treaty of London (April 26, 1915), and the St. Jean de Maurienne agreement of April 17, 1917. The other set of problems concerned the old question of the Straits and Constantinople. Possession of these had been promised to Russia in the Constantinople agreement of March 18, 1915, but this had been denounced by the Soviet government. After the armistice of Mudros (October 30, 1918) with Turkey, Allied forces had taken control of Constantinople, and, pending a decision, which was long delayed because of hopes that the United States would accept a mandate in the area, they remained there. Finally, at a meeting in London in February 1920, Lloyd George and Clemenceau agreed to leave the Sultan in Constantinople, partly at French urging, partly under pressure of the India Office, fearful of the effects of any affront to the Turks on the Moslem population of India.

Meanwhile, all these fine plans had been challenged by the Turks themselves. Under the leadership of an army officer, Mustapha Kemal, a congress at Sivas, in the interior of Anatolia, had formed the 'National Pact' in September 1919, forced the Sultan to call an election, and given place to a Grand National Assembly. In 1920 this established its seat at Angora (Ankara), where a government was organised which, in effect, superseded that at Constantinople. Early in these proceedings, on March 16, 1920, the Allies occupied Constantinople. Kemal, with the forces he had gathered together, then began his work as liberator of his country. He attacked French forces in Cilicia, and Italian forces in Konia, inland from Adalia; Italy then withrew her forces and gave up her claims to any part of the mainland of Asia Minor. In June 1920 Kemal's forces threatened British troops in the occupation zone on the Asiatic side of the Straits. To strengthen themselves,

---

[1] H. Nicolson, *Curzon*, pp. 192, 195–8; Arnold Wolfers, *Britain and France between Two Wars* (New York, 1940), pp. 11–20, 380–1; W. M. Jordan, *Great Britain, France and the German problem*, pp. 1–13, 38–9.

the Allies called on yet another party to the imbroglio, Greece, to launch a major offensive against Kemal. At the Paris peace conference Greece had advanced a claim to a share in the spoils of the Turkish empire, since numbers of her colonists lived on the Aegean coast, especially round Smyrna. With Lloyd George's encouragement the Greeks occupied Smyrna in May 1919 (though it had been previously allotted to Italy). This was partly a tribute to Lloyd George's friendship with Venizelos, the Greek premier, a statesman of great subtlety and charm. Greek forces advanced from Smyrna far into the interior of Anatolia; another Greek army landed in Eastern Thrace (in European Turkey) and occupied Adrianople.

With this encouragement, the Allies were able finally (as they thought) to make peace with Turkey, that is, with the Sultan and the government at Constantinople, and the Treaty of Sèvres was signed on August 10, 1920. Its principal terms had been agreed upon at a conference at San Remo in April at which the Allies had agreed to the internationalisation of the Straits, and to allotment of mandates over Syria to France, Palestine, and Iraq (Mesopotamia) to Great Britain. Under the terms of the treaty, Eastern Thrace, to within twelve miles of Constantinople, Gallipoli, the Aegean islands were ceded to Greece; Smyrna was to be administered by Greece for five years, and afterwards to decide its future by a plebiscite; the Straits and the Dardanelles were to be demilitarised and placed under international supervision. Alas for such plans! By November Venizelos had fallen from office, and events began to move towards the climax which consolidated Kemalist Turkey, widened the rift between Great Britain and France, and overthrew Lloyd George.[1]

By the end of 1920 one other ember of the war was extinguished —Allied intervention against Soviet Russia. When the Soviet government ceased the war against Germany in December 1917, Generals Kornilov and Denikin raised the counter-revolutionary standard on the Don; on November 4, 1918, the British war cabinet decided to help Denikin with arms and equipment. A second front against the Bolshevists was opened in the far north, at Murmansk and Archangel, in June 1918, when British forces landed to protect the stock of munitions previously sent there for the Czarist armies. A third front, in Siberia, became active in November 1918. British, American and Japanese troops had been sent to Vladivos-

---

[1] This account is based mainly on H. Nicolson, *Curzon*, chapters 3, 4, 9, and R. B. Mowat, *European Diplomacy*, pp. 202–4, 287–90.

tock during the summer to aid the Czechoslovak forces, formerly serving with the Czarist armies, whose return to their native land by the Trans-Siberian railway had been blocked by the Bolshevists; the Czechs had taken over most of the railway and its surrounding territory and set up a provisional government at Omsk. The forces on this front were commanded by Admiral Kolchak. In addition, at the end of the war the British occupied Batum and the Batum-Baku railway in the Caucasus, and the French occupied Odessa. The French withdrew in April, 1919 after their troops had been affected by Communist propaganda, and the British forces in the Caucasus were withdrawn a little later.

Early in 1919 intervention was at its height, by the end of the year it was almost over. Churchill, as Secretary of State for War, was its chief advocate, but the Allies would neither send adequate help to the White Russians nor make peace with the Bolshevists. Archangel and Vladivostock were evacuated late in 1919; Kolchak surrendered (and was soon afterwards murdered) in January 1920. The Crimea, the last refuge in the south, was overrun by the Bolshevists in July.

In 1920 the danger-zone was Poland. The Poles, with French encouragement, had invaded Russian territory in the spring of 1920, had occupied Kiev, and were supporting a nationalist government in the Ukraine to form a buffer between themselves and the Bolshevists. This offensive had already roused opposition in the ranks of British Labour, resulting in the *Jolly George* incident in May. In June the Bolshevists were strong enough to begin a counter-offensive; in July they invaded Poland. The Poles then besought the aid of the Allies. A war between the powers and Russia seemed unavoidable, in spite of Labour's 'Councils of Action'. General Weygand, who was already in Warsaw on an inter-allied mission, was ordered to help the Poles in their fight. Weygand was able to inspire them to counter-attack, and Warsaw was saved by the Polish victory in the battle of the Vistula (August 14, 1920)—Poland's 'miracle of the Marne'. Thereafter the Poles and Russians reached agreement in the Treaty of Riga. From this time the Bolshevist scare in England began to die down, though there was plenty of smoke, if not flame, in it for a long time to come.[1]

[1] Churchill's account of intervention in Russia is in his *Aftermath*, chapters 4, 5, 9, 12, 13; suggestions of the other side of the story in K. Zilliacus, *Mirror of the Past* (New York, 1946), pp. 263 ff. See also H. Nicolson, *Curzon*, pp. 202–8.

15. IRELAND: THE WAR OF THE I.R.A. AND THE BLACK AND TANS

All this while a country much nearer home had been writhing in the torments of war: Ireland. The coming of the European war in 1914 had postponed the decision which had then been imminent; between the Liberal government, committed to passing a Home Rule Bill and having the power, under the Parliament Act, to place it on the statute book over the Lords' veto, and the Tories, the party of conservatism and order, treating the English to the spectacle of open encouragement of rebellion in Ulster to prevent it taking effect. From the events of 1914 the Irish drew certain lessons: that the English could not be trusted to honour promises and observe constitutional methods towards them, and that force rather than peaceful persuasion would bring results. On the one hand this led to the decline of Redmond's Irish Nationalist party, pursuing Parnell's old programme of Home Rule, and the growth of Arthur Griffith's Sinn Fein party, with much more sweeping proposals; on the other, it led to the formation of the Irish Volunteers, in direct imitation of Carson's Ulster Volunteers. In 1916, the Volunteers and Sinn Fein came together in the Easter Rebellion in Dublin. Its failure was dismal—until the British government made it glorious by executing in cold blood fourteen of its leaders, and so consecrating with their blood the cause of the Republic they had proclaimed. Then, having arrested scores of the lesser leaders, and presented them with a fine training-ground in which to concert their plans, in the distillery in Frongoch, among the mists of Merioneth, in which they were interned, the government in a gesture of conciliation sent them home again to Ireland. The Irish Convention of 1917, summoned by Lloyd George to work out a solution, was a failure; Sinn Fein boycotted it, the Ulster representatives vetoed everything the other delegates agreed to. To crown these blunders, the government in 1918 decided to impose conscription, hitherto postponed, in Ireland; and arrested the principal Sinn Fein leaders in May on the pretext of their complicity in a mythical 'German plot'. The result was to throw the leadership of the nationalist movement into the hands of the extremists—men less known to the authorities, and so not arrested; while the threat of conscription (which the Armistice averted) brought to the movement hundreds of young men and at least the passive goodwill of their parents.[1]

[1] See Darrell Figgis, *Recollections of the Irish War* (London, 1927), chapter 9.

A new act in the drama opened with the Armistice. Once again the British government provided the opportunity: the coupon election in December, 1918. The election extended to Ireland: the coupon did not. The Sinn Fein party swept the board, electing 73 members (36 of whom were in prison) and winning every seat outside Ulster except four; the Unionists elected 26, the Home Rulers, heir to a great but now bankrupt tradition, six. The popular vote for the whole of Ireland was decisive against the perpetuation of the Union: of 1,526,910 votes the Unionists got only a fifth (315,394).[1] The Sinn Fein candidates had been carefully picked by the new, and extremist, executive; their success presaged the demand for the Republic, and the use of force, if necessary, to secure it.[2]

The victors in the election had pledged themselves not to take their seats in parliament at Westminster; instead they met in Dublin, in the Mansion House, as the self-constituted Irish parliament, Dail Eireann. On January 21, 1919, in proceedings conducted partly in Irish, they issued a declaration of independence, and ratified the establishment of Saorstat Eireann, the Irish Republic, proclaimed at Easter, 1916. This was followed by an appeal for recognition by the nations then assembled at the peace conference in Paris.[3] It was a gallant gesture, but not one from which most people would have predicted success for the cause. Yet within three years the Irish had brought the British Empire, then at the peak of its power after victory, almost to its knees, and had caused a government predominantly Tory to concede far more— though at a certain price—than Carson, 'Galloper Smith', and all the Ulster and Tory rebels of 1914 had fought so bitterly and, it had seemed, successfully to prevent. And by 1949, even the Republic was a reality.

Before seeing how these things could be, we must ask who were the Irish leaders who at this moment of history stood, all too briefly, united by the cradle of the republic. Four stand out: Michael Collins, Cathal Brugha, Eamon De Valera, Arthur Griffith. In these four were represented diverging points of view; the conjunctions and oppositions of the four affected the course of Irish destiny then and for long to come. In them, moreover, the three interlocking but distinct parts of the nationalist movement were represented: the Volunteers, Sinn Fein, and the Irish

[1] Dorothy Macardle, *Irish Republic* (London, 1937), p. 279.
[2] Darrell Figgis, *Recollections of the Irish War*, pp. 229–33.
[3] Dorothy Macardle, *Irish Republic*, pp. 284–8, 959–62.

Republican Brotherhood, the secret society which traced back to the Fenians of the 1860's.

Michael Collins was then adjutant of the Volunteers and director of their organisation and intelligence; he was also, unlike the other three, a member of the Brotherhood. Born near Clonakilty, County Cork, in 1890, he had worked in London as a bank clerk from 1906 until his return to Ireland shortly before the Easter rebellion. He was tall, wiry, fair-haired, broad featured, with humorous grey-blue eyes. An excellent organiser, he inspired devotion both in those around him and in those who knew him only by name. Some found him domineering, and even on occasion something of a bully, but his objurgations and swearing were reserved chiefly for those he knew best. He had at first little interest in politics. 'There were two Micks . . . the jolly, gasconading, hard-swearing good fellow; the other, a dour, quiet man who lived with his life in his hand, heroic, dignified, a thinker, a fighter, a mystery.'[1] He was the principal architect of the victory over England on the military side; his decision to support the treaty made possible the Free State and was paid for with his life.

Even more of a fighter, but with less power of organisation and no spirit of compromise was Cathal Brugha, Collins' bitter opponent within the movement. It is typical of him that while many of the other leaders sometimes used the Irish form of their names, he alone is known by his, and not by his baptismal name, Charles Burgess. 'A little russet-haired man with piercing eyes of blue', he is described; Cosgrave said of him 'except for war he is not worth a damn for anything else'. He was the fighter, bearing the marks of seventeen wounds about his body. He believed passionately in the Republic, and for it he died when the Free State was born. He was president of the Dail in January 1919, when the declaration of independence was made; in the executive or 'cabinet' of the Dail he was Minister of Defence.[2]

In complete contrast with these two was Eamon De Valera, the only one of the four to survive the time of troubles and to dominate Irish politics until after the Republic was formally inaugurated in

[1] Desmond Ryan, *Remembering Sion* (London, 1934), p. 229, also pp. 231–8, the best sketch of Collins. The best life is Frank O'Connor, *Death in Dublin: Michael Collins and the Irish Revolution* (New York, 1937; English edition: *The Big Fellow*); the most detailed account of his times is Piàras Beaslai (Beasley), *Michael Collins and the Making of a New Ireland* (two vols., London, 1926). See also Batt O'Connor, *With Michael Collins in the Fight for Irish Independence* (London, 1929), and P. S. O'Hegarty, *Victory of Sinn Fein* (Dublin, 1924), pp. 23–7, 44, 136–40.
[2] D. Ryan, *Remembering Sion*, pp. 229–30; cf. F. O'Connor, *Death in Dublin*, p. 43 and pp. 62, 70–1, 79, 137, 143; D. Figgis, *Recollections*, pp. 46, 220, 240.

1949. He was born in 1882 in New York, of a Spanish father and Irish mother, and raised on his uncle's farm in Bruree, County Limerick. This young professor of mathematics and physics who dabbled in the study of the Irish language and attended the early parades of the Volunteers in his strange deerstalker's cap, this angular, pedantic recluse, had been the most successful of the Brigade leaders in the Easter Rebellion, and had been spared from execution only because of an American citizenship he disavowed. In person he was alert, tall, spare, with dark hair and rather sharp features; in manner he was austere, dignified, courteous. Leadership had been thrust upon him by his fellow-prisoners in Lewes jail, after the Rebellion, and on his return to Ireland in 1917 he had been elected president of Sinn Fein, largely as a compromise between two factions. He was among those arrested in 1918 in connection with the 'German plot', but Collins engineered his escape from Lincoln jail in 1919. On his return to Dublin he was elected president of the Dail (succeeding Brugha), and immediately left on a mission to the United States. He, too, was a believer in the Republic, but within limits—unfortunately obscured by his almost Jesuitical twists of argument—he was ready to compromise form for reality. He tried to mediate between Collins and Brugha, only making their disagreement worse; subsequently Collins drew away from him, and was drawn instead to the fourth member of the quadrumvirate, with whom at first sight he had least affinity.[1]

This was Arthur Griffith, the founder of the Sinn Fein party. He was a journalist, whose whole life proved that the pen is mightier than the sword, though at times needing the sword's help. Unimpressive in appearance, small though strong, gazing out at the world through thick glasses, he derived his power from clarity of mind and, above all, from his granite-like strength of character. His policies were reflected in the principles of his party; its name meant 'we ourselves', but the independence it sought was to be obtained by peaceful rather than violent means; its object was freedom for Ireland to develop in its own way, including economic and cultural freedom. As far back as 1904 he had drawn up the campaign for Ireland's liberation in his book, the *Resurrection of Hungary*, in which Hungary's winning of freedom

[1] For De Valera see Desmond Ryan, *Unique Dictator: a study of Eamon De Valera* (London, 1936); also Denis Gwynn, *De Valera* (London, 1932), which is critical of him, and M. J. MacManus, *Eamon de Valera* (Chicago, 1946; Dublin, 1947). See also F. O'Connor, *Death in Dublin*, especially pp. 39, 64, 76, 164, and P. S. O'Hegarty, *Victory of Sinn Fein*, pp. 18–21, 148–54.

from Austria under the dual monarchy was pointed to as the way which Ireland must follow; independence within the British Empire was thus, to him at least, a half-way house to the ultimate destination. In the Dail cabinet in 1919 he was Minister of Home Affairs; after De Valera's departure for the United States the real headship of government rested, on the political side, with him, as in the military field it belonged to Collins.[1]

Having proclaimed Ireland's independence, the Dail now had to win it. 1919 was principally a year of preparation. In Paris, Ireland's efforts to win recognition came to nothing. In the United States the Irish Race Convention in Philadelphia sent a committee of three to Paris to assist the Irish cause; the committee visited Ireland *en route*, and on their return to the United States published a lurid account of British terrorism, which was read into the *Congressional Record*.[2]

De Valera's visit to the United States in 1919 was a great personal triumph. He got involved, however, in the factions of Irish-American politics, linked as they then were with the manœuvres preceding the nominating conventions for the coming presidential election and with the opposition to the League of Nations. The Irish organisations in the United States were split in two, and De Valera and one of the leaders, Judge Daniel F. Cohalan, parted after an exchange of letters that were sharp-spoken in the extreme. De Valera's offence was that, in his cele-brated 'Cuba' interview (February 6, 1920) he had suggested that Britain, if it recognised Ireland's independence, might then safe-guard its position by a treaty with Ireland, as the United States had done with Cuba; while Judge Cohalan was anticipating a war between Britain and the United States (over the freedom of the seas) in which case Ireland, under De Valera's policy, would presumably side with Great Britain. It is hard not to agree with Desmond Ryan that some of the Irish Americans hated Britain far more than they loved Ireland, and resented the fact that direction

---

[1] See D. Figgis, *Recollections*, especially pp. 253–9; F. O'Connor, *Death in Dublin*, pp. 17–18, 42, 59, 82; P. S. O'Hegarty, *Victory of Sinn Fein*, pp. 45–8; 127–35.

[2] *Congressional Record*, vol. 58, part 5,. pp. 4650–714 (60th Congress, 1st Session: 1919) are taken up with the report of a hearing before the Senate Foreign Relations Committee on August 30, 1919, on the subject of Ireland's independence. In addition to speeches by Judge Cohalan and others, the Irish declaration of independence is reproduced, and also letters from the 'American Commission on Irish Independence' to King George V, Lloyd George, Bonar Law, Wilson, Clemenceau, and many other public figures. The 'Report on Conditions in Ireland' occupies pp. 4678–81. The bitterness of the attack of the American professional Irish against Britain at this time, ranging over all history, and far beyond the Irish question, has to be read to be believed. It was, of course, bound up with the opposition to the League of Nations.

of Ireland's fight against Britain had slipped from American to native Irish hands. Americans did, however, contribute five million dollars for the Irish National Loan.[1]

At home, Michael Collins and Arthur Griffith were hard at work. The Dail cabinet functioned, not without a certain amount of play-acting by the 'ministers', but still with the framework of a government. Collins, as Minister of Finance, was responsible for raising secretly a loan of £379,000 in Ireland. Arms were smuggled in in cross-channel steamers from Liverpool and Glasgow, and crude grenades and mortars manufactured in the cellar of a bicycle shop in Dublin and in other 'factories'. The Volunteers, after holding a special convention in the spring of 1919, agreed to become the army of the republic, and were henceforth known as the Irish Republican Army (I.R.A.); in effect, the I.R.A. was not much subject to the Dail and to the ministry. Richard Mulcahy was its chief of staff. Collins built up its organisation; brigades were formed in districts across the whole country,[2] with friendly railwaymen and post-office employees serving as links in the communications system. Collins' famed intelligence service owed much of its success to friends in the Dublin police and especially its 'G' squad, who would telephone to tip him off when a raid was imminent, and to agents in the post office, the customs service, and even in government offices in London. One night one of the G men took Collins into the squad's office, where he spent several profitable hours looking through its files. Later, E. J. Duggan, a lawyer, was the actual Director of Intelligence for the I.R.A.

It was at this time that Collins arranged the most sensational of the prison escapes for which he was responsible. Collins himself went to Lincoln to supervise the escape of De Valera and two others from Lincoln jail on February 3. All the elements of melodrama were here: wax impressions of the priest's key smuggled out of the prison, keys smuggled in inside cakes sent to prisoners; in the end complete success was achieved. Elsewhere, four men escaped from the jail at Usk with the help of a ladder fashioned of sheets and faggots. Twenty men got out of the gloomy Mountjoy prison ('the Joy') in Dublin in broad daylight, with the help of a rope

[1] D. Ryan, *Unique Dictator*, p. 102 *seq.*; D. Gwynn, *De Valera*, pp. 79–114; P. Beasley, *Michael Collins*, II, 1–22; D. Figgis, *Recollections*, pp. 248–51; D. Macardle, *Irish Republic*, pp. 289–93, 307–12, 380–5; Patrick McCartan, *With De Valera in America* (New York and Dublin, 1932).
[2] For this subject, see Ernie O'Malley, *Army without Banners: Adventures of an Irish Volunteer* (Boston, 1937; English edition: *On Another Man's Wound*).

ladder thrown from outside over the wall of the exercise yard at a prearranged time when prisoners were exercising. In October six men got out of Strangeways Jail, Manchester, by similar methods, the arrangements being made by code letters and by messages sent in cakes, pots of jam, packages of butter, or simply in the palm of the hand. Which was the more remarkable, the ingenuity of the Irish or the inefficiency of the prison authorities, one is hard put to it to decide.

Meanwhile, Collins led a charmed life in Dublin. Like many of the other leaders, he was for months on end 'on the run'. When men knew that there were orders for their arrest, they would go underground, or in the much more expressive Irish term, 'go upon their own keeping'. Collins' best protection was that for long the police had no photograph of him and he had no specially distinguishing features to aid identification. Bicycles, easily borrowed and as easily jettisoned, served best for locomotion; and if a house was raided, the back door and a leap over the yard wall into a back alley, usually unguarded, provided a frequent means of escape. Meetings of henchmen were often held in Vaughan's Hotel, and if a raid occurred there or elsewhere one could escape through a skylight, walk along the roofs of one of Dublin's terraces, enter another house by skylight, and emerge unconcernedly from a front door some distance from the scene of the raid. Batt O'Connor (who has written a sketch of him) was a builder, and fitted up several houses for Collins and his friends to use as offices: secret cupboards into which papers could be hastily dropped, warning bells, secret escape doors, even secret rooms entered through an innocent-seeming wardrobe, were installed at need.[1]

Slowly, war broke out between the British government and the I.R.A. In the I.R.A. weekly paper, *An t'Oglach*, methods of attack, use of dynamite and the like were described; an editorial on January 31, 1919, declared that a state of war existed, and murder and violence against the English were no crimes until the alien invaders had evacuated the country. There were several isolated episodes: 'executions' of police detectives, caught off guard and shot by gunmen in the street in broad daylight; a few ambushes, a few attacks on police barracks in the country. One of the first incidents was on the day of the declaration of independence, January 21, 1919, when Dan Breen and his men ambushed an

---

[1] The best account of Collins' work and life in Dublin is in P. Beasley, *Michael Collins*, I, 194 *seq.*; cf. B. O'Connor, *With Michael Collins*, and F. O'Connor, *Death in Dublin*.

armed guard of police escorting a cart of gelignite at Solohead-beag, County Tipperary, and killed two policemen. One of the last in 1919 was on December 19, when an unsuccessful attempt was made to ambush Lord French, the Lord Lieutenant, and his party at Ashtown Cross, on the outskirts of Dublin, on the way to the Vice-Regal Lodge. The most successful weapon in 1919 was the boycott, employed against members of the Royal Irish Constabulary (R.I.C.) and their families. This body had always been more than a police force; it was armed, unlike the police in Great Britain, and many of the men were quartered in barracks dotted about the country. A policy of ostracism, including the refusal to sell food to members, demoralised the force far more than a few murders or the threat of more; the men were mostly Irish and resigned in large numbers, and no new recruits came forward. Winston Churchill states that there were 1,500 political offences, including 18 murders and 77 armed attacks, during the latter half of 1919,[1]—a gadfly to a horse, perhaps, but suggestive that British rule was beginning to break down. The government must decide on some policy, and enforce it.[2]

The government decided on war—not openly, but in a manner consistent with the Irish tactics of raids and murders. It would not admit it was a war, or even a rebellion which would have some status in the outside world; but war it was, and nothing is served by calling it anything else. In August Sinn Fein was 'proclaimed' by the British government (i.e. declared illegal), and in September the Dail. On March 23, 1920, General Sir Nevil Macready was called away from his job as Commissioner of the Metropolitan Police and appointed commander-in-chief of the British forces in Ireland. A little later a new Chief Secretary for Ireland was brought into the Cabinet, Sir Hamar Greenwood,[3] a Canadian by birth who had been in parliament as a Liberal since 1906. He had served in the army and at the War Office during the war, and had the reputation of being a 'strong man', tough-minded. Steps were also taken to revitalise the R.I.C. Recruits were sought, by advertisements in England, mainly among ex-soldiers. By the summer of 1920 many of these reinforcements for the R.I.C. were arriving—the notorious Black and Tans, so named after a well-known pack of hounds in County Limerick, because in the absence

[1] W. S. Churchill, *Aftermath*, p. 297.
[2] P. Beasley, *Michael Collins*, I, 319–38, 375–91.
[3] Hamar Greenwood (1870–1948), born in Whitby, Ontario, son of a barrister. Barrister in Australia and in New Brunswick. M.P. (Liberal), 1906–22, (Conservative) 1924–29. Chairman of Dorman Long and Company, Ltd. Created viscount, 1937.

of sufficient R.I.C. uniforms they were given surplus khaki uniforms with the black belts and dark-green caps of the R.I.C. They were paid ten shillings per day. In addition, another force, the Auxiliary Division of the R.I.C., numbering 1,000, was recruited in England from among ex-officers; they received a pound a day. They were often referred to as the cadets or the 'Auxis'. They had a distinctive dark-blue uniform and wore Glengarry caps. While the Irish used the term Black and Tans, or Tans, indiscriminately for all armed police forces in Ireland, the term originally had the restricted meaning just given. A British officer, Major-General Henry Tudor, was appointed Police Adviser to the R.I.C. in May and Brigadier-General F. P. Crozier commandant of the Auxis. Thus did the British government equip itself to fight down Irish aspirations, by all means, fair and foul. This is the greatest blot on the record of the Coalition, and perhaps upon Britain's name in the twentieth century, just as the later settlement was among the best of Lloyd George's achievements. For the means used were bound to defeat themselves, and to yield in time to methods of negotiation and compromise.

Why was the decision taken? The Tories were strong in the Cabinet, including some who had supported the Ulster Volunteers in 1912–14—Lord Birkenhead, Walter Long, Bonar Law; Churchill was not one for half-measures; and the influence of Sir Edward Carson,[1] the grim Dubliner who had organised the Ulster Volunteers and who spared none in the threatening language in which he defended the Union, was potent in the Cabinet, and in the seat of administration in Ireland, Dublin Castle (or the Castle), long reputed to be under the influence of his Ulster Unionist Council. As early as December 1, 1919, *The Times* charged that there was a powerful conspiracy against the prospect of peace in Ireland, and alluded to groups who were 'using' the Irish Executive to arouse a state of rebellion in which a settlement would be impossible. There can be no doubt, also, that Lloyd George was, at the moment, inclined to the use of force, attracted as he was to that clear-headed and persuasive strategist who was his favourite military adviser, General Sir Henry Wilson, the postwar Chief of the Imperial General Staff. An Irishman by birth, Sir Henry had been meddling in politics, on behalf of Ulster, in

[1] Edward Henry Carson (1854–1935), born in Dublin, son of civil engineer. Member of Irish bar. Solicitor-general for Ireland, 1892. M.P., 1892–1921. Called to the English bar, 1893. Solicitor-general, 1896–1905. Leader of the Ulster Unionist Council, 1911, and organiser of resistance to Home Rule. Attorney-general, 1915. First lord of the Admiralty, 1916–January, 1918. Lord of appeal, 1921–29.

D

almost treasonable insubordination to his superiors, even in 1914; the 'greatest political soldier of our day and . . . the greatest mischief-maker and political claptrapper the British army has ever possessed', as General Crozier calls him, not without some justice.[1] He had been prominent in urging Lloyd George to impose conscription on Ireland in 1918, as a war and a peace measure; they were both prepared for rebellion, and his diary (May 7, 1918), referring to Lord French (Sir John French,) who had just been made Lord Lieutenant, says that Lloyd George 'impressed on Johnnie the wisdom of putting the onus for first shooting on the rebels'.[2] The 'rebels' had obliged.

The year 1920 was the year of decision in Ireland—the military decision, at least, just as 1921 was the year in which political strategy resumed the upper hand. The war may be said to have begun on the night before Easter Sunday, April 4, the anniversary of the Easter rebellion, when the I.R.A. raided the income tax offices in Dublin and throughout the country, destroying all records and paralysing the government's tax-gathering machinery, and burned 315 R.I.C. barracks, previously evacuated, destroying the blockhouses for any British counter-offensive.

In the war which followed there were no front lines and, on the Irish side, no uniforms or standardised weapons. It was guerrilla warfare; shootings of individuals from behind hedges or at street corners; ambushes of police convoys by the 'flying squads' of the I.R.A. on narrow country roads; the blocking of roads by felled trees, farm carts, or the digging of holes; midnight raids on houses by the police in search of suspects; kidnappings and holding of hostages; bloodhounds in pursuit of Irish leaders 'on the run', torturings of Irish prisoners by British officers; hunger-strikes by Irish prisoners; curfew at night in Dublin and Cork, where police and rebels walked silently in gum-shoes, and military vans and armoured cars rumbled through the darkened streets; Black and Tan parties roaring into quiet villages at night in their lorries, with searchlights blazing, to turn out the occupants of a few poor cottages and set the buildings afire.

All the time normal life went on: shops were open, trains were running, race meetings were held without interference, by a tacit gentlemen's agreement. Much of Ireland was peaceful throughout the struggle; it was in the south-west, in the counties of Cork,

---

[1] F. P. Crozier, *Ireland for Ever* (London, 1932), pp. 83, 172.
[2] General Sir C. E. Callwell, *Field-Marshal Sir Henry Wilson, His Life and Diaries* (two vols., London, 1927), II, 98.

Kerry and Limerick, that disorder was greatest, and in the cities of Cork and Dublin. The majority of the people, if not ardent supporters of the I.R.A., at least gave no comfort to the Black and Tans; through inclination, fear of I.R.A. 'justice', sympathy with Irish boys under pursuit, or disgust at the Tans, they obstructed all the operations of the British and aided those of the Irish forces; murderers escaped without hindrance in broad daylight, armed men were concealed in cellars or closets, juries would never convict fellow-Irishmen of crimes of violence.

The numbers engaged in the war were estimated as variously as are the incidents of the war. General Macready put the total British forces in Ireland in 1920, military and police, at about 40,000; Irish sources claim that there were 50,000 troops and 15,000 police on the British side. The I.R.A. is said to have numbered about 15,000 men, including 1200 in the Dublin Brigade; it is claimed that there were never more than 5000 men on active service at one time.[1]

The activities of the I.R.A. consisted mainly of ambushes, attacks on police barracks, raids upon the mails, kidnappings and murders. A few examples will suffice. On March 26 an elderly Englishman, Alan Bell, was taken off a tramcar in Dublin while on his way to work and shot dead in the street; with a long experience in intelligence work, Bell had been brought to Dublin to make inquiries through the banks concerning the Dail's finances. On July 17, armed men forced their way into the Country Club, Cork, at 10.30 p.m., and murdered Colonel G. F. Smyth, Divisional Commissioner of the R.I.C., in the smoking room.[2] On 'bloody Sunday', November 21, 1920, at nine in the morning, members of the I.R.A. broke into fourteen houses and hotels scattered throughout Dublin and hauled from their beds and shot, in some cases in the presence of their wives, fourteen British officers and civilians. The most notorious ambush occurred on November 28. A party of seventeen Auxis travelling in lorries along the Dunmanway–Macroom road were decoyed by an I.R.A. man in a British soldier's uniform into an ambush where they were set upon by twenty-seven members of the Cork Number 3 Brigade; all seven-

---

[1] D. Macardle, *Irish Republic*, p. 358; General Sir Nevil Macready, *Annals of an Active Life*, II, 533.

[2] For the provocation, Smyth's orders to his men ('. . . The more you shoot, the better I will like you. . . .') see F. P. Crozier, *Ireland for Ever*, pp. 286–7; 'I.O.' (C. J. C. Street), *Administration of Ireland, 1920* (London, 1921), pp. 218–19; *The Times*, July 30, 1920 (Smyth's own report of his speech, circulated by Greenwood).

teen of the victims of the Kilmichael ambush were left for dead, though one survived to tell the tale.[1]

These and innumerable other incidents were brutal and horrifying enough, even when inspired by revenge, or to silence spies and informers. Why, then, was reprobation principally reserved, not only in Ireland but in England, for the activities of the British forces—the Black and Tans and the Auxis, rather than the military —and not for the I.R.A. ? Both then and later the Irish presented their side of the war much better than the British; the number of accounts published over the years in reminiscences and biographies of Irish fighters has no counterpart on the British side, and at the time Irish papers, like the *Irish Bulletin*, were able to remain in publication and present their version of affairs in vivid terms. British newspapers presented their readers with accounts similarly favourable to the Irish, written by English journalists. The truth would seem to be that the facts, unadorned, were bad enough to discredit both sides, but that sympathy tended to go to the Irish, partly as the underdog in the struggle, partly because of a feeling that it was not for the British government, the custodian of the law, to sully its hands with the terroristic methods of insurgents.

The Black and Tans were accused by the Irish, not only of executions of prisoners and the shooting of prisoners on the fiction that they were trying to escape, but also of cold-blooded murders and random killings of civilians on the streets or in houses when raids were made. A few instances must suffice. In the early hours of March 20, Thomas MacCurtain, Lord Mayor of Cork and commandant of the Cork Brigade of the I.R.A., was shot dead by men with blackened faces who entered his house and called 'Come out, Curtain'. The coroner's jury charged wilful murder against the R.I.C., Lloyd George, Lord French, and others. British writers have ascribed the murder to MacCurtain's fellow-Irishmen, who distrusted him, it is said, as a moderate.[2] At Fermoy one evening the Black and Tans invaded a public house and took out Captain Prendergast, a British ex-officer who lived in the town, dragged him to the river and threw him in, where he

[1] For examples of I.R.A. activities, see 'I.O.' (C. J. C. Street), *Administration of Ireland, 1920*, a very full and careful account of the events of 1920, from the government's side; also P. Beasley, *Michael Collins*, I, 375 ff., II, 23 ff., and E. O'Malley, *Army without Banners*. An account of 'bloody Sunday' by a member of one of the I.R.A. parties is Charles Dalton, *With the Dublin Brigade* (London, 1929), p. 102 *seq.*; cf. I.O., *Administration of Ireland*, pp. 149–57.

[2] D. Macardle, *Irish Republic*, p. 348; N. Macready, *Annals*, II, 442–3; *The Times*, March 22, 29, 1920; 'I.O.', *Administration of Ireland*, pp. 79–80. W. Alison Phillips, *Revolution in Ireland, 1906–1923* (second edition, London, 1926), pp. 175, 313–15, argues weightily for this, though unable to divulge his sources.

drowned. On the night of November 16, 1920, four youths under arrest were shot dead by the Black and Tans on the bridge over the Shannon at Killaloe, on the pretext that they were 'attempting to escape'.[1] Collins' intelligence claimed to have uncovered evidence of a deliberate 'murder plot,' by British secret service men, and the murders on 'bloody Sunday' were carried out to nip it in the bud.[2]

Estimates of casualties in such a war are inevitably fragmentary and conflicting. An Irish source gives the total Irish losses from January 1919 to the truce in July 1921 as 752 persons killed (both civilians and I.R.A. men) and 866 wounded. British losses for 1920 are given by another authority as 176 police and 54 soldiers killed, 251 police and 118 soldiers wounded.[3]

There were also several cases in which towns and villages were raided and 'sacked'; one account lists eighteen.[4] These were cases of deliberate, though unofficial reprisals, condoned as such by the government when they were not blandly denied by Greenwood in the Commons, or sardonically ascribed to the I.R.A. At Tralee, where one policeman had been killed and two wounded, the Black and Tans drove into town on the night of November 1, 1920, and kept up 'a carnival of shooting and shouting' till dawn, and burnt the County Hall. Hugh Martin, an English journalist who visited the place a few days later, saw a typed notice which the Tans had put up: 'TAKE NOTICE. Warning! Unless two Tralee police in Sinn Fein custody are returned, reprisals of a nature not yet heard of in Ireland will take place in Tralee.'[5] More serious for the future of Ireland was the destruction or damaging of many co-operative and other creameries.[6]

It was not so much the individual acts of the Black and Tans and the Auxis which aroused horror in Ireland and in England (where questions were asked almost daily in parliament) as it was the

[1] H. W. Nevinson, *Last changes, last chances* (London, 1929), p. 183.

[2] P. Beasley, *Michael Collins*, I, 448–58, II, 75–86; F. P. Crozier, *Ireland for Ever*, pp. 99–102, 147–9. David Hogan, *The Four Glorious Years* (Dublin, 1953), pp. 90–115, 179, 199–201, gives damning accounts of British atrocities.

[3] D. Macardle, *Irish Republic*, p. 478; W. A. Phillips, *Revolution in Ireland*, p. 174. The figures given by I. O., *Administration of Ireland*, p. 97, for the second half of 1920 are: police killed, 47; civilians killed, 30.

[4] Silvain Briollay, *Ireland in Insurrection* (Dublin, 1922), pp. 91–2.

[5] H. Martin, *Ireland in Insurrection* (London, 1921), pp. 137–48 (it was on this occasion that Martin was threatened with physical violence by the Black and Tans for his frank reports to the *Daily News*; fortunately, he concealed his identity); I. O., *Administration of Ireland*, pp. 299–325, quotes from some of Greenwood's speeches.

[6] H. Martin, *Ireland in Insurrection*, pp. 66, 80; special article on Ireland in *Round Table*, 11: 503 (June, 1921). For a list of creameries attacked, April–November, 1920, see Labour Party, *Report of the Labour Commission to Ireland* (London, 1921), pp. 90–8.

impression of violent, lawless bands actually encouraged by the authorities to bully, pillage, and shoot, and protected from the consequences if they did get into trouble. Lorries of armed men, with rifles at the ready, raced through villages and along the Dublin streets, sometimes trailing the Republican flag in the mud and bawling the song:

> We are the boys of the R.I.C.
> We are as happy as happy can be,

in a way no disciplined force would have tolerated. In Cork the veteran journalist H. W. Nevinson saw a party of Auxis lashing passers-by with whips seized from Irish drivers. Farms were raided, ricks set alight, pigs and geese shot, hens decapitated, furniture smashed, and perhaps the house set alight. Examples of looting were not lacking.[1]

The 'massacre' at Croke Park, Dublin, on the afternoon of 'bloody Sunday', was perhaps eclipsed in horror by the murders of the morning, but it was quite inexcusable; the Labour Party's commission observed that the death-toll was higher than at Peterloo. A large crowd was watching a football game. Soldiers surrounded the field, and gave orders by megaphone that everyone was to file out of the ground to be searched; those with revolvers dropped them. Before the crowd could leave, Black and Tans drove up in lorries, and opened fire into the crowd. A woman was killed at her fiancé's side; a boy was brought down wounded from a tree. Twelve persons were killed and sixty wounded; yet there was no evidence, as Greenwood claimed, that Irish 'gunmen' had shot first; there were no casualties at all from the direction from which the gunmen allegedly fired. General Crozier cites the evidence of his own staff officer, Major Mills, that the Tans opened fire first.[2]

Nor was all this just the result of the men 'seeing red' after their comrades had been attacked or shot by the I.R.A. There was direct encouragement from above. General Crozier tells of discovering that one of his companies at Kilkenny had been ordered

---

[1] This account is based upon Labour Party, *Report . . . Ireland*, pp. 9–13, 21–7, 84; H. Martin, *Ireland in Insurrection*, pp. 106–36; H. W. Nevinson, *Last Changes*, pp. 181–9; F. P. Crozier, *Ireland for Ever*, pp. 116–20, 160; C. Dalton, *Dublin Brigade*, p. 112 *seq.*; E. O'Malley, *Army without Banners*, pp. 226, 289; Douglas Goldring, *Odd Man Out* (London, 1935), pp. 212–19; P. Beasley, *Michael Collins*, II, 59–63, 203.

[2] Labour Party, *Report . . . Ireland*, pp. 40–3, 73–4; F. P. Crozier, *Ireland for Ever*, pp. 104–5.

by a 'highly placed and very senior police official' to conduct a police raiding-party, disguised as 'Shinners' with blackened faces, to the post office, gag the staff, steal the mail bags and rifle them for information, and then attribute the outrage to the Sinn Fein. This was actually done, and much money stolen from the mails. He also recounts hearing that instructions had been given to kill the Bishop of Killaloe by drowning him in a sack thrown from a bridge over the Shannon; this plan miscarried.[1]

Such a reign of terror is not easy to condone. It was the product of guerrilla warfare, protected neither by the rules of war (for instance, regarding the treatment of prisoners) nor by the rule of law. It was the product also of postwar tensions, of companies of junior officers and raw recruits, 'young English boys with the saucy air that is a sure sign of nervousness', as Martin described them. The Black and Tans were under poor discipline, and Macready remarks that, when poorly led and encouraged to take the law into their own hands, they 'became a danger to their friends and a disgrace to their uniform'. As for the Auxis, the Labour party's commission had some justification in referring to them as an undemocratic force, a class weapon which might be turned against England, since they were almost all ex-officers, inflamed with political passion and given a free hand to do as they would. They were independent of other bodies, and tolerated no interference; even Dublin Castle seemed unable to control them.[2] No one, least of all the Irish, denied their bravery. Macready called them a 'tough lot'. Lloyd George, in a public letter to the Bishop of Chelmsford, April 19, 1921, admitted that 'a certain number of undesirables have got into the corps, and in the earlier days discipline in the novel and exacting conditions took some time to establish'. Douglas Goldring recounts a conversation he overheard in the Café Royal, London, in December 1920, which has the ring of authenticity about it: a man was trying to persuade a friend to join the Auxis:

You go to New Scotland Yard tomorrow and see Major ——. He'll give you a form to fill in. You start with two pips and £15 a week. . . . It's a great advantage if you've had colonial experience . . . been used to handling natives. It's a grand life, my dear fella, and a grand country. You can get anything you want if you've a big enough

---

[1] F. P. Crozier. *Ireland for Ever*, pp. 96–9, 107–8.
[2] See General Crozier's experience, *Ireland for Ever*, pp. 99, 107–8; 129–34; also his *Impressions and Recollections* (London, 1930), pp. 257, 264–71, 295 ff. Crozier was a regular army man of good family, a Unionist brought up in Ireland.

revolver (guffaw). All you have to do is to lay it on the counter! . . .
Plenty of girls and lashings to drink.[1]

16. THE PARTITION OF IRELAND

All the while, other things had been occurring in 1920 which
decisively affected the future of Ireland. By the Government of
Ireland Act, which became law on December 23, 1920, the partition of the island was effected; the belligerent Unionists of
Ulster, unable to maintain the whole country in a Union with
Great Britain which had all too obviously been broken, received
their little kingdom in the North as a Unionist stronghold, and
yielded up their hidden control of the rest of the country. Thence-
forth there would be two Irelands: Northern Ireland, a part of the
United Kingdom; and the rest. Partition had been proposed
during the storms over the Home Rule Bill in 1914 as a temporary
solution, and again in 1916 after the Easter Rebellion. In these
earlier proposals the 'excluded' area of Ulster was not to have its
own parliament but to continue to be solely under the parliament
at Westminster. In September 1919 the British Cabinet decided
to introduce a new Home Rule Bill to replace the measure enacted,
and then suspended, in 1914. Under its provisions Ireland was to

[1] Labour Party, *Report . . . Ireland*, pp. 6–7; H. Martin, *Ireland in Insurrection*,
p. 75; N. Macready, *Annals*, II, 483, 522; D. Goldring, *Odd Man Out*, p. 211; C. J. C.
Street, *Ireland in 1921* (London, 1922), p. 35.

Note on Authorities on the Irish War. The works cited have been mainly accounts by
Irish participants in the war, with the virtues and defects of such works. This is true
also of the very detailed narrative to be found in P. Beasley, *Michael Collins*. D.
Macardle's *Irish Republic* is a later work, strongly pro-Republican, but based on many
primary sources in books and newspapers. William O'Brien's *Irish Revolution*
(Dublin, [1923?]) is also useful. Informal Irish narratives of events and episodes are
to be found in Robert Brennan, *Allegiance* (Dublin, 1950), and John McCann, *War by
the Irish* (Tralee, 1946). 'David Hogan's' *Four Glorious Years* is a detailed and weighty
work of reminiscence by Frank Gallagher, member of the staff of *The Irish Bulletin*,
1919–21. Those sceptical of such authorities, and of the very one-sided reports,
having much of hearsay about them, published by the American Commission on
Conditions in Ireland (*Evidence on Conditions in Ireland* [1105 pp.; Washington,
1923]) may turn to narratives biased on the English side: 'I.O.' (C. J. C. Street),
Administration of Ireland, W. A. Phillips, *Revolution in Ireland, 1906–1923*, the
work of a historian, and General Macready's good-natured *Annals of an active life*,
vol. II. The *Report* of the Labour Party's Commission to Ireland may also be judged
unsympathetic to the British side; yet its members were English, and practical men,
and their findings cannot be completely ignored, apart from their influence. General
Crozier was a man with a grievance, but he was in a position to know things from the
inside, and his testimony must be given weight. Most impressive are the accounts of
reporters for English newspapers—not pro-Irish fanatics like Erskine Childers, but
men of unquestioned integrity like Hugh Martin and Henry W. Nevinson: see the
latter's *Last Changes, Last Chances*. The account of the French journalist Sylvain
Briollay, *Ireland in Insurrection*, is also impressive; cf. L. Paul-Dubois, *Irish Struggle
and its Results* (London, 1934), which is partly based on Briollay. Perhaps the most
fair-minded summing up is the special article on Ireland in the *Round Table*, 11:
465–507 (June, 1921).

have Home Rule: remain a part of the United Kingdom, but with local self-government (excluding the power to impose customs duties, income tax and other effective means of taxation). However, the bill provided for two Irish parliaments, not one: at Dublin and at Belfast, for Southern Ireland and Northern Ireland respectively, the latter comprising the much smaller area, and not even the whole of the historic province of Ulster, but only the six counties of Armagh, Antrim, Down, Derry, Fermanagh and Tyrone. Whatever the Tories may have had in mind, it seems clear that it was not Lloyd George's intention permanently to partition Ireland. Indeed, much of the matter of the debates in parliament was over the powers of the Council of Ireland, representative of the Northern and Southern parliaments, which was designed to provide a measure of unity from the start, and the means for its growth in the future. The Council was given powers over railways, fisheries, and contagious diseases, and might exercise additional powers conferred on it by the two parliaments. The bill also provided that partition should end, and a single parliament exercise the powers of the two, whenever the two parliaments should vote in favour of this.

The bill had about it, from the start, an air of unreality as far as it concerned Ireland outside the six counties of the North. Opposition speakers in the debates reminded the government of the fighting in Ireland; and it took little prescience to foretell that Home Rule would no longer satisfy the greater part of Ireland. The bill seems to have been enacted as a temporary shelving of an awkward legislative problem, and as a means of convincing the United States that the government had some Irish policy besides violence; its very slow progress through parliament, occupying much of 1920, seems to suggest this. It was certainly the only bill that the predominantly Tory parliament could have been got to pass at the time. There is no evidence in the debates that it represented a clever and far-seeing design by Great Britain to preserve a strategic toe-hold in the North of Ireland if the rest of the country was lost. The few references to defence in the debates commended the bill because it preserved an indispensable association in such matters between Great Britain and the whole of Ireland.[1] The act, ignored in the South, was accepted only with reluctance by the Ulster Unionists, deserted as they felt themselves to be by the

---

[1] W. S. Churchill, *Aftermath*, pp. 298–9; Nicholas Mansergh, *Ireland in the Age of Reform and Revolution* (London, 1940), pp. 167–76. The debate in the House of Commons on the second reading of the bill is in 127 H. C. Deb. 5 s.

D*

Unionists in England and in southern Ireland. At a meeting of
the Ulster Unionist Council in Belfast on March 4, 1920, Carson
and his friends consented to it or rather to the 'terms', as they
insolently called them, and agreed that Northern Ireland should
consist of the six counties, and not include the other three in
Ulster (Donegal, Monaghan, Cavan), since in the larger area they
calculated that Nationalists would outnumber Unionists. In the
six counties a Unionist and Protestant majority in parliament
could probably be assured (though a large Nationalist minority
was unavoidable), and the area was large enough to be an economic unit.[1]

It remained, if parliament demarcated Northern Ireland, to make
sure that its population was, where not Unionist, at least sub-
missive. As early as February 1920 Sir Henry Wilson records
hearing that the Orange Clubs had been revived, and were ready,
if armed by the War Office, to put a force of some 50,000 men into
the field.[2] Carson characteristically left no doubts as to his views
in his Battle of the Boyne speech on July 12, 1920: 'If you are
unable to protect us from the machinations of Sinn Fein,' he
warned the government, 'we will take the matter into our own
hands. At all costs, and notwithstanding the consequences . . . we
will reorganise . . . the Ulster Volunteers. These are not mere
words. I hate words without action.'[3] On the other side, provocation was not lacking: Sinn Fein and I.R.A. gunmen made
attacks (often fatal) on Protestant workmen and the police.
Riots occurred at Londonderry in May and June, in which twenty
persons were killed.[4] The main outbreaks of violence took place
in Belfast and neighbouring towns in late July and August, leaving 4,000 people homeless and destitute. War was systematically
waged by Orangemen on Roman Catholics, who were branded as
Sinn Feiners; local military forces made no attempt to intervene,
and even fraternised with the victors. The entire Roman Catholic
populations of Lisburn and Banbridge were 'evacuated', and 2,000
men, women and children driven out of the Ballymacarret district
of Belfast. Following Carson's inflammatory speech, a self-

[1] Denis Gwynn, *History of Partition (1912–1925)* (Dublin, 1950), pp. 102 ff.,
146–57, 179–201; Ian Colvin, *Life of Lord Carson* (New York, 1937), III, 375–84;
N. Mansergh, *Ireland in Reform and Revolution*, pp. 175–9; Ronald McNeill (Lord
Cushendun), *Ulster's Stand for Union* (London, 1922), p. 279. Sir James Craig defended the inclusion of the six counties rather than the nine with extreme frankness:
see 127 H. C. Deb. 5 s., 990 (March 29, 1920).
[2] C. E. Callwell, *Wilson*, II, 228.
[3] *The Times*, July 13, 1920; cf. S. Briollay, *Ireland in Insurrection*, p. 108.
[4] *Ireland in Insurrection*, pp. 87–8.

styled Protestant Workmen's Union began to terrorise Roman Catholics in the shipyards. The test of loyalty was simple: 'Curse the Pope'; and those who did not meet it were literally kicked out, and lost their employment. Families driven out of neighbouring towns poured into Belfast as refugees, 150 families being received at one Roman Catholic centre on a single day. One hundred houses were burnt down in Belfast within four days. Hugh Martin, visiting the Ballymacarret district, found the whole of Newtownards Road, one and a half miles long, a line of wreckage, patrolled by Orangemen with piles of stones ready at every corner, and howling 'God Save the King' and 'Kick the Pope o'er Dolly's Brae' in 'delirious triumphal processions'. Casualties included 62 killed and 200 wounded. In these conditions the Ulstermen proposed that a special constabulary of loyal citizens should be formed to preserve order; and in spite of Macready's protests this licensing of Orange zeal was carried out; the Ulster Special Constabulary (the 'B Specials') was formed and paid for by the British government. The Ulster Volunteers had at last achieved official status.[1]

The other development of 1920 was even more noteworthy. The Irish Republic came to have reality, not merely in the 'executions' carried out by the I.R.A., but in the setting up of governmental services alternative to those of Great Britain. Republican courts, first to settle land disputes and to discourage expropriations under the guise of war, later to deal with all types of civil and criminal cases, were established and held in secret, while the British courts remained open but idle for lack of litigants. The British tax-gathering machinery came to a halt. Local authorities (all with Sinn Fein majorities after the local elections held under official auspices in 1920) took their orders from the Dail Ministry of Local Government under W. T. Cosgrave, not from Dublin Castle. British government in Ireland became paralysed, and went into final dissolution. Britain ceased to govern Ireland; the Republic emerged from the shadows and began to take over the functions of government.[2]

The British reply was a public admission of abdication—the

---

[1] Hugh Martin, *Ireland in Insurrection*, pp. 167–76; D. Macardle, *Irish Republic*, pp. 399–401; N. Macready, *Annals*, II, 487–9; I.O., *Administration of Ireland*, pp. 342–53. For a pro-Unionist account, see St. J. Ervine, *Craigavon: Ulsterman* (London, 1949), pp. 397–9, 479.

[2] D. Macardle, *Irish Republic*, pp. 362–6; D. Figgis, *Recollections*, pp. 266–78, 290–300. An amusing account of a meeting of the Boynmore Sinn Fein Parish Court is in Gerald Griffin's 'semi-autobiographical saga', *The Dead March Past* (London, 1937), p. 200 *seq.*

decision to intensify military measures and reconquer the island by force of arms. In August 1920, the Restoration of Order in Ireland Act was passed, extending the powers of the military by providing for courts martial in treason and felony cases, and closed military courts of inquiry in place of coroners' inquests. This proved inadequate, and the step, long urged by Sir Henry Wilson and Macready, of declaring martial law, was finally taken—at first from December 10, 1920, only in the four southern counties of Cork, Kerry, Limerick and Tipperary (extended to counties Clare, Kilkenny, Waterford, Wexford on January 4, 1921)[1] The practice of 'authorised reprisals' followed, beginning on New Year's Day. Sir Henry Wilson had long been arguing with characteristic bluntness against the government's acquiescence in reprisals as long as they were not 'officially' encouraged, as his amazingly frank diary reveals:

> I had 1½ hours this evening with Lloyd George and Bonar Law. I told them what I thought of reprisals by the 'Black and Tans', and how this must lead to chaos and ruin. Lloyd George danced about and was angry, but I never budged. I pointed out that these reprisals were carried out without anyone being responsible. . . . It was the business of the Government to govern. If these men ought to be murdered, then the Government ought to murder them. Lloyd George danced at all this, said no Government could possibly take this responsibility. (September 29, 1920.)[2]

It was almost the last kick in the struggle. There was talk of a truce current in England and Ireland in the autumn. An important 'peace conference' was held in Dublin in August, including both Unionists and moderates of high standing in public life; it had, apparently, the tacit support of Sinn Fein. British opinion was already swinging against the war and its atrocities, moved not only by the reports in the press but by the hunger-strike of Terence McSwiney, MacCurtain's successor as Lord Mayor of Cork and commander of an I.R.A. brigade, a teacher by profession, who had been arrested in August. A long-drawn-out affair such as this always wrings the heartstrings of the great reading public of the sensational press, and MacSwiney's death on October 25, in Brixton jail, after a fast of seventy-four days, was a shocking thing to countless people. The I.R.A.'s rather feeble attempts at terrorism in England may also have moved opinion by bringing the war home to the people, though they amounted to little more

[1] D. Macardle, *Irish Republic*, pp. 395, 431; N. Macready, *Annals*, II, 468, 500–2.
[2] C. E. Callwell, *Wilson*, II, 263; cf. pp. 237, 265, 268–9, 271–3.

than the burning of a few warehouses in Liverpool and a few hay-ricks at farms on the Wirral[1]. In a speech at Carnarvon on October 9, Lloyd George had boasted 'we have murder by the throat'; but he was ready to treat with the enemy even then, if he could overcome the resistance of members of his Cabinet and advisers like Sir Henry Wilson. *The Times* (October 11) declared he was a prisoner of Carson and his forces, and dared not flout them. None the less, there were conversations in December, the intermediary being Archbishop Clune, of Western Australia, who was visiting Ireland. The Labour party's commission in Ireland also engaged in some attempts to negotiate a truce. Father O'Flanagan, the vice-president of Sinn Fein, publicly appealed to Lloyd George for a truce before Christmas. The upshot was, how-ever, to suggest to the government that the I.R.A. was on the run, and the terms were stiffened. Greenwood, in making a statement in the Commons on the subject on December 10, insisted that talks could be begun only if the Irish laid down their arms, and if 'certain individuals who are gravely implicated in the commission of crime' were not included in the discussions.[2]

Instead, December witnessed one of the most disgraceful inci-dents of the whole struggle, the burning of Cork by the Black and Tans and Auxis on the 11th. This appears to have been deliber-ately planned—some thought in order to prevent a truce from being made—rather than being, as Greenwood asserted, a reprisal for a recent ambush of Auxis at Dillon's Cross. It was preceded by some weeks of terror: in November there were 200 curfew arrests; 500 houses were searched, twelve large business premises burnt down, and four notices threatening the citizens of Cork were put up on public placards. On the night of the fire the Black and Tans drove everyone indoors, at revolver point, ahead of the curfew. During the night fires were started at several places, first at a big shop on Patrick Street, then the City Hall and the Carnegie Library, across the river. Banks and stores were robbed. Fire hoses were cut by members of the Crown forces. Yet when it was all over Greenwood declared that the fire had spread itself, even though this involved going against the wind, overleaping several streets and crossing the river. An official inquiry was

---

[1] See P. Beasley, *Michael Collins*, II, 98, and E. M. Brady, *Ireland's Secret Service in England* (Dublin, 1928), whose title is the only sensational thing about it.
[2] P. Beasley, *Michael Collins*, II, 107–38; F. P. Crozier, *Ireland for Ever*, p. 164; Labour Party, *Report . . . Ireland*; I.O., *Administration of Ireland*, pp. 415–26. An earlier attempt to negotiate a truce, which was checked by the murders and the Croke Park affair on Bloody Sunday, is described in the *History of The Times*, IV, ii, 564.

made, but the government refused to publish the report, and found
a scapegoat in an R.I.C. officer, who was suspended. It was in
protest against this that a Black and Tan company paraded in
Dublin with half-burnt corks in their caps. Over the Christmas
holidays there were further incidents: fifteen persons were killed
in widely scattered places, including five persons at a dance in
Bruff, County Limerick, which was raided by the police.

So the third Christmas of the peace passed with war still
darkening much of Ireland's land and England's name.[1]

[1] D. Macardle, *Irish Republic*, pp. 431–4; Labour Party, *Report . . . Ireland*, pp.
35–8; F. P. Crozier, *Ireland for Ever*, p. 174 *seq.*, *Impressions*, pp. 261–3.

CHAPTER TWO

Retrenchment, 1920—1922

1. THE WAR IN IRELAND: THE LAST PHASE

IN 1921 the fighting in Ireland became more desperate. Martial law extended across eight southern counties (elsewhere the civil courts continued to function). The possession of arms and the harbouring or aiding of rebels became a capital offence subject to trial in a military court; and in the spring of 1921 the use of drumhead courts martial for men taken red-handed under arms was authorised, though only used on three occasions before the truce. Only fourteen death sentences imposed by military courts were actually carried out during the seven months of martial law preceding the truce. In the matter of reprisals Macready's order following the proclamation of martial law provided that brigade commanders could authorise the destruction, by explosives, of houses of persons who might be implicated in any outrages against Crown forces, provided notice was given to the occupants, and time to move out valuables.[1]

In these circumstances violence increased on both sides— murders, kidnappings, the execution of hostages, ambushes, raids incendiarism. The most sensational, and costly, exploit by the I.R.A. was the attack on the Dublin Customs House at noon on May 25, 1921. Some 120 I.R.A. men seized the building, ordered the staff to leave, and set it afire. Auxis rushed to the scene, and in the battle which ensued six of the Irish were killed, twelve wounded, and seventy captured. The building was gutted, and with it, unfortunately for historians as well as for government officials at the time, the records of the Local Government Board, Customs and Inland Revenue, Stationery Office, and certain other offices. Macready lists the events of two typical days, March 30 and 31: an officer murdered leaving his hotel in Dublin, a bomb explosion in Amiens Street, a military lorry seized, a retired officer shot in County Cork, rioting in Belfast, an R.I.C. patrol ambushed

---

[1] N. Macready, *Annals*, II, 515–26, 562, 586–94.

and one man killed, an armoured car attacked, an attempt to derail a train, a raid by rebels on a farmer's house in Monaghan, a telephone office burnt and one man killed at Killiney.[1] A British writer gives the number of police killed in the six months from January to July as 223, and the number of soldiers killed as 94; March and May were the worst months.[2] There were also some efforts by I.R.A. parties to terrorise the families of R.I.C. men in England by raiding their houses, firing threatening shots, and attempting arson; these occurred in several suburbs of London, and in Liverpool.[3]

Meanwhile, the provisions of the Government of Ireland Act went ponderously into effect, and partition became a reality. The appointed day for the main provisions of the Act to take effect was fixed as May 3; and elections for the parliaments of Northern and Southern Ireland were held on May 24. The elections were held under the system of Proportional Representation (the single transferable vote), as prescribed in the Act—Britain's gesture towards the electoral reform which it was too squeamish to apply to itself; it survives in Ireland to this day, except in Northern Ireland, where it was abolished for parliamentary elections in 1929.[4] In the South Sinn Fein treated the election, held under British auspices, as a new election of the Dail. All but four of the 128 seats were won by Sinn Fein in uncontested elections. The remaining four members, representing Trinity College, Dublin, met as the parliament of Southern Ireland, along with the senators nominated by the Lord Lieutenant, on June 28, in Dublin; after a brief address from the throne by the Lord Chief Justice they adjourned, unhonoured and unsung.

In the North it was far otherwise: the Unionists (aided, it is said, by many dead voters) elected 40 members, the Nationalists and Sinn Fein 12, including Michael Collins, Arthur Griffith and De Valera (also elected for southern constituencies). Sir James Craig,[5] who had been elected Carson's successor at a meeting of the Ulster Unionist Council in Belfast on February 4, was Prime Minister in the new government (as he remained until his death

[1] N. Macready, *Annals*, II, 549. For the fighting in this period see P. Beasley, *Michael Collins*, II, 181–96.

[2] P. Beasley, *Michael Collins*, II, 219–21, 234; C. J. C. Street, *Ireland in 1921*, p. 7.

[3] C. J. C. Street, *Ireland in 1921*, pp. 23–7.

[4] N. Mansergh, *Government of Northern Ireland* (London, 1936), p. 128.

[5] James Craig (1871–1940), born at Sydenham, near Belfast, son of a wealthy distiller; Conservative M.P. for East (later Mid) Down, 1908–21; parliamentary secretary to ministry of pensions, 1919–20, parliamentary secretary to the Admiralty, 1920–21; created baronet, 1918, Viscount Craigavon, 1927.

in 1940, as Lord Craigavon); and the parliament in Belfast was opened by the King on June 22 in circumstances which proved epochal—for the South, even more than for the North.[1] There had been rioting in Belfast during the election, and again in mid-June, with some loss of life. Earlier in the year there had been disorders in Belfast and Londonderry, and some raids by the I.R.A. in country districts near the border. In one case a party of the Ulster Special Constabulary, intent on reprisal, crossed into Southern territory and was fought and overcome by the R.I.C. in Clones—a nice case of dog eating dog. Disturbances continued until the end of the year, in which both Roman Catholics and Orangemen suffered: 109 persons were killed in Northern Ireland in 1921 in civil disorders, for which I.R.A. gunmen and Ulster patriots were equally to blame. The depression, which at once affected employment in the Belfast shipyards, only made matters worse.[2] Estrangement between North and South was increased in January 1921, when the Dail, at one of its rare meetings, decided on the boycott of trade between Southern Ireland and Ulster. In the opinion of at least one Irish patriot this was disastrous, converting many Ulstermen, hitherto indifferent to partition, into supporters of it; Sinn Fein raids into Ulster had, of course, the same effect. The southern Irish were treating the Ulstermen as foreigners, and spiritual partition supplemented the political.[3]

2. PRELUDE TO A TRUCE

All the while, opinion in England was swinging strongly against the continuance of the war. The Liberal newspapers had opposed it from the start: the *Manchester Guardian*, the *Daily News*, the *Westminster Gazette*; so had Lord Northcliffe's papers, *The Times* and the *Daily Mail*, not only because of Northcliffe's vendetta against Lloyd George but much more because of the constructive ideas of *The Times*' editor, Wickham Steed. Steed did not, in fact, confine himself to helping to shape his paper's policy; he was in touch with members of the Cabinet and with Lord Stamfordham, the King's Secretary, and was particularly concerned that the bearing of Irish policy on Anglo-American relations should never be forgotten.[4] On November 30, 1920, an article in *The Times*, in

[1] C. J. C. Street, *Ireland in 1921*, pp. 17–20, 60–73, 82–3; H. W. Nevinson, *Last Changes*, p. 191.
[2] C. J. C. Street, *Ireland in 1921*, pp. 51–7, 66, 70; St. J. Ervine, *Craigavon*, pp. 431, 437, 442, 457, 460.
[3] P. S. O'Hegarty, *Victory of Sinn Fein* (Dublin, 1924), pp. 49–52; P. Beasley, *Michael Collins*, II, 147–9; C. J. C. Street, *Ireland in 1921*, pp. 11–12.
[4] *History of The Times*, IV, ii, 553–74.

condemnation of the policy of reprisals, contained this cry from the heart from Ireland: 'If only the people in England knew. . . . Everywhere in Ireland today you hear that cry.' 'Why do these things happen?' it continued. 'Why are servants of the Crown charged with pillage and arson and what amounts to lynch law, and even with drunkenness and murder? How can the reign of terror be stopped?' General Crozier's resignation on February 19, 1921, caused a stir; and he followed this up with a letter to *The Times* (April 8), urging a truce, and with a narrative of events in the *Daily News* on May 24.[1] On February 21, Asquith in the Commons denounced reprisals and appealed for a truce. Sir John Simon,[2] a Liberal respected for his legal acumen, was even stronger in his condemnation of reprisals in a letter to *The Times* on April 25: a policy 'politically disastrous and morally wrong . . . intensifying war . . . exposing us to the scorn of the world'.

Conservatives began to come round to the same opinion: Lord Robert Cecil, Lord Henry Cavendish-Bentinck (who 'crossed the floor' of the House of Commons on the Irish issue). Lord Monteagle, in the *Contemporary Review* for September 1920, condemned the government's police action as futile and degrading, and proposed that Ireland be made a Dominion—a solution also advanced by several speakers in the debates in parliament over the Government of Ireland Bill.[3] The *Round Table*, a quarterly representing Liberal imperialism, was coming to favour a negotiated settlement: its June 1921 number had a long special section devoted to a retrospect of Anglo-Irish relations, and proposing colonial autonomy, including fiscal independence, for North and South.[4] This was the work of Lionel Curtis and the editor, John Dove. Sir Horace Plunkett, perhaps the most universally respected Irishman, above politics as founder of the movement for agricultural co-operation in Ireland, was advocating dominion status for Ireland as president of the Irish Dominion League. On February 22, 1921, the Archbishop of Canterbury in the House of Lords condemned the government's policy as morally unjust: 'if it was by

---

[1] F. P. Crozier, *Ireland for Ever*, pp. 144–6; *Impressions*, p. 279; *The Times*, Feb. 23, 1921.

[2] John Simon (1873–1954), son of Congregational minister. Fettes and Wadham College, Oxford; president of Oxford Union. Barrister. M.P., 1906–18, 1922–40. Solicitor-general, 1910–13; attorney-general, 1913–15; home secretary, 1915–16. Foreign secretary, 1931–5; home secretary, 1935–7; chancellor of the Exchequer, 1937–40; Lord chancellor, 1940–5. Knighted, 1910, created Viscount Simon, 1940.

[3] *Contemporary Review*, 118: 305–14 (Sept., 1920); 119: 299–309 (March, 1921); 120: 20–6 (July, 1921).

[4] *Round Table*, 11: 465–534.

wrongdoing that you produced peace, then they had not really won a peace which was worth while.'[1]

From other directions the government was urged to think again. The report of the Labour party's commission on Ireland, published in January 1921, had great influence. 'Things are being done in the name of Britain,' it concluded, 'which must make her name stink in the nostrils of the whole world.' It urged the withdrawal of the British army of occupation, and the holding of an Irish constituent assembly. This policy had been strongly endorsed at a special party conference at Central Hall, Westminster, on December 29, 1920, at which Brigadier-General C. B. Thomson,[2] who had accompanied the commission as military adviser, referred, in an otherwise restrained report, to some Black and Tans as 'drunken, swaggering bullies'. The commission included Arthur Henderson, as chairman, Arthur Greenwood,[3] F. W. Jowett,[4] and W. Adamson. Henderson had moved a resolution in the Commons on October 20, 1920, calling for an independent investigation of the policy of reprisals by those responsible for law and order; it was when this was rejected that the Labour party decided to send its own commission of inquiry to Ireland.[5]

The government had come to the parting of the ways. It could go forward with the policy of force, applying enough, regardless of the consequences, to bring about the end of fighting and the complete restoration of government by Great Britain in Southern Ireland. That was Lloyd George's inclination, and it was supported by many Tory members of the Cabinet. Sir Henry Wilson put it bluntly: the choice was 'to go all out or to get out'. He warned, however, that it was no good 'unless we had England entirely on our side'. In the Cabinet, Churchill urged that this policy could

---

[1] *The Times*, Feb. 23, 1921. In general, see C. J. C. Street, *Ireland in 1921*, pp. 28–49, 110; L. Paul-Dubois, *Irish Struggle*, pp. 73–6; D. Macardle, *Irish Republic*, pp. 446, 448, 460.

[2] C. B. Thomson (1875–1930), born in India, son of a major-general. Served in Royal Engineers from 1894; Boer War; Staff College, Camberley; during the war he served in Belgium, as military attaché in Bucharest, and in Palestine; brigadier-general, 1918. Joined Labour party, 1919. Secretary of state for air, 1924, 1929–30. Created baron, 1924. Killed in the crash of the airship R. 101 at Beauvais.

[3] Arthur Greenwood, (1880–1954), lecturer in economics, Leeds University. Assistant secretary in ministry of reconstruction, 1917–19. M.P., 1922–31 and 1932–54; minister of health, 1929–31; minister without portfolio in war cabinet, 1940–42 (in charge of plans for reconstruction); Lord privy seal, 1945–47.

[4] F. W. Jowett (1864–1944), born in Bradford; city councillor for fifteen years. M.P. for Bradford, 1906–18, 1922–24, 1929–31; first commissioner of works, 1924. Member of the I.L.P. to his death.

[5] Labour Party, *Report of the Labour Commission to Ireland* (1921), especially p. 56 *seq.*; G. D. H. Cole, *History of Labour Party*, pp. 109–10; Fenner Brockway, *Socialism over sixty years: the life of Jowett of Bradford* (London, 1946), pp. 168–74.

only be resorted to if accompanied by the offer of the widest possible measure of self-government; and Lord Birkenhead and Austen Chamberlain, among the Conservatives, supported him.[1]

In deciding to make one last effort of conciliation the government was influenced by the opinion of King George V. The King had frequently sent warnings to ministers against the doings of the Black and Tans and the resort to reprisals. On June 22 he and the Queen were to visit Belfast to open the new parliament of Northern Ireland. Wickham Steed, on hearing of this, went to see Lord Stamfordham, first to pass on to him a warning of the danger the King would be running if he made the visit and then, finding that useless, to urge that the King use the occasion of his speech to call for a truce for the whole of Ireland; he said much the same to Edward Grigg,[2] Lloyd George's secretary, and *The Times* reiterated it in later editorials. Soon after this General Smuts lunched with the King and pressed on him the same idea; and afterwards at the King's request and with Stamfordham's help he put it into writing. Later, at the suggestion of them both, Smuts sent this draft to the Prime Minister, accompanied by a long and persuasive letter. A visit from Stamfordham on June 17 helped to convince Lloyd George; the speech prepared for the King in the Irish Office was scrapped and a new one, embodying Smuts' ideas, was drafted by Grigg, submitted by Lloyd George to the King, and warmly approved by him.[3]

Never, apparently, was there a more sudden and dramatic reversal of policy. On June 21, in the Lords, Lord Birkenhead, on behalf of the government, was declaring that if the Irish were determined to prolong the war until independence was won, Britain would never concede it, but would continue the war at whatever sacrifice. On June 22 the King, in his speech at Belfast, said:

> I speak from a full heart when I pray that my coming to Ireland today may prove to be the first step towards an end of strife amongst her people, whatever their race or creed. In that hope I appeal to all Irishmen to pause, to stretch out the hand of forbearance and con-

[1] W. S. Churchill, *Aftermath*, pp. 303–6; C. E. Callwell, *Sir Henry Wilson*, II, 292, 295–6; N. Macready, *Annals*, II, 562–65.
[2] Edward Grigg (1879–1955). Winchester and New College, Oxford. On staff of *The Times*, 1903–13. Grenadier Guards, 1914. Military secretary to Prince of Wales on his tours to Canada, Australia, New Zealand. Private secretary to Lloyd George, 1921–22. M.P., 1922–25, 1933–45. Governor of Kenya, 1925–31. Minister resident in the Middle East, 1944–45. Created Baron Altrincham, 1945.
[3] H. Nicolson, *King George V*, pp. 346–51; *History of The Times*, IV, ii, 575–7.

ciliation, to forgive and forget, and to join in making for the land which they love a new era of peace, contentment, and goodwill.[1]

The Cabinet, urged on by the King, decided that the universally warm reaction to the King's speech gave them the opportunity they needed; and on June 24, Lloyd George wrote to De Valera and Sir James Craig inviting them to a conference in London. He promised a safe conduct for all concerned—a reversal of the position vehemently and often taken by Sir Henry Wilson, who, when Lloyd George told him he would soon have a chance of talking to De Valera, said he 'did not speak to murderers'.[2]

The suddenness of the reversal of policy was more apparent than real. Long before this, the government had made several conciliatory gestures. In January, after De Valera's return from the United States, it had given orders that he was not to be arrested. In April a new Lord Lieutenant had been appointed, and for the first time a Roman Catholic was selected—Lord Edmund Talbot, member of a prominent English family of Roman Catholics, who was made Viscount Fitzalan. On April 22 Lord Derby, visiting Ireland unofficially and incognito as 'Mr. Edwards', had a long though fruitless talk with De Valera. On May 4 Sir James Craig, visiting Dublin to see the new Lord Lieutenant, had an interview with De Valera, and was taken by car by members of the I.R.A., along a deliberately mystifying route, to a secret rendezvous, where the two talked, though without result. And all the time an English civil servant who had come to Dublin Castle as assistant under-secretary in the summer of 1920, A. W. Cope, had been working, with great skill and persistence, and at some personal risk, to establish relations with the Irish leaders. 'Andy' Cope was Lloyd George's agent in the negotiations in Ireland which led up to the truce.[3] These manœuvres had had their effect on De Valera. At the meeting of the Dail in January he had urged that there should be an 'easing off of their attacks on the enemy', though at the time the proposal was not welcomed.[4] In May, in an interview for the *New York Herald*, he made it clear that he was willing to meet Lloyd George for discussions. In June he made an approach to General Smuts through Art O'Brien, president of

[1] Text of speech is in H. Nicolson, *King George V*, pp. 352–4.
[2] C. E. Callwell, *Sir Henry Wilson*, II, 298.
[3] P. Beasley, *Michael Collins*, II, 223–6, 235; C. J. C. Street, *Ireland in 1921*, pp. 60–3, 101–26; Frank Pakenham, *Peace by Ordeal* (London, 1935), pp. 71–7; N. Macready, *Annals*, II, 456–7, 492, 558; St. J. Ervine, *Craigavon*, pp. 404–13.
[4] P. Beasley, *Michael Collins*, II, 147–8.

the Irish Self-determination League in London; and early that month Smuts paid him a secret visit in Dublin.

3. TRUCE AND PAUSE

Even so, it took time before Lloyd George's letter of June 24 produced any result. De Valera, on receiving it, first consulted the Dail cabinet. He then invited Lord Midleton[1] and four other leading Southern Unionists to a meeting in Dublin before he made reply to Lloyd George 'as spokesman for the Irish nation'. He also invited Sir James Craig to this meeting, but the latter was not to be ensnared into De Valera's subtle scheme to erase partition and refused the invitation. The meeting began in the Mansion House on July 4. De Valera refused to consider going to London unless a truce was first made. The conference adjourned while Midleton went to London and got Lloyd George's agreement on two points: a truce, and direct negotiations between Lloyd George and De Valera (apart from Craig). The truce was also urged upon the government by General Smuts, who visited Dublin on July 5 to help smooth the way of negotiation. The conference was resumed on July 8. At 1.30 p.m. Midleton and the other Unionists called on General Macready to consult him about a truce, and the terms were worked out. The final arrangements were made that same evening in the Mansion House, by then surrounded by an expectant crowd; Macready, Midleton and other Unionists, De Valera and Griffith took part in this meeting.[2]

The truce went into effect at noon on Monday, July 11. It did not include, as Lloyd George had hoped it would, the surrender of arms by the I.R.A. Indeed, as subsequent events showed, such a demand could never have been enforced. As it was, the I.R.A. continued its raids and attacks, not without loss of life among its victims, up to the very hour of the truce.[3]

There followed a long and unexpected delay, chiefly due to De Valera's procrastination. De Valera had written to Lloyd George at the close of the conference on July 8, agreeing to meet him in London to discuss 'on what bases' a conference might be held. He came to London soon enough, on July 12, and had four meetings with Lloyd George, on the 14th, 15th, 18th, and 21st. Lloyd

[1] St. John Brodrick (1856–1942), son of Viscount Midleton, whom he succeeded, 1907 (created Earl of Midleton, 1920). M.P., 1880–1906. War secretary, 1900–3; secretary of state for India, 1903–5.
[2] C. J. C. Street, *Ireland in 1921*, pp. 130–42; N. Macready, *Annals*, II, 569–80; Earl of Midleton, *Records and reactions, 1856–1939* (London, 1939), p. 258 *seq.*
[3] I.R.A. activities on the morning of July 11 are listed in Macready, II, 578; cf. W. A. Phillips, *Revolution in Ireland*, pp. 211–12, 216.

George's concern was to persuade De Valera of the grandeur of the Empire, in whose imperial cabinet he was inviting Ireland to take the vacant seat. De Valera was unimpressed. Lloyd George afterwards said that talking with De Valera was like riding a hobby horse at a fair: you never caught up with the fellow in front. After each meeting, De Valera consulted the men who had accompanied him, Arthur Griffith, Robert Barton, Austin Stack, Erskine Childers. On July 21 Lloyd George gave De Valera the government's proposals, which had been approved by the Cabinet the day before. The Irish delegation then went home.[1]

What the government proposed was almost exactly what finally came about: dominion status for Ireland, with Northern Ireland free to decide its relation to the new dominion.[2] In several meetings of the cabinet of the Dail in July, and in the Dail itself, the terms were discussed and the fatal division among the Irish leaders began to appear. The proposals did not provide for the Republic; and they did not promise the end of partition. For the Republic Stack and Brugha came out as uncompromising champions. De Valera would not go so far. In taking the oath to the Republic at the first meeting of the second Dail, he had made a speech saying he was not a 'doctrinaire Republican' and did not care for 'forms of government as such'. He was already moving, as his letter to Lloyd George on August 11 showed, to the idea of 'external association' (implicit in his 'Cuba' interview): 'a certain treaty of free association with the British Commonwealth group, as with a partial league of nations, we would have been ready to recommend'.[3] Dominion status, for a country as near to Great Britain geographically as was Ireland, would be illusory, no real freedom. As to Northern Ireland's status, no progress was made. Sir James Craig came to London while De Valera was there, and had two meetings with Lloyd George on July 15 and 18, after which he returned to Belfast, having conceded nothing but the right of Southern Ireland to make whatever settlement for itself it could with Great Britain. General Smuts, whose mediation De Valera had sought, advised him in a long letter on August 4 that Craig was immovable, and went on to urge strongly the benefits of Dominion status for the twenty-six counties of the South.[4]

[1] W. S. Churchill, *Aftermath*, p. 312; F. Pakenham, *Peace by Ordeal*, pp. 81–4; A. J. Sylvester, *Real Lloyd George*, p. 64.
[2] Text is given in C. J. C. Street, *Ireland in 1921*, pp. 165–9.
[3] *Ireland in 1921*, p. 176.
[4] C. J. C. Street, *Ireland in 1921*, pp. 161–3, 180–4; F. Pakenham, *Peace by Ordeal*, p. 87 *seq.* Many of the letters and statements during this period of negotiations are reproduced in the *Round Table*, 11: 759–96 (September, 1921), 12: 37–75 (Dec., 1921).

These doubts explain the delay, and the tedious and long-winded correspondence, all published at the time in the press, between De Valera and Lloyd George, beginning on August 11. Early in September Lloyd George, then on holiday in the Highlands, tried to end it by an ultimatum; but by another beneficent intervention of the King it was modified and negotiations were kept open.[1] De Valera was invited to a conference 'to ascertain how the association of Ireland with the community of nations known as the British Empire can best be reconciled with Irish national aspirations' (September 7). To this De Valera seemed to agree, but his reply carried a rider: 'Our nation has formally declared its independence, and recognises itself as a sovereign State . . .' and its representatives could act only as such. Lloyd George cancelled the conference, but the correspondence continued. On September 30 De Valera accepted an invitation of September 29 for a conference on October 11, in London, on the identical terms of the invitation of September 7. A conference and a treaty there were to be, but within the framework of the British Empire. On this Lloyd George had never budged; nor did he.[2]

In this interval between the truce and the beginning of negotiations for a settlement the military situation inevitably disintegrated, particularly for the Irish. Both sides complained of violations of the terms of the truce. The Irish claimed that the British forces were provocative in their attitude, and that plans were being made for a 'round up' of males of fighting age if war was resumed. The deterioration in the I.R.A., which had begun before the truce, proceeded apace. Now that the dangers were over, recruits flocked in, and these sunshine soldiers used their position to bully, to loot, to satisfy personal feuds, and to extort money and supplies. The hundreds of men released from the internment camps returned with a 'mad glitter' in their eyes. Kidnappings and attacks on soldiers and police were frequent. The old, tight organisation, led by men who had braved the early dangers together, had broken up; the intelligence system had to some extent tipped its hand; Collins and other leaders were now well known. Whatever the headstrong ideas of the febrile gunmen, the war could not be restarted; the mass of the people were content with the peace, and would lend little aid to the I.R.A.; and all advantages would lie with the British forces, rested but not disbanded by the truce, with

[1] H. Nicolson, *King George V*, p. 359.
[2] C. J. C. Street, *Ireland in 1921*, pp. 209–24; F. Pakenham, *Peace by Ordeal*, pp. 80–91; D. Macardle, *Irish Republic*, p. 505 *seq.*

plenty of reserves to draw on, and with their old positions intact—
for there was no evacuation following the truce, though some
drafts were made on the military forces, and undesirables were
weeded out of the R.I.C. by Cope. These considerations, even if
unadmitted, must influence both sides in the long negotiations for
the treaty.[1]

4. NEGOTIATING A TREATY

The choice of delegates to the conference was difficult to make.
Eventually, the Dail cabinet selected Arthur Griffith, Michael
Collins, Robert Barton, E. J. Duggan, and George Gavan Duffy.
Collins was most unwilling to go, claiming he was a soldier and
not a politician, but eventually he agreed. Brugha and Stack, his
opponents in the cabinet, refused to go, disclaiming skill in
negotiations, and De Valera sided with them; their presence at
home during the negotiations proved utterly disastrous. De
Valera decided not to go to London, saying that his place was at
home. For this he has been much criticised, on the grounds that
his constant long-range interference in the negotiations was vexa-
tious, as it was, and that he intended all along to disown the results.
which he probably did not. Rather, he stayed at home so that, if
necessary, the delegates could play for time by referring matters to
him, and also in order that, if the negotiations failed he could, with
clean hands, rally the people to a new struggle.[2] One result,
however, was that the delegation was not representative of the
cabinet, consisting of moderates and not extremists. The latter
position was represented only by the secretary of the delegation,
Erskine Childers, whose selection De Valera forced on the unwilling Griffith. Childers, of English birth but of Irish upbringing
in County Wicklow, had had a distinguished career as a clerk of
the House of Commons and as an officer in the navy during the
war, when he won the Distinguished Service Order and took part
with gallantry in the raid on Cuxhaven on January 1, 1915. He
had been secretary of the Irish Convention in 1917, and after this
left British service to work for the cause of Irish freedom. He was
author of the successful novel, *The Riddle of the Sands*, about
counter-espionage before the war. Robert Barton, one of the
delegates, was his cousin, and came of a Protestant land-owning

---

[1] C. J. C. Street, *Ireland in 1921*, pp. 145–57; N. Macready, *Annals*, II, 578–83,
595, 601; D. Ryan, *Unique Dictator*, p. 138; P. S. O'Hegarty, *Victory of Sinn Fein*,
pp. 52, 54–8, 167–9.
[2] D. Ryan, *Unique Dictator*, p. 141.

family in Wicklow. Duggan and Gavan Duffy, the remaining delegates, were lawyers, and chosen as such.

The conference began in London on October 11, 1921. The Irish delegates were lodged in Hans Place, Kensington, and Cadogan Gardens. They took little part in social activities during their stay. The principal meetings were at No. 10 Downing Street, but others were held in private houses, particularly those involving Lloyd George and Arthur Griffith or Michael Collins. The British delegation comprised Lloyd George, Austen Chamberlain, Lord Birkenhead, Winston Churchill, Hamar Greenwood, and Sir Laming Worthington-Evans,[1] and, for constitutional questions, the Attorney General, Gordon Hewart;[2] but the last three took little part in the detailed work. Thomas Jones,[3] the deputy secretary to the Cabinet, and the close confidant and shrewd adviser of Lloyd George, as of subsequent prime ministers, was intermediary in some of the most delicate passages in the negotiations. Lionel Curtis also served as secretary to the British delegation.

Griffith and Collins made the strongest impression on the British ministers, the former for his laconic directness, moderation, and strength held in reserve, which greatly attracted Chamberlain, the latter as a tall, handsome man of the world, honest, and open to persuasion. From the start he and Birkenhead, the 'Galloper' with whom he should have been most at enmity, hit it off superbly; both understood and respected the fighter in the other. It is related that Churchill, also much attracted to Collins, arranged a dinner party, at which Birkenhead talked with the Irish delegates until one in the morning. Afterwards Collins said: 'I trust them. I'm prepared to take their word.'[4] This was crucial for the success of the negotiations. Without the strong and unflinching support of Lord Birkenhead, the Tories, who baulked enough as it was over the negotiations and the treaty, would have hamstrung any settlement. He and Austen Chamberlain—equal in resolution, in willingness to discard ancient hatreds, and in selfless devotion to a

[1] Laming Worthington-Evans (1868–1931), son of a London solicitor. M.P., 1910–31; baronet 1916. Held minor office from 1915; secretary for war, 1921–22, 1924–29; postmaster-general, 1923.

[2] Gordon Hewart (1870–1943). Barrister. M.P., 1913–22; solicitor-general, 1916–19; attorney-general, 1919–22. Lord chief justice, 1922–40. Created baron, 1922, viscount, 1940.

[3] Thomas Jones (1870–1955); lecturer and professor of economics, Glasgow and Belfast; special investigator, Poor Law Commission, 1906–9; secretary of National Health Insurance Commissioners for Wales, 1912–16; deputy secretary of the cabinet, 1916–30; secretary of the Pilgrim Trust, 1930–45; president of the University College of Wales, Aberystwyth.

[4] A. J. Sylvester, *Real Lloyd George*, p. 65.

settlement which helped to rob him of his ambitions for the prime ministership—were the heroes, on the British side, of the conference. Without them Lloyd George, for all his brilliance and finesse in the negotiations—and this conference was his masterpiece, the triumph of his dangerous dexterity as a negotiator— could never have brought the conference safely into harbour. That the conference lasted so long—until the night of December 5–6— was due in part to the many differences separating the negotiators, leading to a succession of crises, and in part to the delays caused by the frequent reference of matters to De Valera by letter, and to adjournments, more than once, while the Irish delegates crossed over to Dublin to consult their colleagues in the cabinet.

Two questions dominated the conference: would Ireland stay inside the Empire as a dominion, or be in 'external association' with it as a republic; and would Ulster be included or not. Ulster, the absent party to the negotiations, dominated them from offstage. Though the Irish were there as plenipotentiaries 'from the elected Government of the Republic in Ireland', the question of the republic was not seriously considered, and the Irish claim to neutrality was also soon thrust aside. The Irish proposal eventually put forward in 'Draft Treaty A' was for external association, and on this De Valera pinned his hopes; Griffith argued for it, but without vehemence—it was not his idea. Lloyd George's determination was, throughout, to get the Irish to accept the status of a dominion—which, at first, was psychologically unattractive, even humiliating, to the Irish, partly since the very conception was, in 1921, still in its infancy, partly because of the feeling that Ireland's proximity to Great Britain would prevent the status of a dominion meaning for her what it might, for example, to Canada. The Irish, never precise during the negotiations as to how far they would go, conceded everything— first the republic, then external association—for the sake of a united Ireland, unpartitioned; Lloyd George, utterly clear about the main objective—Ireland within the Empire—would concede almost anything else to get that, including, what he could not secure, some arrangements about Ulster which might bring it into the new dominion. He half-bartered Ulster for the dominion; the Irish bartered the republic for Ulster and got—only a dominion for themselves, without Ulster.

The climax in the negotiations came on the evening of Sunday, December 4, when the Irish delegates returned to Number 10 Downing Street with the modifications of a British draft of a treaty which they had brought back from Dublin after a meeting of the Dail cabinet—a meeting as stormy as their passage across the Irish Sea which preceded it. Negotiations broke down that evening on the question of Ireland's coming into the empire as a dominion. Next morning they were patched up again when Thomas Jones persuaded Collins to see Lloyd George once more. Collins accepted dominion status in return for Lloyd George's promise— which was surely in part deceitful—that Ulster's boundaries would be so contracted by the award of a Boundary Commission that it would almost certainly have to join Southern Ireland in order to survive. In any case Collins had by now, as a result of his rapid political education in London, come to a decision fateful for the negotiations, for Ireland, and for his life. It was to accept the empire, and Ireland as a dominion within it. A treaty in this sense would give Ireland so much more than it could ever have got in 1919, without fighting, that it was virtually a victory; and it gave, as he said later in the critical debate in the Dail, 'not the ultimate freedom that all nations desire and develop to, but the freedom to achieve it.'

Even then, the final meeting on Monday afternoon, December 5, almost ended in disaster. The question of Ulster was skirted again. A new and looser formula for an oath of allegiance was agreed to. Some further concessions on finance and naval defence were made. This was the limit of what Lloyd George would concede. In return, would the Irish delegates sign the draft treaty now? They had just promised the Dail cabinet to sign no treaty before it had been submitted to the Dail; but Lloyd George was determined to get their signatures at once.

And here the supreme magician produced his last and greatest sleight of hand, and by a stroke of brilliance—or trickery—presented the ultimatum which led to the signing of the treaty. The Northern Ireland parliament was meeting next day, and Lloyd George had promised Craig to let him know the outcome of the negotiations before it met. He had two letters ready, and held them, one in each hand.

> Here are the alternative letters which I have prepared, one enclosing Articles of Agreement reached by His Majesty's Government and yourselves, and the other saying that the Sinn Fein representatives refuse to come within the Empire. If I send this letter it is war, and war within three days. Which letter am I to send? Whichever letter you choose travels by special train to Holyhead and by destroyer to Belfast . . . we must know your answer by ten p.m. tonight. You can

have until then, but no longer, to decide whether you will give peace or war to your country.

Barton, describing the scene subsequently in the Dail, said: 'The English Prime Minister with all the solemnity and the power of conviction that he alone of all the men I ever met can impart by word and gesture . . . declared that the signature and recommendation of every member of our Delegation was necessary or war would follow immediately.' And he convinced them—that all must sign, and sign that night. He had conjured out of existence the telephone to Belfast by which Craig, if he had to have any message at all, could have received it next morning, and the telephone to Dublin by which the delegation might have consulted De Valera.[1]

The Irish left to consider their choice, though Griffith told Lloyd George that he would sign, even if none of the others did so.[2] On their way back to Hans Place, Collins declared that he would sign. After some argument, the others agreed, It was past midnight before they were back in Downing Street.

> As before [wrote Churchill] they were superficially calm and very quiet. There was a long pause, or there seemed to be. Then Mr. Griffith said, 'Mr. Prime Minister, the Delegation is willing to sign the agreements but there are a few points of drafting which perhaps it would be convenient if I mentioned at once.' Thus, by the easiest of gestures he carried the whole matter into the region of minor detail, and everyone concentrated upon these points with overstrained interest so as to drive the main issue into the background for ever.[3]

By 2.30 a.m., December 6, it was all over; all had signed and the meeting broke up. Lord Birkenhead gave the news of the treaty to reporters who had kept the long vigil through the night in the street outside.[4]

What had been signed was curious—actually not a treaty but 'Articles of Agreement for a Treaty between Great Britain and Ireland.'[5] It does, however, say 'Ireland' unequivocally, implying

---

[1] F. Pakenham, *Peace by Ordeal*, pp. 298–302.
[2] Churchill's description of the scene (*Aftermath*, p. 321) should not be missed.
[3] W. S. Churchill, *Aftermath*, p. 321.
[4] This narrative of the treaty negotiations is based on the brilliant account given, with absorbing detail, in Frank Pakenham's *Peace by Ordeal*. It should be supplemented by that in D. Hogan, *Four Glorious Years*, pp. 324–63. An excellent shorter account is in W. K. Hancock, *Survey of British Commonwealth Affairs*, I, *Problems of Nationality, 1918–1936* (Oxford, 1937), pp. 131–46. For Craig's part see St. J. Ervine, *Craigavon*, pp. 444–55.
A valuable list of all meetings, of the whole conference, of subcommittees and of individuals, is given in P. Beasley, *Michael Collins*, II, 446–52.
[5] The text has often been reprinted: see *Annual Register, 1921*. The official version is Cmd. 1560 (1921).

a recognition of the Dail's right to speak for a united Ireland, if
not a recognition of the Republic.[1] It gave Ireland, styled the
Irish Free State, the status of a Dominion within the British
Empire similar to that of Canada. The fateful oath of allegiance
presented for members of the Dail was: 'I do solemnly swear true
faith and allegiance to the Constitution of the Irish Free State as by
law established, and that I will be faithful to H.M. King George V,
his heirs and successors by law, in virtue of the common citizenship of Ireland with Great Britain and her adherence to and
membership of the group of nations forming the British Commonwealth of Nations.' The Free State assumed liability for its share
of the public debt of the United Kingdom, subject to any counter-
claims by Ireland. Coastal defence would be provided by Great
Britain for five years, when the situation would be reviewed in
conference; and the military forces of the Free State were to bear
the same proportion to the population as the military establishments in Great Britain did to the British population. The Free
State granted Great Britain the use of the 'treaty ports', as they
came to be called, in peacetime—Queenstown (Cobh), Berehaven,
Lough Swilly, and Belfast Lough (the last entirely within Northern Ireland), and certain oil storage facilities; in time of war
additional, unstated facilities might be granted. The all-important
clauses regarding Northern Ireland (11–15) maintained the provisions of the Government of Ireland Act, 1920, in force there
until one month after parliament's ratification of the treaty; before
the expiration of that month Northern Ireland, by an address of
both houses of parliament, might contract out of the Free State,
and thus retain its existing status. If it did not do so, it would
retain its parliament at Belfast, but would be subject, in matters
over which its parliament and government did not have authority,
to the parliament of the Free State, under certain safeguards. The
Council of Ireland, as provided for in the 1920 Act, would continue to exist if Northern Ireland remained outside the Free State.
In that case, also, a Boundary Commission of three men, appointed
by the governments of the Free State, Northern Ireland and Great
Britain respectively, would determine the boundary between the
two parts of Ireland 'in accordance with the wishes of the inhabitants, so far as may be compatible with economic and geographic conditions.' (clause 12.)

[1] W. K. Hancock, *Survey*, I, 147.

5. THE DEBATE OVER THE TREATY

It was, however, one thing to sign a treaty in London and quite another to get it accepted in Dublin. De Valera received the news of it on the afternoon of December 6, and seems at once to have set his face against it. The influence over him of the two ministers who had stayed at home, Brugha and Stack, had greatly increased, and they had won him over—Brugha in part because of his intense personal jealousy of Collins, with whom he had, as minister of defence, frequently clashed, Stack partly for a similar reason—Collins' interference with his work as minister of home affairs; Stack was the son of an old Fenian, had taken part in the Easter Rebellion, and made a name for himself as the leader of a hunger strike in Mountjoy prison in 1918. When Desmond Fitzgerald brought in a copy of the treaty and said to Stack: 'I did not think he [De Valera] was against this kind of settlement before we went to London,' Stack replied: 'He's dead against it now, anyway. That's enough.' 'The stress was on the word "now" [Fitzgerald added]; It was a cry of triumph.'[1]

The meeting of the full cabinet took place on December 8, and lasted far into the night. The main issue was not so much the contents of the treaty as the fact that the delegates had signed it (which, as plenipotentiaries, they were entitled to do, in spite of a contrary decision at a cabinet meeting of December 3). It was agreed to submit the treaty to the Dail, but not in the name of the whole cabinet; and De Valera issued a statement to the press, proclaiming the division, and asking for calmness which his words did everything to prevent. Griffith also issued a statement declaring that he stood by the treaty as a 'foundation of peace and friendship between the two nations'.

The split was now complete and open. Its effect on the public was confusion. The great mass of the people in Ireland—as all over the world—had greeted the treaty with thankfulness and relief, as bringing peace and freedom. Now they were told it was not so— but a little late. The supporters of the treaty had a good three days' start over the opponents, and kept their lead.[2]

Thus while the houses of parliament approved the treaty by large majorities on December 16, the Dail debated it long and bitterly from December 14 to January 7, and ratified it only by the

[1] D. Ryan, *Unique Dictator*, p. 142, citing article by Fitzgerald in *Observer*, June 16, 1935.
[2] F. Pakenham, *Peace by Ordeal*, pp. 228-33; P. Beasley, *Michael Collins*, II, pp. 309-13; C. J. C. Street, *Ireland in 1921*, pp. 263, 280.

barest of majorities. Certainly no one loved the treaty and the prospect of continued partition, but most people felt it was a tremendous achievement. O'Hegarty calls the whole debate hypocritical: everyone hoped that the treaty would pass, but by the votes of others; the votes against it were from fear, not conviction.[1] De Valera intervened constantly, interrupting other speakers. His main objection was that the treaty did not reconcile Irish national aspirations with association with Great Britain; the oath of allegiance to the King was a stumbling block. His own proposal, which he circulated, was the celebrated 'Document No. 2': a treaty of association, incorporating, as regards defence, naval facilities, public debt and pensions, and, above all, the freedom of Northern Ireland to contract out of the settlement, the identical provisions of the actual treaty, but making Ireland not a dominion but an associate with the 'States of the British Commonwealth' for matters of 'common concern', including defence, peace and war, and political treaties; 'for purposes of the Association, Ireland shall recognise His Britannic Majesty as head of the Association.'[2] This was, of course, De Valera's external association again—a formula, just as dominion status was a formula, and to most people not worth fighting for. It was, however, exactly what De Valera himself secured for Ireland between 1932 and 1937, and which existed in the main until the Republic was formally established in 1949. Document No. 2 did not mention the Republic.

The defenders of the treaty were not lacking. Griffith argued that some compromise, some association with the British Commonwealth, had been inevitable from the first. Collins tried to keep the peace between the two factions. The opposition, for its part, had nothing positive to recommend: the truce could not continue indefinitely. Griffith, in his final speech, damned the hypocrisy of fighting over an oath, when so many Republicans had already taken one or other of seven different oaths to the King. 'I was told, "No, this generation might go down, but the next generation might do something or other." Is there to be no living Irish nation? Is the Irish nation to be the dead past or the prophetic future?'

When the vote was taken, on January 7, 1922, there were 64 in favour of the treaty, 57 against. Collins again urged harmony— a joint committee of both sides to carry out the treaty. De Valera

[1] P. S. O'Hegarty, *Victory of Sinn Fein*, pp. 83–4.
[2] P. Beasley, *Michael Collins*, II, pp. 462–70. D. Hogan, *Four Glorious Years*, pp. 366–7, explains the genesis of the document.

seemed touched, but before he could speak Miss MacSwiney, sister of the late mayor of Cork, and typical of that bitterness in so many of the women which had much to do with the coming of civil war, was on her feet delivering a 'screeching tirade' against the proposal; there could be no soft talk; the vote was the 'grossest act of betrayal that Ireland has ever endured'.[1] So the treaty was ratified; there was no more war against Britain; instead there was to be civil war, Irishmen and Irish women against their own kith and kin.[2]

First, however, came what in any other circumstances would have been a piece of comedy. De Valera resigned the presidency of the Dail, but was then a candidate for re-election, though his policy had been defeated. He was defeated by 60 to 58; there were some abstentions. Griffith at once rose to say that this was not a vote against De Valera, than whom 'there is scarcely a man I have ever met . . . that I have more love and respect for'; De Valera replied with magnanimity.

6. THE RIFT WIDENS

On the next day, Arthur Griffith was elected president of the Dail, after De Valera and a number of others had walked out. He appointed Collins, Duffy, Duggan, Cosgrave, Kevin O'Higgins, and Mulcahy to his ministry. De Valera returned to the Dail in the afternoon, promised not to stand in the way of Griffith in carrying out his duties, and asked for a statement of policy, which Griffith made. Childers rose to criticise, rousing, for once, Griffith's open anger: 'I will not reply to any damned Englishman in this assembly.'[3]

A curious, second step was necessary, under the terms of the treaty, for its ratification—a meeting of the parliament of Southern Ireland elected under the 1920 Act. On January 14 the members of the Dail who had voted for the treaty met with the four other members of that phantom parliament—the four members for Trinity College, Dublin—and ratified the treaty, also electing, as prescribed, a Provisional Government to take over the administration of the country from the British authorities until the

---

[1] P. S. O'Hegarty, *Victory of Sinn Fein*, pp. 56–8, 102–5, 107–8; D. Hogan, pp. 368–76.
[2] P. Beasley, *Michael Collins*, II, 314–42; F. O'Connor, *Death in Dublin*, pp. 216–26. The debate may be found in Irish Free State, *Treaty Debates*, a volume preceding the series, beginning September 9, 1922, entitled Dail Eireann, *Parliamentary Debates, Official Report*. See also the account in D. Macardle, *Irish Republic*, p. 632 *seq.*
[3] P. Beasley, *Michael Collins*, II, 343–55.

E

government of the Irish Free State had been constituted. Of this Collins was chairman; other members of the Dail ministry who were in it were Cosgrave, Duggan and O'Higgins. These two parallel ministries functioned for several months, the former largely in make-believe, but suggesting that the Republic, whose assembly the Dail was, still had some sort of existence, and so tragically encouraging the movement towards civil war.[1]

To the Provisional Government the Lord Lieutenant formally handed over the government of the country on January 16; but Collins, after taking the 'surrender of the Castle', as he put it, wisely did not install the seat of government in that place of grim memories. The evacuation of the British troops began at once; by May, when the garrison at Cork had left, the only troops remaining were those in Dublin. The task of the Provisional Government was a prodigious one. Among its members a new figure came to the fore, Kevin O'Higgins. Born in 1892, the son of a doctor, he had been elected to the Dail in 1918, and served his apprenticeship as Cosgrave's assistant in the Dail's department of local government. Later, he described the Provisional Government as 'simply eight young men in the City Hall standing amidst the ruins of one administration, with the foundations of another not yet laid, and with wild men screaming through the keyhole'.[2]

Civil war was slow in breaking out, but its coming was inexorable. De Valera formed a new party, the Republican party; and Erskine Childers provided the propaganda for the anti-treaty cause in a paper, *The Republic of Ireland*. De Valera must bear a large responsibility for the civil war. He believed it to be his duty to maintain his stand for the Republic. He was ready, indeed anxious, to have any final decision over the treaty, for example in a general election, postponed until a constitution had been published and tempers had subsided. Yet his speeches in March, on a flying tour of the south, certainly seemed to encourage that violent opposition to the treaty by the dissidents in the I.R.A. which was the root cause of the war: witness his pacificatory remarks in his speech at Thurles on St. Patrick's day, March 17, 1922: 'If they accepted the treaty, and if the Volunteers of the future tried to complete the work the Volunteers of the last four years had been attempting, they would have to complete it, not

---

[1] *Michael Collins*, II, 355–6. P. S. O'Hegarty, *Victory of Sinn Fein*, p. 111; Terence de Vere White, *Kevin O'Higgins* (London, 1948), pp. 78, 82.
[2] T. de V. White, *O'Higgins*, p. 83.

over the bodies of foreign soldiers, but over the dead bodies of their own countrymen. They would have to wade through Irish blood. . . .'[1]

The I.R.A., or a large part of it, was ready for just this. A convention of the I.R.A. was summoned for March 26, but suppressed by the Chief of Staff. The dissidents then held a convention of their own, in the Mansion House, Dublin, on March 18, and appointed their own executive. Thereafter, there were two forces, the Regulars or Dail troops, and the Irregulars, who called themselves 'the Army of the Irish Republic'. Even before this, local commandants had been ignoring official orders from headquarters, and seizing arms and lorries. On February 18, Liam Forde, the Mid-Limerick brigadier, had issued a 'proclamation' repudiating the authority of headquarters. Nevertheless, the high command had made no distinction between loyal and disloyal groups; as the British withdrew, local barracks were handed over to local I.R.A. units, many of them already opposed to the treaty.

The civil war was, in fact, a product of the previous war against Great Britain which had encouraged conduct by the Irish (matched by the Black and Tans) which had at times been more criminal than warlike. It was a product also of the demoralisation of the I.R.A. since the truce. For the later intransigence of the Irregulars, the Irish-Americans had no small share of the responsibility.[2]

The civil war perhaps began on April 14, when the Irregulars, under Rory O'Connor, seized the Four Courts, one of the main government buildings in Dublin. No attempt was made at the time to prevent this. Ambushes and attacks on barracks followed throughout the country. In Dublin, fights broke out in the streets and bombs were hurled, often with more damage to civilians than to the troops. In the town of Kilkenny the Irregulars seized the cathedral, Ormonde Castle and other buildings, and were only dislodged after two days' fighting, though there were no fatalities. At the end of April, a peace conference, summoned by the Archbishop of Dublin, was held, and subsequently a peace was arranged, which lasted, more or less, until after the election.[3]

For a general election there was, as the British government insisted there must be, though De Valera and his followers tried to prevent or postpone it. The issue was to be the treaty; yet so anxious were Collins and the government party to conciliate

[1] D. Ryan, *Unique Dictator*, pp. 169, 195; M. J. MacManus, *De Valera*, p. 155; D. Macardle, *Irish Republic*, p. 683 *seq.*
[2] P. Beasley, *Michael Collins*, II, 426.
[3] *Michael Collins*, II, 381–91. D. Macardle, *Irish Republic*, p. 698 *seq.*

the opposition that Collins entered into a pact with De Valera on May 20 which would have eliminated the issue in order to obtain conditions of peace in which the election, even if robbed of its meaning, might be held. Under the terms of the pact Sinn Fein candidates would be chosen from a panel in proportion to the present strength of the supporters and opponents of the treaty in the Dail; and the new ministry would reflect the same proportions. Naturally, the British government objected to such a curious arrangement, and Griffith and Collins went to London to receive Churchill's admonitions. As it was, the pact permitted other interests to oppose the candidates of the Sinn Fein panel. The result was that peaceful electioneering was constantly interrupted: meetings were broken up, roads and railways were blocked, newspapers were seized. The election was held on June 16. In the event the government party won 58 seats, the anti-treatyites 35, Labour 17, Farmers 7, Independents 7, Unionists (Trinity College) 4.[1]

The election results were interpreted by the government party as giving a 72 per cent majority in favour of the treaty, though the anti-treatyites saw the results as a mandate for a coalition government and the postponement of a decision over the treaty. Thus when the existing Provisional Government and Dail ministry both continued unchanged, without the addition of De Valera and his followers, the latter claimed a breach of promise; and when a meeting of those elected was summoned for July 1, it was summoned as the parliament of the Provisional Government, encouraging the opposition to brand it as unconstitutional, and not the true Dail.

The opposition was, moreover, incensed at the draft of the Free State constitution which was published on the eve of the election. The original draft had contained no reference to the King. The British government insisted on its being drastically revised, not only to reinstate the King and the oath but to make the constitution subordinate to the treaty which, in cases of conflict, was to have priority. These things justified the Republicans, by their own inner light, in making war on the treacherous government; and other events soon brought on full-scale civil war. The meeting of the new Dail, as it called itself, was postponed, and did not occur until September 9. The Republicans (anti-treaty) were then absent; and the constituencies of Northern Ireland un-

[1] P. Beasley, *Michael Collins*, II, 392–8; W. A. Phillips, *Revolution in Ireland*, p. 279; D. Macardle, *Irish Republic*, pp. 735–52.

represented. Debate on the constitution was begun on September 18, and the bill embodying it completed by October 25.[1]

In Northern Ireland the civil peace was hardly less disturbed. Sir James Craig and his cabinet had accepted the news of the treaty in December 1921, with an ill grace, and complained of the financial provisions, the Boundary Commission, and the automatic inclusion of Northern Ireland within the Free State, though with the right to contract out.[2] Thanks to Churchill who, as Colonial Secretary (since January 1921) had become responsible for Anglo-Irish relations, Craig and Collins were brought together on January 21, 1922, at the Colonial Office and agreed, after an all-day discussion *tête-à-tête*, to work together to carry out the settlement. Little, alas, came of this and of subsequent meetings.[3] Not only Belfast but many towns along the border continued to be disturbed by raids, kidnappings, bombings and murders; in all, 294 persons were killed in Northern Ireland in 1922.[4] I.R.A. atrocities were matched by Orange reprisals, with fatal results to both sides: Macready recorded that in one month (February 10 to March 6, 1922) 12 Protestants and 25 Roman Catholics were killed in Belfast and many more wounded.[5]

The existence of the border was an invitation to trouble; indeed, many of the southern Irish hoped to restore unity among themselves by provoking Britain into a new war arising out of border incidents. Sir James Craig bombarded the British government with demands for more troops, while denouncing any move to rectify the frontier through a boundary commission, which led Churchill to write to him officially: 'You ought not to send us a telegram begging for help on the largest possible scale and announce an intention to defy the Imperial Parliament on the same day.'[6] A lilliputian campaign occurred when, at the end of May, Irregulars invaded the Pettigo triangle, a tiny stretch of Ulster territory on the border of Donegal and cut off by Lough Erne from access from Northern Ireland except across Free State territory. The Irish forces occupied Pettigo, a village bisected by the boundary, and seized an old stone fort dominating the village of Belleek. British troops (but surely not '7000 men with cannon and armed launches', as Churchill relates) drove out the Irish with

[1] D. Macardle, *Irish Republic*, pp. 691, 750–7, 797–8, 810–30; W. A. Phillips, *Irish Revolution*, pp. 277–8.

[2] See Craig's letter to Lloyd George, Dec. 14, 1921, in C. J. C. Street, *Ireland in 1921*, pp. 274–7, and St. J. Ervine, *Craigavon*, pp. 461–2.

[3] W. S. Churchill, *Aftermath*, pp. 332–3; St. J. Ervine, *Craigavon*, pp. 467, 472, 475.

[4] *Craigavon*, pp. 460, 467–8.   [5] N. Macready, *Annals*, II, 583, 607, 628.

[6] W. S. Churchill, *Aftermath*, p. 351.

the aid of a few howitzer shells, and afterwards occupied certain villages and maintained a neutral zone along that tricky part of the frontier.[1] In these operations, the pro-treaty and anti-treaty factions of the I.R.A. were more or less acting together, under arrangements made during negotiations which had preceded the pact over the election.[2]

These early months of the new regime in Northern Ireland left an evil legacy: the Civil Authorities (Special Powers) Act passed by the Northern Ireland parliament in 1922 and, after several renewals, made permanent in 1933. This delegated to the Minister for Home Affairs and to the police sweeping powers of search, arrest, summary trial, and imprisonment without trial.[3] In this and other ways order was restored and Protestant and Unionist rule perpetuated among a people of $1\frac{1}{4}$ millions, of whom the Roman Catholics (who were mostly Nationalists) constituted one-third (and in the counties of Fermanagh and Tyrone a majority). The gerrymandering of constituencies,[4] and the large number of the Class B special police (11,514, supplementing 2867 regular police in 1936),[5] kept Nationalist ambitions severely in check.

7. CIVIL WAR

The Pettigo incident, though comical, might have had grave consequences, even more so as it came just before the moment of gravest strain between the British government and the Provisional Government in Ireland in June 1922. The election for the Dail was just over. The Four Courts were still occupied by Rory O'Connor and the Irregulars. On June 22 Sir Henry Wilson, who had retired from the position of Chief of the Imperial General Staff and had been elected to the British parliament for an Ulster constituency, was shot to death on his doorstep in Eaton Place, London, by two Irishmen—not, apparently, connected with either faction of the I.R.A. Sir Henry had been widely credited with organising Ulster's resistance to the still-unborn Free State, though actually he had done no more than give some advice on the reorganisation of the Ulster police.

[1] W. S. Churchill, *Aftermath*, pp. 354–8; N. Macready, *Annals*, II, 644–7.
[2] D. Macardle, *Irish Republic*, pp. 761–2.
[3] Henry Harrison, *Ulster and the British Empire, 1939* (London, 1939), pp. 90–104; text, *ibid.*, pp. 197–227. The report of a commission of inquiry appointed by the National Council for Civil Liberties (London) 'to examine the purpose and effect of the Civil Authorities (Special Powers) Acts (Northern Ireland), 1922 and 1933', published in 1936, strongly condemned this legislation; see *Spectator*, May 29, 1936.
[4] H. Harrison, *Ulster and the British Empire*, pp. 79–81, 194–6.
[5] *Ulster Year Book, 1938*, pp. 231–4. Number of B Specials, 1927, 14,071 (*ibid.*, 1929, p. 156).

In the wave of indignation caused by this event, the British government, apparently at Churchill's urging, sent orders to Macready, still in command of the remaining British troops in Dublin, to drive Rory O'Connor out of the Four Courts. It seemed as if the dearest wish of the Irregulars, to end the civil war, overthrow the treaty and establish the Republic all at once by a new war against England[1] which would unite all factions, was about to be realised. General Macready, in perhaps his greatest piece of public service in a long career devoted, in large part, to directing the military arm in civil affairs, delayed for a day taking action without further orders. The orders were countermanded. Two days later the Irregulars kidnapped J. J. O'Connell, the Commander-in-Chief of the Regulars. Collins and the other leaders then decided to assert the authority of the government, though a virtual ultimatum from Churchill to them, telling them to end this 'gross breach and defiance of the Treaty', almost made them change their minds.[2]

In the early hours of June 28 the attack on the Four Courts began. Macready, under instructions from London, lent the Regulars two eighteen-pounder field guns and some ammunition, and with much noise and firing, but still with tenderness for the rebels, the siege was pressed. By nightfall, ammunition was exhausted and, to Collins' disgust, Macready said he had no more to spare. Next day the government troops gained a footing in the Four Courts, and on June 30 the Irregulars, about 150 men, surrendered. They had mined and fired the buildings, which were largely destroyed. Since part of the edifice housed the Irish Public Record Office, one effect of this military operation was that Ireland's official records, going back to the Middle Ages, were burnt or scattered to the four winds in the burning of the Four Courts.[3]

The capture of the Four Courts marked the formal beginning of war by the Provisional Government against the Irregulars. The Irregulars accepted the challenge: war had been declared against them by their former comrades, and, they said, at Britain's behest. De Valera rejoined his old battalion, now a part of the Irregular forces.[4] The government on its part issued a 'national call to arms'. Collins became Commander-in-Chief of the National Army. On July 12 a proclamation was issued, threatening reprisal

[1] See the evidence given by P. Beasley, *Michael Collins*, II, 400–1.
[2] D. Ryan, *Unique Dictator*, pp. 202–4.
[3] N. Macready, *Annals*, II, 652–9; W. S. Churchill, *Aftermath*, pp. 363–4; D. Macardle, *Irish Republic*, pp. 766–83.
[4] M. J. MacManus, *De Valera*, p. 177.

for all attempts at murder. Gradually the Irregulars were driven out of their hiding places in Dublin. The last group to surrender was at the Granville Hotel, and, fittingly enough, it included Cathal Brugha, who characteristically refused to surrender, and was mortally wounded in trying to fight his way out of the burning building (July 5). He died on July 7.[1]

The civil war was more widespread, but more fragmentary, than the war against the Black and Tans—a matter of murders, raids, arson, ambushes, executions. Collins could no longer rely on his intelligence services; now it was treachery within his own ranks which he had to fear. He had hastily to organise a new army out of remnants of the I.R.A. and new recruits. Nor could he be as tough towards fellow-Irishmen, until recently his comrades, as he had been towards the British. So 'anarchy and the law of the gun reigned, and disorder, loss of life, destruction of property, and crimes of violence steadily increased'.[2] Physical destruction, especially the looting and burning of historic country houses and damage to railway property, greatly exceeded that of the war against the British. Women and children were used as decoys, women as gunmen, as they had not been before; and the bully and the racketeer took over. Gunmen in mufti carried out ambushes and made attacks with pistol and grenade in crowded streets, on foot or from lorries; as often as not the casualties were innocent passers-by.[3]

In July and August the government pressed the attack firmly, but suffered two stunning losses. On July 8, a big concentration of Irregulars at Blessington, outside Dublin, was attacked and driven off. Wexford town was occupied. In the town of Limerick there was fighting for several days. Dundalk was captured by the Regulars on July 16, Waterford on the 20th. Various towns in the west also fell to the government. Cork was occupied on August 11 by some 470 National troops, who made several landings from the sea.[4] Gradually, the government was establishing its authority over the country, and confining the Irregulars to small-scale terrorist activities. Then on August 12 Arthur Griffith died, of heart failure, though suspicions of poisoning were not lacking. The civil war, coming when he had thought his life's work for Ireland's freedom had been crowned with success, had under-

[1]. P. Beasley, *Michael Collins*, II, 407–8; W. S. Churchill, *Aftermath*, p. 365; *The Times*, July 6, 8, 1922.
[2] P. Beasley, *Michael Collins*, II, 403, 409–10, 415–16.
[3] For one tragi-comic incident, see G. Griffin, *Dead March Past*, pp. 286, 296 *seq.*
[4] P. Beasley, *Michael Collins*, II, 413–17.

mined his strength and fortitude. Collins, in his uniform as Commander-in-Chief, delivered the funeral oration. He then resumed a tour of inspection of the south-west, which had been interrupted by the news of Griffith's death. On August 22, when travelling between Bandon and Macroom, near Ballyvourney, his party was attacked by heavy machine-gun and rifle fire from a road higher up the hill. The cars stopped, the men took cover behind a mud-bank at the side of the road, and the machine-gun on the party's armoured car opened up. Firing from both sides continued for some twenty minutes. Collins, who was firing along with the rest, moved to another position up the road, and soon afterwards was found by his companions dying, shot through the skull. The wound was in the back of the head, from a shot fired from a distance, and there were many who suspected foul play from within his own party. He was only thirty-one.[1]

The new Ireland was fortunate in its leaders. Griffith and Collins removed, W. T. Cosgrave and Richard Mulcahy took their places as chairman and minister of defence respectively in the Provisional Government. Cosgrave, who had fought in the Easter Rebellion, and been in De Valera's and Griffith's cabinets under the Dail, had been acting-president of the Dail during Griffith's illness. He was confirmed as President when the Dail met on September 9. The phantom government of the Dail was heard of no more.[2]

Under Cosgrave, Mulcahy, and Kevin O'Higgins (minister of home affairs), the war against the rebels was pressed unflinchingly. Courts martial were freely resorted to; hunger strikes by men and women prisoners were ignored; hostages were taken; reprisals resorted to. The possession of firearms was made a capital offence, for which, among others, Erskine Childers was executed on November 24, an event which stirred the deepest feelings. When a member of the Dail was murdered and another wounded on December 7 as the start of a murder campaign against members of the government, Rory O'Connor and three other prisoners in Mountjoy prison were at once taken from their cells and executed.[3] The burning of houses continued, and the kidnappings, the murders (O'Higgins' father was one of the victims of the rebels), the damage to roads and railways, the seizures of goods and the pistol-backed demands for contributions mounted

[1] P. Beasley, *Michael Collins*, II, 423–40.
[2] See above, p. 100; T. de V. White, *O'Higgins*, pp. 105–7.
[3] D. Macardle, *Irish Republic*, pp. 842–8; T. de V. White, *O'Higgins*, pp. 119–32, 142–6.

E*

week by week. Gradually order was enforced. On April 27, 1923,
De Valera, on behalf of the so-called government of the Republic,
and after a meeting of the Irregulars' executive, issued a proclamation suspending all 'offensive operations'. De Valera's proposals
for peace having been brusquely rejected by Cosgrave's government, an order to the 'Soldiers of the Republic' to cease fire and
dump their arms was issued on May 24. The civil war was over,
though the I.R.A., or gunmen masquerading under its alleged
licence, continued to plague Ireland and England for nearly a
score of years thereafter.[1]

The toll of life taken by the civil war can hardly be estimated.
The Free State government had 11,000 men in internment camps
at the end of the war, and had executed 77 rebels (compared to 24
military executions by the British in 1920–21).[2] The number of
country houses destroyed was put at 139. Destruction of railway
property was especially heavy. The largest railway, the Great
Southern and Western, in 1922 sustained over 400 cases of
damage to tracks; over 300 bridges were damaged, 103 signal
boxes, 36 station buildings, 468 locomotives and carriages. Trains
were stopped in open country, the passengers forced to alight, the
engine uncoupled, run up the line and then sent back, driver-less, to
smash into the empty train. The viaduct near Mallow was blown
up so cleverly that the help of German sappers was suspected.[3]

8. THE IRISH FREE STATE AND THE BOUNDARY

Long before the civil war ended, the Irish Free State had come
into being. The transfer of power to the Provisional Government
was recognised by the Irish Free State (Agreement) Act of
March 1922. The constitution of the Free State, after its acceptance by the Dail, was approved by parliament as embodied in the
Irish Free State (Constitution) Act, passed on December 5. T. M.
Healy, a Home Ruler who had been in parliament from 1880 to
1918, was appointed first governor-general, a choice almost
universally acceptable. On December 6, 1922, the setting up of
the Free State government was proclaimed, and the Provisional
Government came to an end. And on Sunday, December 17,
General Macready and the last of the British forces—the last of
the historic army of occupation—left Dublin and sailed for

---

[1] D. Macardle, *Irish Republic*, pp. 832–91. W. A. Phillips, *Revolution in Ireland*,
pp. 283–303.
[2] D. Macardle, *Irish Republic*, pp. 1021–3.
[3] W. A. Phillips, *Revolution in Ireland*, pp. 288–91.

England. Northern Ireland had exercised its option to contract out of the Free State with precipitate haste on December 7. Ireland was free, but partitioned; and for a time passed into smoother waters.

An early sequel concerning the boundary and certain financial arrangements may be recorded here. The Irish signatories of the treaty had assented to the continuance of partition because they had understood from Lloyd George that the Boundary Commission would so modify the boundary that Ulster would be forced to join the Free State as the price of economic survival. When Collins and Craig met in London in January 1922, they agreed that, instead of the Boundary Commission, negotiations between representatives of their two governments should be resorted to to settle the boundary. Disagreement soon appeared. Collins' understanding was that the Free State was entitled to all of Fermanagh and Tyrone, large parts of Antrim and Down, and the cities of Londonderry, Enniskillen and Newry: Craig's view was that mere minor rectifications of the boundary were involved.[1]

In view of the deliberate ambiguity in the treaty over the boundary, it is not surprising that a solution was delayed and then, eventually, 'cooked'. It was not until 1924, when the Labour government was in office, that the question was reopened; and again, negotiations were first resorted to, this time between Cosgrave, Craig, and British ministers in London. When they failed, and when the Northern Ireland government refused to appoint a representative to a Boundary Commission (whose creation the Free State government now demanded), the Labour government, on the eve of its fall, obtained enabling legislation to appoint a representative for Northern Ireland as well as the chairman; the commission was then constituted with Mr. Justice Feetham, of the South African supreme court, as chairman, J. R. Fisher, a Belfast Unionist, and former friend of Carson, as Northern Ireland's representative, and Professor Eoin McNeill, minister of education in Cosgrave's cabinet, as representative of the Free State.[2]

Subject to much coaching from press and platform as to what, in the opinion of both sides, the treaty's provisions about the boun-

[1] D. Macardle, *Irish Republic*, pp. 628, 684–6, 711–13, 907–9, 1003–5; W. A Phillips, *Revolution in Ireland*, pp. 239–41, 326–30. Denis Gwynn, *History of Partition*, pp. 212–18, gives some evidence to show that at the time of the making of the treaty it was generally understood by all parties that the Boundary Commission would award large areas to the Free State.
[2] D. Gwynn, *History of Partition*, pp. 222–30; D. Macardle, *Irish Republic*, pp. 905–7, 912.

dary had meant, the commission had little hope of reaching an impartial and agreed award. It began work in November 1924, held meetings in London and in Ireland, examined many witnesses, perambulated the border areas, refused, as beyond its competence, to conduct a plebiscite, and a year later was preparing its report. The gist of this was allowed to leak out, and a forecast of it was published in the *Morning Post* on November 7, 1925. It was said that the commission would not deprive Northern Ireland of any large pieces of territory, though in Fermanagh and Armagh parts of the boundary, about forty miles altogether in length, would be moved northwards in favour of the Free State; on the other hand a part of Donegal, near Londonderry, and other places, would be transferred to Ulster.[1]

The reaction of the Free State government was swift and inevitable; it would refuse to cede any territory to Northern Ireland. Professor MacNeill resigned from the commission, and subsequently, from Cosgrave's cabinet. Cosgrave, O'Higgins, and other ministers hastened over to London, and there, on December 3, 1925, signed an agreement with Craig and the British government: the powers of the Boundary Commission were revoked and the boundary of 1920 was allowed to stand unchanged; the Free State, in return, was relieved of its obligations, hitherto undefined, under article 5 of the treaty, for its share in the United Kingdom's public debt less any counter-claims of Ireland against the British government. In addition, the Free State assumed liability for compensation for damage done in Ireland during the fighting in 1919 and 1920 and down to the truce, and promised to repay the British government the sums already paid by the latter for this purpose and to increase by 10 per cent the compensation paid by the Free State for damage to property suffered during the civil war. The agreement gave Northern Ireland an important concession; the powers over it reserved in the treaty for the abortive Council of Ireland were transferred to the Northern Ireland government.[2]

---

[1] D. Macardle, *Irish Republic*, pp. 908–13, 919–20; D. Gwynn, *History of Partition*, pp. 230–5.

[2] St. J. Ervine, *Craigavon*, pp. 498–507 (the fullest account of the negotiations); D. Macardle, *Irish Republic*, pp. 920–31, 1014–15 (text of 1925 agreement); an 'ultimate financial settlement', involving annual payments of nearly £5,000,000 by the Free State to Great Britain in respect of land annuities and other obligations, was signed by Winston Churchill, chancellor of the Exchequer, and Ernest Blythe, Free State finance minister, on March 19, 1926 (D. Macardle, *Irish Republic*, pp. 868, 931, 1016–18).

9. THE CHANGING EMPIRE

The British Empire which the Irish Free State had agreed to join as a Dominion was itself a changing thing. The term 'British Commonwealth of Nations' had come into use during the war to describe the association of Great Britain and the Dominions—a term popularised by the *Round Table* (founded in 1910) and by men such as Lionel Curtis, Philip Kerr and General Smuts. It reflected the independence, strength and nationhood which the Dominions had attained, as shown by their great contributions in the war.

The journeys of Edward, Prince of Wales, during the twenties helped to strengthen the unity of the Commonwealth. The prince's popularity was at its height at this time, kindled by his war service as a staff officer in Flanders as much as by the youthful appearance and enthusiasms of this slender, handsome 'Prince Charming', a people's prince with the common touch and the ability to get on with everyone and set the shyest at his ease. He journeyed to Canada (with a side-trip to the United States) in 1919, then to the West Indies, Australia and New Zealand in 1920, to India in 1922. A tour to South Africa followed in 1925, to East Africa in 1928. Imperial loyalties, not the less potent for being unashamedly sentimental and uncritical, were strengthened by this royal ambassador; the crown became a living, not merely formal, bond of empire.[1]

In the Colonial Empire there were few changes. The idea that native peoples and backward areas constituted 'a sacred trust' of the civilised nations existed long before it was embodied in the Covenant of the League of Nations in the mandates over ex-German colonies. The great administrator of Nigeria, Sir F. J. D. Lugard (later Lord Lugard), gave the idea wider currency as the 'dual mandate': a mandate both for the development of colonial territories in the interests of native and white man, and for the advancement of the native towards the good life by using the best elements in his social organisation alongside the techniques of civilisation—the idea of 'indirect rule' which he pioneered in Nigeria and expressed in his book, *The Dual Mandate in British Tropical Africa*, published in 1922. In its simplest form, this meant that native interests should come first; but this proved

---

[1] Adulatory lives of the Prince of Wales were legion; see W. and L. Townsend, *Biography of H.R.H. the Prince of Wales* (London, 1929). Cf. *Round Table*, 11: 1–9 (Dec., 1920). See also the prince's own account in Duke of Windsor, *A King's Story* (London, 1951).

difficult to apply in the new colony of Kenya (created in 1920 out of the East Africa Protectorate), where some 10,000 white settlers, many of them ex-officers of the war, insisted that their interests came before those of the three million natives and 23,000 Indians in the colony, and demanded 'responsible government', provided that they alone bore the responsibility. After three years of bitter dispute, provoked not by the natives but by the Indians, vigorously backed by the Government of India, the Colonial Office gave judgment: the interest of the natives was 'paramount', and responsible government out of the question, but no drastic change was contemplated—thus in effect preserving the ascendancy of the settlers.[1] Elsewhere, the colonies pursued a slow and uneventful existence under the benevolent autocracy of Government House, Governor, Secretary, Chief Justice, and the ubiquitous, over-worked District Officers; and the slumbers of the Colonial Office in London were seldom disturbed.[2]

With Egypt, a country virtually under British administration since 1882, and over which Britain had proclaimed a protectorate early in the war, the Coalition government attempted to make a settlement in 1920, following a revolt in March 1919. A settlement was prevented by nationalist feeling, whereupon Great Britain, in 1922, unilaterally declared that it recognised Egypt's independence, subject to reservations covering the defence of Egypt and the Suez Canal and the continuation of British administration in the Sudan. Attempts to get a treaty with Egypt on these matters failed.[3] After the murder of the Governor-General of the Sudan, Sir Lee Stack, on November 19, 1924, Britain insisted on the evacuation of Egyptian troops from the Sudan and tightened her control over the country.

It was with India that Britain experienced the greatest difficulties as an imperial power at this time and throughout the interwar years. The war had stirred Indian nationalism, and had brought together, for the time being, the predominantly Hindu Congress party and the Moslems, fired by the Khilafat movement in support of the battered Caliphate and the Turkish empire. As

[1] Colonial Office, *Indians in Kenya, Memorandum* (Cmd. 1922: 1923 [the Duke of Devonshire White Paper]). W. K. Hancock, *Survey of British Commonwealth Affairs*, I, 209–27. Books on Kenya's history are many, bitter and exciting; see especially W. M. Ross, *Kenya from Within* (London, 1927); M. R. Dilley, *British Policy in Kenya Colony* (New York, 1937).
[2] See A. Bertram, *Colonial Service* (London, 1930); C. Jeffries, *Colonial Empire and its Civil Service* (Cambridge, 1938); W. R. Crocker, *Nigeria: a Critique of British Colonial Administration* (London, 1936).
[3] H. Nicolson, *Curzon*, pp. 161–82.

early as August 1917, the government, through the Secretary of State for India, Edwin Montagu, had declared that its object for India was 'responsible government . . . as an integral part of the British Empire'. This sting in its tail robbed the declaration of much of its appeal in India, but the government followed it by an inquiry conducted by Montagu and the Viceroy, Lord Chelmsford, which produced the Montagu-Chelmsford Report of 1918 (the *Joint Report on Indian Constitutional Reforms*, Cd. 9109). Its pro-proposals were embodied in the Government of India Act, completed in December 1919. This reformed the government of the provinces on the lines of Lionel Curtis's ingenious but unsuccessful scheme of 'dyarchy', transferring certain powers to ministers responsible to elected legislative councils, but reserved to the Governor and the officials the powers over justice, police and, in effect, finance. At the centre a bicameral legislature was created, largely elective in composition, but with its authority severely limited by the powers reserved to the Viceroy and his Executive Council, in which Indian members were in a minority.

The effect of these reforms, generous in British eyes but slight to the Indians, was weakened by the contemporaneous Rowlatt acts, the result of the report of an inquiry into sedition by a committee headed by Mr. Justice Rowlatt (Sir Sidney A. T. Rowlatt, a British judge). These gave the government increased powers for the arrest and summary trial of political suspects. Amid a good deal of unrest in 1919 the episode at Amritsar stood forth in unenvied eminence. Following the murder of four Europeans by a mob, an unarmed crowd assembled in an enclosed garden. It failed to disperse when ordered to do so; whereupon Brigadier-General R. E. H. Dyer ordered soldiers to fire upon it. Firing continued for ten minutes. Bullets and panic took the lives of 379, and 1208 persons were wounded. The Amritsar massacre of April 13, 1919, was not soon forgotten, the more so because General Dyer, though relieved of his command and put on half pay, received much support in debates in parliament (in July 1920).[1] Against this background Mahatma Gandhi and the Congress party launched the campaign for India's independence, to be carried out by the weapons of non-violent non-resistance and the boycott. In spite of Gandhi's exhortations, violence inevitably occurred, culminating in a mob attack on a police station at Chauri Chaura in the United Provinces in February 1922, when 21 police officers were killed. Gandhi then called off the civil dis-

[1] *Annual Register, 1920*, pp. 79-80, 273.

obedience campaign; but the government, yielding to much agitation at home, had him arrested and sentenced to 6 years' imprisonment. A calmer period ensued. India remained under the British *raj*, as depicted in E. M. Forster's *Passage to India* (1924):

> 'We're not out here for the purpose of behaving pleasantly' [says Heaslop, a young member of the Indian Civil Service].
> 'What do you mean?'
> 'What I say. We're out here to do justice and keep the peace . . .'
> 'Your sentiments are those of a god . . .'
> 'There's no point in all this. Here we are, and we're going to stop, and the country's got to put up with us, gods or no gods . . .'[1]

10. ECLIPSE OF LLOYD GEORGE'S POLICIES IN EUROPE

In international affairs Lloyd George continued, in 1921 and 1922, his policies of conciliation and personal diplomacy, amid increasing difficulties.[2] Reparations and security were the subject of several conferences. The British and French governments agreed to give Germany the opportunity of presenting proposals of her own regarding the sum total of reparations and the means by which it should be paid. The Germans were invited to the conference of the Allies held in London from February 21 to March 14, 1921, which was partly taken up with the question of Turkey. They met the Allies' leaders on March 1, and immediately put themselves in the wrong. Dr. Simons, the foreign minister, made a speech rejecting the Allies' proposals given on January 28, following a conference at Paris; by putting a high valuation on certain payments already made, and by other arguments, he brought the sum which Germany was ready to pay down to about one-seventh of what the Allies were demanding. In addition, the Germans were already in default over the initial payment of £1,000 million, due from them before the total sum of reparations was assessed. Lloyd George replied in a serious vein: in spite of the moderation of the Allies' demands, the German counter-proposals simply 'mock the Treaty'. Therefore, sanctions must be applied; and this was done on March 8. Duisburg, Ruhrort, and Düsseldorf were occupied, and customs duties levied on certain German imports and exports. Thus, for the moment, Lloyd

[1] E. M. Forster, *Passage to India* (Everyman edition, 1942), p. 39.
[2] For the weaknesses of Lloyd George's personal diplomacy, accelerating the decline of the status and importance of the professional diplomatists, see the shrewd comments of Gordon A. Craig in G. A. Craig and Felix Gilbert (eds.), *The Diplomats, 1919–1939* (Princeton, 1953), pp. 3–10, 17–33.

George swung round to the French position, and supported their policy of severity rather than conciliation.

Germany's total liability for reparations was finally fixed by the Reparation Commission on April 27, 1921, as £6,600 million. Another conference of the Allied governments was held in London (April 29–May 5) to work out a schedule of payments by which Germany might meet this obligation. This provided for payments of £100 millions annually, plus 26 per cent of the annual value of Germany's exports, to cover about one-third of the total sum; Germany was given six days to agree to this, under threat of the occupation of the Ruhr. The terms were accepted, and were carried out until December, 1921, when a default was again threatened by the Germans. This led to a conference between Lloyd George and Briand, who at the time was premier in France, held in London on December 18–22, and to the fatal conference (attended also by the Italian and Belgian premiers) at Cannes (January 6–14, 1922).

At Cannes Lloyd George and Briand, the most conciliatory, the most European-minded, of French statesmen of the period, attempted to come to an agreement not only over reparations but over the future cordiality of the *entente* between Great Britain and France—attempted, and all but succeeded. Briand had broached the question of an Anglo-French pact of security against Germany at the meeting in London in December, to replace the abortive treaties of 1919 between France, Britain and the United States. At Cannes Lloyd George and Briand exchanged memoranda on the conditions for closer association; Lloyd George was ready to agree to a security pact in return for French co-operation in European reconstruction, elimination of naval rivalry, and co-ordination of policies in the Near East. Thus, at last, might France's hunger for security be satisfied. Alas, Briand's position in French politics was insecure, and was completely undermined by the historic game of golf into which Lloyd George inveigled him and Bonomi, the Italian premier, both novices at the game. What was intended to promote feelings of relaxation and cordiality as a constructive interlude in the conference became, to the French public, thanks to the news reporters and photographers, a sign not only of frivolity but of Lloyd George's wizardry, which was leading Briand to sacrifice the interests of his country to British wiles. Briand had to return to Paris next day, January 11, and on the day after he resigned, being replaced by Raymond Poincaré. Lloyd George was left to meet a German delegation, but could make no arrangements with it. The conference broke up on the 13th, having accomplished nothing, except to make plans for a conference at Genoa, and to agree that the Russians should be brought back into the European community by being invited to attend it.

Poincaré's advent to power doomed to failure Lloyd George's last, and most ambitious, conference, the economic conference of all the European powers at Genoa, April 10–May 19, 1922. Poincaré, who soon became England's *bête noire*, was the antithesis of Briand, 'precise, formal, unmagnetic, with an untiring and in-human industry',[1] a narrow lawyer, determined to uphold France's claims against Germany under the treaty to the limit and to use physical sanctions against Germany to guarantee French security. Lloyd George broke his journey from Cannes to meet him in Paris on January 14, but they could come to no common ground; Poincaré insisted on an exact military convention as part of the treaty of guarantee, which Lloyd George rejected as impracticable and insulting. Subsequent negotiations in London were equally futile.

At Genoa, where delegates from twenty-nine European states assembled, including Germany and Russia, and also representatives of the Dominions, the postwar concert of Europe almost achieved reality, only to fade hopelessly away. Lloyd George, in his open-ing speech, hailed the conference as 'the greatest gathering of European nations which has ever been assembled', and laid down the broad conditions upon which the reconstruction of Europe's economic and political harmony could be attained. 'It seemed for the moment that it was the voice of Europe speaking . . . never was an English Prime Minister so nearly Europe's chosen leader. Genoa was the climax and the turning-point of his fortunes—and a turning-point, too, for Europe's policy'.[2] Yet only disappoint-ment followed. The speech of Russia's representative, Chicherin, seemed doctrinaire and conceited, and then and subsequently Russian proposals about disarmament, foreign investment, the settlement of Russia's debts, were unpalatable. The action of the Russian and German delegations in concluding, during the con-ferences, a treaty of recognition and commerce at Rapallo, on April 16, was regarded as a defiance of the other powers.[3] Poin-caré, who had refused to come to the conference, undermined it further by a speech at Bar-le-Duc on April 24, demanding the execution of the Treaty of Versailles against Germany and

[1] J. A. Salter, *Recovery*, p. 158.   [2] Ibid.
[3] Britain and Russia had concluded a trade agreement on March 16, 1921.

threatening, if there was no common action should Germany default on reparations, that France would act alone. The bonds of the *entente* were strained almost to breaking-point. A draft treaty for the resumption of normal relations with Russia was prepared, but it perished when the French and Belgian governments refused to sign it. The failure of the conference, after the high hopes held for it, damaged Lloyd George's position in the long run. Immediately, however, he returned to England better able to face his critics within the Coalition; for hostile and in part exaggerated reports of his diplomacy in *The Times* and the popular suspicions of France led to a revulsion of feeling in his favour.[1]

One international conference of the period did have a great though illusory success, the Washington conference of November 11, 1921 to February 6, 1922. The United States, though it had withdrawn from the Treaty of Versailles, from the League, and in a sense, from Europe, was still concerned with peace and international goodwill, not least in the Pacific. Charles Evans Hughes, Secretary of State in President Harding's cabinet, sent a formal invitation in August 1921 to the major powers to a conference on the limitation of armaments: the United States, Britain, France, Italy, Japan, China, Belgium, Netherlands, Portugal sent delegations, the Dominions being, somewhat to their disgust, included in a British Empire delegation instead of receiving separate invitations. Two subjects were pursued simultaneously at the conference by two committees: one, consisting of delegates from the first five countries named, considered disarmament, the other, representing all nine powers, considered Pacific and Far Eastern matters, whose inclusion in the agenda of the conference had been requested by Great Britain after the Imperial Conference of 1921. Here, as at other conferences, the disagreements between the British and French positions were open and serious and blocked any reduction of land forces. The United States proposed that all capital ships under construction be scrapped and a ten-year holiday on new construction be observed, leaving the existing fleets of capital ships in the ratio of 5, 5, 3, 1·75, 1·75 for the United States, Great Britain, Japan, France, Italy respectively. Balfour, the leader of the British delegation, accepted the Ameri-

---

[1] This account of the diplomacy of these years is based on: W. M. Jordan, *Britain, France, and the German Problem*, pp. 51, 72, 90, 108–9, 193, 200; R. B. Mowat, *European Diplomacy, 1914–1925*, pp. 211–26; H. Nicolson, *Curzon*, pp. 240–5; E. Mantoux, *Economic Consequences of Mr. Keynes* (Oxford, 1946; American edition, *The Carthaginian Peace*), pp. 133 *seq.*; A. J. Sylvester, *Real Lloyd George*, pp. 70–6. See also R. Boothby, *I Fight To Live*, pp. 61–5, 230. On the Genoa conference, see also *History of The Times*, IV, ii, 661–76.

can offer. Thus did Britain's historic naval supremacy become parity, ending a threatened and costly race in naval construction. On submarines and auxiliary craft no agreement was reached. Regarding the Pacific and the prevention of dangerous rivalries among the powers over its many islands, the conference was faced with the hostility of the United States to the continuance of the Anglo-Japanese alliance. The British had no desire to jettison this, regarding it as a guarantee of non-aggression between themselves and a major naval power close to distant possessions of theirs; but the pressure against it was strong, particularly from Canada, in its self-chosen (if seldom effective) role as mediator between Great Britain and the United States. The British agreed to the ending of the alliance only because a Four-Power Treaty (between the United States, Great Britain, Japan and France) replaced it in guaranteeing the *status quo* in the Pacific. The Washington conference was one of the eminences in Balfour's long public career. He received a great welcome on his return to London and was rewarded with the Order of the Garter. Soon afterwards he went to the Lords as the Earl of Balfour.[1]

11. CHANAK

Lloyd George's failure at Genoa was compounded, in the judgment of many, by his policies which in September 1922 seemed to have brought the country to the verge of war over Turkey. Actually the Chanak episode, which led to his downfall, was one of his triumphs, even if its antecedents were not. The fall of Venizelos and the return to the Greek throne of King Constantine at the end of 1920 seemed to have doomed Lloyd George's pro-Greek policy: the British had little enthusiasm for Greece under its old pro-German ruler, and the French, already suspicious of British policies in the Near East, were ready enough for a change. Only Lloyd George held resolutely to his support of Greece, whose army, after its advance in 1920, was occupying lines in the interior of Asia Minor against Kemal's forces. Imperial strategy and naval communications were the grounds for his support of the Greeks and his coolness to the traditional pro-Turkish attitude of his Tory colleagues.[2] Hence, in 1921, when the Greeks could have extri-

[1] R. B. Mowat, *European Diplomacy, 1914–1925*, pp. 227–42; B. E. C. Dugdale, *Balfour*, II, 232–47; H. W. Nevinson, *Last Changes, Last Chances*, pp. 228–49; *History of The Times*, IV, ii, ch. 14, 'The Naval Treaty' (its account of the initiation of the conference should be supplemented by Wickham Steed's letter in *The Times*, May 3, 1952).
[2] W. S. Churchill, *Aftermath*, p. 415.

cated themselves from Asia Minor, they did not do so, in part trusting to Lloyd George's support. They rejected the proposals for the modification of the treaty of Sèvres made at the London conference in February, and in the summer began a new offensive, aimed at Ankara. Already things had begun to turn against them, and against Lloyd George's policy. In March 1921, Russia and Turkey concluded an alliance, and thereafter Kemal received large supplies of munitions from across the Russian border. Still more fatal was France's defection. In October 1921, France and Turkey signed a treaty at Ankara, ending the war between the two and providing that France would evacuate Cilicia and surrender territory in northern Syria to Turkey.

In 1922 events moved towards the climax. On March 4 the Viceroy of India published a memorandum giving sympathetic support to Turkish aspirations as a means of quieting Moslem alarm in India. This, which ran counter to the British government's policy at the time, had been authorised by Montagu, the Secretary of State for India. Curzon, as Foreign Secretary, took up the challenge in the Cabinet, and forced Montagu's resignation. Curzon then attempted mediation between Greece and Turkey. He met Poincaré in Paris on March 22, and together they urged an armistice on Turkey in return for several concessions, including the end of all claims by Greece to Smyrna. The Greeks accepted the terms, but Kemal did not, and the state of war continued. In July Constantine decided on a last fling: to land troops on the northern shore of the Sea of Marmora and occupy Constantinople, even though this involved weakening his front in Asia Minor. The Allies, still in occupation of the zone of the Straits, refused to permit the landing. Kemal seized the chance. He began an attack on the Greeks on August 18, and the weight of his numbers, and the munitions imported from France and Russia, were decisive. The Greek position at Afium Karahissar was broken, and the Greek army streamed back to the coast. Turkish forces entered Smyrna on September 9 ; fire broke out and destroyed much of the town; Greek soldiers and peasants who survived fire and sword found safety in flight across the Aegean Sea, and the Greek adventure in Smyrna came to a desolate close.

A new danger threatened. Flushed with victory, the Turkish forces might invade the neutral zone (stretching from the Black Sea to the Dardanelles along the coast of the Sea of Marmora) and challenge the Allied forces of occupation; they might storm Constantinople, and upset, by violence, not only the prestige of the Allies, but the peace of the Balkans and the peace of Europe. In particular, Turkish forces were advancing towards Chanak, a point on the southern shore of the Dardanelles held by British troops. In this crisis Churchill joined Lloyd George and others in the Cabinet on September 15—Balfour, Birkenhead, Chamberlain—in urging resolute action. A warning, to which Poincaré had agreed, was sent to Kemal to respect the zone of the Straits; telegrams were dispatched to the Dominions outlining the critical position and inviting them to send contingents to aid in the defence of the Straits; and next day a communiqué, drafted by Churchill, was published from No. 10 Downing Street recounting the matters at issue and clearly foreshadowing the possibility of war. The communiqué had bitter results. The Dominion leaders saw it before the telegrams from the Cabinet, sent in cipher, had reached them. They felt they were being asked, imperiously, to send help to Britain in a quarrel into which she had got herself without consulting them; the tender privileges of 'dominion status' seemed to be strangled by the old colonialism. Chanak was thus a crisis in the history of Britain's imperial relations, and ultimately vindicated the independence of the Dominions; for of the replies only New Zealand's expressed moderate enthusiasm, and Canada's was firm in its refusal.

The effect of the communiqué on France was that Poincaré sent orders that the French troops reinforcing the British at Chanak should be withdrawn. This was, as Churchill says, the worst moment in Anglo-French relations after the war. Curzon immediately crossed over to Paris. His meeting with Poincaré was stormy, and he withdrew to shed tears on the arm of Lord Hardinge, the British ambassador: 'I can't bear that horrid little man'. However, an agreement was patched together: the French general at Constantinople was to support the British commander-in-chief, General Sir Charles Harington, in arranging with Kemal a meeting at Mudania to limit the line of the Turkish advance.

The end was not yet. On September 23 Turkish cavalry forces entered the neutral zone at Chanak, but withdrew next day; they returned again, and for some days the situation was tense, nothing but barbed wire separating the lines while each side forbore to take fatal action. Harington's troops had been reinforced, and he had the strength of the Navy behind him. On September 29 the Cabinet sent a telegram to Harington instructing him to give the Turks an ultimatum to withdraw; Curzon opposed this, and was joined, significantly enough, by Stanley Baldwin. Fortunately, General Harington saved the government (and the nation) from the consequences of its intemperate haste, just as another general, Macready, had done over the Four Courts business; he delayed action until the need was past. In this he had the full support of Sir Horace Rumbold, British High Commissioner at Constantinople. On October 3 Harington and other British and French representatives met the Turks at Mudania. The negotiations at first produced no result, since the French representative seemed more concerned to help the Turks than the Allies; a further visit of Curzon to Poincaré in Paris was necessary before new instructions led to agreement embodied in the convention of Mudania on October 11. The Turks agreed to respect the neutral zone; the Greeks were to evacuate Eastern Thrace but the Turks were not to occupy it, pending a final settlement of peace.[1]

The crisis was over: but it had been the last straw for the Tories, and they decided that Lloyd George must go. It is ironic that his final offence had been a last stand, alone and unflinching, on behalf of Britain's influence in the world and of her imperial position—something which should have commended itself to the instincts of the Tories. Deserted by France and Italy at a critical moment, he had, with the support of Churchill and a few others in the Cabinet, 'challenged the armed might and the genius of Kemal with a few battalions—and won. *It was the last occasion on which Great Britain stood up to a potential aggressor before the outbreak of the second World War.*'[2] By an interesting coincidence Mussolini became premier of Italy on October 30, 1922, eleven days after Lloyd George's resignation.

12. ANOTHER COAL CRISIS: BLACK FRIDAY

At home, the last two years of the Coalition were overshadowed by the slump and unemployment, the consequent drive for economy, and the manœuvres and recriminations which prepared the fall of the government. The beginnings of the slump were already apparent before the end of 1920. The government's first response was to hasten the completion of its policy of the decontrol of industry, by advancing the date previously decided on for the decontrol of the coal-mines. The result was a major coal strike, which very nearly became a general strike. It was, with the excep-

[1] H. Nicolson, *Curzon*, pp. 256–76; W. S. Churchill, *Aftermath*, pp. 411–64; R. B. Mowat, *European Diplomacy, 1914–1925*, pp. 292–7.
[2] R. Boothby, *I Fight To Live*, p. 28.

tion of the general strike of 1926, the last, sudden flaming of the fires of labour unrest which had followed the war.

Early in 1921 the coal-owners and the Miners' Federation had begun discussions for a new wages settlement, in anticipation of the ending, on March 31, of the wages agreement made as a result of the strike in October 1920. The miners' prime objective was a national settlement under a National Wages Board, drawing upon a 'national pool' of revenues from coal-mining; coupled with this was the desire for a new system of calculating wages, which would replace the existing confusion of additions to the prewar basis or standard wage in each district and would consolidate some of the wartime additions into the permanent scales. Before these negotiations had got very far the sharp reversal in the fortunes of the industry caused the government to make a sudden change of policy which threw everything into jeopardy. The prosperity of the postwar years was rapidly wearing away. Latterly, the mines had been supported by fantastically high export prices, reaching 115s. per ton when the domestic price was 36s. 7d. This had offset losses on working costs, but only because, under government control, all revenues went into a profits pool which underwrote the unprofitable mines. By now, however, recovery of the continental coalfields, and the beginning of Germany's reparations payments in coal, had caused the export prices of coal to tumble, and what had been a profitable operation for the government became a loss, running in January to over £4¾ millions. The government therefore decided to advance the date of decontrol to March 31; this was not announced until February 22 (though the union and, even more, the owners had been given an inkling of the intention a month or more previously), giving little or no time in which to cushion the shock. A decontrol bill was rapidly passed into law.

The coal strike punctually began on the day when government control ended, April 1. The earlier negotiations between the owners and the Miners' Federation were broken off. The owners posted notices at the collieries, in some cases only a few days before the end of March, of the wages which they were prepared to pay when the contracts expired on March 31. Not merely did the new scales involve very large reductions (reflecting the industry's straitened and unsubsidised circumstances), but they were district scales, abandoning the miners' cherished national agreement. The miners' last-minute reiterations of the plea for a National Wages Board and a national pool of profits met no response; nor did the demand for a subsidy from the government. As for the new scales, the reductions ranged from between 40 per cent and 49 per cent per shift in South Wales to between 10 per cent and 25 per cent in Nottinghamshire; in South Yorkshire the lower-paid men would actually receive small increases. Besides South Wales, the districts faced with the heaviest reductions were Cumberland, North Wales, Forest of Dean, Scotland, Northumberland and Durham. In all cases, the less-skilled workers suffered most: in South Wales the labourer's wage per shift was to be reduced from 14s. 9d. to 7s. 9d. (the average number of shifts worked per week was five). The men refused these terms, and the strike ensued—or rather, as far as the men were concerned, the lock-out.

Within a week the prospect of a general strike began to appear, and what had been threatened in 1920 and was to occur in 1926 came very near to happening in 1921. After meetings of the Transport Workers' Federation and the National Union of Rail-waymen the leaders of the Triple Alliance met on April 8, and issued a strike order to the railwaymen and transport workers for midnight (i.e. 11.59 p.m.) on April 12. This forced the government, which had already declared a 'state of emergency' under the Emergency Powers Act on March 31, not only to issue further royal proclamations mobilising the armed forces, but also to reopen negotiations with the coal-owners and the miners, even offering a subsidy for a short time so that the district wage reductions would be made gradually rather than all at once. The result was that the general strike was postponed; but since the negotiations imme-diately broke down over the miners' stand for a national settle-ment, the strike call was renewed for midnight (i.e. 11.59 p.m.), April 15.

Such an immediate threat of a general strike caused less alarm to the public than to the government, whose counter-preparations, however necessary, were not calculated to produce tranquillity. Leaves of members of the armed forces had been stopped, all classes of army and navy reservists were called up, motor vehicles were requisitioned for emergency distribution of food, public parks like Hyde Park and Regent's Park became huge vehicle depots, and Kensington Gardens blossomed into an armed camp. More serious was the creation of a special Defence Force, for which volunteers were asked for and came forward to the number of 75,000 in ten days, when recruiting was stopped. There were the makings of a civil war. One of Sir Philip Gibbs' novels of this period, *The Middle of the Road*, pictures a defence corps formed of ex-officers by the government to defend 'us' against a revolution fomented by 'Bolshies' and agents paid with foreign gold—the chronic bugbears of those anxious years.

> [Us] . . . meaning the Decent Crowd, Anybody with a stake in the country, including the unfortunate Middle Classes. All of us. Well, we accept the challenge. We're ready to knock hell out of them. . . . This clash has got to come. We must get the working classes back to their kennels. Back to cheap labour. Back to discipline. Otherwise we're done.[1]

Mercifully, the Defence Force was never called into action; but the reservists were not released until June.

The general strike never occurred: 'Black Friday' removed the threat. On Thursday, April 14, an influential group of Coalition members held a meeting in the House of Commons to find for themselves what the positions of the coal-owners and miners were; after hearing from the chairmen of the Mining Association (the owners' body) how large the wage cuts actually were, this group, feeling greater sympathy for the miners than before, invited Frank Hodges, the miners' secretary, who was in the House on other business, to address them that evening. At the meeting Hodges pleaded the miners' case for a national settlement in strong terms. Questions followed, including one, whether the miners would consider a temporary settlement of the wages question, leaving the matters of the National Board and national pool for later consideration. Hodges replied, not unnaturally in a meeting where he sensed a sympathy for his cause, that they were prepared, as always, to consider any offer provided it did not prejudice their fundamental principles. Since this seemed to hold out the possibility of a temporary solution, which might avert a general strike, news of it was taken to Lloyd George. The next day, Friday the 15th, was the last day before the general strike, which was to begin at midnight. That morning, Lloyd George wrote to Hodges inviting the miners' leaders to an immediate meeting to consider a temporary arrangement concerning wages 'without raising the controversial issue of the pool . . . and without prejudice to a further discussion of proposals [for the pool] . . . when a permanent settlement comes to be dealt with'.[2] This proposal the miners' executive rejected at a meeting that morning, on the ground that a temporary settlement could only be made on the

---

[1] Sir Philip Gibbs, *Middle of the Road* (4th edition, London, [1923]), p. 132.
[2] The text in G. D. H. Cole, *Labour in the Coal-mining Industry*, pp. 212–13.

basis of the National Wages Board and the national pool. Hodges offered his resignation, but withdrew it by unanimous request. When word of this decision was sent to the representatives of the Triple Alliance, assembled at Unity House, the National Union of Railwaymen's headquarters on Euston Road, it was sharply challenged, and the miners urged to accept the Prime Minister's invitation to a meeting. This they refused to do. That afternoon J. H. Thomas made the announcement to the assembled news-paper reporters, from the steps of Unity House: 'The strike announced for tonight is cancelled.'

This was 'Black Friday', regarded in the Labour movement as the day of a great betrayal, when not only was a general strike abandoned, the Triple Alliance ruined and the miners sacrificed but the whole structure of united working-class resistance to an expected attack on wages and living standards was demolished at a blow. Yet the weakness it implied had always been present in the Triple Alliance: first, that one of the three groups could commit the others to sympathetic action without surrendering its un-divided control over negotiations, and second that many leaders, such as J. H. Thomas, had no heart in what they saw, if others did not, as an action of potentially revolutionary character against a government ready, and perhaps anxious, for a showdown with labour. Hodges was later regarded as a Judas within the Labour movement: but his extemporaneous reply to a question at a meet-ing in the Houses of Parliament hardly proves that, and he insisted at the time that he never favoured, or meant to imply, anything but a national settlement which, however temporary or however con-fined to wages, would have necessitated something like the national pool or continued government control. The fact that subsequently he resigned from the Miners' Federation (in 1924) and became director of an investment company may have been the result of his experiences over 'Black Friday' rather than evidence of long-concealed original sin.[1]

Once the general strike was averted, the miners' case was hope-less, though they struggled on till June. The threat of the general strike had lost them public sympathy; its failure lost them public notice also. The strike ended on July 1. The men lost their demand for the national pool and a national wages system. The settlement was by districts, but a National Wages Board was set up, though only with limited powers for interpreting district

---

[1] Frank Hodges was later a member of the Central Electricity Board, and died in 1947.

decisions. Wage rates were to be based on a new standard (the pre-war standard with some additions), to which at least 20 per cent was to be added. The owners' standard profit was fixed at 17 per cent of the sum payable as standard wages, and profits beyond this were to be divided between the owners and the men in the proportions of 17 per cent and 83 per cent. The implications of this system of profit-sharing, involving joint audit of the owners' books, were not stressed at the time, and certainly did not contribute to goodwill within the coal industry or industry in general. A government subsidy, to the maximum of £10 millions, was to be used to make the resulting reductions in wages gradual. Actual reductions in wages varied very widely. In South Wales wages fell to about half of the previous level per shift, and in many other coalfields the fall was almost as great, though in the Midlands and South Yorkshire there was very little decline. In January 1922, in Nottinghamshire, where wages were highest, skilled miners were getting 17s. 3d. per shift, unskilled 13s. 7d.; in Durham 8s. and 5s. 10d.; in Bristol, at the bottom, 7s. 4d. and 6s. 4d.[1]

The miners' defeat was followed by that of the workers in the engineering trades a year later, after a strike which lasted from March 11 to June 13. A strike in the shipyards (March 29–May 8, 1922) ended in wage reductions; and during the year workers at the docks, in the building and printing trades, on the railways, and in the cotton industry accepted reductions.[2]

The same spirit and, from the working man's point of view, the same surrender, was shown in the government's jettisoning of wage-fixing bodies. The Agricultural Wages Board (a wartime creation, continued by the Agriculture Act, 1920) was ended, together with minimum wages for farm labourers and guaranteed prices to farmers, in 1921.[3] The Trade Boards (created in 1909 with power to fix wages in industries in which sweated labour was indigenous) were the subject of attacks by the Association of British Chambers of Commerce, and in the press, and were in-

[1] This account is based on G. D. H. Cole, *Labour in the Coal-mining Industry*, pp. 162–263. See also W. A. Orton, *Labour in Transition*, pp. 231–51; *Annual Register, 1921*; J. R. Raynes, *Coal and its Conflicts* (London, 1928), pp. 175–91; W. H. Crook, *General Strike*, pp. 270–82; R. P. Arnot, *The Miners*, pp. 279–331.

[2] L.R.D., *Workers' Register, 1923*, pp. 43–5, 48–9. The course of industrial warfare after the war can be seen in the figures of the aggregate duration in working days of all strikes in progress each year (*Statistical Abstract of U.K., 1930*, p. 112):

1913	9,804,000	1921	85,872,000
1918	5,875,000	1922	19,850,000
1919	34,969,000	1923	10,672,000
1920	26,568,000	1924	8,424,000

[3] L.R.D., *Workers' Register, 1923*, p. 41.

vestigated by a committee headed by Lord Cave.[1] Its report, in
April 1922, recommended the continuance of the boards, but with
limited powers; and no new boards were created.[2] On March 1,
1922, the Civil Service Arbitration Board was abolished. In the
previous July the National Industrial Conference, of which such
high hopes had been held as a parliament of management and
labour, had come to an end.

13. THE SLUMP AND UNEMPLOYMENT; THE DOLE IS BORN

Signs of the slump were only too manifest in 1921 and 1922.
The value of Britain's overseas trade declined: exports by 47·9
per cent, imports by 43·7 per cent, in 1921, as compared with 1920;
in 1922 the value of exports recovered by 1·7 per cent, but imports
declined further by 7·5 per cent. The monthly average production
of pig-iron, which was 669,500 tons in 1920, was 217,600 tons in
1921, 413,700 for the third quarter, 1922; the corresponding
figures for steel ingots and castings were 755,600 tons in 1920,
302,100 tons in 1921, and 519,100 tons in 1922 (third quarter).[3]
The fall in wages was equally great. Wage rates, which reached
their peak in 1920, when the index number was 260 (1913 = 100),
had declined to 170 by 1922. Actual earnings (allowing for the
number of workers unemployed) were 244 in 1920 but 147 in
1922. The Ministry of Labour's cost-of-living index, meanwhile,
which reached 276 in November 1920, was 180 in December 1922.
The *Economist* estimated that the working man had lost three-
quarters of his wartime wage increases by 1922, and commented
that he was waiting for the trade revival which was supposed to
follow the wage reductions. Yet the average of ordinary dividends
was 10·2 per cent in 1921, 8·4 per cent in 1922.[4]

The plight of the man or woman at work was, however, mild
compared with that of the unemployed worker, whose numbers
increased to dimensions of disaster. Unemployment suddenly
became the burning question of the day, as it was to remain, more
or less continuously, for the next two decades; and because it had

[1] George Cave (1856–1928). Barrister. M.P., 1906–18. Solicitor-general, 1915,
home secretary, 1916–18. Lord of appeal (Viscount Cave), 1918; lord chancellor,
1922–24, 1924–28.
[2] L.R.D., *Workers' Register, 1923*, p. 45; *Economist*, Sept. 24, 1921; *The Times*,
April 22, 1922.
[3] *Third Winter of Unemployment* (London, [1922]), p. 333. This was the report of
an enquiry privately undertaken in the autumn of 1922 by a group including J. J. Astor,
B. Seebohm Rowntree, A. L. Bowley and other economists, and based partly on reports
from several areas by local investigators.
[4] *Economist*, Feb. 18, Aug. 5, 1922, Feb. 17, 1923.

been very small in the prewar years and was now very large, it appeared as not only serious but shocking. The number of unemployed persons covered by unemployment insurance, which was 691,103 (5·8 per cent of those insured) in December 1920, was 1,355,206 in March 1921, 2,171,288 (17·8 per cent) in June; thence it fell, standing at 1,934,030 (16·2 per cent) in December, 1,502,955 in June, 1922, and 1,431,929 (12·2 per cent) in December 1922.[1] The industries in which unemployment was heaviest were shipbuilding (36·1 per cent of insured workers in December 1921), iron and steel (36·7 per cent), engineering (27·2 per cent), building (20·5 per cent.);[2] the districts worst affected were Northern Ireland (25 per cent), Scotland (21 per cent), the Midlands and the North-east (18 per cent each).[3] Among the towns hardest hit were Barrow-in-Furness, with 49 per cent of insured persons unemployed in August 1922, Hartlepool with 60 per cent, Stockton with 49 per cent, Jarrow with 43 per cent, Brynmawr with 47 per cent, Handsworth with 44 per cent; in several districts of Glasgow the percentage ranged between 59 and 28.[4]

This heavy and prolonged unemployment produced acts of both protest and alleviation. Demonstrations by the unemployed, at first spontaneous, were later organised by the National Unemployed Workers' Movement (N.U.W.M.), which was founded in 1921 under the inspiration of Wal Hannington, a toolmaker connected with the wartime shop stewards' movement in London. Hannington and other leaders made no secret of being Communists and the N.U.W.M. was considered to be a Communist organisation, and as such was kept at a distance by the Trades Union Congress, though a joint advisory committee of the two bodies functioned rather weakly from 1924 to 1927. The N.U.W.M. oath included the promise 'to never cease from active strife against this system until capitalism is abolished and our country and all its resources truly belong to the people'.

The first big demonstration occurred in October 1920, when crowds of unemployed men, converging on Whitehall to support a deputation of Labour mayors seeking to see Lloyd George, were charged upon by the police, mounted and on foot, and beaten about by police batons—the first of many such attacks in the annals of the unemployed, resulting in broken heads and loss of

---

[1] L.R.D., *Workers' Register, 1923*, pp. 72, 77. Official figures are given in the monthly *Ministry of Labour Gazette* and in the *Abstract of Labour Statistics*.
[2] L.R.D., *Workers' Register*, p. 78.
[3] *Third Winter of Unemployment*, pp. 16, 17. [4] Ibid., pp. 328–30.

blood though not of life. In the winter of 1920–21 there were many demonstrations in London in favour of 'work or full maintenance', particularly before the offices of boards of Poor Law Guardians. During 1921 there were two big demonstrations in London (on July 11 and October 4), the latter ending in a battle in Trafalgar Square. There were similar demonstrations in Sheffield, Dundee, Bristol, Leicester, Cardiff, Glasgow, and several towns in Lancashire. In Liverpool, there was a riot on September 13, 1921, when a crowd of about 5000, refused a hall for a meeting, invaded the Walker Art Gallery. In 1922 the first of the hunger marches of unemployed men took place: delegations, one coming from as far as Glasgow, converged on London on November 17.[1]

The government, on its part, made some efforts to alleviate the plight of the unemployed, and thus advanced further, and without premeditation, along the collectivist path towards the welfare state, though without going nearly far enough to satisfy those who demanded of it work or maintenance. The provisions of the Unemployment Insurance Act of 1920 were never fully enforced; instead, the government, by a series of Acts in 1921 and 1922 (consolidated in the Unemployment Insurance Act of 1922), extended the period during which benefits could be drawn (originally only fifteen weeks in a year), altered the rates of benefit, and increased the contributions. Each step was taken haphazardly, in response not only to the heavy and continuous unemployment and the demands of the unemployed, but also to the pressure from the Poor Law Guardians and the local authorities on whom the burden of relief would fall once the working man had exhausted his unemployment insurance benefits, unless the government assumed the extended responsibility.

The most important of these acts was that of March 1921, which, among other things, provided for two periods of extended benefit of sixteen weeks each, separated by gaps when no benefits could be drawn. This was 'uncovenanted' benefit, beyond what the working man was entitled to from his contributions and in theory an advance against future contributions; for this purpose the Unemployment Fund was given power to borrow up to £30 millions from the Treasury. Thus was born, if not named, the 'dole', ungratefully accepted by those it saved and bitterly condemned by the comfortable classes who saw in it only the symbol

[1] This account is based on Wal Hannington, *Unemployed Struggles, 1919–1936: my life and struggles amongst the unemployed* (London, 1936), pp. 1–107. Cf. L.R.D., *Workers' Register*, 1923, pp. 86–91; *Annual Register, 1921*, pp. 105–9.

of national demoralisation. The principle of insurance, though not abandoned, was strangely transformed. From it sprang another major and unintended change; the unemployment insurance scheme became a form of inquisition. For to limit the numbers to whom aid was extended, it was laid down that payments were to be made only to those 'genuinely seeking' work; and the Employment Exchanges and in time a vast machinery of committees and officials were called upon to make sure that only those thus qualified were granted the aid provided by the law. A secondary consequence was to transform unemployment insurance contributions into a form of taxation by which men in work paid for the support of those out of work: it was discovered in 1926 that 48 per cent of insured workers had drawn no benefits at all in five years, though employees' contributions provided for about one-third of the expenditures of the fund.

The other measure of fundamental importance, and one which caused a scene in the House of Commons in October 1921, was the Unemployed Workers' Dependants (Temporary Provisions) Act (November 1921), which provided payments from the Unemployment Fund, for the wives and dependent children of unemployed workers; the payments (5s. a week for a wife, 1s. a week per child—much lower than the Poor Law scales) were denounced by J. R. Clynes as mocking the poor. On October 26 the Labour members walked out of the House in protest. Actually, they protested too much. The government, in this bill, conceded the whole principle of family allowances, though without admitting it. The precedent was more important than the scales.[1]

The government was, naturally, under heavy pressure to do more than this; indeed, unemployment dominated the autumn session of parliament in 1921. Relief works were only sparingly resorted to by local authorities, whether on their own or with the help of grants and loans advanced by the government; works in the former category employed between 8000 and 10,000 persons in all, and involved chiefly repairs to buildings, roads, tramway tracks and some new construction of schools and public buildings. Some direct grants were also made by the ministries of Transport and Agriculture, under the advice of the Unemployment Grants Committee, for the construction of roads and bridges and for drainage and afforestation schemes.[2]

[1] R. C. Davison, *Unemployed: old policies and new*, pp. 102–12; H. F. Hohman, *Social Insurance in Great Britain*, pp. 233–6; *Third Winter of Unemployment*, pp. 31–40; *The Times*, Oct. 27, 1921.
[2] *Third Winter of Unemployment*, pp. 51–7.

As always, the Poor Law stood as the residuary legatee for cases of distress. Families not covered by the unemployment insurance scheme or insufficiently aided by it, or stranded during the 'gaps' between periods of unemployment benefit 'often about a month), all resorted to the Guardians, and received outdoor relief. The numbers on outdoor relief fluctuated greatly; there were 224,000 persons in March 1921, 831,000 in November (one of the 'gaps'), 732,000 in December, 1,065,000 in June 1922 (another 'gap'), and 861,000 in August 1922. Many Guardians refused outdoor relief altogether; others paid at scales varying from 15s. a week for man and wife and 5s. for each child to Poplar's more generous rate of 33s., plus 10s. for rent (the origin of a new bogey, 'Poplarism'); the Ministry of Health's scale for London was 25s. for man and wife. The burden was, naturally, heaviest on industrial and working-class towns least able to bear it.[1] The Ministry of Health tried to keep the local authorities' expenditures within bounds, and could, under the Local Authorities (Financial Provisions) Act of 1921, refuse permission for increased borrowing. The celebrated protest of the Poplar Council, led by George Lansbury, was against the payment by Poplar to the London County Council of its 'precepts' (contributions for common expenses of the county) as long as its burden of poor relief was so heavy. For this Lansbury and twenty-nine other councillors were sent to prison on September 1, 1921, and not released, embarrassing prisoners as they were, until October 12; a bill was subsequently passed spreading a greater part of the costs of relief over London as a whole.[2]

14. THE ECONOMY DRIVE

Such expenditures, and the general falling-off of business in 1921, led to demands for the classic remedies of economy and deflation. The government, having contributed to the postwar inflation, now deliberately turned to deflation. The budgets of both 1920 and 1921 had provided for surpluses, though the heavy debt incurred during the war, both to the United States and to contributors to the war-savings campaigns at home, remained a burden which the high interest rates, however deflationary in other ways, only made the more serious. In addition the budget of 1921 included the repeal of the excess profits duty; and the income from the sale of surplus war stores was coming to an end. It was in-

[1] *Third Winter of Unemployment*, pp. 41–7.
[2] R. Postgate, *George Lansbury*, pp. 216–20.

evitable that departments would be asked to include large economies in their next year's estimates. Incentive was added, however, by the demand for economy which became the theme of the debates over the Finance Bill during the spring of 1921; for this was taken up by the *Daily Mail* and other papers, and a furious 'Anti-Waste' campaign, pillorying 'squander-mania', was worked up. One hundred and seventy members of parliament signed a manifesto demanding economy; and the City, in the person of Reginald McKenna, chairman of the Midland Bank, called for measures which were 'ruthless, relentless, remorseless'. To fend off the attack, the government on August 16 appointed the Geddes committee to examine next year's provisional estimates and recommend further economies. It was a committee of high business leaders, headed by Sir Eric Geddes, lately Minister of Transport.

The first two reports of the Geddes committee were published on February 10, 1922, and from the many sharp cuts they proposed was immediately dubbed the Geddes axe. The committee recommended savings of £75 millions. The army and navy were the victims of the deepest cuts, £20 millions and £21 millions respectively, including reductions of officers and men numbering 50,000 and 35,000 in the two services. The air estimates were to be cut £5½ millions, education £18 millions, the Ministry of Health £2½ millions, war pensions £3,300,000. The reductions in education were to be made by excluding children under six from school and reducing teachers' salaries; the reductions in expenditures on health services were to be obtained by limiting the state's contribution to the National Health Insurance scheme and to the tuberculosis, maternity and child-welfare services. The pay of the police was to be reduced, and the number of prison warders diminished. It was proposed to abolish the Ministry of Transport, the Mines Department, the Electricity Commissioners, the Department of Overseas Trade, putting their functions under the Board of Trade; and the abolition of the Ministry of Labour and the Employment Exchanges (at a time of acute unemployment!) was even suggested. The third report, published on February 24, recommended further economies of over £11 millions.[1]

Even the government was aghast; and the Admiralty so far broke ranks as to issue simultaneously with the report a furious blast against the proposed naval reductions. The comment of

[1] Committee on National Expenditure, *Reports* (Cmd. 1581, 1582, 1589: 1922).

labour was bitter: working-men were not impressed with the need of economies in the social services 'whilst the rich betake themselves to St. Moritz and the ladies of Mayfair spend extravagantly on dresses . . .'; they objected to 'making the children pay' by the cuts in education.[1] The government accepted cuts of £64 millions. The proposed naval reductions were halved, but further savings were anticipated from the disarmament agreed on at the Washington Conference; and the savings on education were limited to £6½ millions. Since the estimates for 1922 were already £75 millions lower than those for the previous year, the total savings were considerable. A new campaign for economy and against the 'ruinous' income tax preceded the budget. Lord Inchcape declaimed at the Mansion House on April 24 that the country was financially at death's door, facing national bankruptcy.

The budget of 1922, when announced, proved to be the first postwar budget below £1,000 millions; expenditures were put at £910 millions, compared with £1,136 millions in the 1921 estimates (the budget of 1913 was £200 millions). The estimates made possible a reduction of 1s. in the income tax rate (to 5s. in the £) and reductions in the tea duty and postal rates. The economy campaign subsided.[2]

The slump left another mark—the mark of a contracting economy; the beginning of the protective tariff. The war had provided the first whiff of this. In 1915 the McKenna duties (named after the Liberal, Reginald McKenna, Lloyd George's successor as Chancellor of the Exchequer) had been introduced to discourage the importation of foreign luxuries while shipping was scarce: the duties were of 33⅓ per cent on motor-cars and cycles, clocks, watches, musical instruments, and of varying rates on films. These duties were retained after the war, though lowered by one-third for goods of British Empire origin in the budget of 1919—a start towards imperial preference. Wartime embargoes on certain other imports, especially dyes, optical glass and scientific instruments, ran out during 1919, and the plea for protection arose. Words played an important part in the effort to charm the public

---

[1] 'Economy—a Labour view', *Economist*, Feb. 18, 1922.

[2] *Annual Register, 1922*, pp. 14, 28–30, 48–51; *The Times*, April 25, May 2, 10, 1922; F. W. Hirst, *Consequences of the War to Great Britain*, pp. 168–89; P. J. Grigg, *Prejudice and Judgment* (London, 1948), pp. 63–83. Sir James Grigg, secretary of War, 1942–45, had previously a distinguished career in the civil service and from 1921 to 1930 was principal private secretary to the successive chancellors of the Exchequer.

into surrender; for home industry the beguiling phrase 'key industry' was substituted; for protection 'safeguarding'; and if the foreigner's goods were cheaper he was accused of 'dumping', and of benefiting from depreciated currencies, to the detriment of British manufacturers and the sturdy British workman. The war-born, unweaned British dyestuffs industry (in which the government had a large investment) received the protection of the Dye-stuffs Act of December, 1920, which 'regulated' (i.e. restricted) the importation of dyestuffs.

This was prelude to the Safeguarding of Industries Act of 1921, for which the slump, unemployment, the National Union of Manufacturers, and trade associations like the Association of British Toy Manufacturers provided arguments. The Act pro-vided for duties of $33\frac{1}{3}$ per cent on key articles, chiefly from Germany. The list was an anti-climax: optical glass, certain electrical instruments, chemicals, and dolls' glass eyes were apparently what the salvation of British industry depended on (though the Board of Trade, when it compiled the list of articles affected, discovered 6500 items, to the dismay of traders). Manufacturers of other articles might receive similar protection if they could prove that they were suffering from dumping. The Act caused another fissure in the Coalition, dividing Liberals and Conservatives. In a vote upon an order imposing a duty on fabric gloves in June 1922, over half the Coalition Liberals abstained or voted against the government. It was significant of the future that Stanley Baldwin, as President of the Board of Trade, had to bear the brunt of this fight.[1]

15. THE CRISIS IN PARTY POLITICS

The political manœuvres of 1920–22 which preceded the fall of the Coalition mark something both more and less than the government's unpopularity: they mark, rather, a major crisis in party politics. It is easy to exaggerate the Coalition's unpopularity, though it naturally got the blame for the many things which seemed wrong—whether it was in Ireland or in India, whether Bolshevism in Russia or unemployment at home. Right up to its end strong dislike of it among the public at large was lacking. Dislike of it was to be found instead among many of the Con-

[1] R. K. Snyder, *Tariff Problem in Great Britain, 1918–1923* (Stanford University, 1944), pp. 7–10, 21–39, 43, 69–91; *Economist, passim*, especially Feb. 19, May 14, July 9, 1921, Feb. 11, July 29, 1922.

servatives and Liberals in politics; and this was really a sign of their own insecurity. The fundamental thing was that the years since the war had carried away most of the old issues between the Conservative and Liberal parties. On social policy, on education, on questions of empire or foreign affairs nothing now separated them. Most of all, the last great issue, Home Rule or the Union, had been ended by the treaty; the Conservatives had, in fact, dumped the Unionists of the party, much to Carson's disgust,[1] which was anything but salved by their having pensioned off his friends with Ulster.

The logic of events was a fusion of Conservatives and Liberals in opposition to the party of socialism (though not to its policies, since some of them they had already embraced). This was all to Lloyd George's interest, since without it he remained a leader without a party. For the same reason it was all against the interests of Liberals of the Asquithian stripe; and their hopes of the future were rising since Asquith's triumphal return to parliament, as member for Paisley, in February 1920. It was equally against the interests of many Conservatives: the Die-Hard imperialists and Unionists, the managers of the party machine, and a number of younger M.P.'s—all, in fact, whose careers or principles might be compromised by 'fusion'. Two issues united them: first, the character and deeds of Lloyd George, and second, desire for a protective tariff (a real one, not namby-pamby 'safeguarding').

It was easy to find reasons for disliking Lloyd George. He was a Welshman, and one too clever by half; the 'little man' was a dictator who seldom attended parliament but insisted on having a hand in the running of everything, and whose 'garden suburb' interfered even with the proprieties of Curzon's diplomacy. The intellectual arrogance and frank speaking of Lord Birkenhead, one of his chief Conservative allies, was another cause of offence. It was not only the Die-Hards who shared these feelings; many of the junior ministers—under-secretaries and the like—were no less critical: Edward Wood[2] (later Lord Irwin and the Earl of Halifax),

[1] See D. Gwynn, *History of Partition*, pp. 177–8, 199, 207–8.
[2] Edward Frederick Lindley Wood, born 1881, son of second Viscount Halifax, the great churchman. Eton and Christ Church, Oxford; fellow of All Souls. M.P., 1910–25; parliamentary under-secretary for the colonies, 1921–22; president of the Board of Education, 1922–23 and 1932–35; minister of agriculture, 1924–25. Viceroy of India, 1926–31. War secretary, 1935; Lord privy seal, 1935–37; Lord president of the council, 1937–38; foreign secretary, 1938–40. Ambassador to the U.S., 1940–46. Created Lord Irwin, 1925; succeeded father, 1934, created earl, 1944. O.M., 1946.

Philip Lloyd-Greame[1], Leopold Amery,[2] and Sir Arthur Griffith-Boscawen.[3]

A major indictment against Lloyd George was the 'sale of honours'. He had, indeed, been lavish, after the greatest war in history, in the award of honours not only to members of the armed forces, but to politicians, civil servants, businessmen—peerages, knighthoods, decorations had rained down. Some wit chose to dub Cardiff 'the city of dreadful knights'. It was observed, as it had been in many times past, that honours could be bought by the appropriate contribution to party funds: £15,000 for a knighthood, £25,000 for a baronetcy, £50,000 for a barony. In the House of Lords the Duke of Northumberland quoted from letters of touts who claimed to have the means of delivering these goods. Lloyd George was perhaps cynical and careless, but nothing more than that; and awards of honours under the Coalition were at least as much the responsibility of the Liberal and Conservative whips and of Bonar Law, with whom Lloyd George split contributions fifty-fifty for their respective party chests (this was supposed to be the source of Lloyd George's private party chest which caused so much ill-feeling later on). The matter came to a head in 1922 when a peerage was offered, without consultation with the Colonial Secretary, to a South African financier, Sir J. B. Robinson, whose affairs had recently been the subject of litigation. The question was raised in parliament, and debated in both houses in July, when other names were named and the award of honours for party contributions defended. Robinson refused the proffered coronet. A Royal Commission on Honours was created, with a judge, Lord Dunedin, as chairman; its report, which was accepted, recommended that political candidates for honours should be passed upon by a committee of three privy councillors who were not members of the government of the day.[4]

[1] P. Lloyd-Greame, born 1884, took name of Cunliffe-Lister in 1924 and was created Viscount Swinton in 1935. President of the Board of Trade, 1922–23, 1931; colonial secretary, 1924–29, 1931–35; secretary of state for air, 1935–38; minister resident in West Africa, 1942–44; minister of civil aviation, 1944–45.

[2] Leopold S. Amery (1873–1955). Born in India. Harrow and Balliol College, Oxford; fellow of All Souls. On editorial staff of The Times, 1899–1909 (in South Africa, 1900). M.P., 1910–45. Assistant secretary, war cabinet, 1917; parliamentary under-secretary for colonies, 1919–21; parliamentary secretary to Admiralty, 1921–22, and first lord, 1922–23; colonial secretary, 1924–29; secretary of state for India, 1940–45. A lifelong imperialist and protectionist. Married sister of Hamar Greenwood.

[3] Arthur Griffith-Boscawen (1865–1946), born at Trevalyn Hall, near Wrexham. M.P., 1892–1906, 1910–22, parliamentary secretary for pensions, 1916–19, agriculture, 1919–21; minister of agriculture, 1921–22; minister of health, 1922–23. Knighted, 1911.

[4] W. I. Jennings, Cabinet Government, pp. 351–60; H. Nicolson, George V, pp. 511–14; Annual Register, 1922, pp. 72, 79–84; 51 H.L. Deb. 5 s., cols. 475–512

On his side, however, Lloyd George had strong support for continuance of the Coalition either in its present form or under the aegis of some new party. Among the Liberals its chief defender was Churchill, among the Conservatives all the leaders of front rank: Austen Chamberlain, Birkenhead, Balfour, Salvidge, and for a long time Bonar Law, Curzon, Lord Derby,[1] Walter Long. Their arguments were simple: the alternative was Bolshevism, the triumph of the Socialists, perhaps with a minority of the votes in an election fought between three or four parties.

'Fusion', much talked of in the spring of 1920, was thus a counter-attack by the supporters of the Coalition against those who would disrupt it. In February 1920, that shrewd and detached observer, C. F. G. Masterman,[2] sketched out the plan in an article entitled 'The New Democratic Party', but observed that the time for launching it was almost lost, as the government had already begun to go downhill.[3] He spoke by the book, for in that same month the matter was broached at an intimate dinner given by Lord Birkenhead and attended by Lloyd George, Churchill, Chamberlain and Salvidge. Salvidge supported the idea, saying that in future coalitions were inevitable, 'fossilised Toryism' fatal to the party. Bonar Law also favoured it.[4] J. L. Garvin supported the idea in characteristically high-flown articles in the *Observer*, terming the movement 'a landmark in party annals'.[5]

The plan was defeated by the opposition of both Conservatives and Liberals. At the annual meeting of the National Unionist Association in June 1920 a resolution was carried calling on the party to prepare a general tariff scheme. Such a proposal, if pressed, would have split the Coalition; but its force was weakened by Salvidge's warning to the meeting that it was more important

---

(July 17, 1922); 156 H.C. Deb. 5 s., cols. 1745–1862 (July 17, 1922). See below, ch. 4, p. 204.

[1] Lord Derby (17th earl: 1865–1948), war secretary, 1916–18, 1922–24, ambassador to France, 1918–20, was for long a power in Conservative circles and in the life of Lancashire.

[2] C. F. G. Masterman (1874–1927) was a Liberal M.P. intermittently in 1906–14 and 1923–24 and held minor offices: he was mainly responsible for the successful inauguration of the National Health Insurance scheme in 1912 as financial secretary to the Treasury and chairman to the National Insurance Commission. See his books, *Condition of England* (1909) and *England after War* (1922), and his wife's life of him: Lucy Masterman, *C. F. G. Masterman* (London, 1939).

[3] *Contemporary Review*, 117: 153–62 (February, 1920). Cf. Sir Charles Mallet's article, *ibid.*, 18–24 (Jan., 1920).

[4] Stanley Salvidge, *Salvidge of Liverpool*, pp. 180–3; Cf. Viscount Swinton, *I Remember* (London, [1948]), pp. 156–7.

[5] C. F. G. Masterman, 'Fusion: the first phase', *Contemp. Review*, 118: 177–90 (Aug., 1920).

to protect constitutional government through the Coalition than trade through a tariff; and the majority was a small one. The Coalition Liberals were, however, no more solid for 'fusion' than the Conservatives; and with more reason as the junior partners. The pleas of Lloyd George at a meeting in March 1920, and of Churchill at later Liberal gatherings, were equally unavailing. 'Fusion' withered away, but the Coalition lived on.[1]

A change which had large consequences later on occurred in March 1921, when Bonar Law resigned because of his serious decline in health. Austen Chamberlain succeeded him as Lord Privy Seal and Leader of the House of Commons, and was elected leader of the Conservative party; Sir Robert Horne succeeded Chamberlain as Chancellor of the Exchequer, and Stanley Baldwin, hitherto an inconspicuous member of the government as Financial Secretary to the Treasury, succeeded Horne at the Board of Trade. Later in the year, the Irish negotiations and treaty were a severe strain on the loyalty of the Conservative rank and file to the government, though not on the cohesion of its leaders.[2]

At the end of 1921 the leaders, still determined to preserve the Coalition, decided that it was now or never for a general election in which the Coalition, as such, would seek a new term of office. Salvidge travelled to London shortly before Christmas for another dinner at Lord Birkenhead's, which was attended also by Lloyd George, Chamberlain, Churchill, Laming Worthington-Evans, and Lord Beaverbrook,[3] owner of the *Daily Express*. There was much talk in the press at the beginning of January 1922 of an early general election, which *The Times* branded as unwanted. A mutiny thwarted the plan. Sir George Younger, the chairman of the National Unionist Association and head of the Conservative party organisation, revealed and condemned it in speeches and in a circular letter to Conservative candidates and members of parliament.[4] Lord Birkenhead rebuked the 'cabin boy' who was trying to captain the ship, but the letter was an indication of how far differences within the Coalition had gone. Bonar Law's return to London in February 1922, in much better health, marked a further stage, since he was potentially an alternative leader for the

[1] *Annual Register, 1920*, pp. 30–3; C. F. G. Masterman, 'Fusion: the first phase', *Contemp. Review*, August, 1920; S. Salvidge, *Salvidge*, pp. 184–6.

[2] S. Salvidge, *Salvidge*, pp. 193–213.

[3] William Maxwell Aitken, born 1879 in New Brunswick, son of a minister; man of business in Halifax and Montreal until 1910; M.P., 1910–17; knighted, 1911; created Baron Beaverbrook, 1917; minister of information, 1918; minister of aircraft production, 1940–41; minister of supply, 1941–42; lord privy seal, 1943–45.

[4] *The Times*, Jan. 11, 1922, and previous days.

disgruntled Tories. He told friends he detected a complete change of feeling in the party and warned Lloyd George of it, but publicly he kept his peace, above the controversy.

By the end of February Lloyd George came to the conclusion that he ought to resign, and in a long letter to Austen Chamberlain (February 27, 1922) he renewed his offer, previously made to Bonar Law and to Chamberlain, to step down so that Chamberlain could form a purely Conservative government: 'the control [of policy] has been ostentatiously taken out of our hands by men who have no responsibility for the effects . . . without even the formality of consultation among the Leaders.'[1] Chamberlain, with his punctilious sense of honour and his genuine hope that a new national party might emerge from the Coalition, refused. He made the matter public in a speech at Oxford on March 3, saying that he had consulted his colleagues of the party in the Cabinet, and that they had agreed that Lloyd George's resignation would be a national disaster and also an injury to the party. However, Edwin Montagu's resignation as Secretary of State for India on March 9 after his quarrel with Curzon over the Government of India's memorandum on the Turkish situation weakened the government, though he claimed he was a sacrifice to the Die-Hards' hostility to his policies in India. So the Coalition staggered on, muttered against in the drawing-rooms, and decried in parliament by Die-Hards like Sir William Joynson-Hicks[2] and Lord Hugh Cecil, but sustained by the responsible leaders.[3] A motion by Joynson-Hicks condemning the Coalition's 'lack of definite and coherent principle' and calling for a ministry of 'men united in political principle' was defeated by 193 votes in the Commons on April 5.[4]

16. THE FALL OF THE COALITION

In September 1922, events began to move towards the crisis, to the accompaniment of fire and slaughter in Turkey, for which

[1] Letter printed in Sir Charles Petrie, *Life and letters of the Right Honourable Sir Austen Chamberlain* (London, 1939–40), II, 174–8; cf. Malcolm Thomson, *Lloyd George*, pp. 340–3.
[2] William Joynson-Hicks (1865–1932), born in Canonbury, son of a merchant. Solicitor. M.P., 1902–10, 1911–29. Baronet, 1919. Postmaster-general, later minister of health, 1923, home secretary, 1924–29. Viscount Brentford, 1929.
[3] C. Petrie, *Austen Chamberlain*, II, 169–74, 178–81; S. Salvidge, *Salvidge*, pp. 222–34; *Annual Register, 1922*, pp. 2–5, 13, 25, 32–35; B. E. C. Dugdale, *Balfour*, II, 257–8.
[4] *The Times*, April 4, 6, 1922; *Annual Register, 1922*, p. 45. See also the letters from Beaverbrook and Edward Grigg to Lloyd George in *History of The Times*, IV, ii, 652–9.

F*

Lloyd George's Liberal policies, pro-Greek, anti-Turk, were blamed. On the 16th, Sir George Younger wrote to Austen Chamberlain, telling him that Bonar Law was unhappy about the future, but would do nothing which in any way might prejudice Chamberlain's position. On the next day there was a meeting of the Coalition leaders at Chequers (the Prime Minister's country residence in Buckinghamshire, presented to the nation by Lord Lee of Fareham in 1921). Future prospects were considered. The report of the Conservative party managers showed that, if the Coalition broke up, the Labour party might win 300 seats, or even a majority of the House of 613 members, in a general election. Only the Coalition could prevent this, but some 80 Conservative M.P.'s had pledged themselves against any Coalition, and Chamberlain foresaw that they might carry a resolution against the Coalition at the conference of the National Union of Conservative Associations to be held on November 13. Strong speeches from Balfour, Birkenhead and Chamberlain at the meeting might prevent this, but if they failed Chamberlain would have to resign his leadership of the party. Lloyd George refused to accept this, and it was agreed to seek a dissolution of parliament, and face the country as a Coalition, as soon as the Turkish crisis permitted, and before the Conservative conference in November. Only the optimism of Birkenhead, Horne, Churchill and Lloyd George himself prevented, so Chamberlain thought, the Prime Minister's retirement. The party chiefs (Younger, Sir Malcolm Fraser, Sir Leslie Wilson) were indignant at the news of this decision, but it was reaffirmed at a meeting of the Conservatives in the Cabinet on September 25, though Baldwin then opposed it.[1]

The Chanak crisis followed; but it was over before the domestic quarrel reached its climax, though it certainly contributed to it, partly because the Coalition critics feared that a war with Turkey might furnish the pretext for another 'coupon' election. As the criticism of the Conservative rank-and-file increased, the Coalition leaders met at dinner at Churchill's house on October 11, to reconsider their strategy. Meanwhile Curzon had been assailed by doubts. He attended the dinner at Churchill's, and reluctantly agreed to the course there decided on: 'All right, I'm game'. But in the night he wavered between faith on the one hand, resentment and ambition on the other: faith in a great Coalition which would live in history, resentment at Lloyd George's constant intrusion in foreign policy. Ambition called him: he might yet reach the

[1] C. Petrie, *Austen Chamberlain*, II, 192–9.

prime ministership, should the Coalition fall.[1] Next day, when the Conservative ministers met at No. 11 Downing Street, Austen Chamberlain's residence, he said that he thought on reflection that an election before November 13 would endanger the policies being followed towards Turkey, though he did not commit himself against an election. On the 15th, however, after Lloyd George had made a speech in Manchester on the Turkish crisis which irked him, he decided to resign; and he did not attend the second dinner party given by Churchill that evening (Sunday, October 15). At this, the leaders decided to summon a meeting of Conservative M.P.'s at the Carlton Club on October 19, and to demand there a vote of confidence.[2] This climactic meeting was held, therefore, on the initiative of the Coalition leaders, and not, as was afterwards assumed, on the demand of the rebels.

Seldom were rebels less hopeful of success. At a meeting of the executive of the National Union of Conservative Associations on October 18, Salvidge found the Die-Hards very much afraid of the results of the meeting next day at the Carlton Club.[3] The Coalition still had strong support, in parliament and in the country; it still had the Conservative leaders—Chamberlain, Birkenhead, Balfour; and it still had the magic of Lloyd George's name: 'he was still— and none could strip him of his fame—the "pilot who weathered the storm"; he was still the great Lloyd George, the best-known human being in the cottages of Britain . . .'[4]

On the other side were men of little public standing, junior ministers and Tory back-benchers, among whom Amery was prominent. The chief of them, Stanley Baldwin, had entered parliament in 1908 after twenty years in his family's old-established business of iron manufacturing. A country man, devoted to his native Worcestershire, he spoke little in parliament for many years, and had only reached cabinet rank in 1921, at the age of 53. Somewhat awkward in his movements, shy, with round, almost simple features, he gave little impression of ambition or driving force, or of cunning. He had come to distrust Lloyd George and his associates of the 'first-class brains', their 'levity and insincerity, their extravagance and recklessness', but had said little. While on his holiday at Aix-les-Bains (his invariable destination

[1] Wickham Steed, *The Real Stanley Baldwin* (London, 1930), p. 34, states that Curzon had learned, before the Chanak incident, that he was to be replaced as foreign secretary by Birkenhead.
[2] H. Nicolson, *Curzon*, pp. 277–80; Earl of Ronaldshay, *Life of Lord Curzon* (London, 1928), III, 312–19; W. S. Churchill, *Great Contemporaries* (New York, 1937), p. 243; C. Petrie, *Austen Chamberlain*, II, 200; *Annual Register, 1922*, pp. 110–14.
[3] S. Salvidge, *Salvidge*, p. 237.   [4] W. S. Churchill, *Aftermath*, p. 439.

for years) he had decided to resign from the Cabinet and come out against Lloyd George 'in the interests of clean government'.[1] Hurriedly recalled to London during the Chanak crisis, he was alarmed to hear of the plans for an immediate general election to perpetuate the Coalition, feeling that Lloyd George, who had already smashed the Liberal party, was well on the way to smashing the Conservative party also. He listened to friends who urged him to speak out, and did so at a meeting of Conservative ministers on October 16;[2] but did not resign or give Lloyd George any warning of his intentions—not from disloyalty, but because, with characteristic under-estimation of his powers, he expected to fail, and to retire from public life.[3]

All would depend, at the critical meeting at the Carlton Club, on the attitude, even the presence, of Bonar Law. His availability as an alternative prime minister was shown by a letter he had written to *The Times* on October 7 criticizing the government's policy in the crisis over Chanak. He had also sent Salvidge a message: 'My doctors incline to the view that I could resume hard work—if I wished to.'[4] Up to the very last he wavered between deciding to speak out against the Coalition—which would inevitably doom it—and staying away from the meeting altogether. He had told Austen Chamberlain that he thought he would stay away, on grounds of health, since he must speak against him if he came. Chamberlain replied that his speech would be decisive. 'Well, it's a hateful position; I expect that if I had remained in your place I should have acted like you', was Bonar Law's answer. He had drafted a letter to his constituents resigning from parliament.

On the evening before the Carlton Club meeting, Bonar Law was left little peace. His close friend, Lord Beaverbrook, had abandoned his support of the Coalition and was now urging him to return, as a duty, to public life. To his house in Onslow Gardens that evening came first, and by invitation, Sir Archibald Salvidge. Speaking 'in the saddest and most gentle way', he told Salvidge that he had decided to go to the meeting, 'speak in favour of ending the Coalition, and indicate his willingness to resume the leadership and form an independent Conservative Government'. There had grown up in the last few weeks, he said, a 'tidal wave

[1] P. J. Grigg, *Prejudice and Judgment*, p. 88.
[2] C. Petrie, *Austen Chamberlain*, II, 201.
[3] *Lord Baldwin: a Memoir* (*The Times* pamphlet, 1947, enlargement of obituary notice of December 15, 1947), pp. 3–6; R. Boothby, *I Fight to Live*, pp. 26–7.
[4] S. Salvidge, *Salvidge*, p. 236.

of feeling in favour of a United Conservative Party', and to ignore it was to ignore his duty to the state, since 'the disintegration of the Conservative Party would be a national disaster'. Salvidge replied that he found, 'apart from the Die-Hards . . . no overwhelming desire for unadulterated Tory rule'. He reminded him of his own words about Lloyd George at the time of the Armistice: 'We must never let the little man go. His way and ours lie side by side in the future.' 'Bonar flushed deeply and made no attempt to hide how much the reminder had gone home.' But he argued that the party must be kept together; to which Salvidge replied that Lloyd George retained the

> unswerving support of every one of his Conservative colleagues in the Cabinet. Bonar puffed at his pipe for a few moments. At last he said, almost regretfully, without the slightest note of triumph in his voice, 'I may as well tell you that Lord Curzon is here. He is waiting in another room.' It was an absolute bombshell. . . . There was no more to be said and I rose to go. As I reached the door Bonar called me back. He got up and came towards me. 'Tell Austen and F.E. to be moderate,' he said. 'Do you think I or Curzon imagine we can rule the country with the sort of people that will be left to make up a Cabinet after the break tomorrow? I must have Austen and F.E. back at the first possible opportunity. But there will have to be an interval. Tell them not to let it be protracted by unnecessary bitterness.' As Bonar stood there he looked a lonely, perhaps even a forlorn figure. There was nothing suggestive of a man who tomorrow would have reached the very pinnacle of ambition.[1]

After this, Bonar Law talked with Curzon. Another visitor that evening was Sir George Younger.[2] Another was Wickham Steed. And finally Stanley Baldwin, who stayed until midnight and would not leave until Bonar Law promised to come to the meeting.[3] Baldwin had been his associate for two years (1917–18) at the Treasury, when Baldwin was Financial Secretary and Bonar Law Chancellor of the Exchequer.

What brought Bonar Law to this decision? Hardly ambition, if his character is studied, and with but two years to live, according to his doctors. Perhaps the arguments of his friends, and his care for the future of his party; and above all his sense of public duty. But his ideas changed back and forth, now favouring action, now abstention. Next morning he was still undecided, and

---

[1] S. Salvidge, *Salvidge*, pp. 237–8 (extracts from Salvidge's diary notes). Quoted by kind permission of Mr. Raymond Savage.
[2] A. C. Murray, *Master and Brother*, p. 185; Lord Ronaldshay, *Curzon*, III, 319–21.
[3] Letter of Arthur Mann to *The Times*, December 18, 1947; *History of The Times*, IV, ii, 738, 754–5.

Younger found him, about ten o'clock, in his armchair in front of the fire, in carpet slippers. 'Aren't you ready to start?' asked Younger. 'No,' he replied, 'I've changed my mind since last night and I'm not coming.' Younger would not accept this, brought his boots from across the room and helped him put them on; and he left for the meeting without further protest.[1]

At the meeting at the Carlton Club on October 19, Bonar Law, when he came in, was received with enthusiasm, in contrast to the cold reception of Austen Chamberlain. Chamberlain argued for continued co-operation against the Socialists, promising a reconstruction of the government after the election. Balfour also spoke in favour of the Coalition. Baldwin followed. His previous inconspicuousness and his quiet manner made the vehemence of his speech only the more effective: Lloyd George was a dynamic force, and a dynamic force was 'a very terrible thing'. He had smashed the Liberal party, and would if the Coalition continued smash the Conservative party also. There were shouts for Bonar Law. He rose hesitantly, and spoke as if soliloquising, but made it clear that he thought the party should leave the Coalition and go to the country on its own. This decided the issue. The vote in this sense was 187 to 87, nine of the ministers present supporting Chamberlain. Chamberlain and the other ministers then resigned their positions in the government, and Lloyd George an hour later went to Buckingham Palace and tendered his resignation, and that of the government, to the King.[2] Bonar Law formed a government and, on Chamberlain's resignation as leader of the party, was re-elected leader. Chamberlain's scrupulous loyalty to Lloyd George lost him the premiership. As for Lloyd George, when he resigned the King said, 'he will be Prime Minister again'.[3] And so everyone thought. But he never was. The old order had returned.

Thus ended the Coalition. And thus ended the reign of the great ones, the giants of the Edwardian era and of the war; and the rule of the pygmies, of the 'second-class brains' began, to continue until 1940. Lloyd George remained in public life, admired, distrusted, unused, and stonily watched the country sink in the hopeless morass of depression and unemployment, while lesser men frittered away Britain's power in the world. 'We have no one of that calibre now,' sadly remarked a high official in 1938.[4]

[1] Younger's account in A. C. Murray, *Master and Brother*, p. 185.

[2] C. Petrie, *Austen Chamberlain*, II, 203; *The Times*, Oct. 20, 1922; Baldwin's speech is in G. M. Young, *Stanley Baldwin* (London, 1952), pp. 40–2. This account of the fall of the Coalition is corroborated by L. S. Amery, *My Political Life, II, War and Peace, 1914–1929* (London, 1953), pp. 224–39.

[3] H. Nicolson, *George V*, p. 371.   [4] R. Boothby, *I Fight to Live*, p. 27.

CHAPTER THREE

Coming to Rest : 1922—1925

1. THE RETURN OF THE CONSERVATIVES

THE revolt of the Conservative foot-soldiers against most of their leaders—a revolt which became so large as to leave the leaders stranded without a following—had been finally over personality and party rather than principle. It determined for the moment the pattern of politics, the old pattern of Conservative, Liberal, Labour. Whether it would remain, however, depended on the testing of parties and the trial of principles (or at least of slogans) in a general election. In the event this settled little; three elections in as many years were needed to demonstrate that it was the old pattern, its colours now rather faded, that the loom was weaving.

Bonar Law, having been elected leader of the Conservatives on October 23, 1922, formed his cabinet forthwith. Lloyd George's cabinet of twenty members was replaced by one of sixteen, six of whom were peers. The new Prime Minister's freedom of choice was limited by the fact that some of the ablest Conservatives, through their loyalty to the Coalition up to its very end, were unavailable for his ministry, which had to be made up of the 'second-class brains' (though it must be admitted that some of Lloyd George's minor colleagues had been something less than giants). Baldwin was Chancellor of the Exchequer, Curzon Foreign Secretary, Lord Derby Secretary of War, E. F. L. Wood President of the Board of Education, Leopold Amery First Lord of the Admiralty, and Lloyd-Greame President of the Board of Trade. Among ministers outside the Cabinet, and among the under-secretaries, were men like Sir Douglas Hogg,[1] Sir Samuel Hoare,[2]

[1] Douglas Hogg (1872–1950), barrister; M.P., 1922–28; attorney general to Prince of Wales, 1920–22; attorney general, 1922–23, 1924–28, lord chancellor, 1928–29, 1935–38, war secretary, 1931–35; Knight, 1922, Baron Hailsham, 1928, viscount, 1929.

[2] Samuel Hoare, born 1880, son of first baronet (succeeded, 1915). M.P. for Chelsea, 1910–44; air secretary, 1922–23, 1924–29, 1940; secretary of state for India, 1931–35; foreign secretary, 1935; first lord of the Admiralty, 1936–37; home secretary, 1937–39; lord privy seal, 1939–40; ambassador to Spain, 1940–44; created Viscount Templewood, 1944.

Sir Thomas Inskip,[1] Sir William Joynson-Hicks, W. Ormsby-Gore,[2] all members of the Conservative team for the next ten or fifteen years.

The split among the Conservatives which the break-up of the Coalition had caused thus had results which far outlasted it. The breach was healed within a couple of years, but meanwhile the under-secretaries had established themselves on the ladder of office, and were never dislodged. This fashioned the character of the governments of the inter-war years: adequate discharge of routine duties, complacency, the failure of imagination and will.

The breach among the Conservatives affected the leaders rather than the party as a whole. Austen Chamberlain and twelve others signed a manifesto at the fall of the Coalition, condemning the conduct of their fellow-Conservatives, but promising that they need fear no 'factious opposition' from them; the signatories included Birkenhead, Balfour, Horne, Worthington-Evans. Neville Chamberlain,[3] Austen's half-brother, who had been a back-bench Conservative M.P. since 1918, accepted office as postmaster-general under Bonar Law, hoping that this might help to heal the breach. Austen denied that it would, and Neville offered to refuse office, though pointing out that at his age it would end his political career. Austen naturally refused to accept such a sacrifice. He himself largely stayed away from the new parliament, not wanting to oppose the government openly, yet distrustful of its ability and bitter against Bonar Law's conduct towards him. 'If Neville had not joined this Govt. I'd have had them out in six months, for with Neville out none of my people would have joined, and they would be weaker still.' He was still hoping for a reconciliation of Conservatives and Liberals which would restore the Coalition, but gradually he drew away from Lloyd George. Around the beginning of April 1923, he was sounded out by Beaverbrook, on behalf of Bonar Law, about the possibility of resuming office as Lord Privy

[1] Thomas Inskip (1876–1947), born in Clifton, Bristol; barrister; M.P., 1918–29, 1931–39; solicitor general, 1922–23, 1924–28, 1931–32; attorney general, 1928–29, 1932–36; minister for the co-ordination of defence, 1936–39; dominions secretary, 1939, 1940; lord chancellor, 1939–40; lord chief justice, 1940. Knight, 1922; created Viscount Caldecote, 1939.

[2] William Ormsby-Gore, born 1885, son of third Baron Harlech (succeeded, 1938). M.P., 1910–38; under-secretary for colonies, 1922–23, 1924–29; postmaster-general, 1931; first commissioner of Works, 1931–36; colonial secretary, 1936–38; high commissioner in South Africa, 1941–44; trustee of British Museum, National Gallery, Tate Gallery.

[3] Neville Chamberlain (1869–1940), sisal-grower, Andros Island, Bahamas, 1890–97. Business man in Birmingham. Lord mayor of Birmingham, 1915. Director of national service, 1916–17. M.P., 1918–40. Postmaster-general, 1922; minister of health, 1923, 1924–29, 1931; chancellor of the Exchequer, 1923, 1931–37; prime minister, 1937–40; lord president of the council, 1940.

Seal and Leader of the House of Commons, with an implied reversion of the prime ministership in his favour as soon as Bonar Law's poor health compelled his resignation. He distrusted the proposal, coming through a third party, and nothing came of it. Events a month later showed that the breach must get worse before it would heal over.[1]

Bonar Law's first action was to obtain the dissolution of parliament, on October 26, 1922, and the general election was held on November 15. The campaign was quiet; the keynote that of 'tranquillity and freedom from adventures and commitments both at home and abroad', for which Bonar Law had appealed at the time of his election as leader. Issues of principle were, in fact, glossed over. The result was a Conservative majority of 88 over the other parties: 347 Conservatives were elected on a popular vote of nearly 5½ millions. The weakness of the Liberals was increased by the continuing division of the party into two parts: the Liberals under Asquith elected 60 members, the National Liberals following Lloyd George 57; the total Liberal vote was 4·1 millions. Among those defeated was Winston Churchill, turned out at Dundee after a bitter contest which sent E. Scrymgeour, a Prohibitionist, and E. D. Morel,[2] an advanced Socialist, to parliament.

The real significance of the election was in Labour's advance: 142 members were elected, as compared to 59 in 1918, and the popular vote rose from 2·3 millions to 4·2 millions, partly because more candidates were run—414 in all. Two Communists were elected, J. T. Walton Newbold and S. Saklatvala, a Parsee (elected for North Battersea with Labour party endorsement). Labour's principal gains were in Scotland, greater London, Yorkshire, and Durham and Northumberland.

2. THE TRAMP OF LABOUR

The Labour members of the new parliament included almost all the men who were to be prominent in the party during the next generation; Arthur Henderson, frequently unlucky at general elections no matter how successful his planning had been for the party, was alone among the leaders in being out of parliament until returned at a by-election in January. Among the trade-union

[1] C. Petrie, *Austen Chamberlain*, II, 204–13; Keith Feiling, *Life of Neville Chamberlain* (London, 1946), p. 101.
[2] E. D. Morel (1873–1924), took the lead in exposing the scandals of the Congo Free State and wrote several books on the subject and on imperialism and secret diplomacy; one of the founders of the Union of Democratic Control, whose monthly, *Foreign Affairs*, he edited.

men were J. R. Clynes, once a 'piecer' in an Oldham cotton mill, small, quiet, shrewd and respected, and J. H. Thomas, the rail-waymen's leader, genial and easy-going, an opportunist who was not without courage. Philip Snowden was of sterner stuff from the West Riding of Yorkshire, a weaver's son who had entered the excise service, and after an accident which left him crippled had become one of Labour's most fervent evangelists, and, in par-liament, its sharpest debater, particularly on financial questions. His ability, coupled with his biting speech, made him respected by all, but loved by none save those who knew him well. His paci-fism had been deeper than that of Ramsay MacDonald, who had shared defeat with him in 1918 and now also returned to par-liament, carried along partly by the wave of disillusionment over the peace settlement, which made former opponents of the war as popular as once they had been hated. Another of Labour's pioneers who re-entered parliament was F. W. Jowett of Brad-ford, saintly and undeviating leader of the I.L.P.; another of a very different sort was George Lansbury, of Poplar, the burly, warm-hearted countryman who addressed everyone as 'brother'. A new member was Sidney Webb, the party's pedagogue whom the grateful miners of Seaham, remembering his services on the Sankey commission, had sent to represent them. Some recruits from the Liberal party now entered parliament as Labour mem-bers: C. P. Trevelyan,[1] Arthur Ponsonby,[2] Noel Buxton;[3] other newcomers included Clement Attlee,[4] Arthur Greenwood, and A. V. Alexander.[5]

[1] Charles Philips Trevelyan, born 1870, son of Sir G. O. Trevelyan and brother of G. M. and R. C. Trevelyan; succeeded to baronetcy, 1928. M.P. (Liberal), 1899–1918; (Labour), 1922–31. Parliamentary secretary, education, 1908–14; president of Board of Education, 1924, 1929–31.

[2] Arthur Ponsonby (1871–1946), son of Sir Henry Ponsonby, private secretary to Queen Victoria. Member of the diplomatic service. M.P. (Liberal), 1910–18, (Labour), 1922–30; under-secretary for foreign affairs, 1924; under-secretary for dominions, 1929; parliamentary secretary, transport, 1929–31; chancellor of the Duchy of Lancaster, 1931; leader of the Opposition in the house of lords, 1931–35; author, editor of diaries. Created Baron Ponsonby, 1929.

[3] Noel Edward Noel-Buxton (1869–1948), descendant of Fowell Buxton, the anti-slavery leader. Harrow and Trinity College, Cambridge. M.P. (Liberal), 1905–6, 1910–18; (Labour), 1922–30. Minister of agriculture, 1924, 1929–30. Created Baron Noel-Buxton, 1930.

[4] Clement Attlee, born in Putney, 1883, son of a solicitor. Haileybury and Univer-sity College, Oxford. Barrister. Secretary of Toynbee Hall. Served in the war (major). Lecturer in social science, London School of Economics, 1913–23. First Labour mayor of Stepney, 1919, 1920. M.P., 1922–55. Parliamentary private secretary to Ramsay MacDonald, 1922–24; under-secretary for war, 1924; member of Simon Commission (India), 1927; chancellor of the Duchy of Lancaster, 1930–31; postmaster-general, 1931. Deputy leader of the Labour party, 1931–35, leader, 1935–55. Lord privy seal, 1940–42; deputy prime minister, 1942–45; prime minister, 1945–51. O.M. Created Earl Attlee, 1955.

[5] A. V. Alexander, born in Weston-super-Mare, 1885, son of an artisan-engineer.

Labour's new representatives who attracted most attention were, however, the members of the 'Clydeside brigade'. Labour had won 10 out of 15 seats in Glasgow, and 21 out of 28 in the Clydeside area. The Clydesiders formed a loosely-organised group which was out to set the party and parliament afire—or at least so both they and the public thought. Many had earned their passport into politics as agitators among the Clyde workers during the war, and they had no intention of resting on their laurels. 'High explosive, handle carefully', one of them proclaimed on an illuminated button on his coat; and Kirkwood, speaking to the vast crowd which gave them a tremendous send-off at St. Enoch station, Glasgow, promised: 'When we come back, this station, this railway, will belong to the people!' On this night train to London were James Maxton, a school-teacher whose cadaverous features and lank, raven locks prefigured the incorruptible revolutionary; John Wheatley, the most brilliant brain and most uncompromising socialist in the group, benevolent in appearance as he blinked at the world through thick-lensed glasses, a Roman Catholic who had built up a prosperous printing business of his own; Campbell Stephen, a rotund ex-clergyman; George Buchanan, a schoolboy in appearance and a master of 'the more forcible expletives'; Emanuel Shinwell, a Jew of able mind and vigorous speech; David Kirkwood, the engineer, a warm-hearted, sentimental man, devoted to Burns and the Bible, whose natural courtesy and pure Scots speech soon endeared him to all and sundry at Westminster; Tom Johnston, an able journalist, the founder and editor of *Forward*; and L. Macneill Weir, a tall, handsome Bohemian figure in flaming tie, long coat, and striped trousers, 'ex-dominie, ex-actor, journalist, vivacious conversationalist and raconteur of the first order', whom MacDonald picked in 1924, no doubt partly on the strength of his appearance, as his parliamentary private secretary. Of them all Maxton became one of the best-loved figures in the House; he had great powers of emotional oratory, but none of leadership. Unintentionally he destroyed all that he touched: notably the I.L.P.[1]

Baptist lay preacher; served in war (captain); member of staff of Somerset Education Committee. M.P. (Co-operative Party), 1922–31, 1935–50. Parliamentary secretary, Board of Trade, 1924; first lord of the Admiralty, 1929–31, 1940–45, 1945–46; minister of defence, 1947–50. Created Viscount Alexander of Hillsborough, 1950.
[1] The sketch of Weir, as of the other Clydesiders, derives from Gilbert McAllister, *James Maxton: The Portrait of a Rebel* (London, 1935), pp. 13–14, 98–108. Cf. John Paton, *Left turn!* (London, 1936), p. 145.
John Wheatley (1869–1930). Campbell Stephen (1884–1947); M.P. for Camlachie division, 1922–31, 1935–47. George Buchanan (1890–1955); M.P. for Gorbals

The first business of the Labour members was to elect the leader of the Parliamentary Labour Party for the new session. Clynes had been leader in the previous session, and many members thought that he ought to be re-elected, especially Snowden and the trade unionists. But MacDonald (who had been leader before the war) had been campaigning actively for support, and had the Clydesiders solidly behind him. His pacifism had suggested extremist views which were really foreign to him; the vilification he had endured from jingo journalists like Horatio Bottomley even as recently as the bitter Woolwich by-election of 1921, which he had lost by some 700 votes, had seemed to confirm him as a revolutionary leader. Like De Valera, he had leadership thrust upon him, though not averse to it. And he had used his freedom from parliamentary attendance since 1918 to work closely with the I.L.P., and to cultivate the support of the Labour movement in Scotland; in particular his weekly articles in *Forward* played to the gallery of advanced socialists. Hence, at the fateful meeting in Committee Room 14 in parliament on November 21, it was Shinwell who proposed and the Clydesiders who supported MacDonald's election: and he was elected by 61 votes to 56, perhaps because some of the trade-union members were delayed by another meeting from arriving before the vote. Never were enthusiasts so deceived; they had put their worst enemy into the leadership and within two months—less time than Henderson had predicted for the honeymoon—they were in open revolt against him. But he had come to stay, not only as leader, but in the event, Prime Minister.[1]

MacDonald's character, once admired by the many, now slighted, is so much judged by hindsight, that it is hard to reconstruct the impression he made in 1922. His weaknesses, though foreshadowed, were known only to few: his apparent predilection for intrigue and compromise, his jealousy, his hyper-sensitiveness to criticism, his indifference to precise facts and hard theory (worse because never admitted). What people saw was the fine figure with sad, handsome, noble face, brilliant eyes and mass of wavy, greying hair; what they heard was a speaker of exalted and emo-

division, 1922–48; Minister of Pensions, 1947–48; chairman, National Assistance Board, 1948. Thomas Johnston, born 1882; M.P., 1922–31, 1935–45; parliamentary under-secretary for Scotland, 1929–31; lord privy seal, 1931; secretary of state for Scotland, 1941–45; chairman, North of Scotland Hydro Electric Board, 1947. L. Macneill Weir (1877–1939). James Maxton (1885–1946); M.P. for Bridgeton division, 1922–46; chairman of I.L.P., 1926–31, 1934–39.

[1] On MacDonald's election, see especially John Scanlon, *Decline and Fall of the Labour Party* (London, [1932]), pp. 32–5; Philip Snowden, *Autobiography* (London, 1934), II, 573–4; F. Williams, *Fifty Years' March* (London, 1949), p. 298.

tional eloquence, using a voice of great beauty and range in a warm Scots accent to infuse 'a certain poetic quality into his speech and the suggestion of vast depths yet undisclosed . . .'[1] His appearance was aristocratic, his tastes those of the cultivated man of leisure; and to a large section of the party this was no disqualification, even though the nickname 'Gentleman Mac' lacked affection. Towards those he regarded as equals his manner was easy and charming, though never intimate. He looked the part of leader and could carry it outwardly to perfection. His pride commanded respect and his courage admiration. That such a man would be a moderate was in the nature of things—and again, in the present state of the party, this was no disqualification. The rank and file were not socialists, and nor was he. His socialism, as expounded in his books, was based on ideas of natural history imbibed from his early biological studies; society was an organism, and socialism was co-operation, the taking over by society of the economic power which individualism had created but could not control; the enemies of society were the injustices of monopoly, of privilege, of the perpetuation of large fortunes through inheritance. Change, though certain, must be gradual. In one of his earliest works, *Socialism and Society* (1905), he gave as the socialist motto *solvitur ambulando*, 'laboratory experiment, not revolution'; in the preface to the new edition of *Socialism: Critical and Constructive*, written while he was Prime Minister, he proclaimed that the socialist was 'an evolutionist *par excellence*', who 'rejects everything of the nature of violent breaks and brand-new systems'.[2] Lord Inchcape, after meeting him at dinner at Lord Morley's in 1923 ('I was agreeably surprised to find how reasonable he is. He said he was bringing the wild socialist labour members to heel.') shrewdly summed him up as a Whig.[3]

The fact was that the Labour movement was not then, and never

---

[1] W. J. Brown, *So Far . . .* (London, 1943), p. 129.

[2] J. Ramsay MacDonald, *Socialism and Society* (London, 1905), p. 179; *The Socialist Movement* (Home University Library; London, 1911), pp. 247–8 (reference is to New York edition); *Socialism: Critical and Constructive* (London, 1921; revised edition, 1924), p. xii (reference is to 1929 edition). Cf. F. Williams, *Fifty Years' March*, p. 199.

[3] Hector Bolitho, *James Lyle Mackay, first Earl of Inchcape* (London, 1936), p. 226. Impressions of MacDonald are legion: see especially Mary Agnes Hamilton, *J. Ramsay MacDonald* (London, 1929; first published as *The Man of Tomorrow*, 1923), and also her *Remembering my good friends* (London, 1944), pp. 120–30; Sir J. A. Salter, *Personality in Politics* (London, 1947), pp. 54–65; Beatrice Webb, *Our Partnership* (London, 1948), pp. 132, 229, 260, 271, 276 (later, kinder references in her *Diaries, 1912–1924*, especially p. 257). His career to 1919 is fully and sympathetically described in Lord Elton, *Life of James Ramsay MacDonald (1866–1919)* (London, 1939). His views as expressed in speeches and writings are described in Benjamin Sacks, *J. Ramsay MacDonald in Thought and Action* (Albuquerque, New Mexico, 1952).

has been, a single, precise enterprise. In 1922 it was in a particularly fluid state. In parliament it included both the new middle-class recruits from the Liberals and its old working-class members, both the representatives of the I.L.P. and those endorsed by trade unions and the new local branches of the Labour party, both the Clydesiders and the more solid 'southrons'. Yet the lines between such groupings were blurred; most Labour members would be found in several categories either at different times or at one and the same time; and all had caught something of the revolutionary fervour from the Russian experiment, so that even when its magic dissolved for most of them the 'Russia complex' remained—a tenderness towards Russia alternately fanned by Tory gibes and cooled by Russian rebuffs. Always, however, there was a rough line of cleavage which divided what, for want of better terms, one must call the right and the left sections of the party. What made the divisions sharper was that MacDonald, elected leader by the left, at once aligned himself with the right, the more so as the tactics of the left-wingers in parliament became direct, provocative, dramatic.

The cleavage between left and right was actually a projection of the cleavage in international socialism caused in part by the Russian revolution. In Britain, it can be seen most clearly in the I.L.P. This party within the Labour party, far from disappearing once the Labour party admitted individual members and established local branches, grew rapidly after the war: 139 new branches were founded in 1918–19, and the membership reached 45,000. The slump of 1920–21 set it back, but by 1922–23 membership was reported as over 30,000. Its chairman, from 1917 to 1920, was Philip Snowden, and it fell to him to stem the revolutionary tide within it. MacDonald was also very active in the I.L.P. after 1918, using it to build up his own following in the Labour movement, while fighting against those within it who were turning towards the Moscow road. The choice before socialists was clearly posed at the International Socialist Conference held at Berne in February 1919. The main issue was that of 'Democracy and Dictatorship'; whether, in the light of the Bolshevist revolution, socialists could still believe that socialism might be achieved by constitutional, democratic means. With the Soviet Union unrepresented, a majority voted for a compromise resolution equating democracy with socialism; but a substantial minority wished to leave the way open for the Russian revolutionaries to enter the old International.

It was this sentiment, applied to the problems of socialism in Britain, which led the I.L.P., early in 1919, to enter into negotiations for 'Socialist Unity' and a common front against allied intervention in Russia with the British Socialist Party and the Socialist Labour party (forerunners of the British Communist party). These negotiations came to nothing, partly over differences of opinion on the use of parliamentary action. Applying to international socialism the same hopes for unity, the I.L.P. at its conference in Glasgow in 1920 voted in favour of secession from the Second International but at the same time, thanks to Mac-Donald's exhortation and its own divided mind, it rejected a motion supporting affiliation with the Third (or Communist) International founded at Moscow in 1919. It did, however, send delegates to Russia, Clifford Allen and R. C. Wallhead,[1] who joined a delegation of eleven representatives of the Labour party and the T.U.C.—an odd assortment of persons, including Ben Turner,[2] A. A. Purcell,[3] Margaret Bondfield,[4] and Ethel Snowden (Mrs. Snowden)—which descended upon the Soviet Union in May 1920. This visit convinced not only the Labour party but also the I.L.P. that the new Russia was under a dictatorship, with whose Communist International they could have no part; and at its conference at Southport in 1921, the I.L.P. decisively rejected affiliation with the Communist International, and shed its Communist sympathisers.[5]

Differences of opinion on tactics, if not on objectives, remained within the Labour movement. The I.L.P. was until the middle twenties the *avant-garde*, especially under the leadership of Clifford Allen.[5] 'C.A.', as his friends called him, a Cambridge graduate, had been chairman of the No Conscription Fellowship. He was a man of personal charm and striking appearance—a tall,

---

[1] R. C. Wallhead (1869–1934), manager of *Labour Leader*, Manchester, 1906–21; chairman of I.L.P., 1920–23; M.P. for Merthyr Tydfil, 1922–34.
[2] Ben Turner (1863–1942), weaver, president, National Union of Textile Workers; chairman of Labour party, 1911, of T.U.C., 1928; mayor of Batley, 1913–16, 1934–35; M.P. 1922–24, 1929–31; mines secretary, 1929–30; knighted, 1930.
[3] A. A. Purcell (1872–1935), born in London; a french polisher; organiser of Furnishing Trades' Association in Lancashire; president of Manchester and Salford Trades and Labour Council; chairman, T.U.C., 1924. M.P., 1923, 1925–29.
[4] Margaret Bondfield (1873–1953), born near Chard, Somerset; assistant secretary, Shop Assistants' Union, 1898–1908; national officer, General and Municipal Workers' Union, 1908–38. M.P., 1923–24, 1926–31; parliamentary secretary, Labour, 1924; minister of Labour, 1929–31.
[5] G. D. H. Cole, *History of the Labour Party from 1914*, pp. 97–103, 131–40, 149.
[6] Reginald Clifford Allen (1889–1939), born in Newport, Mon., son of a draper, educated at Berkhamsted School and at Peterhouse, Cambridge; supported MacDonald after the formation of the National government in 1931 and was made a peer (Baron Allen of Hurtwood) in 1932.

willowy, attenuated figure, handsome head, wavy auburn hair; he
'looked like a saint; but he was a saint of the militant Jesuit type:
there was a powerful brain and a will of iron behind his apparent
fragility.'[1] He became the treasurer of the I.L.P. in 1922, and
revived its finances with the 'golden stream' of money he attracted
from Quakers and other new converts to socialism. He and
Fenner Brockway[2] and Clement Attlee were for a time a sort of
inner group of leaders, carrying the I.L.P. forward as the exponent of thorough-going socialism to be achieved, not by force,
but by 'persuasion and courage'. In 1923 Allen became chairman,
and Brockway secretary. Impressive headquarters were established in Great George Street, near the Houses of Parliament; a
Guild of Youth and the I.L.P. Arts Guild were started; the *Labour
Leader* was transformed into the *New Leader* which, under the
editorship of H. N. Brailsford, became for a while a weekly of high
literary appeal as well as political force; an Information Department was created, with MacDonald as chairman, Ernest Hunter as
secretary, and Mrs. Mary Agnes Hamilton as one of its members.
Many new branches were founded, the number rising from 637 to
1028 between 1923 and 1925, and the membership to 34,000 (or
by one count to 56,000). Yet the I.L.P., though influential in the
Labour party in these years, and helping to keep it on a socialist
course, never came near to dominating it or making it an out-and-
out socialist party; for the influence of the moderates such as
MacDonald and Snowden was exerted, on the one hand to temper
the enthusiasms of the I.L.P., and on the other to give pre-
ponderance in the Labour party to the moderate and right-wing
sections.[3]

Hence the appearance of shadow-boxing which the Labour performance of 1922–24 presents. There were many strong speeches
and articles, and they were not insincere; but the big battalions
were not behind them. The contrast can be seen in the speeches
of two successive chairmen of the Labour party at the annual conference. In 1922 the chairman was F. W. Jowett, one of the
founders of the I.L.P. in 1893. Speaking at the Edinburgh con-

[1] M. A. Hamilton, *Remembering my good Friends*, p. 116.
[2] Archibald Fenner Brockway, born in Calcutta, 1888, son of a missionary. Editor
of *Labour Leader*, 1912–17; secretary of No Conscription Fellowship, 1917 (served
several terms of imprisonment as pacifist 1917–19); organising secretary, I.L.P.,
1922, general secretary, 1928, 1933–39, chairman, 1931–33; editor of *New Leader*,
1926–29, 1931–46; M.P., 1929–31 and since 1950 (Labour).
[3] Fenner Brockway, *Inside the Left* (London, 1942), pp. 141–6; John Paton,
Left Turn!, pp. 154–5; G. D. H. Cole, *History of the Labour Party*, pp. 142–3,
148–51.

ference (which rejected the Communist party's renewed request for affiliation by a vote of over ten to one), he declared:

Meanwhile, we pay a terrible tribute to Rent, Interest and Profit . . . [which] enrich mainly the class which has already more to spend than it can usefully spend.
It is this class which gives us the spectacles of senseless and wasteful display at race meetings, royal levées and royal weddings, hunting and shooting parties, and the gatherings of the swell mob at continental pleasure resorts.
For the Royal homecoming it is 'roses all the way'. For the miner's wife, trudging to the guardians for relief, it is tears all the way . . .

Hence he demanded redress of immediate wrongs: the party should force upon the government the duty of meeting human needs—maintaining the unemployed, providing decent houses, ensuring for everyone a living income. He wanted a direct attack on the old order, leading to the socialisation of the national income, rather than waiting for the slow effects of reformism and the ultimate nationalisation of industry.[1]

Next year the chairman was Sidney Webb, representative of the Fabian and intellectual, middle-class side of the party. Speaking at the annual conference, in the Queen's Hall, London, he declared that 'from the rising curve of Labour votes it might be computed that the party would obtain a clear majority . . . somewhere about 1926'. 'Socialism,' he continued, 'was rooted in political democracy and every step towards their goal was dependent on getting the support of at least a numerical majority of the whole people.' No one need fear that the British electorate would ever go too fast:

Whilst it would be easy to draft proclamations of universal change, or even enact laws in a single sitting purporting to give a new heaven and a new earth, the result next morning would be no change at all, unless, indeed, it were the advent of widespread confusion. Once they faced the necessity of putting their principles into Bills . . . the inevitability of gradualness could not fail to be appreciated. . . . The whole nation had been imbibing Socialism without realising it. It was now time for the subconscious to rise into consciousness.

The founder of British socialism, he reminded the party, was not Marx, but Robert Owen, who 'preached not "class war"', but the ancient doctrine of human brotherhood (Cheers)'.[2]

[1] F. Brockway, *Life of Jowett*, pp. 180–3. *The Times*, though denouncing Jowett as a 'wrecker' and his proposals as 'naked Bolshevism' in its first leader of June 30, 1922, did not report the speech in its news columns at all.
[2] *The Times*, June 27, 1923.

There was the same contrast in parliament. David Kirkwood used the opportunity of the debate on the King's speech in November 1922 to warn the government that he intended to 'smash' the 'atmosphere of indifference' to unemployment.

It is no new thing for hon. Gentlemen who at the moment are away feasting, while my class are outside starving, to draw tens of thousands a year for doing absolutely nothing. . . . There will be no tranquillity as long as there are children in Scotland starving. . . . No child ought to starve. It should be utterly impossible in this land of the brave and the free. Do you think that we, who come from Scotland . . . from that hardy and intelligent race whom the Romans could never defeat, are going to allow those nincompoops who sit on those benches to efface us? That will not take place. . . .[1]

In a different vein was a debate on socialism which Snowden initiated on March 20, 1923, after winning first place in the ballot for private members' motions. He moved that 'in view of the failure of the capitalist system to adequately utilise and organise natural resources and productive power, or to provide the necessary standard of life for vast numbers of the population . . . legislative effort should be directed to the gradual supersession of the capitalist system . . .' His speech, denouncing capitalism for its inefficiency and its monopoly of labour and land, was answered by Sir Alfred Mond[2] with a panegyric on individual initiative and a condemnation of socialism as a robbing of the rich and the clipping of the wings of enterprise in a 'bureaucratic, soulless machine'. This debate, which had had some publicity in advance, attracted much attention, even though nothing came of it but the exercise of wits and voices.[3] On April 12, in a debate about ex-service men in the civil service, Labour members showed their disgust at the government's complacency by shouts and the singing of the 'Red Flag', so that the House was forced to adjourn.

The most dramatic of these demonstrations of socialist fervour came on June 28. In a debate on Scottish estimates Maxton attacked the Conservatives for supporting economies which, by

[1] 159 H.C. Deb., 5 s., 133–4.
[2] Alfred Mond (1868–1930), son of Ludwig Mond, founder of the chemicals firm of Brunner, Mond and Company. A prime mover of three great combines, Imperial Chemical Industries (I.C.I.), Amalgamated Anthracite Collieries (West Wales), International Nickel Company of Canada. M.P. (Liberal), 1906–23, 1924–28; first commissioner of Works, 1916–21, minister of health, 1921–22. Joined Conservative party, 1926. Baronet 1910, created Baron Melchett, 1928. A devoted Zionist in his later years.
[3] 161 H.C. Deb., 5 s., 2472 ff.

cutting grants to child-welfare centres, had increased the death rate among children.

> In the interest of economy they condemned hundreds of children to death, and I call it murder. . . . It is a fearful thing for any man to have on his soul—a cold, callous, deliberate crime in order to save money. We are prepared to destroy children in the great interest of dividends. We put children out in the front of the fighting line.

Sir Frederick Banbury, crustiest of City Tories, intervened on a point of order: was it in order to call honourable members murderers? Maxton refused to withdraw the implication, and was suspended, as were Wheatley, Campbell Stephen and Buchanan. The 'tumult', as *The Times* called it, lasted an hour and a quarter. MacDonald, it reported, 'sat on the front bench white with anger at the folly of his own followers'.[1]

Such displays served only to sharpen the differences between MacDonald and his own left wingers. MacDonald was determined that the party should be respectable, for if it was to be a national rather than a working-class party it must win the respect of the middle classes. The Conservatives and Liberals at times made this difficult, for it was they who displayed 'class hatred' in the 1923 parliament—contemptuous in their attitude towards trade unionists and bitter towards middle-class members of the Labour party, whom they considered traitors. Sidney Webb was greeted with the cry 'Sit down, Nanny' (his beard giving him a supposed resemblance to a nanny-goat); and Sir Patrick Hastings, a successful and prosperous barrister (and playwright), who had joined the party, was jeered and laughed at when he spoke in condemnation of the government's action in March in arresting and deporting to Ireland some hundred Irishmen who were suspected of plotting against the Free State. No wonder Jowett wrote bitterly of the bad manners of the 'swell mob', and Sir Patrick Hastings deplored the absence of the tolerance and friendliness between the parties which was supposed to exist in the 'best club in Europe'.[2]

Yet in fact the strong spirit of Labour was tamed, partly by the atmosphere of the House and by its social conventions. The 'aris-

[1] 165 H.C. Deb., 5 s., 2377–2402; *The Times*, June 28, 1923. For general accounts of these incidents, see F. Brockway, *Life of Jowett*, pp. 194–202; J. Scanlon, *Decline and Fall of the Labour Party*, pp. 51–3; G. McAllister, *James Maxton*, pp. 113–28; *Annual Register, 1923*; the suspended members were re-admitted to parliament after seven weeks.
[2] F. Brockway, *Life of Jowett*, pp. 196–8; Sir Patrick Hastings, *Autobiography* (London, 1948), p. 229; 161 H.C. Deb., 5 s., 1166–71.

tocratic embrace' was, with occasional lapses, proffered even in these times. Some members merely succumbed to the ease of parliamentary life—the comfortable fire of the Map Room, where Labour members foregathered. Others accepted invitations to parties, sometimes given by Lady Astor. The Clydesiders usually refused such advances. Kirkwood found resistance difficult. At the State opening of parliament he had said to Wheatley: 'John, we'll soon change all this.' Yet he wrote later: 'I had to shake myself occasionally as I found myself moving about and talking with men whose names were household words. More strange was it to find them all so simple and unaffected and friendly.' His pride in Scotland responded when Bonar Law said to him after a debate: 'You Clyde boys were pretty hard on me today. But it's fine to hear your Glasgow accent. It's like a sniff of the air of Scotland in the musty atmosphere of this place.'[1]

3. THE PATCHWORK OF PEACE IN EUROPE

The main problems facing Bonar Law's government and that of his successors were external. The Chanak crisis had brought Anglo-French relations to their lowest point, but the firmness of the British government at the time, under the inspiration of Lloyd George and Churchill, had begun the restoration of Britain's international prestige, weakened by the debacles of the Cannes and Genoa conferences. The year 1923 was Lord Curzon's great and closing year of office as Foreign Secretary, in which this work of restoration—an essential preliminary for Anglo-French reconciliation—was greatly advanced. It marked also the restoration to the Foreign Secretary and to the Foreign Office of authority in the determination of foreign policy.

Curzon's first task, and the one which earned him a triumph, was to get a new treaty with Turkey to replace the shattered treaty of Sèvres; for this purpose he left London for the Lausanne conference on November 17, 1922, just after the government's successes in the general election of November 15. Preliminary agreement on concerted action between Britain and France was reached at a meeting of Curzon and Poincaré in Paris on November 18. Curzon at once established his personal ascendancy over the conference, and by his handling of the negotiations—one of the 'classic examples of expert diplomacy'—not only secured, in all but name, a satisfactory treaty, but re-established British

[1] D. Kirkwood, *My Life of Revolt*, pp. 201–2. After his retirement from the House of Commons he was made a peer, in 1951.

leadership in Europe, broke the recently formed common front of Turkey and Russia, and restored Britain to its old position of friendship with Turkey. Though minor details prevented a treaty from being signed by the day Curzon had set for his departure, February 4, 1923, the agreement completed at the resumed conference (April 24 to July 24), at which Britain was represented by Sir Horace Rumbold, was in all essentials that which he had negotiated. Turkey retained Eastern Thrace (including Adrianople); demilitarised zones were established on both sides of the Dardanelles (including Gallipoli and the Chanak area) and on both sides of the Bosphorus; navigation of the Straits was opened to ships of commerce of all nations in time of peace and of neutrals in time of war involving Turkey, and to warships of all nations (subject to limitations of number and size) in time of peace or Turkish neutrality; and the disposition of the territory of Mosul, with its oil-fields, which was in dispute between Turkey and Iraq, was left for later negotiations (it was ultimately referred to the League of Nations and awarded to Iraq, a decision accepted by Turkey in a treaty in 1926).[1]

It was, however, not on Turkey but on the French occupation of the Ruhr and the chaos in Germany that the attention of Europe was focused during 1923. With Germany in difficulties over reparation payments, the Reparations Commission had in 1922 accepted German treasury bills to meet instalments—in effect a six-months' moratorium. A new German offer was rejected by Poincaré at the London Conference of December 9–11, 1922, and on December 26 the Reparations Commission, at the instance of the French, declared Germany in default on deliveries of timber (72,000 cubic yards of sawn timber and 200,000 telegraph poles): the vote was three to one, the British member casting a negative vote. In this shadow a conference of the Allied premiers was held in Paris on January 2–4; but Bonar Law's proposal of a four-years' moratorium was refused and the conference only recorded, in his words, 'an irreconcilable difference of opinion'. On January 9, the Reparations Commission declared Germany in default on deliveries of coal; on January 11 the French and Belgians began the occupation of the Ruhr, sending troops first to Essen, to support the efforts of a civilian commission, 'Micum' (Mission Inter-

---

[1] H. Nicolson, *Curzon*, pp. 281–350; R. B. Mowat, *History of European Diplomacy, 1914–1925*, pp. 298–308. Further impressions of Curzon and the Lausanne conference are in Harold Nicolson's essay, 'Arketall', in *Some People* (London, 1927). By the Montreux Convention of 1936 the demilitarisation of the Straits was ended and the provisions governing the passage of warships modified.

alliée de Contrôle des Usines et des Mines) in obtaining 'productive pledges' for the actual delivery of reparations.

The French occupation of the Ruhr proclaimed the virtual end of the Anglo-French entente and of the unity of the war-time allies. France's consuming passion for security clashed with Britain's policy of reconciliation; France's need of reparations payments at almost any price to balance her finances clashed with the British thesis that restoration of Germany's financial stability must come first; and France resented the attempts of the British government to link reparations with war debts and to scale down the former to the irreducible claims of the latter. Yet the strands of the entente never completely parted. Though Britain took no part in the occupation of the Ruhr, she did nothing to hamper it. The British zone of occupation in the Rhineland intervened between the French zone and the Ruhr, but French troop trains were permitted to cross it. A state of deadlock lasted through 1923. The government's lack of any firm policy was the subject of much criticism in England, particularly from the Labour party; but it was, perhaps, the best policy which could have been adopted at the time. The British attitude betrayed, perhaps unconsciously, a divided mind. The occupation of the Ruhr was condemned as upsetting the international polity; but to the British economy it brought great, if temporary gains; with the Ruhr coal-mines at a standstill, Britain's coal exports recovered to a high and lucrative volume, and unemployment was diminished.

As the results of the occupation went from bad to worse, Curzon made attempts to mediate between France and Germany. Though some reparations were forthcoming, the cost, both in money and misery, was far greater than the yield. The German population, under the leadership of the government, adopted passive resistance; workers refused to work and government officials to function. France was forced to set up a military regime under General Dégoutte. Disorders in the streets, German lynch law against collaborators, the wrecking of trains, reprisals and counter-reprisals brought much loss of life. Meanwhile to support the population while work was at a standstill the German government resorted to the printing press, and the inflation of the mark reached fantastic heights, spawning present calamity and the future poisons of Nazism. The mark, once standing at twenty to the pound, was already worth 81,200 to the pound in January; by August it was 19,800,000, by September 250 million to the pound. in November 22,300 millions. A lifetime's savings might be reduced in a few hours to the price of a single meal. No wonder that disorder broke out all over Germany, fomented here by the Communists, elsewhere by the National Socialists, reaching in November the climax in the attempted *putsch* in Bavaria led by Adolf Hitler and General Ludendorff.

Curzon's efforts at mediation began in April, when he encouraged the German government to make a new offer to settle the reparations question. An offer was forthcoming, but Poincaré rejected it since it did not provide for the end of passive resistance before the evacuation of the Ruhr began. An exchange of letters between the British and French governments followed, Curzon attempting to find out under what conditions the French would evacuate the Ruhr. The final letter of Curzon's was the long and firm note of August 11: it renewed an earlier suggestion of Curzon's of an 'expert inquiry' into Germany's capacity to pay; it asked whether French demands were not such as to imply the intention to occupy the Ruhr in perpetuity; and it brought in the question of inter-allied debts, offering to receive from the Allies and from Germany no more than was needed to meet Britain's debt to the United States. This note, though much resented in France as accusing her of being a 'bully' and answered in uncompromising terms by Poincaré, had its effect in restoring confidence in Germany, where the Cuno government was succeeded by one headed by Stresemann in August.

The effect of Curzon's note was, however, lost as a result of two developments which weakened Britain's position. The first was the Corfu incident. To avenge the murder by brigands of three Italian officers who were members of an inter-allied commission delimiting the Greek-Albanian frontier, the Italian government under Mussolini had sent an ultimatum to Greece and followed it up by the bombardment and occupation of the island of Corfu. Greece appealed to the League of Nations, whose Assembly and Council were in session in Geneva in September. Lord Robert Cecil, Britain's representative, was given instructions to support the League's authority, which he did tellingly by having articles 10, 12 and 15 of the Covenant read out by the interpreter, and reminding the Council that they were part of the treaty of Versailles.[1] But Mussolini was determined not to be brought to the bar of the League of Nations, and insisted that the matter be handled by the Conference of Ambassadors in Paris, whose agent

[1] Lord Robert Cecil (Viscount Cecil), *A Great Experiment* (London, 1941), pp. 148–51.

the boundary commission had been. This was done. Mussolini accepted from the latter what he had refused the former, thus beginning the undermining of the authority of the League and intruding into international politics once more the doctrine that a dictator's might was right. The effect on the League, in face of the Council's reiteration of its competence to consider the dispute, was at the time little, but on British standing it was immediate. On top of this came the second event; the meeting of Stanley Baldwin, the new Prime Minister, with Poincaré in Paris on September 19, when returning from his annual pilgrimage to Aix-les-Bains. The communiqué issued after the meeting, that the two prime ministers 'were happy to establish a common agreement of views, and to discover that on no question is there any difference of purpose or divergence of principle which would impair the co-operation of the two countries', seemed to be a repudiation of Curzon's policy. Four days later the German government gave way. Passive resistance was abandoned, martial law proclaimed throughout the country, and the currency stabilised by the new *rentenmark*, worth 1,000,000 millions of the paper marks. Poincaré had won, and Anglo-French reconciliation must await a better day.

Yet Curzon's diplomacy achieved two things of importance for the entente and for European stability before he left office. First, when the French, in October 1923, tried once more to promote separatist states in the Rhineland as a means to their own security, and under the protection of their occupying forces, he intervened to nip in the bud efforts which, if successful, would only have added to the turmoil of Germany and of Europe. Second, his advocacy of an expert body to examine the reparations question bore fruit when the Reparations Commission, on November 30, set up two committees of experts to go into the question. This led, in 1924, when Baldwin's government had been replaced by Ramsay MacDonald's Labour government, to the Dawes report and the London conference by which, for the time being, the matter was solved; the device of the committee of experts (first suggested by Charles Evans Hughes, American Secretary of State, in a speech on December 29, 1922, and reiterated by President Coolidge on October 11, 1923) brought back the United States to the European scene, and provided a means by which Anglo-French differences, unamenable to political argument, might be reconciled.[1]

[1] H. Nicolson, *Curzon*, pp. 360–78; R. B. Mowat, *History of European Diplomacy*, pp. 243–59; W. M. Jordan, *Great Britain, France and the German Problem*, pp. 52, 67, 107–30; E. Mantoux, *Carthaginian Peace*, pp. 139–43; P. J. Grigg, *Prejudice and Judgment*, pp. 153–72; *Annual Register, 1923*.

Meanwhile, a debt which was *not* to be put alongside the question of reparations had been settled, and in a way which increased, though in a backhanded fashion, the importance of the chief negotiator, Stanley Baldwin, the Chancellor of the Exchequer. The United States had, in 1922, created a Debt Funding Commission authorised to fund war debts owed by the Allies to the United States on the basis of repayment over 25 years at not less than $4\frac{1}{2}$ per cent interest. Balfour, in temporary charge of the Foreign Office, had in August published the 'Balfour note' (addressed to the French government) renewing an earlier proposal of Lloyd George's for the mutual writing-off of all inter-allied debts 'incurred . . . for a great purpose, common to them all', and observing that 'to generous minds it can never be agreeable . . . to regard the monetary aspect of this great event as a thing apart, to be torn from its historical setting and treated as no more than an ordinary commercial dealing between traders who borrow and capitalists who lend'. Hence, the note continued, what Great Britain would demand from its European debtors 'depends . . . on what Great Britain has to pay America'.[1] This shifting of the onus of debts and reparations on to the United States was hardly calculated to induce American generosity, though its principal effect was to harden French insistence on receiving her due from Germany. However, the United States ambassador in London, George Harvey, had given the government to believe that generous terms could be obtained from the United States for the funding of the British debt, which amounted to £978,000,000. Consequently, Baldwin and Montagu Norman, the governor of the Bank of England,[2] journeyed across the Atlantic, reaching New York on January 4, 1923. In the negotiations in Washington, Andrew Mellon, the Secretary to the Treasury, offered a settlement at $3\frac{1}{2}$ per cent interest on payments spread over 61 years. Baldwin cabled the proposal to the Cabinet, which rejected it. He then proposed a 3 per cent basis, but could win no greater concession from the Americans than interest of 3 per cent for the first 10 years and $3\frac{1}{2}$ per cent for the remaining 52 years. He agreed to urge this on the government, but it was refused and he was ordered to return home. However, the offer had already been communicated to the American press as a generous concession, and Baldwin, on his return, strongly urged the Cabinet to accept it as the best which

---

[1] Text in *The Times*, August 2, 1922.

[2] Montagu Norman (1871–1950). Eton and King's College, Cambridge. Served in Boer War (D.S.O.). Governor of the Bank of England, 1920–44 (previously a director). Created baron, 1944. Rather given to appearing as a man of mystery.

G

could be obtained.[1] He had unintentionally made matters worse by unguarded remarks to newspaper reporters at Southampton, implying that the narrow views of some rural Congressmen made a better settlement impracticable; garbled reports of this statement in the United States aroused indignation and prejudiced the whole issue. In the end the Cabinet accepted the terms, on January 30, though in Bonar Law's case the consent was reluctant and bitter. As a contribution to world stability, the settlement had a good deal of merit; the only trouble was that later the United States made settlements with other debtors more generous than that accorded to Great Britain and did not revise the terms of the British settlement.

4. BALDWIN BECOMES PRIME MINISTER

These circumstances make the selection of Baldwin as Bonar Law's successor as Prime Minister less startling than it has sometimes seemed. Bonar Law's health had been failing, and what eventually proved to be cancer of the throat had weakened his voice, so that Baldwin frequently deputised for him in the Commons; in the early months of 1923 Curzon presided over the Cabinet in his absence, and by reason of his position and prestige might appear to be the obvious successor. A Mediterranean cruise at the end of April brought Bonar Law no improvement in health. On Saturday, May 19, he wrote to Curzon that he was submitting his resignation to the King, and added that he understood that it was 'not customary for the King to ask the Prime Minister to recommend his successor in circumstances like the present'. Most of the Cabinet were out of London at the time for the Whitsuntide recess, but Bonar Law saw Baldwin that day. His resignation was tendered by letter next day, the King being at Aldershot for a review of the troops.[2] Lord Stamfordham, the King's private secretary, returned to London, and summoned Balfour to give the King advice. Whit Monday, a bank holiday (May 21), intervened. On that day Balfour motored up to London from Sheringham, where he was staying, and saw Lord Stamfordham; he advised against the choice of Curzon on grounds of his membership of the House of Lords. Other Conservatives, such as Lord Salisbury, Leopold Amery, and Walter Long, gave similar advice, urging that the Prime Minister should nowadays be a commoner, and that Baldwin was the man. The Labour party

[1] Some details in G. M. Young, *Baldwin*, pp. 44–7.
[2] Bonar Law died on October 30, 1923.

pointed to the difficulties, while it formed the Opposition, of having the Prime Minister in the Lords.

Curzon, however, on receiving Bonar Law's letter on Monday, was convinced of his destiny; and a telegram from Lord Stamfordham, summoning him to London, confirmed him in this. Curzon was staying at Montacute, in Somerset, perhaps the loveliest, though not the largest of the several historic country places which he occupied; there was no telephone to the house, and the telegram was delivered by the policeman on a bicycle, in the stillness of that holiday evening. Lord and Lady Curzon travelled up to London next morning, Curzon talking over his plans as Prime Minister, and receiving the welcome of a battery of photographers on his arrival. At 3.30 Lord Stamfordham came to see him at his house on Carlton House Terrace, and told him that the King had decided to send for Baldwin, who was already at the Palace. Curzon was stunned by this slur, as he regarded it, upon himself and his career, and upon the fitness of a peer for the highest office. Yet he quickly overcame his mortification, accepted Baldwin's invitation to stay on as Foreign Secretary, and proposed him as leader at the meeting of Conservative party members on May 28, observing that he possessed 'the supreme and indispensible qualification of not being a peer.'[1]

Baldwin had, of course, other qualifications, though some of them were not immediately apparent. In the party, in the government, and in the country, he had become increasingly prominent since the Carlton Club meeting, and the American debt settlement, however much open to criticism, had increased his eminence. And some remarks of his, typical of later speeches which gradually built up his popularity as a plain man of common sense and good will, had marked him out for many as the sort of leader which the times called for. Speaking in parliament on February 16 in the debate on the King's speech he had said (rejecting any solution of unemployment by the Soviet system):

Four words of one syllable each are words which contain salvation for

---

[1] H. Nicolson, *George V*, pp. 375–79, quotes Stamfordham's memorandum describing the interview with Curzon, and implies that earlier and more picturesque versions are incorrect, naming his own (*Curzon*, p. 355), where Curzon is described as weeping like a child, and saying of Baldwin: 'Not even a public figure. A man of no experience. And of the utmost insignificance.' It is, however, not true to say that Bonar Law was too ill to give the King advice (*George V*, p. 376); he was not asked. See also Earl of Ronaldshay, *Life of Lord Curzon*, III, 350–3; B. E. C. Dugdale, *Balfour*, II, 266–7. Some gossip about the selection of Baldwin is in Nourah Waterhouse, *Private and Official*, pp. 259–65. L. S. Amery, *My Political Life*, II, 259–60, adds a few details.

this country and for the whole world. They are 'Faith','Hope', 'Love', and 'Work'. No Government in this country today which has not faith in the people, hope in the future, love for its fellow men, and which will not work and work and work, will ever bring this country through into better days and better times. . . .[1]

Baldwin continued Bonar Law's ministry with very few changes, and badly muffed the opportunity to bring about a reconciliation between his supporters (the Die-Hards, as they were rather inappropriately called at this time) and Austen Chamberlain and his friends; though, to do him justice, Baldwin was threatened with the resignation of some of his colleagues if places were found in the government for Chamberlain and his supporters.[2] A curious appointment which Baldwin proposed came to nothing. For the moment he retained the Chancellorship of the Exchequer, while offering it to Reginald McKenna, who was a Liberal. Difficulties arose in finding a parliamentary seat for McKenna, and he eventually refused. Baldwin then offered the position to Neville Chamberlain, who was on holiday fishing in the Highlands; Neville refused, but let himself be over-persuaded—this in August 1923.[3]

Baldwin's government, like Bonar Law's, had little positive achievement to its credit. The Housing Act introduced by Neville Chamberlain, while still Minister of Health, was perhaps the most lasting monument of the period, another step by the Conservatives along the road of collectivism. Reversing the principle of the Addison Act, this measure offered a flat subsidy of £6 a year for twenty years for each house built within certain dimensions by the local authorities or by private enterprise. The bill, introduced in April 1923, had an ill-starred ancestry. The control of rents of working-class houses, beginning with the Rents Restriction Act of 1915, had been continued by an act of 1920, which extended the control of rents to houses of a higher rateable value than those included in the original act but permitted some increase in rent. In Glasgow the increases were resisted at law and by a rent strike, and increases made without a previous notice of eviction were eventually ruled to be illegal (Kerr v. Bryde). Meanwhile, the abandonment of the Addison scheme and the pegging of existing rents while building prices were still high caused building of working-class houses to stop. Bonar Law's government pro-

[1] 160 H.C. Deb. 5 s., 561. The whole speech is worth reading for an expression of Baldwin's style and warm-heartedness. Cf. P. J. Grigg, *Prejudice and Judgment*, p. 111.
[2] For Baldwin's ineptness in these negotiations, see C. Petrie, *Austen Chamberlain*, II, 213–26.
[3] K. Feiling, *Neville Chamberlain*, pp. 107–8.

posed, therefore, to decontrol rents by stages, and to subsidise the building of working-class houses of the smallest type; at the same time it introduced a bill to legalise the increased rents which had already been illegally paid. The resulting outcry cost Sir Arthur Griffith-Boscawen, the Minister of Health, his seat in the by-election in the normally Conservative constituency of Mitcham; and two other ministers lost their seats at the same time. Neville Chamberlain's bill was the result. It was bitterly criticised by Labour for its preference for building by private enterprise and for the miserably small dimensions of the houses which qualified for subsidy (the bill was amended to raise the maximum size of each house to 950 square feet). In the event, the local authorities built little under it: some 436,600 houses were built under the act before the subsidy was withdrawn in 1929, 362,700 of them by private enterprise, mostly for sale and going, since they were beyond working-class means, to white-collar workers. As for rent restriction, the government had to continue it, willy nilly, though the act doing so in 1923 removed the control where there was a change of tenancy. Acts of 1933 and 1938 removed the control from houses above certain values; but the act of 1938 retained the control for houses worth £20 and less (£35 in London), thus leaving intact the mechanism of rent restriction as one legacy of the First World War to the Second.[1]

5. BALDWIN'S STRATEGY: THE ELECTION OF 1923

In the autumn of 1923, the economic scene seemed to be darkening once more. The textile, engineering and shipbuilding industries all complained of depressed trade; and unemployment figures, which had declined to 1,290,947 (11·2 per cent of the insured workpeople) in May, rose slightly, and stood at 1,350,216 (11·7 per cent) in October. Talk of a protective tariff as a means of sheltering the British worker and manufacturer—and also the farmer—began to be heard once again; and received powerful stimulus from the Imperial Economic Conference, held concurrently with the Imperial Conference in October.

Suddenly Baldwin made protection an immediate and burning issue. He was speaking at the National Unionist Association conference at Plymouth on October 25. It was a characteristic speech: apparently the plain thoughts of a simple man of good will,

[1] M. Bowley, *Housing and the State*, pp. 36–40, 271; R. L. Reiss, *Municipal and Private Enterprise Housing*, pp. 33–4, 42–4; *Annual Register, 1923*, pp. 22–5, 43–4; Ministry of Health, *12th Annual Report*, 1930–31 (Cmd. 3937), p. 114.

thinking aloud. '. . . Day and night for long past,' he said, his thoughts had been filled with the problem of unemployment, 'the gravest subject in the country today.' He continued:

> Mr. Bonar Law's pledge given a year ago, was that there should be no fundamental change in the fiscal arrangements of the country. That pledge binds me, and in this Parliament there will be no fundamental change, and I take those words strictly. I am not a man to play with a pledge. But I cannot see myself that any slight extension or adoption of principles hitherto sanctioned in the Legislature is a breach of that pledge [a reference to the Safeguarding of Industries Act]. But at any time that I am challenged I am always willing to take a verdict. . . . This unemployment problem is the most crucial problem of our country . . . I can fight it. I am willing to fight it. I cannot fight it without weapons . . . I have come to the conclusion myself that the only way of fighting this subject is by protecting the home market (loud and continued cheering). I am not a clever man. I know nothing of political tactics, but I will say this: Having come to that conclusion myself, I felt the only honest and right thing as the leader of a democratic party was to tell them, at the first opportunity I had, what I thought, and submit it to their judgments. (Cheers.)[1]

Though protection had already been discussed in the Cabinet,[2] Baldwin's announcement took both the party and the country by surprise. There had been no careful or lengthy planning for a campaign to educate the people in favour of protection—little or nothing since the heroic labours of the tariff reformers of 1903–06. The Conservatives were far from united on the subject. And it was not clear whether Baldwin contemplated an immediate election on the subject or not. His announcement has been often described as a blunder, an 'act of political insanity', or at best as one of the sudden, unpredictable and illogical jumps which seem, in his career, to have taken the place of deliberate and consistent policy. It has even been suggested that Baldwin courted electoral defeat in 1923, foreseeing the troubles ahead, and calculating that, if another party held office and failed to overcome them, the Conservatives would be swept back into power, all the stronger for their brief surrender of it.

The truth was otherwise. Baldwin in 1923 completed the work he had begun at the Carlton Club in 1922, and at the same time repaired the results of the earlier operation. By making protection an issue he restored to the Conservatives a principle dividing

---

[1] *Annual Register, 1923*, p. 122; *The Times*, Oct. 26, 1923.
[2] C. Petrie, *A. Chamberlain*, II, 228–30.

them from the Liberals, but reuniting them among themselves, and he stopped the drift of Austen Chamberlain, Birkenhead, and their supporters towards Lloyd George and the Liberals. This was his own explanation.[1] Whether it brought an immediate electoral defeat mattered little. The chances of avoiding such a defeat were good. Britain's free-trade system had already been breached, and free-trade sentiment was less strong in the constricted postwar economy than it had been before. An electoral defeat on such an issue was not a foregone conclusion. The Liberals, its traditional defenders, were divided. Moreover, it was thought that Lloyd George was about to come out in favour of protection;[2] perhaps the Conservatives ought to come out first and prevent him from stealing their clothes. But win or lose immediately, it offered the Conservatives a reunited party which, having smashed the Coalition which had brought it back to a share of power in 1915–16, could regain power, complete and secure, in the years not far ahead.

The plan worked. Austen Chamberlain was at once active in urging a full-blooded campaign for protection and—what Baldwin seems not to have intended—an immediate election on the subject. As a result, there was a renewed effort to bring Austen Chamberlain and Birkenhead back into the government. The two men met Baldwin on November 12, and though there were difficulties about finding places for them, Baldwin decided to add them to the Cabinet, and even got the King's consent before the scheme was stopped—by a threatened revolt of some of the lesser ministers, which Baldwin was unwilling to face.[3]

An immediate election was, however, still in doubt until parliament met on November 13. Many Conservatives scouted its wisdom.[4] The King was reluctant to grant a dissolution.[5] Yet parliament was dissolved on November 16, and the election held on December 6. The Labour party, after some hurried selection of candidates, entered the fray in strong fighting spirit, and in its manifesto rejected tariffs as being no remedy for unemployment but only an aid to profiteering.

To the Liberals Baldwin's leap in the dark also brought reunion. Several attempts at reconciliation between the Asquith and Lloyd

[1] See Baldwin's statement quoted in *Lord Baldwin, a Memoir* (*The Times*), p. 8; cf. K. Feiling, *N. Chamberlain*, p. 110.

[2] K. Feiling, *N. Chamberlain*, p. 108.

[3] C. Petrie, *A. Chamberlain*, II, 230–38; K. Feiling, *N. Chamberlain*, p. 110; G. M. Young, *Baldwin*, pp. 65–7.

[4] *Annual Register, 1923*, pp. 125–8.   [5] H. Nicolson, *George V*, p. 380.

George wings had come to nothing in 1923. Now, all bickering was banished, at least temporarily. Lloyd George announced himself an unswerving free trader and offered to work with Asquith or anyone else who would serve the country. A united campaign was agreed on, with a single manifesto signed by Asquith and Lloyd George, and all candidates simply designated as Liberals, regardless of past connections. One of the first to rally to the refurbished banner of Liberalism and free trade was Winston Churchill, who stood for West Leicester.

The results of the election confirmed the worst fears of Tory strategists who had denounced Baldwin's plunge; for if they were unclear in other respects, they were a decisive rejection of the policy of protection, and in country districts as much as in the cities. The Conservatives were still the largest party in the Commons, with 258 members compared with 346 before the dissolution; they polled 5,360,000 votes. The Liberals elected 158 members, more from Asquith's than from Lloyd George's wing, where the casualties included Winston Churchill. But their intervention and Baldwin's quixotry had benefited principally the Labour party, which, with only a few more candidates and some 100,000 more votes than in 1922, elected 191 members (as compared with 142 before) and polled 4,348,000 votes. The combined popular vote against the Conservatives was over $8\frac{1}{2}$ millions. Labour's principal gains were in greater London. Eighty-three Labour members were elected in three-cornered contests, but only 19 of these winners had clear majorities.[1]

6. A LABOUR GOVERNMENT IN BEING

What government would materialise from this ambiguous result was not at all clear. Baldwin decided not to resign, but to face parliament when it met on January 8. He was under some pressure to resign; Neville Chamberlain noted that the Cabinet was a 'nest of intrigue', and the *Daily Mail*, which had opposed protection and supported Lloyd George in the election, joined other voices which clamoured for a coalition of Conservatives and Liberals, preferably under some other leader than Baldwin, perhaps Asquith. The City of London professed great alarm at the prospect of a Labour government. There were fears that Labour would tamper with the army and navy and the civil service. Some professed to believe that under Labour the marriage

[1] *Annual Register, 1923*, pp. 139–40; G. D. H. Cole, *History of the Labour Party*, pp. 152–4. The figures for the popular vote are from *The Times*, Dec. 8, 1923.

tie would not be sacred, and that free love would receive official sanction—a revealing misunderstanding of the British working man and of the Labour party. Others twisted a passage from an old book by J. H. Thomas to argue that the people's savings would be in danger of confiscation.[1] Asquith received by every mail 'appeals, threats, prayers . . . to step in and save the country from the horrors of Socialism and Confiscation'.

Asquith was, however, quite clear as to what to do. The country had rejected protection. Labour was the largest anti-protection party, and should be given its chance to take office. Speaking on December 18 he observed that there could be no safer conditions under which to make the experiment. Neville Chamberlain privately reached similar conclusions; a 'merely tactical' alliance to keep Labour out would only strengthen it for the future, whereas in office 'it would be too weak to do much harm but not too weak to get discredited'. It was, in fact, generally assumed by the time parliament met that a Labour government would take office; and by then there was little alarm (though still some theatrical professions of alarm) at the prospect.[2]

For his decision, Asquith has been much criticised. The Liberals, it is argued, by supporting the Labour party committed suicide; Labour used them simply as 'patient oxen' to drag its cart before slaughtering them. But Asquith had very little choice. A coalition of Liberals and Conservatives was made almost impossible by the conflict of personalities. The conflict of principles was equally strong: the Conservatives had campaigned for a protective tariff and been beaten on the issue by the Liberals as much as by Labour. The same conditions applied to a Liberal-Labour alliance: there would have been no agreement on principles behind it. Asquith might, nonetheless, have come to some understanding with Labour over the terms on which the Liberals would support it in office; but this, even if Labour's pride had permitted it, would hardly have benefited the Liberals, who would merely have bartered their life away instead of risking it in independence. It was not Asquith whose decision doomed the Liberal party, it was the electors who refused to make it once again either the largest or the second largest party and to accept its *via media*. The election of 1923 called forth a gallant but futile effort from the

[1] 169 H.C. Deb., 5 s., 422, 662.
[2] J. A. Spender and C. Asquith, *Life of Asquith*, II, 342–4; K. Feiling, *N. Chamberlain*, p. 111; *The Times*, Jan. 8, 1924, and preceding issues; *Annual Register, 1923*, pp. 139–40.

G*

Liberals. Its result could only be the herald of the further decline
of the party.

Labour on its part had little uncertainty what to do. Few
within the party argued that it should refuse office without power
and put the onus of weak and unpopular government upon others.
The Clydesiders and the I.L.P. favoured taking office with an
out-and-out socialist programme and challenging defeat in the
hope that courage would receive its reward in the ensuing election.
The party's leaders, however, were under no temptation, either
from temperament or principle, to follow such a course. The
National Executive voted, on December 12, that 'should the
necessity for forming a Labour Government arise, the Parliamentary party should at once accept full responsibility for the
government of the country without compromising itself with any
form of coalition'. Substantially the same decision had been
reached by the leaders—MacDonald, Snowden, Henderson,
Clynes, Thomas, Webb—at dinner at the Webbs' on December 11.
MacDonald, according to Snowden, did not want to form a
government and was dismayed at the prospect; this is against the
common impression that he badly wanted to be Prime Minister,
and should be read alongside his complaints of the poverty of
material available to him for cabinet-making, and his fear that his
own left wing would expect unattainable results from a minority
Labour government. The leaders' decision was that Labour could
not refuse office without confessing incompetence and disqualifying
itself for the future; but that its policy should be moderate,
eschewing the capital levy and other radical proposals. Some discussion of possible ministers followed, but the final choice was
left to MacDonald. Henderson (who had lost his seat) offered to
go to the Lords as a life peer. It was agreed that if peers were
created they should be men without male heirs (a practice followed
by both the first and second Labour governments). Following
this meeting MacDonald retired, as was his wont, to Lossiemouth,
his birthplace on the remote shores of the Moray Firth; whence
came, during the Christmas season, faint sounds of his joinery.[1]

Parliament met on January 8, 1924. Baldwin's government, in
the King's speech on January 15, was generous with promises it
ran little risk of being asked to honour: increased public works to
relieve unemployment, increased old-age pensions, more housing.

---

[1] P. Snowden, *Autobiography*, II, 594–7; F. Brockway, *Jowett*, pp. 206–7; G. D. H.
Cole, *History of the Labour Party*, pp. 157–9; *Beatrice Webb's Diaries, 1912–1924*,
pp. 255–6.

Clynes on the 17th moved an amendment that His Majesty's present advisers had 'not the confidence' of the House; and Asquith, in a powerful speech, passed sentence on them by stating at once that he would vote for the amendment. The Labour party (he said) as the largest party in the Opposition had an undoubted right to office, and he declined to believe it would bring ruin on the country any more than Gladstone's government of 1892, from which the same had been predicted, had done so. Quoting Adam Smith's refusal to be despondent after Saratoga—'Sir, there is a great deal of ruin in a Nation'—he refused to 'save society' by keeping Labour out. It would not have a 'free letter of licence', and there was no room for any coalition or fusion; but in social legislation and foreign policy there could be real co-operation between it and the Liberals.[1] When the vote was taken on January 21, the government was defeated by 328 votes to 256. Baldwin resigned next day and MacDonald received the King's commission to form a government.[2]

The first Labour government in British history was of curious construction. MacDonald had claimed for himself, some time earlier in 1923, freedom from any commitments, 'except for four or five people, Snowden, Henderson, Morel and Clynes', and had added 'I'm not sure we shouldn't have trouble with Thomas' (this in connection with an abortive attempt by Harold Laski[3] to bring C. F. G. Masterman into the Labour party, with the possibility of his receiving office should it form a government).[4] At Lossiemouth over Christmas, MacDonald had maintained complete secrecy, but had corresponded with Henderson, who came to see Snowden, full of rumours. In a first draft, MacDonald had omitted Henderson altogether—an odd reward to the party's secretary and his faithful colleague from the early days, though one Henderson was ready to agree to, believing he could help the party best, and prevent difficulties he foresaw between party and Cabinet, from outside. In a second draft, MacDonald even more insultingly offered Henderson the position of chairman of Ways and Means—an elective office like the Speaker's, and not part of the government at all. When Henderson angrily refused, MacDonald offered him the War Office, equally inappropriate to

[1] 169 H.C. Deb., 5 s., 310–15.   [2] H. Nicolson, *George V*, pp. 382–6.
[3] Harold J. Laski (1893–1950), lecturer, London School of Economics, 1920, professor of political science, 1926–50. Member of executive committee, Fabian Society, 1922–36; member of executive committee, Labour party, 1936–49, chairman, 1945–46.
[4] L. Masterman, *C. F. G. Masterman*, p. 327.

both Henderson's position in the party and his status as a leader of international socialism; after some insistence, he received the Home Office. MacDonald's first choice for the Foreign Secretary was the wildly inappropriate one of J. H. Thomas; this leaked out and was killed by the scorn of the *Manchester Guardian*, and Thomas, after rejecting the Colonial Office as lacking in prestige, found that it outranked the service ministries in the order of precedence and accepted it. Meanwhile MacDonald was corresponding with men of position outside the party like Lord Parmoor,[1] an ex-Tory and a devout Churchman and ecclesiastical lawyer; he was in consultation with Lord Haldane, the former Liberal Lord Chancellor who was moving toward the party; and he is said to have offered the Admiralty to Lord Chelmsford, ex-Viceroy of India and supposedly a non-party man, at their first meeting. The chancellorship, originally intended for Sankey, was entrusted to Haldane on the latter's insistence (Haldane had been offered Education). J. H. Thomas has a story that the main appointments were made in his house in Dulwich, and that they had to get an almanack to find what offices to fill. At any rate, two days before Baldwin's resignation, MacDonald called into his room in the House of Commons a number of members he intended to include in his Cabinet; and he tossed across the table to Snowden a pencilled note; 'I want formally to ask you to accept the office of Chancellor of the Exchequer'. Snowden nodded acceptance.[2]

The resulting list of ministers was anything but revolutionary. The most unexpected appointments were the two men of the left, John Wheatley as Minister of Health and F. W. Jowett as First Commissioner of Works, with a seat in the Cabinet. Undersecretaries included William Graham[3] (Financial Secretary to the Treasury), C. R. Attlee, A. V. Alexander, Emanuel Shinwell (Mines), Margaret Bondfield, Arthur Greenwood. The Scottish law officers and the officers connected with the royal court were from outside the party. It was a cabinet of moderates, more representative of the upper and middle classes and of new recruits to the party than of the trade-union side and the old-timers and left

[1] Charles Alfred Cripps (1852–1941), married Theresa Potter, sister of Beatrice Webb; father of Stafford Cripps. Barrister. M.P., 1895–1900, 1901–6, 1910–14. Created Baron Parmoor, 1914. Lord president of the council, 1924, 1929–31.
[2] P. Snowden, *Autobiography*, II, 597–601, 604–5; M. A. Hamilton, *Arthur Henderson* (London, 1938), p. 236; F. Williams, *Fifty Years' March*, pp. 303–4; D. Kirkwood, *My Life of Revolt*, pp. 221–2; Eric Estorick, *Stafford Cripps* (London, 1949), p. 70; J. H. Thomas, *My Story*, p. 74; *Beatrice Webb's Diaries, 1912–1924*, pp. 258–64.
[3] William Graham (1887–1932), son of a master-builder of Peebles; M.A., Ll.B., Edinburgh University (honours in economics and statistics); M.P., Central Edinburgh, 1918–31; President of the Board of Trade, 1929–31.

wingers; only five of the twenty members of the Cabinet were trade unionists.[1] Morel was conspicuously absent. Though many supporters of the party were disappointed, the general public was reassured. Snobs were relieved by the presence of men such as Haldane and Chelmsford; and as someone said at the reception on the day before parliament met, 'At any rate, we have the handsomest of all Prime Ministers.'[2] The *Economist*'s prediction of two years before, that the country would be 'astonished at the bourgeois character of a labour administration', was borne out.[3]

The 'new epoch' which Labour writers proclaimed began with a touch of comedy. The wives of some of the new ministers, not unnaturally a little astonished at their translation from everyday life, were provoked by reporters into naïve statements to the press; and the men, privately at least, could not get over the sudden change of fortune. As Clynes (Lord Privy Seal) wrote later:

> as we stood waiting for His Majesty, amid the gold and crimson of the Palace, I could not help marvelling at the strange turn of Fortune's wheel, which had brought MacDonald, the starveling clerk, Thomas the engine-driver, Henderson the foundry labourer and Clynes the mill-hand, to this pinnacle. . . .

The immediate question was whether the new ministers should wear formal dress on going to Buckingham Palace. Many of them possessed none. No difficulty was made when they attended in ordinary clothes; and King George V at once set them at their ease by his genuine friendliness. It was only the snobs who were worried for him; and it was soon clear (what everyone should have known anyway) that the monarchy had no more enthusiastic supporters than the Labour party as a whole. Later, the question of ministers wearing court attire on formal occasions raised a difficulty. MacDonald, not perhaps without some vanity over his own person, was insistent that they should, but some objected, especially Wheatley and Jowett. In the end three sets of the uniforms were obtained, and worn by some of the ministers in turn, when necessary. A dress suit for evening wear was no novelty for many, particularly J. H. Thomas, whom the cartoonists always depicted so adorned; and even Jowett finally agreed to keep one at the office for formal occasions in the evenings. The 'Half Circle Club'[4] of the wives of Labour members started by

---

[1] G. D. H. Cole, *History of the Labour Party*, pp. 156–60; F. Williams, *Fifty Years' March*, pp. 303–4.

[2] H. W. Nevinson, *Last Changes*, pp. 305–8.   [3] *Economist*, October 21, 1922.

[4] *Beatrice Webb's Diaries, 1912–1924*, has several references to it.

Beatrice Webb was a valuable meeting-ground for the new society. Some admirers did not relish the tales of Lord Stamford-ham coaching the ministers about the niceties of court etiquette; downright socialists had hoped that a Labour government would blow away such cobwebs. Pictures of Labour ministers in top hats aroused some ire: 'A workers' government, ye ca' it!' shouted a voice at a meeting of shipyard workers, 'It's a bloody lum hat government like a' the rest.' Others, as Snowden sagely observed, took vicarious pride at seeing their own people arrayed in all their glory while controlling the destinies of empire.[1]

7. THE LABOUR GOVERNMENT'S RECORD

Yet even to its more moderate supporters, the first Labour government was largely a disappointment. Labour was unready. It was a minority government, in office but not in power, shackled to the Liberals and pursuing a policy of moderation. Such a policy was not only one of necessity; it was, for MacDonald, one of choice, so that the lack of a majority suited his book excellently, since it provided the best of excuses against adventures in socialism. MacDonald's main object, as he wrote in a letter to Lord Parmoor, was to 'gain the confidence of the country';[2] and for a time he succeeded. It did, however, put Labour constantly on the defensive, where a more positive, socialist policy would have put the Liberals on the defensive;[3] the result would not inevitably have been a shorter term of office, but it would have been a less disillusioning one. However, in spite of the shabby end, the record of nine months did demonstrate that Labour ministers could govern, and accept all the responsibilities of office, as ably and patriotically as Conservatives and Liberals—and in foreign affairs even more so.

The government's weaknesses were internal. Office united its supporters no more firmly than Opposition had done. To provide liaison between the Parliamentary Labour Party and the Cabinet a new executive committee was chosen, consisting of twelve members outside the ministry; in this the left was well represented, by Lansbury, Johnston, Smillie, Morel, and R. C. Wallhead. Ministers gave explanations of their policies before the committee

---

[1] Snowden, *Autobiography*, II, 605–12,660–63; J. Scanlon, *Decline and Fall of the Labour Party*, pp. 62–68; J. R. Clynes, *Memoirs* (London, 1937–39), I, 343, II, 25; F. Brockway, *Jowett*, pp. 208–9; J. Paton, *Left Turn!*, pp. 168–69 (in Scotland a top hat is a lum hat); H. Nicolson, *George V*, pp. 389–92.
[2] E. Estorick, *Stafford Cripps*, p. 70.   [3] F. Williams, *Fifty Years' March*, p. 306.

but even so some strain between government and supporters was inevitable. The I.L.P. members in parliament formed a group whose secretary, Fenner Brockway (not then in parliament), carried its views to MacDonald. 'Well, Brockway, what commands have you brought me today,' he once asked, magnificent in evening dress, and then gave an engagement as excuse for having 'no time to listen to the view of the Group'.[1] And with the trade-union movement the government had, directly, no liaison at all.

Yet there was much which the government could do as the master, for the time being, of the administrative machine; here parliamentary consent was often not needed. It was early announced that five cruisers would be laid down as replacements for the Navy; the Conservatives had proposed eight, but even the five were criticised by Liberals and several Labour members. On the other hand the later announcement of cessation of work on the new naval base at Singapore evoked stern Conservative opposition. Wheatley, as Minister of Health, cancelled some ineffective restrictions imposed by Sir Alfred Mond on the expenditures of the Poplar Guardians, and successfully stood off the protests which this called forth in parliament. The 'gap' between benefit periods under unemployment insurance was abolished (this required definite legislation), and later, by another bill, benefits were increased and 'uncovenanted' benefits (beyond those covered by insurance) were made a statutory right. The limit on the private means of old-age pensioners (if derived from savings, not from earnings) was raised. The attempt to restore a minimum wage in agriculture failed when the proposed Central Wages Board was eliminated from the bill in committee; but County Agricultural Wages committees were established. In education the minister, C. P. Trevelyan, was able to undo some of the restrictions of the previous economy cuts; progressive education authorities were given greater scope, free places in the secondary schools were increased and the state scholarships to the universities revived, and a survey of obsolete school buildings was begun. The government's failure to find positive means for lowering unemployment was constantly cast in its teeth by Conservatives and Liberals alike; finally, in July, Snowden announced government support, to the tune of about £28 millions, for road-building, standardisation of electricity frequencies, municipal works, and—what became an old stand-by

[1] J. Scanlon, *Decline and Fall of the Labour Party*, pp. 70–2; F. Brockway, *Inside the Left*, p. 152.

of public works programmes of the interwar years without ever being begun—the scheme to construct a barrage across the Severn to enable a road to be carried across the river and current to be generated by it. The government's larger schemes for electricity supply for the country were left as a legacy for the Conservatives. Snowden's budget was a notable, though not a radical one. Estimating expenditure at £790 millions, and anticipating a surplus of £38 millions, he halved the duties on sugar, tea, cocoa and coffee, reduced the duty on dried fruit and reduced the entertainment tax, repealed the corporation profits tax, and repealed the McKenna duties—a return to free trade orthodoxy which won warm endorsement from Asquith and baseless prophecies of ruin from the motor manufacturers.[1]

The greatest legislative achievement of the government was generally agreed to be the product of its most advanced socialist, Wheatley's Housing Act. This increased the state's subsidy to £9 annually for forty years for houses built to rent at controlled rents; it was 'the basis of a vast expansion in municipal house-building':[2] 521,700 houses had been built under it before the subsidy was abolished in 1933. The Act was linked with a scheme to increase the labour force to meet the higher and steady volume of building which it was designed to encourage; Wheatley negotiated with the building trades for an increase in the number of apprentices admitted and a shortening of the period of apprenticeship.[3]

This somewhat meagre record of achievements was made to the accompaniment of constant harassing from within the party, from the Conservatives and from the reluctant Liberal allies. The government sustained a number of defeats on minor issues which MacDonald had announced at the start would not be taken as calling for its resignation. The Liberals, disunited among themselves, not only rallied the government for its failure to fulfil its pledges, particularly regarding unemployment, but often divided in the lobbies, some supporting the government, others voting against it while others, again, abstained. Austen Chamberlain declared that the Liberals were '"visibly" bursting up'; and the Labour party came to hate them more bitterly than it did the Conservatives.[4]

---

[1] G. D. H. Cole, *History of the Labour Party*, pp. 159–62; *Annual Register, 1924*; *Labour Year Book, 1925*, pp. 63–7, 335–9.
[2] Asa Briggs, *History of Birmingham* (Oxford, 1952), II, 232.
[3] G. D H. Cole, *History of the Labour Party*, p. 161; M. Bowley, *Housing and the State*, pp. 40–7, 271.
[4] C. Petrie, *Austen Chamberlain*, II, 241; P. J. Grigg, *Prejudice and Judgment*, pp. 131–3

The Conservatives, on their part, were achieving in adversity the reunion for which Baldwin had hoped. At a meeting of Lancashire and Cheshire Conservatives in Manchester in February, Sir Archibald Salvidge moved and carried a resolution asking that, in view of the country's verdict, protection be dropped from the party's programme. The *Morning Post* chose to regard this as a 'Lancashire plot' against Baldwin's leadership; but Baldwin, in a speech a few days later, followed the suggestion, and later made a few changes in the Conservative Central Office.[1] He emerged, in fact, stronger than before, and with no rival in sight, though criticism of him continued. Moreover, on February 5, Neville Chamberlain effected the reconciliation of Austen and Baldwin at a dinner at his house. Baldwin invited Austen to join the 'shadow cabinet' of ex-ministers and the Opposition front bench and promised, if he agreed, to invite the other Conservative ex-Coalition ministers also; Balfour had already agreed. Austen accepted the invitation and said that he could speak for Birkenhead also in this acceptance.[2] Another ex-minister advanced a stage further on his twenty-year circuit from Conservatism to Liberalism and back again: Winston Churchill. He stood in the by-election in March for the Abbey division of Westminster as an 'Independent anti-Socialist' against an official Conservative candidate, a Liberal, and a Labour candidate. He had much Conservative support, including such men as Balfour and Austen Chamberlain and the press lords (Beaverbrook and Rothermere), but ex-ministers were persuaded not to speak for him. He toured the constituency in a coach and four, and made alarmist speeches. After a hectic campaign he was defeated by the Conservative by 43 votes. But he had won once more his Conservative spurs, and was soon after adopted by the Conservatives of Epping as their candidate, though he was elected in the 1924 election as a 'Constitutionalist'.[3]

Meanwhile, a show of a very different sort, and not one which was the product of the Labour government, was capturing the interest of vast crowds of the British public. This was the British Empire Exhibition, which was opened by the King at Wembley, in the north-west of London, on April 23. This was one of the great international exhibitions of the interwar years, and Britain's

[1] S. Salvidge, *Salvidge*, pp. 257–67. For Baldwin's deductions from the election, see G. M. Young, *Baldwin*, p. 73.
[2] C. Petrie, *A. Chamberlain*, II, 339–40; K. Feiling, *N. Chamberlain*, pp. 111–12.
[3] K. Feiling, *N. Chamberlain*, p. 115; F. Brockway, *Inside the Left*, pp. 153–6; W. S. Churchill, *Thoughts and Adventures*, pp. 214–15.

greatest since the Great Exhibition of 1851. In the grounds (extending over 220 acres) were to be found buildings, estimated to have cost £12 millions, which both in architecture and exhibits displayed the diversity and the natural and industrial opulence of the empire. A West African fort of terra-cotta stucco entranced the panting families, poured forth on to the exhibition grounds by train or charabanc, no less than India's evocation of the Taj Mahal or Australia's mountain of butter; and for those who tired of such educational sights there was always the 'never-stop' railway round the grounds, and the fun fair at the end. By the time 'Wembley' closed on November 1, over 17 million people had visited it; and it was decided to re-open it next year.

8. MACDONALD, THE PEACEMAKER

The Labour party had always claimed that it was better fitted than the older parties to work for international peace;[1] it had condemned the punitive clauses of the treaty of Versailles; it had condemned Britain's inaction over the occupation of the Ruhr. MacDonald, who had taken office as Foreign Secretary as well as Prime Minister, had a great opportunity to improve the country's foreign relations, and, with notable aid from others in the Cabinet, rose nobly to it. Three lines of policy, not all equally fruitful, deserve notice; the improvement of relations with France, and the settlement of the reparations question and the ending of the Ruhr occupation; support of the League of Nations; negotiations with Russia.

For negotiations with the French MacDonald possessed, besides his urbane manner and his graciousness as a host, the inheritance of Curzon's work at the Foreign Office. He began his campaign by a friendly 'personal note' to Poincaré on January 26, followed a month later by a sterner note expressing Britain's anxiety over the apparent determination of France, through the occupation of the Ruhr, to ruin Germany and dominate the Continent. On April 9 the report of the principal committee of experts, headed by the American, General Charles G. Dawes, was published. The Dawes committee's unanimous report, largely written by Sir Josiah Stamp, one of the two British experts, recommended that Germany's currency be stabilised on a gold basis and that Germany

---

[1] See W. P. Maddox, *Foreign Relations in British Labour Politics: a study of the formation of party attitudes on foreign affairs* . . . (Cambridge, Mass., 1934) for Labour's internationalist attitude, its composition and expression.

pay an annual sum for reparations rising from 1,000 million marks in the first year to 2,500 million marks in the fifth and subsequent years. The money was to be obtained from taxation under the ordinary budget (guaranteed by the ear-marking of customs and excise revenues for the purpose), from bonds issued against the German railways, and from certain German industrial debentures. To safeguard the working of the plan, an agent-general for reparations payments was to be appointed (an American, S. P. Gilbert, eventually received the job). In addition, an international loan to Germany of 800 million marks (£40 millions) was recommended.

Acceptance of the Dawes report by the Allies was made more likely by the change of the political weather in France. Poincaré was weakened by the fall of the franc as much as by doubts over his policy towards Germany, and as a result of the elections in May Edouard Herriot, leader of the Radicals, succeeded him as premier. MacDonald at once extended to Herriot an invitation previously made (and accepted) to Poincaré to visit him at Chequers. The visit took place on June 22–23. Cordial relations were at once established; it was agreed that the Dawes plan should be put into operation, and that an inter-allied conference should be held in London in July to settle the procedure; the United States, Belgian, Italian, Japanese and certain other governments were invited to attend. Some confusion resulted from the wording of the official invitations to the conference and from conflicting statements from MacDonald and Herriot, which suggested to ardent French nationalists some undermining of the treaty of Versailles; this led to some criticism in parliament by Asquith of MacDonald's 'new diplomacy', and to a hasty visit of MacDonald to Paris on July 8.

The London conference was opened by MacDonald on July 16, 1924. It worked largely in committees, and after some difficulties reached sufficient agreement by August 2 to invite the German government to send representatives. The German delegates, who included Gustav Stresemann, were naturally chiefly concerned with the time of the evacuation of the Ruhr, and some delicate negotiations were needed before Herriot agreed that it would be completed within a year. With this settled, the conference closed on August 16. For MacDonald, it was something of a personal triumph. He had presided with great skill, and in looks and manner perfectly fitted the part of the magnanimous international statesman, and in private gatherings was able to pour oil on troubled waters with benign effect. Especially was he successful in bringing Herriot and Stresemann together.[1]

Towards the League of Nations the Labour party had always claimed a special and benevolent interest. In its manifesto for the 1923 election it had declared that it stood 'for a policy of International Co-operation through a strengthened and enlarged League of Nations; the settlement of disputes by conciliation and judicial arbitration . . . [and] Disarmament, the only security for the nations'.[2] Lord Parmoor's appointment as Lord President of the Council, with a special interest in foreign and League of Nations affairs (in which he represented the government in the Lords), was an earnest of this policy, in view of his devotion to pacifism and to the League. The government's enthusiasm for the cause was also shown in the delegation sent to the Assembly of the League in Geneva in September 1924. It was headed by Mac-Donald, and included Parmoor, Arthur Henderson, Gilbert Murray,[3] and Mrs. H. M. Swanwick, a leader of the Union of Democratic Control. MacDonald and Herriot were the first premiers of the great powers to attend the Assembly—in whose sessions in 1924 seven prime ministers and sixteen foreign ministers took part. Previous to this, the Labour government had rejected, as had most of the other principal powers, the Draft Treaty of Mutual Assistance (largely the work of Lord Robert Cecil) which the Council had transmitted to the powers late in 1923. In attempting to allay French fears of insecurity and Britain's suspicion of continental entanglements, this proposed that its signatories pledge themselves to come to the help of any of their number who was the object of a war of aggression, and provided that complementary, regional agreements might be signed among smaller groups to give effect to this. The British government's objections turned on the weakness of the guarantees (which would not encourage disarmament), the indefiniteness of the obligations, and the widespread and diverse interests of the British Commonwealth.

At Geneva, MacDonald proposed, instead, that security be

---

[1] *Annual Register, 1924;* Arnold J. Toynbee, *Survey of International Affairs, 1924* (Royal Institute of International Affairs, London, 1926), pp. 340–91; P. Snowden, *Autobiography,* II, 664–79; W. M. Jordan, *Great Britain, France and the German Problem,* pp. 67, 93–5; E. Mantoux, *Carthaginian Peace,* pp. 144–7; G. M. Gathorne-Hardy, *Short History of International Affairs, 1920 to 1939* (3rd ed., Oxford, 1942), pp. 47–8.

[2] Quoted in Lord Parmoor [C. A. Cripps], *Retrospect* (London, 1936), pp. 188–9

[3] Gilbert Murray, born in 1866; Regius Professor of Greek, Oxford University, 1908–36; chairman, League of Nations Union, 1923–38. O.M.

sought, and aggression defined, by the use of arbitration. Herriot's speech carried this further: arbitration, security, disarmament were inseparable. Against this setting, the Protocol for the Pacific Settlement of International Disputes was framed by a number of committees, owing much to the work of Henderson and of Lord Parmoor. It was laid before the Assembly on October 1, and unanimously adopted. It provided for a disarmament conference in June 1925, pledged its signatories to adopt the 'optional clause' (article 36) of the statute of the Permanent Court of International Justice, thereby binding themselves to submit justiciable disputes to the court, and set up means for the settlement, if necessary by arbitration, of other disputes, under the auspices of the Council. If all means of settling a dispute peaceably failed, then the Council of the League was to call upon the signatory states to apply sanctions against the aggressor within the terms of article 16 of the Covenant of the League. Thus the Protocol would impose (except as regards arbitration) no obligations not already borne by members of the League under the Covenant. It was a notable instrument, which the Labour government had every intention of ratifying; but it fell too soon, and its successor killed the Protocol, with dire results for the next generation.[1]

In carrying out its avowed intention to establish normal relations with Russia the government was much less successful than in its other essays in foreign policy; and here foreign and domestic policy impinged upon one another, undermining the government's precarious toe-hold on office. Relations between the British and Russian governments had not been smooth since the signing of the trade agreement on March 16, 1921: continued anti-British propaganda in Russia, outrages against two British subjects, and the insolent tone of official notes had caused Curzon, in a most undiplomatic and stern note of May 2, 1923, to threaten to denounce the agreement unless satisfaction was received.[2] None the less, as soon as the Labour government took office, MacDonald, on February 1, announced Britain's recognition of the Soviet government as *de jure* ruler of the territories of the old Russian empire, and invited it to a conference in London to settle outstanding issues. The conference began on April 14, the principal negotiators being Rakovsky and Arthur Ponsonby, undersecretary for foreign affairs. Negotiations proceeded very slowly,

[1] Lord Parmoor, *Retrospect*, pp. 224-64; A. J. Toynbee, *Survey of International Affairs, 1924*, pp. 16-64. The text of the Protocol, published by the British government as Cmd. 2273, is in the *Annual Register, 1924*, part ii, pp. 88-95.
[2] H. Nicolson, *Curzon*, pp. 357-60.

to the accompaniment in Moscow of press attacks on the British government. By early June there was deadlock; Rakovsky went back to Moscow and returned with new instructions. Negotiations were resumed on August 4. After twenty hours of continuous discussion, and with agreement nearly complete, negotiations broke down at 7.30 a.m. on August 5, almost on the eve of parliament's adjournment for the summer recess. The difficulty was over the wording of the settlement—in itself an evasive compromise—of the claims of British bond-holders. Great pressure was brought on the government to resume negotiations, particularly by left-wing Labour members, A. A. Purcell, E. D. Morel, Lansbury, and R. C. Wallhead, who acted as intermediaries between Ponsonby and Rakovsky. The conference reconvened on August 6, and agreement was announced by Ponsonby in the House of Commons at 7.30 that evening.

Two treaties were initialled, and subsequently signed on August 8. One was a commercial treaty, granting most-favoured-nation privileges and diplomatic status for some members of the Russian trade delegation. The other, the general treaty, left for later negotiation the settlement of the claims of British subjects in respect of pre-revolutionary Russian governmental bonds and of property confiscated under the nationalisation decrees—claims which the Soviet government refused to recognise in principle but over which it was prepared to make exceptions to the decrees of repudiation and nationalisation. Once a second treaty had been completed on these subjects, the British government agreed to recommend to parliament the guaranteeing of a loan to the Soviet government. This, for which the Russians had been pressing throughout the negotiations in return for their concessions to British bond-holders, had been sharply rejected by MacDonald as lately as June 18. A further clause affirmed the intention of the two governments to live in peace and amity and to refrain from acts (i.e. propaganda) endangering the tranquillity of either or embittering their relations with other countries.

The treaty was attacked by Conservatives and Liberals as soon as it was published and especially by the Conservative *Morning Post*. Its very opening, 'between his Britannic Majesty's Government and the Government' of the U.S.S.R. (omitting the King's name out of deference to Russia's republican government) was criticised as unusual and derogatory to Great Britain. The promised loan was strongly assailed. Lloyd George called the treaty a fake. But MacDonald refused to withhold his signature, though he promised that the treaties would, according to custom, come before parliament for ratification. None the less, attacks on them continued during the summer, from business organisations and from political leaders. The government was charged with having now adopted a definitely socialist course, and one which the Liberals would not support. The days of the government were perhaps numbered, even without the Campbell case to bring its downfall.[1]

9. THE GOVERNMENT'S SUDDEN FALL

The end of the Labour government was sudden and messy. Parliament was in recess during August and September, and met on September 30 solely to pass the bill empowering the government to nominate a representative for Northern Ireland on the Irish Boundary Commission.[2] Early in September MacDonald was at Geneva; later, he resumed his holiday in Lossiemouth. The meeting of the Assembly of the League of Nations, the Irish boundary dispute, the Civil War in China occupied most of the public's attention during September; there was a continuing undercurrent of criticism of the Russian treaties and the proposed 'Bolshevist loan', as *The Times* called it, but no talk or suggestion of an imminent political crisis. On September 13, an interview with MacDonald at Lossiemouth was published in which the Prime Minister explained, with evident squeamishness, the circumstances (ferreted out by a newspaper) in which he had received 30,000 £1 shares in the biscuit-manufacturing company of McVitie and Price from a director, Sir Alexander Grant, who had been subsequently given a baronetcy. Grant, a boyhood friend of MacDonald's in Lossiemouth (his father and MacDonald's uncle had both been guards on the Highland Railway) had presented MacDonald with a Daimler motor-car on his becoming Prime Minister, and the dividends on the shares, which were settled on MacDonald for life only, were to be the means by which Mac-Donald could afford the upkeep of the car. Grant's name had been on the waiting list for a baronetcy before MacDonald had become Prime Minister. No one doubted the explanation; but Mac-Donald's sensitive spirit was bruised by criticism of the affair, by anonymous letters, and by cries of 'biscuits' which pursued him

---

[1] A. J. Toynbee, *Survey of International Affairs, 1924*, pp. 233–46; *Annual Register, 1924*, pp. 88–90, 103 (text of general treaty, *ibid.*, part II, pp. 102–7); W. P. and Zelda Coates, *History of Anglo-Soviet Relations* (London, 1944), pp. 129–81.

[2] See above, chap. 2, p. 107.

for a while. Snowden records that MacDonald returned to London in a highly nervous condition.[1] The 'Campbell case', which was to bring the government's downfall, was mentioned in *The Times*, but without much prominence, on September 20. Following a question in parliament on July 29, concerning seditious articles, the offices of the Communist *Workers' Weekly* were raided on August 5 and the acting editor, J. R. Campbell, arrested and charged under the Incitement to Mutiny Act, 1797, as author of an article on July 25 urging soldiers not to fire on their fellow-workers, whether in industrial disputes or in war; it was claimed that copies of the issue had been widely distributed outside military establishments in Aldershot and Farnborough. On August 6, John Scurr,[2] a Labour M.P., had asked questions in parliament about the raid and the charges; and Sir Patrick Hastings, the Attorney General, had replied, admitting the raid and adding that charges were to be pressed against the editor. Other Labour members asked further questions expressive of their dislike of these proceedings—Maxton, Buchanan, Lansbury, Jack Jones.[3] On August 13, after parliament had adjourned, the case was withdrawn, the government counsel stating that 'it had been represented' that the object of the article was to protest against the use of troops in industrial disputes. Now, on September 20, it was reported that Sir Kingsley Wood,[4] a Conservative M.P., intended to ask questions of MacDonald and Hastings concerning the dropping of the prosecution; the texts of his questions were given. Sir John Simon, speaking at Cleckheaton on September 24, also criticised the government for dropping the prosecution.[5] The re-opening of the matter may have been partly MacDonald's own fault. He had talked too freely to a journalist, seeming to protest too much about the case, and to blame it on the Attorney General.[6] Yet there was no public clamour in response to Sir Kingsley Wood's questions or Sir John Simon's

---

[1] *The Times*, September 13, 1924; P. Snowden, *Autobiography*, II, 687–9; *Annual Register, 1924*, p. 100. Grant was a generous benefactor to the endowment of the National Library of Scotland, created out of the Advocates' Library in 1925.

[2] John Scurr (1876–1932), born in Australia, brought up in Poplar (mayor, 1922–23). M.P., 1923–31.

[3] Jack Jones (John Joseph Jones: 1873–1941), M.P. for Silvertown, 1918–40. Born in Tipperary; general organiser, General and Municipal Workers' Union. A wit and genial obstructionist in parliament for many years.

[4] Kingsley Wood (1881–1943), son of a Wesleyan minister. Solicitor; member of L.C.C., 1911–19. M.P., 1918–43. Knight, 1918. Parliamentary secretary, health, 1924–29; postmaster-general, 1931–35; minister of health, 1935–38; air secretary, 1938–40; chancellor of the Exchequer, 1940–43.

[5] *The Times*, September 20, 25, 1924; *Annual Register, 1924*, p. 96.

[6] J. Scanlon, *Decline and Fall of the Labour Party*, p. 79.

charges; and *The Times* on the eve of parliament's meeting carried no hint of crisis.

In parliament on September 30 Hastings gave an apparently satisfactory explanation of his withdrawal of Campbell's prosecution; but the Conservatives decided to table a motion of censure and the Liberals (who were meditating a similar motion over the Russian treaties later on) resolved to propose an amendment calling for a select committee of inquiry. On October 2 there was a scene in the Commons, when Labour members protested against a piece of calculated rudeness by Sir Kingsley Wood—an allusion to MacDonald's motor-car. Next day *The Times'* chief headline was 'The Crisis'. On the 6th the Cabinet decided to treat both Conservative and Liberal motions as matters of confidence. MacDonald explained the decision at the annual conference of the Labour party, in the Queen's Hall, London, next day, damning the Liberal amendment as worse than the Tory censure, since it would put the government on the rack and expose it to a 'packed Committee . . . [with] a roving commission of unjudicial inquiry'— referring to the fact that a select committee, reflecting party strength and appointed by the party whips, would consist of three supporters of the government and seven opponents. Ironically the Labour party, being charged with too much sympathy for the Communists, as shown by the Campbell case, disbarred Communists from its midst more firmly than before at this very Conference; not only was the affiliation of the Communist party once more rejected, but it was resolved that Communists were not eligible for endorsement as Labour party candidates nor even for membership in the party.[1]

The critical debate took place on October 8. It began badly for the government, when MacDonald offered a clumsy explanation of a reply he had given to Sir Kingsley Wood on September 30 which had implied that he had not interfered with the Attorney General over the prosecution of Campbell. Sir Robert Horne, moving the Conservatives' motion of censure, argued that it was pressure from rank-and-file Labour members of parliament which had caused the government to withdraw the prosecution and give the Communists a triumph over the normal course of justice. Hastings' speech—a most able one—made it clear that the final decision had been entirely his own, but that MacDonald and Henderson (Home Secretary) had given him their opinion of the unwisdom of the prosecution before he decided to withdraw it.

[1] *The Times*, October 8, 1924.

'Is it necessary', he concluded, 'to have a vote of censure in order to challenge a minister who makes a mistake?'

MacDonald insisted on making the motion a matter of confidence. 'If this House passes either the resolution or the amendment now,' he concluded, 'we go. It is the end; it will be the end of . . . a high adventure.' Asquith expressed surprise at this 'funeral oration' before the doctor had even pronounced life extinct; and argued that a select committee had not, in the past, been unfair, nor need acceptance of one be grounds for resignation. Meanwhile there had been consultations among the Conservative leaders, and when Baldwin spoke it was to announce that the Conservatives would support the Liberal amendment. Thus, with the government still taking it as a matter of confidence—'a mean and contemptible party manoeuvre', as J. H. Thomas defiantly called it in closing the debate—the government's fate was sealed. The Liberal amendment was carried by 364 votes to 198.[1]

For the fall of the government in these circumstances MacDonald has usually been given all the blame. He has been charged with having had enough of office, of being tired of Liberal jibes from in front, and Labour criticisms from the back benches behind him; he is supposed to have ridden for a fall. It has even been related that MacDonald, in meeting Baldwin, the outgoing Prime Minister, in January, when he consented to take over Baldwin's private secretary and other members of his staff, agreed that a 'reversal of their mutual positions' would take place within nine months.[2] This is to be wise after the event; indeed, after the events of 1931 as much as of 1924. The decision to make the Liberal amendment a matter of confidence was the Cabinet's, not MacDonald's (on October 6), though he may have played the major part in it. The crisis was very brief and sudden, almost a week-end affair. MacDonald is not understood unless his readiness, in an atmosphere of crisis, to come to a sudden, desperate decision is recognised; on such occasions he must have all or nothing. At such a time his irritation with criticism, his feeling of tiredness (increased by the double burden of office he carried), came to the top: best to be rid of it all, go out in the grand manner; and after all, he may have argued, defeat over the Russian treaty was an imminent and less welcome contingency.[3]

[1] The debate is to be found in 177 H.C. Deb., 5 s., 512–694. See also a letter of John Scurr to *The Times*, October 3, 1924.

[2] N. Waterhouse, *Private and Official*, p. 295.

[3] Defeat over the Russian treaty might have given the ascendancy in the Labour party to the left wing, which MacDonald was determined to avert: see G. M. Young, *Baldwin*, p. 83.

10. THE 1924 ELECTION AND THE RED SCARE

Parliament was dissolved on October 9,[1] the third general election in three years was held on October 29. Thus hastily did the country find itself plunged into an election campaign. It began quietly, and at one point *The Times* was talking of the danger of apathy. Baldwin set the tone for many voters with his broadcast address on October 15; he was the first of British prime ministers to master the technique of the microphone, and his quiet voice and simple utterance had very great effect. He appealed for a 'sane, commonsense Government, not carried away by revolutionary theories or hare-brained schemes. . . . We cannot afford the luxury of academic socialists or revolutionary agitation.' By contrast MacDonald's opening speech at Glasgow on October 13, which was also broadcast, sounded the merest ranting; he rounded on the Liberals and Conservatives for turning the Labour government out on a trivial issue and claimed that it was cut short because it had been a success, and had not 'made a mess of things'.[2] Socialism and the Russian treaty were the main issues in the campaign and over them the Conservatives and Liberals drew together: there were local pacts in some cases, and about a hundred Liberal candidates stood down, and threw their weight to the Conservatives.[3]

In the last week, the campaign became more tense. There were complaints of Labour-inspired rowdyism at meetings. *The Times'* headlines of October 23 are a fair sample of the spirit: 'A Bankrupt Party'; '"Red" Designs on Britain . . . Striking through India and Egypt'. This last, which in effect prepared readers for the later bombshell, referred to no more than the revelations in a pamphlet issued by the Russian National Students' Association in Paris. *Punch* had a cartoon, 'On the Loan Trail', depicting a Russian in the guise of a dirty sandwich-man, carrying placards saying 'Vote for MacDonald and me'.[4] There were many rumours that some stunt against the Labour government was being made ready.[5]

[1] The King was, as usual, reluctant to grant a dissolution, and with justice: both because there had already been two general elections in two years, and because the right of a minority party to demand a dissolution was not clear. But to refuse one would suggest discrimination against a Labour government. See H. Nicolson, *George V*, p. 400.
[2] J. A. Salter, *Personality in Politics*, p. 58; *The Times*, October 16, 1924; *Annual Register, 1924*, p. 111.
[3] *Annual Register, 1924*, pp. 111–12.
[4] Cited in L. Macneill Weir, *Tragedy of Ramsay MacDonald* (London, 1938), p. 188; *Punch*, October 29, 1924.
[5] See J. H. Thomas in 179 H.C. Deb., 5 s., 745, citing a *Manchester Guardian* report a few days before the Zinoviev letter was published.

Then it came—just at the right psychological moment, in the newspapers of Saturday, October 25, just before the week-end and only four days before polling (Wednesday, October 29). *The Times* announced it with some restraint: 'Soviet Plot. Red Propaganda in Britain. Revolution urged by Zinoviev. Foreign Office "Bombshell".' Thus was the 'Zinoviev letter' revealed to the world, a perfect example of effective surprise in a political campaign, as one political tactician has called it.[1] This letter, signed by 'Zinoviev', President of the Presidium of the Communist International in Moscow, and by 'McManus', a British member of the Presidium and 'Kuusinen', its secretary, and dated September 15, 1924, was addressed to the Central Committee of the British Communist Party, and marked 'Very Secret'. It urged that the 'proletariat of Great Britain . . . must show the greatest possible energy in the further struggle for ratification' of the Russian treaty, for which purpose 'it is indispensable to stir up the masses of the British proletariat, to bring into movement the army of unemployed proletarians . . .' 'Keep close observation over the leaders of the Labour Party,' it continued, 'because these may easily be found in the leading strings of the *bourgeoisie*. The foreign policy of the Labour Party . . . represents an inferior copy of the policy of the Curzon Government. Organise a campaign of disclosure of the foreign policy of MacDonald.' It went on to offer 'the wide material' in the International's possession 'regarding the activities of British imperialism in the Middle and Far East'. It argued:

a settlement of relations between the two countries will assist in the revolutionizing of the international and British proletariat not less than a successful rising in any of the working districts of England, as the establishment of close contact between the British and Russian proletariat, the exchange of delegations and workers, etc., will make it possible for us to extend and develop the propaganda of ideas of Leninism in England and the Colonies. Armed warfare must be preceded by a struggle against the inclinations to compromise which are embedded among the majority of British workmen, against the ideas of evolution and peaceful extermination of capitalism. Only then will it be possible to count upon complete success of an armed insurrection . . . agitation-propaganda work in the Army is weak, in the Navy a very little better. . . . [There should be cells] in all units of the troops, particularly among those quartered in large centres . . . and also among factories working on munitions and at military store depôts. . . . In

[1] P. Cambray, *Game of Politics* (London, 1932), p. 83.

the event of danger of war, with the aid of the latter and in contact with the transport workers, it is possible to paralyse all the military preparations of the *bourgeoisie* and make a start in turning an imperialist war into a class war.

This extraordinary concoction, linking support of the Russian treaty with plans for the class war in Great Britain, would perhaps have had little effect but for the fact that it was accompanied, in the press, by a letter from the Foreign Office signed by J. D. Gregory, head of its Russian section, to Rakovsky, Russian chargé d'affaires in London, which protested against the letter as propaganda representing a direct interference in British domestic affairs from outside.[1] This covering letter established in the public mind the authenticity of the Zinoviev letter, and ensured that the most serious interpretation would be put upon it.

Here was a stick to beat the government with; its Russian treaty revealed as the harbinger of revolution in Great Britain. 'The Truth at last' was the title of *The Times'* first editorial on the same day; and on Monday a further charge was made against MacDonald (ironic, in view of the perfect timing of the publication for the anti-Labour cause) that his protest was 'tardy', and that he had been trying to hide something. Labour was thrown into dismay.

Yet MacDonald delayed until Monday afternoon, October 27, before making any comment, in a speech at Cardiff. He had been, as he explained, on a campaign tour, moving from one end of the country to the other by car. In spite of the letter's date, the Foreign Office only received a copy on October 10. It was sent to MacDonald on the 15th, and reached him in Manchester on the 16th. He then 'minuted that the greatest care would have to be taken in discovering whether the letter was authentic or not. If it was authentic it had to be published at once'; so, to save time, he instructed a draft letter of protest to Rakovsky to be prepared. He was sent a draft of this on the 21st, received it on the 23rd, revised it and sent it back on the 24th, expecting to receive it back, with the proofs of authenticity, before anything was published. Instead, the Zinoviev letter and the official protest were published on the 25th. (Snowden points out that the Foreign Office must, therefore, have published them before receiving MacDonald's revised draft, which he only sent off on the 24th, and asks why the telephone was never used throughout these proceedings.) MacDonald, though reserving judgment on the

[1] Text in A. J. Toynbee, *Survey of International Affairs, 1924*, pp. 492–3.

question of authenticity, went on to point to the government's prompt handling of the affair, and to the publication of the letter, as evidence that the Labour government was a stout defender of the country against Bolshevism. This was a reasonable line to take; other Labour speakers denounced the letter as a forgery and the affair as a stunt.[1]

Anyway, the Zinoviev letter did its work, or so it was assumed. When the election results were published, the Conservatives had obtained a large majority, 415 seats as compared with 152 won by Labour and 42 by the Liberals. The Conservative vote increased from 5·4 millions to 7·4 millions. It must be noticed, however, that Labour also increased its vote, from 4·3 millions to 5·5 millions, running nearly a hundred more candidates than previously; it had a net loss of 42 seats (64 seats lost, 22 new seats won). Several of the losses were the result of Conservative-Liberal pacts. As usual, it was the Liberals who were the victims of whatever panic the campaign had given rise to; they lost 116 seats, almost all to the Conservatives, and their popular vote dropped from 4·2 millions to just under 3 millions. Asquith, in spite of having a straight fight at Paisley against a Labour candidate, was the most notable of the losers. Winston Churchill returned to parliament; as did Saklatvala, the Communist. Labour's chief losses were in greater London, Scotland, Lancashire, Chesire, and the eastern counties; and the trade-union wing of the party was proportionately stronger in the new parliament, as compared with I.L.P. members and candidates of divisional Labour parties, than in the old.[2]

The Conservative victory has usually been attributed to the Zinoviev letter. It would probably have occurred without it. The letter helped, no doubt, to increase the total poll (from 70·8 per cent to 76·6 per cent of the electorate), and the floating voters doubtless voted safe by voting Conservative, as usual in such circumstances.[3] Baldwin's plea for a 'sane, commonsense Government' was winning votes long before the Zinoviev bombshell. It was Baldwin who sensed the attitude of the majority of the people in the middle twenties, and gave expression to it. Only when he

---

[1] P. Snowden, *Autobiography*, II, 710–15; *Annual Register, 1924*, pp. 115–17.
[2] *The Times*, October 31, 1924; G. D. H. Cole, *History of the Labour Party*, pp. 169–71, 479.
[3] G. D. H. Cole, *History of the Labour Party*, p. 169; P. Snowden, *Autobiography*, II, 716; D. E. Butler, *Electoral System*, p. 172. The average percentage of the vote won by Conservatives in contested seats increased from 42·6 per cent in 1923 (48·6 per cent in 1922) to 51·9 per cent in 1924, chiefly at the expense of the Liberals (Butler, pp. 175, 178).

seemed to have abandoned the policy of moderation which the people came to expect from him did his position become insecure.

11. POST MORTEM ON THE ZINOVIEV LETTER

There remain certain questions to be answered about the Zinoviev letter. MacDonald has been blamed for failing to recognise its importance, for dealing with the Foreign Office over it in a dilatory fashion, and for speaking of it in the campaign only belatedly and ineffectively. What delay there was in publishing the letter was partly the Foreign Office's fault, partly due to MacDonald's election tour—which, in itself, was perhaps a mistake, since he wore out himself and his voice (he once addressed twenty-seven meetings in one day). The tour left him tired, nervous, resentful; he was exposed to bitter attack and, as always, personal criticism touched him on the raw flesh (speaking at Barry he said: 'Why, instead of having a great battle on a political principle, do they [opponents] go about sniffing like mangy dogs on a garbage heap?').[1] He may not have given the letter all the attention it deserved. He may too easily have assumed its authenticity (though he never admitted he was convinced of it); partly because its tone, and particularly its slighting allusions to his foreign policy, were what would strike him where he was most sensitive, in his pride. Yet he did not attempt to suppress the letter. G. D. H. Cole ingeniously suggests that he may, in his correspondence with the Foreign Office, have been playing for time, hoping that the letter would not have to be published until after the election.[2]

At any rate his campaign was a fighting one, not one of a willing loser. His popularity with Labour held. H. W. Nevinson, the distinguished journalist, who accompanied him, records that when he came finally to his constituency of Aberavon, in South Wales, the car was forced to crawl at a mile an hour through dense crowds, who sang a special song for him to the tune of 'Men of Harlech'.[3] He may have mishandled the Zinoviev letter; but he did not sabotage his own cause.

It has been charged that the Foreign Office departed from its role of neutrality in domestic politics and published the Zinoviev letter and its protest to Rakovsky, maliciously, without Mac-Donald's authority, in order to ensure Labour's defeat. Mac-

[1] P. Snowden, *Autobiography*, II, 708–9.
[2] G. D. H. Cole, *History of the Labour Party*, p. 168.
[3] H. W. Nevinson, *Last Changes*, pp. 311–15.

Donald, however, always defended the Foreign Office as having acted correctly and without any disloyalty to him, even though there had been a misunderstanding.[1] For one thing, the *Daily Mail* had also received a copy of the letter, and boasted afterwards of the fact; it had threatened to publish it, and the Foreign Office felt it important to anticipate this. The decision was not that of Gregory (who signed the letter of protest), but of Sir Eyre Crowe, the permanent head of the Foreign Office, who thought the letter genuine (even so, it is not clear why Crowe did not telephone MacDonald, or consult Lord Haldane, who was temporarily handling matters in London). Later, Gregory was involved in the 'Francs case' (in 1928), and it was charged that advance knowledge of the publication of the letter, and of the government's imminent defeat as a result of it, had enabled him to profit in certain foreign exchange speculations. Gregory was dismissed for conduct unbecoming a public servant, but the charges were completely disproved.[2]

The question of the letter's authenticity is less easily disposed of. The bulk of the Labour party never doubted that it was a forgery and has never changed its view; the Conservatives were as convinced that it was genuine. Actually, it mattered little, as to its effect, whether it was genuine or not once it was published with the official protest of the Foreign Office, which made it official also. Rakovsky at once (October 25) replied to the Foreign Office's note, declaring the letter a 'gross forgery' and protesting against its publication without his having been approached first; he complained of the departure from established practice, and of the unfounded accusations, in the note. He pointed out that the titles given for the signatories of the Zinoviev letter were incorrect, and that reference to the 'Third Communist International' was a solecism—there had never been a first or second Communist International. Other protests followed from Zinoviev himself, from Litvinov, assistant commissar for foreign affairs in Moscow, and, later, from the T.U.C.'s delegation to Russia, which had made an investigation in Moscow. The Labour government, before leaving office, appointed a cabinet committee to investigate the letter's authenticity; in the limited time it had it could only report that it could come to no positive conclusion; the original letter had not been produced, or seen, by any government depart-

[1] *Annual Register, 1924*, pp. 116, 134–35.
[2] *Annual Register, 1924*, p. 116; M. A. Hamilton, *J. Ramsay MacDonald*, pp. 261–278; H. Nicolson, *George V*, p. 402; Hugh Dalton, *Call back yesterday: Memoirs, 1887–1931* (London, 1953), pp. 76–7; 215 H.C. Deb., 5 s., 47–72 (March 19, 1928).

ment. The Conservatives, on taking office, appointed a cabinet committee of their own to investigate the matter. Austen Chamberlain, the new Foreign Secretary, wrote to Rakovsky as early as November 21, declaring that the government had 'no doubt whatsoever' of the letter's authenticity. Speeches in parliament by Joynson-Hicks (the Home Secretary) and Austen Chamberlain on December 10 and 15 added a little, though refusing to give the sources of their information, since 'it is of the essence of a Secret Service that it must be secret'. They claimed that the letter reached the government from one source and could be traced from its issue in Petrograd to its arrival in England, and that information had been received about it from three other and mutually independent sources. It had been received by members of the British Communist party, and destroyed by them. To reveal more would endanger individual life. In reply, MacDonald declared that his own position was 'authenticity not proved'. He asked for a proper inquiry. He never got it.[1]

MacDonald, in questioning Austen Chamberlain on this occasion, put his finger on the weak spot in all explanations of the letter's authenticity—the fact that no one had ever seen the original letter; what was published was a translation of a copy. But there were several copies. The Foreign Office got one, the *Daily Mail* had one, the Conservative Central Office was supposed to have had one. Where had they come from? Austen Chamberlain denied that the Foreign Office's copy came from the *Daily Mail*, or the *Daily Mail's* from the Foreign Office.[2] One story was that the Secret Service had intercepted the letter at Riga, copied it and then sent it on.[3] As shrewd an observer as Wickham Steed accepted it as a fact that the letter was a forgery.[4]

A little more light was let in upon the mystery in 1928 after the Francs case. The *Observer* (March 4, 1928) published a letter from Thomas Marlowe, editor of the *Daily Mail* in 1924, stating that he had obtained two copies of the letter from separate sources,

[1] *Annual Register, 1924*, pp. 118, 122–3, 131, 133–4; A. J. Toynbee, *Survey of International Affairs, 1924*, pp. 247–9, 495–6; *Labour Year Book, 1925*, pp. 568–73; 179 H.C. Deb., 5 s., 309–11, 560–3, 671–6, 688–91, 740–6.
[2] 179 H.C. Deb., 5 s., 562–3; N. Waterhouse, *Private and Official*, pp. 317–18.
[3] E. D. Morel, speaking at Dundee, October 24, 1924, mentioned this report but said he had positive information that it was untrue: *Foreign Affairs* (Union of Democratic Control), VI, 129 (December, 1924). E. D. Morel was re-elected for Dundee, but died on November 12, 1924.
[4] Wickham Steed, *The Real Stanley Baldwin*, pp. 78–9. W. P. and Z. Coates, *History of Anglo-Soviet Relations*, pp. 181–97, assumes that it was a forgery and suspects that White Russians in London were responsible; it also claims that they were in touch with Gregory.

H

which he implied were civil servants. The Labour party then demanded a new inquiry. In the debate which ensued in the Commons Baldwin refused an inquiry, reiterated the government's conviction that the letter was authentic, and then took the wind from the Opposition's sails by reading a letter just written and given him by a stranger, a London business man, Conrad Donald imThurn, which declared that the writer had obtained a copy of the letter from a business friend who was close to Communist circles in London on October 9, 1924, and had given the facts to the government department mainly concerned (presumably the Foreign Office) and, through a friend, to the *Daily Mail*.[1] Even this revelation does not, however, completely solve the mystery. (1) The Foreign Office, Baldwin implied, had received another copy or copies of the letter from other sources;[2] (2) the claim of the letter's authenticity still rests only on the government's affirmation, grounded on the information of the necessarily secret Secret Service.[3]

In the matter of the letter's authenticity the historian can only fall back on internal criticism. The style of the letter proves nothing; 'no style could well be simpler to imitate', observes G. D. H. Cole.[4] But its matter tells against it. It is all so pat, as if intended for publication. It contains everything that the professional anti-bolshevist could want, everything that the reader of thrillers about spies and saboteurs would expect—the references to the proletariat and the capitalists and the *bourgeoisie*, to British imperialism in the Middle East, to Ireland and the colonies, to the need for cells in the army (especially at munitions factories and 'military store depôts') and for the finding of 'the future director of the British Red Army'. It doesn't miss a bet. If it was not a forgery, it might just as well have been, for all the credence such a puerile concoction was worth. Not that it matters; it did its work anyway, and that work was much less than many people assumed it to be.

12. BALDWIN AND THE RETURN TO NORMALCY; LOCARNO AND THE GOLD STANDARD

The Conservative government which Baldwin formed on November 7, 1924 was not so very different from that which had

---

[1] 215 H.C. Deb., 5 s., 47–72 (March 19, 1928).   [2] Ibid., 72 (March 19, 1928).
[3] A recent review of the whole affair is R. D. Warth, 'The Mystery of the Zinoviev Letter', *South Atlantic Quarterly*, 49 (1950), 441–53.
[4] *History of the Labour Party*, p. 166.

fallen less than a year before. There were, however, three notable additions. Three members of the Coalition who had been in the wilderness since 1922 were welcomed into the Cabinet, Austen Chamberlain, who became Foreign Secretary, Lord Birkenhead, who became Secretary of State for India, and Winston Churchill (returned to the fold after twenty years as a Liberal) as Chancellor of the Exchequer. Sir Robert Horne was offered and refused the Ministry of Labour; he never held office after 1922. Thus were old wounds healed, though not to everybody's satisfaction. Churchill's appointment was the most surprising and was made on Baldwin's sole initiative; it was far from popular inside the party, particularly among the protectionists, who regarded the new recruit with undisguised suspicion.[1] Nor was it at first sight a very appropriate appointment, since among the many posts Churchill had graced and the many talents he possessed the financial had not hitherto been included. It was said that he accepted with alacrity, thinking that the Prime Minister's offer of the chancellorship was that of the Duchy of Lancaster. Lord Curzon accepted the honorific post of Lord President of the Council (which he held until his death in 1925), Joynson-Hicks was Home Secretary, Amery Colonial Secretary, Sir Samuel Hoare Secretary of State for Air; Neville Chamberlain returned to his old post as Minister of Health.

This began Baldwin's longest term as Prime Minister, which lasted until 1929. In it he impressed his character firmly on the country and, in large part, reflected in turn the national character of those times. The position he created for himself endured until his retirement in 1937; and though (after 1929) he was only Prime Minister for two years (1935–37) he was the chief support of MacDonald in the National government from 1931 to 1935. The strength of his position came partly from the fact that he was not an out-and-out Conservative, but a moderate, representing himself as the plain man, a man of sanity, without art or guile, a country-man puffing slowly on his pipe and (so the cartoonists would have it) gazing pensively at his pigs. He seemed to represent Old England, and his speeches, reflecting on love of country and of countryside, underlined this, just as his indifference concerning foreigners—later a handicap—confirmed it. It spite of appearances, however, he proved himself the ablest politician of his day, and in a crisis fully the master of events; though to him it was a private tragedy that the two crises which tested him to his utter-

[1] L. S. Amery, *Thoughts on the Constitution* (Oxford, 1947), p. 23.

most were ones grievous to him and in his view avoidable: the general strike, and Edward VIII's abdication.

Yet his power and ability came from his apparent lack of them; people trusted him—and they did trust him— because he appeared to be *not* a politician, but the plain man in politics. And in part this was true: his policy was to have no policy; he never had a plan ahead of a gathering crisis; he hated coming to decisions, and to do so made him physically nervous, so that his hands would twitch. He was, in fact, a very sensitive person, behind his bovine mask. When in doubt, he preferred to do nothing, hoping that things would settle themselves. He admitted that he was a lazy man. He liked nothing better than to sit in his inner room, playing patience or doing a crossword puzzle or reading a novel or a biography (not the detective stories to which Balfour and other statesmen were addicted). In a crisis he would withdraw to his sanctum; or if it was acute, go to bed. It was not without significance that he much admired the urbane account of Hanoverian politics in *The Endless Adventure*, by F. S. Oliver, a successful businessman and leisured man of letters. The first volume appeared in 1930. The 'endless adventure' was that of governing men, a task needing craftsmanship, flexibility, and congruence with the needs and tendencies of the times. Oliver's character-sketch of Walpole was a model for Baldwin; and for Walpole's pursuit of a single object, the security of the Hanoverian dynasty, Baldwin substituted the preservation of a balanced and harmonious society, with the scales held even between property and the claims of labour.

In the Cabinet Baldwin seldom gave a lead, sometimes to the annoyance of Neville Chamberlain, who recorded once that he seemed to be paying no attention to him and presently passed an open note across to Churchill bearing these words: 'MATCHES lent at 10.30 a.m. Returned?'—a 'triviality' which 'while a very grave question was being discussed . . . made the most deplorable impression on me'.[1] In keeping with this spirit was his devotion to the House of Commons, and his friendliness and accessibility to all members (except the intellectuals whom, characteristically, he had great contempt for); Labour members, in particular, trusted him and liked him in private.[2] And this, because, essentially, his policy was that of the moderate trade unionist; to prevent the

[1] K. Feiling, *N. Chamberlain*, pp. 164–5.
[2] E.g., J. R. Clynes, *Memoirs*, II, 251; D. Kirkwood, *My Life of Revolt*, pp. 203–4, 219; Lord Snell, *Men, Movements, and Myself* (London, 1936), p. 247; T. N. Graham, *Willie Graham* (London, [1947]), p. 94.

spreading of the class war, to lower the temperature, to achieve, as he put it in his moving speech in parliament in March 1925, 'peace in our time'. Who in England did not want that? Here lay his strength, and his weakness; he would not fight for what he believed, particularly against his own party, until a crisis was upon him, and he tired easily. In both his public and his private character there was much that was endearing; but he lacked the touch of greatness, content to follow events, not to shape them.[1]

For the twenties such a leader was a mixed blessing. His policy was the same as Bonar Law's; tranquillity, a return to the normal conditions of the prewar world. He put it into effect, and by 1925 he had carried it out; the return to the gold standard in that year marks the high-water mark of Britain's attempt in the postwar world to get back to 1914. But it failed in the moment of its success, and in fact contributed to the rapid vanishing of the illusion that return was possible. The general strike of 1926 was an ill omen.

First, to carry out this policy, the more adventurous commitments of Labour's foreign policy must be reversed. As early as November 21 Austen Chamberlain addressed a note to Rakovsky declaring that the government would not recommend the Anglo-Russian treaties to parliament; and thus the treaties perished. This was followed by a critical examination of the Geneva Protocol which the Conservative press in England had denounced and the Dominions had objected to, New Zealand and Australia fearing that it would prevent them from controlling immigration, while others raised objections to its supposedly unlimited and world-wide obligations. The British government's rejection of the Protocol was, therefore, not unexpected when it was announced by Austen Chamberlain in the Council of the League on March 12, 1925. Britain's action killed the Protocol, towards which the other great powers (except France) had reserved their opinion, though the smaller European powers and the Latin American countries had been enthusiastic for it. The last and best attempt to 'put teeth' into the League had failed; and many people dated the decline of the League from this event.[2]

[1] *Lord Baldwin* (*The Times* memoir), pp. 9, 20–22; Wickham Steed, *The Real Stanley Baldwin*; Stanley Baldwin, *On England* (London, 1926; Penguin edition, 1938—the first collection of his speeches); K. Feiling, *N. Chamberlain*, p. 164; R. Boothby, *I Fight to Live*, pp. 33–5; 38–40; N. Waterhouse, *Private and Official*, pp. 267–73; G. M. Young, *Baldwin*, pp. 52–63 (a brief, sympathetic, but strangely uncharitable biography). For Baldwin at his best see Thomas Jones, *Diary with Letters 1931-1950* (Oxford, 1954).
[2] A. J. Toynbee, *Survey of International Affairs, 1925*, II, 2–24; R. B. McCallum, *Public Opinion and the Last Peace*, p. 134.

The Conservatives had, however, an alternative policy—that expressed in the Locarno Pact of 1925. Chamberlain's speech of March 12 had outlined the alternative: limited and special arrangements to supplement the Covenant. A lengthy series of negotiations followed—indeed, they had begun early in the year. What was proposed was a security pact guaranteeing the western frontiers of Germany (principally the German-French boundary); Germany and France would enter into a pact of non-aggression, and this would be guaranteed by Britain and other powers. Thus a compromise between France's quest for security and Britain's reluctance to accept specific commitments in Europe would be achieved, and security and conciliation would advance hand in hand. Stresemann for Germany, and Chamberlain for Great Britain pressed forward this policy, aided by Lord D'Abernon, the British ambassador at Berlin. But it ran into difficulties. It became involved with the final evacuation of the Ruhr and the evacuation of the first zone of the Rhineland occupation, centred on Cologne, which was to have occurred by January 5, 1925, but which was postponed because of Germany's failure to carry out all her disarmament obligations. It became involved with the question of Germany's entry into the League of Nations, to which Germany wished to attach certain conditions, particularly regarding her obligations to take part in sanctions and to permit transit of troops of other countries, under Article 16 of the Covenant, which she contended were incompatible with her disarmed state and her geographical position. And it was involved, most critically, with the question of Germany's eastern frontiers; would any pact govern their future? Germany, with revisionist ideas, opposed the suggestion, but so did the British government, concerned to limit, not magnify its commitments; but France and her allies, Poland and Czechoslovakia, were, of course, correspondingly anxious for guarantees in the east.

Eventually, the diplomatic interchanges of the spring and summer cleared the way for the summoning of the conference at Locarno, on Lake Maggiore, which met on October 5, 1925. Britain, France, Germany, Belgium, Italy, Czechoslovakia, Poland were represented. The chief delegates included Chamberlain, Stresemann, Briand; Benes represented Czechoslovakia; Mussolini attended in the closing stages. In the balmy air of Locarno differences gradually dissolved, with the help of private conversations: for instance, Chamberlain, Briand, the Germans and their staffs combined business with pleasure in a motor-boat excursion on the lake on October 10. The Locarno Pact, announced on October 16, included a treaty of mutual guarantee of Germany's western frontiers and the demilitarisation of the Rhineland: Germany, Belgium and France undertook not to make war on each other, and promised to settle disputes by arbitration; and Britain and Italy promised to come to the aid of any party which was the victim of a violation of these promises. Germany's eastern frontiers were not covered by this treaty, but arbitration treaties were concluded between Germany, Poland and Czechoslovakia, and France entered into separate treaties with Poland and Czechoslovakia. Germany was to be welcomed into the League, and the powers agreed to support Germany's interpretations of her obligations under Article 16.[1]

The Locarno Pact was much more limited than the Geneva Protocol, of which it was an outgrowth. It seemed at the time to guarantee the peace of Europe by an arrangement concerning its most vulnerable area, the Rhineland. French security was bolstered by a treaty with Germany, unilaterally guaranteed by Great Britain and Italy; and Germany, by joining the League, would be received back into the bosom of the European community. Russia and the security of eastern Europe were left out of the negotiations. None the less, the Pact was hailed with enthusiasm in England, and it was generally believed that the 'Locarno spirit' was bringing in a new era of peace. The spell of the war had at last been exorcised. The Pact was the crown of Chamberlain's career, and earned him the reward of the knighthood of the Garter.

The return to the gold standard at the prewar parity, which completed the process of international stabilisation and the restoration of prewar conditions, was announced by Winston Churchill in his Budget speech on April 28, 1925. The government had decided, he said, to allow the act of 1920 which prohibited the export of gold to lapse. This had been the recommendation of the Cunliffe Committee in 1918; and the deflationary policy pursued by the government since 1920 had been directed towards it. Sir Felix Schuster, a leading banker, had called for this at the Institute of Bankers in November 1921: 'Let us have done with short cuts and by-paths and return to the old standard. The road may be long and painful but our fathers trod it before us and we know the way.'[2] Gradually British prices had come down as wages fell;

---

[1] A. J. Toynbee, *Survey of International Affairs, 1925*, II, 25–66; H. Nicolson, *George V*, pp. 406–9.
[2] Quoted in E. V. Francis, *Britain's Economic Strategy* (London, 1939), p. 54.

and actually since 1923 things had been fairly stable: weekly wages slightly rising, wholesale prices still falling, fewer days lost through strikes.[1] The final decision was not a sudden one. It was much discussed in Churchill's circle of advisers. Sir James Grigg describes a dinner given by Churchill at which the return to the gold standard was argued between Lord Bradbury[2] and Sir Otto Niemeyer,[3] who supported it, and J. M. Keynes and Reginald McKenna, who opposed it. The arguments in its favour were that British and United States prices were already almost equal (the discrepancy being estimated at $2\frac{1}{2}$ per cent in favour of the United States), and that a return to the gold standard would be a return to reality, demanding a genuine competitive effort and a switch from basic industries which had lost competitive advantages in export trade to other lines of earning. Against it Keynes argued that the discrepancy between British and American prices was really 10 per cent, so that if the return to the gold standard was at the old parity it would be necessary to deflate domestic prices by that amount—at the cost of unemployment and strikes. McKenna, pressed for his opinion on the matter as a political decision, admitted 'There is no escape; you have got to go back. But it will be hell.'[4]

In parliament, Churchill had to meet much the same arguments. Sir Alfred Mond complained that the return to the gold standard made the City subservient to Wall Street.[5] Hindsight has embroidered much on the decision. It was not the return to the gold standard itself, but the return at the prewar parity which has been criticised. It overvalued the pound, crippling exports and so hampering Britain's trade recovery. London's old prestige and power as the world's money market was restored, but briefly and tragically, since its borrowing and lending policies proved unwise and it was unable to protect itself against the blows of the American stock exchange crash of 1929 and the collapse of the German house of cards which followed. But in 1925 the pound could look the dollar in the face; and outwardly the return to the prewar world was complete.

[1] See table in W. A. Lewis, *Economic Survey, 1919–1939* (London, 1949), p. 44.
[2] J. S. Bradbury (1872–1950), official in the Treasury, principal British delegate to the Reparations Commission, 1919–25. Knight, 1913, baron, 1925.
[3] Otto Niemeyer, born 1883, civil servant (Treasury), 1906–27 (controller of finance, 1922–27); at Bank of England since 1927 (director, 1938); chairman, Bank of International Settlements, 1937–40. Served on several financial missions to countries overseas.
[4] P. J. Grigg, *Prejudice and Judgment*, pp. 180–6.
[5] *Annual Register, 1925*, pp. 40, 42–3.

CHAPTER FOUR

Stability and Change : the Condition of Britain in the Twenties

1. THE RINGING GROOVES OF CHANGE

N O M A N of middle age and comfortable means, contemplating the condition of things in the early twenties, would agree that the postwar England bore much resemblance to the country he had known before the war. The old order had passed away, the halcyon days of the privileged classes. The war had cut across everything. 'Change and decay in all around I see'; it was easy for the casual observer to sum up his impressions in the words of the hymnal, and ignore the manifold evidences of stability which were present also.

A changing spirit was most apparent among writers, less so among artists and architects; it was apparent also in the manners and morals of the younger generation. Here the gap between the generations which the war had caused was most obvious. It was as wide as the gap in political life, but it was the inversion of it: in politics the older generation remained in the saddle, in literature the younger generation, those who had fought in the war and those too young to have done so, quickly thrust its elders into the background. For these reasons the mood of the twenties in society and in the arts was in contrast with that in politics, in looking forward rather than backwards; in the thirties also there was a contrast between the two, but of a different sort; the political mood was one of drawing inward, of insularity, the literary mood was outgoing, inclining towards a world view, social consciousness, a platonic affection for the proletariat.

There were great changes also in the realms of science and learning and in popular ideas about the nature of man and the universe. New knowledge could, of course, spring only from the old, so that its presence was a mark of continuity even when its acceptance was a stimulus to change. For many it was an age of disintegration. The old beliefs, the old props were gone; first religious faith, later faith in reason. Psychology was destroying reason as a guide to conduct, the physicists certainty in the order of the universe.[1]

Yet the greatest changes were those in the material conditions of life. The new technology came bearing many gifts: the most disturbing were motion pictures, wireless broadcasting, and motor buses. These affected all classes of society: but the lower more markedly than the upper. This was true in other things also: the new standards of convenience demanded—and provided—in postwar housing; the demand for inexpensive yet attractive clothes which, particularly for women's dresses, stockings and lingerie, was well served by the new rayon industry. These changes of a materialistic sort tended to bring about a greater equality between the classes in the conditions of life; they suggested a more rapid and complete advance towards equality in general than was actually the case.

The tendency of society was equalitarian; the practice was not. Primacy in politics, the civil service, the professions, business still belonged mainly to the upper and middle classes, protected as they were by the division of education into the public and private sectors. Any analysis of the condition of Britain in the twenties must take account of these two characteristics: stability, more evident in some parts of the national scene than others, but never absent; and change, intruding everywhere, particularly in material conditions, but never all-triumphant. Things seemed the same but were not, as if one was being carried imperceptibly elsewhere while apparently remaining stationary: the opposite of the Red Queen's predicament.[2]

Yet many people disregarded so disturbing a condition and continued to disperse their energies on minor pursuits: such as the crossword puzzle. The passion for this new amusement dated from 1924. It was more than a pastime. It took time and it took ingenuity (as clues became more 'literary' and allusive), diverting energy from more serious matters, distracting the mind from the questions of the day. In a sense the crossword puzzle was the symbol of the age: an inexpensive and ostensibly harmless amusement, leading—nowhere. Utopia in seven letters.

---

[1] E. L. Woodward, *Short Journey*, pp. 123–4.
[2] See the suggestive ideas in Cyril Garbett (Archbishop of York), *In an Age of Revolution* (London, 1952).

2. THE OLD ORDER CHANGETH

In the first years after the war the sense of loss and waste was still strong. Hardly a family but had lost one or more of its sons, often in the first promise of youth. Widows struggling to bring up fatherless children, women in their twenties, their sweethearts killed, facing the long years of spinsterhood, the men with scarred faces or a limping foot or an armless sleeve all carried in their looks, as a reminder to others, the mark of the misery and the exaction of war. Many of the demobilised men took some time to get back into civilian life; ex-officers found that positions in business or the professions equal to their abilities were hard to find. There was restlessness and unease about the future.

By 1925 the war had receded into the background, the changes which it had brought had been accepted. It was taken for granted, for instance, that the old order of high society of the glittering Edwardian days had gone for ever. Great estates were being broken up, great houses sold—in the towns for demolition, in the country for conversion into schools or nursing homes; high taxes and death duties were doing the work of the redistribution of property, whatever the intention of their promoters ten or twenty years before. Evelyn Waugh depicts Colonel Blount in *Vile Bodies* complaining of high bus fares and letting out his house for the filming of an early and amateurish motion picture. For the first time a country house was a problem: the *Spectator* even published two articles on 'How to save the country houses of England' in 1921. A few owners adopted the expedient of showing their houses to the public as a means of meeting part of the cost of upkeep.

More concrete evidence of change was given by the land agents. One firm of auctioneers claimed to have sold within a year the area of an English county. By 1921 land sales fell off, but did not cease. *The Times* published an article in 1922 entitled 'England changing hands', mentioning one firm with 79,000 acres announced for sale in its advertisements and noting that 7650 acres of Lord Manton's land in Suffolk and 31,000 acres of the Duke of Hamilton's properties were up for sale. Farm land, much of it bought by tenants who mortgaged their future to the doubtful rewards of English agriculture, sold at 40–50 per cent above its prewar value.[1] One must not, however, exaggerate the extent of

---

[1] C. F. G. Masterman, *England after War* (London, [1922]; New York, 1923), pp. 45–6, 48–9, 58–60; *The Times*, April 21, 1922; *Economist*, January 17, 1920, January 7, 1922, January 27, 1923.

such changes; witness Shropshire, certainly a remote and slow-moving county compared to the home counties. Of 173 'principal seats' in Shropshire, 53 changed hands between 1922 and 1934, 8 were converted into institutions of one sort or another, and 7 were unoccupied.[1]

Certainly 'society' did not disappear. The *Tatler* and the *Sporting and Dramatic* continued to feast their readers with pictures of titled men and women at meets of the Quorn or the Pytchley, at shooting parties, at Goodwood or Ascot, at the Eton and Harrow match, at Cannes or Biarritz. There was an influx of parvenus (many from the notorious class of war profiteers); but this was nothing new, though it furnished *Punch* with the inspiration for many jokes about clumsy fox-hunters and snobbish lordlings. In 1923 there were 708 lay peers, of whom 198 owed their titles to creations in Queen Victoria's reign, 46 to creations of Edward VII, 176 to creations by George V, since 1910. Between 1917 and 1921, during Lloyd George's prime ministership, 4 marquisates, 8 earldoms, 22 viscountcies and 64 baronies were created. Between 1923 and 1930 the score was 1 marquess, 5 earls, 14 viscounts and 59 barons.[2]

The middle class showed equal vitality, notwithstanding the solemn talk of the 'new poor' in the years immediately following the war. The 'public schools' continued to flourish, in spite of high fees.[3] Certainly prices had increased where salaries had changed little; and the value of savings may well have been reduced to a half or a third of their former worth. One change was inescapable: servants were hard to come by and domestic service on the old scale not to be thought of; however, a 'daily' may even have been less trouble than the housemaid who had previously 'lived in'. In Liverpool the number of domestic servants per 100 families decreased between 1911 and 1921 from 13·5 to 8·3; in Wallasey, a suburb and seaside place, the decline was from 22·4 to 14·5.[4] In London the number of resident servants per 100 families declined in the same period from 57·4 to 41·3 in the West End, from 24·1 to 12·4 in middle-class areas, and from 10·3 to 6·1 in the rest of the metropolis.[5] Life for the middle class was

---

[1] Computed from the 'List of the Principal Seats in Shropshire', in *Kelly's Directory of Shropshire*, 1922, 1934.

[2] *Kelly's Handbook to the Titled, Landed and Official Classes*, 1923, pp. 37–48, 1931, pp. 40–50. See above, ch. 2, p. 134.

[3] Three new boys' public schools were founded: Stowe and Canford in 1923, Bryanston in 1928.

[4] D. Caradog Jones (ed.), *Social Survey of Merseyside* (Liverpool, 1934), II, 301, 306–22.

[5] *New Survey of London Life and Labour*, II (London, 1931), p. 465.

not easy; neither was it penurious. And the middle class had long before begun to limit its families to two or three children.

3. THE DISTRIBUTION OF THE NATIONAL INCOME

Figures showing the distribution of the national income did not suggest that any large change had taken place in society. The proportions of the national income taken by wages and salaries increased. Among wage-earners there was an increase in real earnings between 1914 and 1924, and this movement continued during the next few years. There was also an increase in the number of persons liable for supertax.[1]

The national income of the United Kingdom (excluding the area of the Irish Free State) was estimated to be £1,988 millions in 1911 and £3,887 millions in 1924.[2] Of this, wages took 39·5 per cent in 1911, 42·1 per cent in 1924; salaries 15·6 per cent in 1911, 25·4 per cent in 1924; on the other hand the share of profits decreased from 33·8 per cent to 25·1 per cent, and of rent from 11·1 per cent to 7·4 per cent.[3] The average earnings of all wage-earners on full time rose 94 per cent between 1914 and 1924, while the cost of living rose only 75 per cent; consequently real earnings increased 11 per cent, but if allowance is made for increased unemployment the increase was only about 5 per cent. Between 1924 and 1934 real earnings rose by another 9 or 10 per cent (allowing for unemployment), which was about half as much as the increase in real income per head of population. Meanwhile, the proportion of the national income going to supertax payers was 8 per cent in 1911, 5·5 per cent in 1924. There was an increase in the number and amount of incomes assessed to supertax between 1924 and 1929; the number of persons with incomes over £2,000 increased from 95,296 to 108,891, and their incomes from £549 millions to £593 millions. Professor A. L. Bowley estimated that in 1910 1·1 per cent of the receivers of income took 30 per cent of the national income and 98·9 per cent had the rest; in 1929, according to Colin Clark, 10 per cent of all income

[1] This subject is more fully discussed in Chapter 9, section 3.
[2] A. M. Carr-Saunders and D. Caradog Jones, *Social Structure of England and Wales* (2nd ed., Oxford, 1937), pp. 84–91 (the best brief introduction to the subject of the national income); A. L. Bowley, *Studies in the National Income* (Cambridge, 1942), p. 80. Colin Clark, *National Income and Outlay* (London, 1937), pp. 88–9, gives rather higher figures.
[3] C. Clark, *National Income and Outlay*, p. 94.

receivers took 42 per cent of the national income and 1·5 per cent, with 'four-figure incomes', took 23 per cent.[1]

The national wealth of the United Kingdom in 1914 was £14,319 millions. In 1919 there were 322 persons with fortunes of over £1 million. At that time two-thirds of the wealth was in the hands of 2·5 per cent of the occupied persons over twenty, and one-third in the possession of about $2\frac{1}{2}$ persons per 1000 of the occupied population. The unevenness in the distribution of capital was, however, changing. G. W. Daniels and H. Campion (of Manchester University) estimated that the proportion of persons over 25 with capital of £100 or less declined between 1911–13 and 1924–30 from 88·3 per cent to 78·6 per cent; the proportion owning between £100 and £1000 rose from 8·7 per cent to 15·5 per cent, and there were slight increases in the proportion of people with capital above £1000; however, three-quarters of the people over 25 owned little more than 5 per cent of the capital.[2]

4. EDUCATION: THE CAUTIOUS APPROACH

The same impression of stability, of cautious change and continuing inequality of opportunity and achievement, was given by the system of education. There was an educational ladder, but it was narrow. In 1923–24 only 12·6 per cent of all children leaving elementary schools continued in full-time education.

The waste of ability which this involved for the nation was demonstrated in a pioneer work published in 1926, Kenneth Lindsay's *Social Progress and Educational Waste*. Lindsay's conclusion was that 'proved ability to the extent of at least 40 per cent of the nation's children is at present being denied expression'.[3] Furthermore, he showed that inequality in educational opportunities varied from town to town, and between town and country, between prosperous and poor districts. 'One school in Lewisham wins as many scholarships as the whole of Bermondsey put together, seven poor London boroughs have an average of 1·3 scholars [those with free places] per 1000 children . . . as against 5·3 in seven better-placed London boroughs'.[4] In Merseyside the same variations occurred: in 1927–30 11 per cent of all elementary

---

[1] A. M. Carr-Saunders, *Social Structure* (2nd ed.), pp. 95–8; C. Clark, *National Income and Outlay*, p. 110. *Statistical Abstract of U.K., 1938*, p. 218; R. H. Tawney, *Equality* (London, 1931; 4th ed., 1952), pp. 56–69.

[2] A. M. Carr-Saunders, *Social Structure* (2nd ed.), pp. 102–11.

[3] Kenneth Lindsay, *Social Progress and Educational Waste* (London, 1926), p. 23.

[4] Ibid., p. 8.

school children in Liverpool and Birkenhead went on to secondary schools, 15 per cent in Bootle and 25 per cent in Wallasey.[1] In the universities the odds against an elementary school child gaining a place were, of course, even greater, in spite of the 200 'state scholarships' first offered in 1920 (during H. A. L. Fisher's tenure of office at the Board of Education) and the aid given by Local Education Authorities to students going to the universities.[2] In 1921–24, out of 201,649 pupils leaving the secondary schools of England, about 9750 are estimated to have gone to a university, or 4·6 per cent; since 62 per cent of these had come originally from elementary schools, it was calculated that the number of ex-elementary school boys and girls reaching a university was 4·2 per 1000. For 1920–21 Lindsay calculates that 38 per cent of new students admitted to universities in England had been in elementary schools, 87·4 per cent in Wales, 37·1 per cent in Scotland (or 51 per cent if Edinburgh University was excluded). By 1931–34, out of 225,948 pupils leaving the secondary schools of England, about 14,450, or 6·4 per cent, went to a university; at the universities they formed one-third of all entrants. The proportion of ex-elementary school children reaching the university remained 0·4 per cent.[3]

None the less, the opportunities for secondary education for all children were improved. The number of public secondary schools of the grammar-school type increased from 1205 in 1920 to 1307 in 1931 (England and Wales), and the number of junior technical schools from 84 to 177. The number of free places increased from 113,405 (or 34·2 per cent of all places in the public secondary schools) in 1922 to 131,309 (37 per cent) in 1927–28 and 178,204 (42·7 per cent) in 1930.[4] A child's chance of getting a free place rose from one in 40 in 1914 to one in 21 in 1921 and 1 in 13 in 1929.[5]

In adult education there was a gradual advance. In the twenties the number of three-year tutorial classes of the Workers' Educa-

[1] D. Caradog Jones, *Social Survey of Merseyside*, III, 165.

[2] John Graves, *Policy and Progress in Secondary Education, 1902–1942* (London, 1943), p. 117. The state scholarships were discontinued in 1922–23 for economy reasons, restored by the Labour government in 1924 and increased to 300 in 1930.

[3] A. M. Carr-Saunders, *Social Structure* (1st ed.), pp. 127–8; *ibid.* (2nd ed.), p. 122; K. Lindsay, p. 193.

[4] J. Graves, pp. 146–7.

[5] G. A. N. Lowndes, *Silent Social Revolution: an account of the Expansion of Public Education in England and Wales, 1895–1935* (Oxford, 1937), pp. 113, 115, 119. See also A. M. Carr-Saunders, *Social Structure* (1st ed., 1927), p. 125 (see also diagram on p. 120). For the history of public education in one city between the wars see Asa Briggs, *History of Birmingham*, II, 237 ff.

tional Association nearly doubled and the number of students in adult education courses of all sorts and sponsors increased about 50 per cent (to a total of over 30,000 in 1930). In the tutorial classes (which combined lectures with class discussion) the interest shifted from economics, the subject of greatest appeal before the war, to literature, philosophy, history, sociology, art and music, natural science, though economics remained well represented.[1]

Such moderate progress was in contrast with the high hopes which had been cherished at the war's end. H. A. L. Fisher, Lloyd George's happy choice as President of the Board of Education—no politician but a distinguished teacher of history at Oxford and vice-chancellor of the University of Sheffield—seized upon the opportunity of a time of reconstruction to make plans for a great advance in public education. The Education Act of 1918—the Fisher Act, as it was called—was the result. It gave increased powers to the Board of Education and to the Local Education Authorities (the counties and county boroughs) to develop a comprehensive system of public education from the nursery school to the evening class. It increased the Board's financial aid to at least 50 per cent of the local authorities' expenditures. It outlawed the part-timers and the early-leavers: the exemptions to compulsory schooling for all children under 14 were withdrawn (before the war 40 per cent of the children left school before 14). And it provided, in default of the universal raising of the school-leaving age to 15 (which L.E.A.'s were permitted to do), that day continuation schools should be established which youths between 14 and 16 must attend, if they had finished their full-time schooling, for the equivalent of one day a week (320 hours a year).

The results of the Fisher Act were disappointing. It was a victim of the Geddes axe and the spirit of economy which dominated government after 1921. In particular, the continuation schools were stifled from the start. Their number had increased, and in London and several other places attendance at them was compulsory; but after 1921 compulsory attendance was abandoned (except in Rugby) and their numbers declined.[2]

New hopes for improving public education were raised by the Hadow report in 1926. C. P. Trevelyan, the Minister of Educa-

[1] J. Dover Wilson (ed.), *Schools of England* (London, 1928), pp. 279–87; *Report of the Board of Education, 1922–23*, pp. 102–9 (a brief history of adult education); *ibid., 1924–25*, pp. 127–8; *ibid., 1931*, pp. 169–70; A. Mansbridge, *Trodden Road* (London, 1940); Mary Stocks, *The W.E.A.: the first fifty years* (London, 1953).
[2] J. Graves, pp. 103–12, 118; H. A. L. Fisher, *An Unfinished Autobiography* (Oxford, 1940), pp. 103–9.

tion in the Labour government of 1924, attempted to advance the ideal of 'secondary education for all' (the title of a party pamphlet by R. H. Tawney) by referring to the consultative committee of the Board of Education, whose chairman was Sir Henry Hadow, the question of the best courses of study for children remaining in school till the age of 15. The report, when it appeared, set in train large changes in the elementary schools. Its first recommendation was the 'break at eleven'; that at 11 all children should be sorted out and sent either to the existing secondary and technical schools or to a new type of school to be called a 'modern school' at which they would stay until 15—for the raising of the school-leaving age to 15 was another strong recommendation. It did not balk at the reorganisation of the elementary schools which this would involve; but it insisted that children after 11 should be in separate schools—or at least in senior classes separated as far as possible from the rest—with a curriculum suited to their needs. Only thus, it argued, could there be any remedy for the waste of talent which the nation suffered from the fact that the great majority of all children ended their schooling at 14 and were lumped together in a single kind of school, regardless of their talents, in their last, critical years before they became 14.[1]

There ensued—or rather continued, for it had already begun— the long process of 'reorganisation'—a magic word among school authorities for the next decade. It was no easy task for counties and cities to reorganise their elementary schools so that the children above 11 would be taken from them and sent to other schools—either newly built or adapted from elementary schools whose younger children were now concentrated in the surviving elementary (or 'primary') schools. It was not easy to plan only for groups of schools, as the authorities were instructed to do. In rural districts particularly, the closing of a school, or the sending of older children to a new modern school, was often resented. And the handicap of 'dual control' was always present: many of the elementary schools were 'voluntary schools', provided and partly controlled by the churches. Yet reorganisation went forward. By 1931 one-third of all children over 11 in elementary schools were in reorganised departments.[2]

The raising of the school-leaving age to 15 had to wait much longer. The Labour government announced in July 1929 that

[1] Board of Education, Consultative Committee, *Report on the Education of the Adolescent* (1926).
[2] J. Graves, pp. 129, 131. For comment on this report, *ibid.*, pp. 119–28; H. C. Barnard, *Short History of English Education* (London, 1947), pp. 273–9.

the deed would be done in April, 1931 and later introduced a bill for the purpose, coupled with increased grants to the L.E.A.'s and the provision of maintenance allowances for the children affected. The churches protested that they could not meet the cost of enlarging or rebuilding the voluntary schools which this would necessitate; the government promised help, but went ahead with the bill without making any provision to give it. A Labour member, John Scurr, a Roman Catholic, therefore moved to amend the bill by delaying its operation until building grants for the voluntary schools were authorised. This passed, rendering the bill nugatory; and the Lords rejected it altogether.

Two other changes deserve mention. The School Certificate examinations were brought under the Board of Education in 1918.[1] Teachers' salaries were standardised by the 'Burnham Scales' drawn up by a committee appointed by Fisher with Lord Burnham (owner of the *Daily Telegraph*) as chairman.[2]

In the universities there were greater changes. The number of their students increased immediately after the war, swollen by the ex-servicemen who were aided by government grants; in all, 26,000 students received grants, of whom 6 per cent were over thirty, and 12 per cent were married—circumstances which posed new problems for the academic authorities.[3] By 1925–26 the number of students at the English universities had settled down to 29,275 (20,899 men, 8376 women). London was the largest in numbers, with 8797 students; Cambridge had 5203 (including 475 women) and Oxford 4353 (including 820 women). The others ranged in size from Manchester with 1748 students, to Reading with 558.[4] The Scottish universities had 10,090 students in 1924–25, the federal University of Wales 2750.[5] It was estimated that the number of students per 10,000 of population was 7·8 in England, 21·1 in Scotland and 12 in Wales.[6] Reading received its charter as a university in 1926. University colleges were opened at Swansea (part of the University of Wales) in 1920, at Leicester in 1921 and at Hull in 1928. The administration of the University of London was centralised in 1929 under

[1] J. Graves, pp. 104–7, 151–2.
[2] The scales are given in the annual reports of the Board of Education, 1919–25, and in the Board's *Report of the Standing Joint Committee . . . on a Provisional Minimum Scale of Salaries for Teachers . . .* (Cmd. 443; 1919). See also J. Graves, pp. 101–3; H. C. Barnard, pp. 302–3; A. M. Carr-Saunders and P. A. Wilson, *The Professions* (Oxford, 1933), pp. 260–1.
[3] *Report of the Board of Education, 1921–22*, pp. 5–11.
[4] J. Dover Wilson, *Schools of England*, p. 359.   [5] *Whitaker's Almanack, 1929.*
[6] J. Dover Wilson, *Schools of England*, p. 343.

new statutes promulgated under an act of 1926; the building of the Senate House in Bloomsbury symbolised the change.[1] Several other universities added to their buildings, including Bristol, whose stately tower and buildings at the head of Park Street, in the perpendicular style, were opened by the King in 1925. Nottingham University College moved to its new site outside the town in 1928.

At Oxford, various weighty matters disturbed the meditations of the dons. The admission of women to membership of the university, and to degrees, was conceded in 1920.[2] (At Cambridge, women had to wait another quarter-century for this privilege.) Oxford was more concerned over the abolition of Greek as a compulsory subject for matriculation, another shattering change of 1920. A new Honours School, combining politics, philosophy and economics (P.P.E., or 'Modern Greats') was established in 1921. Another subject of dispute in the senior common rooms was the report of the Royal Commission on Oxford and Cambridge Universities, issued in 1922. The commission recommended the strengthening of the university and its faculties (as opposed to the colleges), the abolition of non-teaching fellowships (except for research fellowships), compulsory retirement at sixty-five and an adequate pension system, an increase in salaries, and an improvement in the allegedly wasteful catering in the college kitchens. These changes (except perhaps the last) were eventually made.[3] At the same time, in 1920, Oxford and Cambridge accepted a share in the grant made annually by the state to assist the universities of Great Britain. The grant was distributed by the University Grants Committee (created in 1911) and after the war was at first £1 million.

5. EAT, DRINK AND BE MERRY

Change of a more sensational sort seemed to mark the manners and morals of the younger generation in society. The postwar years were enlivened by the 'bright young things', whose gay parties and general lack of inhibitions created a legend of the 'roaring twenties' which, for the overwhelming majority of the

[1] W. H. Beveridge, *Power and Influence* (London, 1953), describes the intra-mural battle for the Bloomsbury site (won only through the munificence of the Rockefeller Foundation) and the growth of the London School of Economics after 1919 (chapters 8, 9); see also Lord Macmillan, *Man of Law's Tale* (London, 1952).
[2] See Annie M. A. H. Rogers, *Degrees by Degrees* (Oxford, 1938).
[3] Royal Commission on Oxford and Cambridge Universities, *Report* (Cmd. 1588; 1922); Albert Mansbridge, *Older Universities of England: Oxford and Cambridge* (London, 1923), pp. 196–216.

nation, had no foundation in fact. In so far as there was a spirit of emancipation which affected the conduct of the young, and particularly of young women, it was a product of the feminist movement of the prewar years and of the war itself, which had thrust women into new occupations, including many previously reserved to men. In addition, the toll of war had upset the balance of the sexes. After the war many women could not hope for marriage and many men could not afford it. ·This conjunction of circumstances affected manners—and women's fashions—so that for a time femininity and the maternal instincts were kept under heavy disguise.[1]

Women's fashions in the twenties emphasised this spirit of emancipation and the domination of youth. One writer has described the style as the 'schoolboy shape', placing it in the years 1919–24: dresses were long and cylindrical, with a very low waistline or none at all; thin, sloping shoulders, a flat chest, an entire absence of curves contrived to minimise the normal attributes of the feminine form and to emphasise instead the 'juvenile shape of body'. The habit of wearing the hair cut short, in a bob or Eton crop, and the use of face-powder and make-up in small amounts (lipstick, rouge, mascara and coloured finger nails were seldom seen in good society in the twenties) assisted the illusion. Hats diminished in size until for a time only the close-fitting 'cloche' survived.

Gradually, the cultivation of feminine charms and a more heterosexual standard of taste returned. The historian of women's clothing ascribes to the years 1925–28 the style of the 'schoolgirl shape'. Skirts, which had become shorter and shorter, until in 1926 they were above the knee, became longer once more. Jerseys and jumpers became popular. By 1929 the female body began to emerge from disguise; in the 1930's fashions, though undistinguished, did their best to flatter the figure. What was not lost was the new freedom conferred by a relaxing of older conventions and a use of new materials, above all rayon. Underwear, both for women and men, became thinner, lighter, briefer: in 1928 a woman's entire clothing might weigh no more than one pound. The slip replaced the petticoat. The use of an elastic belt in place of a corset was a boon of the late twenties; the 'two-way stretch' belt first appeared in 1932. Rayon stockings, lighter in shade and weight than the older wool or cotton stockings, were an

---

[1] See the shrewd observations in C. Willett Cunnington, *English Women's Clothing in the Present Century* (London, 1952), pp. 146–7.

important innovation of the early twenties. Sportswear became more rational, but hardly until the beginning of the thirties: shorts for 'hikers' and more elegant shorts for tennis and for the beach, beach pyjamas and slacks for holiday wear began to be popular. Swimming suits were conservative during the twenties; one-piece suits with skirt and knickers reaching towards the knee. The popularity of sunbathing led to suits of greater brevity, either one-piece suits with bare back or two-piece suits which left back and midriff bare—again a fashion beginning with the early thirties.[1]

The new styles and materials assisted another change. The war had blurred class distinctions; and now dress tended to minimise rather than emphasise such distinctions.[2]

Men's fashions benefited, though to less degree, from new materials and conventions. Lighter lounge suits, the soft felt hat, coloured shirts with soft collars became common for everyday wear, outside the higher reaches of business and the civil service. Oxford supposedly contributed the wide-bottomed grey flannel trousers, the 'Oxford bags', which affected the width of trousers generally; brown or suede shoes, brighter ties, and bright knitted pullovers came into common use.[3]

Typical of the time was the 'flapper', the independent, unchaperoned young woman, often supporting herself by a job as secretary, reporter, or salesgirl in a fashionable shop. It was taken for granted that she smoked cigarettes, and in public; she had no reluctance to enter a pub for a drink; she would not refuse a cocktail—more and more the fashionable drink and the fashionable occasion for a party. Her talk was in clichés; cockney accent and phrases were affected on occasion. Or her speech hinted at a lack of reticence about sex which might or might not be true in practice: 'Hello, darling, how's your sex-life?' 'Lousy, darling, how's yours?' was recorded as a fashionable exchange of greetings in 1928.[4]

For science had come to release the younger generation from the old restraints both of morality and of physiology. Dr. Marie

[1] C. Willett Cunnington, *English Women's Clothing*, chapters 1, 5–7 (an admirable work, fully illustrated); C. Willett and Phillis Cunnington, *The History of Underclothes* (London, 1951), pp. 234–6, 241 ff. See also Robert Graves and Alan Hodge, *The Long Week-end: a Social History of Great Britain, 1918–1939* (London, 1940), pp. 39–41, 178–9, 228–30 (a very readable and generally reliable guide to the manners, morals and crazes of the inter-war years).
[2] C. W. Cunnington, *English Women's Clothing*, p. 19.
[3] C. W. and P. Cunnington, *History of Underclothes*, pp. 237–41; R. Graves and A. Hodge, *Long Week-end*, pp. 40, 122, 179.
[4] Nerina Shute, *We Mixed Our Drinks* (London, [1945]), p. 11.

Stopes was blamed for spreading knowledge of contraception in her book, *Married Love*, and in her lectures, beginning with a public meeting in the Queen's Hall, London, in 1922. Those who wished to use contraceptives had on their side the works of Edward Carpenter and Havelock Ellis and Sigmund Freud on the psychology of sex—works, indeed, published in England before the war but only accepted widely after it. Psycho-analysis became a craze as well as a serious study. Nina Blount, in Waugh's *Vile Bodies*, gaily deceives her father into thinking Adam her husband on their Christmas visit (Waugh's satire, brittle, sadistic, and not a little 'bogus'—a favourite word of his characters—attempts more strenuously than other novels of the period to represent the life of the smart young set; just as Noel Coward's plays did in a lighter manner).[1] People were continuously 'popping' in and out of bed with new bed-fellows, though not, apparently, getting much pleasure out of it:

> Bestows one final patronizing kiss,
> And gropes his way, finding the stairs unlit . . .
> T. S. Eliot, *The Waste Land*

The number of divorces increased. The average number per year in Great Britain had been 823 in 1910–12, but was 3619 in 1920–22 and 4249 in 1930–32. The highest number in any year in the twenties was 4522 in 1928.[2] Since desertion or adultery were the only permissible causes, the necessary 'adultery' was usually provided by the husband, for whom the lawyer arranged a blameless night in a hotel with 'a woman unknown'. The newspapers printed the more salacious items of evidence recorded in the court cases, until restrained by the Judicial Proceedings (Regulation of Reports) Act of 1926.[3]

Entertainment the bright young things found in a hectic round of parties, visits to the night clubs (never for long discouraged by the frequent police raids), gate-crashing other peoples' parties, speeding hither and yon in fast sporting cars.

'Oh, Nina, *what a lot of parties.*'
(. . . Masked parties, savage parties, Victorian parties, Greek parties, Wild West parties, Russian parties, Circus parties, parties where one had to dress as somebody else, almost naked parties in St. John's

---

[1] Compare the conduct of Lucy Tantamount in Aldous Huxley's *Point Counter Point*, and of Gumbril and Rosie in *Antic Hay*.
[2] *Statistical Abstract of U.K.*, 1932, p. 23.
[3] With this account of the 'new morality', compare R. Graves and A. Hodge, *Long Week-end*, pp. 100–12.

Wood, parties in flats and studios and houses and ships and hotels and night clubs, in windmills and swimming baths . . .)[1]

Jazz provided the music, the rhythm and the tempo, though this changed frequently. At first the tango, fox-trot and waltz predominated; then the 'shimmy', then the slower Blues, then the Charleston and Black Bottom, and finally the one-step and the waltz once again. Restaurants began providing dance-floors, the Savoy being the first to do so. The even more limited circle of the pseudo-Bohemians indulged in wilder parties in drabber settings— the so-called studios with their flowers in bare earthenware vases, the cushions on the floor, the divans, the drinking of pale tea out of black china cups or whisky glasses. To the Bohemians at home should perhaps be added those 'gone abroad', the expatriates in Paris, the Riviera, Mallorca, Spain, Italy.[2]

6. NEW STYLES, NEW THEMES

Symptoms of the same restlessness were the alarms and excursions of literature. At first the generation which had possessed the field before the war seemed still to be in control: Kipling, Shaw, H. G. Wells, Arnold Bennett, John Galsworthy, Robert Bridges, Joseph Conrad, John Masefield, W. B. Yeats, E. M. Forster. None of these, however, increased his reputation after the war, except Yeats, Forster, Shaw (with *St. Joan*, produced in 1924) and Galsworthy, whose *Forsyte Saga* (1922) enjoyed a large popularity in the twenties, when an examination of the Victorians and their virtues, both sham and solid, was sure of a favourable hearing.[3] The great output of war novels came much later, at the very end of the twenties, though anticipated by a few books like C. E. Montague's *Disenchantment* (1922) and R. H. Mottram's *Spanish Farm* (1924). To these might be added T. E. Lawrence's *Revolt in the Desert* (1927), an abridgement of his *Seven Pillars of Wisdom*, published privately in 1926 (the public edition was published after his death). Lawrence, a mysterious and frustrated figure, had withdrawn from public life, changed his name, and entered the Royal Air Force in the ranks; he was killed while motor-cycling, soon after he had left the service, in 1935.[4]

[1] Evelyn Waugh, *Vile Bodies* (London, 1930), p. 118.
[2] For further pictures of the bright young things, see R. Graves and A. Hodge, *Long Week-end*; Nerina Shute, *We Mixed our Drinks*; D. Goldring, *Odd Man Out* (London, 1935); Hubert Nicholson, *Half my Days and Nights* (London, 1941). For the expatriates and Bohemians, see also D. Goldring, *Nineteen-Twenties* (London, 1945).
[3] Thanks partly to Lytton Strachey's *Eminent Victorians* (1918), and *Queen Victoria* (1921). [4] *D.N.B., Supplement, 1931–40.*

At quite the other end of the literary scale were the writers who catered to the bookstall trade, such as P. G. Wodehouse, the humorist, creator of Jeeves; and Edgar Wallace, fast-living and prodigious creator of plays and thrillers, who published twenty-eight novels in the last six years of his life (1927–32). The craze for detective stories for which dons and statesmen took pride in confessing a taste began in the later twenties.[1]

Much more important, however, were those writers who expressed, in one way or another, a new spirit and made the twenties an extraordinarily vital age in literature, full of the zest for experiment—in marked contrast to the drabness of the politics of the decade. The new literary magazines, the *Criterion*, started in 1922, the *Adelphi* (1923), *Life and Letters* (1928) encouraged much new writing. The new spirit was not entirely a matter of generations, since the leading figures were drawn, some from among those with reputations begun before the war, some from the 'lost generation', and some from those too young to have taken part in the war. All were in some degree in revolt against previous standards, ideas, styles; and particularly against a precious, artificial and ornate style of writing.[2]   Some writers showed a morbid attraction toward violence and sudden death, and a fascination and simultaneous repulsion concerning sex. D. H. Lawrence, unique in his glorification of passionate love, was one of the great figures of the twenties, but never quite regained the power of *Sons and Lovers*, which had appeared as far back as 1913.

Aldous Huxley is perhaps the most representative of the new tendencies, and his novels of the twenties, culminating in *Point Counter Point* (1928), enjoyed great acclaim. Widely travelled, widely read in several languages, pre-occupied with physiology, disease, mortality, putting into the mouths of his characters learned discourses on philosophy—here was a writer to charm and to dazzle; and the interspersing of fashionable seductions amid other episodes kept his novels congruent with the mood of the times. *Point Counter Point* was supposed to contain characters based on living persons—D. H. Lawrence, Augustus John; and in Spandrell's death it combines the violence and the sophistication of the intellectual, as Spandrell waits for death while listening to Beethoven's *heilige Dankgesang in der lydischen Tonart* on the gramophone.

---

[1] R. Graves, and A. Hodge, *Long Week-end*, pp. 50–5, 148, 216–19, 301.
[2] Cyril Connolly, *Enemies of Promise* (London, 1938; revised edition, New York, 1948), p. 58 and *passim*.

Yet Huxley never obtained the dubious flattery of imitation to the extent that T. S. Eliot did, though no one could be harder to imitate than this poet and critic who developed the new and highly intellectual style of poetry and criticism which was dominant throughout the interwar years. *The Waste Land* (1923), from its title and its extraordinary manner, seemed to express the entire postwar age. Symbolic, learned, with its sudden changes of rhythm and its bewildering elisions of thought, it represented an entirely new technique of poetry, and a new content. *The Waste Land*, says Edmund Wilson, expresses 'the terrible dreariness of the great modern cities . . . nameless millions performing barren office routines, wearing down their souls in interminable labours of which the products never bring them profit—people whose pleasures are so sordid and so feeble that they seem almost sadder than their pains. And this Waste Land has another aspect: it is a place not merely of desolation, but of anarchy and doubt. In our post-war world of shattered institutions, strained nerves and bankrupt ideals, life no longer seems serious or coherent . . .'[1]

> . . . bones cast in a little low dry garret,
> Rattled by the rat's foot only, year to year.

Others, in different ways, used the novel to represent life by means of symbolism. James Joyce produced the prose equivalent of *The Waste Land* in what has been called 'the outstanding period-book of the twenties', *Ulysses*, published in Paris in 1922 and banned as obscene in Britain: the experiences in a single day in Dublin in 1904 of Leopold Bloom, his doings and his thoughts. The 'stream of consciousness' technique was also used by Virginia Woolf in *Mrs. Dalloway* (1925) and *To the Lighthouse* (1927). Virginia Woolf was the reigning deity of Bloomsbury in the 1920's before its degeneration into the haven of the pseudo-intellectuals and the arty-crafty crowd.[2]

Among artists there was a contest between the traditionalists who continued to dominate the Royal Academy and the *avant-garde* which believed in modern art and works of abstraction. On

---

[1] Edmund Wilson, *Axel's Castle* (New York, 1931), p. 106; see the entire essay, pp. 93 ff. See also C. M. Bowra's essay in his *Creative Experiment* (London, 1949), pp. 159–88.

[2] For this real Bloomsbury and some of its leaders, including Virginia Woolf, Roger Fry, the art critic, and Lytton Strachey, see Osbert Sitwell, *Laughter in the Next Room* (London, 1949), pp. 17 ff. Cf. M. A. Hamilton, *Remembering my Good Friends*, pp. 137–43; J. M. Keynes, *Two Memoirs* (London, 1949), essay on 'Early Beliefs'; R. F. Harrod, *Life of John Maynard Keynes* (London, 1951), chapter on 'Bloomsbury'; J. K. Johnstone, *The Bloomsbury Group* (London, 1954).

the one hand, popular interest in older works of art was stimulated by a series of special exhibitions held at Burlington House during the winter under the auspices of the Royal Academy, each more crowded than the last. It began with the exhibition of Sargent's portraits in 1926, soon after his death, and was followed by the exhibition of Flemish and Belgian art in 1927, Dutch art in 1929, and the exhibition of Italian art in 1930, which was visited by over half a million people. By contrast, interest in modern art was rekindled after the war by the exhibition of modern French art arranged by Osbert and Sacheverell Sitwell in London in August 1919. With its pictures by Matisse, Picasso, Derain, Modigliani and several others, this exhibition maddened the Philistines. Yet in time the popular taste was won round. Clive Bell's *Since Cézanne* (1922) made many converts. In 1923 came the gift of £50,000 by Samuel Courtauld for the purchase of nineteenth-century French paintings for the Tate Gallery; the first purchases included Renoir, Manet, Van Gogh. 'We are all converted', exclaimed a critic. Soon no would-be sophisticate could afford not to have at least one print of a Van Gogh or a Gauguin upon his walls. In sculpture, the work of Jacob Epstein struck the modern note, and at first provoked lovers of the conventional to tar-daubing expeditions against his works. His plaque to the memory of W. H. Hudson, unveiled by Baldwin in Hyde Park in 1925, represented a flight of birds and Rima, a crude, gaunt figure; many could see no beauty in it.[1] Another sculptor, Eric Gill, contributed to a minor but pleasing advance of the arts by the beautiful type-faces which he designed. The typography of books, newspapers and magazines improved greatly in the twenties, helped partly by the writings and friendships of Holbrook Jackson. 'Gill Sans' was adapted by the London and North Eastern Railway as the standard for its station signs and notices. *The Times* introduced its new type-face with a flourish on October 3, 1932.

In architecture the moderns made little headway in England in the twenties; their turn came rather in the thirties. There was much new building after the war, but mostly in traditional styles. Private houses in brick or stucco were nondescript, though some were Tudor in inspiration, others classical. Neat brickwork, clean rectangular lines, steel-framed windows graced the best of

---

[1] O. Sitwell, *Laughter in the Next Room*, pp. 148 ff., 331–48; R. Graves and A. Hodge, *Long Week-end*, pp. 131, 192–6; *Annual Register*, part ii (annual 'Retrospect of Literature, Science, and Art'); W. A. Propert, 'The Courtauld Gift to the National Gallery', *Contemporary Review*, 125 (1924), 72–7.

them; and larger houses, and buildings for branches of the banks, reflected the Queen Anne style developed by Sir Edwin Lutyens and others before the war. Lutyens' postwar designs included Britannic House, London (1929) and the cenotaph in Whitehall in 1924. Other London office buildings, such as Bush House, showed American influences in their stark lines and lack of ornament. The massive building designed by Charles Holden for the headquarters of the Underground Railways (1929) made effective use of the 'step-back' on a constricted site. In the provinces a number of civic centres were planned, following the example of Cardiff, which had built most of its new centre before the war. Some new churches made effective use of brick in a Romanesque style. One of the largest rebuildings was the most deplored: the rebuilding of Regent Street in a jumble of vaguely classical styles.

Music was considered by some to be in a state of decline. Some composers were neo-classical in style, others moulded form to pictorial effect, such as Ralph Vaughan Williams. Interest in Delius, who by birth was British, was created by Sir Thomas Beecham, the most tempestuous of the many notable conductors of the times. The B.B.C. programmes tremendously enlarged the musical public. For the more eclectic the gramophone was a godsend. Concert-going increased; in London the 'Proms' were at the height of their popularity under Sir Henry Wood's conductorship; and symphonic music in general was put on a less precarious basis with the organisation of the B.B.C. orchestra in 1930. And not all musical enjoyment was passive: local Bach choirs, glee clubs and amateur operatic companies flourished as never before.

7. THE ADVANCEMENT AND DISPERSAL OF KNOWLEDGE

If in society a new generation seemed to be breaking away from the old, in the world of learning the older traditions, the older generation of scientists and historians and classical scholars still held sway, though their ideas, at least in the natural sciences, demanded new revolutions of thought. This was particularly true of the physicists. The mechanistic universe of Newton was, after two hundred years, replaced by one explained by such terms as indeterminacy, relativity, disconnected space. The law of causation was dethroned; there were laws of probability only. The new ideas were gathering strength from the very beginning of the century: from the work of Sir Ernest Rutherford, particularly at

Manchester University, on the disintegration of radio-active bodies and on the nuclear theory of the atom. There followed Rutherford's experiments to split the atom: his paper describing 'the first artificial transmutation of matter' was published in the *Philosophical Magazine* in June 1919.[1] Many others had contributed to the knowledge of the atom: among Rutherford's contemporaries in England Sir J. J. Thomson, Frederick Soddy, H. G. J. Moseley, Geiger.

All this, however, would have made much less impression than it did upon the public but for the extraordinary interest aroused by Einstein's theories. Einstein, as early as 1905, had added the fourth dimension, space-time as one and the same thing, making, with the other three dimensions, the four-dimensional continuum of the universe. His second theory, elaborated by 1917, explained certain observed deflections of light by assuming that space was warped, and took on a non-Euclidean character, in a gravitational field of force. This mathematical explanation was given dramatic proof by the results of the observations of the total eclipse of the sun on May 29, 1919; the verification of Einstein's prediction was announced, in the words of A. N. Whitehead, the philosopher, in an 'atmosphere of tense interest [which] was exactly that of a Greek drama',[2] by the Astronomer Royal at a meeting of the Royal Society in November. The theory of 'relativity' was then generally accepted and gradually digested: the universe is 'a number of different bodies all moving relatively to one another'.[3]

Equally disturbing to older ideas were the advances in biology. The biologists, ignoring the boundaries between their discipline and physics and chemistry, were learning more about growth, about the ductless glands, about genetics, about sex. Each of these studies had a popular application: rejuvenation, eugenics, advances in the study of cancer. Experiments with embryos and living tissues suggested the rather awesome, sanitary, *Brave New World* of Aldous Huxley's novel (1932); they suggested a society of human beings propagated by ectogenesis—the vision of J. B. S. Haldane in *Daedalus, or Science and the Future* (1924). Haldane, in *Possible Worlds* (1928) and Julian Huxley in *Essays of a Biologist*

[1] D.N.B. *Supplement, 1931–40*, s.v. Ernest Rutherford (1871–1937; created Baron Rutherford in 1931).

[2] A. N. Whitehead, *Science and the Modern World* (N.Y., 1925), p. 15.

[3] *Annual Register, 1919*, part ii, p. 49. See also: A. N. Whitehead, *op. cit.*; *D.N.B., 1931–40*, s.v. Ernest Rutherford and J. J. Thomson; Sir James Jeans, *The Mysterious Universe* (New York, 1930); A. S. Russell, 'The Atom', *Quarterly Review*, 241: 311–28 (1924); A. S. Eddington, 'Einstein on time and space', *ibid.*, 233: 226–36 (1920).

(1923) and *Essays in Popular Science* (1926) did much to spread a knowledge of the advances in the biological sciences among the educated public.[1]

Another field in which the layman was given guidance in the understanding of new discoveries was astronomy. He learned that there were countless universes, that 'hundreds of thousands of earths could be packed inside each [star]',[2] that distances in the universe must be measured by light-years. The best-known astronomers were Sir James Jeans and Sir Arthur Eddington: the former for *The Universe around us* (1929) and *The Mysterious Universe* (1930), the latter for *The Expanding Universe* (1933).

Against the primacy of philosophy the newer disciplines could make little headway. Psychology was hardly recognised at the universities as a subject for serious study, and its principal British expositor, William McDougall, resided in the United States after 1920. The pioneer sociologist, L. T. Hobhouse (1864–1929), a philosopher by origin, held the chair of sociology at London until his death; his *Social Development* (1924) was a successor to his work on *Social Evolution* published before the war. A new school of anthropologists was trained at London University by Bronislaw Malinowski and C. G. Seligman. Malinowski's work was more widely known to the general public because of its compatibility with the new morality; for his studies of the sexual life of the Trobriand islanders (*Sexual Life of Savages in North-Western Melanesia*, 1929) demonstrated the conventional basis of any particular code of behaviour.

Never, perhaps, could a smattering of learning be more easily gained by the man in the street. The publication of the *Listener*, beginning in 1929, made broadcast talks available in permanent form. The same year saw the appearance of a new edition of the *Encyclopædia Britannica*, the fourteenth, by some rated below its predecessors, but widely marketed. *Discovery*, a monthly magazine describing in popular but scholarly terms the recent advances not only in the natural sciences but also in archæology, history, economics, politics, first appeared in 1920. A little later, Benn, the publisher, began issuing a series of sixpenny books by scholarly authors which covered a good deal of the same ground. An earlier and not much more expensive venture was that of the

---

[1] Advances in the natural sciences, and the more important works of learning and literature, are described each year in the *Annual Register*, part ii, 'Retrospect of Literature, Science, and Art'. See also J. Arthur Thomson, 'The new Biology', *Quarterly Review*, 240: 215–45 (1923). See also J. G. Crowther, *British Scientists of the Twentieth Century* (London, 1952).

[2] J. Jeans, *Mysterious Universe*, p. 1.

house of Kegan Paul, Trench, Trubner and Company; their 'Today and Tomorrow series', beginning in 1924, had a penchant for Greek titles with an explanatory sub-title: Haldane's *Daedalus*, Bertrand Russell's *Icarus, or the Future of Science*, C. E. M. Joad's *Thrasymachus, or the Future of Morals*. H. G. Wells tried to do the same for history in his *Outline of History* (1920), an essay in universal history, which devoted much space to the origins of the world and of life and to prehistoric cultures. Historical perspective was perhaps also improved by the discovery, in November, 1922, of the tomb of King Tut-ankh-Amen at Thebes by Howard Carter, the archæologist, and Lord Carnarvon. The richness and beauty of the treasures in this tomb, and the dramatic circumstances of its discovery, created a sensation; King Tut became a popular hero, and the Egyptian motif a popular craze.

8. THE CHURCH AND THE CHURCHES

The war increased the difficulties which the churches had been facing long before it began. Church attendance had been declining, and the claims of religion had been challenged by the advance of scientific knowledge and the secularisation of thought. In the Church of England Modernism had grown, in response to the challenge of scientific ideas and biblical criticism; man was made the measure of all things, and Christ accepted as God's son only 'in a *moral* sense'. The high-water mark of the Modernist movement was a conference of Modern Churchmen held at Girton College, Cambridge, in 1921. Some of the addresses given caused an outcry in church circles, and mutterings of prosecutions for heresy; one of the leaders, Dr. H. D. A. Major, principal of Ripon Hall, Oxford and editor of the *Modern Churchman*, was then and for long after a target for attack. Another Modernist, E. W. Barnes, a stout defender of evolution, was, however, made Bishop of Birmingham in 1924. But the foundations of Modernism had been undermined: by the new uncertainties of the scientists, and by the blows which war and depression delivered to the ideas of liberalism in politics, to belief in reason and the perfectibility of man. In the middle twenties a counter-attack was launched, particularly in a collaborative work, *Essays Catholic and Critical* (1926), edited by E. G. Selwyn. A new dogmatism appeared, which poured scorn on the Modernists, liberals and humanists: though several survived.[1]

[1] Canon Roger Lloyd, *The Church of England in the Twentieth Century, II, 1919–1939* (London, 1950), pp. 26–57, gives an account of Modernism and its decline which

The Church of England continued, indeed, to comprehend a diversity of opinions, from those of the Anglo-Catholics to the low churchmen and evangelicals. It continued to lose members to the Roman Catholic church, whose converts included writers such as G. K. Chesterton and Compton Mackenzie and such scholars as Christopher Dawson and Ronald Knox, son of a bishop. The Roman Catholic community in England was growing, according to one estimate, by some 11,000 a year.[1] Among the Free Churches in England the principal event was the reunion of the three largest Methodist churches in 1932. In Scotland an event of the first importance was the reunion of the Church of Scotland and the United Free Church in 1929, by which, in a moving ceremony in Edinburgh on October 1, almost the entire Presbyterian community was reunited. In Wales the (Anglican) Church of Wales was dis-established in 1920, as provided for by the Act of 1914.

The Church of England during these years was fortunate in its leaders. Randall Davidson, the Archbishop of Canterbury from 1903 to 1928, was an ecclesiastical statesman, gifted in reconciling differences, in restraining the extremists on either hand, and in viewing ecclesiastical matters with something of the layman's eye. His successor, Cosmo Gordon Lang, previously Archbishop of York, was a man of many parts, 'never fully reconciled to himself'.[2] Greater than either, and one of the greatest Englishmen of the quarter-century, was William Temple, successively Bishop of Manchester and Archbishop of York and then, all too briefly during the war, of Canterbury. A man of stout frame and tremendous energy, he always did the work of a score. Teacher, philosopher, preacher, leader of retreats, missioner to youth, pioneer of workmen's education, his greatest contribution to the life of his time was to put the Church in the very thick of the movement for a better social order, to convince the great mass of the people that there was someone in high places who felt their sufferings and applied the teachings of Christ to their problems.[3]

---

is decidedly hostile to Modernism and at variance with the spirit of fairness and enthusiasm which in general pervades this attractive book. It should be compared with G. S. Spinks (ed.), *Religion in Britain since 1900* (London, 1952), pp. 172, 179, 186, 188–93.

[1] G. S. Spinks, *Religion in Britain*, pp. 39, 82–3.

[2] G. S. Spinks, pp. 86, 88; cf. R. Lloyd, II, 12–14. See the lives of Davidson and Lang by G. K. A. Bell (1935) and J. G. Lockhart (1949). Lang resigned the archbishopric in 1942 and died in 1946.

[3] William Temple (1881–1944), son of Frederick Temple (1821–1902), Archbishop of Canterbury. Rugby and Balliol College, Oxford; president of Oxford Union, 1904. Fellow of Queen's College, Oxford, 1904–10; Headmaster of Repton, 1910–14. Rector of St. James, Piccadilly, 1914–18; canon of Westminster, 1918–21; Bishop of Manchester, 1921–29; Archbishop of York, 1929–42; Archbishop of Canterbury,

In parish church and in cathedral the lamp of the Church was kept burning. Lincoln Cathedral was rescued from collapse by an appeal which brought in £139,000; and other cathedrals, including St. Paul's, had to be saved from the erosion of time or the death-watch beetle. Old parish churches became the cathedrals of new dioceses and several new churches were built in suburbs and housing estates (as also by the Roman Catholics), usually of brick in severe but effective design. The first part of Sir Giles Gilbert Scott's modern Gothic cathedral at Liverpool was opened in 1924. The building of Guildford Cathedral was begun; the architect was Edward Maufe, one of the most gifted architects of the time, especially in the designing of churches. In the villages many parsons struggled with the indifference of the people and the economic problem of the upkeep of a large Victorian rectory and its grounds. Some stipends were as low as £240; 5000 out of 12,719 were less than £400 in 1939. The union of benefices was almost the only solution possible, and it was frequently taken.[1] In any case, the church's influence was less dependent than before on its services in church. Broadcasting of church services brought countless people within its range, on weekdays and on Sundays. The most popular services, perhaps, were those of the Rev. H. R. L. Sheppard ('Dick' Sheppard), vicar of St. Martin-in-the-Fields, whence the first broadcast of a service by the B.B.C. was made on Sunday, January 6, 1924.[2]

In its own freedom, despite the continuance of the establishment—and dis-establishment, though often talked of, was never a real issue—the Church of England experienced both gain and loss. In 1919 parliament enacted the Enabling Act, which sanctioned the establishment of the Church Assembly, a body including both clergy and laity, and empowered it to make regulations for the church, subject to the (usually formal) approval of parliament. Councils similar to the Church Assembly were established in the dioceses, giving the laity a greater share in the Church's affairs, both financial and spiritual. Temple and Sheppard, as leaders of the Life and Liberty movement started in 1917, had no little share in persuading the Church to make these changes.[3]

1942–44. President of the Workers' Educational Association, 1908–24. See F. A. Iremonger, *William Temple* (Oxford, 1948).

[1] R. Lloyd, II, 149, 184–219, 231 ff. An unfriendly view of the country clergy is given in J. W. Robertson Scott, *England's Green and Pleasant Land* (Penguin Books, 1947; first published 1925), pp. 61–79, 136–47.

[2] R. Lloyd, 15; G. S. Spinks, p. 125.

[3] R. Lloyd, 5–7, 18, 152–4; F. A. Iremonger, *William Temple*, pp. 220–81; G. K. A. Bell, *Randall Davidson, Archbishop of Canterbury* (Oxford, 1935), II, 956 ff.

On the other hand, the Church received a dramatic defeat in the debate in the House of Commons over the 'Revised' Prayer Book. The book stirred the ancient embers of Protestant passion; parts of it, particularly those sanctioning the reservation of the sacrament, were denounced as papistical. Yet many clergy had long been following, without the check of episcopal discipline, rituals not provided for in the Book of Common Prayer. The revised book, whose use was to be merely optional, was designed to remedy the flaw. Against it the evangelical party rallied, led by two members of the government, Joynson-Hicks and Sir Thomas Inskip; and after a debate which included several speeches of deep emotion the book was rejected by 238 votes to 205, on December 15, 1927. It was re-submitted next year, but with even less success. The new book was afterwards published, and its use authorised by Convocation, at the discretion of the bishops, 'during the present emergency'—an illegality for which the church was never brought to account.[1]

9. ALL SORTS AND CONDITIONS OF MEN

The population of Great Britain was increasing slowly during the twenties.[2]

	England and Wales	Scotland	Great Britain	Percentage increase over previous census
1911	36,071,000	4,761,000	40,831,000	10
1921	37,887,000	4,883,000	42,769,000	5
1931	39,952,000	4,843,000	44,795,000	5

The largest increases in the census of 1931 were in the Home Counties surrounding London (Middlesex, Surrey, Herts., Essex, Bucks.) ranging from Middlesex's increase of 30·8 per cent and Surrey's of 27 per cent to Buckinghamshire's of 15 per cent.[3] On the other hand twenty-five towns showed a decline in population, nine of these being in Lancashire and three in South Wales (Rhondda declined by 13·1 per cent, Merthyr Tydfil by 11·3 per cent).[4] The population of Wales declined by 3 per cent, that of Scotland by 0·8 per cent. Since Wales and Scotland had higher

[1] 211 H.C. Deb., 5 s., 2531 ff., 2567; G. K. A. Bell, *Randall Davidson*, II, 1325–60.
[2] A. M. Carr-Saunders, *Social Structure* (2nd ed.), p. 1.
[3] *Census of England and Wales, 1931; Prelim. Report*, p. 62.   [4] Ibid,. p. xix.

I

birth rates than England, their decline showed the results of migration of people to other parts of the kingdom and overseas; Scotland's loss by migration in the decade was 8 per cent. More than that, the census of 1931 demonstrated the drift of population from north to south: Yorkshire, Cheshire and the other northern counties lost on balance 443,000 persons, Wales 259,000, the Midlands 81,000 and the Eastern Counties 41,000; but south-eastern England gained 615,000 persons, and the west of England 32,000.[1]

There was another change: the great days of emigration were over. The total number of emigrants from Great Britain, 389,000 in 1913, declined from a postwar peak of 256,000 in 1923 to 92,000 in 1930; of these the great majority went to destinations within the empire, principally Canada, Australia, New Zealand, South Africa, but were balanced by the return of emigrants, whether from disappointment or home-sickness, so that net emigration to empire countries averaged 74,000 in the later years of the twenties, and was replaced by a net inflow into Great Britain in the thirties. The number of emigrants between 1922 and 1929 who were assisted by the government was 369,000.[2]

The composition of the population was also changing. The ratio of females to males was 1088 to 1000 in England and Wales in 1931; it had been 1096 to 1000 in 1921, 1068 to 1000 in 1911. The population was getting older: in 1911 31 per cent was under 15, 69 per cent over 15; in 1921 the percentages were 28 to 72, in 1931 24 and 76. Persons over 65 constituted 5 per cent of the population in 1911 and 1921, 7 per cent in 1931.[3] As between different social classes the occupied population of Great Britain and Northern Ireland in 1924 was estimated to be made up of wage-earners, forming 76 per cent of the total, salaried persons 14 per cent, independent workers 6 per cent and employers, farmers and professional people 4 per cent.[4]

10. THE CHANGING CITY: SUBURBS AND HOUSING ESTATES

The greater part of the people lived, as their fathers and grand-fathers had done, in the towns. By the time of the census of 1931 only 20 per cent of the population of England and Wales was regarded as rural. A more accurate division would be to count

---

[1] *Census of England and Wales, 1931; Prelim. Report*, pp. xiii–xiv.
[2] Figures in *Statistical Abstract for the British Empire*, 59: 8–9; 60: 8–9; 61: 8–9; Oversea Settlement Committee, *Report* (Cmd. 3589: 1930), p. 31.
[3] A. M. Carr-Saunders, *Social Structure* (2nd ed.), pp. 4–5.
[4] Ibid., p. 60. The subject of population is more fully discussed in chapter 9.

20 per cent of the population as rural, 40 per cent as living in towns with less than 100,000 inhabitants, and the remaining 40 per cent living in the 51 towns with over 100,000 inhabitants. Three cities (Liverpool, Manchester, Sheffield) had between half a million and one million inhabitants each, two (London and Birmingham) over one million.[1]

Of these, London far overtopped the rest. Greater London (the area of the London County Council and the wider area of the Metropolitan Police District) increased in population from 7,251,358 in 1911 to 7,480,201 in 1921 and 8,202,818 in 1931, the increase between 1921 and 1931 being 9·7 per cent. This increase was about three times greater than in the previous intercensal period (1911–21) and twice as great as that of the population of England and Wales as a whole between 1921 and 1931. Greater London now included over a quarter of the urban population, and about one-fifth of the total population, of England and Wales. This was accompanied, however, by a decline in the population of inner London (the L.C.C. area), which between 1921 and 1931 lost 2 per cent of its population (1921, 4,484,523 people, 1931, 4,396,821). The phenomenal growth in 1921–31 was in the 'Outer Ring', which increased by 27 per cent (from 2,995,678 to 3,805,997). Leaving aside the exceptional case of Dagenham, the greatest increase among districts with a population greater than 50,000 was that of Hendon, whose population of 115,682 represented an increase of 101·1 per cent. Three other districts increased by more than 50 per cent, and ten by over 10 per cent. Individual suburbs which mushroomed most sensationally were Kingsbury, whose population increased from 1856 to 16,636 (796·3 per cent), Carshalton (105·2 per cent), Morden (135·2 per cent), Hayes (143·6 per cent), Wembley (199·9 per cent) and Chingford (132·6 per cent).[2]

Already a Select Committee on London Traffic had pronounced conditions intolerable in 1919—and this before the extension of the Tube railways and the electrification of much of the Southern Railway's suburban system. Yet little was done, at least for the benefit of road traffic. The London and Home Counties Traffic Advisory Committee was created in 1924, under the vigorous chairmanship of Sir Henry Maybury.[3] When Waterloo Bridge

[1] A. M. Carr-Saunders, *Social Structure* (2nd ed.), pp. 26–7.
[2] *Census of England and Wales, 1931, Preliminary Report*, pp. xvii–xix, 63–5; somewhat higher figures are given in the *2nd Report* of the Greater London Regional Planning Committee (London, 1933), pp. 23, 24.
[3] W. H. Wickwar, *The Public Services: a Historical Survey* (London, 1938), p. 114.

began to collapse in 1923 there was talk of rebuilding it—but it remained talk, like other schemes for cross-river traffic, including the proposal to put some of the southside railway lines underground and replace Charing Cross station and railway bridge by a road bridge.[1] Meanwhile, the London populace lived in conditions varying from the polite congestion of the service flat to the chronic overcrowding of the slums.[2]

One thing which made nonsense of town-planning schemes was the insatiable desire of the middle class to move out of the older parts of town into new houses in the suburbs. Though London set the pace, the outskirts of any large town showed the encroachment of the businessman's detached or semi-detached 'desirable residence' upon the countryside. From London the season-ticket holder faced longer and longer journeys, often by electric train: to Orpington, or Bexleyheath, Leatherhead or Cobham, Maidenhead or even Pangbourne, Pinner or Cuffley, Leigh-on-Sea or Radlett, or the villas of 'Metroland', the Metropolitan Railway's preserve of 'beechy Bucks'.[3] Most suburban building was without much planning. The idea of the Garden City, illustrated by Letchworth in 1903, produced only one example in this period, Welwyn Garden City, founded by a limited company in 1920. It grew slowly. In the first decade only an engineering firm and the Shredded Wheat company built factories there, so that the desideratum of industry sufficient to employ the local populace was not achieved. For many, Welwyn Garden City was simply another dormitory town, though a very attractive one, with well-built houses, shady, curving lanes, and expanses of lawn in the immaculate shopping centre.

For many working-class families, though not for the poorest, there was also an escape, and one which demonstrated the virtues and limitations of contemporary town-planning: the municipal housing estate. A committee appointed by the Local Government Board, during the era of planning for reconstruction in 1917–18, with Sir John Tudor Walters as chairman, presented specifications for working-class houses to be built with government aid. Not

[1] After much controversy, Waterloo Bridge was demolished (the work beginning in 1934) and a new bridge built: it was opened in August, 1942. Parliament refused to grant funds for the new bridge when its preference for the reconstruction of the old was rejected by the Labour-dominated L.C.C. in 1934.
[2] For a modern and gruesome anatomy of London, see Robert Sinclair's carefully documented *Metropolitan Man* (London, 1937).
[3] For a somewhat different picture, see R. Graves and A. Hodge, *Long Week-end*, pp. 172–3; also J. M. Richards' delicious *Castles on the Ground* (London, 1946). An admirable critique of London's suburbs is to be found in Michael Robbins, *Middlesex* (London, 1953), pp. 182–7 and ch. 14, also plates 68–71.

only were minimum standards of size laid down, but a density of no more than twelve houses per acre was recommended. Two results followed. An entirely new standard of working-class housing came to be accepted: the three-bedroom house, with kitchen, bath, usually a parlour, electric lighting, and gas or electricity for cooking. Such houses were built in very large numbers; in the twenties the majority of new houses were houses of this sort built by the municipalities and the county councils under the various housing acts. Equally important, such houses could not be built in the old, crowded working-class districts: if people must be re-housed close to their old homes they must be moved into flats built on sites from which slum houses had been cleared, as was done in London and elsewhere, though more in the thirties than the twenties.[1]

The result was the construction, by the London County Council and by several other cities, of housing estates in open country on the outskirts—in the case of the L.C.C. far beyond its own boundaries. This policy, as far as the L.C.C. was concerned, had been begun before the war. The new housing estates have been called 'the basic social products of the twentieth century'.[2] One of them alone might be the size of a respectable city; the King-standing estate of Birmingham had a population a little larger than that of Shrewsbury (30,000 in 1932). They were bright, if also somewhat bleak in appearance (for trees, if planted, grew slowly). The houses, in blocks of two or four, of two storeys and built in brick or stucco, were set back from curving streets or circles and had each its long garden strip. A shopping centre grew by degrees, perhaps round a central green, where a new church, a cinema, a public house might also be built. The shops were often small and chilly, with severe plate-glass windows and signs in stiff white letters on a black glass ground. The public house was large and well-appointed, but did not invite conviviality.

Here was the problem of the housing estate. The warmth and neighbourliness of an old community were lacking. The institutions for such a community were lacking, or only slowly provided, either by straining the resources (and inspiration) of the city council or by philanthropic effort: a community hall, sufficient schools, a branch of the public library. Kingstanding in 1932 had one church and one hall; Shrewsbury, with its slightly smaller

---

[1] Typical ground plans of the new houses are shown in L.C.C., *Housing* (1928), pp. 111–62. For details on overcrowding, slum clearance and the construction of working-class houses between the wars, see below, ch. 9, section 7.

[2] Asa Briggs, *History of Birmingham*, II, 228.

population, had '30 churches, 15 church halls and parish rooms, 5 other halls, and 2 public libraries'. The new estates posed other problems to their municipal sponsors: provision of transport services and their fare structures, extension of electricity supply, provision of the normal social services.[1] In time, not only were these problems solved, but a new type of citizen was bred by the housing estates. He was economically in the upper levels of the working population, and the line separating him from the lower middle class could be felt rather than seen. In the twenties the tenant of a council house in Birmingham must have a weekly income of £3 10s. or £4 at least; yet in 1934 78·5 per cent of all families in Birmingham had an income of less than £4 per week.[2]

The largest of all such new communities was Becontree, built by the L.C.C. in the flat Essex country near Dagenham, about 15 miles from Westminster, beyond Barking on the line to Southend. Construction was begun in 1921; by 1924 3296 houses had been built, accommodating 14,564 people; by 1930 17,874 houses had been built, housing 82,689 people (the years of the greatest amount of building were 1926–28); by 1932 there were 22,117 houses and 103,328 people—a town nearly the size of places like Blackburn, Huddersfield, Norwich or Wolverhampton. Most of the inhabitants were not former slum-dwellers (who were rehoused in flats on or close to the cleared sites), but better-class workers, especially those in transport and manufacturing. Thirty-five per cent had to travel 5–10 miles to work, 32·4 per cent 10–15 miles; transport was very limited until the District line's electric service was extended to Upminster (alongside the L.M.S. Barking–Southend line) in 1932. The Ford Company's motor works at Dagenham was established in the vicinity in 1931, but did not draw many of its workers from the estate.[3] The L.C.C. built several other estates, the principal ones being St. Helier, in Surrey (near Morden, south of Wimbledon) opened in 1930–31, Watling (between Hendon and Edgware) built between 1927 and 1930, Downham (near Lewisham) built in 1925–30, and White Hart Lane, near Tottenham, built between 1921 and 1928.[4] All suffered, at least at first, from their artificiality: an early inhabitant of

[1] Asa Briggs, *History of Birmingham*, II, pp. 228, 235, 238, 306–8—pages of shrewd insight and valuable information. Cf. Rosamond Jevons and John Madge, *Housing Estates: a study of Bristol corporation policy* (Bristol, 1946), and for Liverpool D. Caradog Jones, *Social Survey of Merseyside*, I, 275–92.

[2] Asa Briggs, pp. 234, 311.

[3] Terence Young, *Becontree and Dagenham* (London, 1934).

[4] For these and other smaller ones see L.C.C., *Housing* (1928), pp. 67–109; also L.C.C., *London Statistics, 1931–32*, p. 121.

Watling roused her neighbour one morning in 1927 to ask: 'What has happened? Everything is so terribly quiet.'[1] By 1937 Watling had a population of 19,000.

11. THE NEO-TECHNIC AGE: BUSES AND MOTOR CARS

As in housing, so in other things of everyday life the British people after the war were stumbling into a new age, the neotechnic age, as Lewis Mumford has called it, the age of electricity and metal alloys, dependent on science. As in so much else in an unsettled time, the old and the new existed side by side. The big city was the product of the past, but it continued to grow, straining ever more tightly the bands of its roads and bridges and railways, its bricks and mortar, its underground mains and sewers and the labyrinth of electric, telephone and telegraph cables.[2] What did most to strain the bands and break the old ways of life was the internal combustion engine. Before the war a motor car had been a rich man's toy; and the taxi had largely ousted the hansom cab. Now, however, the family car appeared, and added to the traffic which the bus, the lorry and the motor van were already creating. The increase in vehicles on the roads can be seen from the following figures[3] (and they do not include bicycles, whose number was legion):

	Private Cars	Motor Cycles	Commercial Goods Vehicles	Total Motor Vehicles	Horse-drawn Vehicles
1922	314,769	377,943	150,995	975,783	232,865
1927	778,056	671,620	275,831	1,888,726	102,591
1930	1,042,258	698,878	334,237	2,251,142	52,414

The numbers of private cars was equivalent to one per 136 persons in Great Britain in 1922, one per 57 in 1927. In London traffic jams became chronic. A traffic census at Hyde Park Corner showed that in twelve hours 61,454 vehicles passed in 1924, 72,685 in 1929.[4]

[1] Ruth Durant, *Watling: a Survey of Social Life on a New Housing Estate* (London, 1939), p. 1.
[2] See Lewis Mumford, *Technics and Civilization* (New York, 1934), and *Culture of Cities* (New York, 1938).
[3] Licences current in Great Britain during quarter ending August 31 in the years shown: *Statistical Abstract of the U.K., 1930*, p. 282.
[4] Royal Commission on Transport, *Final Report* (Cmd. 3751; 1930), p. 188.

In the towns there was little which could be done. Policemen on point duty controlled traffic by hand signals at busy crossings. Traffic light signals had only begun to come into use in provincial towns by 1929, and in London were later still. Many streets were designated for one-way traffic.[1] In the country a programme of widening and improving the trunk routes was undertaken after the war. The new Ministry of Transport helped to give some coherence to the work. It was authorised in 1920 to classify roads as class I and class II, and such roads were then numbered A1, A4, B1509, etc., the designation appearing on sign posts and road maps. Roads which had been declared 'main roads' were already under the county councils; in 1929 the counties and county boroughs were compelled to take over responsibility for all roads. Towards their maintenance the Ministry made contributions out of the Road Fund, which until 1927 received the proceeds of the motor vehicle taxes introduced by the Finance Act of 1920.[2]

There were several important road schemes in the twenties. These included the reconstruction of General Wade's road from Perth to Inverness; the improvement of the Glasgow–Inverness road and the construction of a new road through the Pass of Glencoe; a new Edinburgh–Glasgow road (using in part existing roads); a new road from Liverpool to east Lancashire towns, begun in 1928; the road tunnel under the Mersey between Liverpool and Birkenhead, completed in 1928; the two great bridges on the Great North Road, opened in 1928, over the Tyne at Newcastle and the Tweed at Berwick. Round London various schemes were carried out, including the North Circular Road, the Kingston bypass (opened in 1927), the Watford bypass, more or less finished by 1927, the Great West Road, built in sections and completed in 1925, Western Avenue—a much more halting project—and other bypasses at Eltham, Sidcup, Croydon, Barking.[3]

In the towns, the buses became larger and more numerous, their routes longer. Gradually they began to oust the tram, though in 86 areas the number of tram-cars actually increased between 1920

---

[1] Asa Briggs, *History of Birmingham*, II, 255.

[2] R.C. on Transport, *Final Report*, pp. 47–9; W. H. Wickwar, *Public Services*, pp. 44–7. For details of expenditures of the Road Fund, see Ministry of Transport, *Report on the Administration of the Road Fund* (annual, 1922–   ). The Trunk Roads Act, 1936, transferred the control of roads designated trunk roads to the Ministry of Transport; the counties continued to maintain such roads as agents for the Ministry.

[3] For the building of new roads, and the failure to build more, see the semi-autobiographical work by Rees Jeffreys, *The King's Highway* (London, 1949). New roads in greater London are listed on pp. 229–31.

and 1928 from 10,600 to 12,000.[1] The trackless trolley-bus, using power from the overhead tram wires, had begun to replace the trams as early as 1911; and many towns by degrees scrapped their trams in favour of buses or trolley-buses in the 1920's—many more in the thirties. Darlington, for example, replaced all its trams with trolley-buses between 1926 and 1929. Other towns which by 1929 had substituted trolley-buses or buses for trams were Chester, Chesterfield, Colchester, Doncaster, Grimsby, Ipswich, Lancaster, Lincoln, Rotherham, Worcester. The large cities remained more faithful to the tram but scrapped some routes and added many bus services, particularly to serve the new housing estates. The increase in town bus services can be seen in the figures for 1920 and 1929: in 1920, 48 municipalities operated buses, owning 649 buses in all; in 1929 100 municipalities were operating a total of 4737 buses.[2] In London the first double-decker buses with covered tops appeared in 1923. The London General Omnibus Company—part of the Underground combine—operated most of the buses but was, in the 1920's, conducting a furious war against fleets of independent buses—pirates, in some cases, operating over the L.G.O.C. routes just ahead of the regular bus, to skim off all the traffic. Dangerous races sometimes occurred.[3] In 1929 London's transport system carried 616 million passengers on the Underground, 346 million on the main-line suburban railways, 1,076 million on the trams and 1,912 million on buses (compared with 936 million in 1920).[4] The problem of handling such a staggering load, and 'co-ordinating' the carriers, led finally to the creation of the London Passenger Transport Board in 1933.

The effect of increased bus services in towns and suburbs was as nothing compared with the effect on the country districts, and in semi-urban areas like South Wales. Buses linked the country towns with the larger cities, and the small villages with the local market town. Shop goods reached the villages in greater amount, also the clothes that copied the London fashions; the village youth could glimpse the life of big cities in visits to the cinema in the

[1] C. E. R. Sherrington, *Hundred Years of Inland Transport* (London, 1934), p. 333.
[2] Ibid., pp. 331–3; R.C. on Transport, *Final Report*, p. 104. Cf. Birmingham's experience (Asa Briggs, *History of Birmingham*, II, 248–54):

		route mileage	miles run	passengers carried
1926:	trams	77	19 millions	238 millions
	buses	63	5 ,,	43 ,,
1937:	trams	65	15 ,,	174 ,,
	buses	153	26 ,,	225 ,,

[3] C. E. R. Sherrington, pp. 326–7, 349; cf. R. Graves and A. Hodge, *Long Week-end*, p. 184. [4] C. E. R. Sherrington, p. 326.

I*

nearest town on Saturday night; and the bus services took children to and from school, enabling small schools to be closed and secondary schools to serve a wider area.[1] The old village carrier, with his slow-moving horse and cart, tended to disappear. Or he might himself purchase a small, single-decker bus and run it himself, as driver and conductor, between his village and the nearest town. Many services grew up in this way, to be later bought and taken over by the large companies. There were 5997 operators of buses in 1931, 5404 in 1933, 4896 in 1935. Small operators comprised 90 per cent of the total number in 1935, but owned only 28 per cent of the vehicles.[2]

The big companies came, naturally, to have most of the traffic. Some of these had begun before or during the war: Scottish Motor Traction (S.M.T.) in 1905, United Automobile Services in 1912, Thames Valley in 1915, East Kent Road Car Company in 1916. Others mushroomed after the war: Eastern Counties, Ribble, United, Southdown, Hants and Dorset, Devon General, Crosville and the widely-ramifying National system, afterwards subdivided. In 56 of the 90 principal companies the controlling interest was owned by Thomas Tilling, Ltd. or by the British Electric Traction Company.[3] The impact of the development of bus services on the railways was heavy. The London, Midland and Scottish Railway calculated that, between 1923 and 1927, passenger receipts for distances up to 10 miles (excepting workmen's tickets and season tickets) decreased 27 per cent, for distances of 11–20 miles 23 per cent, 21–50 miles 9 per cent; but for distances over 50 miles receipts increased 2 per cent.[4]

A slightly different competitor to the railways, first to be seen in 1921, was the long-distance motor coach operating express services between towns 50 to 100 miles apart, and over longer distances—London to Liverpool, London to Edinburgh. These ate into the railways' revenue, particularly for the traffic between London and the south coast and East Anglia seaside towns, partly because the coaches could pick up passengers in the suburbs, where the main-line expresses did not call; in two years the railways had lost between 20 per cent and 40 per cent of this traffic in one area; or a loss of about £23,000 between 1927 and

[1] Cf. C. E. R. Sherrington, p. 329.
[2] Alfred Plummer, *New British Industries in the Twentieth Century* (London, 1937), p. 109.
[3] C. E. R. Sherrington, pp. 328–30; A. Plummer, pp. 131–40.
[4] Wilfred Smith, *Economic Geography of Great Britain* (London, 1949), pp. 620–1. The railways replied by investing over £9 millions in the bus companies under powers obtained in 1928.

1929.[1] Charabancs also took much traffic from the railways with their day excursion trips and weekly circular tours, and their provision for special outings by schools, clubs or business firms; but they also created much of their own business.[2]

Equally challenging to the railways were the road hauliers, with their lorries and vans, many latterly insulated or built as tank-cars, competing for traffic over both short and long distances. Business firms began to maintain fleets of vans for the distribution of their own products. Ex-servicemen bought surplus army vehicles at knock-down prices at Slough, and forced down rates and conditions for the older hauliers before they went bankrupt or sold out. The railway strike of 1919 and the general strike of 1926 provided impressive demonstrations of the power of road transport. The transport of milk, for example, was revolutionised. By about 1930 the old traffic in milk churns on country branch lines had practically ceased. No longer did the farmer drive to the station and unload the churns; instead, the churns were picked up by lorries from a stand at the farm turning, and taken to a creamery, and the milk sent in glass-lined tanks to London or elsewhere, by train or by road.[3]

12. THE RAILWAYS

It would not be fair to say that the railways, by comparison with their newer competitors, remained in the paleotechnic age; though on rural branch lines, where infrequent passenger trains of short six-wheeled stock hauled by diminutive tank engines lingered at flower-embowered stations, it might seem to be the case; as also at begrimed stations in the industrial north and in northeast London. Nor were the large termini in London or the main stations at many provincial cities—Manchester, Liverpool, Birmingham, for example—at all modern, though they were solid and in some cases handsome relics of Victorian architecture— handsome, that is, if properly painted and stripped of the clutter of cheap advertisements.

In the years between the 'grouping' of the railways under the Railways Act of 1921, which took effect in 1923, and the end of

[1] C. E. R. Sherrington, p. 330.
[2] The licensing of bus and coach services was entrusted to Traffic Commissioners by the Road Traffic Act, 1930. See C. E. R. Sherrington, pp. 331, 342–3; W. H. Wickwar, *Public Services*, pp. 92–5; R. C. on Transport, *Second Report* (Cmd. 3416; 1929), and *Final Report*, p. 41; D. N. Chester, *Public Control of Road Passenger Transport* (Manchester, 1936).
[3] Robert Allan, *Royal Road* (London, 1946), pp. 46–62. See Allan also for a description of typical firms of hauliers, pp. 155 ff. Licensing of road hauliers was regulated by the Road and Rail Traffic Act, 1933; see W. H. Wickwar, *Public Services*, pp. 92–5.

the thirties, continuity was perhaps more marked than change. The four groups were fortunate in their general managers—men who combined something of the majesty and the will of the older generation of managers with the imagination which the times called for. Sir Felix Pole of the Great Western, Sir Herbert Walker of the Southern, Sir Ralph Wedgwood of the London and North Eastern and Sir Josiah Stamp[1] of the L.M.S. were an impressive quartet. The old traditions remained strongest at Paddington, since the Great Western alone had preserved its identity in the grouping; only there the sonorous title, Superintendent of the Line, remained in use.

Changes were at first gradual in all four groups: for instance, in the standardisation of locomotives and rolling stock. The variety of colours used by the pre-grouping companies on locomotives and carriages was sadly diminished. The outstanding locomotive designs were those of H. N. Gresley, chief mechanical engineer of the Great Northern, and then of the L.N.E.R., whose Pacifics (which first appeared in 1922) set the standards for speed and efficiency in express train operation. The Great Western 'Castles' (1923) and 'Kings' (1927), in the old Swindon tradition, continued the company's reputation for speed, and did excellently against Gresley's engines in the trials or 'locomotive exchanges' between the two companies in 1925. No use was made of diesel engines on the British railways between the wars, except for the small diesel shunting engines used by the L.M.S., and a number of passenger railcars operated by the G.W.R. after 1933. The 'Sentinel-Cammell' steam railcoach, in which a small steam engine was incorporated in the coach, enjoyed some popularity for branchline services after its introduction in 1923. It was, however, in Ireland that most use was made of light passenger railcars fitted with small petrol or diesel engines. The pioneer was the narrow-gauge system of the County Donegal Railways Joint Committee, under the management of Henry Forbes, traffic superintendent from 1910 to his death in 1943. Its example was copied by the Great Northern Railway of Ireland.

[1] Josiah C. Stamp (1880–1941), economist, prolific writer and lecturer, was in the civil service till 1919 (Inland Revenue and Board of Trade); secretary and director of Nobel Industries, 1919–26; President of the Executive, London, Midland and Scottish Railway (subsequently also chairman of the board) from 1926 to his death in an air raid; served on many royal commissions and on the Dawes and Young Committees; president of at least six professional and learned societies, including the British Association for the Advancement of Science (1936); chairman of the board of the London School of Economics; director of several companies and of the Bank of England. Knighted, 1920; Order of Merit, 1936; created Baron Stamp, 1938. Few men of his generation led a busier, more useful or more serene life.

There were some important developments in signalling. Upper quadrant wire-worked signals were first used in replacement of the familiar lower-quadrant semaphores on the L.M.S. in 1928; they spread to the Southern and L.N.E.R. but not to the Great Western. Colour-light signals were first used by the main line companies on the L.N.E.R. loop serving the exhibition grounds at Wembley in 1924. Power signalling installations were put in at most of the London termini during the thirties, and at some large provincial stations. One of the largest and earliest schemes was the re-signalling of the Southern Railway's London Bridge station, where in 1928 one large, power-worked signal box replaced eight manual boxes. The only applications of colour-light signalling to long stretches of line were on the S.R. Croydon-Brighton line (1932) and the L.N.E.R. York–Northallerton section (1933).

Hardly any new railways were built, and the major new works, apart from the quadrupling of certain sections and the rebuilding of some of the larger stations, were the electrification schemes. There were small schemes in the Wirral peninsula (1938), the Manchester–Altrincham line (1931), the Newcastle–South Shields line (1938); and the electrification of the London and North Western's London suburban lines, begun before the war, was completed. The major schemes were those of the Southern and the Underground. The Southern, which inherited much electrified suburban mileage from the London and South Western (third-rail system) and the London, Brighton and South Coast Railway (overhead system), boldly decided to electrify its entire London suburban network, beginning with the lines to Coulsdon, Sutton, Guildford, Dorking North and Orpington in 1925 (all ultimately on the third-rail system). The entire main line to Brighton was electrified (the electric service started on January 1, 1933), and electrification was carried as far as Hastings (1935), Portsmouth (1937), Reading (1939), Maidstone (1939) and Chatham and Gillingham (1939). The Underground Railways constructed several new lines, some emerging above ground in the undeveloped suburbs: the extension of the Hampstead line to Edgware was opened in 1924, of the City and South London to Morden in 1926. The Piccadilly line was extended westward to Uxbridge and Hounslow over District Railway tracks in 1932, and north-east-wards from Finsbury Park to Cockfosters in 1933; the District from Barking to Upminster (serving the L.C.C.'s new town of Becontree) in 1932. The Metropolitan Railway electrified its line from Harrow to Rickmansworth in 1925 and built a branch to Watford. Other schemes were in progress when interrupted by the Second World War.

The speeds of express trains were only gradually restored, after the wartime decelerations, to the prewar levels; by the summer of 1931 the fastest trains between London and the principal cities were either slightly faster, or only a minute or two slower, than in 1914. In the late thirties there were great accelerations of most of the express train services, until in 1939 116 trains were making scheduled runs at 60 m.p.h. or over, as compared with 65 in 1936 and 9 in 1931. The L.N.E.R. took the lead with the streamlined 'Silver Jubilee' from King's Cross to Newcastle in 1935 (non-stop to Darlington, 232·3 miles in 198 minutes, 70·4 m.p.h.) and the 'Coronation' to Edinburgh in 1937 (392·7 miles in 6 hours, non-stop to York, 188·2 miles at 71·9 m.p.h.). On July 7, 1938 one of Gresley's 'A4' streamlined Pacifics, *Mallard*, on a special test run, covered 5 miles at an average of 120·4 m.p.h. and momentarily touched 126 m.p.h. (on the downhill stretch from Stoke summit, towards Peterborough, on the old Great Northern main line), which was claimed as the world's record for speed with a steam locomotive.[1]

In spite of all efforts, the railways lost ground financially. They did not earn the 'standard revenue' (nearly £51 millions) anticipated in the Railways Act; hence the lower rates which were to follow any earnings in excess of the standard revenue were never introduced, and the attracting back of traffic by lower rates was prevented (except in the case of 'exceptional' rates and excursion tickets). Dividends on ordinary shares continued to be paid until the thirties, though in 1930 they averaged no more than 2·41 per cent.[2] In the thirties passenger service was withdrawn from many branch lines; between 1930 and 1933 some 700 miles of line were closed to passenger traffic.

13. AIRWAYS

The aeroplane, from which most was expected after the war, probably affected the ordinary man least of all the wonders of the new age.

The exploits of the flimsy flying machines of the Royal Air

---

[1] C. E. R. Sherrington, *Hundred Years of Inland Transport*, pp. 317–26, 335–42; C. J. Allen, *Locomotive Practice and Performance in the Twentieth Century* (Cambridge, 1949), pp. 145–51, 163, *passim*; *Railway Magazine*, October, 1939, and other issues.
[2] Statistics of the railways' finances are given in the *Statistical Abstract of U.K.*

Force in the war presaged bold flights over long distances; and many R.A.F. pilots were ready to attempt them. After other attempts had failed two R.A.F. flyers, John Alcock and Arthur Whitten-Brown, made the first flight across the North Atlantic, from Newfoundland to Ireland, on June 14–15, 1919; they flew 1880 miles in 16 hours, 12 minutes. This feat won them a prize of £10,000 from the *Daily Mail*, and knighthoods for both. Charles A. Lindbergh's solo flight, also from west to east across the Atlantic, came later, in 1927. A round-trip crossing of the Atlantic was made by the airship, R34, built by the Admiralty in 1919, but the journey proved too hazardous to be repeated. Official interest was greater in developing air routes between Great Britain and distant parts of the Empire. The Australian government offered a prize of £10,000 to anyone making a flight from England to Australia within thirty days. Two brothers, Ross and Keith Smith, Australian flyers, with the backing of Vickers, Ltd., essayed the task, and completed the journey from Hounslow to Port Darwin, via India, on December 10, 1919, in just under twenty-eight days. Alan Cobham made flights to Capetown and to Australia in 1926. The Australian flyer, Charles Kingsford Smith, made the first flight across the Pacific, from Oakland, California to near Brisbane, in his *Southern Cross* in 1926. The exploit of Miss Amy Johnson, in making a solo flight from England to Australia in twenty days in 1930 excited more attention, as the *Daily Mail* made a great stunt out of it, and gave the aviatrix a prize of £10,000.[1]

Commercial aviation began in 1919, when G. Holt Thomas, an aircraft manufacturer, through a subsidiary, formed the Aircraft Transport and Travel Company and began (August 27) a daily service for passengers and mail from Hounslow to Paris, carrying only two or three passengers a day at first. Other services were flown between London and Amsterdam and Brussels by this and other companies; all were unsubsidised and soon in difficulties. Temporary subsidies to three companies, Handley Page Transport, Instone, and (later) Daimler Airways (the successor to Aircraft Transport and Travel) brought about the renewal of services to the continent in 1921; and for a time there were services also from London to Manchester and Belfast and to the Channel Islands, but these were given up in 1924. In 1923 the Secretary of State for

---

[1] A. E. W. Salt, *Imperial Air Routes* (London, 1930) describes these and several other pioneer flights. Cf. R. Graves and A. Hodge, *Long Week-end*, pp. 84–5, 229, 281–2.

Air appointed a committee on Civil Aerial Transport (the Hambling committee). Its report recommended the creation of a single company to replace the existing ones; and as a result Imperial Airways was formed in 1924, and given a subsidy. Sir Eric Geddes became chairman of the company, and to his vigour it owed much of its success. The government was given the right to appoint certain directors to the company. Imperial Airways began daily services to Paris, Cologne, Zurich, the Channel Islands, and thrice-weekly services to Amsterdam and Berlin. In 1926 it operated three daily services to Paris, and began using three-engined airliners seating nineteen passengers, with a crew of three. The Dutch air service from Amsterdam to London, operated by KLM, began in May 1920. A Belgian service began at the same time; the French and German services to England somewhat later. Internal services in the British Isles were not successfully established until 1930. The development of the imperial air routes by Imperial Airways began, after experimental flights by Cobham and other airmen, with the service from Cairo to Basra in January, 1927—a route over which the R.A.F. had operated a service since 1921. This was extended westward to Karachi and eastward to Genoa in 1929, and the first regular weekly service between Britain and India was inaugurated, though until 1937 part of the journey (latterly from Paris to Brindisi) was made by train. The service was extended to Delhi in 1930. Regular service to Singapore began in 1932, and to Brisbane (at first only for mail) in December 1934. The Alexandria–Capetown service began in January 1932.[1]

14. THE NEW BEHEMOTH

One thing the new technology could do was to spread ideas, news, falsehoods, entertainment more rapidly and to more people than had ever been possible before. The new monster with four heads and many hoarse voices had not yet been named mass

[1] Alfred Plummer, *New British Industries in the Twentieth Century*, pp. 154 ff.; A. E. W. Salt, *Imperial Air Routes*, especially pp. 11–25; Robert Finch, *The World's Airways* (London, 1938), pp. 16–19, *passim*; C. J. Sprigge, *British Airways* (London, 1934). The statistics of air travel reflected an equal transformation. In 1919 British civil aircraft, on all routes, flew 104,000 miles and carried 870 passengers; in 1930 they flew 1,437,000 miles and carried 25,094 passengers (in 1925 the number of passengers was 11,193). The number of passengers between England and destinations abroad was 922 in 1919 (870 in British aircraft); in 1929 it was 26,182 in British aircraft (3244 flights) and 22,071 in foreign aircraft (5992 flights). For 1930 the figures were: British aircraft, 3000 flights, 22,045 passengers; foreign, 6685 flights, 20,390 passengers. (*Statistical Abstract of U.K.*, 1930, p. 293.)

communication; but it already existed. The four heads were advertising,[1] broadcasting, newspapers, moving pictures.

Wireless broadcasting in England, as opposed to the much older wireless telegraphy, began in 1920 when the Marconi Company made experimental broadcasts of speech and music from a station at Chelmsford between February 23 and March 6. Later, on June 15, the *Daily Mail* sponsored a broadcast by Dame Nellie Melba from the same station. Thereafter there was a pause, the Post Office (whose power over wireless derived from the Wireless Telegraphy Act, 1904) having intervened on the ground that the broadcasts interfered with other communications. Amateurs, however, kept up sending and receiving programmes between one another as a means of 'testing' their equipment, and on occasion picked up concerts from the Hague and the Eiffel Tower. During 1921 their organisation, the Wireless Society of London, put pressure on the Marconi Company and the Post Office for the renewal of experimental broadcasts, and as a result the Marconi Company was permitted to make fifteen-minute broadcasts, under the direction of P. P. Eckersley (later chief engineer of the B.B.C.) from the station at Writtle, near Chelmsford, from February 14, 1922, to January 9, 1923. Meanwhile, the radio boom had begun in the United States, where in 1922 sets were being sold at the rate of 25,000 a month; and the Marconi Company announced a plan to set up broadcasting stations and to rent receivers to householders. Other companies which also hoped to exploit the market for receiving sets (and interested, like Marconi, in broadcasting only as a means to this end) protested, and the Postmaster-general, after consulting the Wireless Sub-Committee of the Imperial Communications Committee, invited the various companies to arrange for an efficient service without the danger of monopoly. Two groups were proposed, each of which would operate broadcasting stations.

It was at this point that the Post Office changed its mind in favour of a monopoly. This decision, fraught with the greatest social consequences, was apparently due to a fear of difficulties over the allocation of wave-lengths to rival groups, and to a belief that if many companies wished to put up stations the Post Office would have to choose between the efficient and the inefficient, and would then be accused of favouritism. It also owed much to a recent visit of the assistant secretary of the Post Office to the United

---

[1] For advertising, see E. S. Turner, *The Shocking History of Advertising* (London, 1952), and E. A. Lever, *Advertising and Economic Theory* (Oxford, 1947).

States, where the chaos in early broadcasting by many rival firms was at its worst.

The outcome was that the British Broadcasting Company was formed at the end of 1922 and given a licence, though not necessarily a monopoly, to broadcast from eight stations until January 1, 1925 (later extended to the end of 1926). Broadcasting began from the Marconi Company's station in London on November 14, 1922, and from stations at Manchester and Birmingham next day. In 1925 the government appointed a committee of inquiry under the Earl of Crawford and Balcarres to make recommendations about the broadcasting service after the B.B.C.'s licence expired. Its proposal, subsequently put into effect, was that a public corporation, with a monopoly of broadcasting, should be created. The evidence it heard, from representatives of the press, education and the radio industry, was unanimous in support of this, and the committee was evidently much influenced by the supposedly bad example of the uncontrolled broadcasting industry in the United States.[1]

The most potent influence on policy was, however, that of one man, the creator, for better or worse, of the B.B.C. and its entire philosophy, J. C. W. Reith.[2] Reith, a Scot, son of a minister and an engineer by training, had been general manager of Beardmore's, Coatbridge, before being made general manager (subsequently managing director) of the B.B.C. in 1922, at the age of 33. A man of strong opinions, great force of character, and autocratic methods, he was convinced that broadcasting must be conducted 'as a Public Service, with definite standards . . . not . . . used for entertainment purposes alone . . . [It] should bring into the greatest possible number of homes . . . all that is best in every department of human knowledge, endeavour and achievement . . . The preservation of a high moral tone is obviously of paramount importance.' A monopoly, under public control, was the natural consequence of these views; only with 'unity of control' would there be technical efficiency and economy, but much more the maintenance of standards. The alternative was the American system: ' . . . no co-ordination, no standard, no guiding policy'. Such views no one could propagate better than Reith. In 1924 he gave them to the world in a book, *Broadcast over Britain*; he

---

[1] This account is based on R. H. Coase, *British Broadcasting: A Study in Monopoly* (London, 1950), pp. 3–45, 55–60. Cf. Lincoln Gordon, *Public Corporation in Great Britain* (Oxford, 1938), pp. 157–65; T. H. O'Brien, *British Experiments in Public Ownership and Control* (London, 1937), pp. 96–110.

[2] Knighted, 1927, made a baron (Lord Reith), 1940.

embodied them in his memorandum and evidence to the Crawford Committee; and they were reflected in the memorandum of the Secretary of the Post Office (Sir Evelyn Murray) to the committee. By 1925 they were accepted almost without debate. The Crawford Report (*Report of the Broadcasting Committee*) issued in 1926 (Cmd. 2599) accepted them; witness this passage: 'special wavelengths or alternative services may provide an escape from the programme dilemma, but we trust they will never be used to cater for groups of listeners, however large, who press for trite and commonplace performances'.[1]

This was the parentage of the British Broadcasting Corporation. It was created by a royal charter, issued on December 20, 1926, and to it the old British Broadcasting Company transferred its assets. The part played by the B.B.C. during the general strike influenced opinion in support of such a body. (It is curious that in December 1926 the Conservatives created two public corporations, whose pattern strongly influenced that of other public bodies subsequently brought into being in the 1930's and 1940's; for the Act creating the Central Electricity Board received the royal assent on December 15, 1926.)

The B.B.C. was governed by a board of five governors, appointed by the Crown for five-year terms on the recommendation of the Prime Minister. The Postmaster-general, who was responsible for the B.B.C. in parliament, was given the power of suggesting names to the Prime Minister. In its early years the board included such people as Lord Clarendon, Lord Gainford (the coal-owner), J. H. Whitley, H. A. L. Fisher, Mrs. Philip Snowden, Mrs. Mary Agnes Hamilton, and an ex-headmaster of Winchester. The original board was named in the charter, as was the director-general, none other than Sir John Reith. And in fact for many years he, as much as anyone, fashioned the board's policies.

Broadcasting in 1925 was from nine main transmitters and eleven relay stations; to which the high-power transmitter at Daventry had just been added. The Regional system was put into effect in the years after 1927: the country was divided into five areas, each with its own station transmitting two programmes, the National and Regional, the latter varying in each area and using a good deal of local material and talent. Two more regions, Wales

---

[1] R. H. Coase, *British Broadcasting*, pp. 46–9, 50–5, 60; L. Gordon, *Public Corporation in G.B.*, p. 233. Reith's account of these years is in his autobiography: J. C. W. Reith, *Into the Wind* (London, 1949), pp. 81–134.

and Northern Ireland, were added in 1937. Experiments for short-wave broadcasts to the Empire began in 1927, but the Empire Service only began in December 1932—this on the B.B.C.'s initiative, and without any financial support from dominions and colonies. Experimental television programmes were first transmitted in 1929.[1]

The newspaper press, in spite of broadcasting, more than held its own as a medium of communication. The main changes during the interwar years were the increasing concentration of ownership and the fierce competition among the papers of mass circulation for supremacy in the number of readers. The London press dominated the country—at least as far as morning papers in England (though not in Scotland) were concerned; though a provincial paper like the *Manchester Guardian* continued to be of national importance under the magisterial editorship of C. P. Scott, which lasted until his death in 1932. The war had increased the number of the 'press lords'. Neither they nor the 'trustification' of the press were new; both flourished in the next twenty years, drawing control of both metropolitan and provincial papers into fewer and fewer hands.

Lord Northcliffe's death in 1922 removed the most powerful and ambitious figure among the newspaper proprietors. The ownership of *The Times* then passed, after a keen struggle, to J. J. Astor (younger son of the first Lord Astor) and John Walter, a member of the founding family, and a body of trustees was created, whose consent was necessary for any transfer of shares outside the two families, in order to preserve the paper's independence. Geoffrey Dawson (1874–1944), who as one of Milner's secretaries in South Africa after the Boer War had been a member of the famous 'kindergarten', replaced Wickham Steed as editor (he had had a previous term as editor from 1912 to 1919) and remained so until 1941. Under him the tone of the paper became much more Conservative.[2]

Northcliffe's other papers were taken over by his brother, Lord Rothermere, who in the next few years bought and sold a number of London and provincial papers, though retaining the *Daily Mail*

[1] L. Gordon, *Public Corporation in G.B.*, pp. 165–203; T. H. O'Brien, *Public Ownership and Control*, pp. 110 ff.; W. A. Robson (ed.), *Public Enterprise*, pp. 73–104; R. Graves and A. Hodge, *Long Week-end*, pp. 88–91, 238–9. Accounts of the B.B.C. from the inside are: R. H. Eckersley, *B.B.C. and all that* (London, 1946); Maurice Gorham, *Sound and Fury* (London, 1948).

[2] *History of The Times*, IV, ii, chapters 17, 19, describes the struggle for control. At one time there were plans for Lloyd George to become editor (before Astor and Walter acquired control).

and the *Daily Mirror*. His principal rivals were Lord Beaverbrook, who owned the *Daily Express* and the *Evening Standard*, and a new combination, the Berry brothers, William and Gomer (subsequently Lords Camrose and Kemsley),[1] who between 1924 and 1926 bought a number of newspapers and periodicals from Lord Rothermere, including the entire holdings of the Amalgamated Press (at a cost of £8 millions) and the *Daily Sketch*, and in 1927 added to this by buying the *Daily Telegraph* from Lord Burnham. In 1928 Rothermere, deciding that he had gone too far in building up his rivals, declared war on the Berry empire in the provinces by announcing that he would start a series of evening newspapers, all to be named the *Evening World*. Only two appeared, in Newcastle and in Bristol. The former failed, the latter survived, though only after it had spurred the citizens of Bristol into founding an evening paper of their own. In 1932 a truce was declared in the ruinously expensive war for circulation between the two groups, and an exchange of certain properties was arranged between them.

In the thirties the competition for the largest circulation among the London dailies reached its height. Free gifts and free insurance were offered lavishly to catch new subscribers. The race was won, in 1933, by the *Daily Express*, which first reached a circulation of over two million copies. Its nearest rival was not the *Daily Mail*, but the new *Daily Herald*, Labour's newspaper which in 1929 was taken over by Odhams Press and its manager, J. S. Elias (Lord Southwood)[2] with safeguards to preserve its character as a spokesman of Labour. A substantial rival to all three was the *News Chronicle*, an amalgamation of two Liberal papers in 1930. Other changes of the period were the disappearance of the oldest daily paper, the *Morning Post*, which was absorbed by the *Daily Telegraph* in 1937, and the extinction of three of London's evening papers, the *Globe*, the *Pall Mall Gazette*, and the *Westminster Gazette* (J. A. Spender's old paper, with a great Liberal tradition), all in the twenties. As a result, by 1930 the press, apart from the 'class' papers and numerous provincial papers owned singly or

[1] William Ewart Berry, Lord Camrose, (1879–1954), baronet 1921, baron, 1929, viscount, 1941, owner of Hackwood, formerly Lord Curzon's property. James Gomer Berry (Lord Kemsley), born 1883, baronet 1928, baron 1936, viscount 1945, owner of the historic estate of Dropmore. Their brother, Henry Seymour Berry (1877–1928), created Baron Buckland in 1926, was a large coal-owner, and chairman of Guest, Keen and Nettlefolds. Their father was an alderman of Merthyr Tydfil, where they were born.

[2] J. S. Elias (1873–1947) started his career as an office boy, and made Odhams Press into one of the giants of the industry. Created Baron Southwood in 1937, viscount in 1946.

in groups, was in the hands of seven large combinations—all, but particularly Lord Rothermere's, controlled by financial arrangements between various holding and interlocking companies of baffling complexity. It was estimated that three-quarters of the press was owned by one or other of these groups.[1]

Among the weekly political reviews there were also changes. The *New Statesman*, the Webbs' child, absorbed the *Nation* in 1931. The *Nation*, once a great Liberal weekly, had been in a state of decline since its editor, H. W. Massingham, retired in 1923 when its ownership changed. The *Athenaeum* had disappeared in 1921, absorbed by the *Nation*. A new weekly, *Time and Tide*, was started by Lady Rhondda in 1920. The *Economist* and the *Spectator* continued unchanged through this period; the *Spectator's* famous editor, J. St. Loe Strachey, retired in 1925.

An influence as pervasive though not as potent as that of the press was exercised by the motion picture—the films, 'flicks', or cinema. In spite of its early beginnings and growth before the war, the British film industry was not well established, and during the war it nearly faded away. The American movie industry, by contrast, grew mightily, blanketing not only the American market but much of the rest of the world also. By the end of the war Hollywood had become the centre of production in the industry, and a handful of mammoth concerns, dominating production, distribution and exhibition, had replaced the former chaos of small companies and independent producers. The Hollywood product seemed to satisfy the British public: at least, it saw little else. These were the days of the silent film: of the great screen lover, Rudolph Valentino, of Mary Pickford, the world's sweetheart, of Gloria Swanson, Bebe Daniels, Norma Talmadge, Pola Negri, Clara Bow (the 'It' girl), of Norma Shearer, Janet Gaynor, and Garbo, of Douglas Fairbanks, of Lon Chaney, of W. S. Hart and Tom Mix among the actors of the ever-popular 'Westerns', of the great comedians, Harold Lloyd and Buster Keaton, and above all Charlie Chaplin.

In time, a campaign on behalf of British films, mingled with criticisms of the American product and its influence, had some result. Even the Imperial Conference of 1926 took notice of

---

[1] Kurt von Stutterheim, *The Press in England* (London, 1934), pp. 113–71, 186–211; Lord Camrose, *British Newspapers and their Controllers* (London, 1947); *Economist*, June 13, 1931; P.E.P., *Report on the British Press* (London, 1938), pp. 95–108; R. Graves and A. Hodge, *Long Week-end*, pp. 56–62; Henry Wickham Steed, *The Press* (London, 1938), pp. 86–100; Harold Herd, *The March of Journalism* (London, 1952), pp. 252–83 (includes sketches of some of the chief figures in the newspaper world).

British films, whose poor estate, it was argued, prevented them from being used as propaganda for British trade. In 1927 parliament enacted the Cinematograph Films Act, which established a quota of British films which exhibitors must present: at first it was 5 per cent of the films shown, but it was to rise by 2·5 per cent per year until a figure of 20 per cent was reached. The results were disappointing. Many companies were promoted, but most of them quickly failed. Much of what was produced, the 'quota quickies', was hardly worth showing, and exhibitors compromised between the law and the box office by showing such films at unpopular hours. By the end of the twenties there were two large-scale concerns in Great Britain: Gaumont-British, which had connections with Fox Films in the United States, and British International Pictures,[1] controlling Associated British Cinemas (A.B.C.) and connected with First National (American) and Pathé. Gaumont-British was the creation of Isidore Ostrer and his brothers, sons of a Polish shoemaker of Bow, and included a distributing company started by C. M. Woolf and a chain of cinemas (Provincial Cinematograph Theatres) which Ostrer bought from Lord Beaverbrook. A.B.C. was the creation of a Glasgow lawyer, John Maxwell. By 1929 Gaumont-British owned 300 cinemas (the number of independently owned cinemas was between 2500 and 3000). Both G.-B. and A.B.C. were dependent on overdrafts from the National Provincial Bank, then and later the bank most closely concerned in the film industry. Both companies were producers as well as distributors, the former at Shepherd's Bush, the latter at Elstree; these and other places in London's suburbia were the centres of British production. There were two other important production companies, British Instructional Films, and Gainsborough Pictures (controlled by Gaumont-British), originally started by Michael Balcon in 1924. The most successful British productions were of the educational kind: nature films and documentaries; John Grierson's *Drifters* (1929) marked the arrival of a new director and a new influence in the world of the film.

Talking pictures—the talkies—first appeared in the United States in 1926, but were not taken very seriously. Warner Brothers, to rescue their own struggling concern, produced the first full-length talking picture in 1928, at a time when the film industry was beginning to suffer painfully from the competition of

[1] Later B.I.P. and A.B.C. were merged as Associated British Picture Corporation, Ltd.

radio entertainment. *The Singing Fool*, with Al Jolson, inaugurated the new apparatus in many English cities; and the crowds flocked to it. *Broadway Melody*, released the same year, was the first of a series of successful American musicals. The first important British talking picture was Alfred Hitchcock's *Blackmail*, though Hitchcock had directed good films before, especially *The Lodger* (1926). Films in technicolour had already been made, though colour was still rather a novelty. In the thirties British film companies were more productive and more successful than in the twenties, though like Thursday's child they still had far to go.[1]

15. THE USES OF LEISURE: SPORT, BETTING, GREYHOUNDS, PUBS

If some still found pleasure in solitude, more sought it gregariously, in crowds. Leisure was increasing for the working classes, and entertainment and excitement were provided, on a commercial scale, to prevent it palling.

Sport was a great diversion—not sport one took part in, except for the village cricket matches, but sport one watched or read about. Cricket retained its summer primacy, and the crowds still turned out at Old Trafford or at the Oval, to watch Jack Hobbs score another century or Parker bowl out five men in succession. As autumn approached, however, football resumed sway—soccer, with its scores of professional teams under the Football Association rallying civic loyalty and drawing huge crowds to follow the Arsenal or Sheffield Wednesday, Aston Villa or West Bromwich or Manchester United. For the first Cup Final played in the stadium at Wembley in 1923 a crowd of over 200,000 gathered— nearly 75,000 more than the stadium's capacity—and stormed on to the field itself.[2] The King attended on that and subsequent occasions—a fact not without social significance. In Scotland (as in Wales) it was rugby football which was followed with passionate concern, making the 'international' match against England at Murrayfield the great occasion of the year. Gambling of course gave an edge to the spectators' interest—and increased the sale of evening papers; but the big day of the football pools was in the thirties and later, not in the nineteen-twenties.

[1] Paul Rotha, *The Film till now* (London, 1930), pp. 21–58, 226–34, *passim*; R. Graves and A. Hodges, *Long Week-end*, pp. 133–42, 235–6; A. Plummer, *New British Industries*, pp. 315 ff.; *Economist*, April 20, November 30, 1929; B. B. Hampton, *History of the Movies* (New York, 1931); Alan Wood, *Mr. Rank* (London, 1952), pp. 51–7.
[2] *Illustrated London News*, May 5, 1923.

Betting was as much the twentieth century's vice as drinking was that of the nineteenth. Opportunities for it increased. The totalisator was introduced into England in 1928. It was legalised by the Racecourse Betting Act, 1928, which created the Racecourse Betting Control Board to keep back part of the proceeds for horse-breeding—a worthy object nullified by the tote's high cost of operation. Tote clubs sprang up (there were 284 by the end of 1932, almost all opened that year) and a 'chain-store' totalisator, Tote Investors, Limited, was founded in 1931 with offices in London and the chief provincial cities. Horse-race betting was said to absorb £230 millions in 1929; yet the betting duty (2·5 per cent of the stake) imposed in 1926 brought in so little that it was abandoned in 1929. By comparison, the £8 millions spent annually on greyhound racing and the £3 millions spent on newspaper competitions on football game results (forerunners of the pools) were small potatoes at the end of the twenties.

The racing of greyhounds after a mechanical hare began at Manchester in 1926. The National Greyhound Racing Society was formed to 'control' the sport in 1927. By the end of 1932 there were 187 tracks, 50 under the N.G.R.S., 14 under a rival, and 123 others. Since races could be conducted in the evening under floodlights, opportunities for attending them, or for gambling on them without attending, were much greater than with horse-racing. In 1932 there were seven race courses within 15 miles of London, with 63 days of racing; but there were 23 greyhound tracks with 4000 days' racing. There were 18 million attendances at the N.G.R.S. tracks alone in 1931. In London, attendance was 3 million in 1927, 8 million in 1929. New meccas for the British workman and (more shocking to some moralists) for his wife and children had suddenly appeared: White City, Wembley, West Ham, Harringay, Wimbledon, Catford (all outside London), Belle Vue and White City in Manchester, Powderhall and Stenhouse in Edinburgh, Albion, White City and Carntyne in Glasgow. The first tote on a greyhound track was set up at Carntyne in 1929; many followed, though later they were held to be illegal on greyhound tracks in England, though not in Scotland. Their operation on greyhound tracks (and all other licensed race courses) was legalised by the Betting and Lotteries Act, 1934, subject to a limit of 104 days of racing on each course per year. This was the puny offspring of the deliberations of the Royal Commission on Lotteries and Betting, under Sir Sidney Rowlatt's chairmanship, in 1933. All testimony before the Commission had agreed that the volume of betting had greatly increased since the war; but what could one do? Perhaps it was gambling which kept the people sane and sanguine during the depression, the second war, and the anxieties and austerities of the second peace.[1]

The public house thus came to have a good deal of competition. If still the poor man's club, it was not necessarily his resort. The wireless might keep him at home. Sporting interest might send him to the dogs. A hunger for romance or for excitement might take him to the cinema. Even in silent days the cinema's vogue was growing. In Liverpool the number of cinemas increased from 32 in 1913 to 69 in 1932 (while theatres declined from 11 to 6). In London the number increased from 94 to 1911 to 266 in 1921. It was estimated that 40 per cent of Liverpool's populace went to the cinema in any given week, and 25 per cent of the population went twice a week.[2]

The pub remained one of the distinguishing national institutions; and sobriety increased. Licensed premises in England and Wales numbered 88,739 in 1913 (excluding off licenses), 82,054 in 1922, 77,821 in 1930. Consumption of beer, which had been 35 million barrels in the United Kingdom in 1913 and nearly 13 million in 1918, recovered to 27 million in 1920, and settled at about 20 million barrels after 1927 (excluding the Irish Free State). Consumption of spirits declined in the same period from 31·7 million proof gallons in 1913 to 22 million in 1920 and 10 million in 1930. Convictions for drunkenness declined: in 1913 the number was 153,112 men and 35,765 women in England and Wales; in 1922 63,253 men and 13,094 women; in 1930 44,683 men and 8397 women.[3]

16. ILL FARES THE LAND

In this age of change the land was unchanging, but its fortunes declining. During the war a great concern for farming had appeared, after forty years of agricultural decline had reduced the acreage in England and Wales under cultivation by almost a quarter, as prairie wheat from overseas had replaced home-grown wheat. Arable land in England and Wales had comprised 14¾

[1] Royal Commission on Lotteries and Betting, *Interim Report* (Cmd. 4234, 1933); *Final Report* (Cmd. 4341, 1933); *New Survey of London Life and Labour*, 1, 297.
[2] D. Caradog Jones, *Social Survey of Merseyside*, III, 279–82; *New Survey of London Life and Labour*, I, 286.
[3] *Statistical Abstract of U.K.*, 1930, pp. 88–9, 354.

million acres in 1871 and was just over 11 million acres in 1914; of the land going out of cultivation nearly 2 million acres had been devoted to the raising of wheat. Permanent grassland, meanwhile, increased from 11¾ million acres to 16 million acres, and the cattle carried from 10 to 12 million, though the numbers of sheep declined. In Scotland the changes were less spectacular: arable land declined between 1871 and 1914 from nearly 3·5 million acres to 3·3 million acres, and permanent grassland increased from 1 million to nearly 1·5 million acres.[1] Thus by the time the war came Britain was raising only one-fifth of its wheat; the proportions of its food needs raised at home were, by value, 45·4 per cent in the case of grains, fruit and vegetables, 55·7 per cent of meat, butter, cheese, poultry, eggs, and 43·6 per cent of all foodstuffs.[2]

The war arrested the process. Two million acres of permanent pasture was ploughed, and 1¼ million acres of temporary pasture also ploughed. The wheat harvest increased by 60 per cent; the entire grain crop was increased by 32 per cent, the potato crop by 59 per cent, but home supplies of meat and bacon declined by about 30 per cent. To achieve this, the government, in the Corn Production Act, 1917, guaranteed farmers against losses on wheat and oat crops during 1917–22, and provided for the first time for the fixing of minimum wages for farm workers by an Agricultural Wages Board. After the war Lloyd George announced his agricultural policy in a speech on October 21, 1919; more production at home, for which the farmer must be guaranteed against the violent fluctuations of foreign agriculture. In 1920 the Agricultural Act honoured these promises by guaranteeing the farmer his costs of production for wheat and oats.[3]

Then came the slump. Wheat, which had touched 80s. 10d. per quarter in 1920, fell to 42s. 2d. by 1923; oats fell from 63s. per quarter to 42s. The war had produced an agricultural depression and world-wide shortages, intensified for Britain by the loss of Russian supplies; the high prices had led to an increase in the acreage under wheat until the market was glutted and prices collapsed. The government which (as with unemployment in-

[1] L. D. Stamp and S. H. Beaver, *The British Isles: a Geographic and Economic Survey* (2nd ed., London, 1937), p. 153.
[2] A. D. Hall, *Agriculture after the War* (London, 1916), p. 8; George Walworth, *Feeding the Nation in Peace and War* (London, 1940), p. 20.
[3] G. Walworth, *Feeding the Nation*, pp. 24–42; C. S. Orwin, *History of English Farming* (London, 1949), pp. 82–4; R. J. Hammond, 'British Food Supplies, 1914–1939', *Economic History Review*, XVI (1946), 1–2; *Annual Register, 1919*, p. 124.

surance) had lightly taken on commitments during the boom which
it did not expect to have to honour, found itself faced with meeting
guarantees which might cost between £15 millions and £35
millions in all. Within a year it reversed its field, repealed the
Act of 1920, gave up any guarantees (except for the current crops)
and turned adrift the farmer, the farm labourer, and the whole
state of farming. The Corn Production Acts (Repeal) Bill, introduced in July 1921, produced a bitter debate; but it passed. The
sharpest passages were over the scrapping of the Agricultural
Wages Board and the minimum wage for farm workers, which was
justified on the ground (which was disputed) that they depended
on the guaranteed prices introduced in 1917.[1] The attack on wages
began at once. The farm labourer, who had been receiving 42s.
for a 48-hour week, was offered 36s. for a 50-hour week, and on
very short agreements or none. In many cases wages fell below
30s. a week.

    The crisis came in Norfolk, where the farm labourers were most
strongly organised. In March 1923, the farmers offered 24s. for
a 50-hour week; the National Union of Agricultural Workers
held out for 26s. The farmers seem to have hoped to force the
government into giving them either tariff protection or a subsidy
by precipitating the issue; the union decided to resist in order to
end the decline in wages, for it believed that the outcome in
Norfolk would be decisive for other counties. At the end of March
the men struck; but there was reluctance to push things to
extremities on both sides, and apart from some trouble over
picketing (groups of men were sent out on bicycles to picket farms
where work was going on), feelings did not become very inflamed.
The number of men on strike was about 6000. After various
attempts at negotiation had failed Ramsay MacDonald, then
leader of the Opposition, invited representatives of the National
Farmers' Union to meet him; this led to meetings with representatives of the N.U.A.W. and a settlement on April 18: 25s. for
a 50-hour week. The Labour government restored the wage-
fixing machinery by the Agricultural Wages (Regulation) Act,
1924: county committees were created with power to fix wages,
and a Central Wages Board to supervise (though not, thanks to a
Liberal amendment, to revise) the county awards. Under the
wages committees wages quickly rose to about 30s. a week (higher

---

[1] 144 H.C. Deb., 5 s., 63–179 (especially 66, 91, 142, 155), 249–314; C. S. Orwin,
History of English Farming, pp. 84–5; J. A. Venn, *Foundations of Agricultural Economics* (Cambridge, 1923), pp. 331–5.

in some counties) and remained at that level throughout the twenties.[1]

In these circumstances, the land fared ill. The acreage of arable land in England and Wales resumed its decline, and in 1930 stood at 9,833,000; the number of acres under grass remained almost stationary, but rough grazing increased from just under 4 million acres to 5¼ million. In 1931 the acreage under wheat in England and Wales was 1,197,000, the lowest ever recorded (though the yield, 32·3 bushels per acre, was high). The price of wheat stood at 42s. 9d. per quarter in 1929–30, 26s. in 1930–31. The numbers of cattle, sheep, and pigs remained fairly constant. In the late twenties, however, there was an increase in the production of milk, meat and eggs.[2] With great efforts and large subsidies the growing of sugar beet was encouraged: in 1930 347,257 acres were growing beets (especially in East Anglia) and 8·4 million hundredweight of sugar was being produced (as compared with 26 million hundredweight, imported). Seventeen sugar beet factories were at work.[3] The index of estimated gross agricultural output (1908 = 100) stood at 100 in 1925 but reached 104 in 1930–31. None the less the proportion of Britain's food needs produced at home declined to 39·3 per cent in 1924–28: 15 per cent of the wheat needed was home-produced, 44 per cent of meat, 49 per cent of poultry and eggs, 48 per cent of dairy produce, 70 per cent of potatoes, 44 per cent of fruit.[4]

In the thirties this caused a new stirring of conscience over the nation's use of its land and its treatment of its farms and farmers. Some argued that better farming of existing arable lands would lessen Britain's dependence on imported food. Sir R. G. Stapledon, professor of agricultural botany and director of the Welsh Plant Breeding Station at Aberystwyth, demonstrated and preached that the hill lands of Britain, used (if at all) as rough, unimproved

[1] C. S. Orwin, *History of English Farming*, pp. 106–7; Reg Groves, *Sharpen the Sickle: The History of the Farm Workers' Union* (London, 1949), pp. 170–210; *Annual Register, 1924*, pp. 62, 82; *Economist*, October 22, 1921, March 31, 1923.

[2] Total milk production was estimated to be 1144 million gallons in Great Britain in 1907–8, 1288 million in 1924–25, and 1425·5 million in 1930–31, of which 981·4 million gallons was consumed as liquid milk (899·1 million gallons in 1924–25).

[3] A. Plummer, *New British Industries in the 20th Century*, pp. 269–98.

[4] L. D. Stamp and S. H. Beaver, *British Isles*, pp. 153, 163, 186, 206–7; G. Walworth, *Feeding the Nation*, pp. 126, 136, 331; R. J. Hammond, 'British Food Supplies, 1914–1939', *Ec. Hist. Rev.*, XVI (1946), 1–6; Viscount Astor and B. Seebohm Rowntree, *British Agriculture: the Principles of Future Policy* (London, 1938), p. 53; Sir E. J. Russell, *Farm and the Nation* (London, 1933), pp. 13–37 and *passim* (an excellent brief introduction to the modern farm problem in Great Britain); Lord Ernle (R. E. Prothero), *English Farming, Past and Present* (5th edition, Sir A. D. Hall, ed.; London, 1936), pp. 393–472. Acreage and livestock figures are given in the *Statistical Abstract of U.K.*, e.g., *1932*, pp. 238 ff.

grazings, could be reconditioned by the sowing of rye-grass and clover or reclaimed and put under crops, thus yielding nearly as much meat per acre as the best pastures. Since 32·1 per cent of all of the land of Britain was classified as hill land and rough grazings (or other lands capable of some cultivation), mostly lying above the 700-foot contour, this provided much room for improvement, particularly in mid-Wales, where the hill lands constituted between 39 per cent and 66 per cent of all agricultural land. Stapledon was calling for a general return to the land, and for a much better use of it, both on hill and plain.[1]

Others favoured mechanisation; and it made some progress. The number of oil and petrol engines in use on farms in England and Wales increased from 6284 in 1913 to 65,725 in 1931; the number of tractors from 16,681 in 1925 to 40,000 in 1937.[2] At the same time the number of horses on farms, 1,239,937 in 1914 and rather more in 1920, declined to 961,353 in 1930 and 873,852 in 1935.[3] Some farmers experimented with combine-harvesters and other large pieces of farm machinery, though it was not profitable on farms of less than 500 acres. The principal examples were in East Anglia and Hampshire.[4] A. J. Hosier of Wexcombe, near Marlborough, Wiltshire, developed methods of outdoor dairying, pig-farming and poultry-farming; folding the stock across the fields and employing moveable milksheds and other machines, some of which he began to manufacture and sell.[5] The Agricultural Economics Research Institute at Oxford continued to do valuable work under the direction of C. S. Orwin, as did the various old-established agricultural research stations.[6] Typical of the times were such ventures as the Land Utilisation Survey, begun in 1930 by Professor L. Dudley Stamp of London University, employing school-children in each village to obtain the basic information;[7] the enquiry into British agriculture organised by Viscount Astor and Seebohm Rowntree;[8] and Professor J. A. S.

[1] R. G. Stapledon, *Hill Lands of Britain: development or decay?* (London, 1897), pp. 18, 23, 28, 42; *The Land, Now and Tomorrow* (London, 1935)—a longer and more general work; *A Survey of the Agricultural and Waste Lands of Wales* (London, 1936).
[2] Viscount Astor and B. Seebohm Rowntree, *British Agriculture*, p. 405.
[3] Lord Ernle, *English Farming* (5th ed.), pp. 518–23. For the number of farms in England and Wales see note 3, p. 256, below.
[4] Lord Ernle, *English Farming* (5th ed.), p. 452; M. H. Tiltman, *English Earth* (London, 1935), p. 274; reports in the publications of the Agricultural Economics Research Institute, Oxford University.
[5] A. G. Street, *Farming England* (London, 1937), p. 31.
[6] P.E.P., *Agricultural Research in Great Britain* (London, 1938).
[7] Described in L. Dudley Stamp, *The Land of Britain: its use and misuse* (London, 1948).
[8] Cited above, p. 253, n. 4.

Watson's broadcast talks of a modern version of Cobbett's rural rides which he made throughout Britain in 1933.[1]

17. COUNTRY TOWNS AND VILLAGES

As with the land, so with the country towns and the villages: there was change and no change. The visitor to a village in 1930 might believe that he had returned, as in a dream, to the year 1910; the same men seated on the benches and the settle, the same talk, the same stories, less changed than the ageing villagers who told them. But there was a difference: the young men were not there.

'. . . There's no one between them and old chaps like us.'

'All the rest were killed, you mean?'

'Most of them, sir. Forty-two were killed from this village and they'd be men of thirty-five and forty by now.'

'Ah! That War didn't do any of us any good,' said Mr. Stillaway. 'Nothing's been the same since.'[2]

In many ways the farm labourer had gained little in the amenities of life since the war. Village cottages, however picturesque to outward view, were in many cases the most appalling hovels. They were cold and they were damp; hence rheumatism, tuberculosis, bronchitis. To repair them would necessitate raising the rent beyond the labourer's capacity to pay; for the same reason the new council houses, renting at about 7s. 6d. a week, were usually beyond his reach.[3] Few cottages had a piped water supply, which was lacking in two-thirds of all rural parishes in England and Wales; in a dry summer drought overtook many villages, and water had to be brought round in carts. In a part of North Oxfordshire surveyed in the late thirties, only 6 out of 14 villages had piped water, and in only two were many houses connected to the water-main; only one-third of the farms had piped water. Sewage-disposal systems were, of course, a rarity. Electricity was becoming more widely available: in the North Oxfordshire survey

---

[1] J. A. S. Watson, *Rural Britain Today and Tomorrow* (Edinburgh, 1934). For examples of what could be done in English farming with skill and enterprise see George Henderson, *The Farming Ladder* (London, 1944) for a fascinating account of the success of two brothers who, as very young men, took over a run-down farm in North Oxfordshire after the war, and George Martelli, *The Elveden Enterprise* (London, 1952), an account of Lord Iveagh's rehabilitation of heath lands in Breckland (Suffolk).

[2] A. G. Macdonell, *England, their England* (London, 1933; cheap edition, 1946), p. 235.

[3] J. W. Robertson Scott, *England's Green and Pleasant Land* (Penguin edition, 1947; first published anonymously in 1925), pp. 15–20, 82, 154–5; A. Hutt, *Condition of the Working Class in Britain* (London, 1933), pp. 217–20.

it was available from the 'grid' in eight villages, and on 19 farms.[1] In the country as a whole rural consumers numbered 203,000, or 4 per cent of the potential number, in 1930. Between 1929 and 1936 the mileage of rural mains increased over four-fold, and the number of farms connected with the electricity supply from 600 (1926) to 4000 in 1932 and 30,000 in 1937.[2]

The farmer was not much better off than his labourers. A good farmer, with 350 acres, might have a real income of £1500 a year. In the area of the North Oxfordshire survey, however, half the farms were of less than 150 acres, often poorly laid out, with scattered, non-contiguous fields, half of them less than ten acres each.[3] In England and Wales 37 per cent of the farms (and one-quarter of the total acreage) were owned by the occupier in 1930. Some 250,000 farmers employed labour, and there were 600,000 farm labourers. In other cases the farmer and his family did all the work of the farm, except at harvest time. The population employed in agriculture in Great Britain, which had been 1,429,000 or 7·79 per cent of the employed population before the war, fell to 1,307,000 (6·75 per cent) in 1921 and 1,194,000 (5·67 per cent) in 1931.[4]

Yet the amenities of living in the country were improving in the twenties. The new council houses brought a new standard into rural housing. The effect of country bus services in stirring the life of the villages can hardly be exaggerated. The wireless brought news, dance music, talks, concerts. In the village hall whist drives and dances provided entertainment. The Women's Institutes, dating from 1915, provided for the women not only help and advice on housekeeping, cooking, gardening, child-care, but also lectures and classes in the arts and crafts, in folk dancing, in government. By 1933 they numbered 5000, with 297,000 members.[5] Flower shows, church fêtes and bazaars on the lawn of the rectory or manor house continued older traditions. The

[1] C. S. Orwin, *Country Planning: a Study of Rural Problems* (Agricultural Economics Research Institute, Oxford, 1944), pp. 53–4, 108–22. This was a survey made in the late thirties of the country south-west of Banbury, including Hook Norton, Bloxham, Sibford. It was rather similar to the social surveys of urban areas, but did not identify the villages it included.
[2] H. H. Ballin, *Organization of Electricity Supply in Great Britain*, p. 231.
[3] C. S. Orwin, *Country Planning*, pp. 32–3, 49. In England and Wales there were 892,000 agricultural holdings in 1931, 40 per cent of them under 20 acres (small holdings), 20 per cent (77,400) of 20–50 acres, 25 per cent (94,000) of 50–150 acres, and 47,000 over 150 acres. In Scotland two-thirds of the holdings (59,500) were under fifty acres (L. D. Stamp and S. H. Beaver, *The British Isles*, p. 197).
[4] L. Dudley Stamp and S. H. Beaver, *British Isles*, p. 144.
[5] Inez Jenkins, *History of the Women's Institute Movement of England and Wales* (Oxford, 1953).

simple rustic, never as simple as he had seemed, acted in the plays put on by the village dramatic society, played cricket or tennis, heard lectures on politics, or recklessly rode his motor-bicycle along the winding, deep-set lanes.[1]

With this, though independent of it, was the townsman's new interest in the country—which reached a peak in the thirties when the Youth Hostels movement got under way. J. W. Robertson Scott founded the *Countryman*, and edited it in his house in Idbury, in the Cotswolds, for twenty years from 1927, whetting the atavistic instincts of town-bound Englishmen. S. L. Bensusan's books on the deep peace of his corner of Essex had great popularity; as did A. G. Street's *Farmer's Glory* (1932), and the Batsford books, with their superb photographs, of the Cotswolds, the Lakes, the Marches, the highlands and lowlands of Scotland, the country towns and villages. The resulting exodus from the towns, small though it was, often had good effects. The retired naval officer or businessman often brought new vigour to the life of the village, active as he might be on committees or in organising lectures, or serving as churchwarden or rural district councillor. He might make up for the loss of many of the squires and lesser country gentry of the past, of the former scholar-rector with an independent income, of the schoolmaster or schoolmistress whom the 'reorganisation' of elementary education had banished from many a village. On the other hand, many of the newcomers were mere transients in week-end cottages, adding nothing to local good works and diminishing the stock of the more habitable labourers' cottages.[2]

In the country towns there were also changes, though more noticeable in the thirties, as motor traffic grew year by year. The wide main street, where small half-timbered houses jostled the newer ones of brick, and bowed shop windows of the eighteenth century still displayed the chemist's ointment jars and the carboys of varicoloured waters, had not been transformed. The town hall, the two or three old coaching inns, with panelled smoking-rooms and stables in the yard, the grammar school and the almshouses, the old stone bridge over the river, the side street of Georgian houses of brick or stone, drowsy in the sunlight, the back alleys with their little slums and their pubs with 'spit and sawdust' bars: all this had changed little in a century. The country town was the capital of its part of the county, its grocers' and ironmongers', saddlers' and seedsmen's shops crowded on market day. It had

[1] J. W. Robertson Scott, pp. 91–93, 114.   [2] Ibid., pp. 28–43, 129–35.

K

the cattle market, and perhaps once a year a fair, with roundabouts and coconut shies; it had its annual cattle show, where the brightly-decked shire-horses, gleaming from the currier, were led round by perspiring carters, and the local gentry, ruddy-faced men with neatly clipped moustaches, greeted each other gravely and sat on their shooting sticks. The old order changed little: local society comprised the vicar, the doctor, the solicitor, the auctioneer, a few elderly gentlewomen of private means, and the editor of the weekly paper, with its long advertisements of farm auctions and its accounts of rustic weddings and funerals. The leading tradesmen composed the borough council and took it in turns to be mayor. And in the private bar of the 'Swan' or the 'Three Cups' an odd collection of men, a sort of informal club, would gather nightly, and talk of the weather and the crops, of fishing, and hunting, of people and places and short cuts, and tell and re-tell their stories of the good old days—stories old in Shakespeare's time, and told in his language: 'old, old, Master Shallow—Nay, she must be old'.[1]

[1] John Moore, *Portrait of Elmbury* (London, 1945), p. 189. The whole book is a charming account of a country town between the wars, a breathing likeness; the town, thinly disguised, is Tewkesbury.

CHAPTER FIVE

The World's Workshop on Short Time

1. DIAGNOSIS

IN the economic affairs of the nation, as in its politics and its social structure, the idea persisted that there could be a return to 1914, to 'normalcy'. Calamity only strengthened it. After the war a boom, then a slump, then by 1925 apparent recovery, so that the return to prewar conditions could be sealed by the restoration of the gold standard at the prewar parity of pound to dollar. Next year's setback to trade was dismissed as the effect of the general strike, the more so as conditions were fairly good in 1927 and 1928. When, late in 1929, Britain began to feel the effects of spreading world depression, growing out of financial weaknesses in the United States and continental Europe and the collapse of the prices of primary products, there were still some to argue that her difficulties were temporary, the product of external forces.

Gradually it became clear that Britain had been in a state of depression ever since the war. For a century she had been becoming more and more dependent on foreign trade, exchanging her manufactures and her coal and her shipping and financial services for raw materials and foodstuffs. Her strength as an exporter had been endangered before the war as competition with other countries became keener; the war had disrupted the old courses of trade, had spurred many countries towards self-sufficiency in manufactures, had strengthened new rivals like the Japanese. Britain's advantages in the pioneer age of the industrial revolution were over; and a world turning to oil for power had less need of her coal. Her staple industries were the most affected —coal, iron and steel, shipbuilding, textiles; and these had supplied the bulk of her exports. Their decline should have been offset by the rise of new industries, and to a limited extent it was. But this could not save the old industries, their workpeople and their centres of activity; the staple industries had been highly concentrated, and where they were, there depression and chronic unemployment settled over towns and people. The new industries went elsewhere.

Throughout the twenties, Britain's industrial machine was throttled down; the world's workshop worked only on short time. Even the crude figures of the *Statistical Abstract*, uncorrected for the fall in the value of money and for the increase of population, showed that something was wrong.[1] The number of the unemployed never dropped below one million; imports were higher than before the war, especially imports of 'food, drink and tobacco' and of manufactured goods; exports, which before the war had increased slightly each year, never recovered their prewar volume but remained at best about 80 per cent of the prewar figure, and in several years lower than that.[2]

There were two major public inquiries into this state of affairs, both by committees appointed by the two Labour governments: the Balfour Committee in 1924 and the Macmillan Committee in 1929. The former, the Committee on Industry and Trade headed by Sir Arthur Balfour,[3] a Sheffield steel manufacturer, was directed to inquire into the 'conditions and prospects of British industry and commerce, with special reference to the export trade'. It issued several reports on particular subjects (a survey of overseas markets, studies of industrial relations, of British industrial efficiency, and of the metal and textile industries) before publishing its final report in 1929. The other committee, on Finance and Industry, was presided over by Hugh Pattison Macmillan, a distinguished Scottish lawyer who became a Lord of Appeal, with a life peerage, in 1930.[4] It included a constellation of economists and financial experts—J. M. Keynes, Professor T. E. Gregory, Reginald McKenna, Lord Bradbury, R. H. Brand—and also Ernest Bevin. It was charged with discovering whether the arrangements for banking, finance and credit, internal and international, were

---

[1] See Table 1.
[2] Cf. *Britain's Industrial Future: being the Report of the Liberal Industrial Inquiry* (London, 1928), pp. 21–2.
[3] Created Lord Riverdale, 1935. Served on the Sankey Coal Commission and on very many government commissions and committees over more than three decades.
[4] H. P. Macmillan (1873–1952), successful Scots advocate and later member of the Parliamentary Bar in London; Lord Advocate of Scotland, 1924, in the Labour government (a non-political appointment in this case); Lord of appeal, 1930; minister of information, 1939–40; served as chairman or member of many public committees and charitable bodies; chairman of the court of the University of London; original member and later chairman of the Pilgrim Trust. His busy and useful life may be compared with that of his friend Josiah Stamp. See his reminiscences, *A Man of Law's Tale.* He is to be distinguished from Harold Macmillan, Conservative M.P., 1924–29, and since 1931, minister of health, 1951; author of *Reconstruction* (1933) and *The Middle Way* (1938), two books on economic problems.

Table 1

Trade, Employment, Wages and Cost of Living
1913 and 1919–30

	1913	1919	1920	1921	1922	1923	1924	1925	1926	1927	1928	1929	1930
Total imports (incl. re-exports) £ millions[1]	768	1626	1932	1085	1003	1096	1227	1320	1241	1218	1195	1220	1043
Volume (1924 = 100)[4] retained imports	94·2						100	108·9	108·6	111·2	107·8	114	111·4
Total exports (including re-exports) £ millions[1]	634	963	1557	810	823	885	940	927	778	832	848	839	657
British exports, Volume (1924 = 100)[4]	131·4						100	99·3	88·9	102·3	104·7	108·3	88·7
Number of persons unemployed (thousands)[2], month of December				2038	1464	1229	1263	1243	1432	1194	1334	1344	2500
Cost-of-Living index[3] (1914 = 100)		215	249	226	183	174	175	176	172	168	166	164	158
Wages, money rates[5] (1914 = 100)		215-20	270-80	210	170	165	170	175	175	170	170	170	170

[1] *Statistical Abstract of U.K., 1930*, p. 316 (figures for the United Kingdom; Irish Free State excluded after April 1, 1923).
[2] Ibid., p. 97 (Great Britain and Northern Ireland).
[3] Ibid., p. 115.
[4] G. D. H. Cole, *British Trade and Industry, past and future* (London, 1932), p. 199.
[5] Ibid., pp. 124, 202.

helping or handicapping trade and industrial employment. Its report, largely written by Keynes, was an elaborate and important account of British banking, credit and investment practices; but its recommendations were cautious, and by the time they appeared, June 23, 1931, had been almost overtaken by events.[1] Equally thorough in its investigations, and more widely disseminated, was the work of a committee of Liberals, the Liberal Industrial Inquiry, under Walter Layton, the editor of the *Economist* and subsequently (as Lord Layton) chairman of the *News Chronicle*. Its membership was distinguished, including Lloyd George, Keynes, Seebohm Rowntree, Sir Herbert Samuel, Sir John Simon, Philip Kerr, Ramsay Muir, C. F. G. Masterman, and many leaders in academic, industrial and public life on its special committees. Its report, *Britain's Industrial Future*, was published in a cheap edition with yellow paper covers in 1928, and had a large circulation. The fact that the 'Liberal Yellow Book' was bound up with Lloyd George's bold but unsuccessful programme for the 1929 election gave it an added importance.

2. THE CHANGING CHARACTER OF BRITISH TRADE

By 1929 certain changes in Britain's trade were obvious. The volume of imports was about 20 per cent higher than before the war, and the volume of exports about 20 per cent lower, and this at a time when world trade was rising. True, Europe's share of world trade in 1929 was also less than in 1913; it was the United States and Japan which had increased their share. In 1913 Europe accounted for 58·5 per cent of world trade, in 1929 for 52·2 per cent. Britain took 15·24 per cent of the world's retained imports in 1913, and provided 13·11 per cent of the world's domestic exports. In 1927–29 British imports were 15·5 per cent of the world's total, but British exports had fallen to 10·94 per cent.[2] By 1929 Britain, the world's chief exporter in 1913, was second to the United States, whose share of the world's export trade had risen to 15·77 per cent.[3]

[1] See the summary of the hearings and report in R. F. Harrod, *J. M. Keynes*, pp. 413–26

[2] G. D. H. Cole, *British Trade and Industry*, pp. 127, 129, 214–15.

[3] A. E. Kahn, *Great Britain in the World Economy* (New York, 1946), p. 133. Other accounts of the trends in British and world trade are to be found in Cole, in W. A. Lewis, *Economic Survey, 1919–1939* (London, 1949), pp. 35 ff., and the same author's 'World Production, Prices and Trade, 1870–1960', *Manchester School*, XX (1952), 105–38; also in A. Loveday, *Britain and World Trade* (London, 1931), pp. 147 ff., in André Siegfried, *England's Crisis* (New York, 1931), and in *Britain's Industrial Future*, pp. 21–6. For a general discussion of the international economy after the war, see William Ashworth, *Short History of the International Economy, 1850–1950* (London, 1952), pp. 188 ff.

What made the position even more serious was that by 1927 Europe's recovery had outstripped Britain's, although in the years immediately after the war the recovery of Europe as a whole had been slower than Britain's. In 1927 the value of Europe's exports was 45 per cent higher than in 1913, but Britain's exports were only 35 per cent higher.[1] By 1928 the export trade of France, Italy and Sweden had increased in real value (eliminating price changes) over that of 1913, that of Britain had declined. The index of France's quantum of exports stood at 148 (1913 = 100). Italy's at 132·2, Sweden's at 106·8, Britain's at 84·4. Britain's quantum of exports was lower, compared with 1913, than that of any other country save Russia; she was selling less, compared with prewar, than any other country, and was only partly making up for it in higher prices.[2] Yet the quantum of world trade had greatly increased; if the index for 1913 was 100, in 1929 it was 133.[3]

Two things prevented these changes from being disastrous to the country as a whole, however tragically they affected particular regions and industries. One was the change in the terms of trade, which, after moving slightly against Great Britain just before the war, turned in her favour in the twenties, and even more so in the thirties. The price of primary products, which Britain imported, fell relatively to the price of manufactured goods, Britain's main exports, so that a smaller volume of exports purchased a larger volume of imports. Both import and export prices were higher in the twenties than before the war, but the increase, after the postwar boom, remained much greater in export prices than in imports, and in the thirties import prices, though not export prices, were lower than they had been in 1913. This 'windfall addition to national income' meant that in 1929 a given unit of British labour could purchase 14 per cent more imports than it could have obtained in 1913; the index of the terms of trade (1913 = 100) stood at 114·5 in Britain's favour in 1929.[4] This was no unmixed blessing, for the resulting poverty in the producer countries made them poor markets for British manufactures; this in turn affected Britain's export industries, leading to unemployment and reduced purchasing power of the working population.

[1] A. E. Kahn, p. 158.   [2] A. Loveday, *Britain and World Trade*, pp. 153–5.
[3] W. A. Lewis, *Economic Survey*, p. 79.
[4] A. E. Kahn, pp. 153–4; see also table on p. 144. Cf. W. W. Rostow, 'The Terms of Trade in Theory and Practice', *Economic History Review*, second series, III (1950), 1–20; G. D. H. Cole, *British Trade and Industry*, p. 172. Colin Clark, *Conditions of Economic Progress* (London, 1940), p. 453, gives a table showing a higher and sharply fluctuating advantage to Britain in the terms of trade.

Not over-production but under-consumption was the real trouble. The result was, however, that Britain was able to exist after a fashion; the middle and upper classes fairly comfortably, many of the poor poorly. The general well-being of Britain depended, not only on low prices for farmers overseas, but on the poverty of the 'depressed areas' at home.[1]

The second thing which saved Britain's trading account from disaster was the fact that for at least a century it had never depended on the export of goods alone to pay for what was imported. The invisible exports made up of shipping receipts, income from overseas investments, and income from insurance and other financial transactions had always made up the difference. They continued to do so; but since the export of goods now paid for a

Table 2

Balance of payments: overseas capital investment,
1913 and 1924–30 (£ millions)[2]

	1913	1924	1925	1926	1927	1928	1929	1930
Imports		1291	1331	1253	1226	1206	1229	1053
Exports		953	940	790	839	853	848	666
Balance	− 158	− 338	− 392	− 463	− 386	− 353	− 381	− 387
Shipping receipts ..	94	140	124	120	140	130	130	105
Income from overseas investments ..	210	220	250	250	250	250	250	220
Other receipts (net)	35	50	64	79	79	95	104	89
Balance	181	72	46	− 14	83	122	103	27
New capital issues: British Empire ..	76 (*a*)	134·2 (*c*)	87·8 (*c*)	70 (*b*)				
New capital issues: foreign	100 (*a*)			49 (*b*)				

(*a*) Annual average, 1910–13
(*b*) Annual average, 1926–30
(*c*) E. V. Morgan, *Studies in British Financial Policy*, p. 264.

[1] See R. S. Sayers' review of Kahn's book, *Economic History Review*, second series, I (1948), 73–4, and G. C. Allen, *British Industries and their Organization* (revised edition, London, 1935), pp. 278–80.

[2] A. E. Kahn, pp. 126, 127, 139 (these figures differ slightly from those given in the *Statistical Abstract* and used in Table 1, above). E. V. Morgan, *Studies in British Financial Policy*, gives figures for 1913–25 for capital issues (p. 264), for receipts from shipping and investments (pp. 315–16), for gold movements (p. 335) and for the balance of payments (p. 341). He accepts a figure of about £550 millions for sales of British foreign investments during 1914–19; in 1910 British overseas investments were (Sir George Paish's estimate) £1554 millions within the British Empire, £1638 millions in foreign countries, £3192 millions altogether (*ibid.*, pp. 328–31). G. D. H. Cole, *British Trade and Industry*, pp. 180–1, gives other figures, including overseas capital issues annually for 1924–29. See also *Britain's Industrial Future*, pp. 27–9.

smaller part of the goods imported, the favourable balance created by the invisible exports was much smaller. There was such a balance in the twenties, except for 1926; but it was not large enough to finance new overseas investments on the prewar scale. There was thus a decline in new overseas investments, though not as large as the decline in the trade balance.

The decline in the volume of exports was not matched by a decline in production. Britain's industrial production increased by about 21·5 per cent in value between the two Censuses of Production of 1907 and 1924 (the increase in population in this period was 11 per cent); thereafter production increased, though not consistently, until in 1929 it was about 12 per cent higher than in 1924.[1] This increase matched, but fell below, the increase in the world's industrial production, of which the index (1913 = 100) stood at 139 in 1929, according to the calculations of the Bank of International Settlements.[2] The increase in production, coupled with a decline in exports, would suggest that the home market was receiving larger supplies; and the parallel increase of imports supports the idea that the general standard of living was rising.

The changes in the import trade were symptomatic of the state of the economy. Between 1913 and 1925 the index of volume of net imports rose from 100 to 111.8; but for food, drink and tobacco the rise was from 100 to 123·0, in manufactured articles it was to 117·9, and in raw materials there was a decline, from 100 to 96·9.[3] The increased imports of food were mainly meat, butter, eggs, tea, oranges, bananas; such staples as wheat and other grains, potatoes, sugar, showed slight increases or in some cases, a decline. The figures of imports of raw materials were affected by the large increases in crude petroleum and rubber, and decreases in iron ore and cotton. The manufactured or partly manufactured articles of which the imports increased were those demanded by new technology and new tastes of consumers: iron and steel, copper, lead, cinema films, electrical goods, machinery, cotton goods, petrol, paper, motor cars. The sources of imports in 1929 were much the same as in 1913 as between countries within the British Empire and those outside: the Empire supplied about one-quarter of Britain's imports by value (26·5 per cent in 1929), Europe

---

[1] G. D. H. Cole, *British Trade and Industry*, pp. 147, 202–17; Colin Clark, 'Statistical studies relating to the present economic position of Great Britain', *Economic Journal* 41: 360 (1931). E. V. Morgan, p. 68, gives two indices which show a decline in production in 1919–25 as compared with 1913.

[2] A. E. Kahn, pp. 63, 259.

[3] *Britain's Industrial Future*, p. 22.

supplied 39·8 per cent in 1929, North and South America (including Canada) 32·1 per cent.[1]

The export of all articles increased, between 1913 and 1929, as far as values were concerned, except in the case of coal, whose export declined in both value and volume. The volume of iron and steel exports was below the 1913 figure throughout the twenties; there was a sharp decline in the volume of cotton exports: violent fluctuations in the value and tonnage of shipbuilding for export. The proportion of the volume of exports going to Empire countries increased from 37·2 per cent to 41·5 per cent between 1913 and 1929.[2] Among the continents, Europe was still Britain's largest market: it took 34·7 per cent of Britain's exports by value in 1929, the same proportion as in 1913; Asia stood second as a market.[3] Britain's trade balance with Europe became more adverse than it had been before the war; the increases in Britain's imports of food from the Netherlands and Denmark, the decline in the sale of coal to Italy, the increase in the importation of iron and steel, machinery, electrical goods and rayon from Germany, France, Belgium and elsewhere were not matched by enlarged British exports to the continent. British capital flowed to the continent, but not goods in equal measure.[4]

One remedy for the ailments of trade and industry, dreamed of and expounded by the Conservatives, was a protective tariff. It could not be prescribed, however, except in small doses, after the Conservatives' defeat in 1923. Churchill in 1925 restored the McKenna duties which Philip Snowden had banished: duties of $33\frac{1}{3}$ per cent on motor-cars, watches, films; in 1926 commercial motors, and in 1927 tyres were brought within their scope. The imperial preference of $33\frac{1}{3}$ per cent on dutiable imports was restored in 1925. In that year 'safeguarding' duties (33 per cent *ad valorem*) were conceded, after inquiries by committees of the Board of Trade, on lace, cutlery, gas mantles and fabric gloves; for this purpose a new Safeguarding of Industries Bill was enacted (and extended in 1926), under which industries might apply to the Board of Trade for protection, provided they could show that they were suffering from unfair competition, such as threatened to increase unemployment at home. The protection of safeguarding

[1] Werner Schlote, *British Overseas Trade from 1700 to the 1930s*, tr. W. O. Henderson and W. H. Chaloner (Oxford, 1952), pp. 139–47, 157, 163; G. D. H. Cole, *British Trade and Industry*, pp. 189–200.
[2] For a discussion of the possibilities and illusions of Empire trade, see A. Siegfried, *England's Crisis*, pp. 224 ff.
[3] W. Schlote, *British Overseas Trade*, pp. 147–54, 160, 167.
[4] A. E. Kahn, pp. 237–9; E. V. Morgan, pp. 307–9.

was extended to translucent pottery in 1927 and buttons and enamelled hollow-ware in 1928; and British cinema films given the benefit of a quota in 1927. Liberals and some Labour members protested with ancient vigour; they could not stop these measures but they prevented any more.[1]

3. HANDICAPS TO BRITISH TRADE, PRINCIPALLY MONETARY

The usual explanation given for Britain's difficulties in trade was that she had, by returning to the gold standard in 1925 at the prewar parity of pound to dollar, over-valued the pound—by about 10 per cent, according to Keynes; not the gold standard itself, but the over-valuation of the pound, was the cause of the trouble. The result was not to cheapen imports, but to make exports artificially high-priced. Moreover, the cheapening of imports exposed Britain, if not to 'dumping', at least to the large importations of manufactured goods, a significant tendency in her imports in the 1920's.

Such an analysis of the effects of over-valuing the pound was not just wisdom after the event. It was made, in 1925, by Keynes in a pamphlet, *The Economic Consequences of Mr. Churchill*.[2] It was, of course, much more widely accepted after 1929, when the depression was obvious, and the set-back to trade caused by the general strike could not be used to explain it. In the hearings of the Macmillan Committee in 1930, Keynes and Bevin forced Montagu Norman to admit that the raising of the Bank rate, done for international reasons, had had internal consequences. Norman tried to blame the misfortunes of British industry on bad luck, denied that the return to the gold standard had made wage reductions inevitable, and ascribed Britain's difficulties to 'other factors'; when pressed, he named the stabilisation of French, Belgium and German currencies at low levels. He had, in the end, to admit that the Bank's policy, to save gold, might increase unemployment.[3] In its report, the committee conceded that the over-valuation of sterling had given England a 'competitive handicap' which was 'substantial'.[4]

Economists since then have generally agreed with this con-

---

[1] *Annual Register, 1925*, pp. 5–8, 39–47, 120; A. E. Kahn, p. 108; D. Abel, *History of British Tariffs, 1913–1942* (London, 1945), pp. 24–50.
[2] Reprinted in *Essays in Persuasion* (1932).
[3] Committee on Finance and Industry, *Minutes of Evidence* (1931), I, 210–22, especially questions 3319, 3328–34, 3351, 3360–2, 3393.
[4] Ibid., *Report* (Macmillan Report), Cmd. 3897 (1931), p. 55.

clusion.[1] It can be argued that circumstances were against British trade anyhow: that the world needed less of Britain's staple exports; over-valuation, by keeping up their prices, only made things worse. That it was not the sole cause of trouble is shown by the stagnation of the export trades after devaluation in 1931, though admittedly demand was low all over the world at that time.[2]

With the pound over-valued, two things could happen. Export prices could be forced down, to offset the 10 per cent handicap; apart from savings by improved methods of production, this could only mean a reduction of wages, achieved voluntarily or by the pressure of unemployment. Or the volume of exports could be allowed to fall and the increased adverse balance of payments be met by shipments of gold from England. This second remedy was, however, the last which the Bank of England and the financial authorities would permit to happen, for it would weaken what the return to the gold standard at parity was supposed to produce, the renewed supremacy of the English money market. Hence the Bank rate was raised from 4 per cent to 5 per cent in December, 1925, putting it one point above the New York rate, to attract American short-term funds to London; and at the same time foreign lending was discouraged and credit in Great Britain tightened.[3]

At the same time, the policy of deflation was not followed either, despite the popular impression to the contrary. The return to the gold standard helped to bring on the crisis in the coal mines; and the general strike was the result. After that, however, there was no *general* decline in wages, and in fact real wages rose slightly, as money wages fell less than the cost of living.[4]

Hence British wages remained high in relation to wages in other countries. The International Labour Office index of comparative real wages in July 1928 was: London, 100, Berlin, 66, Paris, 56, Brussels, 55, Warsaw, 43, Vienna, 48, Milan, 45, New

[1] Lionel Robbins, *The Great Depression* (London, 1934), pp. 78–81; W. A. Lewis, *Economic Survey*, pp. 42, 80–1; J. H. Jones, in *Britain in Depression* (London, 1935), pp. 5–12; G. C. Allen, *British Industries and their Organization*, pp. 282–3—four professors of economics. *Britain in Depression* was a collaborative work by a Research Committee of the Economic Science section of the British Association for the Advancement of Science. Cf. E. V. Francis, *Britain's Economic Strategy* (London, 1939), pp. 52–4.

[2] A. Loveday, *Britain and World Trade*, pp. 156–9; A. E. Kahn, pp. 141–2, 170–2; R. S. Sayers' review of Kahn, *Economic History Review*, second series, I, 73–4.

[3] The Bank rate was lowered to 4·5 per cent in April 1927 and raised in 1929 to 5·5 per cent (February), 6·5 per cent (September 26) whence it dropped by stages to 3 per cent in May 1930 (*Statistical Abstract of U.K., 1930*, p. 207).

[4] See Table 1 above.

York, 179, Ottawa, 157. Export prices tended, as a result of all these factors, to remain high in comparison with those of other countries.[1]

Another adverse condition was the shortage of capital. That there was a shortage may seem to be belied by the rate of new overseas investment each year, which greatly exceeded the balance in Britain's trading account (see table 2, above). Much of this, however, was financed by short-term capital attracted to London from other countries, partly by favourable terms intended to offset the postwar financial leadership of New York and Paris. In 1913, a typical prewar year, new capital issues were £242·1 millions, of which £44·6 millions were for domestic purposes. In 1921–25 new capital issues averaged £219·7 millions, of which £97·9 millions were home issues.[2] Though such sums might seem large, they were not adequate for the modernisation of old industries and the development of new ones; and the older industries were turning from internal financing to the floating of new issues. There was traditionally little connection between British financial and banking interests and British industry, as compared to the close connections between the City and foreign enterprises.[3] Yet it was not until the depression that the Bank of England and the other banks came together to form the Bankers' Industrial Development Company, to give industry the benefit of the bankers' advice and aid over 'rationalisation'. The Macmillan Report declared that the supply of credit for industry was generally adequate, except for financing sales abroad, but that there ought to be closer relations between the City and industry.[4]

Much of the new capital investment went into non-productive enterprises, such as entertainment or the production of automatic vending machines. Much was lost in mere speculation, especially in 1928 when Britain experienced a stock-market boom which reflected, on a humbler scale the glittering promotions of the New York market, and ended only a month sooner, when Clarence Hatry's companies collapsed on September 20, 1929. The Macmillan Committee reported that in 1928 £117 millions were

[1] G. D. H. Cole, *British Trade and Industry*, p. 312. See Cole's discussion and tables, pp. 307–15, which minimize the factor of comparative wages as a handicap to British trade. Cf. A. Siegfried, *England's Crisis*, pp. 83–92. Committee on Industry and Trade, *Final Report*, Cmd. 3282 (1929), pp. 94–7, 131, 248; A. E. Kahn, p. 82; A. Loveday, pp. 172–5.
[2] E. V. Morgan, p. 264.
[3] A. E. Kahn, pp. 76–7; Committee on Finance and Industry, *Minutes of Evidence*, questions 3336, 3511–16.
[4] Committee on Finance and Industry, *Report*, pp. 168, 170.

subscribed for new issues in 284 companies; by the end of May 1931 the market value of these issues was £66 millions, a loss of 47 per cent. Seventy of the companies had been wound up, and in 36 others the capital issues had lost all value; the total capital of these 106 companies had been £20 millions.[1] A study by the *Economist* examined 128 new companies formed in 1928, with capital of a par value of £30 millions; at the peak, this capital had a market value of £38½ millions, by August 1929 it was worth £17 millions. The greatest losses were in gramophone companies (whose development had been encouraged by recent successes by the two major companies, His Master's Voice and Columbia), and companies concerned with safety glass, films, artificial silk, and automatic machines.[2]

4. NEW INDUSTRIES FOR OLD?

Financial difficulties apart, there was a new challenge to British industry. New industries were rising alongside the old. The home market was ripe for development. The consumption goods industries, the tertiary or service industries, were expanding. The dependence on foreign trade was declining. Could the new industries compensate for the decline of the old?

The importance of overseas trade to British industry was great, but it was diminishing. It has been estimated, on the basis of the Census of Production for 1924 and 1930, that in 1924–25 27·5–29·5 per cent of national production was exported, in 1930–31 20·5–22·5 per cent. If the products of agriculture and mining, and the manufacture of food, drink and tobacco are omitted, the proportion of the production of the other factory industries going for export was 33–35 per cent in 1924, 25–27 per cent in 1930.[3] Dr. Schlote has calculated an index of relation between the national income (in terms of purchasing power in 1913) and the volume of Britain's overseas trade (on the basis of values in 1913). In

---

[1] Committee on Finance and Industry, *Report*, p. 166.

[2] 'Company Promotions of 1928—an inquest', *Economist*, August 17, 1929. Hatry's promotions included investment trusts, automatic photographic machines, department stores, the steel industry, and municipal loans. The liabilities of the group totalled £29·5 millions, of which £13·5 millions were unsecured. See *Economist*, September 21, 1929–February 1, 1930. The connection of Hatry with United Steel Companies, Ltd., is referred to in P.W.S. Andrews and Elizabeth Brunner, *Capital Development in Steel: a study of the United Steel Companies, Ltd.* (Oxford, 1951), pp. 158–61.

[3] G. W. Daniels and H. Campion, 'The Relative Importance of British Export Trade', *London and Cambridge Economic Service, Special Memorandum* No. 41 (1935), pp. 13–15, 17–18.

this index, if 1913 = 100, the relation in 1927–29 was 83·0, in 1930–33 61·2.[1]

Such a change was bound to cause much discomfort. Britain's past reliance on the export trade was not only great in itself, but was concentrated on a few staple industries, and particularly on the heavy industries. In 1907 about 30 per cent of Britain's industrial output was exported; and of total exports of British production as much as 70·3 per cent was made up of coal, iron and steel, textiles, machinery, cutlery, tools and hardware (in 1913 65·5 per cent). The industries producing these goods accounted for 50 per cent of Britain's industrial production, and employed 20–25 per cent of the occupied population.[2] By 1930 the output of coal had fallen from 266 million tons (in 1907) to 243 million tons, and exports from 82 million tons to 70 million tons; the proportion of output exported had fallen from 30·8 per cent to 28·9 per cent. Output and exports of iron and steel rose, by value, between 1907 and 1930, but the proportion exported fell from 31·6 per cent to 22·7 per cent. In the cotton industry, production declined from a value of £125 millions to £118 millions, exports from £105 millions to £86 millions, the proportion of output exported from 83·6 per cent to 73·1 per cent.[3] In 1913 cotton goods had constituted 31 per cent of all manufactured exports, in 1929 they constituted only 23·5 per cent.[4]

It was unfortunate that it was just those products of which Britain had the most to offer that the world had become least interested in taking. The studies of the Institut für Weltwirtschaft at Kiel University have shown that in 1929 the bulk of the manufactured goods exported by Great Britain consisted of goods for which the world market was growing least rapidly: 42·1 per cent of Britain's exports (of manufactures) were in this class, and only 4·3 per cent in the class of goods for which the world demand was increasing most rapidly. By contrast, Germany's exports consisted largely (55·3 per cent) of goods for which the world market was growing at an intermediate rate; and of the exports of the United States only 17·1 per cent were in the category of goods for which the market was growing slowly, and 28·6 per cent in the class in which world demand was rising most rapidly.[5]

Perhaps the decline in the market for the products of the old, staple industries could be redeemed by the growth of markets,

---

[1] Werner Schlote, *British Overseas Trade*, p. 49.   [2] A. E. Kahn, pp. 66–7.
[3] A. E. Kahn, p. 68.   [4] G. D. H. Cole, *British Trade and Industry*, p. 186.
[5] Cited in W. A. Lewis, *Economic Survey*, p. 78.

both at home and overseas, for the goods of the new and expanding industries, most of them light industries. The most important were the electrical industry, motor cars, bicycles, aircraft, rayon, hosiery, plastics, chemicals, stainless steel, scientific instruments.[1] The value of the output of these industries was only 6·5 per cent of the total output of British industry in 1907, but was 12·5 per cent in 1924 and 16·3 per cent in 1930. Their exports were worth £31·6 millions in 1907, £82·3 millions in 1924, £83 millions in 1930, equivalent to 7·4 per cent, 10·3 per cent and 14·6 per cent of the total of British exports. Such growth, however encouraging, was not large enough to compensate for the decline of the staple exports, and the proportion of the output of the new industries which was exported was lower than was the case with the older industries. Moreover, the imports attributable to the new industries, especially oil, expanded greatly, whereas imports of staple goods remained much smaller in value and became smaller in relation to total imports.[2]

The growth of the new industries can be seen from figures of their average annual increase in output between 1923 and 1935. These were 15·7 per cent for artificial silk, 10·2 per cent for electrical goods, 10·1 per cent for motor cars, 5·3 per cent for dyestuffs, compared with a rate of only 1·9 per cent for British industry as a whole.[3] As exporters, however, their growth was slower than that of their counterparts in the United States, Switzerland, Netherlands, Germany, Canada, and their share of the world market fell between 1913 and 1929, and most sharply in the late twenties, as European recovery from the war was completed.[4]

The reasons for the failure of the new industries to make a larger impression on the world market were various. Lack of capital, lack of good design and of study of the foreign customers' requirements may have held them back. There were charges of poor workmanship and, conversely, of Britain's reputation for solid, everlasting manufactures which prevented her from exploiting a market demanding cheap and flashy articles. In some cases British costs were high, and other countries could produce better and cheaper goods by mass-production methods. Britain

[1] R. S. Sayers, 'Springs of technical progress in Britain, 1919–1939', *Economic Journal*, 60: 275–91 (1950). In 1933 there were estimated to be thirty firms in Birmingham making plastics, most of them started in the previous ten years: Asa Briggs, *History of Birmingham*, II, 291.

[2] A. E. Kahn, pp. 106–9; cf. G. D. H. Cole, *Br. Trade and Industry*, pp. 187, 210.

[3] W. Hoffmann, 'The growth of industrial production in Great Britain: a quantitative study', *Economic History Review*, second series, II (1949), pp. 165, 167.

[4] See A. Loveday, pp. 160–70.

had in the new industries, unlike the old, no advantage from experience, from a head start. The home market was both an advantage and a curse to the new industries: an advantage, since it absorbed most of their products, a handicap, since it discouraged the production of articles which might appeal to the foreign consumer. Here, at any rate, was one great source of Britain's difficulties: the new industries did not grow fast enough to compensate for the decline of the old.[1] 'Today what is really important and significant in England is not the depression of the depressed industries, but the relatively small progress made by the relatively prosperous,' wrote an economist in 1930.[2]

None the less, the shift from old industries to new, and from secondary to tertiary industries, was clear to see. The electrical, automobile, aircraft, rayon, hosiery, chemicals and scientific instrument industries employed 370,500 persons in 1907, 745,000 in 1924, 914,000 in 1930, respectively 5·2 per cent, 10·2 per cent and 12·7 per cent of the working force in British industry.[3] The decline in the numbers and proportions of persons occupied in agriculture, mining, textiles, metal-working and machinery, is matched by the rise in the numbers engaged in commerce, building, personal service, public administration, utilities, entertainment and sport and in the manufacture of food, drink and tobacco, chemicals, bricks, pottery and glass.[4]

These changes were little short of tragic to the men and women whose lives had been committed to work in the older industries. The numbers insured in the coal-mining industry fell between 1924 and 1930 from 1,259,000 to 1,069,000; in iron and steel numbers fell from 313,000 to 287,000, in shipbuilding from 254,000 to 205,000, in cotton from 572,000 to 564,000, in wool from 262,000 to 240,000.[5] And in spite of the shrinkage of the labour force in these industries, the proportion of their workers who were unemployed rose. In 1924 6·9 per cent of the coal miners were unemployed, in 1930 28·3 per cent; in iron and steel (melting, rolling and forging), the proportion of workers unemployed was 20·4 per cent and 32·6 per cent in 1924 and 1930; in

[1] A. E. Kahn, pp. 72–5; G. D. H. Cole, pp. 397–400; E. V. Francis, *Britain's Economic Strategy*, p. 57; G. C. Allen, *British Industries and Their Organization*, pp. 277 ff.
[2] A. Loveday, p. 160.   [3] A. E. Kahn, p. 106.
[4] See tables in A. M. Carr-Saunders and D. Caradog Jones, *Social Structure of England and Wales* (2nd ed., 1937), pp. 36, 39. Annual figures for the number of insured workers in the various industries are given in the *Statistical Abstract of U.K.*, e.g., *1930*, pp. 98–101. See also chap. 8, below, pp. 452–3.
[5] *Statistical Abstract of U.K., 1930*, p. 98.

shipbuilding it was 28·3 per cent and 31·7 per cent; in cotton 15·9 per cent and 44·7 per cent, in wool 7·3 per cent and 26·1 per cent.[1] These figures of course conceal certain fluctuations. Between June 1923 and April 1926, a fairly prosperous time, unemployment averaged 22·3 per cent of the insured workers in iron and steel, 34·5 per cent in shipbuilding, 12·3 per cent in cotton (and much short time in addition), 10·7 per cent in wool. In 1927 unemployment among male insured workers was 15·8 per cent in five industries, coal, metal manufacture, engineering, shipbuilding, cotton and woollens; these industries employed about one-third of all male insured workers. Yet in industry as a whole only 11·3 per cent were unemployed.[2]

In this paradox lay the tragedy of industrial Britain between the wars. The staple industries, which were now contracting, occupied their historic and well-defined areas—the areas of the older coalfields: South Wales, parts of the Midlands, Lancashire and the West Riding of Yorkshire, the Tees-Tyne area of Durham and Northumberland, the isolated industrial area of west Cumberland, and the industrial belt of Scotland. Here they flourished or dwindled together: coal-mining, iron and steel, engineering, shipbuilding, textiles. If the newer and expanding industries had established themselves here, all would have been well. The expansion of the industrial chemicals industry in Lancashire, Cheshire and Durham was some gain; especially the development of the huge plant of Brunner, Mond (later Imperial Chemical Industries) at Billingham, near Stockton-on-Tees, after 1923. But the new industries were mostly light industries, needing little but supplies of power and an abundance of semi-skilled labour; both of which they could get or attract in pleasant surroundings away from the blighted areas of the older industries. New industrial centres grew in the south of England, some in the south Midlands but most of them in London and the Home Counties. Hence the two Englands, or rather the two Britains of the interwar years: chronic depression in the north and in the Celtic fringe, moderate prosperity in the south.

The effects of this can be seen in the incidence of unemployment. In Great Britain as a whole, the number of insured workers increased 10·8 per cent between 1913 and 1930; but in London the increase was 15·7 per cent, in the Midlands 13 per cent, in north-eastern England 6·2 per cent, in Scotland 4·6 per cent, in

[1] *Statistical Abstract of U.K.*, 1930, p. 102 (July figures).
[2] *Britain's Industrial Future*, pp. 23–4.

Wales a decrease of 0·9 per cent. Of these workers the following proportions were unemployed in December, 1923 and December 1930:[1]

| | | *Percentage Unemployed* | |
		1923	*1930*
London	..	9·0	9·8
Midlands	..	9·4	18·6
North-east	..	11·7	24·5
North-west	..	12·7	29·3
Scotland	..	13·5	23·5
Wales	..	5·6	31·2
Great Britain	..	11·2	19·9

BIBLIOGRAPHICAL NOTE ON THE NEW INDUSTRIES

A. Plummer, *New British Industries in the Twentieth Century* (London, 1937) is an excellent introduction; also D. H. Smith, *Industries of Greater London* (London, 1933), and Stephen Miall, *History of the British Chemical Industry* (London, 1931). For the electrical and motor-car industries see the Committee on Industry and Trade (Balfour Committee), *Survey of Metal Industries*, and A. E. Kahn, *Great Britain in the World Economy*, and for motor cars the admirable account in G. C. Allen, *British Industries and their Organization*. Non-ferrous metals are treated in *Britain in Depression*, pp. 313–21, and Winifred Lewis, *The Light Metals Industry* (London, 1949). For the rayon industry see Plummer, Miall, the Balfour Committee's *Survey of Textile Industries*, and H. A. Silverman (ed.), *Studies in Industrial Organization* (London, 1946); Silverman also contains chapters on the hosiery and boot and shoe industries.

The soap and vegetable oils industry was dominated by Lever Brothers, which also expanded into food processing and chains of grocery stores (such as Liptons, Maypole, Home and Colonial). Unilever, a combination of British and Dutch interests, was formed in 1929. See Miall, pp. 237–42; A. Plummer, *International Combines in Modern Industry* (2nd ed., London, 1938), pp. 41–6; and especially the article and chart in *Economist*, June 11, 1932. Also Charles Wilson, *History of Unilever* (2 vols., London, 1954).

There is no satisfactory account of the formation of Imperial Chemical Industries (I.C.I.) in 1926. This merging of several large concerns in chemicals, dyes and explosives, Brunner, Mond, United Alkali, British Dyestuffs, Nobel Industries, with a combined capital of £56 millions, was the work of Sir Alfred Mond and Sir Harry (later Lord) McGowan, chairman of Nobel Industries. See Miall; also A. F. Lucas, *Industrial Reconstruction and the Control of Competition* (London, 1937), pp. 174–89; Hector Bolitho, *Alfred Mond* (London, 1933), pp. 290–304.

5. THE AILING GIANTS

These circumstances discouraged enterprise in the older, staple industries. Some of them—iron and steel, shipbuilding, cotton—had suffered much from the postwar boom: their capacity had been over-expanded, their capital inflated by bonus shares, new flotations, grandiose amalgamations. All of them, but coal-mining

[1] G. D. H. Cole, *British Trade and Industry*, p. 215. Cf. table comparing increases and decreases in the numbers insured in various industries in the north and south between 1927 and 1935 in A. M. Carr-Saunders, *Social Structure* (2nd ed.), p. 43.

more than any, were deficient in their techniques of production. And when they needed help most, to improve their competitive position abroad and at home during the twenties, they lacked the means and the spirit to obtain it.

The coalmining industry was at the end of its pioneering age; its record of 287 million tons of coal raised in 1913 (as compared with about 253 million tons annually in the twenties) had been achieved with the prodigal use of men, brawn and hand picks.[1] Output per manshift in 1927 barely exceeded that for 1914, though by 1932 the increase was significant: 20·32 hundredweight in 1914, 20·61 in 1927 (both for an eight-hour shift), 21.99 in 1932 for a 7½-hour shift. This increase was, however, small compared with that of the continental mines. By 1936, the peak year in every country, Britain's output per manshift was 14 per cent above that of 1927, whereas the increase in the Ruhr mines was 81 per cent, in the Polish mines 54 per cent, in the Dutch mines 118 per cent.[2]

The reason for this disparity was that mechanisation of mining had made less progress in Britain than elsewhere. There was progress, and in difficult conditions: many mines were old (according to the Samuel Commission, the average age of the larger mines was 51 years, and 57 mines, employing an average of 855 men, were over a century old), and in many of them thinner seams were being worked at a greater distance from the surface—the day of easy winnings was over.[3] In 1913 8 per cent of total output was cut by coal-cutting machines; in 1921 14 per cent, in 1925 20 per cent, in 1930 31 per cent, in 1932 38 per cent (80 million tons). There were 1373 conveyors in use in 1924, 3218 in 1929, 4120 in 1932, conveying 53 million tons, or 25 per cent of output. Twenty per cent of the output of coal was washed in 1927, 34 per cent in 1932, the increase in the number of coal-cleaning plants being principally among dry-cleaning plants (27 in 1927, 128 in 1932). The amount of electricity used by the mines above and below ground increased: the number of pit ponies employed fell from 68,000 in 1920 to 41,500 in 1932.[4] There was also an in-

---

[1] W. H. B. Court, 'Problems of the British Coal Industry between the wars', *Economic History Review*, XV (1945), pp. 1–4 (a most enlightening article throughout). See also the excellent account of the industry in J. H. Jones, *The Coal-mining Industry* (London, 1939).

[2] *Coal Mining*: Report of the Technical Advisory Committee (C. C. Reid, chairman), Cmd. 6610 (1945), p. 29; cf. Court, *loc. cit.*, pp. 20–21.

[3] Royal Commission on the Coal Industry, *Report* (Sir Herbert Samuel, chairman), Cmd. 2600 (1926), pp. 46, 123.

[4] A. M. Neuman, *Economic Organization of the British Coal Industry* (London, 1934), pp. 43–5; P.E.P., *Report on the British Coal Industry* (London, 1936), pp. 35, 38.

crease in the use of pneumatic picks, but mainly for ripping and drilling: their use for getting coal, which began in 1928, was limited, since as late as 1934 only 5¾ million tons was obtained in this way.[1] Much coal was still cut by hand, and much of it man-handled for part of its journey underground in the tubs. Where conveyors were used, the lack of loaders (still true in the 1940's) limited their effectiveness. Transport generally was bad: most main haulage (haulage of tubs along the main passages from the workings to the bottom of the shaft) was by endless cable. As late as 1945 the Technical Advisory Committee on Coal Mining (the Reid Committee) declared that 'no single operation associated with coal production in Britain offers more scope for improved efficiency than that of underground transport', and recommended the use of locomotives (electric or diesel) for the carrying of coal, supplies and men underground.[2]

Mechanisation, however good in itself, only increased the disparity between older and newer mines and between the older and newer coalfields. There was an eastward movement in the industry dating back to before the war: seams became thicker, but also deeper, on the eastern side of the country, thus favouring, indeed necessitating, larger and more highly mechanised mines. The coastal workings in Durham and Northumberland were developed while the western coalfield declined; Fife prospered while Lanarkshire suffered; the Barnsley district of Yorkshire was depressed while the new mines in South Yorkshire grew rich from the 'Barnsley' seam, which was there six feet thick and some 700–900 yards underground. Several new, large collieries were developed in South Yorkshire and in the Sherwood Forest area of Nottinghamshire during and after the war (Rossington, Haworth, Thorne, Rufford, Thoresby, Ollerton). The Kent coalfield was another new development, mostly since the war.

Several remedies for the coal industry's sickness were proposed: 'reorganisation', the amalgamation of pits, the closing of uneconomic mines, marketing schemes. The owners preferred the easier method of lower wages and longer hours, and fought the miners on this ground in 1926. Unfortunately they won, postponing the necessary reconstruction of the industry until it came, in the form of nationalisation, to sweep them quite away.

The production of steel in Britain was larger after the war than before, and remained so until 1929, when it reached its postwar

---

[1] Mines Dept., *Annual Report*, 1934, p. 14.
[2] Reid Report, pp. 7–12, 65–7, 78, *passim.*

peak; in 1930 it dropped sharply.[1] Exports of steel after the war
were lower than before the war, though by 1925 the world's
export trade in steel was greater than prewar and Britain's
European competitors had exceeded their prewar exports.[2] British
imports of steel increased, however, until 1930, semi-manufactured
steel being imported for finishing in Great Britain (especially for
the sheet and tinplate trades). These changes might not in themselves have been serious; but they included a sharp decline in the
consumption and export of pig iron, bar iron and acid steel—
products for which Britain had been pre-eminent. Yet the world
production of pig iron in 1930 exceeded that of 1913.[3] Exports
of tinplate and galvanised sheet held up well, especially to Empire
countries and South America. And by 1924 the British home
market for steel was larger than in 1913. These changes meant,
however, that the fortunes of the industry varied between districts:
they were adverse in Scotland and the North, more prosperous in
the Midlands, Sheffield, Lincolnshire and South Wales, where the
finishing trades were strongest.[4]

The industry as a whole was under two handicaps: an excess of
productive capacity, and some technical inefficiency. During the
war and in the succeeding boom Britain's blast furnace capacity
increased from 11 to 12 million tons, steel works capacity from
8 to over 12 million tons. In 1923 there were 482 blast furnaces
in Great Britain, 59 built during and since the war; in 1927 437.
By 1934 the number was down to 308, but 100 of these had been
out of blast for over five years. In 1925 Britain was using only
44·5 per cent of her capacity for the manufacture of pig iron and
58 per cent of her steel-making capacity. At the same time Britain
had shifted from Bessemer to open-hearth steel to such an extent
that Bessemer steel had to be imported: almost no basic Bessemer
was being manufactured, and only 6 per cent of Britain's steel
output was acid Bessemer: yet Bessemer was cheaper to produce
than open-hearth steel (and its production revived in the 1930's).[5]

[1] There are good accounts of the processes of steel manufacture in G. C. Allen,
British Industries, pp. 78 ff., and D. L. Burn, *Economic History of Steelmaking, 1867–
1939* (Cambridge, 1940). British steel production was 7·66 million tons in 1913,
9·64 in 1929, 7·33 in 1930.
[2] Steel exports, 4·98 million tons in 1913, 3·25 in 1920, 4·38 in 1929, 3·16 in 1930.
[3] Pig iron production, 10·26 million tons in 1913, 7·59 in 1929; exports, 11·24
million tons in 1913, 5·45 in 1929.
[4] D. L. Burn, *Steelmaking*, pp. 393–4; G. C. Allen, *British Industries*, pp. 97–101.
Very full statistics of the British iron and steel industry as compared with the industry
in other countries are given in T. H. Burnham and G. O. Hoskins, *Iron and Steel in
Britain, 1870–1930* (London, 1943).
[5] G. C. Allen, *British Industries*, pp. 96–8; Committee on Industry and Trade,
Survey of Metal Industries (1928), pp. 18, 21; 'Ingot', *Socialisation of Iron and Steel*
(London, 1936), p. 46; T. H. Burnham and G. O. Hoskins, p. 49.

By contrast, in the engineering industry there was a fair measure of prosperity. By 1930 production exceeded that of the prewar years. Exports were greater, by value, in 1927 as compared to 1911–13 in boilers, machine tools, textile machinery, locomotives, sewing machines, railway carriages and wagons, cycles, cutlery; less in agricultural machinery. In the export of machine tools Germany and the United States retained their prewar lead over Great Britain; in textile machinery Britain retained its lead, but it was a diminishing one in the face of German and Japanese production. In the trade in all types of machinery (excluding electrical and marine) Britain's exports were £31·7 millions annually in 1911–13, £45 millions in 1923, £46·9 millions in 1925, £45·5 millions in 1930. In 1913 Britain's exports of machinery were 30 per cent of the exports of the seven leading countries; Germany's were 32·5 per cent, those of the United States 25·9 per cent. In 1926 the shares were: Britain, 25·6 per cent, the United States 37·6 per cent, Germany 23 per cent. The British Empire countries had replaced Europe as the largest importers of British machinery.[1]

The fortunes of the shipbuilding industry were more uneven. Before the war British shipyards were building 60·6 per cent of the gross tonnage of shipping launched annually (1·66 million tons out of 2·739 million tons), though in 1892–94 the proportion had been as high as 80·8 per cent. Of the prewar launchings, 22 per cent of the tonnage had been built on foreign order, and this constituted 26 per cent of the tonnage built in all countries for foreign buyers. British shipyards had 580 berths (of a length greater than 250 feet) as compared with 341 in continental Europe (140 in Germany). In 1914 41·6 per cent of the world's tonnage of steam shipping of over 100 tons gross was owned in Great Britain (18·8 million tons out of 45·5 million tons).[2]

After the war the scarcity of shipping and the high freight rates encouraged much new construction and the purchase of old ships at fantastic figures. In 1920 just over 2 million tons of shipping was launched in Great Britain, the largest tonnage ever launched in one year. In 1921 1½ million tons were launched. As a result, by 1921 the tonnage of British-owned shipping exceeded the prewar figure, and in the world as a whole wartime losses had also been more than made good. In 1920 and 1921 41 per cent

[1] *Survey of Metal Industries*, pp. 127–275 (the best account of the engineering industry after the war, down to 1927). Figures for 1930 from *Statistical Abstract of U.K.*, 1930, pp. 375, 381. Cf. G. C. Allen, *British Industries*, pp. 134–42.
[2] Ibid., pp. 372–6, 404–5; *Britain in Depression*, pp. 235, 239, 247, 253.

and 38 per cent of British launchings were for foreign buyers, which was 18 per cent and 17 per cent respectively of the world tonnage launched for foreign buyers. British shipyard capacity increased to 806 berths in 1920; in the other main shipbuilding countries on the continent the increase was much less, from 341 to 451 berths. The price of new ships was on the average three times that ruling before the war, cargo steamers costing £40 per ton in 1920; the highest price for a 7500-ton cargo steamer (dead-weight) was £258,750 in March 1920, as compared to £48,000 in December 1913. Ships purchased second-hand increased in price from £20 per ton at the beginning of 1919 to £31 per ton in December.[1]

On the morning after, the bubble burst. The monthly index number for freight rates fell from 141 in March 1920 (1920 = 100, about six times the prewar figure) to 84 in September, 45 in January 1921, 37 in March. The price of new cargo ships fell to £14 per ton in December 1920, and £8 per ton in September 1921; a 7500-ton freighter then cost £60,000, which remained the price, with small variations, for several years. The slump affected British shipyards at once: 708,000 tons of new construction were begun in the first quarter of 1920, 506,000 tons in the fourth quarter, 51,000 in 1921: 3·3 million tons were under construction in April 1921, 1·1 million tons eighteen months later.[2] Orders for 300 ships were cancelled in 1921.

An uneven recovery followed. The British shipyards continued to launch over 1 million tons of shipping a year, which was equal to 40 per cent of the new merchant tonnage launched in the world in 1920–26. Though the number of berths fell from 806 in 1920 to 686 in 1925, Britain's annual shipbuilding capacity remained around 3 million tons, ½ million tons more than before the war and equal to the entire world's need for new ships each year.[3] In 1925, a fairly good year, 30 out of 96 shipyards had no vessels on the stocks, 15 were finishing orders, the rest were only employing a quarter of their capacity.[4] The proportion of new tonnage consisting of motor ships increased, as did the tonnage of ships driven by steam turbines. In 1926, Parsons, the pioneers of marine steam turbines, began the construction of high pressure marine turbines with the *King George V*, a Clyde steamer with boiler pressure of 550 lb. per square inch.

[1] *Survey of Metal Industries*, pp. 382–4, 406–8; C. E. Fayle, *The War and the Shipping Industry* (Carnegie series; Oxford, 1927), pp. 361–79, 438–43.
[2] A. C. Pigou, *Aspects of British Economic History, 1918–1925*, pp. 85–6.
[3] *Survey of Metal Industries*, pp. 383–7, 394, 402.
[4] E. Wilkinson, *Town that was Murdered* [Jarrow], p. 138.

As with shipbuilding, so with shipping. Britain retained its pre-eminence. World tonnage of merchant shipping had increased to 62 million tons in 1921, 65 million tons in 1923, 66·4 million tons in 1929. In the latter year, Britain's merchant shipping was just over 20 million tons, about 30 per cent of the world's tonnage. Britain's was still the largest merchant marine, followed by that of the United States (13·5 million tons, including Great Lakes and Philippines shipping), Japan and Germany (just over 4 million tons each).[1] Britain retained much of the world's carrying trade; in addition to carrying the lion's share of the trade of Great Britain and the Empire, British shipping carried 50 per cent of the entire seaborne trade of the world, by volume, in 1914 and 47 per cent in 1929. Of the world's seaborne trade in 1929, 45 per cent was outside Great Britain and the Empire, yet British ships carried 25 per cent of it, and this constituted 24 per cent of the carrying done by the British merchant marine.[2]

Last but not least of the staple industries were the textile trades, which, judged by the employment they afforded, stood second to the metal and engineering industry in 1924. These, however, were not one industry but several, of which the cotton, woollen and finishing trades comprised four-fifths of the whole. Cotton, the largest of these, was the most depressed in the twenties, and this almost entirely due to changes in the export markets which had provided the greater part of its demand. This was not a case of an industry rubbing along, and nursing the illusion of recovery, through the twenties; it was in a bad way from 1921 onwards. And since the industry was highly concentrated, the effects of its decline were sharp and not diffused: 85 per cent of those engaged in the industry were in Lancashire and its adjacent areas.[3]

The main change can be concisely shown: in 1912 the United Kingdom produced 8000 million yards of cloth, consumed 1100 million and exported 6900 million; in 1924, when world demand had recovered from the war, Britain produced 5600 million yards and exported 4500 million; in 1929, when world consumption had increased by over 20 per cent and world trade in cotton goods by 5 per cent, British production had declined by 6 per cent and exports by 15 per cent.[4] Yet even then home consumption only took some 30 per cent of the industry's production.[5] In the export

[1] *Lloyd's Register, 1929–30*, II, 1176–7.
[2] C. E. Fayle, p. 6; *Britain in Depression*, p. 240.
[3] G. C. Allen, *British Industries and their Organization*, pp. 205, 210.
[4] G. W. Daniels and H. Campion, 'The Cotton Industry and Trade', *Britain in Depression*, pp. 339–40.   [5] A. E. Kahn, p. 98.

of cotton piece goods Britain still held the leading place in 1923–25 with 50·5 per cent of the world's exports; but in 1909–13 her share had been 69·9 per cent. The United States, France, Italy, India had slightly increased their share of the world's exports; the biggest gains were made by Japan, whose exports of piece goods had increased eight-fold since before the war, and comprised 11·5 per cent of the world's exports of cottons.[1]

The principal markets lost to Lancashire cottons were India and the Far East, the Balkans and the Near East, which had taken 67 per cent of Britain's exports in 1913.[2] By 1929 exports to India had dropped to 42 per cent of the prewar figure, to China and Japan to 29 per cent, to the Balkans and the Near East to 47 per cent. To India alone Britain's exports had declined by 1000 million yards (from 3068 million yards in 1913 to 1883 millions in 1930). This was chiefly the result of the doubling of India's own production, which met 56 per cent of the demand of the Indian market in 1930, as compared with only 27 per cent before the war. Imports into India from Japan had increased meanwhile from 3 million to 243 million square yards (1926–27). The political unrest in India, and the fall in the Indian rate of exchange were other reasons for the catastrophic change in Lancashire's trade with India.[3] In China the trade formerly done by Britain was largely captured by Japan; in East Africa also Japan was increasingly a competitor. In the Balkans trade was lost to Italy, in Canada, Central and South America to the United States, which, before the war, was hardly an exporter of cottons at all.[4]

Lancashire's losses were chiefly in the markets for the cheaper kinds of cottons, those manufactured by the American section of the industry (using American cotton). Here Japanese competition was heaviest, and British costs, partly caused by the high cost of the raw material, were the greatest obstacle to steady trade. Moreover, the countries formerly taking the cheaper cloths in quantity were those most affected by the movement of the terms of trade against producers of primary goods; hence their purchasing power was low. Japan did begin to invade the markets for the better kinds of cottons also, but here Lancashire could hold its own.[5] Hence the Egyptian section of the industry suffered much

---

[1] G. W. Daniels and J. Jewkes, 'The Post-war depression in the Lancashire Cotton Industry', *Journal of the Royal Statistical Society*, n.s., 91 (1928), p. 155.
[2] G. C. Allen, *British Industries*, p. 220; tables in *Britain in Depression*, pp. 347–9; G. W. Daniels and J. Jewkes, *J.R.S.S.*, 91: 156–7; Com. on Industry and Trade, *Survey of Textile Industries*, pp. 54–7.
[3] G. C. Allen, p. 220; *Survey of Textile Industries*, pp. 72, 102.
[4] G. C. Allen, pp. 222–23.   [5] Ibid., pp. 224–6.

less than the American; and this section, having experienced very little 'reorganisation' during the postwar boom, had not the same burdens of large capital and debt charges to carry as had the American section.[1] Employment in the industry fell only slightly in the middle twenties, and unemployment was under 10 per cent of those insured in several years; but, as was traditional in Lancashire in hard times, much short time was worked.[2] The incidence of unemployment was uneven: greater in the spinning section than in the weaving, greater in Oldham, concentrating on the spinning of coarser yarns, than in Bolton, where the finer yarns are spun, greater in Blackburn and Accrington than in Preston, Burnley and Colne, reflecting the different grades of cloth woven in these centres.[3]

[1] G. C. Allen, *British Industries*, p. 226. For a discussion of the effects of reorganization on the American side of the industry, see G. W. Daniels and J. Jewkes in *J.R.S.S.*, 91: 166–206.

[2] Figures in *Survey of Textile Industries*, pp. 32, 307.

[3] G. W. Daniels and J. Jewkes, *J.R.S.S.*, 91: 162–3, 189–90. For the wool textile industry see G. C. Allen, *British Industries*, pp. 251–70D; *Survey of Textile Industries*, 161–5, 193–4; *Britain in Depression*, pp. 353–9.

CHAPTER SIX

Dead Centre: the General Strike and After, 1925—1929

1. CROSS-CURRENTS IN THE LABOUR MOVEMENT

THE general strike of 1926, caused by the bitter coal strike which long outlasted it, was the great and dramatic event of the mid-twenties, interrupting the even tenor of Baldwin's government and the course of economic recovery from the boom and slump which had followed the war. Yet it was an interruption only, and did not change the tendencies of trade and of industrial organisation, the trend in wages and prices, the inexorable advance of social welfare through state action. It made a wound on the body politic and on the economy, but the wound healed, though the scar remained. The reason for this, though it was not immediately apparent, was that the general strike marked the end, and not the beginning, of a time of unrest and possible revolution. The postwar unrest we have already taken note of: the Glasgow general strike, Black Friday, the Councils of Action and the admiration for Bolshevist Russia, the founding of the Communist Party of Great Britain and its offspring such as the National Minority Movement, the arrival of the Clydeside Brigade in parliament, and, in a different way, the Black and Tan war in Ireland. The initial unrest had been allayed by Lloyd George's improvisations and had died away as unemployment brought apathy and the beginning of industrial recovery restored hope. From 1923 onwards there was, to all intents and purposes, a truce: in industrial life between the forces of capital and labour, in politics between the Conservatives and the Liberal–Labour opposition; the history of the first Labour government, though not the circumstances of its defeat, is an illustration of this. The general strike was the result of an interruption of this truce and its ultimate effect was to restore the truce.

That the general strike was a deviation from the main course of events can be seen if we mark the direction which the Labour movement was taking in 1924 and 1925. Labour was definitely moving to the right, away from wartime enthusiasms and from thorough-going socialist policies. There remained, however, tendencies toward the left, and, contrary to what might have been expected, these were clearest in the trade-union side of the movement. When the truce in industry was broken the leftward tendencies became ascendant: for the time being—for the last time between the wars—the counsels of the extremists were followed by Labour, just as, at the opposite end of the scale, the ideas of die-hard Conservatives captured the government and the leaders of industry. The result was catastrophe: the general strike. Once it was over the forces of moderation in the Labour movement regained control: the leadership of MacDonald, Henderson and Bevin, rather than of the I.L.P. and of A. J. Cook.

In the Labour movement the rightward tendencies were to be seen in 1924 and 1925 chiefly in the Labour party. After Labour's defeat in the general election in 1924 there was a good deal of feeling against MacDonald as leader: he had compromised over policy when in office, had humiliated the party and himself over the Campbell case, had led the party to disaster by his attitude to the Zinoviev letter. Snowden urged Henderson to become leader and promised his support, warning that MacDonald, if left in power, would betray the party. Henderson refused, saying that MacDonald was the party's strongest figure and the only one with a real following in the country; a change would only lead to disunity. Since the Clydesiders were also urging the change, Henderson was probably wise to reject it: let them find some other target than him to shoot at, he told their representative, John Scanlon.[1] Hence at the Labour party's annual conference in 1925, at Liverpool, there was no challenge to MacDonald's leadership. There was, however, a heated debate on a motion by Ernest Bevin that Labour should not again accept office as a minority party. MacDonald spoke against the motion, and argued that Labour should keep its hands free to act in future as circumstances demanded. Bevin retorted that MacDonald's speech 'was enough to make Keir Hardie turn in his grave;' but he lost his motion.[2] This conference also continued its efforts to bar members of the Communist party from its counsels. It passed two motions, one declaring Communists ineligible for membership in any 'Individual Section of any affiliated Local Labour Party', the other

[1] M. A. Hamilton, *Arthur Henderson*, p. 256; J. Scanlon, *Decline and Fall of the Labour Party*, p. 85.
[2] G. D. H. Cole, *History of the Labour Party since 1914*, pp. 176–7; F. Williams, *Ernest Bevin*, pp. 122–4.

appealing to the trade unions not to send Communists as their delegates to the annual or local conferences of the party.[1]

In the I.L.P., on the other hand, the rightward tendency was not very apparent. On the suggestion of Clifford Allen, its chairman, the I.L.P. appointed seven commissions to work out the details of socialist policy for a future Labour government. These commissions published reports elaborating socialist policies for agriculture, finance, the empire, India, the trade unions and industrial policy, the reform of parliament. The report which attracted most attention was that on *Socialism in Our Time*, written by J. A. Hobson, H. N. Brailsford, E. F. Wise, and A. Creech Jones,[2] and signed by F. W. Jowett as acting chairman of the I.L.P. Its main author was Wise, an ex-civil servant of brilliant mind; the others were his colleagues on the commission to frame a 'Plan for the speedy Abolition of Poverty and the Realisation of Socialism'. This report was the basis of the I.L.P.'s 'Socialism in Our Time' or 'Living Income' policy, which was persistently pushed, against MacDonald and the Labour party, for the next few years. The policy aimed to advance socialism immediately by securing for everyone, by law, a minimum wage, supplemented by state-provided family allowances. For this purpose it was declared that 'Labour has a claim upon the total pool of the national income'. If a particular industry could not pay the minimum wage which was the recognition of this claim, it would have to re-organise; nationalisation was reserved for 'key' industries. The minimum wage would attack under-consumption and thus improve the home market; but, to avoid being at the mercy of depressions, it would necessitate new policies of credit and banking designed to prevent a slump by the expansion of credit. Thus the whole policy aimed to advance socialism at once, both directly and indirectly, by the immediate imposition of a national minimum wage; hence the two names for this policy, whose essence was: socialism now![3]

[1] G. D. H. Cole, *History of the Labour Party since 1914*, pp. 145-6, 177. See also Carl F. Brand, *British Labour's Rise to Power* (Stanford University, 1941), pp. 239-59; *Report of the 25th Annual Conference of the Labour Party, 1925*, p. 352.

[2] J. A. Hobson (1858-1940), the economist, author of *The Evolution of Modern Capitalism* (1894), *Imperialism* (1902) and several other pioneering works.

H. N. Brailsford, born 1873, veteran socialist journalist, editor of the *New Leader*, 1922-26.

Arthur Creech Jones, born 1891; national secretary, Transport and General Workers' Union, 1919-29; organising secretary, Workers Travel Association, 1929-1939; M.P., 1935-50; secretary of state for the Colonies, 1946-50.

[3] This policy is elaborated in *The Living Wage*, by Brailsford, Hobson, Creech Jones and Wise, published by the I.L.P. and dated September, 1926. The passage concerning the total pool of the national income is on p. 27.

This did not suit MacDonald's book at all. His criticism of earlier manifestations of this policy led to a decision of the National Administrative Council of the I.L.P., in October 1925, to remove him from the editorship of the *Socialist Review*. This caused great distress to Clifford Allen who, though responsible for the appointment of the I.L.P. commissions, had become a great admirer of MacDonald's. Allen therefore resigned the chairmanship of the I.L.P., on the justified plea of ill-health, and was succeeded by F. W. Jowett as acting chairman. When *Socialism in Our Time* was published, MacDonald denounced it before he had read it (as he admitted), and followed this up by an attack in the *Socialist Review* of March 1926, pettishly rejecting 'schemes and proposals . . . [which committees] hand . . . over to a body of unfortunate Members of Parliament, and especially ministers, like orders issued to subordinates by military commanders'. He objected to the 'sanctification of phrases of no definite meaning . . . like "Socialism in our time",' and called such proposals 'millstones for mere show round the neck of the Movement'.[1] Yet at its Easter conference in 1926, just a month before the general strike, the I.L.P. enthusiastically endorsed the 'Socialism in Our Time' report. It also elected James Maxton as chairman, thus emphasising the leftward tendency of the party and setting it on a course which, by putting the Clydesiders and the working-class members in control, and helped on by personal antagonisms, led to the gradual exodus of the intellectuals and the orthodox Labour members from the I.L.P. In 1927 the process advanced farther: the I.L.P. for years had chosen MacDonald as one of its delegates to the Labour party conference, but now refused to do so: Snowden resigned from the I.L.P., as did H. N. Brailsford, at the opposite end of the spectrum, from the editorship of the *New Leader*, after criticism of his salary.[2]

Curiously enough the Trades Union Congress, normally the conservative wing of the Labour movement, was also at this time journeying on a deviation to the left, though it was nearing the end of it. In 1920, after the report, factual but sympathetic, by the delegation sent to Russia by the T.U.C. and the Labour party jointly, the T.U.C. had shown little interest in the Russian experiment. Interest was aroused, however, by the negotiations for the abortive Anglo-Russian treaties in 1924; and from within, the

[1] *Socialist Review*, March, 1926, p. 9; cf. Jowett's reply, *ibid.*, April, 1926.
[2] G. D. H. Cole, *History of the Labour Party*, pp. 149–50, 197–98; F. Brockway, *Jowett*, pp. 225–38, 251–2. Cf. Brockway, *Inside the Left*, pp. 148–50, 157, 185–7; J. Paton, *Left Turn*, pp. 237–43. See above, chap. 3, pp. 150–2.

T.U.C. was prodded by its members who had embraced the National Minority Movement. Resignations of old-time trade union officials like J. H. Thomas, J. R. Clynes[1] and Frank Hodges to take office in the Labour government made room for men of more extreme views, in particular A. J. Cook, Hodges' successor as secretary of the Miners' Federation. At the Trades Union Congress at Hull in September 1924, a Russian trade union leader, Tomsky, was given a 'very hearty reception' as a fraternal delegate and delivered a speech in Russian. Following this the T.U.C. sent a delegation to Russia in November, including A. A. Purcell, Ben Tillett, Herbert Smith, John Bromley, and Fred Bramley, the secretary of the T.U.C. This delegation ran into difficulties in its subsequent attempt to bring about a reconciliation between the International Federation of Trade Unions and the (Communist) Red International of Labour Unions; but at home, in spite of denunciations in the press, it carried the General Council of the T.U.C. into its own *rapprochement* with Russia, an agreement of April 1925 to set up the Anglo-Russian Joint Advisory Council representative of the British and Russian trade union movements, to meet alternately in the two countries.[2]

The Trades Union Congress held at Scarborough in 1925 was the high-water mark of this movement to the left. The *Annual Register* subsequently remarked on its evidences of class-consciousness, its 'strong relish . . . for Marxist phraseology', its hearty applause for the speeches of Harry Pollitt, the Communist, a delegate from the Boilermakers. The presidential address by A. B. Swales of the Amalgamated Engineering Union declaimed the collapse of capitalism and rejoiced: '. . . at last there are clear indications of a world movement rising in revolt and determined to shake off the shackles of wage slavery'. A resolution declaring the Congress' 'complete opposition to Imperialism' was passed, supporting 'the right of all peoples in the British Empire to self-determination, including the right to choose complete separation from the Empire'. Tomsky was once again given an enthusiastic welcome. None the less, when faced with a motion empowering the General Council of the T.U.C. to call and organise a general strike 'to assist a union defending a vital trade union principle',

---

[1] Thomas and Clynes resumed their trade union positions in 1925.
[2] G. D. H. Cole, *History of the Labour Party*, pp. 178–9. Fuller details in *Report of the 57th Annual Trades Union Congress, 1925*, p. 289 ff. The two reports on Russia are: *British Labour Delegations to Russia, 1920, Report* (London, n.d.) and *Russia: The Official Report of the British Trades Union Delegation to Russia and Caucasia, November and December 1924* (London, 1925).

the Congress, on the pleas of J. H. Thomas, Bevin and Clynes, merely referred it to the General Council. Moreover, the three new members elected to the General Council were all from the moderate side: Thomas, Bevin, Margaret Bondfield; and the new president, Arthur Pugh, of the Iron and Steel Trades Confederation, who succeeded Swales, was also of the moderates. A little later the secretary, Fred Bramley (who died in October 1925) was succeeded by Walter Citrine,[1] representative of the new, cautious, efficient bureaucracy of the trade union movement. At the same time, plans for a revived 'Triple Alliance', a Workers' Industrial Alliance to include the miners, railwaymen, transport workers and engineers, came to nothing; though in the event a much larger collective effort took its place.[2]

If the Labour movement was, on the whole, turning to moderate counsels in 1925 the Conservative government was not obviously committed to die-hard policies and hostility towards labour—at least not until the summer. The temper of the government, as shown by Baldwin's leadership and Churchill's social policies, was one of moderate reform, of keeping the peace. Many Conservative extremists were, however, of a different mind, determined to use the large Conservative majority to put Labour in its place. One of them introduced a private member's bill to abolish the trade unions' political levy, which was paid to the Labour party—a crude blow at the party's finances. This Baldwin opposed in a remarkable speech in parliament on March 6, 1925. Some have argued since that the speech was simply a cunning bid for delay until the government could fight the Labour movement from stronger positions. Such an interpretation of the speech (which made a great impression at the time) is quite out of keeping with Baldwin's character. He was a man of good will, who certainly preferred postponing troubles to meeting them, but liked best to avoid them altogether; there was nothing diabolical in his character.

In this speech, Baldwin described the old industrial order he had known as a young man in his family's firm, and its transformation by the great amalgamations of employers and working men. Such organisations were not necessarily bad, but having power they

[1] Walter Citrine, born in Liverpool, 1887; Mersey district secretary, Electrical Trades Union, 1914–20, assistant general secretary of the union, 1920–23; assistant secretary, 1924, general secretary, T.U.C., 1926–46; chairman, British Electricity Authority, 1947. Knighted, 1935, created Baron Citrine, 1946.
[2] *Report of the 57th T.U.C., 1925*, pp. 77, 578, *passim; Annual Register, 1925*, pp. 92–4; G. D. H. Cole, *History of the Labour Party*, pp. 178–9; J. T. Murphy, *New Horizons* (London, 1941), pp. 205–6.

L

must show responsibility in its use. Disaster might come from either side and could be avoided only by both sides learning to understand each other. Any government ought to say that 'nothing shall be done that shall injure the State, which is the concern of all of us and far greater than all of us. . . .' But, having said this, what should the Conservative party's attitude be towards the evolution of a newer state, a partnership, in industry?

> . . . I do not know whether the House will forgive me if I speak for a minute or two on a rather personal note. For two years past in the face of great difficulties . . . I have striven to consolidate, and to breathe a living force into my great Party. . . . We find ourselves, after these two years in power, in possession of perhaps the greatest majority our party has ever had, and with the general assent of the country. Now how did we get there? It was not by promising to bring this Bill in; it was because, rightly or wrongly, we succeeded in creating an impression throughout the country that we stood for stable Government and for peace in the country between all classes of the community. . . .
>
> I want my party today to make a gesture to the country . . . and to say to them: 'We have our majority; we believe in the justice of this Bill . . . but we are going to withdraw our hand, and we are not going to push our political advantage home at a moment like this. . . .
>
> Although I know that there are those who work for different ends from most of us in this House, yet there are many in all ranks and all parties who will re-echo my prayer:
>
> 'Give peace in our time, O Lord.'[1]

That was the end of the bill.

What, then, moved the government from the ways of peace and charged the Scarborough T.U.C. with the heady eloquence of strife and revolt? What ended the truce between capital and labour? Briefly, it was 'Red Friday', a new crisis in the coal-mining industry.

2. RED FRIDAY

The wages settlement in the coal-mining industry in 1921 lasted until 1924, sustained by the 'windfall' of heavy exports in 1923 during the occupation of the Ruhr. The effects of the improved working results of 1923 were, however, imperfectly reflected in higher earnings for the men, owing to certain conditions in the 1921 settlement; and in January 1924, the Miners' Federation gave notice to terminate the agreement. A new agreement was

---

[1] 181 H.C. Deb., 5 s., 839–41. Cf. Stanley Baldwin, *On England* (Penguin edition), pp. 55–9; *Annual Register*, 1925, pp. 16–17; G. M. Young, *Baldwin*, pp. 91–6.

made in May 1924, which raised the minimum addition to the standard wage from 20 per cent to 33⅓ per cent and lowered the owners' standard profit from 17 per cent to 15 per cent of the sum payable as standard wages. The share of net profits to be apportioned to increasing wages beyond the new standard was set at 87 per cent instead of 83 per cent. In addition, the allowances necessary to bring the minimum wage to a subsistence wage, where the former fell below the latter, were increased: the result of this was to put the subsistence wage at between 7s. 6d. and 8s. 9d. per shift, varying according to district.[1]

The 1924 agreement was, unfortunately, out of date before it began. With the end of the occupation of the Ruhr, exports slumped, and profits rapidly became losses. In the first six months of 1925 the loss in working was £2·1 millions, or 0·19 shillings per ton. Between May and July, 1925, nine districts had losses, eight of them of over 1s. per ton. Within five months of the 1924 agreement every district except South Yorkshire was paying no more than the minimum wage; in July 1925 South Yorkshire was in the same condition.[2] On June 30, 1925 the owners served notice to end the 1924 agreement in one month, offering to pay only the standard wage with no minimum addition, though retaining the same ratio of distribution of net profit between addition to wages and profits (87:13). Special adjustments were offered to low-paid men, but the national minimum percentage addition to standard wages was to go. The owners added that better terms could be offered if the miners were willing to return to an 8-hour day. The miners objected that the new terms would reduce wages between 13 per cent and 48 per cent, involving in Scotland a reduction of between 2s. and 3s. per shift; yet at the same time it retained the owners' standard profit regardless of how low wages might fall. Not unnaturally they refused the offer (and ignored the hint about longer hours).[3]

The miners were not, however, going to make their fight alone. Under a new standing order of the Trades Union Congress, the General Council of the T.U.C. was entitled to be kept informed of disputes between unions and employers and to intervene if large numbers of workers were involved; if, none the less, a strike

---

[1] *Report of the Royal Commission on the Coal Industry* (1925) [Cmd. 2600; 1926: the Samuel Report (vol. 1, Report)], p. 133; J. R. Raynes, *Coal and its Conflicts*, pp. 195–9; R. P. Arnot, *The Miners: Years of Struggle*, pp. 339–48.
[2] R. C. on Coal Industry, *Report*, p. 147.
[3] J. R. Raynes, *Coal and its Conflicts*, pp. 202–5; R. P. Arnot, *The Miners*, pp. 362–6.

occurred, the General Council was to organise 'all such moral and material support' as circumstances called for on behalf of the unions concerned.[1] On July 10 the General Council met the Executive of the Miners' Federation, promised whole-hearted co-operation in the 'resistance to the degradation of the standard of life of their members', and endorsed the miners' refusal of the owners' terms. The General Council appointed a special Industrial Committee and called a meeting of the executives of the railway, transport workers' and sailors' unions for July 25. At this meeting an embargo on the movement of coal after the miners stopped work was agreed on. A general strike seemed once more just over the horizon.[2]

Meanwhile, the government had already intervened, and when efforts at mediation proved futile had appointed a court of inquiry, under H. P. Macmillan. This, though boycotted by the miners, reported largely in their favour on July 28: it asked how the miners could keep going without a living wage and questioned the owners' contentions about costs and longer hours of work. Baldwin met the owners' representatives on July 28, and both owners and miners separately on July 29. The owners then offered a national minimum wage, to be a charge upon proceeds before the owners received any profit, but declared that in several districts the minimum would have to be very low if the pits were to continue in operation at all—unless the miners would agree to a temporary relaxation of the 7-hour day. The miners spurned this proposal. The Prime Minister rejected the suggestion of a government subsidy. On July 30, when negotiations were resumed, he accused the miners of being unconciliatory: to their reply that the terms offered meant a reduction of wages he retorted: '. . . all the workers of this country have got to take reductions in wages to help put industry on its feet'. On the same day a conference of one thousand trade union delegates at the Central Hall, Westminster, gave unanimous approval to the General Council's support of the miners. Notices were sent out by the General Council, countersigned by the appropriate trade union officials, ordering the embargo on movement of coal to begin at midnight, July 31 (i.e. 11.59 p.m.), when the miners would cease work.[3]

[1] W. Milne-Bailey, *Trade Unions and the State* (London, 1934), pp. 60–1.
[2] J. R. Raynes, p. 207; R. P. Arnot, *The General Strike, May 1926* (Labour Research Department, 1926), pp. 29–34; R. P. Arnot, *The Miners*, pp. 371–5.
[3] R. P. Arnot, *General Strike*, p. 35; R. P. Arnot, *The Miners*, pp. 376–9; J. R. Raynes, pp. 208–13, 215.

The government backed down. On Friday, July 31 the Cabinet met at 6.30 p.m.; later that evening Baldwin saw the miners' representatives. They agreed to co-operate in an inquiry into means for improving the productive efficiency of the industry provided wages and hours remained unchanged during the inquiry; for that period, expected to be about nine months, the government promised the industry a subsidy, estimated to be not less than £10 millions (in the event it was over £23 millions). On these conditions the strike and the embargo were averted. Under the terms of the subsidy, announced later, the owners were permitted a profit of 13 per cent of proceeds (including the subsidy), provided that when profits exceeded 1s. 3d. per ton the surplus would be used to reduce the subsidy.[1]

This was 'Red Friday', so dubbed by the *Daily Herald* to distinguish it from the earlier 'Black Friday'. The government had surrendered at the threat of united trade union action on behalf of the miners. The *Annual Register* later recorded that the public was 'perturbed' by the government's surrender to trade union 'intimidation', and that many Conservatives were very bitter against the Prime Minister. But it takes two to make a quarrel, and the owners, throughout the sorry months behind and ahead, were no less obstinate than the men. Subsistence wages for labourers in the mines were no more than about 7s. 6d. a shift or 45s. a week, though hewers were earning anywhere from 70s. to 90s. a week. It was hard for the men to understand why the whole burden of ending the industry's working loss should fall on them, and not demand some effort from the owners to reorganise the industry and improve its efficiency.

Baldwin recognised the miners' case indirectly in his speech to parliament on August 6, though he blamed them for refusing to 'move at all', in the negotiations. He justified the government's action to avert the strike on three grounds: hard times, which should not be made worse, the suffering which a strike would cause to the rank and file in industry, and the fact that the public had had no opportunity to think what such a strike would mean. The speech was conciliatory but perplexed, which, surely, was Baldwin's mood. He concluded with a warning to any who might have a 'deliberate and avowed policy to force a stoppage of this kind on the country' that in a free country a minority had never yet coerced the whole community, and 'if the time should come

[1] R. P. Arnot, *The Miners*, pp. 379–87; J. R. Raynes, pp. 213–16; *Annual Register* 1925, pp. 64–6, 77–9.

when the community had to protect itself, with the full strength of the Government behind it . . . [its] response will astonish the forces of anarchy throughout the world'.[1]

Did this mean, as was afterwards assumed, that the government had bought time to prepare for a strike which it could crush? Not necessarily: time can heal as well as abrade.[2] But if the government prepared to meet the contingency of a general strike (as any government must do) while employers and workers remained obdurate, then Red Friday increased, rather than diminished, the possibility of such a strike.

3. SIX MONTHS' DELAY

After Red Friday, everyone went off on their summer holidays. On September 5 the Royal Commission which was to make the promised inquiry into the circumstances of the coal-mining industry was appointed. The chairman was Sir Herbert Samuel,[3] a Liberal who had been Home Secretary in 1916 after holding several lesser offices, and more recently had been British High Commissioner in Palestine; the other members were General Sir Herbert Lawrence, member of the banking firm of Glyn, Mills, Sir William Beveridge, ex-civil servant, economist, director of the London School of Economics, and Kenneth Lee, chairman of the Tootal Broadhurst Lee Company, a large Manchester cotton firm. Its first public hearing was on October 15.

Meanwhile, preparations against a general strike, should there be one, were begun. A private body with an official-sounding name, the Organisation for the Maintenance of Supplies (O.M.S.), was formed late in September. Its object was to recruit volunteers and train them to help maintain supplies and vital services; it disavowed any aggressive or provocative aims. The Home Secretary explained in parliament that the organisation, though independent, could be of help to the government in its own plans; joining it would be a patriotic act. More sinister were the arrogant offers of the newly-born British Fascist organisations to enroll their members as special constables ready to act as a body under

---

[1] 187 H.C. Deb., 5 s., 1581–92, 1684–5, 1691; *Annual Register, 1925*, pp. 80–1. W. H. Crooks, *The General Strike* (Chapel Hill, 1931), pp. 294–8, discusses the government's unpreparedness for a general strike in 1925.
[2] Cf. G. M. Young, *Baldwin*, pp. 99, 103.
[3] Herbert Samuel, born 1870; M.P., 1902–18, 1929–35; parliamentary under secretary, Home Office 1905–09; Chancellor of Duchy of Lancaster, 1909–10 and 1915–16; postmaster-general, 1910–14 and 1915–16; president, Local Government Board, 1914–15; Home Secretary, 1916 and 1931–2; High Commissioner, Palestine. 1920–25. Knighted 1920, created Viscount Samuel, 1937.

their own officers. In general, such offers were refused; though in Liverpool they were accepted.[1]

The government's plans were, indeed, far older. They presupposed the use of powers under the Emergency Powers Act of 1920, but actually went back to the scheme for an emergency road transport system prepared and used by the Coalition government in 1919 at the time of the railway strike, the executive agency then being the Ministry of Food. In 1920 the organisation was worked out in permanent form, and local authorities were notified of it by a circular from the Ministry of Health. Just before Black Friday in 1921 it was ready to go into action. After this it was maintained on a skeleton basis by two civil servants and a clerk—not, one would think, the most exacting of jobs. Now this machine was cranked up. The main responsibility for the plans rested with the Home Office, whose permanent under-secretary, Sir John Anderson,[2] was perhaps the ablest of a distinguished generation of civil servants. The country (England and Wales) was divided into ten divisions, each under a minister acting as Civil Commissioner, to be assisted, if an emergency arose, by a staff of civil servants appointed in advance. Local committees were appointed to work out arrangements for the maintenance of vital services; these were to be assisted by commissioners at the regional headquarters and officers at smaller centres within each region. The Road Officers, for example, were to work with local Haulage Committees made up of representatives of the principal road haulage companies. The plans were sufficiently advanced for the local authorities to be notified of these arrangements by circular 636 from the Ministry of Health, dated November 20. Conferences were held in December and January between national and local officials concerning transport arrangements and routes, and police services. Two more conferences were held early in March, and the road transport officials were asked to keep April 27, 28, clear for further meetings 'in case the threatened emergency materialised on May 1'.[3] The plans were to be put into action on

---

[1] R. P. Arnot, *General Strike*, pp. 47 ff.; A. Hutt, *Postwar History of the British Working Class*, pp. 114–16; W. H. Crook, *General Strike*, pp. 298–302.

[2] John Anderson, born 1882; entered Colonial Office, 1905, subsequently served in shipping and local government; joint under-secretary to Lord Lieutenant of Ireland, 1920, chairman, Board of Inland Revenue, 1919–22; permanent under-secretary, Home Office, 1922–32; Governor of Bengal, 1932–37. M.P., 1938–50; lord privy seal, 1938–39; Home Secretary, 1939–40; lord president of the Council, 1940–43; chancellor of the Exchequer, 1943–45. Chairman, Port of London Authority, 1946. Knighted, 1919; created Viscount Waverley, 1952.

[3] George Glasgow, *General Strikes and Road Transport*, p. 58.

receipt of telegrams from Whitehall containing the single word 'Action'.[1]

To these plans the labour movement opposed very little. The General Council made no real plans as to what the working population was to do in a general strike until the eve of the strike itself, assuming, first, that the deliberations of the Samuel Commission would find a way out of the coal dispute, and later that the threatened strike would somehow be compromised at the last moment. Temperamentally, the majority of its members were against any plans which might seem to challenge the government; and the minority which favoured such plans was hardly more realistic. J. H. Thomas records a discussion about maintaining a food supply for the working class in a general strike. A. J. Cook declared that many families were laying in a secret supply of food, and that his mother-in-law had been bringing back an extra tin of salmon when shopping for weeks past. 'By God,' retorted the irrepressible Jimmy, 'A British Revolution based on a tin of salmon!'[2] More than that, and far from preparing for a strike, the miners, by their record output of coal, had allowed coal stocks to be built up to a high level before the strike began.

The lack of preparation by the T.U.C. only made more unfortunate (but not less maddening to the Conservatives) the speeches of A. J. Cook. In August 1925 he said:

Next May we shall be faced with the greatest crisis and the greatest struggle we have ever known, and we are preparing for it. We shall prepare a Commissariat department. I am going to get a fund, if I can, that will buy grub so that when the struggle comes we shall have that grub distributed in the homes of our people. I don't care a hang for any government, or army or navy. They can come along with their bayonets. Bayonets don't cut coal. We have already beaten, not only the employers, but the strongest Government in modern times.[3]

The government was not so captivated by make-believe. It did one thing which at the least made clear that it was preparing for trouble. On October 14 twelve leaders of the Communist party were arrested, and their houses and the headquarters of the party ransacked by the police for documents. Those arrested included

[1] R. P. Arnot, *General Strike*, pp. 47–62; W. H. Crook, *General Strike*, pp. 303–10; George Glasgow, *General Strikes and Road Transport* (the best account of the government's arrangements, and not confined to road transport), *passim*, especially pp. 55–9; W. Milne-Bailey, *Trade Unions and the State*, p. 73. The text of circular 636 is printed by Milne-Bailey, pp. 74–8; Glasgow, pp. 102–12; W. Milne-Bailey, *Trade Union Documents* (London, 1929), pp. 352–6.

[2] J. H. Thomas, *My Story* (London, 1937), pp. 105–6. See also W. H. Crook, *General Strike*, pp. 310–14.

[3] Quoted in W. H. Crook, p. 295.

Harry Pollitt, the secretary of the party, J. T. Murphy, a member of its executive, J. R. Campbell of the 'Campbell case'. They were tried at Old Bailey under the Incitement to Mutiny Act, 1797, on charges of seditious libel and incitement to mutiny. The judge offered to release the first offenders with a caution if they left the party, but they refused. The trial was the chief instance of a purely political trial in the interwar years. Seven of the men were sentenced to six months' imprisonment, five to twelve months; they were, in fact, put out of the way for the duration of any trouble which might arise.[1]

During the winter everyone marked time, waiting for the proposals of the Samuel Commission. The Commission held 33 public sittings, the last on January 14, and heard 76 witnesses. Its report was completed on March 6, 1926. It admitted that the industry was being operated at a loss, but rejected the remedies proposed by both sides. Nationalisation of the industry was not to be recommended. The continuance of a subsidy would be 'indefensible' and the subsidy should 'never be repeated'.[2] The proposals of the Mining Association, putting the whole burden of the industry's problems upon the miners, were rejected with equal precision: an extra hour's work per shift at no increase in pay; a reduction in rates of pay; other economies equal to 10 per cent of the saving in wages; a reduction in railway rates for coal through a reduction in railwaymen's wages. The Commission crisply replied that the extra hour would only produce more coal which could not be sold—unless the proposal implied the dismissal of miners, so that a smaller working force would produce the same output. And it remarked that 'the owners should discontinue charging the miners as a body with deliberate attempts to destroy the prosperity of the industry, in order to compel its nationalisation . . . and should also cease to countenance accusations against the miners of restriction of output'.[3]

What to do, then? The Commission distinguished between the long-term and the immediate problems. To improve the industry's efficiency it recommended: (1) the nationalisation of the coal royalties—simply a repetition of the unanimous recommendation of the Sankey Commission, which had been ignored ever since; (2) the reorganisation of the industry, under private ownership, and without any 'general measure' of compulsion, through the

---

[1] J. T. Murphy, *New Horizons*, pp. 209–13; Harry Pollitt, *Serving My Time* (London, 1940), pp. 209–48.
[2] R.C. on Coal Industry, *Report*, p. 233.   [3] Ibid., pp. 229–30.

L*

amalgamation of mines to eliminate small units of production, and through co-ordination of the industry with others, and especially with the generation of electricity, under an advisory National Fuel and Power Committee; (3) improved arrangements for research and distribution, with aid from the government; (4) better relations between employers and labour through joint pit-committees, family allowances, profit-sharing, better houses, more pithead baths, annual holidays with pay 'when prosperity returns', and revised methods of pay to give the men not employed at the coal face a 'direct interest in output'.[1] These were all bitter pills for the owners to swallow—if they were really to be made to swallow them.

For the immediate problem, however, the men must provide the solution. Wages must be lowered: 'revision of the "minimum percentage addition to standard rates of wages" is indispensable. A disaster is impending over the industry, and the immediate reduction in working costs that can be effected in this way, and in this way alone, is essential to save it.'[2] This was qualified by insistence that the system of subsistence allowances be continued. The miners were offered three inducements for their sacrifice. The Commission recommended against the lengthening of the working day. It was 'strongly of opinion that national wage agreements should continue'.[3] The third, and more remote, qualification was that the industry be reorganised according to the Commission's proposals: 'before any sacrifices are asked from those engaged in the industry, it shall be definitely agreed between them that all practicable means for improving its organisation and increasing its efficiency should be adopted, as speedily as the circumstances in each case allow'.[4]

4. NEGOTIATIONS AT HALF-SPEED

After the publication of the Samuel Report on March 11 the leisurely pace of negotiation was resumed. The representatives of the Miners' Federation and the Mining Association met on March 25 and 31 and April 1, but were in disagreement from the first. The owners would only talk of lower wages, and to make matters worse, insisted on district agreements, thus denying the men their cherished gains of the war and postwar years, a national agreement and a national minimum wage (the minimum percentage addition to the standard rates). The miners would not

---

[1] R.C. on Coal Industry, *Report*, pp. 233–5.   [2] Ibid., p. 236.
[3] Ibid., p. 236.   [4] Ibid., p. 229.

budge on wages or hours or a national agreement and harped upon 'reorganisation'—about which the owners were openly contemptuous and the Samuel Report unfortunately vague. The government, for its part, did nothing. It gave a grudging acceptance to the proposals of the Report and promised the necessary legislation provided both sides agreed to it. It thus invited them to disagree, in effect giving a veto to the miners over reductions of wages and to the owners over reorganisation. Deadlock came at a meeting on April 13.

The miners were in an unyielding mood: their leaders, Herbert Smith and A. J. Cook, as much as any of them. After the Samuel Report came out a friend told them that it gave them two-thirds of what they wanted: 'It gives us three-quarters,' Cook replied, 'and we can't accept it'.[1] Herbert Smith, born in the workhouse at Kippax (near Leeds) in 1862 and soon an orphan, had entered the pits at 10 and was a member of the local school board at 30. In his youth he had been a fighter at public houses. Short of speech, brave, tough, kindly, he had been president of the Yorkshire miners since 1905, and of the Miners' Federation since 1922. A. J. Cook was a complete contrast: a soldier's son, born in Wookey, Somerset, in 1883, his first experience in mining was in the rural coalfield of Radstock, though he soon moved to South Wales, and was a member of the executive of the South Wales federation of miners when elected secretary of the Miners' Federation in 1924. In his youth he had been, along with his fervid socialism, a rousing preacher in Baptist missions and in the Band of Hope. Utterly selfless, his evangelical fervour was the secret of his appeal as a speaker and a leader; when speaking in the open he would warm to his task and take off his coat, the better to flail the air with his arms to punctuate his eloquence. In 1926 he was certainly the best-hated man to the general public. Trade union leaders such as J. H. Thomas had many bitter exchanges with him; yet they all admitted his sincerity, and grieved for him after his early and painful death in 1931 from cancer, the result of an old mining injury to his leg.[2] 'We are going to be slaves no longer and our men will starve before they accept any reductions in wages',[3] he declared in a speech at the end of March; and this was

---

[1] Cf. J. H. Thomas, *My Story*, p. 111.
[2] Both men are in the *D.N.B.*, *1931–40*. For Herbert Smith (d. 1938), see also Jack Lawson, *The Man in the Cap: The Life of Herbert Smith* (London, 1941); for A. J. Cook, see J. H. Thomas, *My Story*, pp. 95–8, G. McAllister, *James Maxton*, pp. 172–4, and R. P. Arnot, *The Miners*, pp. 350–1, 540–1.
[3] W. H. Crook, *General Strike*, p. 323.

typical of the man, and of the miners who followed him. Cook's slogan was the men's resolution: 'not a penny off the pay, not a minute on the day'.

The owners were equally intransigent. They had not only learned nothing and forgotten nothing since 1919; they now had a friendly government, which did nothing to discourage their determination to obtain an unconditional surrender from the miners. Even their friends found it hard to speak well of them. Neville Chamberlain described them as 'not a· prepossessing crowd'.[1] J. L. Garvin, in the *Observer* on April 25, wrote: 'The owners have been tactless and irritating to the last degree. No responsible body of men has ever seemed more lacking in the human touch. . . . Now, as last July, if they wanted to "get the men's backs up" and keep them up, the owners could not have gone better about it.'[2] Lord Birkenhead wrote that 'it would be possible to say without exaggeration that the miners' leaders were the stupidest men in England if we had not had frequent occasion to meet the owners'.[3] In August 1925, one of the Mining Association's officials had published a statement declaring that the association 'has no illusions as to the possibility of a lasting settlement until the constitutional issue is faced. . . . It will be the endeavour of the Mining Association, during the respite purchased by Mr. Baldwin, to expose to the public the ramifications and activities of our English ".Reds", the methods by which they control the Miners' Federation and other unions and their policy towards industry and the State.'[4]

The owners' stubbornness brought the T.U.C. and the government back to the scene of action. The Industrial Committee of the General Council (often called the Negotiating Committee) had been formed before Red Friday, and had been in touch with the miners during the past weeks.[5] It now called upon Baldwin, on April 14, and urged him to intervene to bring the owners and men together again. He agreed to do so, had a meeting with the miners' executive next day, but let the weekend delay a meeting with the owners until Wednesday, the 21st. Owners and men met together on April 22, but once again found themselves at a deadlock. The owners still insisted on district agreements and

---

[1] K. Feiling, *N. Chamberlain*, p. 156.
[2] Quoted in Wickham Steed, *The Real Stanley Baldwin*, p. 89.
[3] *Lord Baldwin*, (*The Times* memoir), p. 10.
[4] Quoted by Vernon Hartshorn, a miners' M.P., 195 H.C. Deb., 5 s., 358.
[5] The committee consisted of eight members, headed by Arthur Pugh and including Swales, J. H. Thomas and two other railwaymen's leaders, John Bromley and A. G. Walkden. Walter Citrine was secretary. It was essentially a committee of moderates.

lower wages, again talked of longer hours as a means of off-setting lower wages, and even made a new and humiliating proposal, that the subsistence wage (the minimum wage in the industry) should be revised. As for the proposed district wage scales, they simply confirmed the miners in their belief that the owners did not mean to negotiate, but only to insist on unconditional surrender. In Durham and South Wales the rates would be lower than those of 1914. The Durham miner would lose 18s. 4d. a week, the hewer in South Wales would have his weekly earnings reduced from 78s. to 45s. 10d.

The miners, faced by these terms, could only resign themselves to a strike; and the Industrial Committee of the T.U.C. supported them. On Friday, April 23 two large decisions were announced. A delegates' conference of the miners would be held next week, on Wednesday (the 28th), and a conference of trade unions' executives, summoned by the T.U.C., would meet on Thursday 'in order that the trade union movement . . . may be fully informed of the position'. Behind these mild words lay the threat, not just of the coal strike, but of a general strike.

Several meetings between the Prime Minister, the owners' and miners' negotiating committees, and the Industrial Committee, took place during the next and final week before lock-out notices took effect on Friday, April 30. The causes of breakdown were still the same: the owners thought only of longer hours; Baldwin made no proposals of his own, and in particular none about reorganisation which, for the miners, was the fundamental question. Thus the miners were confirmed in their obstinacy by the extravagance of the owners' demands and the government's unwillingness to attempt to get them moderated. They did not believe in the government's impartiality.

On Thursday, April 29, the conference of trade union executives met and adjourned, as the miners' delegates' conference had already done. The most forceful speech at the former was that of Ernest Bevin. He warned that a struggle might be coming in twenty-four hours. All would then have to 'become one union' and join together to save the miners' standards of life; and the miners would 'have to throw in their lot and cause into the cause of the general movement'.

On Friday, April 30, the conference of trade union executives, a thousand members strong, met once again in the Memorial Hall; met, waited for news of the negotiations, adjourned, met, and waited again. There were three adjournments in all before it met at 8.30 p.m., ready to sit tight until the final word came. The owners had that morning produced, at the Prime Minister's request, an offer of a national wages agreement. Two-thirds of the miners had already finished their last shift that afternoon and were already 'locked out', when the Miners' Federation first saw the terms. These offered, not merely the return to the eight-hour day for at least $3\frac{1}{2}$ years, but lower wages for the longer hours; a return to the standard of 1921, which had provided a minimum percentage addition of 20 to the 1914 standard, as compared to the minimum percentage addition of 33 which the miners had had since 1924. These proposals the Prime Minister sent on to the Miners' Federation by letter, which was received at 1.15 p.m. The letter promised, if the miners accepted the longer hours, the necessary temporary legislation for the purpose. It went on to declare that the government had accepted the Samuel Report and was 'willing' to give effect to 'such of [its] proposals . . . as we believe will be of benefit to the industry'. It proposed, therefore, to arrange at once for an 'authoritative enquiry' into the best method of following up the Commission's recommendations regarding selling organisations and amalgamations. Baldwin in fact abandoned at this point the role of arbitrator: he demanded an immediate sacrifice of the miners as to both hours and wages, and offered them in return only another inquiry and a chilly promise of some legislation to help the industry's reorganisation in the future. Of any corresponding sacrifice on the owners' side there was not the shadow of a suggestion.

Though the miners' executive and then the miners' delegates' conference rejected these proposals, as was inevitable, their decision was not given immediately or without qualification to the Prime Minister. After discussion between the miners' executive and the Industrial Committee the miners' reply was taken to Baldwin at 6 p.m. It regretted the owners' offer had come so late, and rejected it. It submitted, however, a copy of the Industrial Committee's proposals, which laid stress on the Samuel Report's proposals of reorganisation, but included the 'revision of the minimum percentage' as one step, though not the first, in this. The miners' letter concluded confusedly:

> Until such reorganisation brings greater prosperity to the industry the miners should not be called upon to surrender any of their present inadequate wages and conditions.

The evening was crowded with meetings. The Industrial Committee, reinforced by Ramsay MacDonald and Arthur Henderson, met Baldwin and, later, other members of the Cabinet, and attempted to get the lockout notices withdrawn so that negotiations could be resumed; incidental to this would be a brief continuation of the government's subsidy. At last the government was brought to talk of the reorganisation of the industry. The miners' executive, which was called in, agreed to consider 'all the difficulties of the industry' (i.e., wage reductions), when schemes for reorganisation should have been 'initiated'. 'Initiated' then became the stumbling block. Would the miners agree to accept reductions now? No, they would not agree in advance of seeing what reorganisation was going to be: 'I want to see the horse I am going to mount,' said Herbert Smith. At this the ministers broke off the meeting.

Immediately after the breakdown the Industrial Committee made their way to the conference of trade union executives at Memorial Hall, which they reached a little before midnight. The delegates had been whiling away the long hours of waiting with singing: Welsh and Scottish songs, music hall songs, solos, recitations and stories told from the platform, singing by three or four groups against each other; and inevitably, 'Lead, Kindly Light'. Down below, members of the General Council played nap or solo whist.[1] Now the audience rallied to hear the Industrial Committee's report. Pugh described the day's negotiations and the breakdown over a 'mere phrase' in the terms for further negotiations. Thomas recounted further details, and declared, as well he might, that he had 'never begged and pleaded like I begged and pleaded today'. The railway strike of 1919 had come, he recalled, over the word 'definitive'; now there was to be a strike over another word, 'initiated'. The general secretaries of the unions represented were then given printed copies of the General Council's plans for co-ordinated action in support of the miners, which had been drawn up by Ernest Bevin and Arthur Purcell. The meeting adjourned until noon next day.

The government had taken two steps already in anticipation of the coal strike and perhaps something more. On this same long day, April 30, the Ministry of Health sent out circular 699 to the local authorities, referring to circular 636 of November 20, and stating: 'It is to be hoped that the present negotiations of the Coal Industry will have a successful issue, but if unfortunately this should not be the case . . . the Government consider it neces-

[1] Hamilton Fyfe, *Behind the Scenes of the Great Strike* (London, 1926), pp. 12–13.

sary that part of the organisation referred to in the above Circular should be set in readiness to operate . . .' Accompanying the circular was a complete list of the civil commissioners and their principal staff members. The whole communication was published in the press on May 1.[1] And, at the time of the negotiations between the Prime Minister and the Industrial Council in the House of Commons, a special meeting of the Privy Council was held in the early evening in Buckingham Palace, with the King, who had motored back from Newmarket, present. A proclamation declaring a state of emergency under the Emergency Powers Act because of 'the present immediate threat of cessation of work in Coal Mines' was drawn up and signed. Though dated April 30, it was published under the date May 1 in the *London Gazette*. It was printed in the Saturday evening papers, the Sunday papers and Monday's *The Times*. All this was before the trade union executives had decided to call a general strike though not, presumably, before the General Council had ordered the printing of the strike instructions. It was simultaneous with the expiration of the owners' notices to the miners, and therefore with the beginning of the coal strike, if negotiations failed. Was the government's action provocative or precautionary? By whom did the offence come?[2]

5. LAST-MINUTE EFFORTS

On the next day, Saturday, May 1 (May Day), the meeting of the trade union executives at the Memorial Hall was resumed at 12.30 p.m. The roll was called and the representative of each executive was asked in turn whether his union approved the General Council's 'proposals for co-ordinated action'. The response was heavily affirmative; executives representing 3,653,527 members voted for the proposals, those representing 49,911 members against. There were three or four speeches—a confused but fighting speech by MacDonald, blaming the government for the breakdown, a speech by Bevin explaining that the proposals for action had only been distributed after the General Council had heard that the proclamation of an emergency had been signed and the O.M.S. had begun to mobilise. 'We are not declaring war on

---

[1] *The Times*, May 1; text in G. Glasgow, *General Strikes and Road Transport*, pp. 112, 137 ff.

[2] This account rests on *The Times*; W. H. Crook, *General Strike*, pp. 320–72; R. P. Arnot, *General Strike*, pp. 110–32; R. P. Arnot, *The Miners*, pp. 408–16; J. H. Thomas, *My Story*, pp. 114–20. There is a useful narrative by the Cambridge economist, D. H. Robertson, in the *Economic Journal*, 36: 375–93 (1926).

the people. War has been declared by the Government,' he said, announcing the General Council's readiness to arrange for the distribution of food, and to continue to negotiate over the coal strike. Curiously, the 'proposals for co-ordinated action', did not mention a general strike; they merely directed that certain 'trades and undertakings shall cease work as and when required by the General Council', giving as reason the failure to get a satisfactory settlement in the coal-mining dispute, and the 'need for co-ordinated action on the part of affiliated unions in defence of the policy laid down by the General Council'. Actually, the General Council issued no instructions calling out trade unionists on strike; that was left to the individual unions. The time set was midnight (11.59 p.m.) on Monday, May 3.[1]

Another decision was taken by the trade union delegates that afternoon, before they sang the 'Red Flag' and dispersed. The vote on the strike proposals was also a vote by the unions to hand over to the General Council of the T.U.C. the 'conduct of the dispute'. This included the Miners' Federation. Did it hand over to the General Council full powers to negotiate and settle the coal strike? The General Council later claimed that it did; the miners denied it. The ambiguity was unfortunate.

Yet there was still no certainty of a general strike. There was an interval for further negotiation in which the General Council was determined to use the powers it had just received to avert the strike, not to bring it off. That afternoon Citrine sent two letters to the Prime Minister; one offering, on the part of the Council, to 'enter into arrangements for the distribution of essential food-stuffs', the other stating that the trade union executives had handed over to the Council the 'conduct of the dispute' and that the Council was 'available at any moment should the Government desire to discuss the matter further'. In spite of the rather tactless combination of letters, Baldwin got in touch with Thomas and met the Industrial Committee at eight that evening (Saturday, May 1). On his suggestion, they formed two sub-committees: Baldwin, Birkenhead, Steel-Maitland (the Minister of Labour)[2] for the Cabinet, Pugh, Thomas and Swales for the T.U.C.; Sir Horace Wilson (the permanent secretary of the Ministry of Labour) and

---

[1] W. H. Crook, pp. 349–51, 373; F. Williams, *Ernest Bevin*, pp. 132–5; text of the 'proposals for co-ordinated action' in Crook, p. 599; W. Milne-Bailey, *Trade Unions and the State*, p. 63; W. Milne-Bailey, *Trade Union Documents*, pp. 342–4.

[2] Arthur H. D. R. Steel-Maitland (1876–1935); Rugby and Balliol, fellow of All Souls, Oxford, president of the Oxford Union; special commissioner to R.C. on Poor Laws, 1906–7; M.P., 1910–35; Minister of Labour, 1924–29. Created baronet, 1917.

Citrine were secretaries. By 1 a.m. (the small hours of Sunday, May 2) this group had agreed on a formula, upon which the negotiators all went home to bed. Thomas went home to Dulwich and told his wife he felt certain of a settlement. The formula ran:

> The Prime Minister has satisfied himself, as a result of the conversations . . . that if negotiations are continued, it being understood that the notices cease to operate, the representatives of the Trades Union Congress are confident that a settlement can be reached on the lines of the Report within a fortnight.

This formula was to be submitted to the Cabinet and to the General Council.[1]

That morning, Sunday, May 2, the General Council met at its headquarters in Eccleston Square at nine. Cook had heard of the last-minute negotiations during the night, and claimed to be surprised at them. He joined the General Council that morning, was shown the formula, and was asked for the miners' consent to it. To the Council's surprise, he told it that the members of his executive had left London last night for their respective coalfields —an action justified by the fact that the coal strike had already begun. He was asked to recall them by telegram, which he did. Unfortunately, in its dismay at this development, the General Council forgot to telephone the Prime Minister of what had happened. Baldwin had, on the committee's assurance last night that they could give him an answer about noon or 1 p.m., called a Cabinet meeting for noon. When no message came (and they apparently sought none by telephone), the members, naturally disgruntled (and perhaps a few of them inwardly elated), dispersed, to meet again later in the day. At 5 p.m., according to J. H. Thomas, the General Council had unanimously decided 'to recommend the acceptance of this formula to the miners and to the Cabinet'. They telephoned No. 10 Downing Street that they were ready to meet the Cabinet, but more delay characteristically ensued to allow time for dinner, for which each side blamed the other.[2] The meeting was set for 9 p.m.

The Industrial Committee, together with MacDonald and Henderson, met the Prime Minister, Birkenhead and Steel-Maitland in the Board Room of the Treasury.[3] At once discussion developed on the meaning of the formula, and whether the miners accepted it. Lord Birkenhead drew up a second formula:

---

[1] W. H. Crook, pp. 361–2; J. H. Thomas, *My Story*, pp. 102, 123.
[2] 195 H.C. Deb., 5 s., 417.   [3] Ibid., 302.

we will urge the miners to authorise us to enter upon a discussion with the understanding that they and we accept the Report as a basis of settlement, and we approach it with the knowledge that it may involve some reduction in wages.

While this was under discussion, word came that the miners' executive had arrived. The Industrial Committee left the Prime Minister to meet the miners and the rest of the General Council to talk over Lord Birkenhead's formula with them, in another room upstairs. Baldwin, meanwhile, went into a meeting of the Cabinet. Half or threequarters of an hour later, according to Thomas, the Prime Minister's secretary came up to the room where the trade unionists were, and said the Prime Minister wanted to see them. They demurred, being apparently near agreement, but on a second request Pugh, Swales, Thomas and Citrine went down, leaving the miners behind. Baldwin, seeming rather ill at ease and jerky, handed the committee a letter and said:

> The task of the peacemakers is hard. Since we were here an hour ago an incident has happened which the British Cabinet takes such a serious view upon that they have instructed me to break off negotiations and convey their decision in this letter which I now hand to you. But I felt, having regard to all that you gentlemen have done to try and effect an honourable peace, courtesy demanded that I should tell you personally. Good-bye. This is the end.[1]

The letter, after declaring that 'no solution of the difficulties in the coal industry' was possible without the 'sincere acceptance of the Report', including both the reorganisation of the industry and the 'interim adjustment of wages and hours', declared that if the miners and the T.U.C.'s committee had accepted this proposal the government 'would have been ready to resume the negotiations and to continue the subsidy for a fortnight'.

> But since the discussions which have taken place between Ministers and members of the Trade Union Committee it has come to the knowledge of the Government not only that specific instructions have been sent . . . directing their members . . . to carry out a general strike on Tuesday next, but that overt acts have already taken place, including gross interference with the freedom of the Press. Such action involves a challenge to the constitutional rights and freedom of the nation.

[1] J. H. Thomas, *My Story*, pp. 125–6; H. Fyfe, *Behind the Scenes of the Great Strike*, p. 23. Baldwin's account (195 H.C. Deb., 5 s., 350) says he said that 'as so often happened the work of the peacemakers had been killed by the action of the hotheads'.

His Majesty's Government, therefore, before it can continue negotiations must require from the Trade Union Committee both the repudiation of the actions referred to . . . and an immediate and unconditional withdrawal of the instructions for a general strike.[1]

When the committee read the letter they were, of course, aghast, not knowing, in the first place, what the 'overt acts' were. They went back to the miners and the General Council and at once decided to repudiate the 'overt acts', drafted a resolution, and returned to the Prime Minister with it. Their letter, published next day, deplored the government's 'precipitous and calamitous decision', which had 'wrecked' the General Council's efforts to obtain a settlement by an 'unprecedented ultimatum'.[2] To their amazement, the trade union leaders found the room where the Cabinet had met, dark; the attendant told them that all the members had gone home. Baldwin had followed his usual custom in a crisis and gone to bed. The government had broken off negotiations and declared war. In this sense Baldwin and the Cabinet were responsible for the general strike. The announcement that negotiations had broken down was made from Downing Street at 1.5 a.m. on Monday, May 3.[3]

And what were the 'overt acts'? There was only one. The machine men, members of 'Natsopa', the National Society of Operative Printers and Assistants, in the *Daily Mail* headquarters in London refused, entirely on their own initiative, to print the Monday issue of the *Daily Mail* unless the editorial was altered. This editorial branded the threatened general strike as a 'revolutionary movement', not to be 'tolerated by any civilised Government', and called on all 'law-abiding men and women to hold themselves at the service of King and country'.[4]

How did the government come to precipitate the general strike over such a triviality, ludicrous if its consequences were not so serious? The Cabinet's decision was hardly made, and the ultimatum written, in the matter of half an hour to an hour. The Cabinet

[1] W. H. Crook, pp. 364–5.

[2] W. Milne-Bailey, *Trade Unions and the State*, gives text, p. 67; also in his *Trade Union Documents*, p. 340.

[3] This narrative is based on the accounts of Baldwin and Thomas in the House of Commons, May 3 and 5 (195 H.C. Deb., 5 s., 67–82, 343–6, 349–50, 408–22), and of Thomas in *My Story*, pp. 122–6. See the critical discussion of different versions of the chronology of the two 'formulae' in Crook, pp. 362–3.

[4] Text in Scott Nearing, *The British General Strike* (New York, 1926), p. 141. See also W. H. Crook, p. 364; H. Fyfe, pp. 22–3; W. Milne-Bailey, *Trade Unions and the State*, p. 67.

had been meeting since 5 o'clock that Sunday evening,[1] and was divided whether to continue negotiations or to take up the challenge of the threatened general strike because of the 'constitutional issue'. Baldwin's subsequent explanation in parliament of his reason for breaking off the negotiations was rather lame: the *Daily Mail* incident was an instance of direct action, the 'beginning of the general strike', which so changed the situation that negotiations could not continue; the General Council had 'lost control'.[2] He was on firmer ground when he claimed that the General Council of the T.U.C. did not have full powers to settle the coal dispute: it could negotiate but not 'take the decision', as Pugh told the Prime Minister on Saturday evening. Hence the Council's acceptance of a formula without the miners' consent would not have satisfied him.[3] He also made much of the risk he took of continuing the negotiations under the threat of a general strike;[4] but it was only that which had caused the resumption of negotiations at all, and the government on its part had taken action which conveyed an equal threat when it proclaimed an emergency and sent out instructions to the local authorities, as early as Friday the 30th.

It seems clear that near midnight, when Baldwin and his colleagues were tired and on edge after a long day of meetings and adjournments, those in the Cabinet who wanted to fight things out seized upon the *Daily Mail* incident, reported to them by telephone, as the excuse for insisting that negotiations be broken off before they robbed them of the expected strike, arguing, no doubt, that the *Daily Mail* incident proved the unreliability of the negotiators. At a late hour a silly argument may sound as good as a sane one, and on one of those points where tired and irritated men dig in their toes—points of pride, of supposed principle, of constitutional rights—the 'wild men' were able to stand and win. Baldwin, the peacemaker, was over-ruled, partly by threats of resignations. The peace party included Baldwin, Steel-Maitland, Birkenhead; but on the other side were ranged Churchill, Neville Chamberlain, Joynson-Hicks, Cunliffe-Lister, Hogg, Bridgeman, Amery. They rejected a settlement with the General Council,

[1] K. Feiling, *N. Chamberlain*, p. 157. G. M. Young, *Baldwin*, p. 114, states that the Cabinet 'approved a note to be issued after that meeting [the meeting at 9 p.m. between Baldwin, Birkenhead and Steel-Maitland and the trade unionists] if Ministers thought it desirable'.

[2] 195 H.C. Deb., 5 s., 70, 345, 350, 351.

[3] Ibid., 410, 418–19 (transcript of part of the discussion on Saturday evening, May 1, read by Steel-Maitland); cf. 348 for a press statement by A. J. Cook on *Sunday* evening reiterating the miners' refusal of any agreement lowering their standard of living.

[4] Ibid., 69, 345, 413.

which would avert the general strike and leave the miners to strike alone, and seized on the constitutional issue. Instead of contributing to another Black Friday, the government solidified the trade union movement by forcing the General Council to go through with the strike.[1] Baldwin, exhausted after days of contendingwith trade unionists, now found himself called upon to fight his own colleagues, and gave way.[2] Yet he showed no enthusiasm for battle: 'everything I care for is being smashed to bits at this moment'.[3] It was the irony of Baldwin's career, both in 1926 and in the Abdication crisis ten years later, that his greatest failure in leadership—the coming of the general strike—was transformed, by the constitutional issue, into one of his greatest successes, when the strike ended in the government's victory nine days later.

6. THE NINE DAYS

On Monday, May 3, the public learned, with little or no real warning, that it faced the unknown dangers of a general strike that very midnight. The meeting of the House of Commons that evening was mostly taken up with speeches rehearsing the events of the last few days and pleading for peace. There were further attempts at negotiation: meetings between the Prime Minister and representatives of the T.U.C. in the House of Commons, which ended only at 11 p.m.[4] The miners' leaders and the Industrial Committee had agreed to a basis for negotiating a settlement of the coal strike: a National Mining Board to determine adjustments in wages, subject to the 7-hour day and 'a national minimum'. Churchill, however, was now setting the government's tune, which was that of 'unconditional surrender', a tune which offered deadlock and the danger of violence and bloodshed, but also the possibility—in the event the fact—of that rare and tragic thing, complete victory for one side. When Henderson and the other negotiators met several ministers that night, Churchill at once asked: 'Have you come to say that the strike notices are with-

---

[1] Scott Nearing, *British General Strike* (New York, 1926), p. 35, quoting H. N. Brailsford in *New Leader*, May 21, 1926. Cf. Thomas in House of Commons: 'At one minute to twelve on Monday night I would have grovelled for peace'; 195 H.C. Deb., 5 s., 421.

[2] 'Should we hang Mr. Churchill or not?' *New Statesman*, May 22, 1926; D. H. Robertson, *Ec. J.*, 36: 383; H. Fyfe, *Behind the Scenes*, pp. 13, 19. See also K. Feiling, *N. Chamberlain*, p. 157; F. Williams, *Bevin*, pp. 136–7. H. Nicolson, *George V*, p. 417, supports by implication the account here given; also L. S. Amery, *My Political Life*, II, 483.

[3] 195 H.C. Deb., 5 s., 73.   [4] W. H. Crook, pp. 367–8.

drawn?' 'No, we——' 'Then there is no reason to continue this discussion.'[1]

On Tuesday, May 4, the first day of the general strike, there was an unwonted stillness throughout the land. Only a few trains were moving, the shunting yards and engine sheds were silent: the docks were still; there were almost no buses, though the increased use of taxis and private cars in London produced spectacular traffic jams.[2] The strike could hardly have come at a better time of year—and in fact at any other time its course might have been much rougher. The weather was good. For the thousands of working men on strike it was a time of holiday; for office workers and others not directly affected by the strike there was the excitement of the unusual, the improvised, the broken routine; for those who volunteered to do the work of the strikers there was the exhilaration of adventure, of incongruity, the spirit of a 'lark'. The subsequent cliché, that strikers and police spent their time playing football matches against each other, had a good measure of truth in it. Parades, meetings, speeches, long hours in committees took up the time of many; other people pursued the daily round as if nothing more than a prolonged Bank Holiday was occurring.

The general strike, which the T.U.C. preferred to call the 'national strike', was general only in two senses: that those workers who were called out on strike came out almost to a man; and that the cessation of work in certain industries and services which resulted did paralyse the normal life of the nation. The General Council's instructions laid down that only the men in the 'first line' industries should go on strike at the start: railwaymen, dockers, road transport workers; the printing trades; iron and steel, metals and heavy chemicals; the building trades; electricity and gas. The unions concerned issued the necessary instructions— the National Union of Railwaymen only after much searching of heart, since their men were much more replaceable than miners and they would bear the brunt of public ill-will. The call-out of the steelworkers and builders was rather an irrelevancy, though they would soon be affected by the stoppage of transport and coal supplies in any case; it was done to give encouragement and a sense of solidarity to the transport men. The only unions which did not join in were the National Union of Journalists, Havelock

[1] W. H. Crook, p. 425, quoting *Lansbury's Labour Weekly*, May 22, 1926.
[2] See G. Glasgow, *General Strikes and Road Transport*, pp. 45–7 for figures.

Wilson's National Sailors' and Firemen's Union, and the Electrical Power Engineers' Association.[1]

The completeness of the stoppage on the railways was attested to by the statements published by the railway companies after the strike, and by their emergency timetables. Passenger service on the L.M.S., maintained by a few of the regular railwaymen, clerks and others pressed into unusual jobs, and volunteers, was 3·8 per cent of normal on May 5 (the lowest ebb) and 12·2 per cent of normal on the last full day of the strike, May 11; freight service was only 1 per cent of normal at the start and 3 per cent at the finish. The other companies' performance was similar, though by the end the G.W.R. and the Southern Railway reported passenger service as 19 per cent of normal.[2] The record on London's underground railways was similar. Of London's 4400 buses, 300 were running on the first day, only 40 by the third; these were all 'pirate' buses. None of the L.G.O.C.'s buses moved on the first day, 526 were running by May 11 out of the fleet of 3293. Altogether 959 buses of all companies were running in London by May 11, after a steady increase on each day of the strike.[3]

Into the gap made by the absence of the railwaymen, dockers, and other transport workers entered a host of volunteers. The O.M.S., having served its purpose of recruiting and training men for service in an emergency, quietly disappeared, merging itself in the local committees of the government's organisation.[4] Undergraduates from Oxford and Cambridge enjoyed a week's holiday and adventure in unloading ships at the docks, most of them hardly realising that they were acting as blacklegs. Their amateur efforts, soon reduced by fatigue, gave amusement to the regular dockers. Other volunteers, undergraduates and members of the general public, acted as drivers and conductors of buses, sometimes causing accidents, though none was fatal. Lorries and vans maintained an emergency system of distribution of food, especially milk. Middle-aged men and women served at canteens kept open day and night in town halls and elsewhere to minister to the emergency lorry drivers. A shut-down of electricity and gas was avoided, partly by the work of naval ratings in stoking furnaces, partly because many of the regular workers remained at work. On

[1] R. W. Postgate *et al.*, *Worker's History of the Great Strike* (London, 1927), pp. 17–32; W. H. Crook, pp. 373–7.

[2] W. H. Crook gives full figures of train services and the numbers of railwaymen on strike, pp. 390–5.

[3] W. H. Crook, p. 390; G. Glasgow, pp. 46–50.

[4] W. H. Crook, p. 388.

the railways many a businessman realised a lifetime's ambition by driving an engine, acting as a guard or manning a signal box.

On the side of labour, where there had been a deliberate avoidance of making arrangements in advance such as the government had made, the strike brought out two things very clearly: the enthusiasm for a common cause, and the genius for improvisation and organisation shown by local trade union groups. For the rank and file the strike was a triumph: for most of its national leaders a humiliation. Many people contrasted the optimism and vitality to be found among the working people all over the country with the pessimism and confusion at the T.U.C. headquarters in Eccleston Square, London. Actually, there was not much for the General Council to do in London except negotiate, when the time came, for ending the strike, and several members of the Council spent part of the strike at meetings in their own districts. Central organisation was in the hands of the Strike Organisation Committee, headed by Bevin and A. A. Purcell; the strike was Bevin's show, and greatly added to his importance in the trade union movement. The General Council's most important task was publishing a daily paper, the *British Worker*, as a counterblast to the government's sheet, the *British Gazette*. It made only three decisions during the strike: to refuse offers of money from Russia, to cancel all permits, and to call out the 'second line' of unions on May 11. Throughout the strike the Council was kept in touch with the districts by dispatch riders travelling by car or motor bicycle; these, all arranged for by the local committees, often carried messages of little importance, both to and from London and from one district to another, but were of the greatest value in keeping up the morale of the men by bringing word from towns both near and distant that they were 'solid'.[1]

In each district, the strike arrangements were made by hurriedly improvised committees, mostly set up by the local Trades Council and called—a significant reminder of the past—Councils of Action in 54 towns; in another 77 towns the names Strike Committee, Emergency Committee or something similar were used. These committees included the Trades Council's executive committee, and representatives of the strike committee of each local union and of other groups such as the Labour party; they in turn set up other committees to deal with the relief of distress, permits,

[1] W. H. Crook, p. 403; R. W. Postgate, pp. 33–4, 38, 60; J. Paton, *Left Turn*, pp. 245–7, 253.

picketing, publicity, dispatch riders, and the like. The publicity committee issued local strike bulletins, either mimeographed or printed; another committee arranged for meetings in the open or in theatres and halls, some of them to enlist the general public's support; another might provide entertainment, such as the football match at Plymouth against the police, arranged at the Chief Constable's request. The most important function of the strike committee and its subsidiaries—apart from the maintenance of morale —was the issuing of permits for work or transport of certain sorts. This was the result of the General Council's offer, spurned by the government, to assist in maintaining the distribution of essential foodstuffs. Many permits were issued, some reading 'By Permission of the T.U.C.', most of them with more elaborate wordings. The sight of these, pasted on the windshields of cars and lorries, was as maddening to the government's supporters as it was heartening to the strikers. In fact, however, the issuing of permits only caused confusion, as decisions to grant or withhold them for particular purposes were difficult to make. On May 7 the General Council ordered that all permits be revoked—a move which brought forth some of the government's most flamboyant pronouncements. The withdrawal of permits led to complaints from the local Co-operative societies, which in many though by no means all towns were helping the strikers by advancing funds for strike pay or receiving credit vouchers for purchases of food. In Newcastle-on-Tyne, where trade union men, with permits, were unloading ships alongside volunteers, the Civil Commissioner, Sir Kingsley Wood, approached the Joint Strike Committee for its help in getting the men to continue the work when they had abandoned it in protest against the presence of two Navy destroyers and submarines which had taken up positions in the river. The proposal for the moving of foodstuffs under the dual control of the committee and the government's organisation made some progress, but was abandoned, after which the committee withdrew all permits and hampered the work of the volunteers by effective picketing.[1]

The government's plans worked smoothly once the strike began. The code telegram, 'Action', was sent out on the night of Sunday, May 2; by then the Civil Commissioners and their staffs in the

[1] The best accounts of local strike organisation are in Scott Nearing, *The British General Strike*, pp. 83–97, and E. Burns, *The General Strike, May, 1926: Trades Councils in Action* (Labour Research Dept., 1926). See W. H. Crook, pp. 371, 402–12 for permits. For the situation in Newcastle, see Crook, pp. 406–10, R. W. Postgate, pp. 67–8, S. Nearing, pp. 148–65, R. P. Arnot, *The Miners*, pp. 436–43.

various areas were at their posts. The emergency arrangements for the movement of food supplies by road proved fairly effective.[1] The Navy was used not only to man power stations and work the docks but to transport mail across the Irish Sea, bring yeast to London and distribute supplies of petrol; and warships were stationed, not only in the Tyne, but on the Clyde and Humber, and at Liverpool, Cardiff, Bristol, Swansea, Barrow, Middlesbrough and Harwich.[2] Troops were moved into London in large numbers, and were doubtless in readiness for service elsewhere also; but except in London their presence was not obtrusive. The only large-scale military demonstration was the convoy of lorries bringing flour from the London docks to the food centre in Hyde Park on Saturday, May 8. A hundred lorries, escorted by twenty armoured cars and detachments of two Guards regiments, were driven from Hyde Park to the docks, returning by noon. Whether the intention was to provoke bloodshed or to discourage it, the result was only ridiculous, for the crowds offered no opposition save curses to the convoy. Next day, Sunday, lorries of steel-helmeted soldiers and squadrons of cars filled with special police were driven from place to place in London to create a feeling of peril; people merely gaped or grinned. Hamilton Fyfe recorded that Churchill's efforts to create a scare by these stunts had definitely failed.[3]

There was little friction between the police and the strikers in the early days of the strike. When violence occurred later it was ascribed to police imported from outside. At Crewe Ellen Wilkinson[4] declared that the strike committee 'simply ran the town'; arriving to make a speech, she was escorted by a procession of trade unionists, with the Red Flag at its head, and preceded by the chief police officials. At Lincoln the police asked the Trades Council to supply it with special constables, which it did. The fact that many of the strikers were ex-service men, and wore their service medals, helps to explain the good order which existed— along with the General Council's specific instructions on this point. In some towns the strikers formed a Defence Corps

[1] G. Glasgow, pp. 34–96; W. H. Crook, p. 373.
[2] W. H. Crook, p. 422; Archibald Hurd, 'The Navy on "Active Service"', *Fortnightly Review*, 120: 87–101 (July, 1926).
[3] W. H. Crook, pp. 387–8, 417–19; H. Fyfe, p. 58; S. Nearing, pp. 45–6; K. Martin, *The British Public and the General Strike* (London, 1926), pp. 90–1.
[4] Ellen Wilkinson (1891–1947), daughter of an insurance agent; graduate of Manchester University; M.P., 1924–31, 1935–47 (Jarrow); Minister of Education, 1945–47; national organiser, National Union of Distributive and Allied Workers, 1915–47.

under ex-N.C.O.'s which prevented police charges on picket lines.[1] There does seem, however, to have been some effort by the militant spirits in the government to produce the revolution they talked of in order to be able to crush it decisively. Special constables were recruited in large numbers, so that their number increased from 98,000 before the strike to 226,000 at the end. In addition, the government on May 8 called for enlistments in a Civil Constabulary Reserve, which soon numbered 18,000 members.[2] Though many of the specials were simply used, sometimes with comical results, on traffic duty, they were intended for strong action. A contemporary picture shows two quite young men in mufti, each equipped with armband, baton, tin helmet and a shoulder-strap carrying what looks like a rifle.[3] O.M.S. instructions had told the volunteers to hit hard, and in some versions to hit to kill.[4] Special constables and their families were promised allowances and pensions in the event of injuries or death.[5] The government's paper, the *British Gazette*, in a characteristic passage on May 6 and 7, declared that the government would 'not flinch from the issue' and would use 'all the resources at their disposal and whatever measures may be necessary to secure in a decisive manner the authority of Parliamentary government'. The same temper was shown in Joynson-Hicks' appeal for 50,000 special constables in London before the week-end, made in a broadcast and followed by a statement in the *British Gazette* on May 10:

> . . . protection is the one thing which will kill the strike and restore England to its normal life. . . . Give the Government enough Special Constables to enable me to allot two to every vehicle . . . thus releasing the regular police for perhaps sterner work. Give us men in numbers that we may have mobile forces of young and vigorous Special Constables available in any London area where trouble is anticipated.

An appeal by the official guardians of the law for men to stir up trouble could hardly be more naked.

The *British Gazette* followed this with an even more menacing notice on May 8:

[1] S. Nearing, pp. xvi (Ellen Wilkinson's introduction), 85 ff.; E. Burns, pp. 70–2; R. W. Postgate, pp. 58–60.
[2] W. Milne-Bailey, *Trade Unions and the State*, p. 73.
[3] See picture in J. H. Thomas, *My Story*, p. 147. H. Fyfe, p. 60, says the 'specials' were armed with a wartime 'trench tool'.
[4] H. Fyfe, p. 60.   [5] W. H. Crook, p. 387.

All ranks of the Armed Forces of the Crown are hereby notified that any action which they may find it necessary to take in an honest endeavour to aid the Civil Power will receive . . . the full support of his Majesty's Government.[1]

The King, with his characteristic sanity, at once caused Lord Stamfordham to send a note to the War Office criticising the announcement as unfortunate.[2] This was at the time of the food convoy from the Docks and the inauguration of the Civil Constabulary Reserve, and followed an 'official communique' in the *British Gazette* which seemed like a declaration of war. Based on the General Council's instruction for the withdrawal of permits to vehicles carrying food, it declared

> the situation is becoming more intense and the climax is not yet reached. Orders have been sent by the leaders of the Railway and Transport Trade Unions to do their utmost to paralyse and break down the supply of food and the necessaries of life. . . .
>
> An organised attempt is being made to starve the people and to wreck the State, and the legal and constitutional aspects are entering upon a new phase.

Extreme measures by the government involved the danger that the moderate trade union leaders would be brushed aside and the extremists take over; and apparently representations of this sort from the Parliamentary Labour Party (and, doubtless, also the views of the King) caused Baldwin to disavow the statement.[3] No wonder Arnold Bennett recorded in his Journal for May 5, after lunching at the Reform Club, 'General opinion that the fight would be short but violent. Bloodshed anticipated next week.'[4]

It is, of course, a fable that there was no violence during the general strike; it is true that there was no loss of life. There were violent outbreaks in Glasgow, where buses were overturned and the police charged the crowds, on May 5; there was trouble in Leeds and Barnsley over attempts to run buses. At Doncaster, on the last day of the strike, a crowd of about a thousand, mostly miners, interfered with traffic, and the police made several baton charges to clear the roads. In many other places, particularly in Scotland and the North of England, pickets interfered with the running of lorries carrying food. In London there were several clashes between police and strikers, in Canning Town, Poplar, Old Kent Road and elsewhere; in the provinces there was violence

[1] W. H. Crook, p. 421; S. Nearing, p. 74.   [2] H. Nicolson, *George V*, p. 418.
[3] W. H. Crook, pp. 415, 419–20.
[4] Quoted in Osbert Sitwell, *Laughter in the Next Room* (Boston, 1948), p. 211.

in Preston, Hull, Middlesbrough, Liverpool, and also in Edinburgh. The police retaliated with arrests. Almost daily raids were made on the Communist Party's headquarters in King Street, London, and on the houses of Communists elsewhere. As a result of the strike there were 3149 prosecutions for incitement to sedition and for violence in the English and Welsh courts. At Glasgow over 200 men were arrested, and 100 sentenced for impeding traffic to terms averaging three months' imprisonment. After the fight at Doncaster 84 men got three months' sentences. Three men at Aberavon received two months' imprisonment at hard labour for having in their possession copies of the *Workers' Weekly* and other Communist literature. At Newcastle, after the breakdown of the negotiations between the strike committee and Sir Kingsley Wood, the police were violent and sentences imposed on strikers were stern. At Birmingham the entire strike committee was arrested.[1]

In its actions the government could draw on almost unlimited powers which it took under the Emergency Powers Act. The various regulations made by Order in Council under the Act were submitted to parliament for approval. Labour members gave them bitter and searching criticism but had no hope of defeating them. The government took power to seize land and buildings, food and other essentials, to commandeer vehicles, issue special drivers' licences, to take over docks, railways, shipping, coal stocks, petrol, to control the supply of electricity, gas and water. Public meetings might be prohibited where there was apprehension of disorder; acts calculated to cause sedition or disaffection among the armed forces, police, firemen or 'among the civilian population' were offences under the Act, and the mere possession of papers which might contribute to disaffection was an offence. A sweeping right of search of premises where such documents might be found was given to the police under directions of the Home Secretary.[2]

The government's justification for such powers was in the 'constitutional issue', that the strike was not an industrial dispute but an attack upon the state. Baldwin's message in the *British Gazette* on May 6 declared: 'Constitutional Government is being attacked . . . Stand behind the Government . . . The laws are in

---

[1] W. H. Crook, pp. 411–12, 415–17; R. W. Postgate, pp. 58–60, 67–8; R. P. Arnot, *General Strike*, pp. 185–204; J. T. Murphy, *Political Meaning of the Great Strike* (Communist Party of Great Britain, 1926), pp. 89, 120–1; K. Martin, pp. 52, 67; *Annual Register, 1926*, p. 61.

[2] S. Nearing, pp. 71–3; W. H. Crook, p. 373; 195 H.C. Deb., 5 s., 453; see also debates of May 5 and 6, 1926, *ibid.*

your keeping. You have made Parliament their guardian. The General Strike is a challenge to Parliament and is the road to anarchy and ruin.'[1] In parliament on May 3 he had said: 'It is not wages that are imperilled; it is the freedom of our very Constitution.' Churchill referred to the General Council's offer to distribute essential foods as that of a 'rival Government', and called the strike a 'conflict which, if it is fought out to a conclusion, can only end in the overthrow of Parliamentary Government or in its decisive victory'. The *British Gazette* on May 5, its first issue, under the headline 'Hold-up of the Nation', roared forth: 'The general strike is . . . a direct challenge to ordered government . . . an effort to force upon some 42,000,000 British citizens the will of less than 4,000,000 others. . . .'[2]

To such charges there were denials in and out of parliament, some of them making pointed references to the quasi-rebellious activities of certain members of the government during the Ulster crisis in 1914. MacDonald, Henderson, Clynes, Thomas and others all denied, as well they might, any thought of revolutionary action, Thomas, in a remark often quoted against him afterwards, saying 'I have never disguised that in a challenge to the Constitution, God help us unless the Government won.'[3] Lloyd George on May 3 ridiculed the suggestion that the trade union leaders who had 'fought the rebellious ones in their own party', and had worked hardest to avert the strike, were making a 'threat to the institutions of the country'. He appealed to the government to negotiate a settlement and warned that a victory would be disastrous to the state, giving 'a sense of superiority to power and wealth' which 'the Prime Minister is the last man I know to want'. Later he supported Henderson and others in their sharp questions over the provocative statements in the *British Gazette*.[4] In the Lords there were some polite passages at arms: Asquith and Birkenhead denounced the strike, but Haldane, to their indignation, refused to join them and besought the government not to call it war. *The Times*, which kept its head, simply remarked in its emergency edition of May 11: 'no one suggests for a moment that any considerable number of men on strike are animated by revolutionary motives'. The General Council of the T.U.C. vigorously denied, in the *British Worker*, that it was attacking the constitution.

[1] Quoted in W. Milne-Bailey, *Trade Unions and the State*, p. 71.
[2] W. H. Crook, pp. 383, 400–1; 195 H.C. Deb., 5 s., 71, 103, 123–4, 337–8. Cf. government handbill reproduced in S. Nearing, p. 142, 'The Great "Hold-up"' which refers to the T.U.C. as 'this alternative Government—this Soviet . . .'
[3] 195 H.C. Deb., 5 s., 81 (May 3).   [4] Ibid., 83–4, 91, 310.

In spreading this message, however, the Council was hampered by a decision of its own taking: that among those industries on strike was the press. In time most newspapers and magazines published emergency editions, mimeographed or in print; but the black-out and the later glimmer of news gave every advantage to the government to spread its version of the news, over the B.B.C., and in the *British Gazette*. The latter, a venture of the government printed in the *Morning Post*'s offices, was an unfortunate excursion by Winston Churchill, its editor, into a new field. Its reporting of the news was one-sided, suggesting, for instance, a gradual weakening of the strike which had little substance in fact. The *British Worker*, published by the T.U.C. in the *Daily Herald* offices, was a much more restrained paper. It never caught up with the government's propaganda; whereas the regular newspapers, had they appeared in full size, could hardly have failed to give all sides of the news, to the strikers' benefit.[1]

The best-known example of the suppression of news and opinion was the refusal to allow the Archbishop of Canterbury (certainly no firebrand nor an unfriendly critic of the government) to broadcast on May 7 an appeal for a settlement drawn up by leaders of the Church and the Nonconformists at a meeting at Lambeth Palace. The appeal (which was finally broadcast on May 11) had been framed after consultation with MacDonald and with Baldwin, though Baldwin objected to part of it. It was Reith, the general manager of the B.B.C., who cancelled the permission previously given to the Archbishop to broadcast the appeal. He was acting, not on any orders from the government, but with the knowledge of Baldwin's attitude to the appeal and the fear that its broadcast might be made an excuse by Churchill for commandeering the B.B.C.—something which was not actually done, and which Baldwin and Reith opposed.[2] The appeal was published in *The Times*, but not in the *British Gazette* until after questions about its omission had been raised in parliament. Other appeals for peace and negotiation by clergy and laity were similarly ignored by the

---

[1] For an analysis of the *British Gazette*, *British Worker* and the other papers, K. Martin, pp. 69–95. Cf. H. Fyfe, pp. 25–38, 44; S. Nearing, pp. 45, 48; W. H. Crook, pp. 421–2.

[2] G. K. A. Bell, *Randall Davidson*, II, 1306–11; J. C. W. Reith, *Into the Wind*, pp. 107–12. The B.B.C. was at the time still a private company. Reith insisted that, as a national institution which had won the public's goodwill, it should not be commandeered or manipulated and, while broadcasting orders and communications from the government, should retain its discretion in its news broadcasts; with the authority of its reputation for impartiality it 'would emphasize and initiate statements likely to counteract a spirit of selfishness and hostility' (Reith's memorandum to Baldwin, *ibid.*, p. 108). Despite Churchill, the Cabinet on May 11 accepted Reith's position.

government, though published elsewhere. The Archbishop himself was untiring in seeing various leaders and working for peace: on May 11 he saw Baldwin at his request to warn him against drifting into an intransigent position and to question the 'truculent and fighting attitude' of some of his colleagues, which Baldwin 'did not in the least deny . . .'[1]

Yet, while the T.U.C. leaders were busy disavowing any revolutionary intentions, many of their followers gladly took up the government's challenge. One Trades Council reported that the strike 'was regarded as a straight fight between the T.U.C. and the Government', and was 'a fine political weapon for Labour'.[2] Ellen Wilkinson related that a meeting cheered for many minutes when a miner said: 'If the British Constitution makes a man work underground for less than £2 a week, it is about time that constitution was challenged!'[3] Another writer quotes an I.L.P. man from the North saying to him: 'Man, John, there's never been anything like it. If the blighters o' leaders here . . . dinna' let us down we'll hae the Capitalists crawlin' on their bellies in a week. Oh, boy, it's the revolution at last!'[4] And, indeed, the revolutionary possibilities of the strike were undeniable: it was realisation of this which increased the leaders' impatience to end it.[5]

7. CALLING OFF THE STRIKE

The dangers in a protracted strike made the more alarming the rigidity which the die-hards in the Cabinet had imposed upon government policy. The *British Gazette* had stated on May 6: . . . there can be no question of compromise of any kind. Either the country will break the General Strike, or the General Strike will break the country . . .'[6] This was the government's position from the start: there could be no negotiations over the coal strike until the general strike was called off unconditionally. Like all such demands it could, if followed literally, have meant only the annihilation of both parties: the General Council, having brought about the strike, could hardly end it without something to show for the miners. Officially, this stand was maintained to the end. In fact, there were constant negotiations behind the scenes, as MacDonald admitted during the strike.[7] Among such efforts was a lunch on Saturday, May 8, arranged by Lord and Lady Wim-

---

[1] G. K. A. Bell, *Randall Davidson*, II, 1312–14; H. Fyfe, pp. 50–1, 59; W. H. Crook, pp. 422, 426; K. Martin, pp. 75–6.
[2] S. Nearing, p. 96.   [3] Ibid., p. xiv.   [4] John Paton, *Left Turn*, p. 253.
[5] W. H. Crook, pp. 402, 414; K. Martin, pp. 24–7.
[6] S. Nearing, p. 73.   [7] W. H. Crook, p. 427.

borne, prominent Liberals, and attended by Lord Reading, recently
Viceroy of India and also a Liberal, J. H. Thomas, Philip Snowden,
J. A. Spender, and two leading coal-owners, Lord Gainford and
Lord Londonderry; this was reported to Thomas Jones, of the
Cabinet secretariat, and to Birkenhead and Churchill by Reading
and Wimborne.[1]

That same evening Baldwin himself opened the way for
negotiations in a notable broadcast, having apparently overborne
for the moment the sterner members of his Cabinet. He promised,
'when the time comes, as I hope it soon may, to discuss the terms
upon which the coal industry is to be carried on . . . to see that . . .
justice is done both to the miners and the owners'. He reasserted
that the general strike was an attack upon the community, but
denied unequivocally that the government was 'fighting to lower
the standard of living of the miners or of any other section of the
workers'. He was ready to parley with anyone—'no door is
closed'; and once the general strike was called off 'absolutely and
without reserve' the mining dispute could be settled. 'I am a man
of peace. But I will not surrender the safety and the security of
the British Constitution. . . . Cannot you trust me to ensure a
square deal for the parties, to secure even justice between man and
man?'[2] This skilful blend of the firm and the conciliatory spirit
was certainly palatable to much of the middle class, as well as to
many of the working people. Meetings were held that week-end
all over the country, calling for negotiations to end the strike;
some of them, in London suburbs like West Norwood and Hampstead, were addressed by trade union leaders, and contributed
large sums of money for the strikers.[3]

At the same time much was being made of a speech delivered
by Sir John Simon in the House of Commons on May 6. In this
he declared that the general strike was not a strike at all, and that
men out on strike had broken their contracts, were taking part in
an utterly illegal proceeding, and were liable to be sued for
damages. The protection of trade union funds given by the Trade
Disputes Act of 1906 was, he implied, sacrificed in an unlawful
strike; and 'every trade union leader who has advised and promoted that course of action is liable in damages to the uttermost
farthing of his personal possessions'.[4] This weighty pronounce-
ment was, of course, given full play in the *British Gazette*, and

---

[1] These negotiations are described by Osbert Sitwell, who helped to instigate them,
in *Laughter in the Next Room*, pp. 212–29.
[2] *The Times*, May 10.   [3] H. Fyfe, pp. 50–1, 64.
[4] 195 H.C. Deb., 5 s., 583–6; W. H. Crook, pp. 470–1.

must have made many of both strikers and leaders falter. In law his opinion commanded little respect. It was demolished by A. L. Goodhart, the editor of the *Law Quarterly Review* (subsequently appointed Professor of Jurisprudence at Oxford in 1931) on the ground that the general strike was simply a sympathetic strike, which was legal under the Act of 1906; pressure on a third party was implicit in any sympathetic strike and the fact that that party was now the government made no difference. Nor was it possible to bring the strike under the laws of treason or seditious conspiracy. To this reasoning the working man was apt to add two more points: if the general strike was illegal then there was something wrong with the law—the old story of one law for the rich and one for the poor; and (later on), if it was illegal, why was a new act of parliament needed in 1927 to make it so?[1]

At the time, however, Sir John Simon's opinion was accorded respect and fear—the more so since a decision given by Mr. Justice Astbury in the Chancery Division of the High Court on May 11 coincided with it. In granting an injunction to prevent officers in one of the London branches of the sailors' union from calling out members on strike, the judge added certain *obiter dicta* branding the 'so-called general strike' as 'illegal and contrary to law' and not protected by the Trades Dispute Act of 1906, since no 'trade dispute' could exist between the T.U.C. and 'the Government and the nation'.[2]

Rumours were also current as early as Sunday, May 9 that the government intended to arrest the members of the General Council and of the local strike committees, to impound trade union funds and to call up the army reserves.[3] Neville Chamberlain, Hogg, Balfour were pressing Baldwin for strong action: 'the best and kindest thing now is to strike hard and quickly', wrote Chamberlain.[4] On May 11 the Cabinet decided to introduce a bill immediately to define illegal strikes ('. . . intended to intimidate or coerce the Government or the community') and make the use of trade union funds in such a strike an indictable offence. Again the King intervened, unknown to the public, warning the Home Secretary and the Attorney-General that 'anything done to touch the pockets of those who are now only existing on strike pay might cause exasperation and serious reprisals on the part of the

[1] Goodhart's article is in the *Yale Law Journal*, 36: 464–85 (February, 1927), cited in W. H. Crook, pp. 473–7, who also cites other opinions contrary to Sir John Simon's. See also K. Martin, pp. 96–109; D. H. Robertson, *Ec. J.*, 36: 389.
[2] W. H. Crook, pp. 472–3.
[3] Ibid., p. 421; H. Fyfe, p. 69; R. P. Arnot, *General Strike*, p. 201.
[4] K. Feiling, *N. Chamberlain*, pp. 157–8.

sufferers', and counselling the Prime Minister not to provoke the strikers 'who until now had been remarkably quiet'.[1] Private members, employers, the party whips gave similar advice; and the proposal was abandoned.

By now the *deus ex machina* which the General Council—and the government—so desperately needed had appeared: Sir Herbert Samuel. He was staying in Italy when the strike began, but returned to England on Thursday, May 6.[2] He got in touch with J. H. Thomas, recalled the members of the defunct Royal Commission (who felt their intervention would be useless), and saw Baldwin and Steel-Maitland. Appalled at the deadlock which prevented negotiations, he decided to do what he could on his own initiative. He met the Industrial Committee of the General Council; since secrecy was deemed essential, they met in the sumptuous mansion of Sir Abe Bailey, a South African mining magnate, in Bryanston Square, which Sir Abe offered to Thomas. The plan was to bring attention back to the coal strike: Sir Herbert was to draw up a statement filling out some of the Samuel Report's recommendations; if this was agreed to by the General Council and the miners it could then be the basis for calling off the strike, it being understood that Sir Herbert would 'strongly recommend' its acceptance by the government as the basis of a settlement. The negotiations ended on Monday, May 10 after the miners' leaders, Herbert Smith, A. J. Cook, and W. P. Richardson, had been called in. After the General Council had been consulted, and some changes made, the Samuel Memorandum, as it came to be known, was put in final form. It proposed that negotiations in the coal dispute should be resumed and the subsidy renewed for the time being; that present and future disputes should be referred to a National Wages Board representing owners and miners under an impartial chairman; and that there should be no revision of wages until the Board was convinced that there were sufficient assurances that the Samuel Report's reorganisation proposals would be 'effectively adopted'. Then and only then should wages be considered, subject to the condition that the wages of the lowest-paid men should not be lowered and that a reasonable minimum wage should be fixed.[3]

[1] H. Nicolson, *George V*, pp. 418–19.
[2] Viscount Samuel, *Grooves of Change* (Indianapolis, 1946), p. 226 (English title: *Memoirs*).
[3] Text in W. H. Crook, pp. 602–3; R. P. Arnot, *General Strike*, pp. 225–6, W. Milne-Bailey, *Trade Union Documents*, pp. 348–50. For the negotiations see Crook, pp. 429–30; R. W. Postgate, p. 79; S. Nearing, pp. 46–7; J. H. Thomas, *My Story*, pp. 106–7, 129–31; Viscount Samuel, *Grooves of Change*, pp. 226–30.

The General Council was prepared to accept the Samuel Memorandum as a basis for reopening the negotiations in the coal dispute and calling off the general strike. On Monday, and again on Tuesday (May 10, 11) it besought the miners' executive to accept it. The miners refused; the leader in this being not Cook but Herbert Smith. The miners pointed out that the Memorandum implied that there would be some reductions of wages, which was undeniable, and asked what assurances there were that the government would adopt it and the lock-out notices be withdrawn. There were none and could be none in advance; Thomas was reduced to saying, 'You may not trust my word, but will you not accept the word of a British gentleman who has been Governor of Palestine [Samuel]?' The miners' obstinacy forestalled the General Council's plan to call off the strike on Tuesday evening, May 11. Word of this had reached Downing Street through Lord Wimborne's secretary; hence a telephone call to the T.U.C. at Eccleston Square just after midnight from the Prime Minister's secretary which mystified some of the General Council. The Council adjourned at 1 a.m. (Wednesday, May 12) after agreeing on a final (and as it proved futile) meeting with the miners on the morning of the 12th before going to Downing Street to announce the end of the general strike.[1]

At 12.20 p.m. on Wednesday, May 12 a deputation of the General Council met Baldwin at No. 10 Downing Street. The farce of 'unconditional surrender' was kept up to the end: the deputation was not admitted to the Prime Minister's presence until Sir Horace Wilson had received it to be sure that its object was solely to call off the strike. With the Prime Minister, to accept the surrender, were Birkenhead, Steel-Maitland, Neville Chamberlain and some other ministers. Arthur Pugh began with a long statement leading to the announcement: 'we are here today, sir, to say that this general strike is to be terminated forthwith in order that negotiations may proceed, and we can only hope may proceed in a manner which will bring about a satisfactory settlement'. Baldwin replied that there was a great deal for them both to do: 'All I would say in answer to that is I thank God for your decision. . . . I shall lose no time in using every endeavour to get the two contending parties together and do all I can to ensure a just and lasting settlement.' Thomas asked the Prime

---

[1] W. H. Crook, pp. 430–1; S. Nearing, pp. 49–53; J. H. Thomas, pp. 131–4; A. J. Cook, *The Nine Days* (London, [1926]), pp. 20–2; Lord Samuel, p. 230; Ben Turner, *About Myself* (London, 1930), pp. 311–13; O. Sitwell, *Laughter in the Next Room*, pp. 237–8.

Minister's help to get 'things on the right road again', to prevent
'guerrilla warfare'. Bevin followed this with a longer speech of
shrewd realism, asking the government to give employers a lead
in reinstating the strikers without difficulty; victimisation, though
not named, was the Council's great fear. He also asked if the
mining lock-out would continue while negotiations were resumed.
Baldwin gave no satisfaction on these points, beyond saying he
would consider them. 'You know my record. . . . I think you
may trust me to consider what has been said with a view to seeing
how best we can get the country back into the condition in which
we all want to see it. You will want my co-operation and I shall
want yours. . . .'[1]

The news was at once broadcast that the strike had ended, the
B.B.C. adding at the General Council's request a statement that
the Council had decided to terminate the strike 'in order to resume
negotiations', and that telegrams were being sent to the secretaries
of all unions, from whom members must await definite instructions. (The miners' executive, however, sent out telegrams that
it was no party to the General Council's decision and that miners
should not resume work until after a delegates' conference, called
for May 14.) The General Council's announcement, printed in
the *British Worker* on May 13, went even farther in misinformation:
the Council 'has obtained assurance that a settlement of the mining
problem can be secured which justifies them in bringing the
general stoppage to an end'. With this it published the Samuel
Memorandum and an exchange of letters between Sir Herbert and
Pugh, the former emphasising his entirely unofficial character, the
latter agreeing to this but adding: 'they [the General Council]
assume that during the resumed negotiations the subsidy will be
renewed and that the lock-out notices to the miners will be
immediately withdrawn'. Though such wide assumptions may
seem disingenuous, the members of the Industrial Committee of
the General Council really believed them.[2] Throughout the
country the announcement was read as implying that the General
Council had obtained 'terms' in ending the strike. More significantly, the Council nowhere mentioned that the miners had
rejected the Samuel Memorandum.[3]

[1] The stenographic report of this meeting has been often printed. See W. H.
Crook, pp. 432, 604–8; S. Nearing, pp. 172–4; R. P. Arnot, *General Strike*, pp. 221–4;
R. P. Arnot, *The Miners*, pp. 446–9.
[2] Ben Turner, *About Myself*, p. 314.
[3] W. H. Crook, pp. 436–40; R. P. Arnot, *General Strike*, pp. 224–5. See also
Samuel's statement to the press, May 12, in Arnot, pp. 226–7, and his correspondence
with Steel-Maitland, May 8–9, published May 14, *ibid.*, pp. 237, 240–1.

At strike headquarters and in working-class houses throughout the country the news of the strike's sudden ending was received with shock and disbelief. In spite of the government's news-stories to the contrary, the strike was still solid, with little sign of any drift back to work. Moreover the General Council, only the day before, had issued orders for the 'second line' of workers to be called out: the engineers and shipbuilders.[1]

Disbelief soon gave way to dismay and anger. Not only, it soon appeared, had the miners been betrayed, but all those who had joined in the general strike also. On May 13 the *British Gazette*'s headline was: 'Unconditional Withdrawal of Notices by T.U.C. . . . Surrender Received by Premier'. The *Daily Mail* exulted: 'Surrender of the Revolutionaries . . . Revolution Routed'. Baldwin's broadcast message on the evening of the 12th stated that the strike had ended 'without conditions entered into by the Government', though he added that he would keep to his speech of the 8th in 'the spirit and the letter'.[2] Working men were already finding themselves faced by victimisation and reprisals. Then began a second, shorter and more bitter general strike— one hardly recognised by the general public but not soon forgotten by working people. Here, for a day or so, smouldered the fire of possible violence and civil war.

The second general strike began on May 13, when men going back to work found themselves refused, or accepted only on terms which might include reduction of wages, loss of seniority, or in some cases an engagement to leave their unions. Railwaymen on the Great Western were asked to sign this statement: 'You are hereby engaged on the understanding that you are not relieved of the consequences of having broken your service with the Company.' As if to fan the blaze, the government sent a long food convoy through London on May 13, protected by armoured cars and soldiers; and that evening the police broke up a peaceful meeting in Poplar with savage charges.[3]

The result was a sudden, sullen closing of ranks. The men who had gone out on strike to help the miners now found the miners deserted and themselves left to strike anew for their very livelihood in the future. The General Council had betrayed them, breaking the clause in its own strike instructions of April 30: that 'in the event of any action being taken and Trade Union agree-

[1] W. H. Crook, pp. 393–6, 423–5, 436–46; R. W. Postgate, p. 87.
[2] W. H. Crook, pp. 438–41.
[3] Ibid., pp. 232, 441–4, 453–4; J. H. Thomas in House of Commons, May 13, 195 H.C. Deb., 5 s., 1053–5.

ments being placed in jeopardy, it be definitely agreed that there will be no general resumption of work until those agreements are fully recognised'.[1] Instead, the men were forced back on their own resources. The local strike committees at once took control and decided to continue the strike until all men were taken back unconditionally. On May 13 the strike was more solid than ever; over 100,000 more men were out. The Cardiff committee telegraphed the General Council calling upon it to order the resumption of the general strike; Bristol railwaymen reported on the 14th, 'Position splendid; all out; all in together'. The railwaymen forced the hand of their executives: on the afternoon of the 13th the secretaries of the railway unions wired a call to all members to stay out on strike 'until we receive satisfactory assurances'. The General Council published a somewhat prevaricating statement headed 'Stand together'.[2]

Meanwhile, the leaders tried to avert the new strike. MacDonald raised the question in parliament on the evening of May 13, describing what had happened since the official end of the strike, and contrasting the conciliatory broadcast message of Baldwin with the provocative tone of the day's *British Gazette*. He also mentioned the King's message, published that morning:

> At such a moment it is supremely important to bring together all my people. . . . This task requires the co-operation of all able and well-disposed men in the country. . . . Let us forget whatever elements of bitterness the events of the past few days may have created, only remembering how steady and how orderly the country has remained . . . and forthwith address ourselves to the task of bringing into being a peace which will be lasting.

Baldwin's reply was in the same spirit, and declared specifically: 'I will not countenance any attack on the part of the employers to use this present occasion for trying in any way to get reductions in wages. . . .'[3] There had been other approaches to Baldwin, who had now regained control of the Cabinet and was determined on peace.[4] Next morning the newspapers gave prominence to Baldwin's speech in parliament and published conciliatory editorials.

In the next few days settlements were made in the industries

---

[1] W. H. Crook, p. 601.
[2] Ibid., pp. 446–55; S. Nearing, pp. xix–xx; R. P. Arnot, *General Strike*, pp. 230–9.
[3] 195 H.C. Deb., 5 s., 1042–51.
[4] See the article in the *New Statesman*, May 22, 1926, cited above, p. 310.

concerned, and the men returned to work, most of them on the old conditions, after an admission of wrongful action in joining the strike. In some cases non-union men were retained alongside trade unionists; in Brighton busmen and tramwaymen and printers were forced to leave their unions.[1] The hardest struggle for reinstatement was that of the railwaymen. Even after an agreement reached, at the price of humiliating concession by the unions, on May 14, there was delay in taking the men back, so much so that a second agreement was made on May 21, by which the 'guaranteed week' was temporarily suspended except for men who had not gone on strike. After enforcing this reduction of earnings on the men—necessitated in part by slack trade, made worse by the strike—the companies did not take all of them back: some 45,000, nearly a quarter of the N.U.R.'s membership, had not gone back to work by October.[2]

Thus ended the general strike, though not the coal dispute which was its immediate cause. Its cost in money was great, but such figures are always without real meaning. Its cost in goodwill, in encouraging class-consciousness and ideas of class war, was soon forgotten by the middle classes, who had tasted only the excitement of the strike and none of its bitterness. Then and later the nation, through its writers and chroniclers, congratulated itself on the strike, turning it from a disgrace to a minor national triumph: that for nine days the country had been at a standstill, without bloodshed and with all difficulties overcome by the invincible good humour and the sporting instincts of the British people. The truth was otherwise. There had been violence, and would almost certainly have been much more—real trouble, in fact—if the strike had not ended when it did. The General Council's 'betrayal' of the strike saved, not only trade unionists, but the whole nation from the brutal consequences which the government's intransigence over 'unconditional surrender' would soon have produced. It was afterwards said that the strike was defeated by the community; by the ordinary people rallying to support the government. In such a context 'ordinary people' means the middle classes. As one writer put it, the strike only showed what was known already, that people who dress like gentlemen will instinctively take sides against people who commonly work with their coats off; if such people, and the armed forces, had beaten the working class, it was not much to boast

---

[1] W. H. Crook, pp. 462–5.

[2] Ibid., pp. 452–60, 609–12; J. H. Thomas, *My Story*, p. 135.

M*

about.[1] Even so, the bitterness left by the strike among working people would have seeped away had not the government, instead of binding up the nation's wounds, deliberately reopened them by its legislative revenge next year. Here was the paradox of Baldwin's statesmanship once again: he had turned the strike, in its coming a tragedy, into a triumph for himself; within six months he had thrown all this away and found his reputation lower than it had ever been. Thus, strangely, the strike led, with no long delay, to Labour's success in the general election of 1929.

The perverseness of the Tories after the strike was all the more odd when the reactions of the leaders of the Labour movement to it are considered. Among the rank and file feelings about the strike were a compound of bitterness and pride: pride in the unselfishness of it, in the skill in organisation which their people had shown, in the sense of standing together in a noble cause of their own, not one thrust upon them from above, as in a war. 'We showed them what we could do', was the way of putting it;[2] and the 'them' is not to be overlooked. The leaders' verdict was, however, quite different: the strike had shown them the 'limitations of industrial power';[3] 'Never again' was their cry. The nobility of the strike was lost in recriminations against the miners' stubbornness, both for causing the strike and for refusing to consent to its ending. The *post-mortem* was protracted. A conference of union executives was summoned for June 25 to consider action on behalf of the miners, but it was cancelled because of the continuance of the coal strike. At the year's T.U.C., at Bournemouth in September, Pugh spoke of the strike in his presidential address and there was some angry discussion from the floor.[4] The General Council's report, prepared for the June meeting, was not published until January 1927, when a special conference of executives was held upon the strike. Here the whole story was retold, the old arguments threshed over: C. T. Cramp of the N.U.R. called it a 'great disaster', Ben Turner 'a great movement and a great effort'. The Council's report was accepted by a vote of 2,840,000 to 1,095,000.[5] The minority was not insignificant, but the strike was buried. Its failure had two results for the Labour movement: superficially it weakened it, bringing apathy, an

---

[1] *G.K.'s Weekly*, May 22, 1926.   [2] S. Nearing, p. xx.
[3] F. Williams, *Bevin*, p. 145.   [4] S. Nearing, pp. 106–28.
[5] T.U.C., General Council, *Report of Proceedings at a Special Conference of Executives, January 20–21, 1927.*

unwillingness to strike,[1] and a great decline of trade union membership (caused also by hard times), but at bottom, and over the years, it strengthened the working man's loyalty to his own movement and his own party; and for the leaders it confirmed and strengthened all the conservative, rightward tendencies which were manifest before it.[2]

8. TO THE BITTER END: THE COAL STRIKE

Though the coal strike continued, Baldwin lost no time in attempting to end it. On May 14 he sent to the Miners' Federation and the Mining Association new proposals which partly reflected Sir Herbert Samuel's Memorandum: a national agreement, an immediate reduction of wages by negotiation but leaving subsistence wages intact, a National Wages Board under an

---

[1] Aggregate duration of strikes each year in working days, 1925–30 (*Statistical Abstract of U.K., 1930*, p. 112, *1938*, p. 152; for earlier figures, see above, chap. 2, p. 124):

1925	7,952,000	1929	8,287,000
1926	162,233,000	1930	4,399,000
1927	1,174,000	1931	6,983,000
1928	1,388,000	1932	6,488,000

For 1933–8 the figure was under two million each year except 1937 (3,413,000) In 1934 it was 959,000.

[2] NOTE ON BOOKS ON THE GENERAL STRIKE. The best account is that given by Professor W. H. Crook, *The General Strike* (Chapel Hill, 1931); though it deals with the idea of the general strike and several of its manifestations, the greater part of it is taken up with a detailed and well-documented account of the British general strike. Its author's viewpoint is independent. R. P. Arnot, *The General Strike, May 1926*, is a full account published by the Labour Research Department, left-wing in attitude. R. W. Postgate, E. Wilkinson and J. F. Horrabin, *A Workers' History of the Great Strike*, is also valuable, especially for its reliance on bulletins and reports from local Labour groups. Hamilton Fyfe, *Behind the Scenes of the Great Strike*, is the account of events, as seen in London, by a man of independent judgment and wide experience who was then editor of the *Daily Herald*. A. J. Cook's *Nine Days* is mostly concerned with the beginning and end of the strike. Scott Nearing's *British General Strike* is a contemporary compilation of printed materials and interpretations of the strike by an American. Kingsley Martin's *British Public and the General Strike* is excellent for its account of the press and its part in the strike. J. H. Thomas, *My Story*, and the debates in the House of Commons (195 H.C. Deb., 5 s.) yield various points of detail. Emile Burns, *The General Strike, May 1926: Trades Councils in Action*, and George Glasgow, *General Strikes and Road Transport*, have already been mentioned for their special information. A good general account, based on the work of others, is in Allen Hutt, *Postwar History of the British Working Class*, chapter 6. John Murray, *The General Strike of 1926* (London, 1951) is based on earlier narratives and adds nothing to them. The T.U.C.'s side is to be found in the General Council's three reports: *Report of the Special Conference of Executive Committees, April 26—May 1, 1926; Report to the Conference of Executives of Affiliated Unions, June 25, 1926; Report of Proceedings at a Special Conference of Executives, January 20–21, 1927*. The second of these was printed by J. Bromley in the *Locomotive Journal*, June 1926. The miners' position was given in *Statement of the Miners' Federation of Great Britain on the occasion of the Conference of Trade Union Executive Committees* [January 1927] (printed in R. P. Arnot, *The Miners*, pp. 507–19). The British Library of Political and Economic Science at the London School of Economics has a large collection of pamphlets, books and newspapers on the general strike.

independent chairman to frame a new national wage agreement and to prevent future disputes, and a grant of £3 millions to the industry to mitigate the reductions in wages pending the new agreement to be worked out by the Board. He also promised legislation to give effect to the Samuel Report's recommendations regarding amalgamations and other matters; but omitted mention of the nationalisation of the royalties. The miners' reply, a few days later, though accepting the other proposals, fastened inevitably on the proposed wage reductions as a reason for rejecting the plan. The owners went much further: not only did they continue their opposition to the Samuel Commission's proposals for re-organisation, but with characteristic rudeness added that it would be 'impossible to continue the conduct of the industry under private enterprise unless it is accorded the same freedom from political interference as is enjoyed by other industries'. Baldwin's reply to both sides was sharp, particularly to the owners. He 'greatly regrets' that they had 'thought it necessary to adopt the uncompromising attitude' their letter conveyed, and observed that 'political interference' had been caused solely by 'the incapacity of the industry, unlike other industries, to settle its disputes for itself'. To the miners he replied that their rejection of his proposals restored the government's freedom regarding the Samuel Report, parts of which it had only accepted with reluctance, and that the offer of a continued subsidy could not be held open beyond the end of the month.

This was brave speaking, but it was also Baldwin's last shot. He had made his proposals; both sides rejected them; he sank back, to let them fight it out between themselves. In fact he went further, by introducing, in June, a bill to suspend the 7-hour day in the mines—something for which the owners were pressing and to which the Samuel Report was specifically opposed. This was followed by a Mining Industry Bill to give effect to some of the Report's positive proposals: it facilitated, without making likely, amalgamations, and it imposed a levy on royalties for miners' welfare. Both these were passed, the former against the heated opposition of the Labour party. They did nothing to improve the atmosphere for negotiations. Quite the contrary; the 8-hour day equipped the owners with 'knuckle dusters', observed MacDonald.[1] Meanwhile, the regulations under the Emergency Powers Act were renewed by parliament from month to month.

[1] 198 H.C. Deb., 5 s., 1745 (July 26, 1926).

During the summer the opportunities for a harmonious ending of the dispute slipped away. The miners' executive, approached by a group of three men, including Seebohm Rowntree and Walter Layton, and by the Industrial Christian Fellowship, representing both the Church of England and the Free Churches, seemed in July to be ready to negotiate over wages. A deputation of the I.C.F., including William Temple, waited on Baldwin on July 19 with the proposal of a subsidy for four months to maintain the old wages while the reorganisation of the industry and a new wages agreement were worked out. Baldwin and his fellow-ministers rejected this hopeful approach immediately: they would consider no subsidy or loan; the owners and miners must settle the dispute by themselves.[1] The government professed to doubt that the miners were ready to negotiate; and a ballot in all districts, followed by a national delegates' conference on August 16–17, did reject any compromise, in spite of the advocacy of Herbert Smith and A. J. Cook. But the majority was a narrow one, and the executive asked the Mining Association for a new meeting. It took place on August 19; but the owners were now sure that the government was on their side and that they had only to wait until the men were forced to surrender. They would concede nothing: longer hours and district agreements were all they would consider. The miners were, however, persistent. Smith, Cook, and Richardson obtained an interview with Churchill (in Baldwin's absence on holiday) and Steel-Maitland on August 25; and though Churchill bluntly rejected all talk of a subsidy, he declared that the government preferred a settlement by agreement to a fight to the bitter end.

At last the government seemed to be resuming the initiative. The delegates' conference of the miners (September 2) responded by empowering the executive to make proposals for a settlement, provided only that it was national: A. J. Cook followed this with a letter to Churchill asking him to summon a meeting of the miners and the Mining Association to begin negotiations for a new national agreement 'with a view to a reduction in labour costs'. It was now the owners' turn to be intolerably adamant. First by letter, and then in a meeting with Churchill on September 6, Evan Williams and his associates declared that the Mining Association would not enter into national negotiations, and was legally incapable of doing so; power rested in the district associations,

[1] F. A. Iremonger, *William Temple*, pp. 337–43; W. H. Crook, *General Strike*, pp. 465–6.

although the national body had, in the exceptional conditions during and since the war, reluctantly made national agreements. Churchill was furious, declaring that the Association was 'narrowing . . . the possibilities of peace', and that had the government known that the introduction of the 8-hour bill 'would synchronise with a decision on your part the moment you got it to close the national door, never should we have allowed ourselves to be placed in that position.'[1] The government backed down, and let itself, the miners, and the country be beaten by a handful of stubborn coal-owners, 'discourteous and stupid', Baldwin called them in parliament (September 27), and unrepresentative of employers as a whole. In so doing it repudiated the Samuel Report and its previous acceptance of it, including insistence on national agreements in coal-mining as in other industries.

After this, all was anti-climax. On September 17 Baldwin proposed district agreements under the national supervision of an arbitration tribunal; the miners rejected this. On November 6, following an intervention by the T.U.C., the government made a rather similar proposal, which the miners also rejected. By then the drift back to work, which had begun in a small way in July, mainly in Warwickshire, and had grown in August in Nottinghamshire, Derbyshire and Cannock Chase, was getting large. In the Midlands a miners' M.P., G. A. Spencer, and other miners' delegates had withdrawn from the Federation and formed a union of their own, the Miners' Industrial Union. With the blessing of a delegates' conference on November 19, the miners sought agreements with the owners in each district; between November 29 and December 23 these were concluded and the men returned to work. The strike did not so much end as crumble away. The terms varied, but in general included the 8-hour day (7½ hours in Yorkshire, Kent, Notts. and North Derbyshire), the minimum percentage addition to the standard wage ruling under the 1921, rather than the 1924 agreement, and the division of net proceeds in the ratio of 87:13 between miners and owners (85:15 in South Wales, Yorkshire, and the Midland fields). The owners had won and the miners lost on all counts: the miners lost the national agreement, and had to work longer hours for lower wages; in 1927 the reduction in average earnings per shift was put at 7d., from 10s. 5d. to 9s. 10d. In 1928 there were further reductions in some dis-

---

[1] *The Coal Situation; Stenographic Notes of a meeting between His Majesty's Ministers and the Mining Association . . . September 6, 1926* (London School of Economics collection); *Annual Register, 1926*, pp. 101–2.

tricts; and unemployment among miners, reaching the proportions of tragedy, called forth the public's charity in support of a Miners' Relief Fund started by the Lord Mayor of London.[1]

The effects of the strike were wholly disastrous, and not only for the miners and, ultimately, the owners. British industry and trade, already in difficulties, suffered a set-back; over half a million men, besides the miners, were thrown out of work during the strike because of the shortage of coal. The year's output of coal was about half the previous year's; the loss in coal exports was about 28 million tons, and coal was imported, chiefly from Germany and Poland, at a cost of £42 millions. The cost of the strike, in loss of coal production, was put at £97 millions and in miners' and others' wages £75 millions; another estimate of the loss caused by the strike was between £216 millions and £270 millions.[2] How far the miners and their wives and children suffered from the strike can hardly be known. Contributions from other trade unions and from the general public raised large sums for their support (£1·8 millions, of which about a million pounds was contributed by Russian trade unions).[3] An appeal was made for help from the American trade unions, but met with little response, partly because of an unkind statement by Baldwin at the time of its launching that there was no serious distress among the miners. The poor-law authorities did not pay relief to miners on strike, but they did to miners' wives and children: the amount expended on poor relief in the six months ending September 30 was £6 millions more than for the same period in the previous year (£13 millions as compared with £7 millions).[4]

9. THE GOVERNMENT BLUNDERS

The government's retreat before the coal-owners was followed by its capitulation to its own right wing in two measures, the Trade Disputes Act and the breaking of relations with Russia after the Arcos raid, which in 1927 helped to prolong the bitter feelings which the events of 1926 had left in the Labour movement.

[1] This account is based chiefly on the full narrative in the *Annual Register, 1926*, pp. 56–130, and on J. R. Raynes, *Coal and its Conflicts*, pp. 247–82. See also R. P. Arnot, *The Miners*, pp. 457–506.

[2] *Annual Register, 1926*, p. 130, pt. ii, pp. 85–6; J. R. Raynes, *Coal and its Conflicts*, p. 283.

[3] The government made a protest to the Russian government about the contributions of the Russian trade unions, under pressure from indignant Conservatives. The King expressed his disapproval of this protest against money being sent to save miners' women and children from starvation: H. Nicolson, *George V*, p. 421.

[4] *Annual Register, 1926*, pp. 94, 126, 129–30; R. P. Arnot, *The Miners*, pp. 479–486, 495, 498, 520.

The bill to change the law concerning strikes, decided upon by the Cabinet during the general strike, was merely postponed, not abandoned. Debate on it occupied most of May 1927. As finally enacted, the Trade Disputes and Trade Union Act, 1927, had four main parts:[1]

(1) it declared illegal any strike (or lockout) which 'has any object other than or in addition to the furtherance of a trade dispute within the trade or industry in which the strikers are engaged' (thus banning sympathetic strikes), or which was 'designed or calculated to coerce the government either directly or by inflicting hardship upon the community';

(2) intimidation was made illegal, and was defined;

(3) trade union members were not to be required to contribute to the union's political fund (the political levy paid to the Labour party) unless they gave written notice of wishing to do so; i.e., they must 'contract in', not, as previously, 'contract out' of paying the levy;

(4) 'established civil servants' were forbidden (saving existing members) to be, in effect, members of trade unions or associations connected with the T.U.C.; their associations must consist of employees of the Crown alone (this was explained as ensuring that they would owe no other loyalty than to the government).

The bill aroused bitterness in the Labour party and among the trade unions, though less in the country at large. It was condemned by moderate opinion as insulting the responsible trade union leaders and encouraging the extremists, and as resting solely on the government's majority, without any consultation with the trade unions.[2] Interruptions during debate were frequent. The guillotine was resorted to in the committee stage (for the first time in six years); in protest the Labour members, led by Clynes, walked out of the House in a body. Some improvements were made in the text, but it remained from its very nature vague and provocative of trouble: to define strikes, lock-outs, intimidation was harder than squaring the circle; a phrase like [causing] 'grave inconvenience to the community' might mean almost anything.[3]

[1] 17 & 18 Geo. 5, ch. 22. The text may conveniently be found in W. H. Crook, *The General Strike*, pp. 614–22.

[2] *Spectator*, February 12, April 9, 30, 1927. Ramsay Muir, 'Trade Union Reform', *Contemporary Review*, 131: 409 (April, 1927) called the bill ill-timed, unjust, unnecessary and 'wicked folly'. Muir, professor of history at Liverpool and Manchester (until 1921), M.P., 1923–24, was chairman and president of the National Liberal Federation, 1931–36. See Bevin's similar reactions: F. Williams, *Bevin*, p. 141.

[3] 205 H.C. Deb., 5 s., 1669 (Baldwin), 1786–1801 (Snowden). Cf. Lord Reading's strictures in the House of Lords, 68 H.L. Deb., 5 s., 73, 79. W. H. Crook, *General Strike*, pp. 481–5.

The Act's effects were hardly what the more sober of its supporters can have expected. Its clauses outlawing general and sympathetic strikes were never invoked. The change in the machinery of the political levy reduced the Labour party's income from affiliation fees by over a quarter; the fall in trade union membership in 1926–28 was less than the fall in the number of trade unionists affiliated with the party (from 3,352,347 to 2,025,139).[1] On the other hand, the Act increased working-class support for the Labour party by providing a first-rate grievance. Nothing annoyed the Conservatives more in the debates on the bill than Labour's pledge to repeal it whenever the party gained power. It had long to wait. A bill introduced by the second Labour government was abandoned because of the combined opposition of the Liberals and Conservatives to it. Proposals to amend the Act during the Coalition government of 1940–45 were rejected by Winston Churchill. As a result, when Labour gained both office and power it repealed the Act in 1946—simply, brusquely, triumphantly.

The denunciation of the trade agreement of 1921 with Russia, which had survived the Zinoviev letter, and the withdrawal of the diplomatic recognition given by the Labour government in 1924, was the result of a long campaign by right-wing Conservatives. Russian actions after the revolution, and Russian propaganda over the years, gave some justification to the 'Red obsession' of the Tories, though their own language against Russian agents ('scum of our gutters', 'outpourings of foreign sinks', 'microbes of Bolshevism') provided plenty of ammunition to the Russians in the various diplomatic exchanges concerning propaganda. The prolonged civil wars in China, with their demonstrations of Chinese hostility to foreigners, in which Communist influence was not lacking, were another cause of exasperation. Attacks on the British concession at Hankow in January 1927 were ascribed to the influence of a Russian agent.[2]

At four in the afternoon of May 12, 1927, a large force of police, reported as about 200, descended on the offices of Arcos Ltd., a British company organised to carry on trade with Russia, and the Russian Trade Delegation, which shared the same building at 49 Moorgate, in London. The police were seeking a particular document which was believed to be improperly in the possession of an employee in the building; but they found neither it nor

[1] G. D. H. Cole, *History of the Labour Party*, p. 195; *Labour Year Book, 1930*, pp. 9, 12.
[2] W. P. and Z. Coates, *History of Anglo-Soviet Relations*, pp. 197–266 (pro-Soviet); *Survey of International Affairs, 1927*, pp. 256–66.

anything else of importance, their haul consisting of a list of 'cover' addresses for letters for Communists in the United States, Mexico, Canada, a letter of trivial news from Moscow, and other letters complaining of the difficulties of recruiting British seamen for Soviet merchant ships. Baldwin, asked in parliament if further documents might be printed before a debate, replied 'We will do the best we can to produce something . . . [interruption].'[1]

The government had blundered. The decision to make the raid was taken by Joynson-Hicks, Baldwin and Chamberlain, not by the Cabinet. The raid had uncovered nothing. Yet it had to be justi- fied; and breaking off diplomatic relations was the only way of doing so. On May 24 Baldwin announced that the trade agree- ment would be ended and the British mission recalled from Moscow, and that the Russian government would be requested to withdraw its mission and trade delegation from London.

10. TORY SOCIALISM

In the midst of these aberrations the government pursued the policies of social amelioration and of nationalisation which embodied its ideas of national unity, progress and efficiency. The government's record of useful social legislation was greater than that of any of the interwar governments save Lloyd George's coalition of 1918–22.

The two members of the government who were most responsible for its progressive policies in social legislation were Neville Chamberlain, Minister of Health, and Winston Churchill, the Chancellor of the Exchequer, both identified among the more vigorous proponents of its policies antagonistic to Labour. Nor was this any accident. Neither was a Tory, save as the term im- plied that 'Tory democracy' which their fathers had done much to fashion. 'Our policy is to use the great resources of the state, not for the distribution of an indiscriminate largesse, but to help those who have the will and desire to raise themselves to higher and better things,' declared Chamberlain in the second reading of the pensions act of 1925. He was also, like his father, an expert administrator, trained in the schools of local government and of business. It was, therefore, typical of him that on taking office in 1924 he should have sketched out a programme of legislation, including twenty-five bills to be introduced, under a definite time-table, in the next three years. Here was the nearest thing to

---

[1] 206 H.C. Deb., 5 s., 1842–51. The government published the documents sup- porting the break in Cmd. 2874 (1927).

a programme which Baldwin's government had; moreover, twenty-one of the bills were enacted.[1] His partner, Churchill, expounded in his first Budget speech on April 28, 1925, a financial programme which was largely carried out: redistribution of the burdens of taxation to aid industry and reduce unemployment, and help from the state to give the wage-earner security in his own home. With these objects income tax was reduced by sixpence, the supertax was lowered, death duties increased, and provision was made for the new pensions scheme announced by the Chancellor.[2]

Subsequently, Neville Chamberlain introduced the Widows', Orphans' and Old Age Contributory Pensions Bill. It owed much to the success of National Health Insurance and its use of the contributory principle. It provided pensions of 10s. a week for widows (and also allowances for widows' dependent children) and 7s. 6d. per week for orphan children, and 10s. a week for insured workers and their wives at the age of 65. The scheme was tied to National Health Insurance and applied only to those covered by it; for this purpose the weekly contributions paid by workers and employers were increased. Non-contributory old-age pensions at 70 were not affected, save that those receiving contributory pensions at 65 continued to receive the same pension at 70 at the cost of the state, as under the 1908 act, but without the means test. The pensions under the 1908 act had already been increased to 10s. a week by an act of 1919.[3]

In dealing with unemployment insurance the government was, inevitably, less happy. The continuance of large-scale unemployment which had prevented the scheme from being solvent, and dissatisfaction with supposed frauds upon the scheme by the undeserving, led the government, in 1925, to appoint a departmental committee under Lord Blanesburgh (a law lord). Its report, issued in January 1927, was unanimous, and recommended some lowering of benefits and contributions, and the abolition of extended benefit, to be replaced by granting standard benefit to any unemployed person as a statutory right for an indefinite period

[1] K. Feiling, *N. Chamberlain*, pp. 129–31, 459–62.
[2] Churchill's Budgets are discussed and summarised in P. J. Grigg, *Prejudice and Judgment*, pp. 114–205. Churchill's later Budgets were less successful, and were balanced only by the abortive tax on betting and by raids and windfalls: two raids on the Road Fund; changes in the times of payment of the beer duty and income tax which gave windfalls by collecting, for once only, part of two years' revenues in one financial year.
[3] Sir Arnold Wilson and G. S. Mackay, *Old Age Pensions* (Oxford, 1941), pp. 72–96, 106.

provided he or she could show evidence at every three months' review of having been in insurable employment for thirty weeks in the previous two years, and could satisfy the old requirement of 'genuinely seeking work'. Labour criticised the report, but Margaret Bondfield, one of its signers, defended its recommendations as the best to which the majority would agree, and declared that a minority report would have been useless. The government's Unemployment Insurance Bill, introduced in the autumn, included the substance of the recommendations. The bill provoked Labour opposition, both because of its reductions of benefits and because it represented no constructive policy of finding employment for those out of work. The committee stage was protracted, in spite of the use of the guillotine, and was marked by several interruptions and the suspension of four members.[1]

In yet another way the government's social legislation, though in general not illiberal, provoked Labour's ire. The matter of 'Poplarism'—the generous scales of relief adopted by certain boards of Poor Law Guardians, and paid with the help of borrowed funds—had long been an irritant to the Conservatives. In July 1926, soon after the general strike, Neville Chamberlain introduced a bill giving the Ministry of Health authority to supersede Guardians who misused their powers by others appointed by the Ministry. It was aimed at the Guardians in West Ham, and first applied there; in 1927 it was invoked also in two mining districts, Chester-le-Street (Durham) and Bedwellty (Mon.).[2]

Local-government reform was the largest of Chamberlain's ventures. His Local Government Act of 1929 had a long and varied ancestry. Its provisions for the Poor Law went back to the majority report of the Royal Commission on the Poor Laws of 1909 and to the report of a sub-committee on local government, with Sir Donald Maclean as chairman, made to the Ministry of Reconstruction in 1918. Its other administrative changes came mostly from the second report of the Royal Commission on Local Government (Cmd. 3213, 1928) which had been at work under Lord Onslow since 1923, supplemented by negotiations between the Ministry of Health and the local authorities. The arrangements for derating and for block grants originated with Winston Churchill and the Treasury: derating was announced in Churchill's 1928 Budget as a measure to relieve industry of some of its burdens of

[1] R. C. Davison, *The Unemployed*, pp. 117, 139–56; H. F. Hohman, *Development of Social Insurance in Great Britain*, pp. 238–40; *Annual Register, 1927*, pp. 39, 110–14.
[2] K. Feiling, *N. Chamberlain*, pp. 139–42; S. and B. Webb, *English Poor Law History*, II, ii (London, 1929), pp. 851–934.

taxation and so combat depression.[1] The resulting bill had 115 clauses and 12 schedules, several of them the size of a normal bill. A similar bill applied the same principles to Scotland, transferring most powers of local government, including those over education, to the county councils, partly at the expense of the burgh councils (only the four county burghs of Edinburgh, Glasgow, Dundee and Aberdeen were outside the counties' jurisdiction).

Chamberlain introduced the bill on November 27, 1928, in a speech of $2\frac{1}{2}$ hours. He observed that 'gigantic changes' had taken place in the country since the acts of 1888 and 1894, but there had been 'no serious or radical attempt' to reform local government since then. The 635 Poor Law Unions and their Guardians were abolished and their powers and buildings were transferred to the counties and county boroughs, to be managed through their public assistance committees. Urban and rural district councils were to be regrouped, following a review of their work by the counties every ten years.[2] The counties received additional powers over roads, public health, maternity and child welfare, town and country planning; in some cases these powers could be shared with or delegated to the urban or rural district councils and the municipal boroughs. The derating provisions carried much further the special treatment which had been long accorded to agricultural land subject to local taxation. Agricultural land and farm buildings were now to be entirely exempt from payment of rates, and industrial property and the railways were in future to be relieved of three-quarters of the rate levied against them—the railways on condition that the money saved was used to reduce the freight rates on coal and steel. Finally, the counties and county boroughs were to receive from the Treasury the amounts lost to them through derating, estimated at £24 millions, and a further £16 millions representing the grants formerly paid by the Treasury for public health, roads and other services. The new grant was, however, to be a 'block grant' superseding the old percentage grants in which the Treasury contributed a proportion of the local authorities' expenditures, thus favouring the more prosperous areas whose rates brought in larger revenues. The block grant was calculated according to a formula, subject to

---

[1] C. H. Wilson (ed.), *Essays on Local Government* (Oxford, 1948), pp. 29-30, 72-5, 128-33 (essays by V. D. Lipman and Maureen Schulz); *Annual Register, 1928*, p. 40; K. Feiling, *N. Chamberlain*, pp. 143-8.

[2] By 1939 the number of rural districts had been reduced from 652 to 475 and of urban districts from 783 to 572, and 33 new municipal boroughs had been created.

quinquennial revision, which took account of each area's population, number of children under five, rateable values, proportion of unemployment, and population per mile of roads. Existing grants from the Treasury for education, police, housing, and part of the expenditures on roads were outside the block grant and not affected by it.[1]

Two measures, the Electricity (Supply) Act and the issuing of a charter to the B.B.C. as a public corporation, both dating from December 1926, are measures of nationalisation typical of the empiricism of Tory policy during these years. Both are really measures of rationalisation rather than of socialism. The Electricity Act was the response to the state of electricity supply which, with its high costs, many local generating stations and varying frequencies, was a handicap to British industry in its struggle against depression. It owed something to the work of a private committee under Lloyd George's sponsorship, which published a report, *Coal and Power*, in 1924; more to a recent report by a committee appointed by the government under the chairmanship of Lord Weir. It was, however, a precedent for later measures of nationalisation, in that it put a business enterprise under the management of a public board appointed by a minister—in the case of the Central Electricity Board by the Minister of Transport after consulting bodies representing local government, electricity, industry, labour, and other interests. The Board was a thing without precedent; the Port of London Authority, cited by Baldwin as an example, was made up of members elected or appointed by the port users and certain official bodies.

The Electricity Act transferred the wholesale distribution of electricity to a national body, the Central Electricity Board. The Board's function was to buy power at cost from selected generating stations, distribute it over transmission lines acquired or built by it, and sell it to the existing private or municipal undertakings for retail distribution. There would thus be a national system, with the advantages of generation in large stations, interconnection of plants, and standardisation of frequencies, but existing interests in retail distribution would be unaffected. The Board controlled the location, design and, in part, the operation of the selected stations, but did not construct or own them. The bill ran into the opposition of several Conservatives, some sniffing a socialist scheme, others representing the resistance of some of the power

[1] C. H. Wilson, *Essays on Local Government*, pp. 74–87, 133–6, 248; K. B. Smellie, *Hundred Years of English Government*, pp. 387–9; *Annual Register, 1928*, pp. 109–10.

companies. Labour condemned it as not going far enough, but its support helped the government to pass it more or less intact. The results justified the expectations of it. Between 1927 and 1936 the C.E.B. laced the country with the high-voltage transmission lines of the 'grid', whose pylons outraged some lovers of the countryside. The grid, largely complete by 1933, extended over 4,000 miles, and distributed power from 130 selected stations to 630 local plants through which the retail distribution was carried on. When war came in 1939 this national system, though designed for other ends, was of incalculable value.[1]

A very different measure deserving notice is the Representation of the People (Equal Franchise) Act of 1928. This removed the unequal treatment of the sexes in the Act of 1918 by giving the vote to all women at the age of 21, subject only to the three months' residence qualification which applied to the male voter. The 'flapper vote', as it was dubbed, was criticised by some as a party manoeuvre by the government, by others as endangering the state since women voters would outnumber the men by two millions. Labour criticised the bill because it did not end plural voting. In general, however, the measure was accepted calmly as inevitable; and it even passed the Lords, though not without causing great discomfort to many of their lordships.[2]

11. FOREIGN AND IMPERIAL AFFAIRS: A HALTING-PLACE

In foreign affairs the record of the closing years of the Conservative government did little to strengthen its reputation. There was, it is true, the illusion that all was well in Europe. Germany was admitted to the League of Nations, with a permanent seat on the Council, in 1926, though not until the jealousy of certain other countries which were not entitled to permanent seats had been appeased by enlarging the Council and creating three semi-permanent seats in it. The result of these manoeuvres was to delay Germany's admission for six months, and to cause Brazil's resignation from the League. The accord which existed, however, between the foreign ministers of the three leading powers in Europe—Austen Chamberlain, Briand, Stresemann—during the

[1] H. H. Ballin, *Organization of Electricity Supply in Great Britain*, pp. 184–208; W. A. Robson, *Public Enterprise*, pp. 105–42; A. Plummer, *New British Industries*, pp. 21–23. The *Architectural Review* for November, 1933, is devoted to an excellent account of the grid.
[2] For the interesting history of this bill and its unsuccessful predecessors since 1919, see D. E. Butler, *Electoral System in Britain*, pp. 15–38. The residence qualification had been reduced from six months to three in 1926.

long period when they held their offices simultaneously and met frequently at Geneva seemed to promise well for the future, and led people to forget that problems had not been solved but merely shelved. Germany, for instance, was punctual in the payment of reparations under the Dawes plan, but it was her large borrowing from abroad which was sustaining her economy.

The civil war in China continued to cause concern. In 1927 the government dispatched British troops to Shanghai to help in the defence of the International Settlement, an action much criticised by Labour. During that year, however, the Nationalist government at Nanking, eventually under Chiang Kai-shek's leadership, was enlarging its authority. In 1928 the civil war came to an end.[1]

The brittleness of goodwill was shown by the failure of the disarmament conferences of 1927. The League had appointed a Preparatory Commission for the intended Disarmament Conference in December 1925. Differences of opinion soon appeared: the difference between France, demanding that security precede disarmament, and Britain pressing for disarmament yet standing closely to a policy of no commitments; French insistence that disarmament demanded international supervision, the refusal of Italy and the United States to accept this; the discussion of war potential and of trained reserves of troops, in which France, weak in one and strong in the other, was at loggerheads with the British and German position. Things were made worse by negotiations between the British and French governments to resolve their different views; a compromise was reached in July 1928, but announced by Chamberlain in such guarded terms as to arouse great suspicion that secret clauses must exist in it. Moreover, its naval clauses aroused resentment in the United States and put a strain on Anglo-American relations. Thus little or no progress was made towards disarmament in general.

The three-power conference on naval disarmament at Geneva (Great Britain, the United States, Japan) in June–August 1927 was equally barren. The French and Italian governments refused the invitations issued by the United States. At the conference the British and American representatives were soon in disagreement. Britain, because of her special needs in protecting her sea communications, was opposed to the American proposal that all categories of naval vessels should be reduced in the 5, 5, 3 ratio (as between Britain, the United States and Japan) which had been

---

[1] G. M. Gathorne-Hardy, *Short History of International Affairs*, pp. 100–1, 230–45, 250.

applied in the Washington treaties to capital ships; she favoured instead a general reduction in the size of ships and the calibre of guns. The main clash was over cruisers, the Admiralty contending for 70 cruisers (15 of 10,000 tons and 55 of 7,500 tons), while the United States proposed a limit of cruiser tonnage which it intended to use chiefly for building 25 heavy cruisers, leaving provision for only 20 light cruisers. Britain, if concerned to maintain 'parity' with the United States in heavy cruisers, would thus have been left very short of light cruisers on which she depended for the protection of convoys. Behind this lay the belief that 'mathematical' parity with the United States meant in effect American superiority. On this point the conference foundered. One result of it was the resignation of Lord Cecil, one of the British representatives at the conference, from the government, in which he was Chancellor of the Duchy of Lancaster and Britain's representative at the League. He claimed that on the policy of disarmament he and the majority of the Cabinet were not in agreement; the breakdown at the naval conference, for which he blamed the influence of Churchill in the Cabinet, was in sequence with the failure to make real concessions to the French point of view in the Preparatory Commission, and with the unconditional rejection of the Protocol.[1]

Happier, but in the event no more productive of concrete results, was the Kellogg–Briand Pact for the Renunciation of War, signed at Paris by fifteen powers on August 27, 1928. It grew out of a proposal by Briand to the United States that it and France should mutually outlaw war between each other; through the efforts of F. B. Kellogg, the American Secretary of State, this became a pact open to all governments which agreed to renounce war as an instrument of national policy. The renunciation did not involve wars of self-defence; the pact outlawed wars of aggression, but signatories could avoid even this prohibition by making war without declaring it at all.[2]

In the history of the British Empire the later twenties were also years of apparent quiet. The main event was the Imperial Conference of 1926. It busied itself with the usual speeches and dis-

---

[1] *Annual Register, 1927*, pp. 78–85, 117–18; *Survey of International Affairs, 1927*, pp. 21 ff.; Lord Cecil, *All the Way* (London, 1949), pp. 190–1; Lord Cecil, *A Great Experiment* (London, 1941), pp. 185–9, 358–66 (text of correspondence between Cecil and Baldwin over the resignation; also in *The Times*, August 30, 1927).

[2] This discussion of foreign policy rests chiefly on G. M. Gathorne-Hardy, *Short History of International Affairs*, pp. 163–76, and W. N. Medlicott, *British Foreign Policy since Versailles* (London, 1940), pp. 86–104. See also Elaine Windrich, *British Labour's Foreign Policy* (Stanford, 1952), pp. 57–66.

cussions on consultation and communication between Great Britain and the Dominions, on foreign policy, imperial trade, imperial air communications. Its most notable work was to accept a report analysing, from the standpoint of the relations of Great Britain and the Dominions, what the British Empire had come to be. The report was drafted by a strangely-named committee on Inter-Imperial Relations presided over by Lord Balfour. It eschewed attempting to lay down a constitution for the Empire, but explored the meaning of the equality of status which now existed between Britain and the Dominions. In the process it produced a cumbersome and oft-quoted definition, dignified in the report by italics, stating that Britain and the Dominions were 'autonomous Communities within the British Empire, equal in status, . . . united by a common allegiance to the Crown, and freely associated as members of the British Commonwealth of Nations'.[1] In due course this was given legal effect by the Statute of Westminster in 1931—with certain results hardly to be anticipated in 1926.

12. THE CONSERVATIVES' DECLINE, THE LIBERALS' RENAISSANCE, LABOUR'S QUANDARY

From early in 1927 the government was in a state of decline and all parties were looking towards the next election. The authority which the government had possessed for much of the populace after the general strike was dissipated when it failed to act decisively to end the coal strike. As early as February the *Spectator* was calling upon Baldwin to reconstruct the Cabinet, which was 'not one of marked distinction'. By midsummer a series of by-election defeats was adding weight to the plea.[2] A plan to reform the House of Lords, announced on June 20, 1927, seemed designed only to entrench the power of a Conservative House of Lords, and was abandoned in the face of general criticism from both Opposition and Conservatives.

The government was suffering from its own divisions and a paucity of able men. When there was talk in 1927 of a successor to Baldwin, Baldwin let it be known he favoured W. C. Bridgeman, the First Lord of the Admiralty, a true patriot but hardly a leader.[3]

---

[1] For the conference, see *Annual Register, 1926*, pp. 116–19; the Report of the Committee on Inter-Imperial Relations (Cmd. 2768) is printed *ibid.*, part ii, pp. 93–107.

[2] *Spectator*, February 12, June 11, 1927; *New Statesman*, June 11, 1927.

[3] Wickham Steed, *The Real Stanley Baldwin*, p. 103. William Clive Bridgeman (1864–1935), son of a clergyman; Eton and Trinity College, Cambridge; M.P., 1906–29; Mines secretary, 1920–22; Home Secretary, 1922–23; First Lord of the Admiralty, 1924–29. Created Viscount Bridgeman, 1929.

The other heirs apparent were Sir Douglas Hogg, Edward Wood, Joynson-Hicks. The real measure of the decline of the Conservatives is that by 1928, with Wood's departure to India as Viceroy (as Lord Irwin, in 1926), Hogg's elevation to the Lord Chancellorship as Lord Hailsham, and Birkenhead's retirement from politics, the next in line of succession for the leadership seemed to be Neville Chamberlain; unless Churchill should vindicate his orthodoxy to the party.[1] At the same time, the changes in the Cabinet meant a weakening of the die-hard influence; there were no more bold measures of provocation after 1927; and Joynson-Hicks found the outlet he needed for his zeal for righteousness in helping to defeat the revised Prayer Book in the two debates upon it.

Outside the Cabinet there was greater diversity of opinion. House of Lords' reform, disarmament, the Trade Disputes Act, above all the means of reducing unemployment, whether by a general tariff, by mild measures of 'safeguarding', or by derating —all caused divisions within the party. Younger Conservatives, restive at the party's leadership, and nicknamed the Y.M.C.A.— men like Robert Boothby, Oliver Stanley,[2] Harold Macmillan— advocated a new Conservatism, using the power of the state to aid both industry and the working man by the control of credit, marketing schemes, wages boards, and workers' representation on boards of directors.[3] There was agreement only on one thing: the ineffectiveness of Baldwin's leadership. Yet as long as he was in place, quarrels and rivalries stayed in the background; and if ever he should take up a strong position, his doing so would end his power and usefulness in the party. Hence he did nothing—which suited his genius well enough. To the country, however, the impression he gave was of hanging on, waiting for something to turn up.[4] By 1929 the government would have by law to go to the country; and by then it had manifestly outstayed its welcome.

The Liberals were also divided, but into two parts only: those supporting, and those hating Lloyd George. With Asquith's retirement to the Lords in 1925, several Liberals in the Commons were reluctant to accept Lloyd George's leadership; and ten of

[1] See discussion in K. Feiling, *Neville Chamberlain*, pp. 149-50, 160-7.

[2] Oliver F. G. Stanley (1896-1950), son of 17th Earl of Derby, married daughter of Lord Londonderry; served in war as major; Military Cross; barrister; M.P., 1924-50; Minister of Transport, 1933-34, Labour, 1934-35, Education, 1935-37, Board of Trade, 1937-40, Secretary of State for War, 1940, Colonies, 1942-45.

[3] See R. Boothby, *et al.*, *Industry and the State: a Conservative View* (London, 1927).

[4] See, for instance, Baldwin's refusal to speak during a Labour vote of censure on the government regarding its policies towards coal-mining, November 16. 1927: *Annual Register*, 1927, pp. 114-16.

them, led by Walter Runciman,[1] formed a 'Radical Group' in opposition to him. In the complex structure of the Liberal party organisation the Asquithians were stronger. The Lloyd George Fund, or rather Lloyd George's control over it (it was actually administered by trustees), was a stumbling block to Liberal reunion. So was the difference between Lloyd George and Asquith over the government's policy during the general strike, which led to Lloyd George's departure from the Liberal 'shadow cabinet'.[2] However, in October 1926, after his first illness, Asquith resigned the party leadership;[3] the shadow cabinet ceased to exist, and Lloyd George's leadership was, in effect, unchallenged.

In 1927 a more united party began to gain strength. Sir Herbert Samuel, who had, while in Palestine as High Commissioner, kept clear of the party's dissensions, became chairman of the Organisation Committee. Lloyd George offered to finance Liberal party candidates out of his fund; the offer was accepted, and the party announced that it would put 500 candidates into the field at the next election. Some disgruntled Liberals formed an independent body, the Liberal Council, with Lord Grey as chairman; but it gained little following. Signs, not merely of reunion, but of renaissance, multiplied. In the summer of 1927 the Liberals won three out of five by-elections. In its meetings and addresses throughout the country the party showed great activity. Much of this came from the spirit of inquiry which the annual Liberal Summer School at Oxford, an innovation when it began in 1922, had brought about. Much of it came, however, from Lloyd George's own efforts. In the twenties he was a giant out of work; and he poured forth his energies (and some of his Fund) in promoting inquiries and shaping policies concerning the country's major problems. In so doing he hoped, of course, to regain office in 1929. In this he failed; but in the process he influenced public policy for the next decade. And it was his policies—the Liberal party's policies—which dominated the general election of 1929.[4]

Lloyd George's policies are embodied in five works. His *Coal and Power* we have already noticed. The Land Enquiry Com-

[1] Walter Runciman (1870–1949), born in South Shields, son of a shipowner (created Baron Runciman, 1933); M.P. (Lib.), 1899–1900, 1902–18, 1924–31, (Lib.Nat.) 1931–37; parliamentary secretary, Local Government Board, 1905–7; financial secretary to Treasury, 1907–8; president, Board of Education, 1908–11, Agriculture, 1911–14, Board of Trade, 1914–16 and 1931–37; lord president of the Council, 1938–1939. Succeeded father and created Viscount, 1937. Mission to Czechoslovakia, 1938.
[2] J. A. Spender and C. Asquith, *Asquith*, II, 362–6.
[3] He died on February 15, 1928.
[4] For the fortunes of the Liberals in these years, see the *Annual Register* and M. Thomson, *Lloyd George*, pp. 381–96.

mittee produced *Land and the Nation* in 1925, proposals for developing agriculture, partly by a controversial scheme of state purchase of land, to be leased to working farmers at fixed rentals. This was followed by *Towns and the Land* (1925), which was concerned with town planning on regional lines. Overshadowing these three, however, was the famous Liberal 'yellow book', *Britain's Industrial Future*, published in 1928 by the Liberal Industrial Inquiry. Its recommendations sound commonplace only because in the intervening years they have come to be taken for granted: the putting of industries of public concern under public boards; an Economic General Staff within the government; the expansion of joint industrial councils and other employer-worker organisations; the use of the Bank of England's powers over credit so as to maintain steady trade; and a large programme of national development—more roads, houses, garden-cities, electricity, reclamation, afforestation. The nation was creating capital at the rate of £500 millions a year and should put it to use, thus employing labour to improve 'our national equipment'.

Here was the basis of the Liberals' programme in the general election of 1929: *We Can Conquer Unemployment* and Lloyd George's pledge (March 1, 1929) to reduce unemployment to normal proportions within a year by schemes of work, ready to be put into immediate operation and involving no increase in taxation. It was a large, deficit-financed,[1] public works programme intended to restart the economic machine and pay for itself out of the increased revenues which recovery would bring; it would also use unemployment funds to support the men at work on the new schemes. The principal item was the building of a national system of trunk roads, of which the actual routes were shown; this was to cost £42 millions. Ring roads round cities (£20 millions), building of some 7,500–10,000 new road bridges (some to replace level crossings over railways) at a cost of £37 millions, London traffic improvements (£16 millions) were also proposed. The road schemes would employ, directly or indirectly, 350,000 men in the first year. A larger housing programme, a doubling of the rate of providing additional telephones (of the principal countries of the world Great Britain was at the bottom of the list in number of telephones per 1000 of population in 1927: 36, as compared with 160 in the United States, at the top of the list), more elec-

[1] See Keynes' support of the scheme: 'Can the Liberal Pledge be Carried Out?' *Evening Standard*, March 19, 1929 (Liberal party pamphlet) which points out that saving and investment are not equally balanced in a time of unemployment.

trical transmission lines and generating stations, land drainage—
all were part of the plan. Later, in response to criticism, capital
schemes for improving the railways were added.

In 1927 the Labour party began to draft a new programme,
partly spurred to this by the I.L.P. The result, however, only
caused dissension, not only with the I.L.P. but among the party
leaders.[1] *Labour and the Nation* was the final product. It was
drafted by R. H. Tawney, and approved in principle at the Labour
party conference at Birmingham in 1928. This was a revised,
longer, and more imprecise version of *Labour and the New Social
Order*. It declared the party to be a socialist party. Its aim was
the 'organisation of industry . . . in the interest . . . of all who
bring their contribution of useful service to the common stock'.

> Its Socialism, therefore, is neither a sentimental aspiration for an
> impossible Utopia, nor a blind movement of revolt against poverty
> and oppression. It is the practical recognition of the familiar common-
> place that 'morality is in the nature of things', and that men are all,
> in very truth, members of one another. It is a conscious, systematic
> and unflagging effort to use the weapons forged in the victorious
> struggle for political democracy to end the capitalist dictatorship in
> which democracy finds everywhere its most insidious and most
> relentless foe.[2]

13. THE GENERAL ELECTION OF 1929

The long-awaited general election took place on May 30, 1929,
parliament's session having ended on May 10. For once in the
interwar years the election was held, not in the autumn, but in late
spring, amid fine weather which Labour believed to be to its
advantage, particularly on election day when it had fewer cars
than its opponents in which to take voters to the polls. Unemployment and policies for world peace dominated the campaign. Lloyd
George's pledge to conquer unemployment gave the Liberals great
confidence. Labour, however, simply annexed Lloyd George's
programme, claiming that it could carry it out better than he. The
Conservatives were left rather short-winded. Speaking on April
18, Baldwin claimed that the country's trade was recovering and
that the gravity of unemployment was exaggerated. He promised
slum clearance, more technical education, better maternity welfare
schemes. This was hardly heroic. His pledge to retain Austen

---

[1] For some examples, see Hugh Dalton, *Call back yesterday: Memoirs, 1887–1931*
(London, 1953), pp. 173–6.
[2] Labour Party, *Labour and the Nation* (revised edition); cf. G. D. H. Cole, *History
of the Labour Party*, pp. 205–9.

Chamberlain at the Foreign Office promised no change where many people thought change was most needed—in the Conservatives' support for the League and for peace through collective security. To make matters worse, the Conservatives placarded the country with large pictures of Baldwin, with the legend 'Safety First' underneath. It is a question how safe some of the acts of his government had been; after five years, the electorate was looking for something more dramatic.

Yet it was a dull campaign. Stunts and alarms were lacking. The increased electorate (from $21\frac{3}{4}$ millions to nearly 29 millions), made for uncertainty.[1]

Nor was the result decisive. Labour won 287 seats, and for the first time was the largest party; the Conservatives 261, the Liberals, for all their efforts, only 59. Labour was once again in a minority if the Conservatives and Liberals should vote together in parliament. It was in a minority also in the popular vote: the Conservatives polled 8,664,243 votes, Labour 8,360,883, the Liberals 5,300,947.[2] The Communists fought 25 seats against Labour and lost them all, most of them badly. Labour's largest gains were in Lancashire, Cheshire and greater London, and also in Yorkshire and the West Midlands. Within the party the trade union M.P.s increased from 88 to 114, those sponsored by divisional Labour parties from 25 to 128. The I.L.P. ran 52 candidates and elected 37, 17 from Scotland, into which more and more it was being driven back.[3]

Labour's supporters in the crowd in Trafalgar Square watching the election results being flashed on a screen greeted the repeated note, 'Labour gain', with mounting enthusiasm. Analysis next morning produced more sober thoughts. If the Conservatives had been defeated, Labour had not won, and many of Labour's successes were ascribed to the Liberals' splitting of the anti-Labour vote. This is, of course, uncertain: Labour won 118 seats on a minority vote but the Conservatives won 150 in this way, the Liberals 40.[4] Most seats were contested by three candidates. As in the other elections since the war it was the Liberals who suffered. They had made the running, but the race was not to them. For the Conservatives the setback was much less serious. They suffered both for their pugnacity in 1927, their flabbiness since, especially concerning unemployment and disarmament. They

[1] For the campaign, see *Annual Register, 1929*, pp. 32, 34, 39, 42–5; *New Statesman*, May 18, 1929.
[2] *Annual Register, 1929*, pp. 45–6.
[3] G. D. H. Cole, *History of the Labour Party*, pp. 219–21.   [4] Ibid., p. 219.

offered safety, but so did Labour which, since the general strike, had cold-shouldered its extremists and grown eminently respectable. Why not have a change, after five years? But not to Lloyd George and his dynamic spirit. So let it be Labour, but Labour still hobbled. If this was the country's mood, it was certainly MacDonald's also. The stage was set for the drift into the thirties.

CHAPTER SEVEN

The Turning Point : 1929—1931

1. LABOUR ACCEPTS THE CALL

THE ambiguous result of the general election produced momentary uncertainty. MacDonald made a curious, and some thought later a prophetic, statement at his house in Hampstead: 'If I can prevent it there shall be no disturbance of the country by an election within two years': an implied warning to members of the party who might wish to force a second election; and a plea for sufficient time for the development of his policies. 'I wish to make it quite clear that I am going to stand no "monkeying". It will rest with the other two parties and not with us whether there is to be an election sooner than in two years.'[1]

The immediate uncertainty was resolved by Baldwin, who resigned on June 4, having advised the King to send for MacDonald. By doing this, Baldwin ignored those who advocated a Conservative-Liberal combination to avert the menace of socialism, and he also avoided any association with Lloyd George in a coalition such as Lloyd George had sketched in a talk with Churchill the previous February.[2]

MacDonald accepted the call to duty, and soon announced the composition of his Cabinet. The details were decided upon by the 'Big Five', MacDonald, Henderson, Snowden, Thomas, Clynes. The main internal dispute concerned, as it had in 1924, Arthur Henderson. Henderson wanted the Foreign Office, MacDonald, as before, favoured Thomas for the position and wanted Henderson to take charge of plans for employment and industrial reconstruction. Henderson refused. Thomas, at a second meeting, agreed to take the Colonial Office, thinking MacDonald would again be Foreign Secretary, and was astounded when Henderson shook him warmly by the hand, saying 'that leaves me the Foreign Office'. On the third day of discussions Thomas announced that he had decided to accept the position of Lord Privy Seal in charge

---

[1] *The Times*, June 3, 1929. [2] M. Thomson, *Lloyd George*, p. 399.

of schemes for employment; and Henderson was then gratified in his ambition to be in charge of the Foreign Office.[1] For once, Henderson had insisted that his devoted services to the party receive recognition in office—and no minister better justified himself in the ensuing government. Thomas, who had apparently been captivated by the opportunities open to the man who would meet the great challenge of unemployment found, by contrast, nothing but trouble in his position. More important was the decision to exclude the party's left wing from the Cabinet: John Wheatley and F. W. Jowett, members of the Cabinet in 1924, were both left out. As compensation George Lansbury was given the office of First Commissioner of Works, with a seat in the Cabinet. Snowden claimed to have proposed him for this position where he could 'do a good many small things' without the 'opportunity of squandering money' (thus did the government assure for itself one lasting memorial, the popular 'Lansbury's Lido' in the Serpentine in Hyde Park).[2]

The resulting tone of the government was that of the right wing of the party, even though, unlike the 1924 ministry, it contained no members from outside. Almost all the principal ministers had held office—some of them the same office—in 1924. A newcomer was Sir John Sankey, who became Lord Chancellor; another was Wedgwood Benn,[3] an ex-Liberal, who was Indian secretary. Snowden was again Chancellor of the Exchequer; Sidney Webb (ennobled as Lord Passfield) became Colonial Secretary. Margaret Bondfield achieved fame as the first woman to become a Cabinet minister and privy councillor; but was unpopular in her office as Minister of Labour. Herbert Morrison[4] was Minister of Transport, but without a seat in the Cabinet. As Attorney-General MacDonald obtained W. A. Jowitt,[5] a successful barrister who had been elected to parliament as a Liberal; Jowitt's rapid 'cross-

---

[1] P. Snowden, *Autobiography*, II, 759–64. See also Hugh Dalton's account in his *Memoirs*, pp. 213–17.

[2] Snowden, pp. 759–60.

[3] W. Wedgwood Benn, born 1877, served in Air Force, 1914–18 and 1940–45; M.P. (Lib.), 1906–27; (Lab.), 1928–31, 1937–42; secretary of state for India, 1929–31, for Air, 1945–46. Created Viscount Stansgate, 1941.

[4] Herbert Morrison, born 1888; secretary, London Labour Party, 1915–47; mayor of Hackney, 1920–21; member of L.C.C., 1922–45 (leader of the Council, 1934–40); M.P., 1923–24, 1929–31 and since 1935; Minister of Transport, 1929–31, Supply, 1940; Home secretary, 1940–45 (War Cabinet, 1942–45); Lord President of the Council and Leader of the House of Commons, 1945–51; Foreign secretary, 1951.

[5] W. A. Jowitt, born 1885, son of rector of Stevenage; barrister; M.P. (Lib.), 1922–24; (Lab.), 1929–31, 1939–45; Attorney-General, 1929–32, Solicitor-General, 1940–42, various offices, 1942–45; Lord Chancellor, 1945–51; created Baron Jowett, 1945, viscount, 1947, earl, 1951.

ing of the floor' raised some criticism against him, though he re-submitted himself to his constituency and was re-elected.[1]

Such a Cabinet of moderates made it likely that MacDonald would gain in effect what he had not secured formally, support from outside the party in carrying on the government. But whose support? He told Snowden that he had arranged to see Baldwin after Baldwin's resignation was announced. Snowden suspected MacDonald of attempting to make a bargain to stay in office; MacDonald explained it as a mere courtesy call. When the Big Five were discussing the membership of the Cabinet, however, Snowden insisted that there must be no understanding with the Conservatives, because of the irreconcilable difference between their support of 'safeguarding' and Labour's belief in free trade; and others agreed.[2] This left the Liberals. The Big Five agreed to make no arrangements with the other parties, but to depend on the Liberals for support; and when parliament met the Conservatives made sure of this by moving an amendment to the King's speech on the matter of safeguarding, which the Liberals had perforce to join Labour in defeating. Thus Lloyd George was put in the position of doing what he had sworn before the election not to do, putting a 'purely Socialist Government in power'.[3] He made the best of it by declaring, before parliament met, that the election had really endorsed the Liberals' programme and that they would support the government in carrying it out. The party was, for the time, united under him, and elected him its leader in parliament on June 13.[4]

In the programme which it announced in the King's speech on July 2 the government accepted the Liberals' invitation, though not in so many words. A good deal of legislation was promised; schemes of economic development at home and overseas were to be prepared; and there were to be inquiries into the steel and cotton industries. There was certainly little socialism in this. MacDonald, during the debate, went far—some thought too far— to appeal to both parties for support. Referring to 'the very serious problems that this country has to face' he asked:

I wonder how far it is possible, without in any way abandoning any of

---

[1] Details of the ministry are in the *Annual Register, 1929*, and in G. D. H. Cole, *History of the Labour Party*, pp. 225-8. The *Annual Register* and Cole are also the main sources of the account of the second Labour government's career given in this chapter.

[2] P. Snowden, *Autobiography*, II, 757-9.

[3] See his letter to C. P. Scott, April 30, 1929; M. Thomson, *Lloyd George*, pp. 398-9.

[4] *Annual Register, 1929*, pp. 50-1.

our party positions . . . to consider ourselves more as a Council of
State and less as arrayed regiments facing each other in battle . . . so
far as we are concerned, co-operation will be welcomed . . . so that by
putting our ideas into a common pool we can bring out . . . legislation
and administration that will be of substantial benefit for the nation as
a whole.[1]

2. THE CHALLENGE OF UNEMPLOYMENT:
AN OPPORTUNITY MISSED

It was not to be. The government faced the steady opposition
of the Conservatives and in several cases obstruction from the
House of Lords, with only the halting support of the Liberals.
For this it was itself largely to blame, though it could blame in
turn the cruel web of fate. Few governments have entered office
with higher hopes and wider goodwill, few have fallen less
lamented by friends as well as foes. It entered office just as the
illness of the British economy, chronic since the war, took a
desperate turn, brought on by the widening world depression.
Labour, by desperate remedies, might have saved the day. Instead,
it followed the half-measures of its predecessors. When these
failed, it forfeited the nation's confidence and opened the gate once
more for the Conservatives. It was weakened from within, by
resignations, and by criticism from the Left. It fell a victim of its
own shortcomings as much as of some strange political manoeuvres.
The failure left its mark equally upon the Liberals, aggravating
their internal divisions even while they took out upon the government in scornful speeches and grudging votes their own feelings
of frustration.

Thus was lost a great opportunity—the last one offered for the
building of a better nation out of the calamities and transforma-
tions of the war. Two years' stalemate made possible the return
of the sort of government which had already, in the twenties,
failed to promote economic recovery and succeeded only in
aggravating social discontents. Yet such a government could only
offer more of the same: more evasions, greater insularity, policies
which defeated their own objects and would have been even more
ruinous if wholeheartedly pressed, and which as it was helped
bring on the next calamity in the world's history. In this sense
Labour's failure was the turning point in Britain's history between
the wars.

The chief failure was over unemployment, which all parties had

[1] 229 H.C. Deb., 5 s., 64–5.

made the main issue of the election. Actually, unemployment was a little lower when the government took office than it had been a year before, and this was true for each month until December 1929: in June there were 1,164,000 insured workers unemployed, in November 1,326,000, as compared with 1,453,000 a year before. It was in 1930 that the figures began to be alarming, for instead of the usual drop in unemployment as winter changed to spring there was a steady rise, which was unchecked throughout the year: 1,520,000 unemployed on the registers in January, 1,761,000 in April, 2,070,000 in July, 2,319,000 in October, $2\frac{1}{2}$ millions in December.[1] Even by running, the government could not stay in the same place, but was carried backward, conquered by the unemployment it was to conquer.

It was the victim of circumstances. It was the government's misfortune to take office just as the unsound structure of the postwar international economy began to crumble. The German economy had been sustained by large loans, three times the amount paid out by the Germans in reparations. Much of these came from the United States, some from Great Britain. By 1928 the heavy lending since the war by the American investor had come to an end, and in its turn the great speculative boom in American stocks and bonds had begun, drawing gold, hot money and the funds of normally prudent Europeans to the United States. The flow of gold to the United States, in purchase of its exports and in payment of war debts, had increased credit and the money in circulation, though prices, because of improved efficiency in production, had not risen correspondingly. There seemed no end to the pot of gold; so why not invest, and get one's share? The classic remedy, the raising of the bank rate, was only taken sparingly in 1928 and then proved ineffective. Hence when confidence gave way and heavy selling began the crash came quickly, on October 29, 1929. In a week 240 securities had declined in market value by $15,984 millions. The American crash immediately affected investment and trade the world over. In England, the almost simultaneous Hatry crash, in September, similarly discouraged new investment. The price of primary products whose production had greatly increased in a time of high consumption fell heavily, ruining the producer countries as markets; the price of manufactured goods, kept high by the industrial rigidity of the times, did not fall nearly as much and so tempt the reluctant consumer to buy. Britain's total exports fell

[1] *Statistical Abstract of U.K., 1930*, p. 97.

from £839 millions in 1929 to £666 millions in 1930 and £461 millions in 1931. And once trade fell off, public policy only discouraged it further: the raising of tariffs, the abandonment of the gold standard, the instability of foreign exchange. The full effect of all these things was only seen in 1931–33; the immediate effects were bad enough. It was with growing unemployment caused by these circumstances that the luckless Jimmy Thomas was called upon to deal.[1]

As 'minister of employment' Thomas was given three assistants, George Lansbury, Thomas Johnston, under-secretary for Scotland, and Sir Oswald Mosley, a new and wealthy recruit to the party from Birmingham, once a Conservative M.P. but now Labour's Chancellor of the Duchy of Lancaster. Thomas set about his task with great energy. In the debate on the King's speech, on July 3, he was ready to report much done in a single month—railway managers, business leaders, civil servants interviewed, large plans drafted. He talked of the building of roads, of improvements on the railways. He also mentioned colonial development schemes, including a bridge across the Zambezi; and plans for attracting new industries into distressed areas in Great Britain. In practice, this involved a limited commitment to a programme of public works, aided by grants or guarantees for loans. The Development (Loan Guarantees and Grants) Act, 1929, and the Colonial Development Act, 1929, were the result.

From here Thomas' performance, and the government's, tailed off. Thomas made a trip to Canada in August to try to enlarge the Canadian market for British exports. He received a fine welcome, and on his return claimed to have stimulated increased orders for British coal and ships (Wheatley unkindly called them 'ships that pass in the night'). When he reported to parliament on November 4, Thomas stated that the public works schemes which the government had already stimulated involved an expenditure of £42 millions. Both Lloyd George and Conservative speakers criticised the programme as including little that was really new; and Maxton called on Thomas to try socialism instead.

Thomas could not explain a failure which he himself hardly understood. There was no lack of ideas. Johnston was pushing national relief schemes, such as the building of a road round Loch Lomond (he did succeed in getting the coach road from Aberfoyle

---

[1] J. P. Day, *Introduction to World Economic History*, pp. 84–95; J. A. Salter, *Recovery* (second ed., London, 1933), p. 24.

to the Trossachs reconstructed). Lansbury proposed retirement pensions for workers at sixty, a colonising scheme in Western Australia, land reclamation in Great Britain. These and all such schemes failed in the Unemployment Committee where the four ministers were confronted with bleak negatives from the top civil servants from the various departments. If this was not sufficiently discouraging, the Treasury watch-dog was always at hand; and no Chancellor of the Exchequer was more economy-minded and less sympathetic to any proposals of a socialist cast than Philip Snowden. Thomas would not fight him, and Lansbury, the only other member of the Unemployment Committee in the Cabinet, could not do so single-handed.[1]

In January 1930 MacDonald announced the creation of the Economic Advisory Council, outgrowth of an earlier, informal body. It had a staff of five, including three economists, Hubert Henderson, H. V. Hodson, Colin Clark, and included some ministers and a number of men from outside politics, such as Sir Arthur Balfour, Keynes, Tawney, G. D. H. Cole, Sir Josiah Stamp, Ernest Bevin, Citrine, and several businessmen. It met every month under MacDonald's chairmanship, but accomplished little.

By the spring of 1930, unemployment policy was threatening to produce a rift within the ministry itself. Sir Oswald Mosley, ostensibly Thomas' lieutenant in the fight against unemployment, chafed at the slow and orthodox policies being followed. He was ambitious but clear-headed. He drew up a programme of action.

It included increased pensions and allowances to induce earlier retirement from industry and to enlarge purchasing power, protection of the home market by tariffs, import restrictions and bulk purchase agreements with foreign, and especially Empire producers, the development of British agriculture, rationalisation of industry under public control, and much greater use of credit to finance development through the public control of banking.[2] These proposals were embodied in what became known as the 'Mosley memorandum', and were submitted by Mosley, Lansbury and Johnston to the Cabinet in February, without having been seen first by Thomas. Thomas naturally took offence, but was mollified by MacDonald.[3] In any case the character of the proposals, in-

[1] R. Postgate, *George Lansbury*, pp. 252-6; Thomas Johnston, *Memories* (London, 1952), pp. 103-6 (some amusing stories); Hugh Dalton, *Memoirs*, p. 260.
[2] G. D. H. Cole, *History of the Labour Party*, p. 237. See Mosley's speech in parliament after his resignation: 239 H.C. Deb., 5 s., 1348-72 (May 28, 1930).
[3] J. H. Thomas, *My Story*, pp. 169-74.

volving breaches with free trade and orthodox banking policies, doomed them in the eyes of Snowden, whose word on economic policy was law in the Cabinet. After gathering dust for some months, the memorandum was definitely rejected in May. As a Cabinet document, however, it had become secret, and its details were never published though the gist of them leaked out. When, on May 19, the Conservatives renewed their attack on the government's failure over unemployment, this time through Neville Chamberlain, advocating the application of safeguarding—for the Conservatives had begun a new round in their fight for Protection —Mosley took occasion to resign his office. Soon after this, on June 6, Thomas gave up his thankless task and became Secretary of State for the Dominions—the combined office of Dominions and Colonial Secretary being now divided, with Sidney Webb remaining as Colonial Secretary. Vernon Hartshorn succeeded Thomas as Lord Privy Seal and Clement Attlee succeeded Mosley; but MacDonald announced that he himself would take general responsibility for unemployment policy.[1]

Mosley followed up his resignation by moving a resolution condemning the government's policy at a special meeting of the Parliamentary Labour Party which was held soon afterwards. His speech won much sympathy, and Henderson, who replied in conciliatory fashion, urged him to withdraw his motion, since he had made his point and would accomplish nothing further by it. Mosley persisted; whereupon party loyalty caused its defeat by 202 votes to 29.[2] Nothing daunted, he took his case to the Labour party's annual conference at Llandudno in October; and a motion that the National Executive should go fully into his proposals and report on them was only very narrowly defeated. Maxton, supporting the proposition that the government's failure rose from its not applying socialist remedies was, by contrast, heavily defeated. MacDonald reminded the conference that the progress of socialism must be slow and evolutionary, but that they were 'moving, as it were, in a great eternal ocean of surge towards righteousness, towards fair play, towards honesty . . .'[3] Mosley ought to have noticed, not the ovation his speech received, but the cheers which greeted the Prime Minister's two speeches—the first drawing on the grief which all felt at the death two days

---

[1] Hartshorn and Attlee had been members of the Indian Statutory Commission (the Simon Commission) at the time of the government's formation. Hartshorn, Welsh mining leader and postmaster-general in 1924, died in March, 1931.
[2] G. D. H. Cole, *History of the Labour Party*, p. 241; *Annual Register, 1930*, p. 48.
[3] *Report of the Annual Conference of the Labour Party, 1930*, p. 193.

before (October 5) of Lord Thomson, the Air Secretary, and 48 of the 54 persons on the airship R101 when it burst into flames and was wrecked near Beauvais, in northern France, while on a test flight to India. Instead, Mosley believed, as Lord Randolph Churchill had done over forty years earlier, that he had a real party following, and prepared to lead it. In December he published his manifesto, which was signed by A. J. Cook and 17 M.P.'s., including John Strachey,[1] Aneurin Bevan[2] and W. J. Brown.[3] This was enlarged in February 1931 into *A National Policy*, and Mosley announced that he was forming the New Party to campaign for its adoption. At this point most of the seventeen took alarm, suspecting the autocratic tendencies which soon carried Mosley into the leadership of the British fascist movement; only four Labour members, including Mosley's wife and Strachey, joined. The Labour party expelled him, though he had been elected a member of the National Executive at Llandudno. It was easy, afterwards, to say that he had never been a true supporter of Labour or a believer in parliamentary methods; the fact was, as he told the Llandudno conference, that the Labour party had a great opportunity, in attacking unemployment, to remodel the country; when it shrank from it, he recoiled, disillusioned, into bolder and more dangerous courses.[4] The immediate effect was that any vigorous Labour programme to deal with unemployment, making use of public works and novel credit policies, was ruled out not so much on its merits as through Mosley's tactics.

Mosley's resignation from office in May 1930, coupled with Conservative and Liberal attacks on the government's unemployment policies in two debates (May 19, when the government's majority sank to 15, and May 28), led MacDonald to seek more definitely than hitherto the co-operation of the other parties. In June he invited the Conservatives and Liberals to a meeting. Baldwin refused. Lloyd George accepted, and meetings followed, the Liberals represented by Lloyd George, Lord Lothian and Seebohm Rowntree. In a debate on October 28 the government's majority was 31; most Liberals abstained under a party decision.

[1] John Strachey, born 1901, son of J. St. L. Strachey, editor of the *Spectator*; Eton and Magdalen College, Oxford; M.P., 1929-31 and since 1945; wing commander, R.A.F.V.R., Second World War; Minister of Food, 1946-50; Secretary of State for War, 1950-51; author of *The Coming Struggle for Power* (1932).
[2] Aneurin Bevan, born in Tredegar, 1897; coal miner; M.P. for Ebbw Vale since 1929; Minister of Health, 1945-51, Labour, 1951. Married Jennie Lee in 1934.
[3] W. J. Brown, general secretary, Civil Service Clerical Association, 1919-42; M.P. (Lab.), 1929-31, (Indep.), 1942-50.
[4] G. D. H. Cole, *History of the Labour Party*, pp. 239-43; W. J. Brown, *So Far*, pp. 156-62.
    N*

This, however, led to Liberal dissensions: the chief whip resigned, and his successor, Sir Archibald Sinclair,[1] could get no assurance from members that his instructions would be followed; Sir John Simon, still one of the party's chief figures, published a letter to Lloyd George declaring that he had no confidence in the government and would vote on each issue according to his conscience.

In the related problems of unemployment insurance and relief the government was no happier. Here, however, the attack from within, from Maxton and the I.L.P., and from other back benchers, was stronger than that of the Opposition; within the Labour party Margaret Bondfield was the least popular minister, though her record was as good as the hard times permitted. At the very start of the government's career, in July, she had introduced an interim measure increasing the Treasury's contribution to the Unemployment Insurance Fund, which had nearly reached the limit of its borrowing powers (£40 millions) owing to the large number of men receiving 'transitional' benefits; this evoked Labour complaints that the party had promised more than this, namely work or maintenance.

In November 1929, came the Unemployment Insurance bill, which increased the number of persons who might obtain 'transitional' benefits although lacking the minimum number of insurance contributions and again enlarged the Treasury's expenditure for this purpose. The bill also provided for the training of young persons in receipt of benefit and it increased slightly the rates of benefit for young persons and for wives. Its biggest innovation was to reverse the obligation that an applicant for benefit must prove that he was 'genuinely seeking work'; it became the responsibility of the official to prove that the applicant had refused reasonable offers of work if he was to be denied benefit. This righting of what had been a great grievance among working people was not, however, enough to satisfy Maxton and his friends. While the Conservatives attacked the bill for extravagance, Maxton and 30 others introduced an amendment condemning the bill's 'omissions'.[2] To meet the Conservative strictures on extravagance the government appointed a Royal Commission under a judge, Holman Gregory, to examine the workings of unemploy-

---

[1] Archibald Sinclair, fourth baronet of Ulbster, Caithness, born 1890; M.P. for Caithness and Sutherland 1922–45; chief Liberal whip, 1930–31, leader of Parliamentary Liberal party, 1935–45; secretary of state for Scotland, 1931–32, for Air, 1940–45; created Viscount Thurso, 1952.

[2] The bill was amended by the House of Lords to include, among other things, a time-limit. The Commons accepted this, but extended it from one year to three. As such the bill became law as the Unemployment Insurance Act, 1930.

ment insurance. On the basis of its report, the government introduced in July 1931 the 'Anomalies' bill to end certain abuses in the system, depriving some classes of unemployed persons, mainly married women, of benefit. The bill was bitterly attacked by I.L.P. members and others, and also by Mosley, but it was passed.

The rifts which these measures revealed were not so much between Labour and the I.L.P. as within the I.L.P. itself. There were 140 M.P.'s who belonged to the I.L.P., but only 37 of these had been elected with the financial support of the I.L.P. At the I.L.P. Conference at Birmingham at Easter, 1930, Maxton obtained passage of a resolution that the I.L.P. Group in parliament should be reconstructed on the basis of acceptance of I.L.P. policy. This was done, but only 18 of the 140 accepted membership on these terms.[1] Between this smaller I.L.P. Group and the rest of the Labour party differences became strained and personal. At the time of the 1931 general election an 'uneasy truce' still existed; but the current carrying the rump of the old I.L.P. toward disaffiliation from the Labour party in 1932 was already strong. Wheatley, who might have held it back, had died in 1930. And in 1930 MacDonald had at last resigned his membership of the I.L.P., which he had held since 1894.[2]

3. THE COAL MINES ACT AND OTHER HAZARDS

The retort of Labour ministers to critics within the party was usually that circumstances denied the means for a better policy; but behind this lay the argument that the government was a minority government at best. Some of the government's policies came close to the limits of Liberal tolerance and its fate was in the balance more than once. The Liberals, however, were as much the prisoners of circumstance as Labour, and were no more anxious than Labour for a new election, however great the strain of supporting unpalatable policies.

An example of the difficulties involved is the Coal Mines bill, introduced in December 1929. The government was committed to doing something for the miners, at least to the extent of restoring the 7-hour day. Its original proposals, made in

[1] The group included Maxton, Jowett, Brockway, W. J. Brown, John Strachey, E. F. Wise, R. C. Wallhead, and the Clydesiders Kirkwood, J. McGovern, Campbell Stephen, and Jennie Lee, a miner's daughter who had been elected to parliament, for North Lanark, in 1928, at the age of twenty-four.
[2] F. Brockway, *Jowett*, pp. 264–9, *Inside the Left*, pp. 207–9; G. D. H. Cole, *History of the Labour Party*, pp. 246–8.

November, included the acquisition of the royalties, but this part was postponed for a subsequent bill (which never materialised). The bill provided for a 7½-hour shift instead of one of 8 hours. To prevent the lowering of wages for the shorter shift the bill offered the owners a cartel arrangement: production quotas, set for each district by a central council of owners, would be divided among the collieries by district boards, thus preventing prices (and so wages) from falling through cut-throat competition between districts or collieries. Minimum prices were to be fixed by the district boards, and the boards might also permit the transfer of quotas from one colliery to another. This proposal, which hardly represented orthodox socialism, was admittedly modelled on the voluntary Five Counties scheme which had had a brief life in the previous year;[1] it was accepted by the owners, and became Part I of the eventual Act. The restrictionist schemes, making use of quotas and levies, which formed so large a part of Britain's programme for recovery in the thirties, were really inaugurated in this bill. The remaining provision, a National Wages Board without compulsory powers, became Part IV of the Act, but lapsed through the owners' arrogant refusal to have anything to do with it. The marketing and quota proposals of the bill were strongly criticised by the Liberals, and to a less extent by Churchill and other Conservatives. On the second reading, just before Christmas 1929, the government came close to defeat. Conservatives, many of whom had returned to town for the purpose, voted in unexpectedly large numbers against it, as did 40 Liberals; but with 2 Liberal votes and other Liberal abstentions the government had a majority of eight, 281 to 273.

In these circumstances, the government's fall was generally predicted early in the new year. However, both it and the Liberals took the lesson to heart. The government brought in amendments to the bill (Part II of the Act) which, on the basis of Labour's passion for 'reorganisation' of the coal-mining industry in 1926, it should have included in the first place. By this part of the bill a Coal Mines Reorganisation Commission would be established to prepare and promote schemes of amalgamation. Following this, Lloyd George announced in a speech on January 20, 1930 that the Liberals would continue to co-operate with the government if the government reciprocated with concessions to its views and either refrained from assailing Liberals in their constituencies or agreed to a real measure of electoral reform.

[1] For this scheme see J. H. Jones, *Coal Mining Industry*, pp. 88–107.

Certain other measures of the government had an easier passage. Among these were the Housing Act, 1930, introduced by Arthur Greenwood, the Minister of Health, which dealt mainly with slum clearance and provided subsidies for the purpose. A bill for the operation of London's passenger transport services by a single public corporation was introduced by Herbert Morrison, the Minister of Transport, in 1931, but was still incomplete when the government fell. The Agricultural Marketing Act, 1931, was the work of Christopher Addison, the former Liberal minister, who had become Minister of Agriculture in 1930. It provided for the creation of marketing boards of producers to grade and sell agricultural products or to fix their prices; a board could be created only after a majority of the producers had voted for it, but its powers then extended over the minority also. Here again Labour provided a precedent which was followed by the National government.

Other measures were less fortunate. The bill to raise the school-leaving age to fifteen, as promised by the Labour party, was not introduced until 1930, and after drastic amendment in the Commons was rejected by the Lords in February 1931. Over this, the minister, Sir Charles Trevelyan, resigned on March 2, though he made it clear that his disagreement with the government concerned more than education; he was 'very much out of sympathy' with its method and believed that the crisis in trade required 'big socialist measures' in which it seemed to show less and less belief.[1] Dr. Addison's Land Utilisation bill was another which suffered at the Lords' hands. It proposed to establish an Agricultural Land Corporation to acquire and operate demonstration farms; but the Lords left very little when they had finished with it.

The bill which the government introduced in 1930 to amend the hated Trade Disputes Act of 1927 met a different fate. It aimed to make legal the sympathetic but not the general strike, to restore 'contracting out', and to give civil servants their freedom in the trade-union movement which the 1927 Act had taken away. The Conservatives had, naturally, no sympathy for the bill at all, and many Liberals, notably Simon, were as uncompromising. But it passed its second reading in January 1931, after long debate, only to be so amended in committee that the government abandoned it. The amendment which wrecked it—a Liberal one defining a general strike—was apparently made with the approval of the Attorney-General and the Cabinet. Presumably the govern-

[1] *The Times*, March 3, 1931.

ment preferred no bill to one which could not meet all the wishes of the trade unions.

The history of electoral reform was more complex, since it involved the always-delicate relations of the government with the Liberals. An all-party conference on the subject, presided over by Lord Ullswater, a former Speaker, was appointed in December 1929, but came to an end the next July, unable to reach agreement, mainly because neither Labour nor the Conservatives would accept the Liberals' darling, proportional representation. None the less, the government promised a bill in the King's speech in October 1930, and published the text on January 17, just when its future was most precarious because of the revolt of many of the Liberals over the Trade Disputes bill. The bill was introduced in February 1931, its main provision being that the alternative vote should in future be used in all parliamentary elections. The main parts carried, but in committee a clause abolishing the university representation was defeated with the aid of some Liberal votes. Consultations between Lloyd George and Mac-Donald followed—the relations between the parties, if indeed they existed, being strained also by the economy campaign of the time. When on March 24 Lloyd George proposed to the Liberals continued co-operation with Labour (the Protectionist Tories being the alternative as a government), many, including Simon, refused, being ready to oppose the government on all points. An unsteady co-operation continued—made no stronger by a later amendment to the electoral bill abolishing plural voting rather than the university representation. This gave the Lords their opportunity. By July they had amended the bill so that little remained: plural voting was restored, and the alternative vote limited to London and the larger boroughs. The bill was in this state when the government fell.[1]

4. PROTECTION OR FREE TRADE:
TORY TROUBLES AND THE 1930 BUDGET

During these months the Conservatives had their troubles no less than Labour and the Liberals. The focus of them was Baldwin's leadership, under fire after the Conservatives' failure in the 1929 election; the main issue was the party's stand on Protection and imperial trade. Baldwin, who had lost an election in 1924 for advocating Protection too broadly, now almost lost the leadership of his party for not supporting Protection broadly enough. Yet

[1] D. E. Butler, *Electoral System in Britain*, pp. 58–83, gives a full account of this unhappy bill.

he emerged from the test stronger than before; and the issue also decided who would be his successor.

The crisis over the party's leadership was brought about from outside, by Lord Beaverbrook. In July 1929, he began in his newspapers his campaign for 'Empire Free Trade' as a means of overcoming the country's chronic economic ills: complete freedom of trade between all the countries of the British Empire, with a tariff wall around the Empire, shutting out the rest of the world. A campaign for Protection with such powerful backing should have been meat and drink to most Conservatives; but Beaverbrook's 'Crusade', as he soon called it, was too much of a good thing; it was quickly pointed out that the Dominions would be the first to refuse freedom of entry for British manufactures competing with their own. Early in 1930 Baldwin tried to stem the flood by proclaiming safeguarding and imperial preference as the party's policy, but rejecting any tax on food. This was not enough for Beaverbrook, who replied that his crusade would now become a party, soliciting campaign funds and running candidates: the United Empire Party was born, with the help of his fellow press lord, Lord Rothermere. Baldwin then tried a direct approach to Beaverbrook, and on March 4 announced that he would submit the question of a tax on food to the people in a referendum—a favourite though radical proposal of the Conservatives. Beaverbrook then made his peace with the party, but Rothermere did not, and continued the United Empire Party.

Snowden's Budget, opened on April 14, lent no balm. Faced with a deficit of over £40 millions, on an estimated expenditure of £782 millions, partly because revenue had fallen far short of Churchill's estimate in the previous Budget, partly because of the added charges for pensions and unemployment relief, Snowden balanced the Budget with some transference of funds from one account to another and a decrease in the amount budgeted for debt redemption, and with increases in direct taxation which fell almost entirely on the well-to-do. He raised the income tax from 4s. to 4s. 6d. in the £, but altered the exemptions so that persons with the lower incomes (about three-quarters of the taxpayers) paid no increase; he increased the surtax rates, and he increased the death duties, which on estates of over £2 millions would now demand 50 per cent rather than 40 per cent of the capital. Only one indirect tax was increased: the beer duty was raised by a penny a gallon. On the other hand the Safeguarding duties on lace, cutlery, fabric gloves and gas mantles, which were due to expire, were not renewed; though the Chancellor regretted that he could not also sacrifice the revenue of the McKenna and silk duties. To add insult to injury he announced that a separate bill would be introduced providing for a valuation of all land, as a preliminary to a land values tax. And on top of this there were to be measures to prevent tax evasion by the larger taxpayers.

Here was a Budget to rouse the Tory thunder. Investment funds would dry up, the depression would grow worse. The gestures toward free trade menaced the programme of Protection and the cultivation of the Empire's markets. Generally the Liberals supported the Budget, but on July 9 they almost defeated the government on an amendment; some fifty Conservatives, who had been kept in wait in a nearby building, came into the division lobby 'at the double' and with the Liberals reduced the government's majority to three. Yet it was really a conservative, orthodox budget: it was balanced, and the increases in taxation were not large, and were placed on the shoulders best able to bear them.

Meanwhile, in May 1930, the Conservatives began an 'educational campaign' up and down the country in favour of Safeguarding and Imperial Preference: 'Home and Empire' was the slogan. But it lacked the indispensable ingredient for the Empire Free Traders, the promise of duties on food, without which little real preference could be given to the Dominions; and Beaverbrook joined Rothermere once more in threatening to oppose Conservative candidates who would not give such a promise. The first victim of the new attack was not Baldwin, but J. C. C. Davidson,[1] the chairman of the party organisation, who was compelled by party mutterings to resign. His successor was Neville Chamberlain, who had recently become chairman of the party's research department and had infused a new energy into it.

Fate was carrying Neville Chamberlain more and more into the lead in the party. Any controversy involving Protection was bound to arouse him and to make him a pivotal figure. He was efficient; he was in many ways a moderate. As the 'Crusade' kept up the criticism of Baldwin, Chamberlain saw clearly that the leadership might fall to him. Loyalty kept him beside Baldwin; and also his fear that a change might put Churchill, rather than himself, in power. Churchill had been the most constant, the most aggressive

---

[1] J. C. C. Davidson, born 1889; barrister; private secretary to Bonar Law, 1915–20, parliamentary private secretary to Bonar Law and Baldwin, 1920–23; M.P., 1920–23, 1924–37; chancellor of Duchy of Lancaster, 1923 and 1931–37; chairman of Conservative party, 1927–30; created Viscount Davidson, 1937.

of the Conservatives in the opposition in parliament to the Labour government; there were many in the party who might support him, especially for his views about India and the Empire. But Churchill not only opposed any taxes on food, but had kept in contact with Lloyd George; and a Conservative-Liberal agreement based on those two, besides being personally obnoxious to Chamberlain (who never forgave Lloyd George for his brusque dismissal of him as Director of National Service in 1917 and was always a good hater), would certainly prevent any far-reaching measures of Protection. Thoughts such as these kept Chamberlain beside Baldwin, and so gave him, though late rather than soon, his mantle.

Immediately, Chamberlain's hand at the party helm and new vigour on Baldwin's part kept the leadership unchanged. Baldwin always acted strongly only after great provocation, or at a crisis. Now Rothermere supplied the provocation. In June Baldwin called an extraordinary meeting of Conservative M.P.'s and hit back at his critics. His trump card was a letter from Lord Rothermere to a Conservative member stating that in no circumstances would he support Baldwin or any other leader unless he knew exactly what his policy was going to be, had guarantees that it would be carried out in office, and 'unless I am acquainted with the names of at least eight, or ten, of his most prominent colleagues in the next Ministry'. Baldwin's comment, after pointing to the way in which this would nullify the King's role in the making of a Prime Minister and Cabinet, was uncompromising: 'a more preposterous and insolent demand was never made on the leader of any political party. I repudiate it with contempt and I will fight that attempt at domination to the end.'[1] He received a vote of confidence. The press lords had saved him.

In October the Imperial Conference was held, with most of the Dominion prime ministers in attendance. Though it was partly concerned with constitutional questions, which had important results next year, its main preoccupations were economic. R. B. Bennett, the Canadian Prime Minister, made an offer: in exchange for like preference from Britain and the other Empire countries, Canada would give an Empire preference in her market based on the addition of 10 per cent in her existing or future tariffs. The government's reply was naturally non-committal, and in parliament on November 27 Thomas called Bennett's offer 'humbug': it would not lower Canada's tariffs against Britain, which were

[1] Wickham Steed, *The Real Stanley Baldwin*, pp. 183-4.

already far too high for British goods to surmount. Baldwin welcomed Bennett's offer (at Chamberlain's prodding) but refused to do more than promise proposals for imperial preference, an emergency tariff on manufactures and a quota system for wheat with guarantees for the home farmer at the next election. This was not good enough for the press lords. In October they challenged his policy anew by running an Empire Free Trade candidate, Vice-Admiral E. A. Taylor, against the Conservative candidate in a by-election in South Paddington; the admiral won. On the same day, October 30, Baldwin again defended himself before a special meeting of Conservative peers, M.P.'s and candidates and offered to resign if it was the party's wish. Colonel Gretton, one of the die-hards, moved a resolution proposing a change of leadership, charging Baldwin with lack of vigour and with subservience to the 'old gang'. It was defeated by 462 votes to 116; whereupon the meeting voted unanimous confidence in Baldwin.

This was not the end. The final crisis came in March 1931. The press lords' campaign continued, in spite of conversations between Chamberlain and Beaverbrook. Conservatives such as Churchill continued to denounce the prospect of dominion status for India, which Baldwin supported. Late in February the party's chief agent reported to Chamberlain that without a change in leadership there was a real doubt whether victory could be expected at the next election. Chamberlain consulted the party's senior figures; all except Bridgeman thought Baldwin 'would have to resign', and advised Chamberlain to show Baldwin the agent's memorandum. On March 1, he sent it to him; and later that day Baldwin told him he was going at once. Again the press lords saved him. In a by-election in St. George's, Westminster, Sir Ernest Petter, a Conservative, announced his candidacy and made his challenge to Baldwin's leadership the main issue. It was with difficulty that a Conservative was found to oppose him, but eventually Duff Cooper[1] agreed. Bridgeman then persuaded Baldwin not to resign till the fight was over. The by-election campaign was a violent one—all the more because it was within the family. Baldwin intervened, and in a speech in the Queen's Hall on March 17 named Beaverbrook and Rothermere and challenged their pretensions. Their newspapers, he said,

are not newspapers in the ordinary acceptance of the term. They are

[1] Alfred Duff Cooper (1890–1954); Eton and New College, Oxford; M.P., 1924–29, 1931–45; War secretary, 1935–37; first lord of Admiralty, 1937–38; Minister of Information, 1940–41; chancellor of Duchy of Lancaster, 1941–43; ambassador to France, 1944–47; created Viscount Norwich, 1952.

engines of propaganda for the constantly changing policies, desires, personal wishes, personal likes and personal dislikes of two men. What are their methods? Their methods are direct falsehood, mis-representation, half-truths, the alteration of the speaker's meaning by putting sentences apart from the context, suppression, and editorial criticism of speeches which are not reported in the paper . . . What the proprietorship of these papers is aiming at is power, but power without responsibility—the prerogative of the harlot throughout the ages.[1]

Duff Cooper won the election by 17,242 votes to Petter's 11,532, and Baldwin stayed on. There was a momentary breach between him and Chamberlain, especially when Chamberlain resigned the chairmanship of the party organisation in mid-March to be available for the party leadership which the inner circle expected to be vacant for him to fill. The breach soon healed. Chamberlain was able to arrange a truce with Beaverbrook, and the campaign against Baldwin died down.[2]

These events had consequences both immediate and remote. Baldwin was strengthened in his leadership of the party. The challenge had made him fight back; and his rebuke to the press endeared him anew with the public as the plain man arrayed against the forces of selfishness. And Chamberlain, forced into the role of his principal defender, became, though denied the immediate succession, the undisputed heir apparent. But why not Churchill? It was just at this time, on January 27, 1931, that he publicly withdrew from the Conservative 'shadow cabinet', because he bitterly opposed the Labour government's current policy towards India, which Baldwin and the party supported.[3] Thus was the stage set for the thirties: the clash of personalities and policies had blindly decided who was to dominate the policy and character of the British government in the tragic decade, and who was to be left out of office.

In another way the stage was being set also. During 1930–31 the barriers of ideas against Protection were breaking. Bankers' meetings, chambers of commerce (even that of Manchester), the Federation of British Industries, industrialists like Morris, the motor manufacturer, called for Safeguarding and imperial pre-ference. So did voices from the other side: Mosley's manifesto

[1] Quoted in D. Abel, *History of British Tariffs*, p. 61.
[2] The facts of the Conservative party's troubles in 1929–31 can be found in the *Annual Register*; for what lay behind them K. Feiling, *Neville Chamberlain*, pp. 170–87, is invaluable. See also D. Abel, *History of British Tariffs*, pp. 51–62, and G. M. Young, *Baldwin*, pp. 142–62.
[3] See below, pp. 377–8.

and his New Party; and, even more important, the T.U.C. which, at its meeting in September 1930, gave serious thought to the development of trade within the Empire. And the Liberal bastions were falling. On March 3 Sir John Simon, though not committing himself to a tariff, called on his fellow Free Traders to consider 'fiscal methods'. In higher circles ideas were changing. In the discussions within the Macmillan committee in 1930 Keynes had been moving towards belief in a tariff. In March 1931, he set a debate going by letters and an article in the *New Statesman*, the *Daily Mail* and *The Times*. He proposed a temporary revenue tariff. His argument was only partly protectionist. He wanted to increase the demand for home manufactures and so provide employment; he wanted revenue to balance the budget without increasing direct taxation; and he wanted—part of the new theory he was beginning to refine—a programme of expansion, which would be achieved by capital freed for investment by the reduction of Britain's adverse trade balance. Fellow-economists might refute his ideas as mutually contradictory; the layman might miss the qualifications in his arguments. The effect of his advocacy remained—not that Keynes was then the force and symbol he later became. Another revolution in British policy was in the making; and indeed had long been.[1]

5. AFFAIRS FOREIGN AND IMPERIAL

The Labour government took office at the time when the postwar peace settlement and international goodwill were at high tide. The Kellogg Peace Pact had recently been signed. This was followed, in 1929, by a new settlement of German reparations, under the Young Plan, and by the evacuation of the Rhineland by the occupying forces, including British troops, completed by June 1930. In May 1930 Briand circulated among the European governments his plan for European union, a United States of Europe. Though this reflected France's continual preoccupation with the problem of security it also put into words what countless men of goodwill had long thought in their hearts. The golden age was at hand! But the responses of governments varied from enthusiasm to chilly criticism, the British government being sceptical of an exclusively European grouping which might conflict with its world-wide interests. The matter was considered by

[1] *Annual Register, 1930*, pp. 55, 70–1; *1931*, p. 34; D. Abel, *History of British Tariffs*, pp. 63–70. Keynes, McKenna, Bevin and three other members of the Macmillan committee signed an addendum in favour of a tariff: Com. on Finance and Industry, *Report*, pp. 199–203; cf. R. F. Harrod, *J. M. Keynes*, pp. 424–31.

a commission of the League, and nothing more was heard of it. In the same year a draft disarmament convention was agreed to by the Preparatory Commission, and the Disarmament Conference was summoned for February 1932.

The ebb was at hand, none the less. The draft disarmament convention and agenda for the conference were passed by a majority vote which left many countries, if not all, dissatisfied: notably Germany, Russia and the United States. Already, on October 3, 1929, Stresemann had died, and with him any sustained will in Germany to tread the path of peace and reconciliation. By 1930 the end of foreign lending had brought the collapse of Germany's synthetic prosperity; governmental economies brought resistance; the chancellor, Bruening, was forced to rule by emergency decree; and in the elections in September the National Socialist party enlarged its representation in the Reichstag from 12 to 107 seats. 1930 was also the year of Mussolini's boast (May 17):

> Words are a very fine thing; but rifles, machine-guns, warships, aeroplanes, and cannon are still finer things . . . right unaccompanied by might is an empty word.

Neither for the hopeful spirit of 1929 nor for the gloomy forebodings of 1930 was the Labour government responsible, but it did much to encourage the first and to allay the second. *Labour and the Nation* had made much of Labour's devotion to peace— greater than that of the Conservatives—through the methods of conciliation, arbitration, disarmament, co-operation with the League. Arthur Henderson not merely believed in such things, he acted upon them. His genuine goodwill, his readiness to talk things over, his lack of stiffness or national pride, his very 'bourgeois' qualities made him popular at Geneva, where he was assiduous in attending the meetings of the League. Many described him as the most successful British Foreign Secretary since the war; and the tribute to his international reputation was his election as president of the Disarmament Conference in 1931. MacDonald rather grudged him his personal success at the Foreign Office; but he himself attended the Assembly of the League in 1929 and played the chief part in the negotiations for naval disarmament in 1929–30. And the government's acts certainly bore out its good intentions. In September 1929, Britain signed the Optional Clause of the Statute of the Permanent Court of International Justice, binding itself to submit all disputes (with certain reservations) to the court's arbitration; all the Dominions followed. In 1931, following discussions at the Imperial Conference of 1930, the government adhered to the General Act for the Pacific Settlement of International Disputes, which was aimed at creating machinery to carry out the Kellogg Pact. In this also the Dominions (with the exception of South Africa) followed. Soon after it had taken office, in 1929, the government announced, to the Conservatives' disgust, the slowing-down of work on the naval base under construction at Singapore, and the suspension of work on two new cruisers and two submarines. And—another controversial measure—diplomatic relations with Russia were resumed in October 1929, and a commercial agreement signed in April 1930.[1]

At the conference at the Hague in August 1929, however, the Labour government's goodwill seemed to be rather lacking. This conference was to settle the future of Germany's reparations and other economic problems remaining from the war, and to make possible the ending of the Allied occupation of the Rhineland. The Young Plan, drawn up by a committee of experts and named after the American representative, Owen D. Young, replaced the Dawes Plan. Germany's obligations were lowered, and were to be paid off by annuities by 1988; Allied controls on Germany's economic life were ended, and Germany herself assumed the responsibility for making the reparations payments. The trouble was that the Plan altered Britain's share in German payments (while not, of course, lowering the debts she owed as a result of the war); hence to the Hague went Philip Snowden, determined to get better terms for his country. His plain speaking, of a sort seldom heard in international conferences, his Yorkshire stubbornness, won him most of what he wanted—an adjustment of the terms, giving Britain a guaranteed annuity of £2 millions—a trivial victory in the light of circumstances a brief two years later. Snowden's firmness gained the unlikely applause of Conservatives, and indeed of the general public in Britain, for a man who neither courted nor received popularity as a rule; but now he was the 'iron Chancellor', an unfortunate addition to his vanity. He had, however, almost wrecked the conference by his incursion into diplomacy; it was the good sense and geniality of Henderson which saved it.

[1] For Henderson's work as Foreign Secretary see Mrs. Hamilton's excellent biography of him: M. A. Hamilton, *Arthur Henderson* (London, 1938), pp. 283 ff. There is a useful commentary in Hugh Dalton's *Memoirs*, chap. 11 (Dalton was undersecretary), and a judicious account by Henry R. Winkler in G. A. Craig and F. Gilbert, *The Diplomats*, pp. 311–43.

The London Naval Conference of 1930 was another passing triumph of Labour's, and particularly of MacDonald's diplomacy (MacDonald insisted on keeping the conduct of Anglo-American relations in his own hands). After the failure of the Naval Conference of 1927 the question of naval disarmament was dormant until 1929. It was then revived by the new President of the United States, Herbert Hoover, who brought to his office fresh zeal for the promotion of peace and economy. His ambassador to London, General Charles Dawes, pursued the matter in his brisk and forthright manner immediately after his arrival on June 16, 1929. He paid a visit to MacDonald in Scotland, and propounded a new method of deciding on points of mutual disarmament, a 'yardstick' or scientific formula by which 'parity' could be accurately assessed. Much was hoped for from the yardstick, which was, however, never produced. Long weeks of negotiation in person and by letter only revealed old differences, chiefly concerning the actual strength of the British and American fleets and the British need for at least seventy light cruisers compared with American insistence on fewer but heavier cruisers (of which one consequence would be a larger fleet of heavy cruisers for Japan). MacDonald paid a quick visit to the United States in October; he received a lion's welcome, addressed the Senate, exchanged ideas with the President on a log beside the Rapidan River; but the question of cruiser strength, unsettled before the visit, remained unsettled at the end, however much goodwill had been generated. However, a naval conference was summoned to meet in London in January 1930, and representatives from the United States, Japan, France and Italy attended. MacDonald presided over the conference. Britain agreed to accept 50 cruisers rather than 70 as its minimum need; it then became possible to agree on the tonnage to be allotted to cruisers, destroyers and submarines in the British, American and Japanese navies, keeping roughly to the overall 5:5:3 ratio. A five years' holiday in the construction of capital ships was agreed to, and also the early scrapping of a few battleships. There was agreement on the tonnage and armament of submarines, and on aircraft carriers. France and Italy could not come to any agreement over their rival claims and needs in the categories of smaller ships, nor was France ready to concede Italy parity with her, unless her security was guaranteed by a Mediterranean pact including Great Britain. In the end both countries remained outside the main treaty which was signed on April 22. Once again French security clashed with British conciliation—a warning that even among friendly powers the road to peace was still not an easy one.[1]

Events elsewhere reinforced the lesson. In Egypt Arthur Henderson showed that Labour had entered the holy of holies of imperial policy by demanding the resignation of Lord Lloyd,[2] the British High Commissioner, whose firm policies were out of harmony with Henderson's intentions, as they had been also with those of Austen Chamberlain. The Tories, Birkenhead and Churchill in particular, raised a storm of protest, but Henderson successfully defended himself in one of his most effective speeches in the Commons, on July 26, 1929.[3] The Labour government was, however, no more fortunate than the Conservatives in its attempt to negotiate a treaty with Egypt; the British reservations on Egyptian independence (security of communications, continuance of the existing regime in the Sudan) remaining as unacceptable to the new Egyptian nationalism as they had been since Britain offered independence in 1922.

In Palestine also Britain found the avuncular role hard to sustain. The Mandate (allotted to her in 1920) was an impossible one: to allow the free development of the indigenous Arabs and at the same time to build the Jewish 'national home' through large immigration, land purchase and settlement. At the Wailing Wall in Jerusalem, ground equally sacred to Arabs and Jews, a long series of incidents ended in the disorders of August 1929, in which 133 Jews and 116 Arabs lost their lives. Pressed on all sides, by the guarded censure of the League of Nations Mandates Commission, by Arab demands and Zionist indignation, the government, after considering two official reports, attempted to give judgment in the Passfield White Paper of October 1930 (Cmd. 3692): until Palestine's productivity was improved (with the aid of a British loan of £2½ millions) new Jewish settlement must be confined to the reserve lands already in Jewish possession, and

---

[1] G. M. Gathorne-Hardy, *Short History of International Affairs*, pp. 176–86, 249–58, 335–38; W. N. Medlicott, *British Foreign Policy since Versailles*, pp. 105–21; E. Windrich, *British Labour's Foreign Policy*, p. 71 ff. For Snowden at the Hague see his *Autobiography*, II, 778 ff. Studies of the London Naval Conference based on recently published British and U.S. documents are: Conyers Read, 'Recent United States and British Government Publications on the London Naval Conference of 1930', *American Historical Review*, 54 (1949), 307–14; B. E. Schmitt, 'British Foreign Policy, 1919–1939', *Journal of Modern History*, 21 (1949), 320–6; J. L. Godfrey, 'Anglo-American Naval Conversations preliminary to the London Naval Conference of 1930', *South Atlantic Quarterly*, 49 (1950), 303–16.

[2] George Ambrose Lloyd, Baron Lloyd (1879–1941), M.P. (Conservative), 1910–18, 1924–25, Governor of Bombay, 1918–23, High Commissioner for Egypt, 1925–29, secretary of state for colonies, 1940; created baron, 1925.

[3] M. A. Hamilton, *Arthur Henderson*, pp. 296–304.

eviction of Arabs elsewhere must cease. This foreshadowed the later curtailment of Jewish immigration but did not bring it about; indeed, the harshness of the White Paper toward the Jews was mitigated, as a result of criticism of it by Jews and non-Jews, by a statement made by MacDonald on February 14, 1931.

In India also the government had to deal with the consequences of inflamed nationalism. Through the twenties disorder was endemic, though not as convulsive as it had been at the war's end. Communal outbreaks between Hindus and Moslems took the lives of 450, and injured over 5000 persons, between 1923 and 1927; and great strikes, particularly in Bombay, in the Tata steel works, and on some of the railways, added their toll. The government countered with a Public Safety Bill to curb Communist activities, and in March 1929, arrested over thirty trade-union leaders and sent them up for the long trial of the 'Meerut conspiracy case'. Clearly the Act of 1919 was not working well; and two years before the appointed time the Conservative government consti-tuted the Indian Statutory Commission, in 1927, a body made up of members of the two houses of parliament under the chairman-ship of Sir John Simon, to examine it. The Simon Commission had great difficulty, when it visited India, in obtaining co-opera-tion in its inquiries. The Indians turned to the drafting of a con-stitution of their own at an all-parties conference in 1928. In the summer of 1929 Lord Irwin, the Viceroy, paid a visit to England to consult the government; from this came the Irwin declaration of October 31 that the 'natural issue of India's constitutional pro-gress . . . is the attainment of Dominion status'. This was much criticised in England, as intended to allay strife by deceiving Indian opinion while really implying, as was officially admitted, no change in policy. It did not, in any case, satisfy the Congress party, which at its meeting late in December adopted and pub-lished an Indian 'declaration of independence', in whose vindica-tion a boycott of the central and provincial governments and a contingent campaign of civil disobedience and non-payment of taxes was proclaimed.

In these inauspicious circumstances the Simon Report appeared in June 1930: a magisterial survey of India's past and present, and recommendations for an enlarged electorate, responsible govern-ment in the provinces and a conference between representatives of the British government, the government of India, and the ruling princes of the native states on the future form of the central government. The misfortune of the Report was to have been overtaken by events. In India the widespread disorders of civil disobedience had broken out. Gandhi had led his march to the sea, to challenge the government's salt monopoly by occupying a salt marsh; in May he had been arrested, as had the two Nehrus, father and son, and other Congress leaders. The government, by mass arrests, tried to control the disorders: in nine months 54,000 persons had been convicted of offences of civil disobedience. That this should happen while Labour was in office in Britain was too much for many of Labour's supporters; two members of parliament, Fenner Brockway and John Beckett, were suspended in July, the one for persisting in questions against the Speaker's ruling, the other for the 'rape of the mace', his seizure of the Commons' mace as a means of terminating the proceedings.

Yet the government at home continued its policy of conciliation. As MacDonald had promised before the Report was issued, in response to a suggestion from Simon, the government called a Round Table Conference in London (the first of three, as it proved) at which British and Indians might discuss India's future government before any decisions were taken. The conference began on November 12, 1930—another of the great gatherings over which MacDonald could preside so well. The weakness of the conference was that its Indian delegates included no members of the Congress party, which had boycotted it; its strength that the Indian princes were represented. From this came its only success: the princes agreed that the states should come into an all-India federation of the future. With this encouragement the government, in January 1931, invited support for further consultations with Indians before a new constitution was framed; and this the Conservatives gave. This, however, exasperated opinion at the other pole. Churchill, in the debate in parliament, denounced the government's policy as premature and dangerous: concessions to nationalism would only increase disorder, and the struggle would go on for 'the complete severance' of every tie between Britain and India, '. . . a frightful prospect to have opened up so wantonly, so recklessly, so incontinently and in so short a time'.[1] It was on this issue that he took the fateful step of resigning from the Conservative shadow cabinet. By the time the second Round Table Conference met, in the autumn of 1931, with the presence of Gandhi to represent the Congress interest, the Labour party was out of office; and Churchill also.

[1] 247 H.C. Deb., 5 s., 702 (January 26, 1931).

6. THE FINANCIAL CRISIS

The government's weakness, and the precarious support it was receiving from the Liberals, made its end seem likely early in 1931. A crisis threatened in February, when the Conservatives moved a vote of censure on the government's wasteful expenditure and borrowing, particularly for the unemployment insurance fund. A Liberal amendment called for the appointment of a special committee to review government expenditures and recommend economies—another Geddes axe, in fact. The amendment was accepted by the government and supported by Snowden, who admitted that the situation was extremely grave—an unpalatable warning to his own party. Following this, he appointed a Committee on National Expenditure, presided over by Sir George May, recently the secretary of the Prudential Assurance Company; of the other six members two represented Labour and the remainder the business community, including the heads of the Hudson's Bay Company and the Cunard Steamship Company, and Lord Plender, the accountant. Until it and the concurrent Royal Commission on Unemployment Insurance reported there was nothing to do but wait. This was underlined by Snowden in his second Budget, introduced later than usual, at the end of April, because of his absence through illness. He balanced a Budget of £803 millions by raids and anticipations reminiscent of Churchill's, and with no increases in taxation except in the petrol tax: but goaded the Conservatives with the inclusion of a tax on land values to be imposed once the necessary valuation was completed. At the time he called the Budget a makeshift; and in his *Autobiography*[1] he explained that he anticipated a second Budget in the autumn, when the report of the May committee might have converted his party and the public to the economies and increases in taxation which the times called for, and when he hoped to carry out a large conversion of maturing War Loan certificates.

By the time that the May committee reported, however, things were getting out of control. Unemployment had touched the mark of 2½ millions in December 1930; for the next three months it was over 2,600,000 though in April and May it was just under that figure. In June 1931 it was 2,707,000, and threatened to be higher next month (as it was by some 100,000). In that month the government had to seek parliament's approval for an increase in the unemployment insurance fund's borrowing powers (it had been

---

[1] P. Snowden, *Autobiography*, II, 900–4.

increased by £30 millions in 1930). The report of the Macmillan committee on Finance and Industry was published on July 13. Though in tone reassuring, its documentation of Britain's plight in the world economy—lack of balance between demand and supply, the decline of international lending, the fall in prices, the decline of British exports—only made present difficulties seem insuperable. André Siegfried's *England's Crisis*, published in the spring and widely read, was also discouraging, as it made much of the high level of costs, wages and taxes in Great Britain as an obstruction to exports.

Yet until late in July any financial crisis seemed to be a matter for the countries of central Europe to worry over; Britain was not apparently affected and could even help the weaker brethren. Thus when the Vienna bank, the Credit Anstalt, failed in May through the depreciation of its holdings (ultimately because Austria's banking facilities were too large for its truncated territory), the Bank of England, in June, made an advance of £4·3 millions to the Austrian National Bank, which was guaranteeing the Credit Anstalt's foreign liabilities. Austria's financial weakness rapidly reacted upon Germany; persons affected by the Austrian failure and those who now became anxious about foreign balances anywhere began to withdraw their short-term credits from Germany. Here politics were closely bound up with economics; the strength of the Nazis since the elections of September 1930, Communist riots in the Ruhr in June, and stern governmental measures in finance imposed by decree all made the investor nervous. The Reichsbank lost 150 million marks in gold and bills of exchange in the first week of June, 540 millions in the second, 150 millions in two days, June 19–20. Collapse was at hand; when a rescue was offered from the United States: President Hoover's proposal for a year's moratorium on all inter-governmental war debts and reparations (June 20). At this point intransigence came to block the path to safety. France's position in international finance was strong; at the same time her need and her moral claim to German reparations—the unconditional annuities of the Young plan—were great, and her suspicion of Germany even greater, particularly because of the proposed Austro-German customs union, secretly negotiated and suddenly announced in March, which foreshadowed a political *anschluss*. She used her strength to exact terms immediately favourable, ultimately fatal to her, since in accelerating Germany's financial collapse they played into the hands of Hitler and the Nazis. The Hoover

Moratorium was not finally accepted by all the powers until July 6; a conference in London on July 20 over Germany's financial crisis produced no positive results; on August 19 a standstill agreement accepted the freezing of Germany's foreign liabilities for six months; and in September the customs union was publicly abandoned.

Long since the damage had been done. Despite new credits from New York and Paris, the Bank of International Settlements and the Bank of England (which further weakened Britain's own position in the near future) the run on German funds continued. In July the German crisis became internal also: the failure of an industrial concern, the Nordwolle (North German Wool Combing Corporation) affected several banks, particularly the Danat (Darmstadter und National) bank. German depositors became alarmed, and a flight from the mark began. Despite efforts by the Reichsbank, the Danat bank closed its doors on July 13, and a two-day holiday of all banks followed. Later in the month there were further failures. In Rumania and Hungary there were similar happenings in this fatal month of July.[1]

Britain's turn must have come sooner or later; but it came sooner, and with large consequences, because of the special circumstances which surrounded it. Just before parliament's adjournment for the summer recess, on July 30, Neville Chamberlain, by prearrangement with Snowden, drew attention to the serious position the country was placed in by the international crisis, her own heavy expenditures, and the resulting lack of confidence in British finance. Snowden's reply admitted that things were serious and hinted at unpleasant economies. The government's sole action was to appoint an Economy Committee of the Cabinet to consider the May report's proposals; the members were MacDonald, Snowden, Henderson, Thomas, Graham, and it was to meet first on August 25.

Next day, a few hours after parliament had risen, the May report was published.[2] Even with Snowden's warning, the public was unprepared for its diagnosis and prescription. A government deficit of £120 millions was estimated by April 1932, and to meet it new taxation totalling £24 millions and economies amounting

[1] G. M. Gathorne-Hardy, *Short History of International Affairs*, pp. 261–3 (an excellent brief account); H. V. Hodson, *Slump and Recovery, 1929–1937* (London, 1938), pp. 64–76 (a much fuller narrative).
[2] Cmd. 3920 (1931). The report commonly called the May report is a majority report. The two Labour members of the committee issued a dissenting report, which was almost completely ignored.

to £96 millions were proposed; of the economies £66½ millions were to be found in reductions in unemployment expenditures, including a 20 per cent reduction in benefit payments. The alarmingly large deficit was chiefly a matter of accounting; for the majority made the extravagant demand that all unemployment expenditures be met out of income and not by further borrowing for the unemployment insurance fund.

The May report brought the centre of the financial crisis at once to England. The headlines it drew in the press were not offset by any official statement of reassurance; and the normal forum for discussion had just closed, the members of parliament having all dispersed for their summer holidays. Foreigners with funds in London, already nervous from the past month's events, at once drew the worst conclusions, that Britain was on the verge of bankruptcy, and heavy withdrawals began. Whether the May report's diagnosis was correct or not (the *Economist* for August 8 stated that it 'rather seriously overpaints the gloom of the immediate budgetary position') the result was the same: the impairment of confidence and a crisis. Here the May report was in contrast with its predecessor, the Geddes axe: it brought down a government; the axe prolonged one.

London's financial crisis had already begun: from July 15 to the end of the month the Bank of England was losing gold at the rate of £2½ millions a day. The raising of the bank rate by two stages from 2½ per cent to 4½ per cent served to confirm suspicions rather than to reassure. On August 1 the Bank announced that it had obtained credits of £25 millions each from the Bank of France and the Federal Reserve Bank of New York; and the fiduciary note issue was raised by £15 millions. Yet after a lull in the first week of August the drain was resumed, and it was clear that in less than a month the new credits would be exhausted. It was this which led the leaders of the Bank of England to give Snowden a warning which he relayed to MacDonald, who had gone as usual to his remote holiday retreat in Lossiemouth. MacDonald's sudden return to London by the night train—he was in London early on August 11—suggested that something was wrong, and marked the beginning of the August 'crisis' which in less than two weeks, by Sunday, the 23rd, had brought the Labour government to an end.

In the days intervening there were meetings between MacDonald, Snowden and the Bank of England's representatives, Sir Ernest Harvey, the deputy governor, and E. R. Peacock, a director

(Montagu Norman was away). The bankers told MacDonald (according to Neville Chamberlain)

> (1) that we were on the edge of the precipice and, unless the situation changed radically, we should be over it directly, (2) that the cause of the trouble was not financial but political, and lay in the complete want of confidence in H.M.G. existing among foreigners, (3) that the remedy was in the hands of the Government alone.[1]

The 'remedy' was a balanced budget to restore foreign confidence and save the pound, and it was over the means of attaining this, and particularly whether a cut in unemployment benefits should be part of the economies, that the Cabinet was divided and resigned, to be replaced by a 'National' government under MacDonald.

These circumstances, amid others which gave the political crisis the smell of conspiracy, gave rise to the later charges of the Labour party that the government had been the victim of a 'bankers' ramp', by which was meant that financial interests had engineered (or were to blame for) the crisis and by the pressure they exerted ensured the actual outcome. The charges need to be separated. There was a financial crisis, and financiers were naturally consulted by the government when it occurred. But the financiers had not caused it except as they had played a part in an international financial system which was collapsing. That they put pressure on the government to economise, and especially to reduce the 'dole', is equally certain;[2] but this was only reiterating the advice of the May committee and that of Treasury officials who had testified before the Royal Commission on Unemployment Insurance that the 'stability of the British financial system is in danger of being undermined'. This was orthodox advice, accepted by an orthodox Chancellor of the Exchequer; to blame the bankers for giving it is to blame them for lacking a belief in economic theories which only became fashionable later.

A more specific charge was that French and American bankers insisted that governmental economies include reductions in unemployment payments as a condition of advancing the new credits to save the pound. The Bank of England officials spoke of the possible need of credits of £80 millions when they saw MacDonald and Snowden in the first days of the August crisis, and after the crisis these credits were actually granted by the Federal Reserve Bank of

---

[1] K. Feiling, *N. Chamberlain*, p. 191.
[2] See reports in *New York Times*, August 30, 1931.

New York and the Bank of France to the British government. The
report that, before the Labour government fell, the French and
Americans had attached these conditions to the new credits
originated with the *Daily Herald* on August 25, and was at once
denied both in London and New York. MacDonald himself, however, repeated the charge, partly as a means of excusing his
actions.[1] In parliament in September 21 he claimed that reductions in unemployment payments could not be reversed because of
'special conditions of the borrowing', though later parliamentary
questions brought firm denials of this, including one from Snowden
himself. The explanation of these conflicting statements lies in
the meaning of words like 'advice' and 'dictation'. Obviously
foreign bankers did not dictate to the British government; no
government would have accepted dictation. The bankers gave
advice about the conditions under which loans would be rapidly
and generously obtainable; and these included a balanced budget
and savings at the expense of the unemployed.[2] In any case, denials
that there had been a 'bankers' ramp' occupied much of the
speeches of government leaders during the election campaign in
October.

A different charge was that the City's inept financial policy,
that of 'lending long and borrowing short', had brought on the
crisis; that if foreign short-term deposits and bills had not been
used to make long-term loans abroad Britain's great financial resources would either have been available at home or could quickly
have been 'mobilised' to save the pound without wrecking the
government. One answer to this charge is that in so far as London
had accepted many short-term foreign balances, this was part of
her traditional function as a money market and reflected foreign
confidence such as the return to the gold standard had been
intended to justify; it was also a deliberate policy to restore world
trade and British prosperity.[3] In this view, London's short and
long-term investments and loans to Germany and other countries
were not, by 1931, unusually large, and the margin by which she
was a short-term debtor not great.[4] But whatever foreign credits
Britain had were either frozen by the preceding crisis in Central
Europe or could be liquidated only at the risk of extending the

[1] L. M. Weir, *Tragedy of Ramsay MacDonald*, pp. 386–95; P. Snowden, *Autobiography*, II, 947; *Daily Herald*, August 27, 1931.
[2] 256 H.C. Deb., 5 s., 282, 1272, 1460, 1645, 2010–13. Cf. W. A. Morton, *British
Finance, 1930–1940* (Madison, 1943), pp. 62–70.
[3] L. Robbins, *The Great Depression* (London, 1934), pp. 89–91; J. B. Condliffe,
The Commerce of Nations (New York, 1950), pp. 504–25.
[4] H. V. Hodson, *Slump and Recovery*, pp. 81–5.

world crisis; hence when foreign balances in London were called there was nothing for it but to try to stop the process by restoring confidence or admit the inability to discharge obligations. This was admitted in September, when the gold standard was abandoned after the budget had been balanced; but to do so in August, under a Labour government which, by the orthodoxy of the time, was in bad financial odour, was unthinkable as long as traditional policies were followed. And traditional policies were insisted on by Snowden; none of whose colleagues had the knowledge or skill to overrule him.[1]

There is another view which makes the bankers of the City of London both more culpable and more heroic. An economist as uncompromising as T. E. Gregory expressed soon after the crisis the suspicion that many British loans to Germany, enticed by high interest rates, had been unsound. Other loans, especially to Germany, were excessively large. The Macmillan report gave cautious support to the view that London's short-term foreign liabilities, much of them in the form of deposits, were dangerously large in relation to assets; on March 31, 1931, the excess of these liabilities over current assets was over £250 millions, though it had been higher in previous years. More than that, the joint-stock banks and acceptance houses had decreased their prewar ratio of capital to circulating acceptances.[2] When for any reason foreign balances and credits were drawn on they turned to the Bank of England to discount the paper they held. The Bank could have refused, and preserved its own resources and the gold standard at the cost of the failure of several of London's financial houses. When it chose the alternative, of sustaining its weaker brethren in London, it was caught by another difficulty arising from recent policy; that instead of large holdings of short-term foreign bills such as it had held in times past it had large quantities of Treasury bills which could not readily be marketed abroad. The Bank itself was frozen. Its instinctive reaction was then to turn to the government to save it by restoring confidence and thus encouraging the foreigner to leave his money in London.[3]

Yet if finance did cause the crisis, it did not determine its outcome. That was shaped by politics and personalities; to which we now turn.

[1] Actually the Bank of England had done a good deal to control investment and to manipulate credit: see L. Robbins, *Great Depression*, p. 85.
[2] Committee on Finance and Industry, *Report*, pp. 42–3, 112, 149.
[3] W. A. Morton, *British Finance*, pp. 30–7, 51–2.

O

7. THE GOVERNMENT PETERS OUT

The political crisis of August 1931 was peculiar for its form and its outcome. Hence the later talk that it had been plotted, with MacDonald as the chief plotter. Three things at the outset support the idea: that the crisis came in August, the 'silly season', when parliament was adjourned, so, that all was done without parliamentary debate and was over before parliament met, to the injury of the constitution; that the publication of the May report seemed curiously timed, to occur just as parliament dispersed; and that the press, by its shading of news and editorials, helped greatly to work up the atmosphere of crisis. These things, however, only explain the form, not the outcome, which might easily have been otherwise; as a chronicle of events will show.

When MacDonald arrived back in London on August 11 there was no obvious sign of a crisis, though the newspapers of the previous week had been conducting an economy campaign (seasoned by the May report) and two, the *Daily Mail* and the *Sunday Times*, had talked of a possible National Government. In London MacDonald met the Bank's representatives and received from them, as we have seen, some plain advice. It was they who proposed that, to strengthen the government's hand, the leaders of the Opposition parties should be consulted. MacDonald agreed, and the first of the meetings between MacDonald and Snowden and the Opposition leaders—meetings of great importance in the development of the crisis—took place on August 13. Indeed, Chamberlain recorded that it was at the invitation of the deputy governor of the Bank that he went to London.[1] At this meeting Neville Chamberlain and Baldwin represented the Conservatives, Baldwin having interrupted his customary journey to Aix-les-Bains to return to London; Sir Herbert Samuel and Sir Donald Maclean represented the Liberals, for by a fateful coincidence Lloyd George was laid up during the crisis, recovering from an operation performed at the end of July. This meeting was rather premature, since the ministers had as yet nothing definite to offer except their intention to secure large economies in government expenditures; but they set the pattern for the future: consultations which compromised the Cabinet's decisions, and which were attended and reported upon by two ministers only, MacDonald and Snowden. By this time MacDonald had also seen Sir Clive Wigram, the King's private secretary. And the Cabinet's Economy

[1] K. Feiling, *N. Chamberlain*, p. 191; cf. Viscount Samuel, *Grooves of Change*, p. 243.

Committee, which had been hurriedly summoned, had had two meetings, and considered a tentative list of economies, totalling £78½ millions, drawn up by the government departments; it was agreed to submit this for the Cabinet's discussion at a meeting called for August 19. On the 13th, therefore, ministers and Opposition leaders dispersed once more for the week-end (and Baldwin for Aix); the committee issuing a statement promising that the government would balance the budget, including unemployment charges, and calling for equality of sacrifice from all for this purpose.

Over the week-end the *Daily Mail* and the *Observer* made more mention of a National Government, though rather by denying its possibility (J. L. Garvin pronouncing 'there is not to be a National Government—not yet'[1]). While the *News Chronicle* (August 13) decried rumour as responsible for 'this latest "crisis"', *The Times* lent its authority to a continuous campaign against the government's extravagance which did much to build up the crisis (and discourage the foreign creditor). In a typical leader on August 12 it declared: 'Every hour which passes without some check upon the flood of national expenditure, and without some decision in national policy . . . delays, by a period which may be disastrous, the return of confidence at home and abroad in this country's will and power to set its financial house in order.' Nor did it improve matters by propagating, by means of denying them, tendentious reports of a Cabinet split (which had not yet begun).

On Monday, August 17, the political drama was resumed by another meeting of the Cabinet's Economy Committee in the evening. On the 19th came a long meeting of the Cabinet, from 11 a.m. to 1 and from 2.15 to 7 (tea being served during the meeting) and again after dinner from 8.15 to 10.25 p.m. At this, economies amounting to £56¼ millions were provisionally agreed on, subject to later discussion of the possibilities of converting part of the national debt and reducing the amount put into the sinking fund, and, according to Snowden, to further discussion of an additional saving of £20 millions in the 'transitional' unemployment payments. As it was, £22 millions of the savings provisionally accepted came from savings in the unemployment insurance scheme, though without reducing the standard rate of payments.

Next day, Thursday, August 20, was devoted to meetings outside the Cabinet. MacDonald and Snowden, with the Cabinet's consent, met the Opposition leaders (Chamberlain, Sir Samuel

[1] *Observer*, August 16, 1931.

Hoare, Samuel, Maclean) to tell them the results of the Cabinet's meeting;[1] but, curiously, the figure which they mentioned for proposed economies was £78 millions (the figure which the Cabinet Economy Committee had discussed) and not the £56 millions provisionally accepted the previous evening. Moreover, Snowden for the first time gave the Opposition leaders an alarmist figure for the anticipated deficit: £170 millions, £50 millions higher than the May committee's estimate. The Opposition leaders accepted the economies of £78 millions as a bold and courageous scheme, and adjourned to prepare detailed proposals for a later meeting.

That afternoon, the Cabinet Economy Committee met a joint gathering of the National Executive of the Labour party and the General Council of the T.U.C. This meeting, proposed by Henderson, was a natural corollary to the meetings with the Opposition leaders at a time when parliament was not in session. Economies were discussed, and an assurance given by Snowden that no reduction in unemployment allowances was proposed. Later there was controversy over this statement: what the T.U.C. took as a positive assurance implied, according to Snowdon, only that no decision had yet been reached. The General Council followed this with a four-hour meeting, as a result of which Walter Citrine and Ernest Bevin were sent to represent to the Cabinet the Council's objections to many of the proposed economies; they saw MacDonald and Snowden at 9.30 p.m., just after a Cabinet meeting, and became convinced that the ministers' minds were made up to accept, at the dictation of outside forces, proposals which the T.U.C. would find intolerable. These meetings later received great prominence, being the basis for Conservative charges that the T.U.C. had 'dictated' to the government (the obverse of Labour charges of dictation by the bankers).

On Friday the 21st, there was another long Cabinet meeting. Agreement on economies to be proposed to parliament was reached, the crisis was apparently over, and the members dispersed to their week-end retreats. The economies, however, still amounted to only £56 millions. MacDonald and Snowden made their report to the Opposition leaders at five that afternoon; and the apple cart was upset again. For now they admitted that the Cabinet had modified its previous plans and accepted economies of £56 millions—actually, the only figure ever accepted by the

[1] Hoare states that Thomas was present also: Lord Templewood, *Nine Troubled Years* (London, 1954), p. 17.

Cabinet—instead of the £78 millions; and the Opposition leaders, who had come (by the testimony of Chamberlain and Samuel) to propose larger economies, especially over unemployment payments, were naturally indignant at the apparent diminution, the more so as it provided under half the savings on unemployment charges which the economies of £78 millions had included. The meeting adjourned. The Liberals consulted Lord Reading and Lloyd George, presumably by telephone, and they and the Conservatives returned to MacDonald late that evening, and told him that the economies were quite inadequate, and unlikely to be accepted by parliament or to restore confidence. Chamberlain told MacDonald that, in such circumstances, the financial crash would come before parliament met, and it was therefore his duty to avoid it; for which purpose the Conservatives (and Samuel endorsed this for the Liberals) would give him all their support in the present government or in a 'reconstructed' government. MacDonald spoke of his difficulties with characteristic self-pity, but said he would not resign, but go on with those of his colleagues who would follow him.[1]

Hence another Cabinet meeting on Saturday, the 22nd, for which the members were mustered by phone and wire and even with the help of the police, to try to agree on additional economies which would win Opposition support. These, so MacDonald and Snowden told their colleagues, must amount to £25–30 millions, the bulk of them to be found out of unemployment charges, if the Opposition was to be satisfied. From this came later charges of an ultimatum delivered by the Opposition leaders. Both Chamberlain and Samuel denied this in parliament; and clearly they had not so much demanded specific economies in unemployment charges or anything else as given their opinion of the need for greater reductions, particularly in unemployment expenditures.

By now the crisis had been worked up to the highest pitch (though had the apparent settlement on Friday endured it would have subsided at once). The newspapers reported that Baldwin, after telephonic communication with friends in London, was returning post haste from Aix; and more significantly that the King was interrupting his stay at Balmoral (to which he had only just travelled, arriving on Friday) and would be back in London on Sunday morning (the 23rd). Rumours of splits in the Cabinet and of resignations were reported. 'Cut the talk and get on with it', was the *Daily Mail*'s advice on the 22nd. This was mild, however,

---

[1] K. Feiling, *N. Chamberlain*, pp. 191–3; P. Snowden, *Autobiography*, II, 938–40; Samuel in parliament, September 14, 1931, 256 H.C. Deb., 5 s., 546 ff.

in comparison with the bolts of the old thunderer, *The Times*. On the 20th it had given the Cabinet the choice of 'the path of courage or the path of cowardice'; next day its leader was headed 'A Matter of Hours'; next day 'Another Day Gone' headlined talk of a race against time. On August 24, when the battle was actually over, the leader, with icy patience, was entitled 'Still Waiting', and gave, with a twisted kind of loyalty, the information that the Bank of England's credits of £50 millions were almost exhausted. It was in an atmosphere of tension, hardly conducive to clear thought and sober action, that the Cabinet met on the climactic days, Saturday and Sunday, August 22–23:

> headlines, crowds, police, hectic movements, day and night meetings, the door of Downing Street loosened on its hinges by the constant passage of leading figures of all three parties as they hurried by the ever-present battery of photographers

as a contemporary described it.[1]

It is not surprising that at the Cabinet meeting on Saturday morning, August 22, signs of a split appeared. The members had done their work, as they thought, and gone home. Now they had been brought back again and were told that they must find further economies, including a reduction in unemployment payments. The terms of their discussions seemed to have been changed completely; and while they twisted and turned to find other economies and expedients (suspension of the sinking fund, re-examination of the gold standard, higher taxation of the wealthy, a revenue tariff—all, though later adopted, ruled out at once, and particularly the last, by the flinty Chancellor of the Exchequer) they were always brought back by MacDonald and Snowden to the point that only reductions in unemployment payments would satisfy the Opposition and resolve the crisis; yet this would at the same time betray the hopes of the party's supporters and probably split the party itself. Hence Henderson, who had hitherto left the fighting to others, notably Lansbury, Greenwood and Johnston, now led in opposing these proposals, perhaps influenced in part by the vehemence of Bevin and his colleagues on the General Council of the T.U.C. The meeting did, however, authorise MacDonald and Snowden to submit to the Opposition hypothetical economies of £68½ millions, including £12¼ millions saved by a 10 per cent reduction in unemployment allowances. This was done at a meeting at 12.30 p.m. that day; and to such economies the

---

[1] Lord Ponsonby, 'The National Government', *Contemporary Review*, 140 (1931): 417–18.

Opposition leaders gave a grudging support, confirmed by representatives of the Bank of England, who stated that with these economies new credits would doubtless be granted in New York. The Cabinet met briefly that afternoon, and then adjourned to meet again on Sunday.

MacDonald saw the King at Buckingham Palace at ten o'clock on Sunday morning (August 23). He explained the need for further credits from New York, and said that he was waiting for a reply to the question whether economies (and again the rejected figure of £78 millions appeared) which included a 10 per cent cut in unemployment payments would be sufficient to restore confidence and induce the flow of credit. He warned, however, that some of the ministers, and especially Henderson and Graham, would not accept such economies, and that their resignations would necessitate the resignation of the entire government. On hearing this, the King decided to consult the leaders of the Opposition parties, Baldwin and Samuel.[1]

At noon the King saw Sir Herbert Samuel at the Palace (Baldwin for the moment could not be found). Samuel strongly advised that MacDonald should be persuaded to stay on as head of the existing government or some 'reconstituted' Labour Cabinet or, failing these alternatives, of a National government made up of members of the three parties; the necessary but unpalatable economies affecting the working class could best be imposed by a Labour government. Baldwin, when the King saw him at three that afternoon, declared his readiness to serve the country, either in a National government under MacDonald or in a Conservative government with Liberal support.[2]

The critical meeting of the Cabinet was held at seven that evening (Sunday, August 23). No word had yet come, however, from New York in reply to a query from the Bank of England to J. P. Morgan and Company, the bankers, about the possibility of raising a loan to tide over the Bank's difficulties—now, of course, transformed into the government's difficulties. So the meeting adjourned, and for an hour or more the ministers strolled in the garden of No. 10 Downing Street in the cool of the evening. At 8.45 a telephone message came from the Bank, followed by Sir Ernest Harvey, bearing the telegram from New York. MacDonald read it to the members of the Cabinet; Sir

---

[1] H. Nicolson, *George V*, pp. 460–1.

[2] Ibid., pp. 461–2; Lord Samuel, *Grooves of Change*, p. 246. L. S. Amery states that Baldwin's decision rested partly on his determination to exclude Lloyd George —and Churchill—from office: *My Political Life*, II, 240.

Ernest, waiting outside, thought that 'pandemonium had broken loose'. The telegram stated that the prospects of a loan subscribed to by the American public would not be good unless parliament should already have enacted economy legislation; and it asked whether the Cabinet's present proposals had the sincere approval of the Bank of England and the City as likely to be sufficient to restore confidence.[1]

MacDonald appealed to his colleagues to accept the larger economies, including the 10 per cent cut in unemployment payments. The alternative, if any senior ministers wished to resign, was the resignation of the whole Cabinet.[2] The figure involved was a paltry £12¼ millions. Yet it involved a principle which many could not accept: regardless of the sacrifices demanded of the rest of the community, it seemed to ask too much of the poorest of the poor. There was complete deadlock. Eleven ministers were ready to support the reduction in unemployment payments; ten were not. The eleven were MacDonald, Snowden, Thomas, Webb, Sankey, Lord Amulree, Tom Shaw, Wedgwood Benn, Parmoor, Margaret Bondfield, Herbert Morrison; but the ten included men who could not be ignored: Henderson, Clynes, Graham, Alexander, Greenwood, Johnston, Addison, Adamson, Lansbury, Lees-Smith.[3]

During these discussions MacDonald had nothing to contribute. He sat back, absent-mindedly doodling on a blotter, waiting wearily for the end.[4] 'When this final disagreement occurred,' wrote Snowden, 'it was evident that the Prime Minister had anticipated such a development and had made his plans to deal with it.'[5] He asked the members of the Cabinet to place their resignations in his hands, which they did. He then left at 10.10 p.m., to see the King, saying that he would advise him to summon Baldwin and Samuel to a meeting next day of all four (the King, MacDonald, Baldwin, Samuel). After a brief audience with the King[6] he was back in the Cabinet room, and told his colleagues that the meeting would take place at ten next morning. The Cabinet then dispersed, expecting that next day another government, presumably a Conservative-Liberal coalition, would be formed. Following this, Baldwin, Samuel, and Chamberlain arrived at No. 10 Downing Street, entering by the garden

---

[1] H. Nicolson, *George V*, pp. 462–3.   [2] Ibid., p. 463.
[3] I have constructed this list from *The Times*, August 25, 1931, and Hugh Dalton, *Memoirs*, p. 271. The authority for the inclusion of Lees-Smith among the ten is Harold Laski: Kingsley Martin, *Harold Laski* (London, 1953), p. 81.
[4] L. M. Weir, *Tragedy of Ramsay MacDonald*, p. 382.
[5] P. Snowden, *Autobiography*, II, 950.   [6] H. Nicolson, *George V*, p. 464.

entrance and so escaping recognition by the large crowd which remained in Downing Street until midnight.[1]

On Monday, August 24, after the meeting with the King in the morning, MacDonald met his Cabinet once more, at noon. He told it, to its utter stupefaction, that though it was out, he was in; that he had agreed to head a National government composed of individuals rather than parties, as a temporary expedient for the sole purpose of settling the financial crisis; Baldwin and Samuel were prepared to join.[2] By this time an official announcement had been made that the formation of a National government was under consideration. MacDonald formally tendered the Labour Cabinet's resignation to the King at 4.10 that afternoon. The establishment of the National government, with MacDonald as Prime Minister, was announced at 9.15 that evening. The other members of the small Cabinet were Baldwin (Lord President), Neville Chamberlain, Samuel, Lord Reading,[3] Hoare, Cunliffe-Lister (four Conservatives, two Liberals), and three Labour men, Snowden, Thomas, Lord Sankey.[4]

8. THE NATIONAL GOVERNMENT: WHOSE CHILD?

The dramatic ending of the August crisis set going a controversy about its inner causes, and diverted attention from one of the main

[1] For details of this meeting, see below, p. 398.

[2] Nicolson's account (*George V*, p. 467) states that each member in turn, round the cabinet table, refused to join the National government (except Thomas, Sankey and Snowden). Snowden's account (*Autobiography*, II, 954) states that MacDonald asked the three of them to stay behind at the end of the meeting and then invited them to join the new government. Henderson told Dalton that morning, before the cabinet meeting, that MacDonald was determined to have a National government, with himself as prime minister (*Memoirs*, p. 271).

[3] Rufus Isaacs, first Marquess of Reading (1860–1935); barrister; M.P. (Lib.), 1904–13; solicitor-general, 1910, attorney-general, 1911–13; lord chief justice, 1913–21; ambassador to U.S., 1918–19; viceroy of India, 1921–26; foreign secretary, 1931.

[4] This account of the crisis rests on that given in my article, 'The Fall of the Labour Government in Great Britain, August, 1931', *Huntington Library Quarterly*, VII (1944), 353–86, where full references will be found. The principal source is Snowden's account in his *Autobiography*, II, 929 ff., supplemented by the newspapers for the month. There is a careful account, containing much new information, in Harold Nicolson, *George V*, pp. 453–69; and some useful sidelights in Hugh Dalton, *Memoirs*, pp. 266–88. R. Postgate, *George Lansbury*, pp. 268–71 adds little (see the curious tale of the commandeering of Lansbury's papers from Postgate by the government in 1944: pp. vii–viii). Keith Feiling's *Neville Chamberlain*, pp. 189–93, gives valuable information. Much detail came out at the time in the form of revelations of cabinet discussions in speeches made by ministers and ex-ministers in parliament in September, 1931 (256 H.C. Deb., 5 s.). Of other references the chief are an article by Sidney Webb: 'What happened in 1931', *Political Quarterly*, III (1932), 1–17 (republished by the Fabian Society as Fabian Tract No. 237 [1932]); M. A. Hamilton, *Arthur Henderson*, pp. 371 ff.; and L. Macneill Weir, *Tragedy of Ramsay MacDonald*, a bitter attack on MacDonald by his parliamentary private secretary, who was out of London during the crisis but seems to have obtained some inside information.

O*

facts about it. This was that in the crisis the Labour Cabinet had been found wanting. Its failure was not, as was relentlessly charged by Conservative and other apologists for the National government, that it had 'run away' from the crisis by refusing to accept unpleasant economies; it was ready enough to economise, though not necessarily according to someone else's pattern. Its failure lay months back in timid measures to deal with unemployment and a weakening trade balance, and in ignorance of the workings of finance. For this some of the blame lay on its leaders, MacDonald and Snowden; but much on the other ministers who in the past had offered no alternative proposals, and in the crisis accepted the pronouncements of MacDonald and Snowden, and resigned rather than insist on different measures.

Yet this does not absolve MacDonald for much of the responsibility for the failure, though to the public at large his translation to National leadership wiped off all old scores in the instant. Who makes a government, its leader or its followers? MacDonald, as leader, was doubly responsible for the fate of his government. Before the crisis he moulded it; at the crisis he determined it. He was not open in consulting with his colleagues; on the contrary, he seems to have avoided all of them save Snowden during the crisis. Instead, he compromised them by his meetings with the Opposition leaders, and by the misleading reports of Cabinet discussions which he gave them. He then delivered an ultimatum to the members of the Cabinet, for which he and not the Opposition leaders was responsible, and offered them no alternative but resignations which he seemed only too ready to accept. And if they had not agreed to resign, he could have brought about the same result, and was clearly ready to do so, by his own resignation. A Prime Minister's right to resign is absolute, and involves (save when it occurs through illness on his part) the fall of his government.

It was at this stage that the resolution of the 'crisis' departed from the normal pattern. MacDonald advised the King to consult the Opposition leaders in company with him; and when this was done agreed to form a National government in association with them. A Conservative government or a Conservative-Liberal coalition would have been a more conventional sequel. When MacDonald, Baldwin and Samuel met the King at Buckingham Palace at 10 o'clock on Monday morning, August 24, the King, in reply to MacDonald's statement that he had the resignation of his Cabinet in his pocket, 'trusted there was no question of the

Prime Minister's resignation: the leaders of the three parties must get together and come to some arrangement'.[1] He told them of his hopes for a National government, and urged MacDonald to stay at his post in the crisis. Baldwin and Samuel said they were willing to serve under MacDonald; and after consultation among the three for over an hour an agreement to form a National government was reached.[2]

In this the King's intervention was both constitutional and decisive. Constitutional because in a crisis he must get the best advice he can (usually from the various party leaders), and must commission the strongest government obtainable in the minimum time.[3] Decisive because without the King's appeal MacDonald, whatever day-dreams of a National government he may have had in the past, would never have been persuaded to try to form a coalition; and, even more important, he could not have suggested that the Opposition leaders serve under him, whereas the King could and did. The King's experience, going back to the constitutional crises in the first years of his reign, before the war, predisposed him in favour of such a solution; indeed, 'the royal belief in coalitions is almost a family inheritance'.[4]

MacDonald's intentions before the final decision on August 24 are much more difficult to disentangle. The theory of a deep-laid plot on his part began with Sidney Webb's article on the crisis in the *Political Quarterly* for January 1932, was greatly strengthened when Snowden's *Autobiography* appeared in 1934, and was given definite form in L. Macneill Weir's *Tragedy of Ramsay Mac-Donald* in 1938. Snowden, who claimed to have had no inkling of MacDonald's intentions until MacDonald asked him to join the National government after the meeting of the Labour Cabinet at noon on Monday, the 24th (though often suspicious of Mac-Donald's consultations with the other parties in the months before), gave it as his opinion that MacDonald had 'deliberately planned the scheme'; so did Sidney Webb.[5] And, apart from the fact that so complete a change of face on MacDonald's part, such a betrayal in Labour's eyes, naturally inspired the belief in the Labour party

[1] H. Nicolson, *George V*, p. 465 (memorandum of Sir Clive Wigram, who had become the King's private secretary on Lord Stamfordham's death on March 31, 1931).

[2] Ibid., pp. 465-7; John Gore, *King George V* (London, 1941), pp. 406-9.

[3] W. Ivor Jennings, *Cabinet Government* (Cambridge, 1936), pp. 36-40. Herbert Morrison, *Government and Parliament* (Oxford, 1954), pp. 79-80, criticises the King's wisdom in preferring the controversial National government to a Conservative-Liberal Coalition.

[4] W. Ivor Jennings, *Cabinet Government*, p. 66.

[5] P. Snowden, *Autobiography*, II, 954; S. Webb, *loc. cit.*, p. 9.

that it must have been planned long in advance, there were MacDonald's actions immediately after the crisis. He showed, according to Snowden, no regret over the end of the Labour government, and much enthusiasm over the new one. When Snowden, on the day after the National government was formed, remarked that he would now find himself popular in strange quarters, he replied, 'gleefully rubbing his hands: "Yes, to-morrow every Duchess in London will be wanting to kiss me"!'[1] On the other hand, he showed some sympathy with the feelings of his former colleagues when he held a farewell meeting with the junior ministers of the Labour government on the afternoon of Monday, August 24. He spoke of the seriousness of the crisis as the justification for forming the National government, but did not ask his hearers to join him in it. They were most of them young men and must think of their careers; he was committing political suicide. Yet he hoped that some of them would follow him.[2] He refused to attend meetings of the National Executive of the Labour party on the 26th and of the Parliamentary Labour Party on the 28th: 'Do you think I am going there to be shot at by those fellows?'[3]

More suggestive was the long history of the idea of a National government; the talk of it in the press in August was only the upper part of the iceberg, which was much larger underneath. J. L. Garvin had pressed the idea in two editorials in the *Observer* on January 25 and February 22, 1931. Low, the cartoonist, and no friend of the Tories, published a cartoon in December 1930, showing MacDonald at the head of the Cabinet table, at which Baldwin was also sitting; this new year's prophecy was entitled 'The unemployment question having produced a crisis, Mr. MacDonald forms a "National Government".' Rumours of a National government were rife in the spring and summer. J. H. Thomas (though later disclaiming foreknowledge) was said to have boasted that he would be in a National government when it was formed, and to have put the date in September.[4]

Behind the journalists' smoke-screen were a few facts. There was MacDonald's 'council of state' speech in 1929, and his mention at that time of a government lasting two years. There were meetings between MacDonald and Baldwin as early as

---

[1] P. Snowden, *Autobiography*, II, 957.
[2] Hugh Dalton, *Memoirs*, p. 272; H. Nicolson, *George V*, p. 467.
[3] L. M. Weir, *Tragedy of Ramsay MacDonald*, pp. 386–8, 392–3.
[4] J. H. Thomas, *My Story*, pp. 192–6; L. M. Weir, *Tragedy of Ramsay MacDonald*, pp. 121 (Low's cartoon), 294–316, 420; S. Webb, *loc. cit.*, pp. 3–4.

November 1930, when the leaders were in growing difficulties with their own followers; after one of these MacDonald told Mrs. Hamilton that Baldwin had suggested that they should get together to solve their common difficulties, and asked her to sound out people in the party. Neville Chamberlain recorded in July 1931, that MacDonald had talked to some Conservatives of a National government, but added that he and Baldwin had agreed that the party 'would not stand it for a moment'; two weeks later, however, he admitted the possibility in a financial crisis (July 24).[1] There was also the testimony of Sidney Webb. He wrote to MacDonald in June, stating that he wished to retire; MacDonald asked him to stay on a little longer, since he was planning to reconstruct the government, 'and I may soon take a decision that will surprise you'.[2] Yet all this does not prove that there was a plot; it proves only that a National government of some sort had been discussed in high political circles for some time, and that MacDonald expected some crisis. With the chronic weakness of the Labour government's majority, speculation about its future was not unnatural.

MacDonald's affinity for a National government is equally clear from any study of his character, inward and contradictory as it often seemed. A moderate in his views, only turning to the I.L.P. in his early days when rebuffed by the Liberals, a man whose lowly birth only made his ambition greater, his pride more defensive, a man of solitary spirit after his wife's death, with no close friends but many acquaintances, a cultivated man, lover of the society of people of taste and charm and breeding, a jealous man,[3] despising colleagues of narrower views, a natural autocrat, better in office than in opposition, he had become more and more withdrawn from his Labour colleagues in his second government, seldom or never meeting them socially[4] and retreating more frequently to Chequers. He may well, as Nicolson suggests, have resented what he felt to be the 'dictation' of the T.U.C. during the crisis.[5] He found it easier to talk with the Opposition leaders. And in a crisis his temper demanded a clear decision. He must have

[1] K. Feiling, *N. Chamberlain*, p. 189; H. Dalton, *Memoirs*, pp. 285–7.
[2] M. A. Hamilton, *A. Henderson*, p. 394.
[3] For his jealous criticism of Henderson, see H. Dalton, *Memoirs*, pp. 225–8; H. Nicolson, *George V*, pp. 440–3 (over Egyptian negotiations); M. A. Hamilton, *Arthur Henderson*, pp. 326–8.
[4] H. Dalton, *Memoirs*, pp. 179–80, gives examples. When MacDonald went to No. 10 Downing Street in 1924 he kept the door communicating with No. 11 permanently locked.
[5] H. Nicolson, *George V*, p. 458.

his way or go out; he must have all or nothing. This was 1924 over again, except that the circumstances were more dramatic. Hence he was certainly ready to present the Cabinet with an ultimatum, and if it was rejected to resign.[1]

Resign? Or only step out to return in triumph as head of another government, far more popular with press and society, made up of men of birth and manners, his bitter enemies the day before, it was true, but now his friends, and much more so than his wooden, bourgeois Labour brethren? Should he not put country before party? He certainly liked to be Prime Minister. Now he could continue in office, and save the country to boot. What a triumph for the Lossiemouth outcast of sixty years before! Such thoughts must have been in his mind on the night of August 23; and reinforcing them were the flattering appeals to his patriotism, his pride, his indispensability, by the King, by Chamberlain and Baldwin, by Samuel.[2] His decision then, at the height of the crisis, is not hard to understand. That he had decided upon it earlier, as opposed to being vaguely predisposed towards it, cannot be proved.

And for two reasons. First, supposing one can start a crisis (and MacDonald had not started this one), one cannot be sure how it will develop. Things might so easily have gone otherwise in August, and ended simply in Labour's fall (before or after parliament met) and a Conservative-Liberal coalition. Not that MacDonald would have regretted that much: better out than in under restraint, though in opposition he would still be chained to the Labour party. Second, and more important, there seems to have been no anticipation of the solution actually followed, on the part of the Conservatives, until Sunday, August 23. On August 16, Neville Chamberlain recorded that to get the relief from the financial crisis through economies (such as the first meeting between MacDonald and the Opposition leaders seemed to promise), 'and to do it through a Socialist government', was so important 'that we must give it our support'. On Friday evening, August 21, MacDonald was telling the Opposition leaders he would not resign. Two nights later, at the meeting at No. 10 Downing Street at 11 o'clock (after the Cabinet had agreed to resign and had dispersed) he told them that he would help them to put through the proposals his Cabinet had split over, 'though

---

[1] See my article, *Huntington Library Quarterly*, VII, 383–5, and M. A. Hamilton, *Remembering My Good Friends*, pp. 120–30.
[2] Hoare stresses MacDonald's reluctance—and Baldwin's—to form a National government: Templewood, op. cit., pp. 18, 21.

it meant his death warrant', but that 'it would be no use for him to join a government' since it would only bring odium on it. It was then that Chamberlain intervened, urging that though he lacked votes in the House he 'might command much support in the country'.

> And would not a government including members of all parties. hold a much stronger position? . . . Finally I asked him if he had considered the effect on foreign opinion.[1]

MacDonald made no answer at that time. Chamberlain a few days later said (according to Snowden) that he went to bed expecting that Baldwin would be called on to form a government next day.[2]

Next morning MacDonald had been persuaded. Who was responsible? MacDonald and the King. They and to a less extent Baldwin, Chamberlain and Samuel were the makers of the National government. There is no proof that MacDonald, or any of the others, had planned it so beforehand. But they were perhaps not very surprised at the outcome.

9. THE CONSEQUENCES

The crisis was over. Fond illusion: it had just begun. The financial crisis was not solved. Within a month, and in spite of the National government and a balanced budget, Britain was forced off the gold standard; the pound was saved, but not in the way intended. The consequences of the political crisis, or rather of its solution in the National government, were more long-lasting. First, the crisis transformed the balance of parties, weakening though not really splitting Labour, sapping the Liberals of their partly-recovered influence, and strengthening the Conservatives, to whom, as the self-proclaimed true-blue party, the National label was both a natural addition and a convenient mask. The August crisis alone might not have worked this transformation; but when the National government decided to call a general election in October to confirm its existence, the transformation was complete. Labour was routed, independent Liberalism almost blotted out, the National government, which meant Conservative policies and, in the main, Conservative members, was triumphant. From this came a second result: the change in economic policy from free trade to a protective tariff. The importance of this can be exaggerated, in view of the restrictionist character of the

[1] K. Feiling, *N. Chamberlain*, p. 193.   [2] P. Snowden, *Autobiography*, II, 952.

economy in the twenties; but it seemed almost a revolution, and one which the Conservatives had hitherto quite failed to accomplish single-handed.

Some would deduce consequences more remote. To the extent that the events of August 1931 shaped the form of British government and British policy for the next nine years they did constitute the great turning point in the twenty years between the two world wars. The years ahead were dominated by two things: depression and military aggression. Both, but particularly the latter, were not opposed with strength by the British governments of the thirties. Partly this was because depression breeds not strength but weakness, retreat. Perhaps, however, a government with a smaller majority and a stronger opposition would have followed firmer policies. Taking advantage of the financial preoccupations of the Western powers in September 1931, Japan chose the moment to stage the Mukden incident and begin the conquest of Manchuria, the first open breach of the League system of collective security and the first challenge to the Kellogg pact. Hitler's advance to power and the aggressions of the Nazis in Germany and Mussolini's Fascists in Italy were not far behind. Obviously the crisis of August 1931, caused none of these things. The times were out of joint. Britain's circumstances perhaps made them worse. Or so it seemed to critics who noticed that the new government included most of the old familiar faces, but lacked the country's two masters of decision, Winston Churchill and Lloyd George. 'It was no "National" government. It was simply a get-together on the part of the Boys of the Old Brigade, who climbed on to the bandwagon and sat there, rain or shine, until they had brought the British Empire to the verge of destruction.'[1]

The immediate consequences to the parties deserve a word more. Nine more years of Conservative rule was one. The Labour party's weakness was another. The party held together under Henderson's leadership, opposed the National government and expelled those who had joined it. Its weakness was not apparent until the elections of October 1931. Thereafter it was clear; it had lost in numbers (though the decline in voters was far less than the decline in its representation in parliament), but much more it had lost its soul. MacDonald and Snowden had taken away the remains of its evangelical fervour, of its old faith in itself. Yet very few left its ranks. In August 1931, besides the four in the new

---

[1] R. Boothby, *I Fight to Live*, p. 93. Cf L. S. Amery, *My Political Life*, III, 55–7.

Cabinet, only one other ex-cabinet minister (Lord Amulree),[1] two non-cabinet ministers, and eight other members of parliament (including MacDonald's son, Malcolm)[2] supported the National government; fifteen in all. The smallness of the number surprised and embarrassed MacDonald. Yet he appealed to few to stay with him. He invited Shinwell to stay on as Mines Secretary and was angrily refused; he invited Sir Stafford Cripps,[3] Lord Parmoor's son and the new Solicitor-General, but Cripps, after returning to England from a sanatorium in Germany, refused. Of the three Cabinet members who followed MacDonald, Lord Sankey, though greatly respected, was not as Lord Chancellor a close party man. J. H. Thomas, on the other hand, was a life-long trade unionist, a Labour member since 1910, and one of the party's chief figures. His decision was not an easy one: though he, like MacDonald, enjoyed office, liked wearing a dress shirt, and was by temper a moderate, his working-class ties were real; he regretted the parting with friends of half a century and the loss of his position as general secretary of the National Union of Railwaymen (and the pension to which it had entitled him). For Snowden there were few personal ties to snap; his part in the crisis and his financial orthodoxy easily persuaded him to stay on and give the country the balanced budget he had hoped for, though of sympathy and respect for MacDonald he had not a shred.

As in every crisis since 1910 it was the Liberals who suffered most. Had Lloyd George not been ill he would have had to have a place in the National government and he might, as his biographer suggests, have insisted that it be a genuinely national government, including the bulk of the Labour party, with the alternative a purely Conservative Cabinet. However, he sent MacDonald his good wishes, and allowed his son Gwilym to take minor office. And the Liberals (like the Conservatives) approved what had been done at a party meeting on August 28.

[1] William W. Amulree (1860–1942), graduate of Edinburgh University, barrister, president of the Industrial Court, 1919–25, chairman of numerous arbitration and wages committees and royal commissions (licensing, London motor coaches, Newfoundland); Air Secretary, 1930–31; created baron, 1929.

[2] Malcolm MacDonald, born 1901; M.P., 1929–35, 1936–45; secretary of state for Dominions, 1935–38, Colonies, 1935 and 1938–40; Minister of Health, 1940–41; High Commissioner in Canada, 1941–46; governor-general of Malaya, 1946–48; Commissioner-general for U.K. in S.E. Asia since 1948.

[3] Richard Stafford Cripps (1889–1952), barrister, M.P., 1931–50, solicitor-general, 1930–31, ambassador to Russia, 1940–42, mission to India, 1942, lord privy seal, 1942, minister of aircraft production, 1942–45, president of the Board of Trade, 1945–47, minister for economic affairs, 1947, chancellor of the exchequer, 1947–50.

10. OFF GOLD ANYWAY

On September 8 parliament met to ratify what had been done in its absence. MacDonald asked for a vote of confidence, and received it by 311 votes to 251 in the Commons. Henderson, now leading the Opposition, sorrowfully admitted what MacDonald's speech had coldly ignored and what many Labour men now denied, that the loss of three or four colleagues who had been in the forefront of Labour's battles, and especially of two who had helped in building up the movement from its early days, was a 'direct loss to the Labour movement'. He argued that the crisis could have been overcome in other ways, without depressing further the low standard of the unemployed; and he denied that a government could be 'national' which was opposed by the largest party in the House.

Snowden's Budget followed on September 10. He now estimated a deficit of £74 millions in the current year and £170 millions in the next full year, partly explained by the insistence that all borrowing for the Unemployment and Road funds must cease. To meet the deficit, the appropriation for the sinking fund was reduced from £50 millions to £32½ millions (an economy which the Labour Cabinet had not been allowed to touch), direct taxes were increased by £51½ millions in a full year (income tax raised from 4s. 6d. to 5s. in the £, exemptions and children's allowances reduced, surtax increased), and indirect taxes (mainly on beer, tobacco, petrol) were raised by £24 millions. The balance was to come from economies, which were the subject of a separate bill: reductions in the salaries of ministers, judges, members of parliament and teachers, and in the pay of the police and the armed services, and in the allowances of the unemployed, which averaged 10 per cent. Teachers were, however, to lose 15 per cent of their salaries; and unemployment charges were to be reduced not only by the 10 per cent cut in benefit rates (Labour's sticking-point), but by increased contributions, the limiting of the benefit period to 26 weeks per year, and by a needs test for 'transitional' payments. Thus would £22 millions be saved in the current year (by all the economies), and £70 millions in a full year. The fact that these economies were only £14 millions more than the savings of £56 millions tentatively accepted by the Labour Cabinet became a two-edged argument: of the National government's moderation or of the lack of any justification for its existence at all: it led also to the 'revelations' of Cabinet discussions by present and past members, to the benefit of historians later. At any rate the budget was balanced, and Snowden a hero in circles where he had usually been anathema. Nor was he slow to accept his new role as the nation's saviour; as if to prove that water could come from a stone, the 'iron Chancellor' ended his budget speech with poetry, reciting lines from Swinburne:

> All our past proclaims our future:
>   Shakespeare's voice and Nelson's hand,
> Milton's faith and Wordsworth's trust in
>   this our chosen and chainless land,
> Bear us witness: come the world against her,
>   England yet shall stand.

Yet all in vain, in one sense. Before budget and economy bill were even passed, the country had abandoned the gold standard which the National government had been formed to save; and without disaster ensuing. On August 28, after the National government's birth, credits amounting to £80 millions had been granted in New York and Paris, though not to the Bank of England but to the British government. Yet the drain on the Bank's gold reserves and foreign currency continued, partly as German finances continued unstable, with effects which began to appear in the Netherlands, partly through uneasiness caused by Conservative efforts to work up an early general election. Then, in the week of September 14, came the news of a mutiny in part of the British navy stationed at Invergordon, in Scotland (whether really a mutiny or not mattered little; any news that the British navy, of all things, was faltering was enough to make the nervous foreigner decide that Britain was really near its last gasp). The drain on funds became an avalanche: £5 millions in gold withdrawn on the 16th, £10 millions on the 17th, £18 millions on Friday the 18th. The credits of £80 millions were almost exhausted. Over £200 millions had been withdrawn from London since mid-July; the Bank's gold holdings were down to £130 millions. The Bank of England, previously so tenacious of the gold standard (and Montagu Norman's immovable testimony of its supreme importance had been confirmed more moderately by the Macmillan committee as recently as July), suddenly swallowed its scruples and on the 19th advised the government to suspend the Bank's obligation, under the Act of 1925, to sell gold at a fixed price. A half-hearted attempt was made to raise new credits from France and the United States—gold-standard countries presumably not indifferent to the standard's fate—but nothing came of them. With singularly little demur the government accepted the advice; by a bill rushed through parliament on September 21 Britain went off the gold standard. At the same time the bank rate was raised from 4·5 per cent to 6 per cent.[1]

Hardly a leaf stirred. The pound fell from around $4.86 to $3.80, then fluctuated between $3.90 and a low point of $3.23 on December 1 before settling at around $3.40 by the end of the year. There was no disaster, at least immediately, for reasons which we shall explore later. There was little public alarm in England, and none among the economists; but foreign opinion was shocked. The strangest event of a year of surprises was perhaps this; that a revolution, or what would a month before have been thought one, took place without arousing more interest in England that that of a passing sneeze. That is not to say, however, that similar 'confidence' would have sustained the change had unregenerate Labour still been in office.

In fact, with an unsound Labour government banished, 'unsound' financial policies could be safely followed. The orthodoxy which had won its last victory in August capitulated in September. The alternative would have been a much higher bank rate and a much more severe deflation, until the reduction of costs and of imports forced a new balance in the British economy.[2] Because the policy of the National government was partly deflationary—reduction in salaries and in unemployment benefits—people failed to see how much of it was borrowed from the new school of thought. The 'dole' was continued, wage-rates remained fairly stable, cheap money brought about some recovery; and a devalued pound was of some help to the export trades. 'Going off gold' was the signal of the new policy. Labour had stuck to old policies, and had been pushed aside when it shied at modifications, both deflationary and expansionist, which the National government unhesitatingly and even unconsciously accepted.

There was even a scapegoat at hand, to take all guilt away from the new government for this apparently unfortunate beginning: Invergordon. Through over-hasty decisions at the Admiralty and delay in explaining them, the men of the fleet in harbour at Invergordon, awaiting naval exercises, first heard of the way in which

---

[1] H. V. Hodson, *Slump and Recovery*, pp. 78–80, 85–6; H. F. Fraser, *Great Britain and the Gold Standard* (London, 1933), p. 101.

[2] H. F. Fraser, *Great Britain and the Gold Standard*, pp. 114–15.

the reductions of pay in the armed services would affect them by wireless broadcasts and by Sunday papers (including the sensational *News of the World*), and by an unusually large supply of the (Communist) *Daily Worker* on Monday, September 14. Some of the news may have been garbled; the facts were bad enough, and gave rise to the grievances. The cuts brought daily pay down to a level proposed by an official committee in 1925 but not applied, except to new entrants, as a result of the intervention of Lord Beatty, the First Sea Lord; thus the men felt that an implied contract with them had been broken. And the cuts seemed very uneven: 7 per cent for admirals, 3.7 per cent for lieutenant-commanders, 7.7 per cent for a chief petty officer, 10.5 per cent for an able seaman (married, with children) and 13.6 per cent for an unmarried A.B. (the latter figures included the men's allowances, which were not reduced; without them, the men's cuts ranged as high as 25 per cent for an able seaman). A typical seaman faced a reduction in pay from 31s. 6d. to 25s. 1d. a week. Such things, talked over in the large canteen in Invergordon on the evenings of the 13th and 14th, when alternate watches of the crews had shore leave, gave rise to decisions for collective action; some of the leaders were Communists, but 'cells' and 'agitators' were not needed to spur men worried about insurance premiums, furniture being bought by instalment payments, and even possible imprisonment for debt. Next day, September 15 (so it was decided), the men would refuse orders to fall in for work, to take the ships out of the harbour for the exercises; this passive resistance was to begin on the battleships *Valiant* and *Rodney*, and to be shown by cheering, which would be the signal to the men on the other ships to follow suit. A moderate and loyal manifesto petitioning the Admiralty to review the reductions in pay was drawn up.

All went according to plan. On the 15th 12,000 men refused to obey orders to fall in for work; three battleships, two battle cruisers—all the ships at Invergordon—were affected; elsewhere throughout the fleet there were no manifestations. There was no disorder; the normal housekeeping of the ships was carried on by the men themselves. Their chief expedient was the obstinate refusal to muster, so that officers, deprived of the quarterdeck whence to address them, could only attempt to reason with the men on their own ground, in the mess decks. The admiral in charge cancelled the sailing orders. The Admiralty ordered all the ships to return to their home ports for inquiries, and began to review the reductions, until the government made this unnecessary by announcing, on September 21, that no reductions would exceed 10 per cent, whether in the services or among the police and the teachers (whose campaign against the proposed 15 per cent reduction in their pay had won the public sympathy). The proposed reductions in navy pay and pensions would, at best, have produced little over £1½ millions in savings; over this trifle Britain had its 'mutiny' and lost the gold standard. There were no court martials after the mutiny. Thirty-six 'ringleaders' were dismissed the service, but with no charges brought against them; and some officers were punished by premature retirement for having saved the Admiralty, by their moderation, from the savage consequences which might have followed on its own blunder.[1]

11. CASHING IN

As soon as the National government had been formed, and even before parliament met, talk began about a general election. At the meeting of the Conservatives on August 28, when they endorsed the new government, Lord Hailsham called for an early election. One theme captivated the Conservatives: now was the time to smash socialism and give the country the only true remedy for its ills, a protective tariff. As early as September 3 Chamberlain recorded an intrigue among Conservatives outside the Cabinet to get their colleagues within to insist on an election, at which the tariff would be presented as the only means of avoiding the unpopular economies which would otherwise be necessary.[2] It was Churchill, however, who was outside the government, who brought the issue clearly into the open in a speech in parliament on September 8. It was essential, he argued, to make the government truly National (which Labour's abstention prevented it from being) by basing it on a popular majority. There should be an early election, before the new government had to bear the unpopularity for new discontents; and the time was now ripe for the indispensable policy of Protection. Yet moderate opinion, as reflected in the *Economist* and the *Spectator*, deplored the campaign for an election as inflaming the crisis and dangerous while the crisis lasted; the only danger to the government came from its strongest party, the Conservatives.

[1] Kenneth Edwards, *The Mutiny at Invergordon* (London, 1937), a full account by a retired lieutenant-commander; Fred Copeman, *Reason in Revolt* (London, 1948), pp. 40–53, is the account of an ordinary seaman.
[2] K. Feiling, *N. Chamberlain*, p. 194.

Soon, however, the Conservatives carried their persistence a step further. Why not an election in which the National government appealed to the country for support, its programme being, of course, the Conservative nostrum of the tariff? Pressure for this course became so great that on September 18 Samuel wrote to MacDonald on behalf of his Liberal colleagues protesting against such a move (to which Snowden was also opposed). MacDonald replied on the 20th that the objections to an election were so overwhelming that he could not have agreed, and, with the gold standard crisis upon them, 'there is not even a theoretical justification for an Election now'.[1] Brave talk! The Conservatives were not to be put off. On the 21st the '1922 Club', commemorating another Tory revolt, met and decided that there should be an immediate election on the issue of the tariff; next day Baldwin told Snowden that the pressure was too great for him to withstand.[2] By the 24th the Conservative business committee had fallen in line, supporting 'a national appeal by a national government under MacDonald, provided the programme embodied the full tariff'. It was agreed, if the appeal was successful, to continue to accept MacDonald as Prime Minister; on which Chamberlain with rare naïveté commented: 'Truly, the Conservative party is a wonderful embodiment of good sense, patriotism, and honesty.'[3]

MacDonald, Snowden and the Liberals were then in a dilemma. It was clear now, if it was not in August, that MacDonald was a prisoner of the Conservative majority in his own government, and could regain his freedom only by resigning. Snowden, to prevent the government adopting the abomination of a tariff, as he regarded it, had no weapon but resignation also. And for Samuel and his colleagues the situation was even worse: they were free traders or they were nothing; they represented a small, even forlorn party; and if they would not go along with the Conservatives, Sir John Simon and his 'Liberal Nationals' would—and this band of twenty-five or so, virtually outside the Liberal party already, formally proclaimed its separate existence on October 5. True, they could also resign. This would not prevent an election (though it might have made the actual result less one-sided); and it would be interpreted as demonstrating the Liberal party's final worthlessness, that it was ready to desert the government in a time of

---

[1] Viscount Samuel, *Grooves of Change*, p. 252.
[2] Ibid., p. 251; P. Snowden, *Autobiography*, II, 989; J. E. Wrench, Dawson, pp. 292–3.
[3] K. Feiling, *N. Chamberlain*, p. 195.

crisis over a mere point of doctrine. Yet Lloyd George at least was clear that resignation from the government was the right course to follow. Samuel and Sir Walter Layton went down to Churt, in Surrey, where he was convalescing on his farm, to consult him on October 4. He insisted that the Liberals should leave the government if an election was forced: 'If I am to die, I would rather die fighting on the Left.' Allied with the Conservatives on the issue of the tariff, the Liberals would have nothing distinctive left about them, and would lose their independence and any claim to support from the people. Events proved him right, of course; though the unfriendly could argue that he had himself compromised Liberalism's independence thirteen years before, and was now anxious only to postpone the election until he was strong enough to fight it as a leader. Next day MacDonald came down to see him; but his blandishments were unavailing, and after he had left, Lloyd George rang up Samuel and tried to get him to pledge to stand firm.[1]

The fight was lost, the decision already taken, by Samuel and by Snowden and MacDonald All yielded to the Tory pressure, backed by the King's conviction that the continuance of the National government was essential.[2] The only thing remaining at issue was whether the government would publish a single 'National' manifesto. This, since it must submit to Conservative stubbornness by including the tariff, was more than the Liberals could stomach; so that at the last moment the Conservatives' hope to cash in on the National government's popularity with their own party programme seemed doomed. But a 'formula' was found, by Neville Chamberlain—to have no programme; or rather that each party should issue its own manifesto, and that the general manifesto, signed by the Prime Minister, should simply appeal for a free hand, free to consider every proposal, including tariffs, to deal with the problems of the times. Thus was MacDonald's pledge of the previous August abandoned. Once the emergency was over, he had said, the parties in the government would 'resume their respective positions. . . . The election which will follow will not be fought by the Government. There will be no coupons. . . .'[3] And the justification? That the emergency still existed, and that only national co-operation between the parties,

[1] Viscount Samuel, *Grooves of Change*, pp. 254–5; M. Thomson, *Lloyd George*, p. 408.
[2] H. Nicolson, *George V*, pp. 492–3.
[3] Official statement, August 24, and MacDonald's broadcast, August 25; *The Times*, August 25, 26, 1931.

with a new lease of power from the people, could grapple with it. Parliament was dissolved on October 7, the general election to take place on October 27.

It was the coupon election all over again, though, let it be granted, without the coupons. As in 1918, the lion's share of the National candidates was taken by the Conservatives. Pacts were arranged where possible to prevent a Conservative opposing a loyal Liberal or Labour candidate, but in some cases local feeling was too strong. The self-sacrificing Samuel found himself opposed by a Conservative at Darwen, and four other Liberals in the government were similarly opposed and, unlike Samuel, defeated; yet Conservative ministers faced no Liberal opposition. There were 517 Conservative candidates, 39 Simonite Liberals, 121 Liberals, 21 National Labour candidates.[1]

The stridency of the campaign was another unpleasant reminder of 1918—and of 1924. Lacking any common programme, lacking any programme at all except a belief in their own indispensability, the various supporters of the National government followed two courses: first they confused the voter with their divided voices, proclaiming rival programmes and contradicting their allies; then they united in abuse of their Labour opponents and appeals to the voters' fears if Labour were victorious. Such a campaign gave no mandate for the tariff which the Conservatives later claimed as the price of victory. MacDonald, contesting his constituency at Seaham, asked for a 'doctor's mandate', to diagnose and to prescribe. If the Conservatives tried to put something over, he warned, 'I am not their man. I am going to enquire into tariffs with an open mind' (October 24). Snowden was more positive in his broadcast on October 17: a majority would not be a 'mandate to carry a general system of protection in the new Parliament'. The Liberal manifesto, signed by Samuel and five others, declared that 'freedom of trade is the only permanent basis of our economic prosperity'; in a speech at Bradford on October 9 Samuel followed this by denouncing tariffs as a patent medicine, though he promised to consider every proposal for the improvement of trade. Baldwin and Chamberlain tried to conjure the issue away; they were 'convinced of the supreme value of the policy of tariffs', as Baldwin put it on October 24 and as he and countless other Conservatives had declared during the campaign. That, however, was not the issue to be decided now; it would be decided after the election, after impartial examination. Other Conservatives, however, were

[1] *Annual Register, 1931*, p. 87.

less guarded; Austen Chamberlain, for instance, called on his constituency to win 'a triumph' for Protection.

Only Lloyd George and the Labour party were consistent in their opposition to the tariff. Lloyd George's letter to his constituents in the Carnarvon Boroughs denounced the election as the most 'wanton and unpatriotic' ever imposed on the country, intensifying differences when co-operation was essential. It was a 'mere Tory ramp to exploit a national emergency for Tory ends . . . to smash the political influence of organised labour' and to obtain a mandate for a protective tariff, which would only make things worse.[1] The Labour party's manifesto, 'Labour's call to action', declared that the capitalist system had broken down and socialism was the only solution. Banking and credit must be brought under national ownership and control, and power, transport and steel reorganised as public services. Tariffs were no cure; instead there should be national planning of industry and trade, and the creation of import boards. A balanced budget was essential, but not by the means of the Economy Act; the 'harsh policy' of reductions of unemployment benefit must be reversed.

Where all the National candidates differed on policy, all could agree on abuse. Snowden, though not himself standing for re-election, set the tone in his broadcast on October 17, and in statements to the press; and the bitterness with which he denounced life-long colleagues of a bare two months ago, though thought by some to be in questionable taste, undoubtedly convinced many independent voters, and many Labour men and women, to vote against Labour as untrustworthy. 'Bolshevism run mad' was his description of Labour's programme; it would 'plunge the country into irretrievable ruin'. Others were not behindhand. The Labour ministers were damned as the men who ran away from the crisis, men ready to put the country under the dictatorship of the T.U.C. Class propaganda was thus turned against them, and feebly answered by Labour taunts of the 'bankers' ramp'. Patriotism was enlisted on the side of the 'National' government; and even the Archbishop of Canterbury, addressing a diocesan conference on October 19, left no doubt which side he was commending to the faithful: he praised the Prime Minister's courage and stated the issue as finding 'men whom we could trust to see the country through' its difficulties.

The most powerful weapon against the Labour party was fear. MacDonald irrelevantly brandished a handful of German paper

[1] *The Times*, October 10, 1931.

marks from the time of inflation before an audience. Walter Runciman started the Post Office Savings Bank scare: that depositors would lose their hard-earned savings, which would be squandered by a Labour government to pay for the dole—regardless of the fact that past governments for many years had followed orthodox financial practice in using the funds in the Savings Bank for loans to the Treasury. Everything was done to create panic. One Conservative minister declared: 'Tomorrow there will be a new England or no England.' No wonder the *Manchester Guardian* called it 'the most fraudulent election campaign of modern times'. The dominant mood, as in 1918, was one of sullenness, of meetings of grim, silent audiences; though on both sides there was also a good deal of organised rowdiness at meetings.[1]

The resultant victory of the National government was no surprise, though its dimensions were, and *The Times* called it 'astounding'. Driven by patriotism and fear, as the *Economist* summed it up, the people had decided to play safe, and vote National, which usually meant voting Conservative. Labour lost two million of its voters of 1929, though its solid core of support was unmoved. In returns from the constituencies this meant a landslide victory for the National government, the enormous majority of 497 seats. Of its supporters, 472 were Conservatives, 33 were Liberals, 35 Simonite Liberals, and 13 National Labour, a total, with certain Independent members, of 556. The National government, with 14½ million votes, had a popular majority of almost 7½ million votes; the Conservative poll rose by over 3 millions, to 11·8 millions; the Liberals' fell by nearly 3 millions, to 2½ millions. The Conservatives lost no seats, and won over 200. The Liberals increased their representation from 59 to 72 (including Lloyd George's followers) but were divided, and a handful in the government compared to the Conservatives. As in every election since the war, they were the real losers; for now they had lost independence as well as votes. MacDonald's Labour supporters were an even more pitiful remnant.

In the landslide, Labour was swept under. All the former Labour ministers were defeated, except Lansbury, and among the minor ministers C. R. Attlee and Sir Stafford Cripps. Arthur Henderson, defeated at Burnley, was desperately ill on the day of the election, having caught a chill during the campaign; and he

---

[1] For the election campaign and speeches see *The Times* and the *Annual Register*, *1931*, pp. 84–6. A good collection of statements on the tariff issue is in D. Abel, *History of British Tariffs*, pp. 80–3. An excellent summary of the campaign, will be found in the issues of the *Economist* for October 17, 24, 31, 1931.

never properly recovered, though his public (and later his parliamentary) career continued for four years longer. The Labour party, with a total poll of 6.6 millions, returned only 46 members, as compared with 287 in 1929. Its heaviest losses were in Scotland and the Midlands, but those in London, Lancashire, Yorkshire were hardly less severe. Not only did it lose all the marginal seats it had picked up in 1929, but many solidly working-class constituencies also. Only Wales and Durham stood firm. From Scotland Labour had three members, from the Midlands three; from the South of England none. To the Labour survivors should be added five I.L.P. members of parliament, now virtually severed from the Labour party; this was in effect the old Clydeside brigade under Maxton, but woefully shrunk in numbers. The Opposition included Lloyd George's party of four—a family party consisting of Lloyd George, his son Gwilym, his daughter Megan, and Gwilym's brother-in-law, Goronwy Owen—all representing rural Welsh constituencies. As for the Communists and Mosley's New Party, they too were swept away, and returned no members to parliament.[1]

The results of the election reached far beyond the immediate future. It was not that, as in previous elections, they showed how violently the electoral system registered swings of opinion, so that the popular vote of the minority was grossly under-represented in parliament; this lesson in the virtues of the Liberal proposals for electoral reform was little marked by Labour members who had scorned it earlier. The importance of the election was that it gave the Conservatives, under false colours, an overwhelming strength in parliament which they could hardly have won unaided. Once again, whatever the popular tides of feeling since the war, they were in power, and contrary to the tendencies which were carrying governments in the United States and France in the opposite direction. The old ministers were back, the humdrum figures of the twenties, without even the need now of seeking new blood or caring about Opposition efforts. And behind them were the solid ranks of Conservative members: unknown men most of them, a mere name to their constituents, many put up as candidates in hopeless seats and now suddenly picked up and planted at Westminster in the general panic. The government had nothing to fear behind it or in front.

[1] Figures in 1931 election as given in *Whitaker's Almanack, 1932*.

CHAPTER EIGHT

Sitting it Out: Economic Recovery and Political Apathy, 1931—1935

1. THE NATIONAL GOVERNMENT

T HE history of the National government was one long diminuendo. From its triumph in 1931 it shambled its unimaginative way to its fall in 1940, when the failure of the campaign in Norway and the Nazi invasion of the Low Countries brought Great Britain to the crisis of the new world war. Its origin was an emergency which was financial and domestic; its tasks were to overcome a series of catastrophes which were international and military. Its responses were not bold. It retreated before aggression; it rearmed, but at first too slowly. In fact it was not unsuccessful in its economic policies but fatally narrow in its political conduct. Failure in the latter sphere darkened its reputation in the former; in retrospect it has been blamed for all the misfortunes of the time, partly because its opponents rose to power by reiterating their version of its history and its period.

The mood of the early thirties was not heroic. Gone was the hopeful internationalism of the twenties, the return to the gold standard, the restoration of world trade. Britain, beset by depression, turned inward, like every other country, and concentrated on internal problems and domestic solutions. In time the mood changed, but the government remained the same; 1935 was the year of decision. Other countries might have new and adventurous governments: Germany the Third Reich, France the Popular Front, the United States the New Deal, Russia another Five-Year Plan. Only in Britain did the Conservatives remain in power; hence the Second World War, restoring conservatism in other countries, could only dethrone it in Great Britain.

That the National government was in harmony with the national mood could not be doubted. MacDonald and Baldwin, having alternated in office in the twenties, shared it in the thirties, and combined their talents for calming the passions and rubbing the sharp edges off awkward questions. MacDonald should not be judged by these last years as Prime Minister. Prisoner of the Conservatives, he could have given a lead to the government only if he had been a stronger and younger man than he was. His health was failing; his speeches, never crystal-clear, became more and more difficult to follow; only his courage, sternly tested by trouble with his eyes, remained with him to the last. He had the misfortune, it has been said, to outlive himself not in retirement but in office.[1]

The one strong man in the government was not of the sort to endear it with the people: Neville Chamberlain, the Chancellor of the Exchequer. It was he who largely directed its domestic policies and more and more dominated the Cabinet. In the day of the lesser men he was outstanding, with his clear, civil-service mind, high principles, narrow but progressive views, great energy and self-confidence. What he lacked was warmth. He repelled Labour men by his scorn, Conservatives by the discipline he demanded of them.[2] 'Weaned on a pickle', a normally generous. Labour observer called him;[3] the rasping voice seemed symbolic of the man.

Of the other members of the government little need be said. The Cabinet, unlike the emergency Cabinet of August 1931, was of normal size—twenty members. It contained at first eleven Conservatives, four Labour members, and five Liberals (three from the official party, two from Sir John Simon's group). Of the Labour members MacDonald, Thomas and Lord Sankey retained their former positions: Snowden became Lord Privy Seal, and went to the Lords with a viscountcy. Sir Herbert Samuel was Home Secretary, Sir John Simon Foreign Secretary—an unexpected and unfortunate choice. Another Simonite, Walter Runciman, went to the Board of Trade at Snowden's insistence that it and the Treasury should not both be in the charge of protectionists. Seldom was Snowden so mistaken. The Conservative ministers included hard-working men, such as Sir Samuel Hoare, Cunliffe-Lister, Lord Hailsham, Lord Londonderry (1878–1949). They were not men to inspire others. It was the omissions which were conspicuous; Winston Churchill, Leopold Amery, Austen Chamberlain (who stood down in favour of younger men).

[1] See Pierre Maillaud, *The English Way* (Oxford, 1945), pp. 145, 155–68 (the acute observations of a Frenchman resident in England since 1932).
[2] K. Feiling, *N. Chamberlain*, brings out the best in him and also shows his weaknesses; see pp. 81–3, 104, 118–24, 130, 135, 142.
[3] Lord Snell, *Men, movements and myself* (London, 1936), p. 248.

To oppose this government of all the talents the Labour remnant elected George Lansbury as chairman; his unorthodox but effective discharge of the duties of leader of the Opposition received the praise of Baldwin.[1] Clement Attlee was vice-chairman of the party. On occasion, after his recovery, Lloyd George was also to be found on the front Opposition bench.

2. THE TRIUMPH OF THE TARIFF:
THE END OF THE HONEYMOON

The first important measures of the government were those taken to promote recovery by fiscal means. In November 1931, Runciman introduced the Abnormal Importations bill to give the Board of Trade power for six months to impose duties up to 100 per cent *ad valorem* on manufactured articles which were entering the country in 'abnormal' quantities. There had been no inquiry, such as had been promised during the election campaign; no justification for the measure was made save that the country was suffering from the 'dumping' of foreign goods in 'abnormal' amounts—words of undefined but pejorative meaning; and even the fact of 'dumping' was not proved. Such a bill was a stern trial of the patriotism of the Liberal free traders; but they accepted it, and despite Labour opposition it was quickly passed. Duties of 50 per cent were at once imposed on imported pottery, cutlery, typewriters, woollen goods, paper, gloves, followed soon by others on bottles, cameras, cotton goods, electric lamps and radio parts. The Horticultural Products (Emergency Duties) Act, passed soon afterwards, gave the Minister of Agriculture similar powers to hamper the importation of fresh fruits, flowers and vegetables.[2]

With these new precedents in their hands, the Conservatives advanced towards a general tariff. The Cabinet appointed a Balance of Trade Committee under Neville Chamberlain's chairmanship; Snowden and Samuel were members, but the protectionists, among whom Runciman was now included, were in a majority. Again, despite all promises, there was no exhaustive, impartial enquiry. All the Board of Trade's evidence, under Runciman's leadership, was directed to the support of a tariff; no other expert opinion was sought; Samuel later described the whole inquiry as 'merely perfunctory'.[3]

[1] G. M. Young, *Baldwin*, pp. 202–3.
[2] D. Abel, *History of British Tariffs*, pp. 87–91; *Annual Register, 1931*, pp. 94–8, 103.
[3] P. Snowden, *Autobiography*, II, 1007–8; Viscount Samuel, *Grooves of Change*, p. 260.

Before the committee's recommendation of a general tariff was accepted a Cabinet crisis occurred. The Liberal ministers, Samuel, Maclean, Sir Archibald Sinclair, threatened to resign, and so did Snowden. Following a lengthy Cabinet meeting on January 21, 1932, MacDonald reasoned with the dissentients at Snowden's flat during the evening, though more concerned with his personal position in the government than with its principles. Next day a solution was announced: the 'agreement to differ', first proposed by Chamberlain and pressed by other Conservatives. 'Because of the paramount importance of maintaining national unity in the presence of the grave problems that now confront the country and the whole world', the dissenters would remain in the Cabinet, bowing to the majority's decision in favour of a tariff but free to express their opposition to it. This breach with constitutional practice, incompatible with the party system and the collective responsibility of the Cabinet, was greeted by some with ridicule and by most with indifference. It did not last long.[1]

This settled, the Import Duties bill was introduced on February 4, by Neville Chamberlain, speaking in the presence of Joseph Chamberlain's widow and children, and claiming, with a show of emotion hitherto rare with him in public, that the measure vindicated his father's work and would have been a consolation for 'the bitterness of his disappointment'. The main provisions of the Act, which went into operation on March 1, were (1) the imposition of a general customs duty of 10 per cent on almost all imports, those already dutiable being exempt from the new duty; (2) the exemption from the duty of goods from within the Empire, pending the Imperial Economic Conference to be held in Ottawa in the summer; (3) the exemption of certain other goods, which were placed on a free list; (4) the creation of a committee, the Import Duties Advisory Committee, on whose recommendation the Treasury could order the imposition of additional duties. The free list included wheat and maize, meat and animals (but not all foodstuffs), iron and tin ores, scrap steel, zinc, lead, rubber, pulp and newsprint, pit-props, cotton, wool, flax, hides and skins. Despite vigorous opposition from Samuel in the Commons and Snowden in the Lords, the bill passed: in the Commons the vote was 454 to 78, the opposition comprising all the Labour members and 32 Liberals.[2]

[1] P. Snowden, *Autobiography*, II, 1010–12; D. Abel, *History of British Tariffs*, pp. 92–5.
[2] D. Abel, *History of British Tariffs*, pp. 95–103; J. H. Richardson, *British Economic Foreign Policy* (London, 1936), pp. 93–5.

The Import Duties Advisory Committee was at once constituted: it consisted of Sir George May, as chairman, and two other members. Its first work was a report, published on April 21, 1932 (Cmd. 4066), recommending as a general policy that duties on manufactured goods should be raised to 20 per cent *ad valorem*, on luxury goods to 25 per cent or 30 per cent, and on bicycles, bicycle parts and some chemicals to $33\frac{1}{3}$ per cent. Certain goods used in British manufactures were put under a duty of 15 per cent. These recommendations were at once adopted. During the next three years the Committee considered some 300 applications concerning duties, and about 100 orders were issued, some raising, others lowering duties on particular imports. A tariff which was nearly all-embracing but also generally moderate was thus constructed. Its most tangible results were in the iron and steel industry, as will be seen later. Its effect, coupled with the Ottawa agreements, was to leave about a quarter of Britain's imports free of duty, and half paying duties of 10–20 per cent.[1]

There followed the Imperial Economic Conference, held at Ottawa from July 21 to August 20, 1932. It was not the love-feast for which Conservative imperialists and protectionists had hoped. The British delegation, headed by Baldwin and including Chamberlain, Thomas and four other ministers, was made up of protectionists; accompanying it was a large body of civil servants, industrialists and journalists. The hope was that mutually advantageous means for increasing trade within the Empire might be found. Britain now had a tariff, and could offer more imperial preferences in return for concessions by the Dominions for British manufactures. On the other hand, the ministers' freedom in negotiation was limited by the policy of protecting the British farmer, and the desire not to damage Britain's trade with foreign countries. The Dominions could offer little in the way of real help to British manufacturers without hurting their own carefully-nursed 'infant industries', however much they desired concessions from Great Britain for their own primary products. 'Empire free trade' suited them only as a one-way proposition.[2]

Hence from the start the British and Dominion delegates were at cross-puposes. The British ministers found themselves amateurs at the game of bargaining over tariffs. The fighting, haggling and snubbing to which they were subjected even

[1] J. H. Richardson, pp. 96–9, 127; F. C. Benham, *Great Britain under Protection* (New York, 1941), pp. 25–8.
[2] See W. K. Hancock, *Survey of British Commonwealth Affairs*, II, part i (Oxford, 1940), pp. 214–20.

P

threatened their own unity. They were exposed to sharp attacks in the Canadian press. Even civil servants such as Sir Horace Wilson, adept at the production of mollifying 'formulas', were not spared from criticism. At the end, the conference almost broke down at an all-night session which Chamberlain left in disgust (August 19–20).[1]

Twelve agreements were signed, of which seven were between Britain and the other Dominions, the Irish Free State excepted. Britain promised to continue and in some cases to increase the imperial preference already given to foodstuffs and other products coming from the Dominions. In return, British imports into the Dominions were to receive preference, but chiefly by increasing the tariff against foreign goods, leaving untouched the rate against British goods, already impossibly high in many cases. British traders and the British government were given the right to make representations to the tariff boards in the Dominions about particular duties.[2]

The news of these agreements was too much for the free traders in the Cabinet. Snowden and Samuel exchanged letters at the end of August; both of them, and also the other Liberal ministers, were ready to resign in protest. MacDonald, alarmed at the threat to the unity of the National government, attempted to dissuade them. 'He was disturbed about his personal position,' wrote Snowden, 'and kept on repeating, "I do not know what to do".' To Samuel he argued that Britain's strong position in the world was due to 'our present political combination'; were the Liberals to end it, his own influence as head of such a combination would be destroyed ('I should be regarded as a limpet in office'), and with the ending of the 'national effort in co-operation' the country would be 'grievously damaged'. Action was delayed until the Cabinet could meet. Samuel made a counter-proposal; that 'further progress' with the Ottawa agreements should be suspended until after the World Economic Conference. This received short shrift from the Tories. Snowden, in a letter to MacDonald on the 15th, protesting against the appeal to personal loyalty, asked why the Tories should not be asked 'to subordinate personal views on principle' in the national interest. Too late he was tasting the bitter fruits of his own conduct:

[1] D. Abel, *History of British Tariffs*, pp. 104–8; K. Feiling, *N. Chamberlain*, pp. 213–15.
[2] The terms of the agreements are to be found in J. H. Richardson, *British Economic Foreign Policy*, pp. 138–56; D. Abel, *History of British Tariffs*, pp. 108–10; W. K. Hancock, *Survey*, II, i, pp. 222–30.

They have sacrificed nothing, but have used the enormous Tory majority we gave them at the Election to carry out a Tory policy and to identify us with it. We have sacrificed our Party and ruined the political careers of a score of young Labour M.P.'s.

When the Cabinet met on September 28, Snowden resigned, as did the Liberal ministers (Samuel and Sinclair) and Lord Lothian and Isaac Foot among the under-secretaries. MacDonald, Thomas and Sankey stayed on.[1]

Precious little National flavour was left in the government. Sir William Jowitt, the Attorney-General and a Labour member, had resigned in January (lacking a seat) and was replaced by Inskip, a Conservative. A Liberal, Sir Donald Maclean, had died in June and been replaced at the Board of Education by Lord Irwin, the ex-viceroy, who was a Conservative. Snowden's cherished land valuation had been suspended as early as December 1931, by Neville Chamberlain, though the *coup de grâce* was not given to the elusive land tax until 1934. Of course, the Prime Minister was left, and his two colleagues. And Simon and his loyal band of Liberal Nationals were still on hand.

3. THE PARALYSIS OF FOREIGN POLICY

In the event, the most important decisions which the National government had to take were those of foreign policy. The first large violation of the peace of the world since the war of 1914–18 occurred in Manchuria on September 18, 1931. It came at the worst possible moment for stern action by Great Britain. The National government was not a month old, and was fully occupied in balancing the budget, saving—and then abandoning—the gold standard, and caballing about a general election. When Japanese soldiers suddenly occupied Mukden, following a well-timed explosion on a length of railway track, and gave the signal for the Japanese army rapidly to take over the whole of Manchuria, the Chinese government appealed to the League of Nations under Article 11 of the Covenant and to the United States as a signatory of the Nine-Power Pact and the Kellogg Treaty. The matter was debated in the Council of the League on September 22. The Japanese representative was conciliatory. Lord Cecil, for Great Britain, proposed an inquiry, and persuaded the Council to appeal to both Japan and China to stop fighting and to return their forces to their own frontiers. No one seemed to be very much worried.

[1] P. Snowden, *Autobiography*, II, 1020–30, 1081–5; Viscount Samuel, *Grooves of Change*, pp. 273–80; *Annual Register*, 1932, pp. 82–5.

There was a good deal of sympathy in Great Britain for the Japanese, whose economic rights in Manchuria had been impaired by Chinese anarchy and the recurrence of incidents involving Japanese troops stationed in the country. The *Spectator*, for example, hardly alluded to the Manchurian crisis until October 3, when its tone was reassuring: Japan was complying with the League's appeal. In the contest which followed, the League and the ideas of collective security and the rule of law were defeated; partly because of indifference and of sympathy with the aggressor, but partly because the League powers were unprepared, preoccupied with other matters, and too slow to perceive the scale of Japanese ambitions.

Already the League had lost the first round. The proposed inquiry was abandoned by the Council on September 25, when H. L. Stimson, the United States Secretary of State, published a note which, though warmly supporting the League's appeal, advised against holding an inquiry contrary to the wishes of Japan. Hope of co-operation between the League and the United States over the crisis perhaps faded as early as this, encouraging the Japanese government—or rather the army—to go ahead in Manchuria. By the time the Council met again in mid-October, with the American consul at Geneva present, not much could be done. Japan was asked to evacuate the territory she had occupied by November 16. When that day came, she had not done so, and the Council then accepted a Japanese proposal of a commission of inquiry (November 21), and on December 10 postponed indefinitely any coercive measures against Japan. This was the critical decision, and its significance was not unnoticed at the time. On October 31, the *Spectator* had declared that the League was 'facing the most critical moment of its career'; on November 14, when urging Sir John Simon to propose strong action at Geneva, it said that if the appeal to Japan was in vain 'that is an end of any pretence that war as an instrument of national policy has been renounced . . . war is re-enthroned . . . a straight road back to 1914 lies open'.

Early in 1932 the pace quickened. On January 29 China invoked Articles 10 and 15 of the Covenant, which would normally lead to the application of sanctions against Japan by members of the League. At the same time fighting between Chinese and Japanese broke out in Shanghai, Japanese reinforcements were landed and the Chapei area bombed. A month's fighting followed, as the Chinese forces in Shanghai made a strong resistance to the

Japanese. The Asiatic squadron of the United States navy was despatched to Shanghai. The British and American consuls worked together to secure a truce, which was arranged on May 5. The Japanese withdrew from the parts of Shanghai which they had occupied.

If the interest of the public was then centred on Shanghai, the interest of students later was centred on the Anglo-American diplomatic exchanges of the time. On January 7, 1932, Stimson published a note enunciating the doctrine of 'non-recognition', which would apply to Japanese conquests in Manchuria and to any territorial changes effected by force. He hoped for the support of other powers in this policy; instead he received the frigid reply on January 9 that since Japan had promised to maintain the 'open door' in Manchuria, the British government 'have not considered it necessary to address any formal note to the Japanese Government . . .' Both then[1] and later it was argued that Simon, by this communiqué, squashed a proposal for joint British-American action which would have brought the Japanese to heel, restored the strength of the League and reversed the fatal courses which led to 1939. Neither country, however, then contemplated economic or military action. What Simon's rebuff to Stimson accomplished was the stiffening of Japanese contempt for the League and the great powers, and the frustration of co-operation between Britain and the United States, which might have led, however unintentionally, to strong measures against Japan. On February 8 a second episode of the same sort occurred. The United States proposed that the Nine-Power Pact be invoked against Japan. Transatlantic telephone conversations followed. The Foreign Office drafted a statement on 'non-recognition' which, on February 16, the Council of the League adopted; but the British reply, urging that other League powers should join in invoking the Pact, chilled Stimson's resolution even though it involved a difference of method and not of end.

In any case, what was the invoking of the Pact to mean? Nothing, the Japanese decided. Being now sure of Manchuria, they inaugurated their puppet state of Manchukuo on March 9 and recognised it on September 15, 1932. The League, waiting for the report of its commission of inquiry under Lord Lytton, did

[1] See an article by Alfred Zimmern on 'The United States and Manchuria' in *Spectator*, January 16, 1932. Cf. ibid., March 5, 1932: 'It is by no means a question today of whether the United States would be willing to keep pace with the League, but whether the League is prepared to take steps sufficiently decisive to satisfy the United States.'

nothing. The Lytton report, published on October 2, was sympathetic with Japanese grievances in Manchuria, but condemned the Japanese invasion, refused to accept Manchukuo's independence as genuine and proposed for Manchuria an autonomous regime under Chinese sovereignty. More delay followed while the report was considered. In February 1933, when the League adopted the report, Japan gave notice of its resignation from the League and launched its attack on Jehol, part of China proper. The League did nothing. Japan's war against China was to drag on for years of nominal peace, until it became part of the greater world war of the forties. The League was to blame, the National government was to blame, Sir John Simon was to blame. 'The British representatives at Geneva seem intent on consulting Tokyo's convenience in all things', complained the *Spectator* (April 30, 1932). There was no strong body of opinion in the country which wanted anything very different.[1]

In 1932 and 1933 pacifist sentiment, a vague belief in the League as the guardian of peace, a disbelief in the possibility of a European war were still dominant among the British people—indeed, they remained so until 1935. The Peace Society was strong, and held large meetings addressed by men of eminence. The famous resolution in the Oxford Union, that 'this House will in no circumstance fight for its King and Country', was passed by 275 votes to 153 on February 9, 1933, and received world-wide notice out of all proportion to its importance, as a sign of Britain's pacifism and decadence which was an encouragement to dictators abroad. More potent in influencing policy was the by-election in East Fulham in October 1933. The Conservative candidate, advocating an increase in the strength of the army, navy and air force, was defeated by the Labour candidate who accused him of preparing for war; a Conservative majority of 14,521 was replaced by a Labour majority of 4,840.

Despite the portent of Manchuria, hopes for peace in Europe persisted. The postwar occupation of the Rhineland had been ended, reparations were finally abandoned at a conference at Lausanne in June 1932, after having been suspended for a year by

---

[1] W. N. Medlicott, *British Foreign Policy since Versailles*, pp. 145–57; G. M. Gathorne-Hardy, *Short History of International Affairs*, pp. 303–20. For a summary of the controversy over the parts of Stimson and Simon in the Manchurian crisis see Sara R. Smith, *The Manchurian Crisis, 1931–1932* (New York, 1948). R. Bassett, *Democracy and Foreign Policy: a case history: the Sino-Japanese Dispute, 1931–33* (London, 1952), exhaustively examines the Manchurian crisis in the light of contemporary and later opinion in Great Britain (for critical comment, see Salvador de Madariaga in *Manchester Guardian Weekly*, September 3 and 11, 1952).

the Hoover moratorium. After token payments in 1933, Britain in 1934 ceased to make payments on her war debt to the United States; the other European debtors, saving only Finland, were already in default. It remained only to complete the pacification of Europe by holding the long-awaited Disarmament Conference and carrying out in all countries a programme of disarmament already imposed upon Germany.

The Disarmament Conference opened at Geneva, under the presidency of Arthur Henderson, on February 2, 1932—just after the Japanese attack on Chapei. It soon ran into familiar difficulties. The fact of German rearmament beyond the limits prescribed in the Treaty of Versailles was already well known. Hence the French demand for security clashed with the British instinct for conciliation. Germany was demanding in armaments the equality with the other powers which she had already won at all other points; either the powers must disarm to her level or she must be allowed to rearm to theirs. The British were prepared to concede this, the French were not. For the British public had long been ashamed of the Treaty of Versailles, had long been ready to treat the Germans as equals.

> Sir John Simon could have said in three sentences what the country, if it had been consulted, would have required him to say—that Great Britain admits in principle, without cavil or reserve, the justice of the German claim to equality status; that equality must be achieved not by the re-armament of Germany, but by the reduction of the armaments of other countries.[1]

The conference soon came to a standstill. To disagreement over principle was added disagreement over detail—British experts being as stubborn as those of other countries in refusing to give up their favourite weapons, especially on the sea. The moderate Chancellor in Germany, Bruening, having failed to win concessions from the powers, fell from office in May 1932, to be replaced by the wily von Papen, who in turn gave place to General Schleicher in November. It was von Papen's government which announced Germany's withdrawal from the conference on September 16; but Germany returned later, after a Five-Power conference at Geneva in December (Britain, France, Italy, Germany, the United States)

---

[1] *Spectator*, September 24, 1932, 'Sophistry and statesmanship'. Cf. ibid.: 'the mind of the vast majority of the British people is made up [that] Germany cannot be held down by force; she cannot be treated thirteen years after the War as a conquered nation; she cannot be tied hand and foot in the matter of armaments while other countries are left free.' For the evolution of British sentiment towards Germany see R. B. McCallum, *British Opinion and the Last Peace*, 'The retreat from Versailles'.

had found a formula which ingeniously combined the incompatible; Germany was conceded 'equality of rights in a system which would provide security for all nations'.

It was too late. On January 30, 1933, Hitler became Chancellor in Germany, von Papen having persuaded President von Hindenburg that office would either tame or discredit him. The strength of the Nazis had apparently been waning. In the elections of November 1932 their number had fallen from 230 to 196 among the 584 members. The Nazis prepared for new elections on March 5, particularly by exploiting (if not arranging) the firing of the Reichstag building on the night of February 27 as a Communist conspiracy. Even so, the Nazis won only 288 seats, and with their allies, the Nationalists, had a majority of 33 in the Reichstag— enough, however, to seize dictatorial powers by a bill passed on March 23. The *gleichschaltung* of the states, the liquidation of opposition, the persecution of the Jews followed without delay.

Despite these unfavourable events, a new start was made in the Disarmament Conference. On March 16 Ramsay MacDonald brought to the conference a plan (the work of Anthony Eden, Under-secretary for Foreign Affairs, and of civil servants) which included, along with several proposals made previously, actual figures for the armed forces of the various countries, and limits on the size and type of armaments. The proposals would have reduced the size of the French army, and permitted Germany to attain parity with it; which led Winston Churchill to condemn them in the House of Commons (March 23) as 'somewhat unseasonable' while he exclaimed, to the annoyance of many, 'Thank God for the French Army.'[1] None the less, in spite of some obstruction by Germany, the proposals were approved in principle before the conference adjourned in June and Henderson set off on a pilgrimage of the capitals on behalf of disarmament.

Meanwhile, the powers had made an attempt, on the initiative of Mussolini, to appease Germany by an agreed revision of the peace treaties. Mussolini proposed to MacDonald and Simon, when they were at Rome on March 18, a Four-Power Pact (Britain, France, Italy, Germany) for this purpose. Its method was hardly admirable since it involved, in effect, circumventing the League and reducing the influence of the smaller powers (and especially Poland, the principal intended victim of revision) at the expense of the great ones, among which Mussolini was anxiously ranging Italy. France, with her all-important association with the Little Entente,

---

[1] W. S. Churchill, *The Gathering Storm* (new ed.; London, 1949), p. 68.

was only lukewarm in her support, and the plan was so modified as to come to nothing. Hitler, however, had taken notice, and on May 17 soothed the apprehensions of the powers by the first of the conciliatory speeches which marked his path of terror down to 1940: a European war would be 'madness'; Germany would do her part for international security, and was ready to dissolve all her military forces and destroy her weapons if other nations would do the same; but if the others did not disarm, 'Germany must at least maintain her claim to equality'. What could be more reasonable than that?

Hopes were high, therefore, when the Disarmament Conference resumed on October 14, 1933. Sir John Simon offered a plan, concerted with France, that for five years there should be international supervision of arms, without disarmament or rearmament; after this probationary period there would be disarmament, bringing all to an equality with Germany. Germany, it seemed, might accept—and was even committed to doing so by Hitler's speech of May 17. In the nick of time Hitler slipped out of the trap, summoned his cabinet, telegraphed his representative at Geneva, and on the afternoon of October 14 gave notice of Germany's withdrawal from the conference and of her intended resignation from the League of Nations. This was a 'momentous date in world history'; the Locarno period was over, and 'the world entered upon an uneasy progress towards a new conflict'. It was the first of Hitler's gambles; he expected dire consequences: a French invasion of the Ruhr, a Polish invasion of East Prussia. Nothing happened. He had won his first diplomatic victory, and could expect several more such easy triumphs.[1]

The Disarmament Conference was dead, though not formally pronounced so until May 1934, when it adjourned *sine die*. Rearmament was beginning. The necessary efforts for peace, whether in Europe or the Far East, were inhibited by the depression, by the lack of harmony between Great Britain and France, by apathy and by pacifism among the British people, by the opportunism of Sir John Simon at the Foreign Office.[2] From early in 1933 the tone of articles in periodicals like the *Contemporary Review* was more and more pessimistic: it was an age of disintegration; international co-operation was gone; Britain lacked any policy; war lay not far ahead. The *Spectator* had bidden farewell to 1932 'unmourned and unregretted, with its memories of inconclusive disarmament

[1] J. W. Wheeler-Bennett, *Munich: Prologue to Tragedy* (London, 1948), pp. 213–14.
[2] M. D. Stocks, *Eleanor Rathbone* (London, 1949), pp. 227–9.
    P*

discussions, nerveless Manchurian discussions, its currency crisis, its tariff increases . . .'[1] Yet 1933 had been far worse. What hope was there for 1934?[2]

4. IMPERIAL INTERLUDE

During these years much of the attention of parliament and of the intelligent public was directed to the future of the Commonwealth and of India; and in its imperial policies the National government was, with one exception, to be seen at its best. In November 1931, parliament passed the Statute of Westminster, which gave legislative recognition to the freedom from parliament's control which the Dominions already possessed. This was an agreed measure, implementing Lord Balfour's definition of the status of the Dominions in 1926, and approved by the Imperial Conference of 1930. The statute had been debated in the parliaments of the Dominions, and came to parliament with their resolutions asking for its enactment. It recognised the freedom of the Dominions to make laws regardless of their repugnance to British legislation; it removed the application of any British act to a Dominion except on the Dominion's request; it gave the Dominions power to legislate concerning their own nationals outside their boundaries. The preamble recognised the crown as the 'symbol of the free association of the members of the British Commonwealth of Nations', and declared that it would 'be in accord with the established constitutional position of all the members' that changes in the law regarding the succession and the royal titles should have the assent of the parliaments of the Dominions: a matter of some importance later.[3]

The Government of India Act of 1935 was perhaps the greatest product of the partnership of Baldwin and MacDonald. Baldwin was unwearied in supporting the new policy toward India (strengthened, no doubt, by the part in framing it taken by his friend Lord Irwin) and in resisting Conservative attempts to weaken it.[4] MacDonald gave much thought and energy to the work of making India's new constitution; indeed, the conviction

[1] *Spectator*, December 30, 1932.
[2] For general accounts of international affairs see G. M. Gathorne-Hardy, *Short History*, pp. 342–64; R. W. Seton-Watson, *Britain and the Dictators* (Cambridge, 1938), pp. 68–101.
[3] For text and commentary, see K. C. Wheare, *Statute of Westminster* (Oxford, 1933), and his *Statute of Westminster and Dominion Status* (London, 1938; 5th ed., 1953); cf. W. K. Hancock, *Survey of British Commonwealth Affairs*, I, pp. 273–94.
[4] G. M. Young, *Baldwin*, pp. 187–9.

that he must do so may well have been one of his main reasons for agreeing to form and to continue the National government.

The path was not smooth. A second Round Table Conference was begun in London in September 1931, having been planned before the change of government. It followed a pact made in the spring between Gandhi and Lord Irwin, by which the civil disobedience campaign in India was to cease and the Congress Party join in the Round Table Conference. Gandhi's presence in London was, however, more amusing to the public and pleasing to anti-imperialists than productive of agreement at the conference table. His demands included dominion status, but went beyond it: India (like De Valera's Ireland) must have partnership with Great Britain, and immediate control of foreign policy and defence; and India apparently meant the Congress Party. Moreover, the proper representation of the different communities in India remained an unsolved problem, and in the end MacDonald had to make his own Communal Award, published in August 1932.

The government's policy remained, however, unchanged. In debates in parliament in December the die-hards made a great effort to get the government to abandon the policy of its predecessor, a minority government and a Socialist one to boot. Lord Lloyd in the Lords, Winston Churchill in the Commons, spoke vehemently of the dangers of the new policy which was far beyond that of the Simon report: the withdrawal of the British raj would lead to bloodshed and civil war. Churchill spoke for an hour and a half: his warning of violence in India was vivid, and, after many years, justified only too grimly:

> There are mobs of neighbours . . . who, when held and dominated by these [communal] passions will tear each other to pieces, men, women and children, with their fingers. Not for a hundred years have the relations between Moslems and Hindus been so poisoned as they have been since England was deemed to be losing her grip and was believed to be ready to quit the scene if told to go.[1]

Churchill mustered only 43 votes for his amendment to the government's 369. The typical attitude of Conservatives was expressed by the *Spectator*: the government must not be deflected by 'die-hardism' from the object of a Free India as a Free State in the Commonwealth.[2]

Yet the wheels ground slowly. A third Round Table Conference

[1] 260 H.C. Deb. 5 s., 1298 (December 3, 1931).
[2] 'India—the Immediate Task', *Spectator*, November 7, 1931.

was followed by the deliberations for eighteen months of a Joint Select Committee of both houses of parliament under the chairmanship of Lord Linlithgow. A bill was introduced in parliament late in 1934. It provided for an all-India federation, and for greater autonomy—in effect, a cabinet system of government—in the Indian provinces (from which Burma was separated, to have a government of its own). The bill was piloted through the Commons with great skill by Sir Samuel Hoare, and passed its second reading by 404 votes to 133. In the Lords, where the debate was unusually well-attended, the vote in favour of it was 236 to 55. It received the royal assent as the Government of India Act on August 4, 1935.[1]

The immediate effects were not dramatic. The provisions in the act for federation never went into effect; but new Indian governments took office in the provinces after elections and, following some tussles over their constitutional limitations, in April 1937. War came before the act had had a fair trial, and made it seem old-fashioned. During and after the war India demanded greater freedom; and got it in 1948 at the price of partition and bloodshed. Yet both Pakistan and the Republic of India remained in the Commonwealth; thanks not only to the leaders in India at the time—Gandhi, Nehru, Jinnah, Lord Mountbatten—but perhaps also to the work of Irwin, MacDonald and Baldwin in the thirties and to the fact that one member of the Simon Commission was Prime Minister of Great Britain, in a Labour government, after the war.

5. COLD WAR WITH IRELAND

Toward Indian aspirations for freedom the National government was too complaisant for the liking of Tory critics; towards Irish aspirations it went for some years to the opposite extreme. The trouble was not of its making, though its aggravation was. In 1932 the moderate government of Cosgrave in the Irish Free State was replaced by one led by De Valera; and De Valera at once began to cut several of the links between the Free State and Great Britain, carrying out with equal logic but greater skill the programme he had announced but failed to fulfil by persuasion or by force ten years earlier. In the interval, the Free State's independence, which De Valera had scorned, had been increased by the passing of the Statute of Westminster; and this advantage, given

---

[1] This account rests mainly on Reginald Coupland, *India: a re-statement* (Oxford, 1945), pp. 136–43.

to the Free State on the eve of Cosgrave's fall, was exploited to the full by the new government.[1]

De Valera was not slow to make use of his opportunity. After preliminary warnings, he introduced in the Dail on April 21, 1932, a bill to abolish the oath of allegiance and to remove the Treaty from its position in the constitution of the Free State (hitherto the constitution must be construed with reference to it and any laws repugnant to it were void). The Senate found this circumvention of the Treaty too much to swallow and amended the bill to provide for prior agreement with the British government; this delayed the bill until after the general election of January 1933, when it passed in its original form under the deadlock provisions of the constitution, and went into effect in May. In the same first spring of power De Valera announced, in accordance with his election promises, that the land annuities due to the British government would be withheld, and this was done when they fell due on July 1, 1932.[2] Meanwhile the Governor-General, James MacNeill, appointed under the previous government, was first insulted by being left out of official ceremonies for the Eucharistic Congress in June, and was then removed (or allowed to resign) in October 1932, before his normal term was over. As successor Donal Buckley, a retired shopkeeper and member of the Dail, was appointed at a reduced salary; he was enjoined to perform no public or social duties and was accommodated, not in the Vice-regal Lodge, but in a suburban villa. His formal powers of recommending appropriations and vetoing legislation were abolished. The office of the King's representative was made ludicrous and empty, though not accorded the dignity of being extinguished.

In 1933 a bill was passed abolishing appeals from the Free State to the Judicial Committee of the Privy Council. In April 1934, the Dail passed a bill abolishing the Senate. Its demise

[1] W. K. Hancock, *Survey of British Commonwealth Affairs*, I, 320–30; Tom Ireland, *Ireland, Past and Present* (New York, 1942), pp. 489–584. See also Donal O'Sullivan, *The Irish Free State and Its Senate* (London, 1940) which, despite its title, is a comprehensive political history of the Irish Free State, and a very good one. The I.R.A. continued a secret existence and disturbed the public peace with periodic proclamations and murders. Kevin O'Higgins was assassinated on July 10, 1927. De Valera's government 'proclaimed' the I.R.A. in June 1936.

[2] The land annuities continued to be collected by the Free State government; at first they were paid into a suspense account; in March 1935, they were halved and applied to ordinary exchequer purposes. They represented repayment of principal and interest on sums advanced by the British government under the land acts of 1870–1909 for the purchase of land by Irish tenants. For legal aspects of the dispute, see W. K. Hancock, *Survey*, I, 341–4, 371.

occurred in May 1936. Finally, before this stage of De Valera's programme was completed, the law of Irish citizenship was transformed; the most fundamental, if least noticed change of this period, and one which the other dominions (and Great Britain itself) followed after the Second World War. The Irish Nationality and Citizenship Act of 1935 repealed the British Nationality Acts as they applied to the Free State, deprived (in so far as the Free State could deprive) Irish citizens of their status as British subjects, and provided for them and for persons naturalised the status of Irish citizens. The accompanying Aliens Act made all persons who were not Free State citizens aliens.[1] The proud status of British subject, the common citizenship of the Empire, was repudiated in favour of a more limited but Irish nationality; 'reciprocal citizenship', the fellow of external association, was offered instead, and British subjects in Ireland were exempted by executive order from the provisions of the Aliens Act.[2]

With these measures De Valera reached the limit of his attack on the constitution and Ireland's place in the Commonwealth, until the abdication of Edward VIII in December 1936, opened the next act of the play. De Valera's programme, in this first act, was essentially moderate: the Free State still stood, a member of the Commonwealth, acknowledging in a whisper the Crown as the symbol of its free association. It was, none the less, fought with great determination by the National government. Why was this? From pride? From insistence on precarious legality? Perhaps it was because De Valera made no effort to conceal his ultimate objective: the republic, and external association with the Commonwealth. Unprepared to swallow so much at one gulp, the British government refused to take morsels bit by bit, unaccompanied by any soothing syrup.

The National government's resistance to De Valera's policies was concentrated on two issues: the oath and the land annuities. J. H. Thomas, the Dominions Secretary, insisted that the treaty (which included the oath) could only be altered by the consent of both sides.[3] The legal argument was demolished by the Judicial Committee of the Privy Council in 1935 when it recognised the

[1] Great Britain recognized no change in the status of Irish persons in the United Kingdom before the Republic of Ireland was established in 1949; after that, by the Ireland Act, 1949, Irishmen resident in Great Britain were not to be classed as aliens and might even vote in British elections.
[2] W. K. Hancock, *Survey*, I, 161–2, 337–40, 378–80; T. Ireland, *Ireland*, pp. 609–11. D. O'Sullivan, *Irish Free State*, pp. 286 ff.
[3] W. K. Hancock, *Survey*, I, 330–7.

legality, under the Statute of Westminster, of the Free State's abolition of the right of appeal to the Privy Council.[1]

This left the British government with nothing but the moral argument for the sanctity of treaties. Yet it abandoned this by resorting to economic sanctions against the Free State. When the land annuities were withheld on July 1, 1932, the National government hurried through parliament a bill to impose special duties on Irish imports into Great Britain, to recoup the Treasury for the sums withheld. By an order of July 12, duties of 20 per cent were imposed on Irish live animals, meat, bacon, poultry, butter, eggs, cream. The Free State retaliated by duties of 20 per cent on British coal, cement, iron and steel.

There were several attempts at negotiation during the five years of the trade war. De Valera was willing to submit the dispute over the land annuities to arbitration, but rejected any tribunal made up only of members of the British Commonwealth. Any other tribunal the British government refused as a 'point of principle'. 'We will take every step we can to prevent Southern Ireland going out of the British Commonwealth,' declared J. H. Thomas, on July 10, 1935.[2] All that was accomplished was the 'coal-cattle pact' of December 21, 1934: Britain increased the quota of cattle to be imported from Ireland, Ireland increased its purchases of coal from Britain; the duties remained on both sides. The pact was extended by an agreement of February 8, 1936, which also enlarged the Irish market for British cement.[3]

[1] Moore & Others vs. Attorney-General for the Irish Free State, 1935: W. K. Hancock, *Survey*, I, 372–3; Henry Harrison, *Ireland and the British Empire, 1937* (London, 1937), pp. 181–201 (a discussion of the legal aspects of De Valera's disputes with the British government which is quite as ingenious as Hancock's).

[2] W. K. Hancock, *Survey*, I, 344–9.

[3] For the trade war and its results see W. K. Hancock, *Survey*, I, 354–68; T. Ireland, *Ireland*, pp. 605, 650, 667–70; Cicely Hamilton, *Modern Ireland* (London, 1936), chapters 1, 2. The sum withheld annually by the Free State, including the land annuities, R.I.C. and other pensions, and public works and local loans repayments, was a little over £4,800,000. The British government collected slightly more than this by the duties on imports from the Free State (Hancock, I ,350–51). The effects of the trade war are shown in the following table, based on Hancock, I, 356, 367.

FREE STATE EXPORTS (£000)

	1929	1931	1933	1934	1935	1936 (10 months)
To United Kingdom	43,466	34,944	17,940	16,422	17,991	16,654
To other countries	3,338	1,332	1,129	1,152	1,624	1,553
Percentage of total *British exports* taken by Irish Free State	4·8 (4th)	7·8 (2nd)	5·2 (5th)	4·9 (5th)	4·7 (6th)	

6. CONDITIONS OF RECOVERY

Meanwhile, the nation's economy fared a good deal better. Recovery, despaired of in 1931, was in the air by 1933, obvious by 1935. The National government got little thanks for it, partly because it did not deserve it—its policies, as will be seen, neither helped nor hindered very much—partly because recovery, like the depression, was uneven, so that the misery of the depressed areas drew attention away from the return of prosperity elsewhere. This was the basis for the myth, sedulously propagated later, of the 'hungry thirties'. The reality was rather different.

The signs were clear enough. Employment, which fell from 1929 to September 1932, had recovered to its earlier level by the autumn of 1934 and was 10 per cent higher by 1937, though the increase of population was only 3·5 per cent. The number of insured persons unemployed in the United Kingdom was just under 3 millions from August 1931, to January 1933, when the peak, 2,955,000, was reached. It fell steadily thereafter, and was below 2·5 millions in August 1933, below 2 millions for the first time in July 1935, and stood at about 1,600,000 after July 1936. The proportion of insured persons unemployed was 9.7 per cent in May 1929, 23 per cent at the peak, 12 per cent in 1936. In other industrial countries, the proportions were higher, at the bottom of the depression, and recovery slower.[1]

Figures of production and foreign trade showed the same tendencies. Production declined by about 15 per cent between 1929 and 1932, but by 1937 was 20 per cent above the level of 1929.[2] Imports dropped only 11 per cent in volume but 40 per cent in value; by 1936 they had returned to the old level in volume, though still 32 per cent less in value. Exports, on the other hand, fell 32 per cent in volume and 50 per cent in value, and made only a slight recovery after 1932. Since world trade dropped by over a quarter of its previous volume between 1929 and 1932, Britain did not do too badly; in fact her share in world trade rose slightly.[3]

---

[1] *Britain in Recovery* (London, 1938), pp. 4–8, 91–5, 104, for a fuller discussion of the facts and figures; this is an invaluable collaborative work by a Research Committee of the Economic Science and Statistics section of the British Association for the Advancement of Science, a companion volume to *Britain in Depression*. See also *Statistical Abstract of U.K., 1936*, pp. 132–3, and Table 2, below. Allowing for uninsured persons out of work the number of unemployed persons over fourteen in Great Britain may have been as high as 3,747,000, at the peak (*Britain in Recovery*, p. 95).

[2] Ibid., pp. 6–11, and Table 2, below.

[3] See W. A. Morton, *British Finance, 1930–1940* (Madison, 1943), pp. 202, 206, 210, and Table 3, below. Cf. J. B. Condliffe, *Commerce of Nations* (New York, 1950), p. 495; *Britain in Recovery*, pp. 13, 17; A. E. Kahn, *Great Britain in the World*

Table 1
Unemployment in Great Britain and Elsewhere[1]

Year	No. of Insured Persons Unemployed in Great Britain in January (millions)[2]	Percentages of Unemployment (Yearly Averages)					
		Great Britain	Australia	Canada	Germany	United States	Sweden
1932	2·85	21·9	29·0	22·0	30·1	23·8	22·8
1933	2·95	19·8	25·1	22·3	25·8	24·3	23·7
1934	2·40	16·6	20·5	18·2	14·5	20·9	18·9
1935	2·29	15·3	16·5	15·4	11·6	18·5	16·1
1936	2·13	13·0	12·2	13·2	8·1	13·3	13·6
1937	1·67						
1938	1·81						

Table 2
Index of Production in Great Britain, 1929–37[3] (1929 = 100)

1929	..	100	1933	..	93
1930	..	92	1934	..	104
1931	..	84	1935	..	110
1932	..	85	1936	..	118
			1937	..	124

These figures pointed the moral. In depression and recovery the standard of living fell but little in Great Britain—for those in work. Imports were maintained, but cost much less than before; exports languished. Much of Britain's recovery was at the expense of the foreign producer and of the unemployed, particularly those in the depressed areas which were dependent on the export trades.

Economy, pp. 126, 132. For a general account of British recovery see F. C. Benham, Great Britain under Protection, pp. 218 ff.—an admirable book; and for an excellent contemporary survey, Herbert Heaton, British Way to Recovery (Minneapolis, 1934).
[1] Britain in Recovery, p. 104, based on International Labour Review.
[2] Statistical Abstract of U.K., 1938, p. 134.
[3] London and Cambridge Economic Service: Annual Index of Production, as given in table in Britain in Recovery, p. 6. This same table gives other indices: the Board of Trade's is quite similar to that of L.C.E.S., one based on Colin Clark, National Income and Outlay, tables 91, 93 (national output of goods and services, excluding invisible exports) shows a smaller fall (1931 and 1932: 93; 1933: 98).

At the same time, and for the same reasons, the cost of living fell, providing the margin for increased investment at home: the result was the housing boom, which had a good deal to do with the process of recovery, and took the place of a large public works programme, such as the United States adopted. Other factors were the continuing growth of the consumer industries and the home market, and the beginning of rearmament (which had little effect until quite late). There was also some industrial expansion—more than was usually recognised—both in older industries such as steel, china, railways, and in the new industries: chemicals, rayon, motor cars. Beside all this the government's policies—tariffs, import quotas, marketing schemes, devaluation, exchange control, cheap money—made very little difference.

Table 3

Britain's Share of World Trade[1]

Year	Value of World Trade (1929 = 100)	Share of U.K. (per cent)	Value of U.K. Imports (1927 = 100)	Volume of U.K. Imports (1927 = 100)	Price of U.K. Imports (£ millions)	Share of World Imports (per cent)	Value of U.K. Exports (£ millions)	Value of U.K. Exports (1927 = 100)	Volume of U.K. Exports (1927 = 100)	Share of World Exports (per cent)
1929	100	13·1	100·2	101·4	1112	15·24	729·5	100·9	104·0	10·76
1930	93·0	13·4	85·7	98·8	957	16·11	570·6	79·0	87·3	10·51
1931	85·5	13·3	70·7	101·0	798	17·18	389·2	54·6	69·4	9·36
1932	74·6	13·4	57·6	88·9	702	16·43	365·0	50·0	68·1	10·06
1933	75·4	13·5	55·4	89·5	675	16·58	367·9	50·1	68·8	10·37
1934	78·2	13·8	60·1	93·9	731	17·05	396·0	53·8	72·2	10·47
1935	81·8	13·9	62·1	95·4	756	17·46	425·8	57·8	78·6	11·08
1936	85·8	14·5	69·6	101·5	848	18·22	440·6	60·3	79·6	10·61
1937	96·8	13·6	84·4	107·8	1028	17·03	521·4	71·7	86·4	9·87

In part, Britain's recovery was of a piece with the general recovery in world trade which began, for no apparent reason except to confirm the theory of the trade cycle, in 1933. Britain's balance of payments in these years was an indication of the country's fortunes. In 1931 there was an unfavourable balance of £104 millions, in 1932 a smaller deficit, in 1933 an exact balance, in 1935 a favourable balance (as there had been in the twenties). Improved income from shipping and overseas investments, reflecting the recovery in world trade, contributed most.[2] Danger

[1] W. A. Morton, *British Finance, 1930–1940*, pp. 202, 206, 210, based on League of Nations, *Review of World Trade*, and *Board of Trade Journal*.
[2] See Table 4 below; also A. E. Kahn, p. 126; W. A. Morton, pp. 201, 223 ff.; *Britain in Recovery*, pp. 18–23; W. A. Lewis, *Economic Survey*, p. 85.

signals were still there for those who would read them: the export of gold, and the decline in new overseas capital issues, which was all the greater if the sums coming in as repayment of past loans and investments were placed alongside.[1] At certain times between 1931 and 1934 new overseas investments were actually prohibited by the government.[2] More than ever, the country was living on its fat.

And on the difficulties of others. In the thirties the terms of trade, already in Britain's favour, became even more so. The fall in world commodity prices, which was greater than the fall in export prices, meant that Britain could import the former volume of goods at two-thirds of the former cost, a saving of about £400 millions annually.[3]

Table 4

Britain's Balance of Payments[4]

1930–37 (£ millions)

	1930	1931	1932	1933	1934	1935	1936	1937
Imports (−) (a)	1053	870	710	685	754	797	865	1048
Exports (a)	666	461	422	422	460	536	519	606
Balance	− 387	− 408	− 287	− 263	− 294	− 261	− 345	− 442
Shipping receipts ..	105	80	70	65	70	70	85	130
Income from overseas investments	220	170	150	160	170	185	200	210
Other receipts	89	54	16	38	47	38	42	46
Balance on current account ..	27	− 104	− 51	0	− 7	32	− 18	− 56
Net gold movements ..	− 2	31	− 15	− 195	107	− 115	− 166	− 190
New overseas capital issues (b)	98	41	37	83	63	51	61	60
Repayments	39	27	48	67	42	81	107	61

(*a*) Kahn's figures for imports and exports, being based on those of the *Board of Trade Journal*, are different from those used by W. A. Morton and cited above, Table 3.

(*b*) 1928: £143 millions.

[1] Sir Robert Kindersley's annual articles on British foreign investments in the *Economic Journal*, 1929–38; A. E. Kahn, p. 139; W. A. Morton, p. 304; J. H. Richardson, *British Economic Foreign Policy*, p. 73.
[2] J. H. Richardson, pp. 69–75, gives particulars.
[3] See Table 5, below; also A. E. Kahn, pp. 144, 153; *Britain in Recovery*, pp. 14–17; F. C. Benham, pp. 237–9; W. A. Lewis, p. 81; G. L. Schwartz, 'Terms of Trade', *Sunday Times*, June 6, 1948.
[4] Based on A. E. Kahn, p. 126.

Table 5

Britain's Terms of Trade, 1929–38[1]
(1913 = 100) (a)

1929	1930	1931	1932	1933	1934	1935	1936	1937	1938
114·5	121·6	134·2	134·5	139·7	136·4	134·0	130·1	123·6	133·3

(a) I.e. 100 export units bringing in 100 import units.

7. TARIFFS, QUOTAS, CURRENCIES

Not that the National government did not attempt directly to regulate trade in the interests of recovery. Such policies had two features: they were restrictionist; and they were a part of the economic nationalism which had become even more fashionable than before.

One such policy, devaluation, had little lasting effect. Sudden fluctuations in exchange rates were prevented by the Exchange Equalisation Fund, opened in July 1932; but the attempt to use it also to buy gold and keep the pound down in value was countered by the new government in the United States, under President F. D. Roosevelt, which revalued the gold reserve and devalued the dollar in 1933. The Fund was later used against the franc, until France went off gold in September 1936 and joined a tripartite agreement with Britain and the United States to use equalisation funds to maintain stability. Actually the pound, which fell from $4.85 to $3.37 after devaluation, rose to $5.13 and settled down to around $4.99 by the end of 1933.[2] One result of Britain's devaluation was the formation of the sterling bloc, consisting of Britain, the Dominions and the Scandinavian countries. Britain, the great free trader, had started the vogue for managed currencies.

The Ottawa agreements helped to reshape Britain's foreign trade without increasing it. Their effect was limited by the seventeen trade agreements which Britain concluded between 1932 and 1935 with other countries, the most important being those with Argentina, Norway, Sweden, Denmark, Poland, Germany, Russia (one was made also with the United States, but not till 1938). By these agreements Britain gave quotas for the importation of meat, butter and other natural products, in return for con-

---

[1] A. E. Kahn, p. 153.
[2] See table in W. A. Morton, p. 124, and his discussion, pp. 121–74; also N. F. Hall in *Britain in Recovery*, pp. 149–61.

cessions for British exports (especially coal in the case of the
Baltic countries). The bargaining power of the tariff was thus put
to use, at the expense of the privileges won by the Dominions for
their exports to Britain at Ottawa.[1]

The general effects of these policies are shown in the table
below. Britain in the thirties obtained more of her meat, bacon,
butter and grain than previously from the Dominions, at the
expense of Denmark and Argentina; British consumption increased, but former suppliers shared only slightly in the enlarged
market. British exports of machinery, motor cars and textiles to
the Dominions benefited. The increase in exports of coal to the
Baltic countries, which helped the east coast ports and coalfields,
was paid for by the loss of markets for British coal in France,
Italy and Belgium, which were supplied with German coal thrust
away from the Scandinavian countries. South Wales, the great
exporting coalfield, was the sufferer.[2]

Table 6

Proportions of British Trade with Empire and Foreign Countries[3]
1929–38

	1929	1930	1931	1932	1933	1934	1935	1936	1937	1938
Imports: (a) from Empire	25·7%	25·0	24·5	31·6	34·3	34·7	35·1	36·8	37·3	37·9
from foreign countries ..	70·6%	70·9	71·3	64·6	63·1	62·9	62·4	60·8	60·6	59·6
Exports: (a) to Empire	39·6%	37·5	35·9	38·2	39·2	42·0	43·3	44·4	44·2	45·6
to foreign countries ..	55·5%	56·5	56·3	54·7	55·6	53·1	52·0	50·8	51·7	50·1

(a) Trade with the Irish Free State is excluded: hence the combined percentages do not come
to 100 per cent.

The counterpart to the tariff and the trade agreements was the
series of measures designed to help the British farmer. In the
beginning the state's intervention was limited to the setting up of
marketing boards to regulate the grading and pricing of certain

[1] J. H. Richardson, *British Economic Foreign Policy*, pp. 101–21; F. C. Benham,
pp. 128–45; H. Heaton, pp. 101–11.
[2] For fuller details, see F. C. Benham, pp. 102–9, 145–8; J. H. Richardson, pp.
121–9, 147–55; W. K. Hancock, *Survey of British Commonwealth Affairs*, II, i, 230–60.
[3] Based on table in F. Benham, pp. 256–7 (source: *Statistical Abstract of the British
Empire*). W. Schlote's figures (*British Overseas Trade*, p. 163) are about 1 per cent
higher for the proportion of British imports and exports within the Empire; see
above, chap. 5, pp. 265–6.

products, with coercion applied to the recalcitrant minority once two-thirds of the producers had accepted the scheme. This was an inheritance from the Labour government, Addison's Agricultural Marketing Act of 1931, which was put to use vigorously by Walter Elliot, the Minister of Agriculture after 1932. Regulation of the home market was, however, ineffective if imports remained uncontrolled; hence the addition, in the Agricultural Marketing Act of 1933, of powers for the fixing by the Board of Trade of quotas for the importation of certain products from abroad. When quotas and tariffs failed to give the British farmer the protection and incentive he needed, subsidies were resorted to. The results in some instances were not without absurdity.

Marketing boards were created for milk, bacon, potatoes, hops. Of these the Bacon Marketing Board was the least successful in raising prices for the farmer, in spite of the limitation of imports of Danish bacon by a quota scheme to 64 per cent of their previous volume; in 1938 bacon producers were given a subsidy. The producers of eggs and poultry rejected a marketing scheme, but were protected by quotas and import duties. The livestock farmer was supposed to be helped by the reduction of imports of frozen and chilled beef from Argentina, Australia and New Zealand; but the Dominions balked at reducing their exports for his benefit and he was eventually helped by a subsidy from the government, first given in 1934 and renewed by the Livestock Industry Act of 1937. The growers of fruit, flowers and vegetables were given the protection of import duties, but were not subject to marketing schemes. Fishermen were helped by the imposition of quotas for the importing of foreign-caught fish in the Sea-Fishing Industry Act of 1933.

The largest marketing scheme was that for milk, inaugurated in 1933. The Milk Marketing Board, with subsidiary boards for eleven regions into which England and Wales were divided (Scotland had a scheme of its own), was the intermediary in all contracts for the sale of milk by farmers to the milk companies, and paid to the farmers a 'pool price' which was roughly midway between the wholesale price of liquid milk and the price of milk sold for manufacture and destined to become butter, cheese, dried or condensed milk, cream or plastics. Farmers who sold their milk retail were obliged to pay a levy to the Board. The scheme was an extension of that previously sponsored by the National Farmers' Union, by which milk prices had been negotiated annually between the producers and the large distributors. Milk production increased, but its consequences were checked by another intervention; rather than see the farmer receive a lower price, the government tried to encourage people to 'drink more milk' by subsidising its distribution at low prices to mothers in the depressed areas and to children in the state schools. Even so, the consumption of milk rose only slightly, from 0·38 pints per head daily in 1933–34 to 0·42 pints in 1936–37. A disastrous fall in the price of 'manufactured' milk was prevented by quotas and duties on the importation of butter, cheese and dried milk from foreign countries; but New Zealand would submit to no such restrictions, and the government had to subsidise the price of 'manufactured milk' also. The *Economist* made merry at the 'economics of Bedlam', by which the low price of milk sold for the manufacture of umbrella handles, 5d. per gallon, was held to justify keeping the price of milk for mothers at 2s. or more per gallon.

The production of wheat and sugar beets was encouraged in other ways. By the Wheat Act of 1932 a processing tax was levied on every sack of flour milled in Great Britain, and the money used to pay the farmer a deficiency payment covering the difference between the actual price of wheat and a guaranteed price of 10s. per hundredweight (45s. per quarter). There was a low duty on wheat imported from foreign countries, and also on imported barley. Acreage subsidies were given to the growers of barley and oats. Land under wheat increased from 1,200,000 acres in 1932 to 1,700,000 acres in 1937, and production from 20 million hundredweight to over 30 million; but even the bumper harvest of 1934 of 36 million hundredweight supplied only a quarter of Britain's needs.[1] The scheme was not an unmixed blessing: it encouraged the least efficient producers, and by diverting wheat from feed it increased the need for imported feeding stuffs for cattle. As for sugar beet, long the pampered child of British farming, its subsidy, due to end in 1934, was continued by the Sugar Industry (Reorganisation) Act of 1936 despite the adverse report of an official committee of inquiry; about one-third of the country's sugar came from its own soil, at an annual cost of £5·5 millions in subsidy and abatement of excise.

Partly as a result of these measures, British agricultural output increased in volume by one-sixth between 1931 and 1937. The

---

[1] A quarter = 8 bushels; 1 bushel = 60 lb. of wheat; one hundredweight = 112 lb., one-twentieth of a ton. Thus one quarter (measure of capacity) = a little over 4 hundredweight of wheat in weight.

number of pigs and poultry had increased by 50 per cent; the number of dairy cows increased, but not the herds of cattle and sheep. Farm prices increased, to the benefit of farmer and labourer, and also of landlords and those concerned in land values. The cost to the state of assistance to agriculture, which was estimated at £45 millions a year in 1934, was put at £100 millions by 1939; of this nearly £24 millions was accounted for by subsidies, £17 millions by derating, and £60 millions by the increased cost of raising at home what would otherwise have come from abroad. To the consumer the programme had at least not raised prices, thanks to the low level of the prices of primary products the world over and the lowering of prices by foreign exporters to offset the protection given to British and Dominion foodstuffs. The index number of retail food prices (1914 = 100) was 131 in 1931, 120 in 1933, 130 in 1936.[1]

With such policies in the ascendant, there was little prospect that a great international conference would succeed in reconstructing world trade or a free world economy by arranging for the reduction of tariffs, the raising of commodity prices and the stabilisation of currencies and exchange rates. These were the objectives of the World Economic Conference of 1933, long prepared for, and freighted with high hopes, the more so because, for once, the United States was a full participant. It was, in fact, the last of the great international conferences of the interwar years; its success a desperate hope, now that economic nationalism and militarism were increasing their sway, and the Nazis were already in power in Germany; its failure prophetic of doom. It was opened in London by the King on June 12, and was presided over by MacDonald. It ended in fact, though not in ceremony, on July 3 when it received President Roosevelt's 'bombshell' message rejecting the idea of an agreement for the international stabilisation of currencies because it would hamper national policies designed to raise the purchasing power of the people at home by currency regulation. For the conference's failure Roosevelt was given the blame; but Great Britain, by abandoning the gold standard, creating the Exchange Equalisation Fund, and enacting

[1] The fullest accounts of the marketing schemes and other measures of agricultural assistance are in *Britain in Recovery*, pp. 165–230; cf. *Britain in Depression*, pp. 89–151. For maliciously witty comment, see A. S. J. Baster, *The Little Less*, pp. 36–49. Other good accounts are in J. H. Richardson, pp. 156–98; F. Benham, pp. 48–58, 62–9, 202–14; H. Heaton, *British Way to Recovery*, pp. 78–98; A. F. Lucas, *Industrial Reconstruction and the Control of Competition*, pp. 228–58. For reactions in the Dominions to these policies see W. K. Hancock, *Survey of British Commonwealth Affairs*, II, i, 239–44.

the new tariff, was as much to blame, the temper of the times even more so. In the rest of the agenda, including the reduction of tariffs, the conference was no more successful. *Sauve qui peut* was the new motto; collective action by the nations not even a pious hope. The new rulers of Germany were not slow in making and following their own deductions from the conference's outcome.[1]

8. THE OLD INDUSTRIES: RESTRICTION AND EXPANSION

Meanwhile there were signs of recovery among the heavy industries which had been longest and deepest in the slough of depression. The pattern was strangely varied: schemes for the restriction of output on the one hand, programmes of expansion on the other; the help of the government, in finance or in legislation, sometimes sought, sometimes refused or ignored.

The iron and steel industry illustrates the several responses of heavy industry to the depression. Production of steel dropped from 9·6 million tons in 1929 to 5·2 millions in 1931. By 1933 it had recovered to 7 million tons, by 1936 to 11·8 million tons, reaching 13 million tons in 1937. Unemployment in the industry claimed 47·7 per cent of its insured workers in June 1932, only 10·7 per cent of a slightly larger number of workers in June 1937.[2] Exports had declined to less than half their previous volume between 1929 and 1933; imports, until 1931, remained steady at the pre-depression figure of about 2·8 million tons.[3] Billets and bars and other semi-finished products, much of them of Bessemer steel, came in, chiefly from Germany and Belgium; they had always been important to the British re-rollers, and had become even more so since production of Bessemer steel in Britain had almost ceased. These imports were thus both normal and necessary; but on the ground of abnormality they found themselves opposed, after April 1932, by a 33⅓ per cent tariff on semi-finished products, and a lower tariff of 20 per cent on finished goods—a curious discrimination against the raw material of many British manufacturers.

The Import Duties Advisory Committee's report recommending these tariffs made them temporary and conditional upon 'a considerable measure of reorganisation' of the industry, arguing that protection alone would not 'enable it to play its proper part

---

[1] H. V. Hodson, *Slump and Recovery*, pp. 172–206; *Annual Register, 1932*, pp. 52–9, 288–92; Jeannette P. Nichols, 'Roosevelt's monetary diplomacy in 1933', *American Historical Review*, 56 (1951), 295–317.
[2] *Britain in Recovery*, pp. 102, 364.   [3] *Britain in Depression*, pp. 271–3.

in the national economy'.[1] Yet the industry, though thus offered, in effect, a cartel with the government's blessing, was reluctant to reorganise. Eventually, in February 1934, the National Federation of Iron and Steel Manufacturers accepted a reorganisation of the Federation into the British Iron and Steel Federation, with a new constitution, an independent chairman (Sir Andrew Duncan, previously chairman of the Central Electricity Board), and some powers of co-ordination over the associations controlling the various sections of the industry. On the strength of this, the I.D.A.C. recommended that the tariff on steel become permanent.[2]

This paper reorganisation soon involved a real cartel. Though imports fell after the imposition of the tariff, dropping to one million tons in 1933, they began to rise in 1934; exports remained nearly stagnant. The B.I.S.F. demanded a higher tariff; the government instead recommended a bargain with the European steel cartel, *Entente Internationale de l'Acier*, comprising the producers of Germany, France, Belgium, Luxembourg. Bargaining proved difficult, until the government helped with a temporary increase of the tariff to 50 per cent *ad valorem*. This led to an agreement made in July 1935 between the British steel industry and what became the International Steel Cartel. British import duties were lowered to 20 per cent on a quota of imports set, at first, at 670,000 tons of 'cartel products' (imports from outside the Cartel would, with certain exceptions, be subject to the duty of 50 per cent). Britain, in turn, received export quotas for the continental markets. This involved secondary arrangements with the existing international cartels for tin-plate, rails and ship-plate.[3] Quotas for the production and export of British steel and for the supply of imported steel to British users, administered by the B.I.S.F., were a necessary consequence.[4]

Amalgamations and the closing of steelworks were characteristic of the industry in the thirties; but there were schemes of expansion also. Richard Thomas and Company continued to absorb tin-plate works in South Wales; United Steel Companies increased their interests in Lincolnshire. In Scotland Colvilles, by new purchases, enlarged their empire until it included virtually the entire Scottish industry except the Scottish Iron and Steel Company (which in 1939 joined with Bairds, the coal combine).

---

[1] Cmd. 4066 and 4181 (1932), quoted in F. Benham, *Great Britain under Protection*, p. 181.
[2] *Britain in Depression*, pp. 277–9; 'Ingot', *Socialisation of Iron and Steel*, pp. 96–8.
[3] F. Benham, pp. 182–4, 188–91.
[4] Ibid., pp. 184–5; I.D.A.C., *Report on Steel Industry*, pp. 64–5.

Colvilles closed the large Mossend works at Coatbridge. Dorman Long closed the Bell works at Clarence. Guest Keen closed the great works at Dowlais, leaving of the cradle of the Welsh iron industry nothing more than a triumphal arch of coal leading to a vast emptiness and a few crumbling foundations on a hillside. These were grievous blows to the districts concerned, even though counter-balanced by new plants elsewhere.[1]

One glaring example of the discouragement of new enterprise on the part of the British Iron and Steel Federation coloured its reputation with the public: the more because it concerned the best-known, if not quite the saddest, of the towns laid low by depression, Jarrow. This Tyneside town, dependent on Palmers' shipyards for employment, was reduced to destitution when the yards were closed as part of the restrictionist programme of the shipbuilders. In September 1935, 72·9 per cent of its insured workers were unemployed. A company proposed to construct on the site of the shipyards an integrated steelworks designed on the principles of Henry Brassert, a well-known consultant. The scheme came to nothing because of obstruction from the Federation.[2] Thereupon, the townspeople and the town council organised a march of 200 Jarrow men to London in October 1936, with the aid of Ellen Wilkinson, the local M.P.; they carried petitions asking the government to provide work for the area. New efforts followed. The people of Surrey had adopted the town in 1934, thanks to the enthusiasm of Sir John Jarvis, the sheriff, and Chuter Ede, chairman of the county education committee (Home Secretary in the Labour governments of 1945–51), and subscriptions had helped to start relief schemes. Jarvis founded Jarrow Metal Industries, Ltd., bought part of Palmers' shipyard and the Close works of Armstrong, Whitworth at Gateshead, and established in Jarrow in 1938 a foundry, a tube mill, a ship-breaking yard, and engineering works. In 1939 the Consett Iron Company, with some help from the Bankers' Industrial Development Corporation, began the construction of a new steelworks in Jarrow. Those of Jarrow's unemployed who did not find work in these concerns were soon absorbed by the yards elsewhere along the Tyne, busy on armaments.[3]

---

[1] *Britain in Depression*, p. 277; D. L. Burn, *Economic History of Steelmaking*, p. 451.
[2] Ellen Wilkinson, *The Town that Was Murdered*, pp. 172–86, has a full account, which may be compared with D. L. Burn, p. 461, and I.D.A.C., *Report on the Iron and Steel Industry* (Cmd. 5507: 1937), pp. 23–9.
[3] E. Wilkinson, pp. 194–211; I.D.A.C., *Report on Steel Industry*, p. 29; information from Jarrow Metal Industries, June, 1948.

By the late thirties the steel industry could claim without pre-varication that expansion rather than restriction was its chief characteristic; and in fact in the 'gloomy thirties' little is more remarkable in British industry than the construction of several large steelworks of heroic conception. Three large schemes were begun in 1937: the construction of new blast furnaces and coke ovens by United Steel Companies at Frodingham (Lincs.) and at Workington, the enlargement of Colvilles' plant at Clyde-bridge, and the construction of the John Summers' sheet-making plant at Shotton (near Chester) with a broad strip mill, opened in 1939. Altogether, steel-furnace capacity was raised from 11 million tons in 1929 and 13·5 million tons in 1937 to 14 million tons at the end of 1939.[1]

To this expansion two large enterprises made further contribu-tions. In 1932 Stewart and Lloyds began the construction of a huge integrated steelworks at Corby, Northamptonshire; two years later the first steel was made in the plant. The works at Corby were an epic of pioneering. Corby was a small village in open country, near large ironstone deposits which had attracted several small blast furnaces to it. Here were constructed, to Brassert's specifications, blast furnaces, coke ovens and by-pro-ducts plants, a blooming mill, strip mills, and tube works; most of the steel, made from local ores won by open-cast mining, was used on the spot for the making of tubes, replacing imported strip. By an interesting reversion to older British practice, the steel used was basic Bessemer rather than open-hearth steel. By November 1936, nearly 4000 persons were employed at the works. Half of the workers were recruited locally, but one-third were Scots, uprooted from the derelict steel towns of Lanarkshire and the Clyde, and moved, with the help of the Ministry of Labour, and accompanied by their own butchers, to this strange southern countryside.[2]

The setting of the other large enterprise was more sombre: the narrow, steep-sided valley of Ebbw Vale. Richard Thomas and Company bought the works of the Ebbw Vale Company, a coal and iron concern which had failed, demolished them, and built along the valley bottom, strung out over a length of two miles, a series of works including blast furnaces, coke ovens, steel furnaces (three Bessemer, four open-hearth), rolling and cogging mills, cold

---

[1] *Britain in Recovery*, p. 371; D. L. Burn, p. 464; P. W. S. Andrews and E. Brunner, *Capital Investment in Steel*, pp. 187–234.
[2] I.D.A.C., *Report on the Steel Industry*, pp. 71–5; information from Stewart and Lloyds, Corby, April, 1948.

reduction mills and a wide-strip mill, the first in the country, used for making strip for tinplate. Much of the heavy machinery came from the United States. The works were opened in 1938. Ebbw Vale was not an ideal site, distant from ore deposits or ports though near to coal. The original intention of Sir William Firth, the driving force of Richard Thomas and Company, was to construct the strip mill at Redbourn, Lincolnshire. The pressure of the government, and the public campaign to help South Wales in its distress, led him to choose the site at Ebbw Vale.[1]

In contrast with the steel industry, shipbuilding produced no examples of expansion but a striking instance of restriction. Since the postwar over-expansion of shipyard capacity and the record tonnage, over 2 millions, built in British yards in 1920, orders had fallen off, though in 1930 Britain still launched over 1·4 million tons. Next year the tonnage launched was about one-third of that; in the worst year, 1933, it was 133,000 tons. Over 60 per cent of shipyard workers were unemployed, though the total number of workers had fallen. A plan to reduce shipyard capacity, leaving surviving yards to compete for the reduced number of orders at higher prices, was not unnatural. It came early, however, and owed nothing to the government though much to the banks which had lent heavily to shipbuilding companies. A company, National Shipbuilders' Security, was formed in February 1930 under the leadership of Sir James Lithgow, head of a Port Glasgow shipbuilding firm and connected, as a director, with several other Scottish shipbuilding companies and with Colvilles. The capital came from the shipbuilding companies and the Bankers' Industrial Development Corporation; and N.S.S. also received a levy of 1 per cent on the sale or contract price of all ships built by its members. Its purpose was to buy up shipyards and sterilise them from shipbuilding for forty years. In four years it had acquired 137 berths with a capacity of one million tons; thereafter its efforts slackened. This left a capacity of about 1,400,000 tons, about 40 per cent above the estimated demand, based on Britain's share in the world demand of 900,000 tons of new construction annually. Among the victims of N.S.S. were several Scottish shipyards and several on Tyne and Tees, including Palmers' at Jarrow, which launched its last ship in 1932, went into receivership in 1933 and was sold to N.S.S. in 1934.[2]

[1] D. L. Burn, p. 459; E. Wilkinson, p. 187; information gathered at Ebbw Vale, April, 1948.
[2] E. Wilkinson, pp. 145–64; *Britain in Depression*, pp. 250–6.

A revival in shipping and shipbuilding was helped by the intervention of the government. By the British Shipping (Assistance) Act of 1935 a subsidy was granted to tramp shipping; and the building of new ships was encouraged by government loans under a 'scrap and build' scheme. The tonnage of new ships launched in British yards rose to 856,300 in 1936, 920,800 in 1937, and the proportion of shipyard workers unemployed fell to 24·4 per cent.[1]

Table 7

Britain's Merchant Marine

Year	Million Tons	Percentage of World Tonnage
1913	19	39·2
1929	20	29·6
1937	17·5	26·5

Of a different character was the government's intervention, after earlier and uncharitable refusals, in the North Atlantic Shipping Act, 1934. This made available government loans up to £9·5 millions for capital and construction of ships for the North Atlantic service. There were two principal objects: to help the merger of Cunard and White Star and keep the latter from falling into American control; and to re-start construction of Number 534, the Cunarder later named *Queen Mary*, which had been rotting on the stocks at Clydebank for many months. David Kirkwood's agitation, public pressure for work for the unemployed, and the desire to regain the 'blue ribbon' of the North Atlantic were thus all gratified.[2]

The coal-mining industry followed yet another pattern. By act of parliament (Part I of the Coal Mines Act of 1930) it had obtained authority for production quotas. A central council set the tonnage of coal to be raised each year, and gave quotas to the districts, which in turn, under the control of district boards, allotted tonnages to individual collieries. The district board also fixed

---

[1] E. Wilkinson, pp. 167–70; *Britain in Recovery*, pp. 341–59 (both this section and the preceding one on shipping (pp. 325 ff.) have excellent tables on British and world shipping and ship-building); F. Benham, pp. 58–60; E. Davies, '*National*' *Capitalism: the Government's Record as Protector of Private Monopoly* (London, 1939), pp. 161–84.

[2] F. Benham, p. 58; H. Heaton, pp. 114–17.

minimum prices. Control of selling, either by selling syndicates or, more usually, by selling committees which issued permits for individual sales, was a development of 1936. The scheme was amended from time to time. It was not so much restrictive as distributive—an early application of 'fair shares' for all. Though it kept alive the production—and resulting employment—of inefficient mines and certainly penalised some of the efficient companies whose output was curtailed, it did not block efficiency altogether; for unused quotas within each district could be bought by the more ambitious concerns. Moreover, the annual national tonnage permitted was never quite reached.[1] A time of peace and equilibrium had come for the harassed industry. Output fell from 244 million tons in 1930 to 207 millions in 1933, and recovered to 241 millions in 1937. Exports (including bunkers) had been 75 million tons in 1930 and reached their lowest figure, 50 million tons, in 1936, recovering to 56 millions in 1937. The labour force declined; of the smaller number of miners 18·9 per cent were unemployed in June 1937, as compared with 40·6 per cent in 1932.[2] In 1935 the miners asked for a wage increase of 2s. per shift (the 'miners' two bob'); by a settlement in January 1936, they received half of this. The selling agencies, which were to raise prices to support the wage increase, were a result.

So far would the coal-owners go in tolerating the interference of the government. To schemes of reorganisation involving compulsion they opposed all the rugged individualism which other industrialists eschewed. The Coal Mines Reorganisation Commission, created by Part II of the Act of 1930, ruefully reported in 1933 that it had failed to promote voluntary schemes of amalgamation of collieries in any district, and in 1936 that out of four schemes which it had prepared, one, for West Yorkshire, had been rejected by the Railway and Canal Commission in a test case in 1935, leaving all its work at a standstill.[3] The National government decided to intervene. A bill was introduced in 1936 to strengthen the powers of the Commission. Against the coal-owners' opposition the government yielded; it first announced large amendments and then withdrew the bill altogether. It was not until 1938 that a new bill was introduced, and again the fury of the owners was aroused. Again the government yielded to its friends: the pro-

---

[1] *Britain in Recovery*, pp. 239–44; W. H. B. Court, 'Problems of the British Coal Industry between the wars', *Econ. Hist. Review*, XV (1945), 15–17.
[2] *Britain in Recovery*, pp. 56, 102.
[3] Mines Department, Coal Mines Reorganisation Commission, *Reports*: Cmd. 4468 (1933), 5069 (1936).

cedure for amalgamations was made so difficult as to be almost unworkable.[1]

However, the owners had to swallow, in another part of the Coal Act of 1938, the nationalisation of royalties. In itself a small matter, this was a milestone in the history of nationalisation; it was reached by the National government which the Conservatives dominated; and it made easier, and brought nearer, the nationalisation of the mining of the coal to which the state had now resumed title. In the matter of compensation the Act set precedents for the future. When government and owners failed to agree on a figure, the matter was arbitrated. The owners were awarded nearly £66·5 millions—fifteen years' purchase of the estimated income, or rather over half the £112 millions which they had demanded, and less than the £75 millions the government had offered. The government increased the award by £10 millions. By this award individual bargains were refused: a 'global' sum was given, to be distributed among the royalty owners. A new Coal Commission was given control of the royalties and also the revised powers of reorganisation deriving from the Coal Mines Reorganisation Commission.[2]

9. AIR SERVICES AND LONDON'S TRANSPORT: TWO CASES OF NATIONALISATION

There were two other industries in which the intervention of the National government took the form of nationalisation. The first was civil aviation. Imperial Airways, with the aid of subsidies from the government, had successfully pioneered the routes of empire, but had failed to profit from its European services. In 1935 it faced a rival, British Airways, formed by a merger of Hillman Airways, started in 1932 by Edward Hillman, founder of a successful motor-coach business, with two other companies, and also enjoying a subsidy. British Airways was given a monopoly for the British service to Scandinavian countries and to Berlin, and competed with Imperial Airways in the lucrative London-Paris service. The results were disastrous; and in 1938 an official report recommended a division of empire and European services between the two companies and an expansion of both. Imperial Airways was then reorganised by Sir John Reith, who reluctantly left the B.B.C. for the purpose and brought to civil aviation the B.B.C.'s gospel of a single chosen instrument exer-

[1] E. Davies, *National Capitalism*, pp. 139–45; W. H. B. Court, *loc. cit.*, pp. 18–19.
[2] E. Davies, ibid., pp. 127–39.

cising public responsibility for an industry dependent on public money. The government decided to merge Imperial Airways and British Airways into a public corporation, British Overseas Airways Corporation, whose directors would be appointed by the Air Secretary. The necessary bill was introduced in July 1939, and the new corporation came into being in April 1940.[1] The arguments for this piece of 'Tory socialism' were quite empirical: the new corporation would put national interests first, advance Britain's position in overseas civil aviation services, encourage the production of British aircraft, and end the competition between two heavily-subsidised private companies.[2]

During these years there was progress towards the establishment of transatlantic air services. The Germans operated a service by airships in the summer of 1936, but abandoned it after the accident at Lakehurst, New Jersey, which destroyed the *Hindenburg* by fire on its maiden voyage in May 1937. Imperial Airways and Pan American Airways made experimental flights by aeroplane across the Atlantic in 1937, and agreed on the use of airports at Foynes, Ireland, and Botwood, Newfoundland for the route. The first commercial flight was made by Pan American in the summer of 1939, followed by a flight by Imperial Airways' flying boat, *Caribou*, with mail in August; but regular commercial services had to await the end of the Second World War.

Within the British Isles there was a large increase in internal services. In the summer of 1932 'ferry' services were given to the Isle of Man, the Isle of Wight, between Romford and Clacton and between Bristol and Cardiff. In 1934 internal mail was regularly flown, first between Inverness and the Orkneys, later on the London–Belfast–Glasgow route and to the Shetlands and Isle of Man. In 1935 there were 76 services flown by 19 companies, in 1936, 54 services flown by 16 companies; route mileage was 4019 in 1936, compared with 5810 in 1935, 3265 in 1934. The number of passengers carried on internal services was over 72,000 in 1934, 121,000 in 1935. The most successful services were those to islands attractive to summer holiday-makers; especially the service to the Channel Islands.[3]

[1] A. Plummer, *New British Industries of the Twentieth Century*, pp. 160–85; E. Davies, *National Capitalism*, pp. 245–64; Lord Reith, *Into the Wind*, pp. 294, 307–34.
[2] 349 H.C. Deb., 5 s., 1831 (July 10, 1939).
[3] For internal services, see Air Ministry, *Report of the Committee to consider the Development of Civil Aviation* (Sir Henry Maybury, chairman), Cmd. 5351 (1937), and R. Finch, *The World's Airways* (London, 1938), pp. 109 ff.
The increase of air travel between Great Britain and destinations in continental Europe is shown by the following figures (*Statistical Abstract of U.K., 1938, p. 345*):

The other instance of nationalisation was that of London's passenger transport services. The London Passenger Transport Act of 1933 had a curious ancestry. Much of London's transport— the 'tube' railways and the District Railway, the L.G.O.C. buses and several of the trams—had long been operated by the Underground group of companies developed by the genius of Lord Ashfield and Frank Pick. Proposals to give to the Underground group a complete monopoly were made in 1927 by an official body, the London and Home Counties Traffic Advisory Committee, which argued that the construction of new electric railways which were badly needed in the northern and north-eastern suburbs could only be financed if all transport services were consolidated, the cheaper buses helping to pay for the expensive but indispensable trains. A bill for this purpose was before parliament in 1929. The Labour government produced its own alternative: a monopoly under a public corporation; and had almost enacted such a measure, thanks to the energy of Herbert Morrison, the Minister of Transport, when it fell.[1]

The National government decided to revive Morrison's bill, though some Conservatives opposed it as a socialist scheme and a dangerous precedent. Again, the arguments of the government's spokesmen were entirely empirical. Much time and money had already been spent on the bill, and lengthy negotiations with the companies completed. Co-ordination of London's transport was indispensable for a 'cheap, efficient and financially sound' service, and co-ordination without common ownership was inadequate.[2] The Act created the London Passenger Transport Board, and gave it a monopoly of all public passenger services within a specified area and the right to operate services in a larger area. The suburban services of the main line railways were left outside, but their

---

AIRCRAFT FLIGHTS AND PASSENGERS CARRIED BETWEEN
THE UNITED KINGDOM AND THE CONTINENT

	British Aircraft		Foreign Aircraft	
		Passengers		Passengers
	Flights	carried	Flights	carried
1930	3,000	22,045	6,685	20,390
1934	6,820	58,125	7,862	44,542
1937	12,608	77,967	11,285	81,184
1938	14,222	69,565	13,152	91,655

Fuller figures and reports on the various companies flying internal services are in Air Ministry, *Report on the Progress of Civil Aviation* (annual).

[1] Herbert Morrison, *Socialisation and Transport* (London, 1933), pp. 1–80; L. Gordon, *Public Corporation in Great Britain*, pp. 245–63; T. H. O'Brien, *Public Ownership and Control*, pp. 202–20.

[2] 269 H.C. Deb., 5 s., 1255 ff. (October 27, 1932); 274: 843–5, 924 (February 14, 1933).

receipts were pooled with those of the Board and the pool divided in the proportions of 62 per cent to the Board and 38 per cent to the railway companies. The Board's operation of the 'tubes', buses and trams began on July 1, 1933. Lord Ashfield and Frank Pick presided over its destinies unchanged,[1] and carried forward the building of new lines, partly by electrifying certain suburban lines of the Great Western and London and North Eastern railways and connecting them with existing 'tubes'. The routes to Ruislip, Barnet, Loughton, Epping and Newbury Park were completed, though not all brought into use, by 1940.

One concession was made by the government to Tory critics. The Board was left largely independent of the Minister of Transport, and its members were appointed, not by the Minister, but by five 'appointing trustees', the chairman of the L.C.C., the heads of the London bankers, the chartered accountants and the Law Society, and a representative of the London Traffic Advisory Committee. The Board was superseded in 1948 by the London Transport Executive, one of the executives entrusted with the management of Britain's land transport under the British Transport Commission when transport was nationalised by the Transport Act of 1947.[2]

10. THE SOURCES OF RECOVERY:
INCREASING CONSUMPTION

What, then, were the sources of recovery? Some said the tariff, though the trade figures did not bear them out. Others pointed to the policy of cheap money and to the housing boom. Before the question can be answered, some further analysis of the country's economic condition is necessary.

Two things stand out in the economy of the thirties: increasing consumption and the development of the home market and the consumer and service industries. These were the tendencies of the twenties. The depression made remarkably little difference, and any setback had been more than made good by 1934. The cost of

[1] See F. A. Menzler, 'Lord Ashfield', *Public Administration*, 22 (1951): 99–111. A biography of Frank Pick (1878–1941) is being written by Christian Barman.

Albert Stanley (1875–1948), born in Derby but spent his early years in the United States, and had been manager of electric tramways in Detroit and New Jersey before returning to England in 1907. He then became general manager of the Metropolitan District Railway and several of the London 'tube' railways; managing director of the Underground group of companies in 1912; chairman 1919–33. President of the Board of Trade, 1916–19. Knighted 1914, created Baron Ashfield in 1920. Chairman of the London Passenger Transport Board throughout its existence (1933–47) and subsequently of the London Transport Executive. A completely self-made man.

[2] For other accounts of the L.P.T.B. see E. Davies, *National Capitalism*, pp. 215–42; W. A. Robson (ed.), *Public Enterprise*, pp. 155 ff.; W. H. Wickwar, *Public Services*, pp. 105–18.

living fell heavily in the thirties, thanks to the fall in world commodity prices, but wage rates fell very little; consumption by the
working classes fell only slightly, and by 1934 had recovered to
the level of 1929. In spite of the low incomes of the unemployed
and of workers on short time the real income of the working classes
was on the increase.[1] For the middle classes the fall in spendable
income between 1929 and 1932 was greater than for the working
classes, but their consumption was not greatly affected.[2] The
supply of food per head of population increased between 1929 and
1932 in all the main commodities except beef and flour, and the
increase was substantial in mutton and lamb, pork and bacon, milk,
eggs, bananas. The growth of the home market was shown by the
number of workers in the distributive trades, which rose every
year during the depression, from 1·5 millions in 1929 to 1,879,000
in 1937. The figures for wireless sets, telephones, new car regis-
trations, the number of cars in use, the number of letters and postal
matter delivered in a year, were all evidence of increasing consumption.[3]

Table 8

Indices of Consumption and the Cost of Living[4]

	1929	1930	1931	1932	1933	1934	1935	1936	1937
Wage rates ..	100	100	98	96	95	96	97	99	103
Cost of living ..	100	96	90	88	85	86	87	90	94
Consumption by per- sons with incomes of less than £250 ..	100	98	97	94	96	100	104		
Total value of con- sumption (entire population) ..	100	98	95	94	94	97	102	110	118
Prices of consumption goods and services	100	95	93	92	90	90	91		

The progress of the service industries was shown by the
increased numbers of persons employed in laundries and dry-
cleaning works, hotels and restaurants, entertainment and sport.[5]
In the main groups of industries the largest increases in employ-

[1] See Table 8 above; further discussion in chap. 9.
[2] *Britain in Recovery*, pp. 30–1.   [3] Ibid., table on p. 37.
[4] Ibid., pp. 26, 27, 33: based on Ministry of Labour indices and Colin Clark's
National Income and Outlay, tables 12, 72, 89.
[5] Ibid., p. 37. Laundries and dry cleaning: 1930, 130,000 persons employed, 1937,
163,000; hotels and restaurants: 1930, 302,000, 1937, 379,000; entertainment and
sport; 1930: 65,000, 1937, 116,000.

ment between 1929 and 1937 were in the service industries (an increase of 33 per cent), followed by gas, water and electricity supply (32 per cent), building and contracting (26 per cent), government service (22 per cent), transport and distribution (18 per cent), commerce, banking and insurance (17 per cent). For all industries and services the increase in employment was 13 per cent, for manufacturing 10 per cent. There was a decline in employment only in mining and agriculture. The tertiary industries (transport, distribution, public utilities, personal services, commerce, government) absorbed 33·4 per cent of the insured population in 1929, 36 per cent in 1937.[1] It is true that part of this increase did not really represent an increase in employment: some of the occupations under the umbrella of the service industries were parasitic; for example, touting for newspaper subscriptions, which gave part-time 'employment' to the unemployed.

At the same time there was a continuous increase in the productivity of British industry. Between 1929 and 1936 output per person employed in Great Britain in manufacturing industry rose by 20 per cent, at a time when it increased only 13 per cent in Germany and fell in the United States (though American industrial efficiency, measured by this standard, remained about twice as high as that of Great Britain). Beyond this, as Colin Clark has shown, the higher the proportion of workers in tertiary production as opposed to primary production and secondary industry, the higher the average of real income per head;[2] and this was the tendency in production and employment in the thirties even more than in the twenties.

Table 9

Productivity in Manufacturing Industry[3] in Great Britain
(output per head)

1929	..	100	1934	..	111
1930	..	99	1935	..	117
1931	..	97	1936	..	120
1932	..	98	1937	..	120
1933	..	103	1938	..	111

[1] *National Income and Outlay*, tables on p. 39.

[2] Colin Clark, *Conditions of Economic Progress* (London, 1940), pp. 176–80, 289, and chaps. 9, 10.

[3] L. Rostas, 'Industrial Production, Productivity and Distribution in Britain, Germany and the United States', *Economic Journal*, 53 (1943), 46–9.

The expansion during the thirties of those industries most closely concerned with the increase of consumption shows the same pattern. Production of motor cars, vans and buses, for example, was a little below that of 1929 in 1930–32, but exceeded the previous record in 1933 and increased from year to year until 1937. Imports of cars dwindled to a few thousand in 1931–33, and then increased, though never to the volume of the twenties; exports after 1933 rose to double what they had been in the twenties, though representing about the same proportion of production. The number of private cars registered in the United Kingdom, which was just over 1 million in 1930, was 1,834,248 in 1937.[1]

The record of the engineering trades benefited from the strength of demand for electrical and constructional equipment during the depression; marine engineering and the branches concerned with railway carriages and wagons suffered most. Enterprising firms repaired their fortunes by new undertakings: for example a very old firm, Newton, Chambers of Thorncliffe, added the manufacture of excavators to its production of light and heavy castings; Mather and Platt of Manchester opened a new works at Radcliffe in 1932 for the making of food-processing machinery, supporting its older lines of pumps, electric motors and fire extinguishers.[2] Similar enterprise was shown by the best-known firm in the Potteries, Wedgwood, which opened its new works in the country at Barlaston, some miles from Stoke-on-Trent, in 1940 and transferred to it most of the production of the historic Etruria works.

Depression even increased the demand for the cheaper consumer goods—rayon stockings and dresses, chocolate bars, ice cream. In the rayon industry, Courtaulds continued to expand, opening a new works for the manufacture of viscose staple fibre at Greenfield, Flint, in 1937.[3] Only the millers, among the food industries, were in difficulty. They followed the method of the shipbuilders: formed a Millers' Mutual Association, with production quotas, penalties, allocation of markets, and a Purchase Finance Company to buy and close mills. This industry was an example of concentration of control also: one firm, Rank, accounted for one-third of total production, and two other giants, Spillers and the Co-operative Wholesale Society, were not far behind.[4]

[1] A. E. Kahn, *Great Britain in the World Economy*, p. 111; *Britain in Recovery*, pp. 302–9. Production of motor vehicles was 238,800 in 1929, 507,700 in 1937 (Kahn's figures).
[2] *Britain in Recovery*, pp. 377 ff., has a survey of the engineering trades.
[3] H. A. Silverman, *Studies in Industrial Organization*, pp. 322 ff.
[4] A. F. Lucas, *Industrial Reconstruction*, pp. 136–7; M. Compton and E. H. Bott, *British Industry: its changing Structure in Peace and War* (London, 1940), p. 75.

The electricity supply industry was in a state of constant growth throughout the thirties. The construction by the Central Electricity Board of the grid of overhead transmission lines was carried on through the early thirties, and there was much building of new power stations and enlargement of old ones. Production of electricity doubled in six years, from 11,413 million kilowatt hours in 1931 to 22,877 million in 1937. New consumers were supplied to a number as high as 800,000 per year, the total number of consumers reaching 9 million, as compared with 2 million in 1923. By 1938 over a million electric cookers were in use, and other appliances, such as vacuum cleaners, stoves, irons, wireless sets and even refrigerators were adding to the demands for power in homes and public buildings; electrification of railways and the use of electric motors in place of belts from overhead shafts to drive machines were increasing the demand from industry.[1]

11. DEFLATION OR CHEAP MONEY?

With all this, government policy had rather little to do. In so far as it helped to promote recovery, it was not because, as was usually thought, it was deflationary, but because it was rather the opposite. The deflationary phase of the National government's policy was short-lived. The economy cuts lasted, it is true, until 1934; but the inflation represented by an unbalanced budget was present during 1932, in spite of all the hullaballoo about balancing the budget which had brought about the fall of the Labour government. The Budget for 1933, by failing to provide moneys for the sinking fund for debt reduction, and by meeting the past year's deficit by borrowing, continued this tendency. The National government's financial policies made the best of both worlds: they seemed sufficiently deflationary to restore confidence; they were in fact sufficiently inflationary to assist recovery by maintaining the purchasing power of the people. Of course the very fact that a Conservative government—even better, a 'National' government—was in office instead of Labour, was in itself enough to restore business confidence, whatever policies it pursued.

Neville Chamberlain's record at the Treasury thus proves to be rather different from what it was thought to be. His first Budget, in 1932, provided for estimated expenditures of £766 millions, compared with £803 millions in Snowden's Budget of April 1931, and £818 millions in the emergency Budget of the following

[1] *Britain in Recovery*, pp. 257–77, has full particulars of the electricity supply industry.

September. He budgeted for a small balance of revenue over expenditure, but next year had to admit that a deficit of £32 millions had been incurred, partly through miscalculations of revenue. The 1933 Budget provided for expenditures of £697 millions, a reduction caused in great part by savings on debt charges through the conversion of war loan and lower rates of interest. No provision was made for the sinking fund for debt redemption, and the deficit was met by borrowing. However, the 1934 Budget, setting expenditures at £706 millions, anticipated a surplus of £29 millions and reported an actual surplus of £39 millions from the previous year. As a result, the cuts in unemployment allowances were removed and one-half of the reduction in government salaries was made good, the old scales being fully restored in 1935. In addition, the standard rate of income tax was lowered from 5s. to 4s. 6d. in the £. The country had left 'Bleak House', the Chancellor observed, and might now begin 'Great Expectations'. The final Budget of the reign, that of 1935, estimated expenditures at £729 millions.

The government's policy was, in fact, more modern than its critics supposed. It included the promotion of low interest rates, 'cheap money'. The motive was, apparently, not so much one of promoting recovery as of reducing debt charges; and the policy was questioned as being inflationary by several bankers and economists.[1] It had, however, the benefit of the change of opinion which had begun in the interrogation of Montagu Norman by Keynes and the redoubtable Bevin in the Macmillan committee regarding the effects of the Bank of England's bank-rate policies on unemployment, and which Keynes, Bevin and their colleagues in Addendum I of the committee's report had strengthened by their recommendation of a more flexible use of low interest rates to stimulate borrowing and employment.[2]

The lowering of the rate of interest began as early as February 1932, when the Bank of England first lowered the bank rate. By June it had fallen from 6 per cent, the rate adopted on September 21, 1931, to 2 per cent, where it stayed until 1939.[3] The conversion of £2,087 millions of 5 per cent war loan to 3·5 per cent in the summer of 1932 carried on this policy. The plan had been Snowden's, prepared for in his emergency Budget of 1931, and now realised by Chamberlain with the aid of patriotic propaganda

[1] W. A. Morton, *British Finance, 1930–1940*, pp. 243, 246.
[2] Committee on Finance and Industry, *Report*, Addendum I, pp. 190–1; R. F. Harrod, *J. M. Keynes*, pp. 415–18. Cf. above, chap. 5, p. 267.
[3] W. A. Morton, p. 244.

and the favouring breezes of financial opinion. The saving to the government in interest was £23 millions annually.[1]

The cheap money policy played a part in helping to bring recovery, but perhaps a rather smaller part than was generally assumed.[2] Until 1934 capital investment remained small despite the low interest rates. New issues (including overseas issues) fell from £236 millions in 1930 (a figure fairly typical of the previous decade) to £89 millions a year later, and recovered only to £150 millions in 1934, £217 millions in 1936.[3] Increased investment after 1934 was the product of the recovery in the domestic market and in world trade, rather than of cheap money; some of it was in the new industries—motor cars, electrical goods, aircraft manufacture.

Nor did cheap money bring about large-scale assistance by the government in the creation of employment. British policy, unlike that in the United States, did not include large programmes of public works. Three things damned such policies for the National government:[4] that Lloyd George proposed them, that Labour favoured them, that the passion for economy (which must not be openly flouted) condemned them. The government did, however, encourage some important works of construction by guaranteeing the interest on the sums needed: reconstruction on the railways (the Railways [Agreement] Act, 1935), and in London's transport, and the construction of the *Queen Mary*. The building of the new steelworks was helped by semi-official bodies, the Bank of England and its offspring, the Bankers' Industrial Development Corporation. The same cautious policy was followed by the local authorities responsible for the construction of roads, bridges, schools, government offices and houses. Such local work undoubtedly provided some employment directly and indirectly; but not consistently. Capital expenditure for roads and bridges was £16 millions in 1930, £19 millions in 1931 and 1932. It then fell to £10 millions in 1933, £8 millions by 1936. The lag between the coming of depression and the reduction of these expenditures

---

[1] W. A. Morton, pp. 71–2, 244–5.

[2] See Morton's arguments, ibid., pp. 290–7; cf. F. Benham, *Great Britain under Protection*, pp. 227–33.

[3] Midland Bank's figures, cited in Morton, pp. 300, 304. Colin Clark's figures in *National Income and Outlay*, p. 185, and *Economic Journal*, September, 1938, cited *ibid.*, p. 300, and based on the production of capital goods, show a smaller decline and a greater recovery (after 1934) in gross investment.

[4] Though the Macmillan committee had given much thought to the matter, and Keynes, Bevin and the other signatories of Addendum I of the report recommended public works financed by government borrowing: Com. on Finance and Industry, *Report*, Addendum I, pp. 203–8; R. F. Harrod, *J. M. Keynes*, pp. 420–2.

Q*

meant that they were greatest when the need was greatest (though not necessarily where it was greatest). The current expenditures by the local authorities also helped to keep places and people alive.[1]

Another kind of government spending which stimulated production and employment was that for rearmament. This, however, only began seriously after the depression had lifted in 1936. The Budget for 1936 was the first which included a large increase for the armed services; a sharp rise in the index of industrial production in the last quarter of 1935 suggests that the effect was already being anticipated.[2]

None of the government's policies, in fact, was the main source of recovery, though all contributed their share towards it. The most important thing was the pattern of income and consumption. While prices were low, those persons who were in regular employment—after all, the great majority—had a greater margin than before between their income from wages or salary and their basic needs for food, clothing, shelter—a margin estimated to be £250 millions more in 1932 than in the twenties.[3] They had more to spend on consumer goods and, perhaps, for a better house which they might even 'own'. Hence the continuing growth of the consumer and service industries; hence the housing boom which was not so much the cause as the symbol of recovery.

12. THE HOUSING BOOM

The boom in the construction of houses and flats was the chief feature of economic activity in Great Britain during the thirties, though the fact that the greater part of it was to be seen in London and the home counties may have exaggerated its extent to the casual observer. It absorbed at least a quarter, perhaps half, of all capital investment.[4] Between 1920 and 1930 about 1·5 million houses were built in England and Wales, two-thirds of them with state assistance. In the next ten years about 2,700,000 houses were built in England and Wales, the great majority without public aid. Altogether over 4·5 million houses were built in Great Britain between the wars (4,172,000 in England and Wales, 336,000 in Scotland); of these over a quarter in England and

[1] W. A. Morton, pp. 332–3.
[2] Ibid., p. 286; H. V. Hodson, *Slump and Recovery*, p. 472: index of industrial production (1929 = 100); 1934, 97·8, 1935, 1st quarter, 104·1, 3rd quarter, 102·1, 4th quarter, 111·2.
[3] W. A. Morton, p. 323, citing *Economist*, October 26, 1935.
[4] Ibid., p. 318; cf. Colin Clark, *National Income and Outlay*, p. 193.

Wales, and two-thirds in Scotland, were built by the local authorities.[1] The construction of new houses in these twenty-one years provided one-third of all houses existing in England and Wales at the beginning of the second war.

The extent and progress of the housing boom can be seen from the annual figures of houses built. In the twenties the annual average for England and Wales was 150,000 houses; new construction rose, during the depression years of 1931 and 1932, to over 200,000 houses, jumped to 266,000 in 1933 and 329,000 in 1934, remaining around this figure for every year until 1939. The year of greatest activity was 1936, when 346,000 houses were built.[2]

Most of the houses constructed in such numbers were built without assistance from the state: over 2 million out of the total of 2·7 million.[3] Private enterprise, assisted by some of the government's financial policies, thus came to the rescue of the state and saved it from the worst effects of those other policies of the government which enforced economy and brought the building programmes of the municipalities and counties almost to a standstill between 1931 and 1935.[4] Several circumstances favoured this. Building costs fell during the depression years, partly because the price of materials (such as Swedish timber) was low, partly because wages remained stationary but the efficiency of the building industry increased. A typical working man's non-parlour house cost £350 in 1931, under £300 in 1933, and not until 1937 did it begin to approach the higher figure again.[5] Some of the saving in costs was at the expense of the men in the building trades: much building was done at cut rates, by men who camped out in the

---

[1] R. L. Reiss, *Municipal and Private Enterprise Housing*, p. 15 (these figures include all houses completed by March 31, 1940). For figures relating principally to working-class houses see chapter 9, section 8.

[2] Figures from *Annual Abstract of Statistics, 1948* and *1949*, cited by A. P. Becker, 'Housing in England and Wales during the business depression of the 1930's', *Economic History Review*, second series, III (1951), p. 322 (figures relate to England and Wales and refer to housing units; the year ends March 31: i.e., 1933 = April 1, 1933–March 31, 1934). The best account of the housing boom (down to 1936) is by Sir Harold Bellman in *Britain in Recovery*, pp. 397–437; see also W. A. Morton, *British Finance*, pp. 318–29; F. Benham, *Great Britain under Protection*, pp. 223–7.

[3] For the detailed annual figures, see A. P. Becker, *Econ. Hist. Rev.*, 2nd ser., III, 322, and *Britain in Recovery*, pp. 399, 435 (half-yearly figures).

[4] For the cycles of municipal and private-enterprise building between the wars see Asa Briggs, *History of Birmingham*, II, 229–34.

[5] W. A. Morton, *British Finance*, p. 322, *Britain in Recovery*, p. 428. R. L. Reiss, *Municipal and Public Enterprise Housing*, p. 51, puts building costs of a 3-bedroom, non-parlour house as follows:

	1925	1931	1935	1938
Cost of building per sq. ft.	11s. 0d.	8s. 9d.	7s. 10d.	9s. 2d.
Building cost	£440	£350	£320	£365

half-finished houses they were constructing. At the same time (and thanks in part to the 'council houses' constructed during the twenties) the standards of housing demanded by working men and their wives had risen. If they could borrow at low rates over long terms to buy a house of their own, the demand for new houses ought to rise spectacularly.

And they could, thanks to the building societies, which took credit for 75 per cent of the houses built in the thirties. The building societies had increased their capital greatly since the war, attracting investors in their shares and small savers to their deposit accounts; after 1932, when interest rates fell, they combined security with rates more attractive than previously.[1] They, in turn, gradually reduced their mortgage interest rates, from 6 per cent to 5·5 per cent in September 1932, then to 5 per cent in June 1933 and 4·5 per cent in April 1935. At the same time they increased the terms of repayment of mortgages from an average of sixteen years to twenty-one or twenty-five years, and often increased the amount lent from 80 per cent to 90 per cent of the cost of the house. These changes reduced the monthly repayments of the proud house-owner from 16s. 6d. per £100 on a sixteen-year mortgage at 6 per cent interest to 11s. 3d. on a 25-year mortgage at 4·5 per cent interest. At this rate his monthly payment might be as low as £2 14s. 9d., the lowest average payments arranged by one building society; and this payment of about 14s. per week, was no more than the weekly rent of a larger council house. One society found that the proportion of wage-earners among its borrowers rose from 34·8 per cent in the twenties to 50·5 per cent in 1936. Even so, it was chiefly the 'clerical workers and better-paid artisans' who became the society's clients; the ordinary working man's best hope of a good new house was a council house, renting from 7s. 3d. to 15s. a week in Birmingham, and from 8s. to 13s. in York.[2]

The same circumstances favoured the building of blocks of flats, especially in London—the 'service flats' designed for the childless couples and small families of the middle class. Here was another source of the building boom: low interest rates encouraged companies to finance the building of flats by bank overdrafts, repaid by the sale of debentures (for example, to insurance companies) when the flats were completed.

---

[1] For the building societies' finances and their sources see Morton, pp. 324–7, and Sir Harold Bellman (head of one of the largest of them, Abbey Road) in *Britain in Recovery*, pp. 417–22.
[2] *Britain in Recovery*, pp. 422–9; R. L. Reiss, pp. 57, 63–4.

The effects of the housing boom upon recovery cannot be gain-said. The building of 200,000 houses is estimated to have pro-vided work for one-quarter of the building industry. Employment in building increased by 13·5 per cent in 1934, as compared with an increase of 6·8 per cent in all other industries; and the fall in un-employment among bricklayers, carpenters and plasterers in 1934 was comparable. The effect of the boom on industries indirectly affected by it was of the same character—employment increasing in them by 8·1 per cent in 1933, 9·9 per cent in 1934. The building industry's index of employment (1931 = 100) rose to 130·4 in 1936 though the index in all other industries rose only to 113·9 and the index of business activity to 121·1.[1]

13. THE NEW ECONOMICS, AND THE IDEA OF 'PLANNING'

Britain's recovery seems, therefore, to have owed most not to governmental policy nor the application of new economic theories but to the combination of low prices, increasing consumption and rising productivity which were partly world-wide, partly domestic in their origins and which had existed to a smaller extent in the twenties as well. None the less, the depression gave apparent confirmation to new economic theories; especially the new analysis of unemployment and investment developed by J. M. Keynes—the 'Keynesian revolution' in economic theory.

Keynes expounded his ideas in two books, the *Treatise on Money* (1930) and the *General Theory of Employment, Interest and Money* (1936). Employment is determined (he argued), not by the level of wages, but by two rival motives in each person, the pro-pensity to consume and the propensity to invest. Investment to be effective in stimulating employment need not be in useful goods nor promise a high rate of interest: it may just as well be in digging holes in the ground or building the pyramids of Egypt. It depends on the 'liquidity preference' of each person—his preference for assets which can be quickly or slowly converted into spending power. This in turn is affected by the supply of money and credit. If the banking system increases the supply, the preference is altered, and investment increases; if the supply is low, the pro-pensity to consume and the propensity to invest are both lowered and unemployment rises: there is too much 'saving'. Four conse-quences follow: the control of policies influencing credit and investment should not be left in private hands; low interest rates

[1] *Britain in Recovery*, pp. 409–16.

should be the rule when employment falls off, but even they will be insufficient to restore it; investment should be stimulated by programmes of public works; and the unequal distribution of income being an obstacle to the propensity to consume, a more equal distribution would increase employment.

What was Keynes' achievement, admitting that much in his theory was not new? He gave the economists 'a new method of classifying the forces determining the level of output as a whole',[1] —a new general theory, a new set of tools. To the public he gave the idea that nations were not helpless against the automatic workings of economic laws, thus strengthening, however unintentionally, the tendency towards nationalism and collectivism. He made people think about economics, and helped to illustrate his contention that men of ideas were far more powerful than the 'practical' men of affairs:

> . . . the ideas of economists and political philosophers, both when they are right and when they are wrong, are more powerful than is commonly understood. Indeed, the world is ruled by little else.[2]

Keynes' ideas were in harmony with another tendency of the times: the belief in planning. Planning as a faith derived partly from the earlier talk of 'rationalisation', partly from Labour's interest in nationalisation.[3] The 'Russia complex' of the thirties was another inspiration. Russia was briefly popular: it was open to visitors, shepherded around by Intourist; it was visited and written about by the great—Bernard Shaw, Lord Lothian, Lady Astor, the Webbs; its demonstration of a planned society, and the success claimed for the 'Five Year Plan', made their appeal.

The vogue for planning deserves illustration. 'Political and Economic Planning (P.E.P.) was founded in 1931, as an anonymous group of civil servants, businessmen and academic and professional people interested in politics and economics and devoting themselves to the impartial study of the problems of industry. In 1935 a catholic group of 152 men and women—trade unionists, members of parliament, professors, churchmen, businessmen, Conservative, Liberal, Labour—published, under the banner of

---

[1] R. F. Harrod, *J. M. Keynes*, p. 465.
[2] J. M. Keynes, *The General Theory of Employment, Interest and Money* (London, 1936), p. 383. See Roy Harrod's brilliant *Life* of him, especially chapters 10 and 11; also R. Boothby, *I Fight to Live*, pp. 233–45; J. B. Condliffe, *Commerce of Nations*, pp. 604–12; H. Feis, 'Keynes in Retrospect', *Foreign Affairs*, 29: 564–77 (July 1951).
[3] See, for example, G. D. H. Cole, *Principles of Economic Planning* (London, 1935).

'Liberty and Democratic Leadership', a book entitled *The Next Five Years: an essay in political agreement*. Part I was devoted to economic policy, and recommended a 'plan for Britain'. Harold Macmillan, a Conservative M.P., published *Reconstruction: a plea for a national policy* in 1933, and *The Middle Way* in 1938; Sir Arthur Salter's *Recovery* (1932) is almost as sweeping in its call for planning and for government interference in business. From the Labour side came Barbara Wootton's *Plan or no plan* (1934), advocating a planned economy and contrasting the Russian economy favourably with unplanned systems.

There was another source of interest in planning: the depressed areas. Once the depressed areas became a national problem it was seen that they could not be relieved without a national plan. The new phrase which started ideas in motion was the 'location of industry'; to whose study the problems of overcrowding and housing, the growth of London and the danger of air raids also contributed. It was Sir Malcolm Stewart, the Commissioner for the Special Areas in England and Wales, who drew attention in his final report in 1936 to the connection between the location of industry and unemployment. A Royal Commission to study the question was appointed under the chairmanship of Sir Montague Barlow in 1937.[1]

14. THE DISTRESSED AREAS

The Barlow Report was the last echo of the industrial problem of the interwar years: the problem of the distressed areas. It was they which tarnished the picture of recovery and were the basis for the myth of the 'hungry thirties'. They were fairly well defined: industrial Scotland, South Wales, west Cumberland, the Tees–Tyne area in northeast England; the areas of the old, staple industries, heavily dependent on exports, the trinity of coal, steel and ships. Two other areas were badly off: industrial Lancashire, concerned with cotton textiles, coal, and engineering, and Northern Ireland, dependent on agriculture, linen manufacture, and ship-building; but they were never classified as 'special areas'. Nor were the distressed areas uniformly afflicted: in South Wales, for example, the inland valleys were in greater distress than the coast, the eastern side of the area as compared with the west, with its interest in anthracite and tinplate.[2]

[1] Royal Commission on the Distribution of the Industrial Population, *Report* (Barlow Report: Cmd. 6153: 1940). Cf. P.E.P., *Report on the Location of Industry* (London, 1939).
[2] H. A. Marquand, *South Wales Needs a Plan* (London, 1936), pp. 35–8.

The marks of the distressed area were easily recognisable. The proportion of insured workers who were unemployed was higher than elsewhere, and this despite the fact that the number of their insured workers had increased much less than in the more prosperous regions. In London the number of insured persons in employment rose by 27 per cent between 1923 and 1934, in southeast England by 43·8 per cent; in northeast England it fell by 5·5 per cent, in Scotland by 1·7 per cent, in Wales by 26·2 per cent.[1] The eastern section of South Wales, despite heavy emigration, had 46 per cent of its adult male workers unemployed in 1934, its surplus labour force being estimated at 39,000 men.[2] Scotland never had less than 10 per cent of her insured workers out of work between 1923 and 1938, and the proportion was always higher than that of Great Britain as a whole.[3] The cost to the country of keeping derelict communities in suspended animation by payments from public funds was very heavy: Merthyr Tydfil, in 1937–38, was costing £830,000 or £1 per family per week, which was £200,000 more than Coventry, a town three times as large; yet on top of this Merthyr was levying a local rate of 27s. 6d. in the £, which was not an encouragement to new industries to move in. It was estimated that the cost in interest

Table 10

Unemployed as Percentage of Insured Workers in Various Regions[4]

	1929	*1932*	*1937*
London and S.E. England	5·6	13·7	6·4
S.W. England	8·1	17·1	7·8
Midlands	9·3	20·1	7·2
North, N.E., N.W. England ..	13·5	27·1	13·8
Wales	19·3	36·5	22·3
Scotland	12·1	27·7	15·9
Great Britain	10·5	22·2	10·8
Northern Ireland	15·1	27·2	23·6

[1] Ministry of Labour, *Report for the Year 1934* (Cmd. 4861; 1935), p. 9.
[2] H. A. Marquand, *South Wales Needs a Plan*, pp. 40–1.
[3] J. A. Bowie, *The Future of Scotland* (London, 1939), p. 102; C. E. V. Leser and A. H. Silvey, 'Scottish Industries during the Inter-War Period', *Manchester School*, May, 1950.
[4] M. P. Fogarty, *Prospects of the Industrial Areas of Great Britain* (London, 1945), p. 5; *Ulster Year Book, 1932, 1935, 1938.*

and sinking fund of moving away the entire community of 63,000 would be less than the annual charge for maintaining it in idleness.[1]

Table 11

Percentage of Insured Workers Unemployed
in Distressed and Prosperous Towns, 1934[2]

Jarrow ..	..	67·8	Greater London ..		8·6
Gateshead	..	44·2	Birmingham	..	6·4
Workington	..	36·3	Coventry	..	5·1
Maryport	..	57·0	Oxford ..	..	5·1
Abertillery	..	49·6	Luton ..	..	7·7
Merthyr	..	61·9	High Wycombe ..		3·3
Greenock	..	36·3	St. Albans	..	3·9
Motherwell	..	37·4	Watford ..	..	7·0

Attention was first focused on the special problems of the distressed areas in 1932. Industrial surveys of several areas were made by the local universities and published by the Board of Trade, but little followed from them. In March 1934, harassed by hunger marches and spurred by three articles by a special correspondent in *The Times* on the depression in County Durham ('Places without a Future'),[3] the government decided to see for itself how things were, and appointed four men—two members of parliament, two men of business—to investigate conditions in Scotland, west Cumberland, Durham and Tyneside, and South Wales.[4]

The government was finally stirred to action. A bill, the Depressed Areas (Development and Improvement) bill was introduced in November 1934. It provided for the appointment of unpaid commissioners, one for the depressed areas in England and Wales (South Wales, Tyneside, west Cumberland), one for Scotland, to initiate and aid measures for the 'economic development and social improvement of the depressed areas'. A grant of £2 millions was to be given. The bill was criticised from both sides of the House of Commons on the score of its inadequacy, Lloyd George comparing it unfavourably with the programmes of

[1] P.E.P., *Report on the Location of Industry*, pp. 17, 19, 44.
[2] Ministry of Labour, *Report . . . 1934*, p. 5.
[3] *The Times*, March 20, 21, 22, 1934; *History of The Times*, IV, ii, 884–6.
[4] Ministry of Labour, *Reports of Investigations into the Industrial Conditions in Certain Depressed Areas* (Cmd. 4728; 1934). The investigators were J. C. C. Davidson, M.P., Euan Wallace, M.P., Sir Wyndham Portal, Sir Arthur Rose.

the New Deal. In the Lords the depressed areas were renamed Special Areas; and with this change the bill became law. It was another act of state intervention, empirically taken.

The immediate results were not spectacular. Grants by the commissioners to local authorities and to private bodies such as the National Council of Social Service, helped to start improvement schemes for water supply and sewage disposal, the building of hospitals, the repair of harbours; and the amenities of the distressed areas were improved by parks, swimming pools, social centres. A little help was given to housing schemes. Much help was given, with small results, to plans to transfer unemployed families on to the land.

Larger schemes were frustrated by circumstance. The commissioners' powers were limited by their small funds, and by the fact that they could not assist in programmes of public works for which other grants were payable. Sir Malcolm Stewart, the first Commissioner for the Special Areas in England and Wales, had much to do with the location of Richard Thomas' new steel works at Ebbw Vale. His other efforts, including approaches to no fewer than 5800 firms, to induce industries to move into the distressed areas, had 'generally speaking . . . failed'.[1]

When he resigned in November 1936, Sir Malcolm Stewart pointed out the difficulties which had confronted him, in his third report as Commissioner. He urged a 'second experiment . . . to deal more directly with the problem of unemployment', adding: 'We must not fear making a break with the traditions and practices of the past.' The government, with the icy Runciman at the Board of Trade, tried to ignore the report; but, coinciding with the march of the men from Jarrow to London, it raised a clamour which could not be gainsaid. One of Sir Malcolm's proposals was accepted in the Special Areas (Amendment) Act, 1937, which offered remission of rates, rent and income tax, even up to 100 per cent for five years, to firms which would establish works in the distressed areas; for this purpose a treasury fund of £2 millions was set aside. The main result was the establishment of trading estates, where firms could lease premises, both large and small, with power, heating and other services already laid on. The estates

---

[1] *Reports of the Commissioner for the Special Areas (England and Wales)*, Cmd. 4957 (1935), 5090 (1936), 5303 (1936), 5595 (1937), 5896 (1938); *Report of the Commissioner for the Special Areas in Scotland*, Cmd. 4958 (1935), 5089 (1936), 5245 (1936), 5604 (1937), 5905 (1938); H. A. Marquand, *South Wales Needs a Plan*, p. 87; R. C. Davison, *British Unemployment Policy: the modern phase since 1930* (London, 1938), pp. 94–106.

at Treforest in South Wales, Team Valley, near Gateshead, and North Hillington, outside Glasgow, were all begun by 1937; in Scotland there were also smaller estates at Larkhall, Chapelhall and Carfin. By 1939 there were 85 works established at North Hillington making such things as neon signs, clothes, ice-cream; at Treforest 32 factories were in production. The estates only attracted light industries, mainly employing women, and the total number of workers on any estate was only in the hundreds.[1]

What had such busy, if cautious, efforts produced? In the Special Areas in England and Wales the number of unemployed persons fell from 361,993 (36·8 per cent of the insured population) to 207,896 (21·7 per cent) between January 1935 and August 1937. The proportion of insured persons unemployed in Great Britain had, however, declined from 18·2 per cent to 10·4 per cent in the same period.[2] By this time rearmament was affecting employment. There had also been years of industrial transfer: the uprooting of Welsh youths to become waiters in London instead of

Table 12

Movement of Population within Great Britain, 1931–38[3]

	1931	1938	Increase or Decrease (−)
Great Britain	44,795,000	46,208,000	—
England and Wales ..	39,952,000	41,215,000	—
Greater London	8,204,000	8,700,000	496,000
Rest of S.E.	5,274,000	5,790,000	516,000
Northumberland, Durham (North I.)	2,243,000	2,204,000	− 39,000
W. Midlands (Midland I.)	4,534,000	4,751,000	217,000
South Wales	1,898,000	1,783,000	−115,000
Rest of Wales	696,000	683,000	− 13,000
Scotland	4,843,000	4,993,000	150,000

In all other regions there were moderate increases of population.

[1] P.E.P., *Location of Industry*, p. 11; J. A. Bowie, pp. 240–7.

[2] *Reports* of Commissioners for Special Areas, appendices.

[3] National Register, *Statistics of Population on September 29, 1939, Report and Tables* (1944), p. xv (explanation of regions, p. xxxii; detailed tables, p. 1). The figures for 1938 are the Registrar General's estimate. Use of the National Register's figures for September 29, 1939, is vitiated by the movement of population from evacuation to reception areas which had already taken place. Cf. R. M. Titmuss, *Poverty and Population* (London, 1938), chapter 13.

miners in the Rhondda. From the Special Areas in England and
Wales over 21,000 persons were transferred in 1935, 28,000 in
1937, and 18,000 in 1938. The number of persons moving without
official aid was not known; in 1937 it was put at nearly 15,000.[1]

15. SCOTS WHA HAE

One consequence of the depression was the rise of the Scottish
nationalist movement, which attracted a good deal of attention in
the early thirties. It had, of course, several roots. Some of its
leaders were looking for a revival of a distinctive Scots literature,
and Scottish art, of which the signs were disappointingly few: the
novels of Lewis Grassic Gibbon and Neil Gunn alone had much
reputation outside Scotland, and C. M. Grieve's poetry in an
adaptation of the Scots vernacular had few important rivals.[2]
Others deplored the inequality in social conditions between England and Scotland: the figures of malnutrition, illness, infant and
maternal mortality, overcrowding and slum housing remained
very much worse than in England.[3] Scotland was bearing more
than her share of misery and depression; with a government and
parliament of her own she could work vigorously to put her own
house in order.

Certainly Scotland's economy had been at a low ebb since the
war; for which England was given the blame. When steelworks, shipyards, railways, textile mills, banks were more and more controlled
by English companies and directed from head offices in London,
Scotland's interests came last. The Calico Printers' Association
closed all its Scottish works by 1929; the workshops of the old
Scottish railways were closed or much reduced in their operations;
the naval dockyard at Rosyth was closed; steelworks were abandoned, shipyards left silent, rusting, grass-grown. The production
of coal fell by 24 per cent, and employment in coal-mining by 36
per cent, between 1913 and 1937; in Lanarkshire, previously the
source of more than half Scotland's coal, production was almost

---

[1] *Reports of the Commissioner for Special Areas in England and Wales*, Cmd. 5090
(1936), p. 106; *1937*, p. 192; *1938*, p. 105.

[2] Ian Finlay, *Scotland* (Oxford, 1945), chapter 10 (the book is an excellent brief
introduction to Scotland). The Welsh, with their more widely spoken language and
the annual Eisteddfod, were less concerned about their cultural independence:

WALES (1931 Census)

Population:	South Wales	1,898,000
	Rest of Wales	696,000
	Speaking Welsh and English	811,329
	Welsh-speaking only	77,932

[3] See below, chapter 9.

cut in half.[1] Scottish shipping declined by 25 per cent while England's increased slightly. In Dundee the jute industry, on which half the industrial population depended, recovered in the thirties to half its prewar production after drastic reorganisation had restored some of the advantages it had lost to Indian competition.[2] Altogether the volume of Scottish production declined by about 12 per cent between 1907 and 1930 at a time when England's rose by 20 per cent; Scotland's share in Britain's production fell from 9·9 per cent in 1924 to 8·2 per cent in 1935.[3] Unemployment, despite an increase in employment, was greater in 1938 than in 1923; in the years between it was always higher than in Great Britain as a whole. At the worst period, in 1932, Scotland had 27·7 per cent of her workers unemployed; in 1937 15·9 per cent.[4] And Scotland was thought to be still losing her people; though actually the decline in Scotland's population between 1921 and 1931 was reversed after 1931, and natural increase and some further influx from Ireland raised the population by some 155,000, to just over 5 million, by 1939.[5] One child in five born in Scotland was said to be an Irish Roman Catholic; and in some of the industrial areas the Irish constituted 25 per cent of the population.[6]

The Highlands and the Western Isles were a special problem. Their population had declined from one-fifth of that of Scotland (or about 300,000) in 1801 to one-twentieth (293,000 persons) in 1931; in the twentieth century some 32,000 persons were leaving each decade, moving southward to the industrial belt or to England or overseas. None of the occupations open to the Highlander promised much: crofting agriculture, sea fishing, forestry. The tourist industry grew slowly. The only large new industry, aluminium manufacture at Foyers and Kinlochleven, contributed only slightly to the economy of the region, and this was true also of the hydro-electric power stations completed at Lochaber in 1929 and at Loch Rannoch and Tummel Bridge in 1930 and 1933.[7]

---

[1] Production of coal in Scotland in 1937, 32,242,000 tons; employment in coal-mining, 90,592 (*Stat. Abstract of U.K.*, 1938, p. 311).

[2] H. A. Silverman, *Studies in Industrial Organization*, pp. 238–40.

[3] J. A. Bowie, *Future of Scotland*, pp. 97, 108; G. M. Thomson, *Scotland, that Distressed Area* (Edinburgh, 1935), pp. 37, 54 (cf. his *Re-discovery of Scotland* (London, 1928) for earlier, similar complaints); A. M. MacEwen, *The Thistle and the Rose* (Edinburgh, 1932), pp. 43–6; A. D. Gibb, *Scotland in Eclipse* (London, 1930).

[4] J. A. Bowie, pp. 100–3.   [5] Ibid., pp. 18–23.

[6] 272 H.C. Deb., 5 s., pp. 245, 261 (November 24, 1932).

[7] Hugh Quigley, 'The Highlands of Scotland: proposals for development', *Agenda*, III (1944), 83–95; J. Gollan, *Scottish Prospect* (Glasgow, 1948), pp. 180 ff. The Hydro-Electric Development (Scotland) Act, 1943, created the North of Scotland Hydro-Electric Board, a public corporation with a monopoly of the future develop-

The Scottish nationalist movement took form in the National Party of Scotland, founded in 1928. The nationalists contested several parliamentary elections in vain; their main success was Compton Mackenzie's victory over Sir Robert Horne in the rectorial election at Glasgow University in 1931. The only result of their agitation was that in 1938 the various Scottish offices were regrouped in four departments and concentrated in a brand-new Scottish Whitehall on the Calton Hill in Edinburgh, St. Andrew's House, opened in 1939.[1]

16. UNEMPLOYMENT RELIEF: THE GOVERNMENT'S PRIDE AND FALL

There was one reason for the government's limping efforts to conquer unemployment, whether in the distressed areas or elsewhere—one, that is, apart from its failure to comprehend the psychological condition of the British people in the thirties, ready for a bold lead yet apathetic when left without one. The reason was the existence of unemployment insurance. Not to end unemployment but to relieve the unemployed as economically as possible was the great preoccupation.

The results were not ungenerous, after a fashion, but they were maladroit. When the National government imposed the cut of 10 per cent in unemployment payments as part of the economies of September 1931, it also introduced the means test which, because of the inquisition it involved, was bitterly resented by working people. For convenience, the responsibility of passing on applicants' needs was placed upon the Public Assistance Committees (P.A.C.) of the local authorities which were already experienced, as successors to the old Poor Law, in assessing the needs of those applying for outdoor relief. The funds used for transitional payments came, however, not from the local authorities but from the Treasury. This curious and temporary system was first established by Orders in Council under the National Economy Act, 1931, and was modified, and the conditions of the means test relaxed, by legislation in 1932. It meant that the scales of unemployment relief (the transitional payments) were not uniform; yet

---

ment of hydro-electric power in the Highlands. This was linked with the British Electricity Authority by the Electricity Act of 1947. For other accounts of the Highlands problem, see A. G. Macdonnell, *My Scotland* (London, 1937), pp. 128–30; the works of Quigley and MacEwen, and Alexander Maclehose, *The Scotland of Our Sons* (Glasgow, 1937). The Gaelic-speaking population (1931) numbered 137,000, all but 7000 being bilingual.

[1] For books on Scotland see the bibliography in Bowie; also A. D. Gibb, *Scotland Resurgent* (Stirling, 1950).

the system worked smoothly, and only two P.A.C.'s, out of many dominated by Labour, were superseded by commissioners appointed by the Ministry of Labour: at Rotherham and in County Durham. The means test reduced the payments of half a million persons and removed a quarter of a million from the registers, as well as deterring thousands more from applying; thus perhaps £12 millions was saved, and the number of the unemployed kept officially below three million, even at the worst time, January 1933. The actual cost of transitional payments, which had brought the Labour government down, fell only by £24 millions in 1932-33, to £101 millions.[1]

Such an emergency system could hardly last. It affronted the tidy mind of the Treasury, giving large sums for disbursement to committees outside the government's control. The Royal Commission on Unemployment Insurance, under Holman Gregory, in its final report in November 1932 (Cmd. 4185), proposed that the existing scheme of contributory unemployment insurance should continue, and that unemployment assistance (the new term for transitional payments) should be provided by a separate service. With this the government concurred, and thanks to Neville Chamberlain[2] an attempt was made to remove unemployment assistance from local control and party politics by putting it under a statutory commission, the Unemployment Assistance Board (U.A.B.).

This was the genesis of the Unemployment Act, 1934, a notable piece of social legislation, by which the Conservatives consolidated the welfare state, though in ways which robbed them of any gratitude. Part I of the Act concerned unemployment insurance. Part II created the Unemployment Assistance Board, a body of six members modelled on the B.B.C., and independent of the Ministry of Labour. The U.A.B. would have its own offices throughout the country, and its own staff, which soon numbered 6000. To it was given the responsibility for all able-bodied unemployed: not only those receiving transitional payments, but ultimately also all other unemployed persons who, being outside unemployment insurance and the system of transitional payments, had hitherto been an actual charge on the P.A.C.'s. This was a further nail in the coffin of the Poor Law, for the P.A.C.'s were left with little more than the sick and aged and the transients of the casual wards in the

[1] R. C. Davison, *British Unemployment Policy*, pp. 14–16, 21–6; cf. P.E.P., *Report on the British Social Services* (London, 1937), p. 134; H. F. Hohman, *Development of Social Insurance in Great Britain*, pp. 248–50.
[2] K. Feiling, *N. Chamberlain*, pp. 230–2.

workhouses. The Act widened eligibility for relief, and prescribed a needs test on a family basis, but with certain alleviations. The cost would be borne by a new Unemployment Assistance Fund, provided by the Treasury, but with a contribution of £2 millions from the local authorities in return for their savings on public assistance.[1]

What damned the Act in the eyes of the working people were the U.A.B. scales of relief payments which were to go into effect on the first appointed day, January 7, 1935, when the U.A.B. was to take over from the P.A.C.'s the administration of what had been the transitional payments. The scales were to be national and uniform, and there were new provisions regarding rent and the needs of a household as opposed to individuals. It was said that many persons would benefit, but when the actual scales were published it was clear that many people would suffer. In all innocence the U.A.B. began life with a first-class political crisis, from which only the government, eschewing its self-denying ordinance against politics in relief, could save it.

The protests against the U.A.B. scales were not peculiar to the time. With the advent of the National government Wal Hannington and his friends of the National Unemployed Workers' Movement (N.U.W.M.) had redoubled their efforts. Nineteen-thirty-two was perhaps the year most disturbed by hunger marches and other demonstrations, countered by frequent baton charges by the police and by numerous arrests.[2] In 1935 the protests came from all quarters: from town councils and trade unions, from members of parliament of all parties in the distressed areas. In South Wales there were several large demonstrations in January and February; others occurred in Glasgow, Maryport, Sheffield. More effective were the questions put to the government and the debates in parliament on January 28 and 29 and February 6.

The government gave way. On February 5 a standstill order was issued. It was not until November 1936 that the U.A.B.'s revised scale was put into effect. Very few cuts were actually made. Local advisory committees were appointed. Finally, on April 1, 1937, the second appointed day, the U.A.B. took responsibility for the unemployed previously maintained by the P.A.C.'s.[3]

[1] R. C. Davison, *British Unemployment Policy*, pp. 35–46.
[2] A. Hutt, *Postwar History of the British Working Class*, pp. 216–29, and W. Hannington, *Unemployed Struggles*, pp. 219–97, describe many of these events.
[3] R. C. Davison, *British Unemployment Policy*, pp. 65 ff.; *The Times*, January 28, 29, February 5, 6, 1935; A. Hutt, *Postwar History of the British Working Class*, pp. 263–5.

This crisis coincided with the easing of the burden of unemployment. The flaring-up of violence, reminiscent of the troubles of 1918–21, died away. There was an embittered strike at Harworth colliery, Nottinghamshire, for several months in the winter of 1936–37. In November 1936, the N.U.W.M. staged the biggest of the hunger marches, against the means test; it ended in the familiar kind of mass meeting in Hyde Park. As international tension increased and political controversy grew sharper, direct action faded. Yet for a while it had seemed that Communists and Fascists might involve the country in violence and bloodshed; and the period, brief as it was, left its mark on the statute book.

17. FASCISM FOR BRITAIN?

The British Fascist movement had its beginning in this same period of distress, in 1931–32, and reached its height of menace in 1934. Sir Oswald Mosley and his New Party were left in the wilderness in the general election of 1931; and next January Mosley's restless spirit led him to Mussolini at Rome. The birth of the British Union of Fascists (B.U.F.) under Mosley's leadership followed, some earlier British Fascist organisations rallying to the new standard. Mosley's programme was published in September 1932, in his book, *The Greater Britain*. Britain was to become a corporate state, parliament being transformed for this purpose and liberty made subordinate to service to the state. Anti-semitism was not at first part of the programme, and became prominent after the death of Mosley's first wife, Lady Cynthia (a daughter of Curzon) in 1933; in 1936 Mosley married at Munich, in Hitler's presence, Lady Diana Guinness, sister of Unity Mitford, whom Hitler called a 'perfect Nordic type'.

Mosley, with his proud bearing and confident manner, impressed many people with his sincerity and ability.[1] The members of the B.U.F. came mainly from among young men of the middle class, and from the black-coated workers—two groups whom the depression denied employment or importance. At his headquarters in King's Road, Chelsea, Mosley maintained a number of his blackshirts in a sort of barracks. Branches were established throughout the country, numbering about 400 by 1934, when the total membership was estimated to be 20,000. Huge meetings were held in the large towns, sometimes out of doors, sometimes in public halls; contingents of blackshirts were transported to them.

[1] See the writer, Beverley Nichols, in *News from England* (London, 1938), for an account of a visit to him.

Violence became the principal technique of agitation, reaching its climax at a mass-meeting held at Olympia on the evening of Thursday, June 7, 1934, and attended by 15,000 people, with another 5000 outside. Mosley, trim in his black shirt, and illuminated by spotlights on the stage, made an address which was frequently interrupted. On each occasion the spotlights were turned on the hecklers, and he (or she) was set upon by several Fascist stewards and brutally kicked and beaten as he was removed from the hall. No interference from the police checked these un-English atrocities; indeed the police were busy that evening arresting Communist and anti-Fascist demonstrators outside the hall. Next day's report in *The Times* merely mentioned that interrupters had been 'ejected', and a leading article criticised the movement mildly for its theatricality. The truth soon came out: in protests by Conservative M.P.s and others, and in letters from correspondents. Geoffrey Lloyd, Baldwin's parliamentary private secretary, an eye-witness, told of single interrupters being attacked by ten to twenty Fascists, and deplored their 'unmerciful brutality'; another spectator condemned the 'disgusting display of force'. The Home Secretary was closely questioned about the conduct of the police on Monday, the 12th, and the whole affair debated in the Commons on the 14th.[1]

The Olympia meeting tore away the movement's veil of respectability. People were shocked and angry. Lord Rothermere, whose *Daily Mail* had given the B.U.F. support earlier in 1934, drew back. Three weeks later came the news of Hitler's bloody 'purge' of his fellow-Nazis, which destroyed any lingering appeal which British fascism might have for the public at large. Violence continued to accompany the movement, and was deliberately sought in provocative Fascist marches through districts in the East End of London, where attacks and counter-demonstrations could be expected and the police seemed more concerned to protect the Fascists than to curb their brutalities or defend their victims. In 1937 the movement began to decline: the police, thanks in part to new legislation, began to restrict its demonstrations; the public was becoming too pre-occupied with Fascism abroad to give it much support at home.[2]

Twice the National government intervened to restrain the tendencies to public violence. In 1934 the Incitement to Disaffec-

---

[1] *The Times*, June 8, 9, and later issues, 1934.
[2] James Drennan, *B.U.F., Oswald Mosley and British Fascism* (London, 1934), is a laudatory sketch. Frederic Mullally, *Fascism Inside England* (London, 1946) is a hostile account, with full particulars of the Olympia meeting and other incidents.

tion bill was enacted, in 1936 the Public Order bill. Both, however, seemed almost as bad as the disease, and were thought by many to be a deliberate attack by the government upon the liberty of the subject. The Public Order Act prohibited the wearing of political uniforms, gave the police new powers for banning processions, and extended outside London the offence of 'using insulting words and behaviour'. The Incitement to Disaffection Act strengthened earlier measures against the possession and dissemination of seditious literature and extended the powers of the police for searching for such documents under a search warrant and for confiscating them. Opposition to the bill came from many quarters, and though it was passed, it was only after a good deal of amendment.[1]

18. THE BEGINNING OF REARMAMENT: THE RESIGNATION OF MACDONALD

Meanwhile, in this same year of 1934, the sickness of Europe, with its fever of arming for a new war, was growing worse. Hitler, having broken up the Disarmament Conference, announced on December 18, 1933, his terms for returning to it, including permission for Germany to have a conscript army and many types of arms hitherto denied it. German rearmament was accelerated, with little pretence of concealment. Britain's disarmament, on the other hand, had reached its nadir; the appropriations for the armed services, which had been £116 millions in 1926–27 and £110 millions under the Labour government in 1930–31, were £102·7 millions in the economy year of 1932–33.[2] The campaign waged for two years, almost single-handed, by Winston Churchill on behalf of rearmament now at last, in 1934, began to have some success.

Churchill's warnings to parliament and people of the dangers of disarmament had begun, as the first volume of his memoirs later reminded them, as early as May 1932, when he asked those who favoured the approximation of French and German military strength: 'Do you wish for war?'[3] It was in this year that the government abandoned the 'ten-year rule' (that war was not to be expected within ten years), and began a survey of what was needed to meet the 'worst deficiencies' in armaments.[4] Churchill repeated his warnings of Britain's inferiority in the air, and of German

---

[1] *The Times*, May 7, October 27, 29, 30, 1934.
[2] J. W. Wheeler-Bennett, *Munich*, p. 230.
[3] W. S. Churchill, *Gathering Storm*, p. 66.
[4] W. K. Hancock and M. M. Gowing, *British War Economy* (History of the Second World War: United Kingdom Civil Series: London, 1949), p. 63.

rearmament, in March and November 1933.[1] In 1934 his interventions became more frequent. For the first time, on February 7,
he sketched the danger of a sudden outbreak of war, accompanied
within a few hours by destruction from the air: 'the crash of bombs
exploding in London and cataracts of masonry and fire and smoke
will warn us of any inadequacy . . . in our aerial defences'.[2] The
air estimates in March provided for four new squadrons, increasing the first-line air strength from 850 to 890 planes. Churchill
complained that Germany, now 'arming fast', would within a year
or eighteen months be strong enough in the air to threaten 'the
heart of the British Empire', while Britain was 'the fifth air Power
only—if that'.[3] Replying for the government, Baldwin gave a
pledge:

> . . . any Government of this country—a National Government more
> than any, and *this* Government—will see to it that in air strength and
> air power this country shall no longer be in a position inferior to any
> country within striking distance of its shores.[4]

The government began to stir itself. On July 20, 1934 it
announced a new programme: within five years the R.A.F. was to
be increased by 41 squadrons (820 planes) to a first-line strength
at home and overseas of 1304 planes. Liberals and Labour opposed
the measure, the Liberals deploring a new arms race, Labour
protesting that rearmament would not increase security but
'jeopardise the prospects of international disarmament'. Baldwin
rejoined in an oft-quoted passage on July 30:

> When you think of the defence of England you no longer think of the
> chalk cliffs of Dover, you think of the Rhine. That is where our
> frontier lies.

Yet it was Germany which continued to forge ahead. On November 28 Churchill told the House that not only did Germany have a
military air force but that within a year it would be as strong as
Britain's and by 1937 twice as large. Baldwin denied this flatly.
Germany's air strength was not 50 per cent of Britain's in Europe,
and a year hence Britain's margin in Europe would still be nearly
50 per cent. On May 22 of the following year he had to eat his
own words.[5]
     Other events in Europe in 1934 were not reassuring. In words
and action German official policy was quiet, and nothing was done

---

[1] W. S. Churchill, *Gathering Storm*, pp. 66, 77.   [2] Ibid., p. 84.
[3] Ibid., p. 101.   [4] Ibid., p. 102.   [5] Ibid., pp. 107, 111.

to endanger the peaceful return of the Saar to Germany. The territory was under the administration of the League of Nations, but by the treaty of Versailles a plebiscite in 1935 was to decide its future. The plebiscite, held on January 13, 1935 under the supervision of an international force, was overwhelmingly in favour of the reunion of the Saar with Germany. At home it was another matter. Hitler's 'purge' of June 30, 1934, in which Roehm, Karl Ernst, Schleicher, and other close associates of the Fuehrer were murdered in the night, and many more, probably over 200 persons, shot by firing parties during the day, gave new notice of the ruthlessness of the dictator and the bestiality of his regime.

Elsewhere there was turmoil. Dollfuss, the dictator of Austria, having on February 12 liquidated the Socialist opposition and bombarded the new blocks of municipal flats in Vienna where many Socialists lived, was himself murdered by the Nazis on July 25, 1934, in an ill-planned attempt at a *coup* by which the *Anschluss* would be accomplished. For the time being, Hitler drew back in his plans for Austria while France and Italy, foreseeing a common danger, became momentarily more friendly towards each other in opposition to Germany. France, however, was weakened by internal strife. The Stavisky scandals in December 1933 had revealed the extent of corruption in high places; the rioting in Paris and the shots of the police when a Fascist attempt at a *coup d'état* on February 6, 1934 was suppressed at a cost of sixteen lives showed how bitter and violent the political and social divisions within the nation had become. A strong government was formed under Doumergue, with Louis Barthou, a vigorous statesman of the old school, as foreign minister. Barthou brought a new virility to French foreign policy. He opposed condoning German rearmament, repaired the Little Entente, and by a series of visits to foreign capitals attempted to forge an Eastern Pact of Mutual Guarantee against Germany. It was perhaps not without Nazi connivance that he (and King Alexander of Jugoslavia) were murdered by a Croatian assassin at Marseilles on October 9, 1934, and his policies brought to an end. His successor was a more supple contriver, Laval. But Barthou's work left important results. With French support, Russia was admitted to the League of Nations, with a permanent seat on the Council, on September 18, 1934; and a treaty of mutual assistance between France and Russia was signed on May 2, 1935.[1]

[1] J. W. Wheeler-Bennett, *Munich*, pp. 240–2; G. M. Gathorne-Hardy, *Short History of International Affairs*, pp. 366–73.

A new period of crisis began early in 1935. France, under Laval, remained friendly towards Italy (thus encouraging Mussolini in sinister plans of his own). Simon and Laval met on February 3 and published a joint statement on behalf of Britain and France in favour of 'a general settlement freely negotiated between Germany and the other powers' and an armaments agreement replacing the Treaty of Versailles. Essential parts of the plan were an air convention by which the western powers would promise immediate assistance from the air to the victim of aggression, and the making of pacts embracing the countries of eastern and central Europe. This repudiation of Versailles by the powers most concerned in the maintenance of the treaty was an invitation to Hitler to flout it; but, coupled with the hint of an 'air Locarno', it threatened his future plans.[1] It was followed on March 4 by the publication of a White Paper, *Statement Relating to Defence*, issued in advance of a debate on the subject in the Commons.

The White Paper, only nine pages long, was a document of epochal significance. Much of it was devoted to a defence of past policy and a pledge of its continuance: support of the League and collective security, efforts to bring about a reduction of armaments. But, it continued, the government 'can no longer close its eyes to the fact that adequate defences are still required'. The Disarmament Conference was at a standstill, Germany and Japan and other countries were rearming, and in Germany the 'spirit in which the population, and especially the youth of the country, are being organised [lends] colour to . . . the general feeling of insecurity . . .' The government must put Britain's defences in order. The needs of each branch of the services were discussed, and the paper concluded with the words: 'An additional expenditure on the armaments of the three Defence Services can, therefore, no longer be safely postponed.'[2]

This was Hitler's cue. On March 9 his government admitted officially the existence of the German air force; on March 16 conscription was reintroduced and a peace-time strength of the German army of 550,000 men provided for. On March 12, France doubled the period of service of its conscripts. Disarmament had ended in Great Britain, and rearmament became the official policy there as in Germany.

MacDonald's career as head of the state ended with these

[1] G. M. Gathorne-Hardy, pp. 391–3; R. W. Seton-Watson, *Britain and the Dictators*, pp. 232–3.
[2] *Statement Relating to Defence* (Cmd. 4827; 1935), pp. 4, 6, 10.

events. By one of the many ironies in his life, the White Paper on defence bore the initials J.R.M. The apostle of peace signed as one of his last state papers the announcement that Britain must rearm. His health was failing; the government's popularity was very low. Simon at the Foreign Office, and Lord Londonderry at the Air Ministry, were the targets for much criticism. The Conservatives had long been chafing for a change. The celebrations of the silver jubilee of George V's accession to the throne in May formed a fitting conclusion to his last prime ministership. On June 7 Stanley Baldwin succeeded him as Prime Minister. The old government had sat out most of the dance, and must now retire. The new one was not very different, but events forced it to measures more vigorous, if not more fortunate, than its predecessor's.

CHAPTER NINE

The Secret People and the Social Conscience: the Condition of Britain in the Thirties

1. INTROSPECTION

THE THIRTIES have a bad name in people's memory of them: the gloomy thirties, a 'devil's decade'. It was certainly not a heroic time, and there was much gloom overhanging it, particularly in the distressed areas. One circumstance, however, both increased and lightened the gloom. This was the time when the country turned inward, and concerned itself more with its own ills than with the cares of the world. More was written and more was read about the 'condition of England question' than in the twenties. This introspection aroused a social conscience which had been sluggish in the more hopeful twenties. It was a time of social surveys, of 'mass observation', of public alarm about the nation's future. Social consciousness was also stimulated by the divisions over the Spanish civil war, and inevitably took on a political cast.

The political intensity of the last few years before war began had its counterparts elsewhere: in the new spirit in literature, in greater adventurousness in architecture, in the passion for ballet, in the search for new life in religion, in the journeyings on foot or on bicycle by the town-bred 'hikers' whom the Youth Hostels tempted forth to roads and footpaths. There was dreariness but there was also hope. There were strange flowers blossoming on the slag heaps.

2. OUT OF WORK

There were several Englands, and their differences had never been more sharply drawn. J. B. Priestley, whose *English Journey*, made in the autumn of 1933, gives one of the best pictures of the time, discovered four. One was the old England of the southern counties and the guide books. The second was nineteenth-century

England, the industrial north, the country of coal tips and silent blast furnaces and 'thousands of rows of little houses all alike'. Twentieth-century England was the England of the bustling home counties, of by-passes and housing estates and suburban villas and cocktail bars gleaming with chromium trim. The fourth England was the England of the dole.[1] Its boundaries were much the same as those of nineteenth-century England; and if one's view took in the whole of Great Britain, it would include all of industrial Scotland, all of South Wales and parts of North Wales, as well.

This sad, unemployed Britain was only dimly known to many in the comfortable classes in the south, though it could be seen almost anywhere in London and in the back streets of any of the larger towns; nor could anyone long miss the seedy beggars selling matches or shoe laces, or the Welsh miners, with mufflers round their throats, singing 'Land of our Fathers' by the kerbside. The stricken areas were, however, a land apart: much written of, but seldom visited by outsiders, save for the devoted social workers and the thoughtful undergraduates who played the Good Samaritan in the community centres and club houses. The Welsh mining valleys were numb with distress. Industrial Lancashire was at a standstill, though not officially classified as a special area. In Wigan one man in three was on the dole. The mining villages of county Durham, the steel works and shipyards of Tyne and Tees were derelict: Gateshead, Hebburn, Jarrow, Wallsend, Crook. Of Stockton-on-Tees Priestley wrote 'the real town is finished. It is like a theatre that is kept open merely for the sale of drinks in the bars and chocolates in the corridors.'[2] So it was in west Cumberland. So it was in Scotland: in Glasgow perhaps half the population was unemployed.[3]

Consider the Bishop Auckland area of southwest Durham. It had had 33 coal pits employing 28,000 miners. By 1935 17 pits were abandoned, three more closed and unlikely to reopen, and the remaining 13, where work dragged on with small and irregular

[1] J. B. Priestley, *English Journey* (London, 1934), pp. 397–408.
[2] Ibid., p. 342.
[3] Descriptions of several distressed areas exist. For London, Lancashire, Scotland, see A. Hutt, *Condition of the Working Class in Britain* (1933); for the Tyneside, Priestley's *English Journey* and Ellen Wilkinson's *Town that was Murdered* (Jarrow: a Left Book Club book); for Lancashire, Priestley's *English Journey* and George Orwell's *Road to Wigan Pier* (Left Book Club: London, 1937); for South Wales, Hilda Jennings, *Brynmawr* (London, 1934), and Philip Massey, *Portrait of a Mining Town* (*Fact*, November, 1937; describing the Blaina-Nantyglo area). More vivid and penetrating than a score of studies is Walter Greenwood's novel of Manchester, *Love on the Dole* (1933: references to 1945 edition). See also the figures and references (including government reports) given in chapter 8, section 14, above.

R

shifts, employed 6500 men, though often not on full time. Despite the fact that many families, and particularly the younger men, had moved away, unemployment was very high: 80 per cent or more of the workers in Tow Law were unemployed, almost 100 per cent of those in Shildon; at West Auckland only one hundred men out of a thousand had had work in the last seven years.[1] In a street of sixty cottages in one of the mining villages you would hardly find one where the man was at work.

The appearance of the derelict towns varied little. Everywhere you saw shops closed and boarded up, houses with peeling paint and broken slates. Only the pawn shops and the cinemas flourished, only the Labour Exchange drew its shabby crowd. Only Sam Grundy, the bookie, prospered, able to win Sal Hardcastle for his lust and find jobs for her family through his pull with the bus company; able also to get a job in the police for an informer like Ned Narkey.[2] The only sign of life was the men standing at the street corners, with nothing to do, nothing to say.

> He was standing there as motionless as a statue, cap neb pulled over his eyes, gaze fixed on pavement, hands in pockets, shoulders hunched, the bitter wind blowing his thin trousers tightly against his legs. Waste paper and dust blew about him in spirals, the papers making harsh sounds as they slid on the pavement.[3]

The unemployed fell into three categories: those out of work for a few weeks or months at a time, or drawing partial unemployment relief (those working three days or less per week); the young men who had never had work, or who had worked as youths only until they qualified for a man's wage; and the long unemployed, those who had been out of work for a year or longer and were unlikely—particularly the older men—ever to find work again. Those long unemployed were the most to be pitied. There were 300,000 of them in Great Britain in January 1932, 480,000 in July 1933, 337,000 or 23·9 per cent of those receiving unemployment pay, in July 1936. Their numbers were greatest among the men aged 60 to 64 (at 65 unemployment relief ceased), and diminished in each lower age-group;[4] they were most numerous among miners, shipbuilders, cotton trade operatives, and therefore most numerous in the areas of greatest distress: 57 per 1000

---

[1] T. Sharp, *A Derelict Area: A Study of the South-West Durham Coalfield* (London, 1935), pp. 23, 33–9.

[2] Walter Greenwood, *Love on the Dole*.   [3] Ibid., p. 254.

[4] In July 1935, 105 per 1000 workers aged 60–4 had been unemployed for over a year as compared with 80 per 1000 aged 50–9, 54 per 1000 aged 45–53, 31 aged 25–34, 29 aged 21–4: *Men Without Work*, p. 20 (see next note).

workers in 1936 were long unemployed in northeast England, 123 per 1000 in Wales, 281 in the Rhondda, where their actual number was nearly 11,000.   Among these long unemployed in Great Britain, 52,900 had been out of work over five years in 1936, 205,000 for two years or longer.   In Crook 71 per cent of the unemployed had been unemployed for over five years; in the Rhondda, 45 per cent.   And as men returned to work these, who were the last to be taken on, increased in proportion to the short-time unemployed.   By 1936, 77 men in every 100 thrown out of work between 1929 and 1932 had found work, by 1937, 94; this meant that 27 per cent of the remaining unemployed were long-term unemployed.[1]

What did the state do for these redundant working people? It did not provide relief work, though it did try to stimulate employment on public works by guaranteeing loans.   The government's chief policy was simply to maintain the unemployed man and his family by payments of one sort or another from public funds.

Between 1931 and the beginning of 1935 a man, wife and three young children could expect to receive 29s. 3d. a week as unemployment insurance benefit or as 'transitional payments' (subject to the means test) after benefit rights were exhausted; or they might receive payments (which varied from place to place) from the local Public Assistance Committee.   The economy cuts in the benefit rates were ended in July 1934.   The Unemployment Assistance Board's revised scale in 1936 gave the same family about 36s. a week.   In 1936 43 per cent of the unemployed were drawing insurance benefits, 37 per cent were receiving payments from the U.A.B.; most of the remainder (some 334,000) were at that time still being maintained by the P.A.C.[2]

For being subsisted the unemployed man and his family had to prove need, once insurance benefits were exhausted.   No doubt any means test would have been resented by men who believed, not without justice, that their lack of work was not their own

[1] See text and tables in *Men Without Work: a Report Made to the Pilgrim Trust* (Cambridge, 1938), pp. 6–46, 65, 74.   This is the best social study of unemployment made in the thirties, and was the work of enquirers in Deptford, Leicester, Rhondda, Crook, Liverpool, Blackburn, under the auspices of a committee on unemployment convened by Archbishop Temple. See also that vade-mecum of the social condition of Britain: G. D. H. and M. I. Cole, *Condition of Britain* (London, 1937; Left Book Club), pp. 219–33.

[2] For scales and other matters, see R. C. Davison, *British Unemployment Policy since 1930*, pp. 15, 36, 125; G. D. H. and M. Cole, *Condition of Britain*, pp. 212, 228–30; G. Orwell, *Wigan Pier*, pp. 76–8. See also Polly Hill, *Unemployment Services* (London, 1940) and Eveline M. R. Burns, *British Unemployment Programmes, 1920–1938* (New York, 1941).

fault; what made the means test hated and loathed by the working classes was its form and its administration. It was a household means test. It took account of any earnings by members of the household (sons and daughters, for instance) as well as of savings, pensions, income from house property or other assets.[1] Thrift was penalised and improvidence rewarded. Family solidarity was undermined: growing sons and daughters were forced to support their parents in a way which frayed the tempers of both generations and might break up the family: sons and daughters would move into lodgings in order not to be 'dragged down' by having to support their parents. The test was an encouragement to the tattle-tale and the informer, the writer of anonymous letters and the local blackmailer; to all sorts of unneighbourliness.[2] It stimulated petty tyranny and insolence on the part of Labour Exchange clerks and managers; the weekly visit to the Exchange would bring the sudden, curt announcement by the clerk: 'They've knocked you off dole.'[3]

Yet, however frustrating to the individual, the dole kept people alive, and it kept them on the safe side of discontent and thoughts of revolution. Many people, particularly the young married men, were better off on the dole than on the low wages which they could earn if employed—especially if work was intermittent. For one thing, unemployment payments involved the whole system of family allowances, to which industry was a stranger. In a study of young men in Cardiff it was found that 34 per cent of the single men and 45 per cent of the married men had received in their last job less in wages than they were then receiving in unemployment allowances.[4]

It was the social and psychological effects of unemployment which left the most lasting marks. Many men out of work accepted their fate, shrugging their shoulders: 'Lots worse off than them. They all say that.'[5] To such men a spell of unemployment was a holiday, patched clothes a mark of honour. Some might join a W.E.A. class, like the Durham miner who took a five-year course in English literature; others found a use for their leisure in reading,

[1] For scope of the means test regulations see the Coles, p. 214.
[2] G. Orwell, *Wigan Pier*, pp. 78–9; A. J. Lush, *The Young Adult* (Cardiff, 1941), p. 36.
[3] W. Greenwood, *Love on the Dole*, pp. 191–3. See also E. W. Bakke, *The Unemployed Man* (London, 1933: a useful study made in Greenwich by an American observer).
[4] A. J. Lush, *Young Adult*, p. 28; cf. R. C. Davison, pp. 72–3; *Disinherited Youth* (Edinburgh, 1943), pp. 44–5; *Men without Work*, pp. 164–71, 201–12.
[5] J. B. Priestley, *English Journey*, p. 281.

or in taking part in plays or joining in the other activities of a community house or unemployed men's club. Some went for long walks—a week's walking holiday on 3s. 5d. was the recollection of one; others played football, even if it meant a seven-mile walk to the game. Some worked in an allotment, others kept poultry, others did amateur carpentry in their back yards or at the club. In summer they might pick blackberries or mushrooms, and the younger ones might go for a swim. In the mining districts men often scrabbled for coal on the tips or pilfered it from stacks or railway wagons. Many found odd jobs canvassing for newspaper subscriptions or running with betting slips; others pursued the will o' the wisp of earning some money by succumbing to shady 'make and sell' schemes advertised in the personal columns in the newspapers: send 2s. 6d. for a kit for making shoe polish to sell to your friends.[1]

To the large majority unemployment meant apathy. The young men had never known steady work and did not fret at the lack of it. They 'were undisciplined and carefree, the dingy butterflies of the back streets. They had no sense whatever of waste and tragedy in themselves . . . they lived below the level of worry.'[2] In many families the main problem was to keep warm, and to conserve low energy. This was best done by staying in bed late and going to bed early; fuel, light and effort were all thus saved. Going to the cinema served these purposes also, as well as providing a passing distraction from boredom. In Cardiff, 52 per cent of the unemployed youths interviewed visited the cinema once a week, and almost half of these twice a week; in Liverpool and Glasgow as many as 80 per cent went to the cinema at least once a week.[3] Others resorted to the many licensed clubs which existed in the cities, where billiards, gambling and raffles flourished.[4] For many there was nothing to do, when their wives drove them out of doors, but to sit in the public library or to loaf at street corners, smoking fag ends of cigarettes or the used tea-leaves they stuffed into their pipes. Even the queue 'at the Labour' (the Employment Exchange) brought variety and companionship.

Life was, in fact, sustained by the weekly round of existence, by indulgence in cheap luxuries, by the excitement of small bets.

[1] Information (some of it statistical) on the more serious pursuits of the young unemployed in Lush, *Young Adult*, and *Disinherited Youth*. Personal information from Durham miners, June 1948, and from Mr. T. Brennan, University College of Swansea, May, 1952. See also John Hilton, *Rich Man, Poor Man* (London, 1944), pp. 158–9.
[2] J. B. Priestley, *English Journey*, p. 306.
[3] A. J. Lush, *Young Adult*, p. 80; *Disinherited Youth*, p. 104.
[4] *Disinherited Youth*, pp. 113–15.

Friday brought the week's money and a slightly better dinner; Saturday evening the football scores. As George Orwell so profoundly observed, people *settled down* to living on the dole; they did not go to pieces, they did not turn to revolution. They cut down on necessities and concentrated on luxuries.

> You can't get much meat for threepence, but you can get a lot of fish-and-chips. Milk costs threepence a pint, and even 'mild' beer costs fourpence, but aspirins are seven a penny and you can wring forty cups of tea out of a quarter-pound packet. And above all there is gambling, the cheapest of all luxuries. Even people on the verge of starvation can buy a few days' hope ('Something to live for,' as they call it) by having a penny on a sweepstake. . . . When you are unemployed, which is to say when you are underfed, harassed, bored and miserable, you don't *want* to eat dull, wholesome food. You want something a little bit 'tasty'. There is always some cheaply pleasant thing to tempt you. Let's have three pennorth of chips! Run out and buy us a twopenny ice-cream! Put the kettle on and we'll all have a nice cup of tea! *That* is how your mind works when you are at the P.A.C. level.[1]

Others, again, felt lost, hopeless. Time was heavy when there was nothing to do. 'It's like as if you were dead.' Friends drop away, or one is ashamed to meet them in one's old, shabby clothes. Many came to a feeling not only of uselessness but of bitterness; the youth, thwarted of his manhood,[2] the old man, robbed of the respect of his children, deprived of his self-respect as head of the household. Thus Mr. Hardcastle faced the ruin of his family. 'What had he been *able* to do other than what had been done? The responsibility wasn't his. He'd worked all his life; had given all he had to give . . . Oh, why the devil couldn't they give him work? The canker of impotence gnawed his vitals.'[3] Some listened to the organisers of the unemployed, the Wal Hanningtons, and went on hunger marches or attended unemployed men's meetings, despite the ubiquitous constables and plainclothes men, taking their notes, spotting agitators for black-listing, arresting leaders or breaking up meetings with their batons.[4]

---

[1] G. Orwell, *Road to Wigan Pier*, pp. 89, 95–6. Quoted by kind permission of A. M. Heath and Company, Ltd.
[2] E. W. Bakke, *The Unemployed Man*, pp. 62–3; A. J. Lush, *Young Adult*, pp. 42–5; W. Greenwood, *Love on the Dole*, p. 150.
[3] W. Greenwood, p. 247.
[4] Ibid., pp. 193–202; Wal Hannington's two books, *Unemployed Struggles*, and *Problem of the Distressed Areas* (London, 1937). For typical left-wing criticisms of the 'justice' meted out to working men, see A. Hutt, *Condition of the Working Class*, pp. 242–9.

Yet it was the women who suffered more than the men. Unemployment brought leisure for the men, if they chose to regard it so; it brought no rest to the wives and mothers. They must scrape and scrimp to feed and clothe the family, usually on less money than before, even if what there was was now fixed and regular. Very often the children were well cared-for and healthy. If anyone in the family went short on food and clothes, it was the mother. For her the bitterness was unrelieved. In Durham it took the form of a resolve: no son of mine shall go into the pits; I'll see those children dead first.[1]

For many of the young men who were unemployed, life was not as bitter as this. The 'disinherited youth' had grown up on the dole, after holding some blind-alley job[2] or serving a barren apprenticeship. Many had come to accept this existence: in Liverpool—a black spot, admittedly, for the young unemployed—30 per cent of the unemployed men aged 20–34 could be classed as work-shy, a higher proportion than among the middle-aged and the older men in Liverpool.[3] Many of them had married on the dole: 35 per cent of the unemployed men between 18 and 25 in Liverpool, 31 per cent of those in Glasgow.[4] It was to the credit of the state that it did not discourage such marriages. In fact, it encouraged them, for two could live better than one on the scale of unemployment allowances. Often the wife would continue at work, supporting the husband. The newer industries employed more women than the older and declining industries had done (except the cotton trades); hence the impression in the depressed areas that there was only work for women, and for boys and girls just out of school.[5] 'Why don't you get wed. They're all doin' it. Tarts go out to work, nowadays, while the owld man stops at home.'[6] The habit of marrying on the dole shocked members of the comfortable classes; but, as one writer observed, 'it would be far more disturbing if the youth of today, as a consequence

---

[1] Durham miners, to the author, June 1948; *Men without Work*, pp. 126–7, 139–41; J. B. Priestley, *English Journey*, p. 333.

[2] In the Merseyside survey it was found that 72 per cent of the adolescent boys in work were in blind-alley jobs, e.g., as errand boys, office boys, messengers: *Social Survey of Merseyside*, III, 208.

[3] For a discussion of the numbers of unemployed who were work-shy, see *Men without Work*, pp. 144, 164–78.

[4] *Disinherited Youth*, p. 54.

[5] A. Hutt, *Condition of the Working Class*, pp. 201–3. An excellent study of working-class girls, which brings out the terrible monotony of their jobs, is A. P. Jephcott, *Girls Growing Up* (London, 1942).

[6] W. Greenwood, *Love on the Dole*, p. 228. In Lancashire, ' "tart" is a general term for all femininity', ibid., p. 6.

of unemployment, actually did give up the desire for family life.'[1]

To keep men in condition for work, and to re-train them for new jobs, the Ministry of Labour operated Government Training Centres and Instructional Centres. Attendance was voluntary, though sometimes 'encouraged'. The Instructional Centres were intended to rehabilitate men in physical condition and morale by twelve weeks' hard work and solid meals. In summer their number was increased by the use of tented camps, where the men did forest clearance for the Forestry Commission, or dug ditches, made roads, levelled land or worked at stone-breaking. For women there were Domestic Training Centres, but domestic service, though often resorted to, was not popular among girls from the factories and the industrial areas.

In alleviating the distress of unemployment the state's efforts were dwarfed by those of a voluntary character. Unemployed clubs, community service clubs, occupational centres sprang up by the score, both in the smaller towns and in the large cities. By 1935 there were some 400 in all, with 250,000 members. Cardiff had 21 clubs, Liverpool and Glasgow nine each. They were, of course, part of the long traditions of self-help and of charitable social service: they had connections with, and sometimes grew out of, older settlement houses and clubs in working-class districts; they paralleled the work among the unemployed of bodies such as the Y.M.C.A. and the Salvation Army; they had links with the adult education movement. There were also some shelters maintained by the National Unemployed Workers' Movement.

The origins of the clubs were various. Many sprang from local initiative or some isolated effort. The movement became a national one in January 1932, when the National Council of Social Service held a meeting at the Albert Hall, at which the Prince of Wales spoke. The National government, under pressure to do something for the unemployed, decided to support the Council's efforts with a grant, initially, of £20,000. Thereafter the N.C.S.S., through its paid organisers and its local councils, helped in the starting of many clubs. The custom of adoption spread. Surrey adopted Jarrow, Bath adopted Redruth, the B.B.C. staff a club in Gates-

---

[1] A. J. Lush, *Young Adult*, p. 46. This study, and the report entitled *Disinherited Youth*, were both made for the Carnegie United Kingdom Trust on the basis of a survey in 1937–39 of unemployed men aged 18–25 in Liverpool and Glasgow and in Cardiff, Newport and Pontypridd. *Disinherited Youth* deals with the results of all three surveys, Lush's *Young Adult* with the survey in the three last-named towns. See also *Men without Work*, especially pp. 220–9.

head, the Ministry of Health staff in London adopted a club in Crook. Towns, schools, staffs of banks and business firms joined in the movement, sometimes with more zeal than discretion, which risked pauperising the club which was being helped.

Some of the less usual efforts of voluntary bodies to help the unemployed achieved some renown. One of the earliest, which began in 1926, before the depression was acute, was the educational settlement of Maes-yr-Haf, at Trealaw in the Rhondda, founded by the Quakers and inspired by its warden, Emma Noble. Its chairman was A. D. Lindsay. It became the 'spiritual powerhouse' of the Welsh valleys. It had its own buildings and a permanent staff of lecturers, physical-training instructors, craftsmen and social workers, as well as extra help in the summer from Oxford undergraduates. It established a holiday camp on the Glamorgan coast; it started another settlement at Bargoed; it stimulated the growth of the club movement throughout the valleys. A later institution on the same model was the Pontypool Educational Settlement, founded in 1937 through the efforts of a local minister, Rev. G. S. Burden, and aided by the Commissioner of the Special Areas. It had its own new building, with lecture rooms and a library. Residential adult education centres were another product of the movement. The best known, Coleg Harlech, in North Wales, was founded in 1927 and took in working men on scholarships (not necessarily unemployed men) for a year's further education. It was one of Thomas Jones' happy inspirations, carried out by its warden, Ben Bowen Thomas.[1] Others were founded with the prime object of training unemployed men as club leaders and teachers. The N.C.S.S. organised three in country mansions: King's Standing, near Burton-on-Trent, Hardwick Hall, County Durham, and Wincham Hall in Lancashire.

Elsewhere the Quakers were concerned with schemes of subsistence and beautification. At Brynmawr they first formed a Community Study Council. From this came a social survey and a town development scheme which made a famous swimming pool and park (the labour of the unemployed made waste land into parks in several other places, including Tow Law and Jarrow). At Brynmawr the Quakers' efforts also forwarded the work of a co-operative society which made furniture and woven goods and worked an old coal mine. All over the country the unemployed

---

[1] Thomas Jones, *Welsh Broth* (London, [1952]), pp. 162–3. Coleg Harlech inspired a similar college in Scotland at Newbattle Abbey, given by Lord Lothian and opened in 1937.

R*

were encouraged to grow vegetables on allotments, with tools, seeds and fertilisers supplied by the Allotments for the Unemployed scheme which the Quakers organised. A larger undertaking was the Eastern Valleys Production Society, organised in South Wales by Peter Scott with the aid of a grant from the Commissioner of the Special Areas. From its farms and workshops its products were distributed among its members, the 'unemployed' who worked in it as co-operators. A similar scheme was the Upholland Experiment, near Wigan, aided by a gift from Lord Nuffield. Here a fluctuating number of members, some two hundred or more, worked on four farms raising pigs, growing vegetables and producing milk, or were employed in an industrial centre where tailoring, baking, jam making and the like were done.[1]

3. CLASS AND INCOME

Any estimate of the condition of Great Britain in the thirties is bound to be affected by the numbers and fortunes of the unemployed. It is affected also by the continuing evidences of inequality between the classes, including both those in work and the unemployed, in matters of income and capital, nutrition, the death rate, infant and maternal mortality, and shelter. True, a picture drawn in 1933, in the depth of the depression, was darker than one painted in 1936 or 1937, in the time of recovery. Three things must be borne in mind in examining the social conditions of the decade. There was, except for 1931–32, a rise in real income for the entire population. There was a small diminution of inequality of incomes as a result of the depression, but this was disappearing by 1937. And inequality of condition remained: a little less perhaps, than in the twenties, but still far too large for the conscience of a troubled and introspective generation.

It is well to have some idea of numbers. Counting by families in Great Britain in 1934, some three-quarters of all families (73·5 per cent, or 8,600,000 families) were working-class families, with an income of £4 a week or less. The middle class, if possession of an income of £4–£10 a week is the criterion for membership, consisted of 2½ million families, or 21·3 per cent of all families.

---

[1] Voluntary work among the unemployed, and its impact, is best studied in *Men without Work*, Part V, and in H. A. Mess, *Voluntary Social Services since 1918* (London, 1948), pp. 40–54. See also *Disinherited Youth*, pp. 109–12; Hilda Jennings, *Brynmawr*; E. Wilkinson, *Town that was Murdered*, pp. 227–30; R. C. Davison, *British Unemployment Policy since 1930*, p. 101. There are good accounts of clubs in Blackburn and Seaham Harbour in J. B. Priestley, *English Journey*, pp. 282–4, 325–6.

The remaining upper class comprised 617,000 families, 5·2 per cent of all families.[1]

The national income fell from 1929 to 1932, but then recovered, and by 1936 was above that of 1929, and therefore above that of 1924 also by about 7 per cent. The proportions distributed between wages, salaries, profits and interest and rents remained very stable, save that the share of profits dropped sharply between 1931 and 1933.[2]

Wage rates remained rather steady. From 1924 to 1929 they fell by 6 per cent, and from 1929 to 1932 by another 4 per cent, thus standing 10 per cent below the 1924 figure; by 1937 they were almost back to the level of 1924. The average depended, however, on the inelasticity of the rates in the sheltered industries; in the cotton, woollen and coal-mining industries the fall by 1932 was about 15 per cent. Earnings, however, fell by less than wage rates, partly through upgrading of workers and some change from time to piece rates.[3] Thus in the last quarter of 1935 the average weekly earnings of a miner were 49s., and this was about the average for workers in all the main industries; for the textile worker this meant average weekly earnings of about 36s. The sum is larger if the earnings of men only are considered. The average number of hours worked per week in all industries was then 47·8.[4]

National Income, 1924–38 (Great Britain and Northern Ireland)

	1924	1929	1931	1932	1933	1934	1935	1936	1937	1938
National income (Bowley),[5] £m.	3887	3926	3438	3327	3533	3713	3919	4151	4351	4362
National income (Clark)[6], £m.	3529	3912	—	3349	—	3694	3909	—	—	—
Income per head (Clark), £	78·6	85·5	—	72·4	—	79·0	83·5	—	—	—
Income per occupied person (Clark), £	172·6	183·8	—	154·7	—	168·3	177·7	—	—	—

[1] Cole, *Condition of Britain*, p. 64.

[2] See above, chapter 4, section 3, and chapter 8, section 10; and table below.

[3] A. L. Bowley, *Studies in National Income*, pp. 62–3; A. C. Pigou and C. Clark, *Economic Position of Great Britain*, pp. 29–31.

[4] See tables and discussion in H. Macmillan, *The Middle Way*, pp. 50–6, quoting *Ministry of Labour Gazette*, July, 1937. Agricultural wages ranged from 30s. to 38s. for a week of fifty hours or more; in most counties they were about 32s.

[5] A. L. Bowley, *Studies in the National Income, 1924–1938*, p. 81.

[6] A. C. Pigou and C. Clark, *Economic Position of Great Britain* (London and Cambridge Economic Service, Special Memorandum No. 43; 1936), p. 18. (Reproduced in Carr-Saunders and D. Caradog Jones, *Social Structure of England and Wales* [2nd ed.], p. 93.) Clark gives rather higher figures for the years 1924–33 in *National Income and Outlay*, p. 88.

Distribution of Home-Produced Income, 1924–35[1]

	1924	1929	1931	1932	1933	1934	1935
Wages %	42·1	41·8	42·8	42·5	42·0	41·5	40·5
Salaries ..	25·4	26·6	27·8	28·3	28·0	26·5	25·0
Profits ..	25·1	23·1	19·5	18·8	19·8	22·4	25·4
Rents ..	7·4	8·5	9·9	10·4	10·2	9·6	9·1

Meanwhile prices fell steadily until 1932, and then rose only slightly. The net result was an increase of real income per head of population of about 24 per cent, or 20 per cent per occupied person. Real wages per head had risen about 17 per cent, or allowing for the unemployed, by about 9 per cent.[2] With this may be compared the findings of the Bristol social survey in 1937. Of all working-class families 68 per cent had an average income of 75s. 10d. per week, enough for 'sufficiency', raising them above the standard of minimum needs by from 50 to 200 per cent. And 12 per cent of the families, with an average income of £5 17s. 7d., had enough to live on in comfort.[3] Even the unemployed man with a family was better off in the thirties than the unskilled labourer in full work in 1913.[4] For a time of depression this was a remarkable and unexpected phenomenon.

Apart from the rise of real wages, the betterment of the working class was helped on by the transfer from rich to poor effected by taxation and the social services. In 1913 the working class paid in taxes more than it received in social services, but in 1925 it received in social services more than it paid in taxes by £55 millions (contributing 85 per cent of the cost), and in 1935 more by £91 millions, when its contribution to the cost of the social services was 79 per cent.[5] Calculations based on taxation, contributions to national insurance schemes, and expenditure in 1937 showed that between £200 millions and £250 millions was redistributed from rich to poor by taxation and social expenditure, or 5–6 per cent of the national income. The effect was to raise the income of the working class by 8–14 per cent.[6]

[1] C. Clark, *National Income and Outlay*, p. 94.
[2] A. C. Pigou and C. Clark, *Economic Position of Great Britain*, pp. 20, 33, 39. See table below.
[3] Herbert Tout, *Standard of Living in Bristol* (Bristol, 1938), pp. 26–8.
[4] C. Clark, *National Income and Outlay*, p. 270.
[5] A. M. Carr-Saunders, *Social Structure* (1st ed., 1927), p. 158; (2nd ed.), pp. 147–54; C. Clark, *National Income and Outlay*, pp. 142–8.
[6] Tibor Barna, *Redistribution of Incomes through Public Finance in 1937* (Oxford, 1945), pp. 233–4. Mr. and Mrs. Cole think that the amount redistributed was somewhat less: *Condition of Britain*, pp. 322–49.

Real Income, Real Wages, Wage Rates and Earnings, Prices, 1924–38

(1924 = 100)	1924	1929	1931	1932	1933	1934	1935	1936	1937	1938
Wage rates[1]	100	96	—	90	—	90	90·5	94	98·5	99·5
Earnings[1] ..	100	98	—	89	—	93	97	98·5	102	103
Prices, Board of Trade index[2] ..	100	82	62·5	61	62	63	64	68	78	73
Real income per head[3] ..	100	114	—	106·8	—	118·8	124·3	—	—	—
Real income per occupied person (incl. unemployed)[3]	100	111·8	—	103·7	—	115·5	120·9	—	—	—
Real income per head (excl. unemployed)[3] ..	100	108·3	—	110·0	—	116·4	120·7	—	—	—
Real wages[4]	100	104	114	116·5	116	115·5	—	—	—	—
Real income per person in work, £[5] ..	203·8	226	218·3	217·4	221·9	228·8	237·2	—	—	—
Real income per person in work at consumption prices (allowing for terms of trade), £[5]	202·4	221·9	219·4	220·4	228·8	235·2	240·8	—	—	—
Real income per occupied person (incl. unemployed), £[5] ..	185	203·4	184·4	183·4	194·2	204·8	211·8	—	—	—

Inequality and its diminution can also be seen in one of Sir Josiah Stamp's studies. The number of persons with incomes over £5000 more than doubled between 1913 and 1921, and was even higher in 1929, but by 1934 had dropped by nearly a third. There were 206 persons with an income of over £100,000 in 1921, only 65 in 1934. Taking the income of the person 10,000th in the list from the highest, he found it to be £10,410 in 1921,

[1] A. L. Bowley, *Studies in National Income*, pp. 62–3, using for wage rates the figures of E. C. Ramsbottom in *Journal of the Royal Statistical Society*, 1935, 1938, 1939.
[2] Ibid., p. 192.
[3] A. C. Pigou and C. Clark, *Economic Position of Great Britain*, p. 20.
[4] Ibid., p. 33, citing E. C. Ramsbottom, *J.R.S.S.*, 1935.
[5] C. Clark, *National Income and Outlay*, p. 208.

£7459 in 1934, a fall rather greater than that of the cost of living.[1]

Part of the change Sir Josiah Stamp attributed to the effect of death duties over a long period: 'the degradation of the taxable corpus under the influence of the heavy duties'. An estate might increase through interest at the rate of 4 per cent per year, but income tax and supertax of 60 per cent would reduce this increase to 1·6 per cent, which was insufficient to pay death duties of 50 per cent once in 25 years. 'The rate of subtraction exceeds the rate of addition by 0·4 per cent per annum and the corpus of wealth must slowly diminish.'[2] This did not prevent Sir John Ellerman, a shipowner and recluse, from leaving an estate of over £36 millions when he died in 1933; his successor as the richest man in the country was Joseph Rank, the miller.

By the later thirties, however, the number of the well-to-do was recovering. There were more people with incomes of £2000–£7000 in 1937 than in 1924. Those with incomes above £7000 were fewer in 1937 than in 1924, but in every bracket their number was greater in 1937 than it had been at the bottom of the depression.[3]

Higher Incomes and the Price Level, 1913–37

	No. of persons with incomes exceeding £5000[4]	No. with incomes exceeding £100,000[4]	Income of 10,000th person[5]	Cost of living index[6]
			£	
1913	13,664	75	6,170	63
1921	28,803	206	10,410	142
1929	29,846	166	9,986	95
1932	22,953	95	8,166	84
1934	19,713	65	7,459	80
1937	26,114[3]	99[3]	—	—

[1] Sir Josiah Stamp, 'The Influence of the Price Level on the Higher Incomes', *J.R.S.S.*, 99: 643, 649 (1936). See table above. Cf. A. M. Carr-Saunders, *Social Structure* (2nd ed.), p. 97.

[2] J. C. Stamp, *loc. cit.*, pp. 654–5. For the distribution of property as shown by death duties in 1934 see Cole, *Condition of Britain*, pp. 72–6.

[3] *Statistical Abstract of U.K.*, 1938, p. 218.

[4] J. C. Stamp, *J.R.S.S.*, 99: 643.　　　　[5] Ibid., 649.

[6] *Statistical Abstract of U.K.*, 1938, p. 218.

4. THE WELFARE STATE IN SCAFFOLDING

Extensive though they were in the thirties, the social services left many gaps where people crouched unprotected.[1] The independent worker was not included in unemployment insurance or assistance; youths of 14–16 were brought in only in 1934, agricultural workers in 1936, domestic servants in 1938. Any system of family allowances was lacking, with the curious exception of payments under unemployment assistance and public assistance—the back of the coin whose obverse bore the inscription 'means test'. The welfare state was standing, but still incomplete and in scaffolding. All was ready for Sir William Beveridge and his report in 1942, and for the revolutionary change in attitudes towards the services of the state which the blitz (being no respecter of persons) introduced.[2] By the legislation of 1945–48 the gaps were filled, the walls finished, and a roof put over all. The difference between the old social services and the new was that the latter formed a nearly coherent system and included all people 'from cradle to grave', rich and poor alike: national insurance, national assistance, family allowances, the national health service. And being all-inclusive, they no longer put a stigma on those they helped.

It was in the system of national health insurance that the gaps were most obvious in the thirties. Wives and mothers were not provided for at all, except at the time of child-bearing. Children between one and five were left out and during their school years were only inspected, seldom treated, by the school medical and dental service. Of the adult population, only wage-earners were included in national health insurance, which meant that not only were dependents left out, but also all independent workers; and it was not until 1938 that youths of 14–16 were included. In 1936 the number covered by national health insurance in Great Britain was just over 19 millions, or rather over half the population above the age of 14. The medical service provided under public assistance was, however, available to those in need, as was treatment for tuberculosis, venereal disease and insanity. The growth of

[1] Accounts of the social services include W. H. Wickwar, *The Social Services* (London, 1936, rev. ed., 1949); E. W. Cohen, *English Social Services* (London, 1949); P.E.P., *Report on the British Social Services* (London, 1937). See also Arnold Wilson and G. S. Mackay, *Old Age Pensions* (Oxford, 1941). For the social services as seen in one district see A. F. C. Bourdillon (ed.), *Survey of the Social Services in the Oxford District* (2 vols., Oxford, 1938–40).

[2] R. M. Titmuss, *Problems of Social Policy* (History of the Second World War: United Kingdom Civil Series: London, 1950), esp. p. 506.

public hospitals in the thirties, including many transferred from the old Poor Law, increased the opportunities for hospital treatment for people not covered by the contributory schemes of the voluntary hospitals.[1]

Calculations of the cost of the social services depended partly on what was included in the term. The net expenditures by the government and the local authorities on unemployment benefits and relief, old age pensions, widows' and orphans' pensions, public assistance, national health insurance, education, housing, hospitals and child welfare, rose from £74·6 millions in 1913 to £376·8 millions in 1931 (or about £9 per capita). In 1913 such expenditures were about a quarter of the public revenue and about 3 per cent of the national income; in 1931 they constituted rather less than a third of the public revenue and about 10 per cent of the national income.[2] About a third of the cost of insurance payments, public assistance and pensions was met by the contributions of employers and employees, and about half of this share was contributed by the working men.[3] All but one-sixth of the cost of national health insurance was met by employers' and workers' contributions.[4] The effect of the social services upon poverty was less clear. In the Bristol survey it was estimated that if public assistance was abolished the proportion of working-class families below the poverty line would rise from 10·7 per cent to 12·1 per cent; on the other hand one-third of all the families below the line had no help from the social services at all.[5]

The growth of the social services provided by the state ended neither the need nor the zeal of private charity. The vast conglomeration of the voluntary social services continued to flourish, often in partnership with the state. Half of the nursery schools (there were only 115 by 1939) were provided by voluntary effort; a quarter of the maternity and child welfare centres were run by voluntary committees, though receiving 80 per cent or more of their expenses from public funds. Approved schools for delinquent children, district nurses, the Workers' Educational Association, unemployed men's clubs—all represented voluntary effort in

[1] For criticism of national health insurance, see P.E.P., *Report on the British Health Services* (London, 1937), esp. pp. 206–29, and Hermann Levy, *National Health Insurance* (Cambridge, 1944).

[2] See table below. Figures based on C. Clark, *National Income and Outlay*, pp. 140–41. Higher figures are given in A. M. Carr-Saunders, *Social Structure* (2nd ed.), p. 150; and in P.E.P., *Social Services*, pp. 12, 38–40.

[3] Cole, *Condition of Britain*, p. 330. For the costs of the social services in relation to revenue, ibid., pp. 323–48.

[4] P.E.P., *Health Services*, p. 199.

[5] H. Tout, *Standard of Living in Bristol*, pp. 29, 48.

Expenditure on the Social Services in Great Britain, 1913–35,
Compared with Revenue and National Income

	1913	1924	1930	1931	1932	1933	1934	1935
Expenditure on social services by the government and local authorities,[1] £m.	74·6	225·4	354·2	376·8	374·7	368·3	376·2	382·4
Total expenditure of the government and local authorities,[2] £m.	257	880	982	1005	968	919	941	993
Total income of same,[3] £m.	281	932	1022	1047	1035	1017	1037	1068
Workers' insurance contributions,[1] £m.	8	31	38	40	42	43	46	46
Employers' contributions,[3] £m.	9	40	48	49	51	51	53	54
National income,[4] £m. ..	1988[5]	3887	3812	3438	3327	3533	3713	3919

partnership with the government and the local authorities. Private
charity provided for the blind and the halt, the unmarried mother,
the discharged prisoner; it provided the lifeboat service, the
missions to seamen, the funds for aged governesses. Youth
organisations drew in one-third of the nation's youth.[6] Older
bodies like the Charity Organisation Society and Dr. Barnardo's
Homes continued to flourish; new ones appeared, such as the Save
the Children Fund—largely international in purpose—founded by
Eglantyne Jebb in 1919.[7] The National Council of Social Service,
also founded in 1919, sponsored local councils in urban districts
and worked alongside the village hall committees and the
Women's Institutes in the rural areas. The provision of hospital
accommodation was still largely in the hands of the voluntary
hospitals: of some 3029 hospitals in Great Britain in 1935, 1013
were voluntary, 116 were general public hospitals, 523 were Poor
Law hospitals, and the remainder were lying-in hospitals, fever
hospitals and tuberculosis sanatoriums provided by the local

[1] Unemployment benefits and assistance, old age pensions, contributory old age and widows' pensions, public assistance, sickness benefit, education, housing, hospitals, maternity and child welfare service: based on table 59 in C. Clark, *National Income and Outlay*, pp. 140–1. I have excluded war pensions (£52·1 millions in 1931).
[2] C. Clark, *National Income and Outlay*, pp, 140–1 (sinking funds excluded).
[3] Ibid., pp. 140–1.   [4] A.. L. Bowley, *Studies in National Income*, p. 81.
[5] Bowley and Stamp's figure for 1911: in A. M. Carr-Saunders, *Social Structure* (2nd ed.), p. 91.
[6] H. A. Mess, *Voluntary Social Services since 1918*; A. F. C. Bourdillon (ed.), *Voluntary Social Services: their place in the modern state* (London, 1945); W. H. Beveridge, *Voluntary Action* (London, 1948); *Annual Charities Register and Digest* (C.O.S.).
[7] See Edward Fuller, *Right of the Child* (London, 1951).

authorities. The raising of money was a perennial vexation: the soliciting of subscriptions, the bazaars, the flag days (London had 133 in 1935). In 1937 some 900 charitable organisations raised over £4¾ millions, of which rather under half was for hospitals and dispensaries.[1]

In one branch of the public service, the educational system, the thirties brought little change. Inequality between public and private education persisted, prolonging the line between the classes. The economy campaign showed itself chiefly in the 10 per cent cut in teachers' salaries, which was partly ended in 1934, wholly in 1935, and in delay to the building of new schools until late in the decade. The 'reorganisation' of the elementary schools on the lines of the Hadow report continued, until by 1938 63·5 per cent of all children over 11 in elementary schools were in reorganised ('Modern') schools. The number of children in the public secondary schools of England and Wales increased from 394,105 in 1930 to 470,003 in 1938, a rise from 10 to 11·4 per 1000 in the whole population. The proportion of children in the secondary schools rose during the depression years and then fell a little: in 1930 it was 17·8 per cent of the total population aged 14–17; in 1934, 22·8 per cent; in 1937, 19·2 per cent. The number staying at school after 16 rose and fell similarly. The provision of free places was replaced by 'special places' (dependent on the parents' income) in 1933, but the proportion of pupils in the secondary schools who paid no fees at all fell only from 49·4 per cent to 46·9 per cent (in 1938).[2]

The one big change which the decade ought to have seen was eventually frustrated: the raising of the school leaving age to 15. Parliament finally enacted this long-deferred measure in 1936. It was to take effect in September 1939; and to prevent the difficulty which had balked the Labour government's bill in 1931 the voluntary schools were offered grants of 50–75 per cent of the cost of the necessary enlargements of their buildings. Alas for vain hopes! The second war postponed the appointed day once again. It also produced a more comprehensive reform of public eduation: the Butler Act of 1944.

[1] P.E.P., *Health Services*, p. 257; *Annual Charities Register, 1938*, p. 469; A. M. Carr-Saunders, *Social Structure* (2nd ed.), pp. 165–6.
[2] *Statistical Abstract of U.K., 1938*, pp. 54–65; J. Graves, *Policy and Progress in Secondary Education*, pp. 142–7. There is a useful survey of the educational system in Cole, *Condition of Britain*, chapter 6.

5. 'THAT'S THE WAY THE MONEY GOES'

In this enlightened age between 15 per cent and 30 per cent of the people of Great Britain were in poverty or near it. John Hilton estimated that two million families, or 17 per cent of all families, had no margin whatever for saving; another six million families were worth less than £100—what could be realised, in property, furnishings, savings, at the death of the head of the family. This left four million families worth more than £100, of which half ranged from the comfortable middle classes to the very wealthy.[1] Eight million families lived with little or nothing between them and destitution but the weekly sum of wages or unemployment relief or old age pension; or if the income-receiving population was examined two-thirds of it (11½ million persons) was found to receive less than £2 10s. a week in earnings (omitting pensions and relief payments). This same two-thirds received only one-third of the aggregate income.[2]

Many working-class families were forced to spend their meagre income uneconomically. Any unusual expense, even for clothes or shoes, demanded credit or a loan. The moneylender's business was declining, and the pawnbroker's also, though he still accommodated one family in three in a sample of three hundred families.[3] More commonly a mother needing to buy clothes for her family would buy a 'clothing club' check from an agent, paying so much a week for it, and using it at one of the designated shops to buy what she needed. The checks were themselves used as security for small-scale borrowing among neighbours in which as much as 6s. 6d. might be paid for a loan of 3s.[4] The hire-purchase system of buying furniture and clothing was another old snare in a new disguise, and had multiplied twenty-fold between 1918 and 1938. It involved about £50 millions in goods at any one time, and probably two-thirds of all mass-produced articles

---

[1] John Hilton (1880–1943), professor of industrial relations at Cambridge, began his career in his native Bolton as a mill mechanic, and was later foreman and manager in engineering works. In the thirties he was a popular speaker on the B.B.C. In *Rich Man, Poor Man*, written and delivered as the Halley Stewart lectures in 1938 (published in 1944), he tried, by a combination of statistics, case studies and his own insight into the lives of working people, to discover why the poor were poor, and how poor they were. Though he answered many questions, his own conclusion stands: 'I have been coming to the view since I began these investigations that as regards social conditions and business practice affecting the common people of this land of ours, no one knows anything about anything that really matters.' (p. 133). His figures are only intended to be approximate, but are close to those of Orr, Clark, and the Coles (above, p. 491); I have combined his figures given on pp. 23–6, 110–11.

[2] John Hilton, *Rich Man, Poor Man*, p. 38.

[3] Ibid., pp. 98–104; *Our Towns: a close-up* (Oxford, 1943), pp. 18–21.

[4] *Our Towns*, pp. 58–9; J. Hilton, p. 130.

such as furniture, bicycles, motor-cycles, wireless sets and cars.[1] The life-insurance policies for which the agents of the industrial insurance companies collected a shilling or two every week, even from the poorest families, were not economical. This burial insurance took in some £60 millions a year, but paid back to its holders, after allowing for overhead costs of 35 per cent or more and the legion of lapsed policies, only half that sum.[2]

Another 'investment'—and thought of as such by the investor, though deplored by his critics—was the weekly entry in one of the football pools on the results of a combination of the principal professional association football matches each Saturday. By 1936 between five and seven million people were sending in their forecasts each week, and paying about 3s. for their entries; about £800,000 was taken in each week, or £30 millions a year. The pools promoters—Littlewoods and Vernons at Liverpool, Shermans at Cardiff, others in London, Edinburgh and elsewhere—worked on the principles of the tote: they kept back 5 per cent of the pool as commission or profit, which made them fortunes of £2 millions or more a year—new and almost anonymous millionaires; another 5–15 per cent paid for their expenses in postage, printing, advertising and the hiring of some 30,000 people to sort coupons and lick envelopes in converted warehouses; the remainder they distributed to their investors, in sums as high as £22,000, as low as a few pounds or shillings. The growth of the pools was the great social phenomenon of the thirties, testified to by the five-fold increase in the sale of sixpenny postal orders and three-fold increase in the sale of shilling orders. Their popularity sprang partly from the boredom of many lives, but also from the fact they were fair, taking money from the poor but also returning it, and offering to the working man, who would never inherit a tidy legacy or make a killing on the stock exchange, the only opportunity of making a fortune and putting by a little money.[3]

---

[1] J. Hilton, p. 133.

[2] J. Hilton, pp. 163–4; *Our Towns*, pp. 10–11. Of the £3198 millions of 'small savings', £385 millions in 1938 (£300 millions in 1934) was represented by industrial insurance. P. Massey, *Portrait of a Mining Town*, gives the budgets of four families (pp. 62–6): insurance cost one family 3s. 2d. out of an income of 26s., another 1s. 8d., another 2s. 8d. out of incomes of 52s. 9d. and 47s. 8d.; another family 8d. out of 39s. B. S. Rowntree found that a great majority of the York families spent 10 per cent of the family income on insurance (*Poverty and Progress*, pp. 212–13). The subject was one of the many concerns of Sir Arnold Wilson and Professor Hermann Levy: see their *Burial Reform and Funeral Costs* (1938) and *Industrial Assurance* (1937).

[3] John Hilton, *Why I Go in for the Pools* (London, 1936), based on responses to a broadcast request for letters; *The Public and the Pools: an Inquiry* (1938: reprint of

What of other pleasures? The consumption of beer declined during the years of depression, and by 1938 had still not quite reached the figure of 1930.[1] Smoking increased steadily, apart from a slight fall in 1931–33: in 1930 the nation's consumption of tobacco was 150 million pounds; in 1938, 189 million pounds.[2] The cinemas took in some £40 millions annually and sold 20 million tickets a week, which meant that 40 per cent of the people went to the pictures once a week, and 25 per cent went twice a week or more.[3]

A form of recreation which grew greatly in popularity in the thirties, particularly in Scotland, was dancing. Large dance halls (the 'Palais') were built in the big towns, and smaller halls and dancing schools also provided opportunities for dancing, especially on Saturday nights. Dancing was a serious business, following a variety of jazz steps which were elaborated by the dancing schools into the complicated 'English style'; local competitions led the successful pairs on towards the national championship and a brief day of glory.[4]

One other sign of the times was the increase of holidays. A committee under Lord Amulree's chairmanship was appointed by the Minister of Labour to examine the question of holidays with pay. It reported in 1938, recommending that a week's holiday with pay ought to be the standard practice.[5] In the twenties some 1½ million wage-earners were entitled to such a holiday annually; by 1938, 3 million; in 1939, under the spur of the Holidays with Pay Act, 1938, some 11 million.[6] Some took their families to the new holiday camps which were springing up among the sandhills near Skegness and Pwllheli and Ayr and Lowestoft and in countless places round the coasts. The Civil Service Clerical Association claimed to have started the first, at Corton, near Lowestoft, in 1924.[7] Many camps and holiday homes were managed by business

---

articles in the *Daily Telegraph*). By 1938 it was estimated that ten million people regularly went in for the pools, spending £40 millions annually. Littlewoods and Vernons used their profits to establish mail-order stores and also retail chain stores dealing in clothing, hardware, novelties, in many towns.

[1] Consumption of beer: 19·9 million barrels, 1930; 14·1 million barrels, 1932; 18·7 million barrels in 1938 (*Statistical Abstract of U.K., 1938*, p. 406).

[2] *Statistical Abstract of U.K.*, 1938, p. 406. Consumption of tobacco in 1924, 128 million lbs.; 1913, 92 million lbs.

[3] J. Hilton, *Rich Man, Poor Man*, p. 120.

[4] 'Saturday night at the Palais', *Economist*, February 14, 1953.

[5] *Report of the Committee on Holidays with Pay* (Cmd. 5724: 1938).

[6] A. F. C. Bourdillon, *Voluntary Social Services*, pp. 151–2. Under the Act power was given to Agricultural and Trade Boards to fix holidays with pay.

[7] W. J. Brown, *So Far*, p. 113.

firms, staff associations and professional organisations for their own members. The first commercial holiday camp was opened at Skegness in 1937 by Butlin's, the largest company in the business. By 1939 there were over 100 commercial camps, ready to accommodate half a million people during the season. Older bodies, such as the Workers' Travel Association (founded in 1922), the Holiday Fellowship, the Co-operative Holidays Association, arranged tours and maintained hostels. It was estimated in 1937 that 15 million people took a week's holiday—a figure which would include many working-class families; but only one-third of those who earned less than £4 a week could afford this.[1]

6. ILL FED

Here was the rub. No matter how much the statistics pointed to a general increase in real income there was no doubt, as the uneasy social conscience discovered, that very many families were still, in the thirties, ill fed, ill housed, ill cared for when illness struck.

Several social surveys were made to determine the extent of poverty and malnutrition, all applying different standards of the minimum needs of a family. In Bristol—a rather prosperous city—10·7 per cent of the working-class families studied in 1937 were below the poverty line. This meant that some 16,000 children, or one child in five among working-class families, was in poverty amid a total population of some 452,000 persons.[2] On a more rigorous standard in 1928, 9·1 per cent of all working-class people in London were found to be in poverty.[3] In the Merseyside survey of 1928–32, 16 per cent of working-class families were adjudged to be in poverty, or 30 per cent on B. Seebohm Rowntree's more generous 'Human Needs' standard.[4]

More elaborate data was provided by Seebohm Rowntree, who in 1935–36 did what it was given to no one else to do: he repeated the survey of the working population of York which he had made

---

[1] Elizabeth Brunner, *Holiday Making and the Holiday Trades* (Oxford, 1945): a mine of information, not only about holiday-makers but about the great increase in the number of persons employed in the holiday trades between 1921 and 1939. See also R. Graves and A. Hodge, *Long Week-end*, p. 381. For an excellent survey of one aspect of the problem of leisure, see Donald Pilcher, 'Leisure as an architectural problem', *Architectural Review*, December, 1938.

[2] H. Tout, *The Standard of Living in Bristol* (Bristol, 1938), pp. 25–36 (briefest and best of all the social surveys of the time).

[3] M. Abrams, *Condition of the British People, 1911–1945*, pp. 104–5.

[4] D. Caradog Jones, *Social Survey of Merseyside*, I, 149–56; figures for other towns in F. LeGros Clark (ed.), *National Fitness* (London, 1938), pp. 154–5, A. M. Carr-Saunders, *Social Structure* (2nd ed.), pp. 168–81.

over thirty years before, in 1899, when he wrote his classic, *Poverty*. In his second survey he used a rather more liberal standard of needs than in his first: his 'Human Needs' standard (based on the 1937 revision of his book, *The Human Needs of Labour*) demanded for a family of man, wife and three children an income, after paying rent, of 43s. 6d. per week. On this basis he found 31·1 per cent of the working population, and 17·7 per cent of the total population, to be below the poverty line (14·2 per cent of the working population being in abject poverty, with an income of under 33s. 6d. per week). Over half the working-class children under one (52·5 per cent) were under the poverty line, and this same proportion of working-class people would, so Rowntree calculated, be in poverty at some time during their lives—usually twice, in childhood and old age, and a quarter at a third period in early middle life (25–44), when the burden of a family was greatest. Had there been progress, none the less, since his first survey? On the standard he used in 1899 he had found 15·5 per cent of the working class (9·9 per cent of the population) in poverty; in 1936, on the same standard (an income of 30s. 7d. per week after rent) 6·8 per cent of the working class (3·9 per cent of the population) were in poverty.[1]

The causes of continuing poverty were not difficult to find. Of the people in York below the poverty line, 28·6 per cent were doomed because the head of the family was unemployed; but another 32·8 per cent were doomed although the head was in regular employment, but at earnings inadequate for the family's needs. Another 9·5 per cent were dependent on inadequate earnings in casual employment. 14·7 per cent were poor because old: the poverty of old age was found to be more acute than that due to any other single cause.[2] The Bristol survey ascribed unemployment as the cause of poverty in 32·1 per cent of the families in poverty, insufficient wages as the cause in 21·3 per cent of the families, old age in 15 per cent, sickness in 9 per cent. The first two causes explained 80 per cent of all the poverty affecting children. The size of a family contributed to its poverty: 24·8 per cent of all families with three children were in poverty, 51·5 per cent of all families with four children or more; yet only 9 per cent of all families had three children or more.[3] Similar evidence was used by Rowntree to reinforce the arguments for a system of

---

[1] B. Seebohm Rowntree, *Poverty and Progress* (London, 1941), pp. 32, 96–102, 156–50, 451.
[2] Ibid., pp. 39, 66–71.
[3] H. Tout, *Standard of Living in Bristol*, pp. 37–46.

family allowances.[1] For the striking conclusion of these surveys was that unemployment alone was not the trouble. In York 72·6 per cent of the unemployed families were in poverty. In the cases studied in *Men without Work*, 30 per cent of the unemployed men were in poverty, and another 33 per cent were living on a level of bare subsistence.[2]

'Poverty', 'subsistence': what did such words mean? How much would a family need, if it spent its money wisely, to have sufficient food?[3] How many families were undernourished? Sir John Boyd Orr published some sensational findings under the title *Food Health and Income* in 1936. The study was a semi-official one, made by the Market Supply Committee of the Ministry of Agriculture and the Rowett Research Institute at Aberdeen. It took into account the country's food supply, the distribution of the national income, and the diets of different income groups revealed in 1152 family budgets from several parts of the country. The standard of nutritional needs which it applied was the Stiebeling standard compiled in the United States by the government Bureau of Home Economics. Sir John divided the population of the United Kingdom into six groups:[4]

Group	Income per head per week	Est. expenditure in food (average)	No. in group	Per cent of total population
I	Up to 10s.	4s.	4,500,000	10
II	10s. to 15s.	6s.	9,000,000	20
III	15s. to 20s.	8s.	9,000,000	20
IV	20s. to 30s.	10s.	9,000,000	20
V	30s. to 45s.	12s.	9,000,000	20
VI	Over 45s.	14s.	4,500,000	10

He found that group one (4½ million people) enjoyed a diet which was inadequate for perfect health in all the constituents (proteins,

[1] B. S. Rowntree, *Poverty and Progress*, pp. 35–7, 161–8.
[2] Ibid., p. 46; *Men without Work*, p. 423. See also J. Hilton, *Rich Man, Poor Man*, esp. chapter 3, 'Why are the Poor, Poor?'
[3] The standard most commonly used was a minimum diet drawn up in 1933 by a committee of nutrition of the British Medical Association. This provided 3400 calories per day for an average man, at a cost of 5s. 11d. per week. It was modified, principally by an increased milk allowance, in a standard worked out by R. F. George in 1936. See R. F. George, 'A New Calculation of the Poverty Line', *Journal of the Royal Statistical Society*, 100 (1937), 74–95—an excellent review of the subject; also H. Tout, *Standard of Living in Bristol*, pp. 15–20.
[4] John Boyd Orr, *Food Health and Income: A Survey of Adequacy of Diet in Relation to Income* (London, 1936), p. 21.

fats, calories; calcium, phosphorus, iron; vitamins A and C); group two's diet was inadequate save in protein and fat, group three's inadequate in minerals and vitamins, group four's inadequate in calcium. Only groups five and six could afford a really adequate diet. Thus 10 per cent of the population (including 20 per cent of the country's children) was very badly fed, and as much as half the nation ill-fed.[1]

Sir John Boyd Orr's findings were open to both criticism and qualification. The sample was small and the standards of nutritional needs it assumed were not accepted by all authorities.[2] Moreover, Orr himself gave figures showing that the annual consumption of food per head had increased between 1909–13 and 1934 in everything save flour. The consumption of fruit had increased by 88 per cent, vegetables by 64 per cent, butter and margarine together by 50 per cent, eggs by 46 per cent, meat by 6 per cent, potatoes by 1 per cent.[3] None the less, Sir John's work caused a stir, one result of which was the government's Physical Training Act of 1937, which provided grants for physical training classes and for the development of playing fields, summer camps and recreation centres.

[1] John Boyd Orr, *Food Health and Income : A Survey of Adequacy of Diet in Relation to Income* pp. 5–6, 33, 36, 49; tables and charts on pp. 32, 34–7. The tables are reproduced in simplified form in Cole, *Condition of Britain*, pp. 129, 131. Another widely-read study, by the medical officer of health of Stockton-on-Tees, was G. C. M. M'Gonigle and J. Kirby, *Poverty and Public Health* (London, 1936).

[2] See P.E.P., *British Health Services*, p. 325, for the criticisms of Professor A. L. Bowley and others. Orr recognized the strength of such criticisms: see *Food Health and Income*, pp. 61–8. Colin Clark (*National Income and Outlay*, pp. 111–13) calculated the proportions of the population possessing weekly incomes classified into Orr's six classes, using particulars of 23,000 families taken from the 1931 census. These differ, as he showed, between London and the larger and smaller towns. His weighted average of all districts gave results a little less gloomy than Orr's in the distribution of income per head, but darker in the distribution among children under fourteen.

Distribution of Population by Income Groups (England and Wales: weighted average of all districts):

Income per head per week	All persons (per cent)	Children under 14 (per cent)
Up to 10s.	13·7	25·3
10s. to 15s.	16·9	26·7
15s. to 20s.	16·5	20·2
20s. to 30s.	25·3	19·0
30s. to 45s.	19·4	7·3
Over 45s.	8·1	1·5

[3] Details in Table II in *Food Health and Income*, p. 18 (Cole, p. 124), which also give figures for 1924–8. For butter and margarine the figures are:

	1909–13	1924–28	1934
Butter (lbs. per head, per year)	16	16	25
Margarine (lbs.)	6	12	8

Even larger increases in consumption of food per head between 1920–23 and 1935–38 are shown in Richard Stone, *Measurement of Consumers' Expenditure and Behaviour in the United Kingdom, 1920–1938*, I (Cambridge, 1954).

Even more difficult to judge was the improvement in the well-being of the school children. Cleanliness had increased. In London in 1912, 39·5 per cent of the school children had been found to be verminous; in 1937 the proportion was only 7·9 per cent. In Carlisle 9·3 per cent of the entering children had lice or nits on their heads in 1926; in 1935, 1·3 per cent.[1] (Yet during the second war, when 1½ million people, mainly children, were evacuated from London and other large cities, the nation was shocked to the core by the reports of the habits of many of the slum families which their hosts in the reception areas discovered: slatternly women, verminous children sewn into their clothes, families with the eating habits of animals, bed-wetting by grown boys. Cleanliness is not easy when a whole family must share one bed and seven or eight families a single foul, distant lavatory.)[2] There had been an improvement in physique, though wide variations remained. In Lincolnshire the average height of a boy of 12½ increased from 55·4 inches in 1910–13 to 56·8 inches in 1933, and his weight from 74·9 lb. to 80·1 lb.; in Northampton the boys' height rose from 55·4 inches to 57·3 inches, and their weight from 72·4 lb. to 79·9 lb.[3] Sir John Boyd Orr gave the average heights of boys at a public school, at Christ's Hospital, and at a council school: at the age of 14 these were 63·7 inches, 61·1 inches and 58 inches respectively. A similar variation had existed as far back as 1883.[4]

7. ILL HOUSED

If many people were still ill fed, fewer were ill housed than in previous times. In his second survey of York, in 1936, Seebohm Rowntree found that a great improvement had taken place since 1900 in the houses in which working people lived. In 1900, 5·7 per cent of the working-class population of York lived in overcrowded houses, in 1936 only 1·7 per cent (or 2·9 per cent under

[1] Sir George Newman, *The Building of a Nation's Health* (London, 1939) pp. 183 ff., esp. 210; F. Le Gros Clark, *National Fitness*, p. 53.
[2] *Our Towns: A Close Up* (Oxford, 1943), gives full details: this study was made in 1939–42 by the Hygiene Committee of the Women's Group on Public Welfare, in association with the National Council of Social Service. It shows that the fairly satisfactory results of the school medical service's inspections need considerable qualification, and not only for pre-school children: ibid., pp. 66–80. In Liverpool in 1938 the school *nurses* found 20·8 per cent of the children unclean; the doctor's examinations found only 4·5 per cent of the boys and 13·1 per cent of the girls (p. 68).
[3] F. Le Gros Clark, *National Fitness*, pp. 33–4, 117–35, esp. 124.
[4] J. B. Orr, *Food Health and Income*, pp. 39, 69. Further information on the health of school children (showing the continuing prevalence of rickets and bad teeth) is in M'Gonigle, *Poverty and Public Health*, pp. 38 ff., and P.E.P., *Health Services*, p. 322. The chief source is the annual reports of the Chief Medical Officer of the Board of Education entitled *The Health of the School Child*.

a stricter standard); in 1900, 26 per cent lived in slum houses; in 1936, 11·7 per cent. In 1900 only 12 per cent had comfortable and sanitary houses, in 1936 at least 30 per cent. By 1939 almost every house had its own water supply and its own water closet, and a third of them had baths. Moreover, by 1939 the city council had nearly completed its slum clearance programme of 1933, by which 1032 houses were to be pulled down and some 1000 reconditioned; only 423 slum houses remained.[1]

Many other cities made progress in housing. In 1936 a census of overcrowding was made by the local authorities as required by the Housing Act of 1935. Of nearly 9 million working-class houses inspected in England and Wales 341,554, or 3·8 per cent, were found to be overcrowded on a not-too-rigorous standard which included living and sleeping rooms, normal segregation of the sexes, and a maximum of two persons over 10 years old per room, or five persons in three rooms, ten persons in five rooms, and so on. Leeds, which made a second count which included only rooms used for sleeping, found 21·1 per cent of its houses overcrowded instead of 3·3 per cent on the official standard. Over the whole country such a standard would have shown some 853,000 houses to be overcrowded.[2] Variations between districts were, of course, very great. In Shoreditch 17·2 per cent of the families were overcrowded, in Sunderland 20·6 per cent, in Hebburn 25·2 per cent, in county Durham 12 per cent, in Anglesey 9·5 per cent; on the other hand in Kent only 1·3 per cent of the families were overcrowded, in Bournemouth 0·3 per cent, in Oxford 1 per cent. Superficially, the big cities were not the worst offenders in overcrowding their people: in London 7 per cent, in Liverpool 7·4 per cent of the families were overcrowded, in Birmingham 3·7 per cent, in Bristol 2·1 per cent.[3] In Liverpool this meant, however, that 11,500 houses were overcrowded, in London, 70,000. A correlation between overcrowding and mortality rates was easily demonstrated.[4]

Quite another problem was the abolition of slums. Until 1930 slum clearance was hardly tackled at all; catching up with the

---

[1] B. S. Rowntree, *Poverty and Progress*, pp. 223–85. For earlier discussions of the housing problem in Great Britain, see chapter 1, pp. 43–4, chapter 3, pp. 164,176; chapter 4, pp. 228–30; chapter 8, pp. 458–61.

[2] Ministry of Health, *Report on Overcrowding Survey in England and Wales* (1936), quoted in Cole, *Condition of Britain*, pp. 158–9; cf. P.E.P., *Health Services*, p. 35. A 'house' is any separately occupied dwelling or apartment.

[3] Cole, *Condition of Britain*, p. 162.

[4] P.E.P., *Health Services*, p. 37; R. M. Titmuss, *Poverty and Population* (London, 1938), pp. 221–5.

deficiency in the absolute number of houses needed was a large enough task. During the twenties only some 11,000 slum houses were demolished and 17,000 people rehoused.[1] It was the second Labour government, with Arthur Greenwood as Minister of Health, which took up the question. The Housing Act of 1930 provided for slum clearance by the local authorities, aided by a subsidy which depended on the number of families rehoused and the cost of rehousing them, particularly in the cleared areas. Each local authority was charged with producing a five-year plan for clearing its slums. The new programme had hardly been begun before it and other housing plans were brought almost to a standstill by the economy drive of 1931–33. The building of houses under the Wheatley Act (which Greenwood had rescued from the extinction which the Conservatives had intended for it) was brought to an end in 1933.[2]

Instead, the National government, with Sir E. Hilton Young as Minister of Health,[3] decided to concentrate on slum clearance under the Greenwood Act. New programmes were drawn up by the local authorities under the Housing Act of 1933: under them 266,851 houses were to be demolished, 285,189 built in their place and 1,240,182 persons rehoused.[4] Such figures were a fraction of the true dimensions of the slums. In Manchester the corporation proposed to demolish 15,000 houses, though as many as 30,000 had been estimated to be unfit for human habitation and 80,000 more not very much better. Sir Ernest Simon calculated that there were actually about one million unfit houses in England and Wales.[5] Birmingham, in 1935, had 38,773 back-to-back houses and 51,794 without separate water closets. In North Battersea 60–70 per cent of all water closets were shared by more than one family.[6]

The National government's plans were enlarged in Hilton Young's Housing Act of 1935: local authorities were obliged to make plans to end overcrowding, which would ultimately become a legal offence. The Overcrowding Survey of 1936 was one result. In 1938, as a measure of economy, the subsidy for slum clearance was reduced.[7]

The effect of these measures, and of the boom in building by private enterprise during the thirties, was large. In one sense there was no housing question by 1939. In 1918 there had been a

[1] Marian Bowley, *Housing and the State, 1919–1944* (London, 1945), pp. 135, 147.
[2] Ibid., pp. 46, 135–40, 153.
[3] Minister of Health, 1931–35; created Lord Kennet, 1935.
[4] M. Bowley, *Housing and the State*, p. 153.
[5] Ibid., p. 140; Cole, *Condition of Britain*, p. 175.
[6] *Our Towns*, pp. 87, 93.   [7] M. Bowley, *Housing and the State*, pp. 140–3, 168.

deficiency of 610,000 houses in England and Wales as compared to the number of families; despite the building of the twenties there was still a deficiency, although a smaller one, in 1934, allowing for the increased number of families then existing. By 1939 there was no deficiency; there were 90,000 more cheap houses, and 585,000 houses of all sorts, than there were families. For the more prosperous families of the working class, and for the middle class, there need no longer be a housing problem.[1] Overcrowding had also been reduced. Only 23,651 houses had been built specifically to rehouse overcrowded families, but the effect of new building in general was estimated to have reduced the overcrowding recorded in 1936 by one quarter.[2] And many of the slums *had* been abolished. The local authorities had rehoused over a million people, leaving only some 239,000 in their old quarters among those whom the five-year plan was to have rehoused.[3] London, Leeds, Liverpool, Manchester and Sheffield, which together accounted for 43 per cent of the people to be rehoused, failed to complete their programmes; most of the other county boroughs and smaller towns did so.[4]

Houses built in England and Wales, 1919–39[5]

Numbers built by local authorities—

Under Addison Act, 1919 ..	170,100	
Under Chamberlain Act, 1923	75,300	
Under Wheatley Act, 1924 ..	504,500	
Under slum clearance acts ..	265,500	
Under overcrowding acts ..	23,600	
Under other housing acts ..	72,700	
Total built by local authorities ..		1,111,700
Number built by private enterprise with subsidy (*a*) ..		430,400
Number built by private enterprise without subsidy (*b*) ..		2,455,600
Grand Total		3,997,700

(*a*) Of these the great majority, 362,700, were built under the Chamberlain Act.

(*b*) Excluding houses with a rateable value exceeding £78 (£105 in London).

[1] M. Bowley, *Housing and the State*, pp. 24, 49, 172, 173–9.   [2] Ibid., p. 160.
[3] Ibid., p. 160: houses built, 255,701; deficit, 29,488 houses.   [4] Ibid., pp. 154–8.
[5] Based on table, *Housing and the State*, p. 271. One cannot be too grateful for Miss Bowley's admirable book.

Housing in Scotland was, historically, another story. Over-crowding was worse than in England and Wales, even on a lower standard; for in Edinburgh and Glasgow, the only really large cities, a 'house' generally meant an apartment of one, two or more rooms in a tenement. Between 1919 and 1931 new building, mostly by the local authorities with the aid of subsidies, hardly kept pace with the growth of population. The overcrowding survey of 1935 showed that almost 260,000 houses were over-crowded; this was 22·6 per cent of all Scotland's working-class houses, whereas in England and Wales the proportion of such houses overcrowded was 3·8 per cent. In some places the pro-portion was appalling: in Lanarkshire (outside the burghs) 36·79 per cent of the families were overcrowded; in Coatbridge and Motherwell over 40 per cent, in Clydebank 44·9 per cent, in Edin-burgh 17 per cent.[1]

The number of slum houses made matters more urgent. In 1919 there were 60,000, but only some 12,500 houses had been built by 1930 in replacement of slum property. In 1934 the local authorities proposed, in their slum clearance programmes, to demolish 63,000 houses; by 1938 they had demolished 55,000 and built 40,000 houses under this programme. During the housing boom of the thirties building proceeded at a slower rate in Scotland than in England, and in contrast to England most of it was done by the local authorities. By 1939 a total of 303,576 working-class houses had been built in Scotland since the war. There were still 66,000 houses in use which were unfit for human habitation, and 200,000 houses needed to end overcrowding.[2]

Building of Working-class Dwellings in Scotland, 1919–38[3]

Dwellings built by local authorities with state assistance—	
(a) general, and to relieve overcrowding	136,241
(b) for slum clearance	67,524
Built by local authorities without state assistance ..	4,572
Built by private enterprise	95,239
Total working-class dwellings	303,576
Total, including larger houses built by private enterprise	311,510

In Scotland, as in England, many of the new houses built by the

[1] P.E.P., *Health Services*, p. 36.
[2] M. Bowley, *Housing and the State*, pp. 261–8 (a very condensed survey); J. A. Bowie, *Future of Scotland*, pp. 74–80.
[3] Dept. of Health for Scotland, *Annual Report, 1938* (Cmd. 5969; 1939), p. 177.

large cities were on housing estates in what had been open country. In 1937 the Glasgow corporation began the development of an estate at Pollok, planning to build 3780 houses at a density of no more than 5½ per acre. Aberdeen was planning a slightly larger estate at Kincorth.[1]

Typical of municipal housing in England was the work of Bristol's corporation, which built 14,610 houses between 1920 and 1939, nearly two-thirds of them after 1930. During the same period some 36,000 houses were built privately in Bristol, and 5000 demolished; the total number of houses in the city in 1939 was 108,000. Nearly all of the council's houses were built on estates: Fishponds, Sea Mills, Bedminster, Knowle, Filwood Park (Knowle West), Southmead, Horfield. The largest development (Knowle-Bedminster) comprised a housing estate twice as large as Welwyn Garden City.[2]

Another progressive city was Manchester, home of Sir Ernest and Lady Simon, two of the country's most zealous advocates of better housing and public education. Plans were made for a garden suburb to house 100,000 people, and include, like Welwyn, some new factories. In 1925 the Wythenshawe estate of 2500 acres was bought, just across the city's southern boundary. By 1934, 4600 houses had been completed.[3] In Leeds a plan to demolish and replace all the back-to-back houses by five-year stages was accepted by the council in 1933 under the inspiration of the Rev. Charles Jenkinson,[4] the vicar of Holbeck, who was a member of the Labour party and leader of the council when Labour won control of it in 1933. Leeds had 72,000 back-to-back houses, of which 33,000 were deplorably bad. The first 8000 were to be replaced by 1935, partly by houses on estates, partly by a magnificent group of blocks of flats built at Quarry Hill in the heart of the city, and containing 938 dwellings.[5]

London continued in the thirties its large housing programmes

[1] J. A. Bowie, *Future of Scotland*, p. 81.
[2] R. Jevons and John Madge, *Housing Estates: a study of Bristol corporation policy*, is an excellent illustrated account of Bristol's housing estates, their inhabitants, amenities, cost of living. In the same period (1919–38) Birmingham built 50,268 municipal houses, housing about 200,000 people, nearly the size of the population of Plymouth; another 54,536 houses were built by private enterprise: Asa Briggs, *History of Birmingham*, II, 228–9.
[3] E. D. Simon and J. Inman, *Rebuilding of Manchester* (London, 1935), pp. 36 ff.; Cole, *Condition of Britain*, pp. 184–5.
[4] Charles Jenkinson (1887–1949) was born in Poplar, son of a stone-mason, and was a book-keeper in early life, later (1912) lay secretary to the Rev. Conrad Noel at Thaxted. He was ordained after the war. See the life of him: H. J. Hammerton, *This Turbulent Priest* (London, 1952).
[5] R. Lloyd, *Church of England in the 20th Century*, II, 128–37.

of the twenties. Slum clearance involved the building of lofty blocks of flats, by the L.C.C., by the metropolitan borough councils, and by housing societies and private estates, such as the Duchy of Cornwall, in or near the former slum areas; such blocks were to be seen towering above the pygmy buildings of earlier generations in Southwark, Lambeth, Shoreditch, Wandsworth, St. Pancras, Clapham Park, Camberwell, and elsewhere. The second policy was the building of housing estates outside London. Older estates, such as Becontree, Bellingham, Watling and St. Helier were completed; new ones were begun by the L.C.C. at Mottingham, Thornhill, Hanwell, Kenmore Park. Some of the metropolitan councils built estates of their own, the largest being that of Woolwich at Middle Park.[1]

8. THE CHANCES OF SURVIVAL

We may now ask how far the people of Britain were healthier than before. The expectation of life had increased since 1871 at all ages except in the first week of life and beyond the age of 75 (or 80 in the case of women).[2] A boy had a life expectancy of 40·4 years at birth in 1871, 58·7 years in 1931.[3] The results of the medical examinations of men eligible for military service seemed to show an improvement in health between the wars. In 1920 the Ministry of National Service reported on 2,425,184 men examined for military service between November 1917 and October 1918. Of every nine men of military age three were 'perfectly fit and healthy; two were upon a definitely infirm plane of health and strength . . . three . . . could almost (in view of their age) be described with justice as physical wrecks; and the remaining man as a chronic invalid with a precarious hold on life'.[4] In 1947 the Ministry of Labour and National Service reported on the examination of 7,177,774 men for military service by medical boards

---

[1] Full details, with pictures, dates, size, of building by the various local government bodies and by private agencies, are given in L.C.C., *London Housing, 1937*. See above, chapter 4, pp. 230–1.

[2] P.E.P., *Health Services*, p. 24.

[3] See tables in *Statistical Abstract of U.K., 1936*, p. 40. The figure quoted is for England and Wales: for Scotland the comparable figures are 41·1 years (1871), 56 years (1931).

[4] Ministry of National Service, *Report upon the Physical Examination of Men of Military Age . . .* (Cmd. 504; 1920), p. 4, quoted in G. C. M. M'Gonigle, *Poverty and Public Health*, p. 31. The report is of great value, giving results by districts and occupational groups. It argues that, despite the numbers of men who enlisted before 1917, those examined in 1917–18 fairly represented 'the manhood of military age of the country in the early part of the twentieth century'. (p. 5.)

between June 8, 1939 and December 31, 1946. Of these 70 per cent were placed in grade 1, consisting of 'men who, subject only to such minor disabilities as can be remedied . . . attain the full normal standard of health and strength, and are capable of enduring physical exertion suitable to their age.' The words used in defining the four classes were the same in 1917–18 and in 1939–46; if the standards were the same, the improvement in twenty years was remarkable indeed. The significance of the figures for 1939–46 is increased by the division of the men (and also the women) examined into age groups, since it shows the effects of the years of depression upon the generations which they produced. And the effects seem slight. Of the men under 21, 81 per cent were placed in grade 1, 71 per cent of those aged 21–25, and 62 per cent of those aged 26–30. The figures for women were slightly better than those for men.[1]

Men examined for Military Service, 1917–18 and 1939–46:
Per cent in each grade

Grade	1917–18	1939–46				
		Under 21	21–25	26–30	31 and over	Total
I	36	81	71	62	43	70
II	22·5	10	14	17	22	14
III	31·5	4	8	10	15	7
IV	10	5	7	11	20	9
Total (numbers)	2,425,184	3,240,906	1,085,908	2,045,480	805,480	7,177,774

When we turn to the figures of mortality we again find that there has been improvement, though to some extent the appearances are deceptive. There were great variations between different regions and different classes, as several contemporary critics pointed out. For England and Wales the standardised death rate was 13·5 per 1000 persons in 1911–14, 9·7 in 1931–34, 9·3 in

[1] Ministry of Labour and National Service, *Report for the Years 1939–1946* (Cmd. 7225; 1947), pp. 140, 358–9. The grades are defined on p. 336. Grade II includes men 'able to undergo a considerable amount of physical exertion not involving severe strain'; those with defects of feet and vision were separately enumerated within this grade. Grade III included those with 'marked physical disabilities', grade IV, those unfit for any form of military service.

S

1937; the crude death rate was 13·8 in 1913, 12·3 in 1931, 12·4 in 1937.[1] For Scotland the crude death rate was 15·7 in 1911–15, 13·2 in 1931–35 and 13·8 in 1937; the standardised rate was 13·2 in 1931, 13·3 in 1937.[2]

Standardised Death Rates per 1000 Persons[3]

	England and Wales	L.C.C. area	County boroughs*	Other urban districts*	Rural districts*
1911–14	13·5	14·5	15·9	13·0	10·9
1931–34	9·7	10·1	10·9	9·7	8·7
1937	9·3	9·5	10·4	9·3	8·2

* Outside Greater London from 1931 onwards.

More striking are the differences between various towns, crowded districts and suburbs. Thus, the index number of Bermondsey's standardised death rate in 1937 as compared with that of England and Wales, was 113, Finsbury's 128, Stepney's 115, Croydon's 90, Ealing's 78, Harrow's 73. Outside London the rate for Birmingham was 106, Manchester 128, Rhondda 134, Burnley 135, Wigan 138, as compared with Bournemouth 88, Exeter 90, Oxford 80, Cambridge 73.[4]

Another indication of the nation's health might be found in the death rate from tuberculosis. In 1922–24 it had been 1066 persons per 1 million population (standardised rate for all ages, England and Wales); in 1935 it was 687, in 1937, 657.[5] Once again, the death rate was much higher in Durham, Northumberland, and South Wales—the black spots of unemployment—than elsewhere.[6]

Infant mortality (the number of infants under one year dying per 1000 live births) also justified both satisfaction that it was less than it had been, and shame that it was still great, particularly

[1] *Registrar-General's Statistical Review of England and Wales, 1937*, Text, p. 17, tables, Part I, Medical, p. 4.
[2] *Annual Report of the Registrar-General for Scotland, 1937*, pp. xv, lxiv.
[3] *Registrar-General's Statistical Review of England and Wales, 1937*, text, p. 17.
[4] Ibid., pp. 21–4. Cf. R. M. Titmuss, *Poverty and Population*, chapters 3, 6. For the effects of unemployment on the death rate, see G. C. M. M'Gonigle, *Poverty and Public Health*, pp. 264–71; *Registrar-General's Statistical Review of England and Wales, 1934*, Tables, I, Medical, pp. 4, 70B, 79.
[5] *Registrar-General's Statistical Review of England and Wales, 1937*, text, p. 94.
[6] R. M. Titmuss, *Poverty and Population*, pp. 169–72; death rate among men, 15–35, from respiratory tuberculosis, 1931–35 (England and Wales = 100); West Ham 153, South Shields 280, Sunderland 192, Cardiff 197, Merthyr Tydfil 160.

in certain places. For England and Wales the rate was 62 in1931–1935, 57 (the lowest figure ever reached) in 1935, 59 in 1936, 58 in 1937. The rate had averaged 153 in 1871–75, 110 in 1911–15, 76 in 1921–25.[1] The rate for Scotland, which had been 127 in 1871–75, was 91·8 in 1921–25, 80·8 in 1931–35, 76·8 in 1935, 80·3 in 1937.[2] Other countries had done better. In 1935 the infant mortality rate in New Zealand was 32, in Australia 40, in Sweden 47, in Ontario 56, the United States 60, Germany 68.[3] Chicago reduced its infant mortality rate from 74 to 38 between 1925 and 1937; Liverpool's rate, in the same period, fell from 99 to 82.[4] Some towns and counties had done well: the rate for Coulsdon and Purley in 1935 was 32, for Surrey 41, for Greater London 51. It was safer to be born in the south-east of England (where the rate

Infant Mortality by Class of Father, England and Wales[5]

	1911		1921–23		1930–32	
	A	B	A	B	A	B
Class I, II	95·8	77	53·8	68	43·1	70
Class III	130·2	104	76·9	97	57·6	94
Class IV, V	134·6	108	92·5	117	72·1	117

A. Infant mortality rate per 1000 *legitimate* live births.
B. Per cent of Registrar-General's rate for all classes.

The Classes are those used by the Registrar-General in the 1911 census, modified in the 1921 census : viz., I, Upper and Middle classes; II, Intermediate; III, Skilled labour; IV, Intermediate; V, Unskilled labour.

[1] *Registrar-General's Statistical Review of England and Wales, 1937*, text, p. 31.
[2] *Annual Report of Registrar-General for Scotland, 1937*, p. lxiv. In Kilmarnock the rate in 1937 was 114, in Glasgow 104 (ibid., lxvi). Cf. J. A. Bowie, *Future of Scotland*, pp. 59–63.
[3] Table in R. M. Titmuss, *Poverty and Population*, p. 80.
[4] R. M. Titmuss, *Birth, Poverty and Wealth* (London, 1943), p. 73. Other countries had not always had better rates than England and Wales: Titmuss (ibid., p. 88) gives the comparative figures for Holland and England and Wales:

Infant Mortality per 1000 Live Births

	Holland	England and Wales
1880–90	183	142
1910–20	95	100
1936–38	37	56

[5] Ibid., p. 31. Illegitimate births were a little over 4 per cent of total births in England and Wales per year: *Statistical Review of England and Wales, 1938–39*, text, p. 181. The same disparity between the classes existed and increased in the death rate for infants under one month and at other intervals during the first year: see tables in Titmuss, *Birth, Poverty and Wealth*, p. 38.

was 47) than in the midlands (59) or the north (68) or in Wales (63). The rate in county Durham was 72; in Sunderland it was 92, in Gelligaer 85 (1936), in Jarrow 114.[1] It was safer, also, to get one's self born into the upper or middle class. The infant mortality rate of the upper classes was lower, and as the rate had fallen for all classes the difference in the chance of survival during the first year of life between the upper classes and the working class had actually increased.

Yet another index of a nation's health are the figures of maternal mortality. In England and Wales the rate of maternal mortality from all causes, per 1000 live births, averaged 4·03 in 1911–15, 3·90 in 1921–25, 4·30 in 1931–35. It began to rise in 1925, and was worst, 4·60, in 1934. The rate for 1937, 3·26, was the lowest recorded. The rate per 1000 live and still births, recorded after 1928, was a little lower (3·78 in 1934, 3·16 in 1936, 2·78 in 1937).[2] For Scotland the rate per 1000 live births was 6·4 in 1921, 6·1 in 1931–35, 5·6 in 1936 and 4·8, the lowest recorded, in 1937.[3] Sir George Newman complained that there had been no improvement in England and Wales comparable to the lowering of the death rate in general since the beginning of the century, though countries like Holland, Denmark and Sweden had rates of 2 per 1000 births; yet the rate of some English hospitals was 1·3, and of mothers attended by Queen's Institute midwives between 1924 and 1933 it was 1·9. A committee of the Ministry of Health appointed by Neville Chamberlain in 1929 carried out a large investigation, and reported that half the deaths in maternity cases were preventable by better ante-natal care, better training of midwives, improved obstetrical techniques and antiseptic methods.[4]

One thing more was needed: more food for mothers. Sir George Newman prescribed a diet of milk, cheese, butter, eggs, liver, fish, fresh fruits and vegetables for a pregnant woman; the cost of the milk alone—two pints per day—would have been 4s. a week when the British Medical Association's minimum diet allowed only 4s. 11d. per head per week for everything. The effects of unemployment on maternal mortality were, in fact, clearer than on other mortality rates. The Pilgrim Trust's inquiry compared

[1] R. M. Titmuss, *Poverty and Population*, pp. 80–1.
[2] *Registrar General's Statistical Review of England and Wales, 1937*, text, pp. 152–3.
[3] Registrar-General of Scotland, *Annual Report, 1921*, p. cxxvii; Department of Health for Scotland, *Annual Report, 1937* (Cmd. 5713; 1938), p. 66; J. A. Bowie, *Future of Scotland*, p. 91.
[4] Sir George Newman, *Building a Nation's Health*, pp. 281–308.

maternal mortality rates in two groups of county boroughs in 1928–34, those with heavy unemployment and those with little, and found that the rate was 19·8 per cent higher in the former than in the latter. Later, in 1935–37, an experiment was made by the National Birthday Trust Fund with two groups of pregnant women, one (10,384 women) of which was given special food during pregnancy (at a cost of 13s. 4d. per woman), while the other group of 18,854 women was not. The maternal mortality in the first group was 1·63 per 1000 births, in the latter 6·15.[1]

9. ... AND MEN DECAY'

It was not death rates which aroused concern in the thirties, it was the birth rate. The number of births had been falling since 1903 in Great Britain, as in most of the countries of western and northern Europe, though the date at which the decline began had varied; in France it was as early as 1859. The birth rate had been falling in England and Wales since 1877; the natural increase in population had declined also, despite the fall in the death rate.[2] In England and Wales 948,271 babies were born in 1903, and after the war years of fewer births, 957,782 in 1920. In 1925 the number was 710,582, in 1931, 632,081. The lowest figure was that for 1933, 580,413; by 1938 it was 621,204. The natural annual increase of population (excess of births over deaths) had been over 400,000 at the beginning of the century, 140,451 in 1931, 83,948 in 1933. The crude birth rate (live births per 1000 population) had been 33·5 in 1881–5, 23·6 in 1911–15, 15·8 in 1931; it was 14·4 in 1933, 15·1 in 1938. For Scotland the rate was 33·3 in 1881–5, 25·4 in 1911–15, 19 in 1931, 17·6 in 1933, 17·7 in 1938.[3] To offset the lower rate of natural increase the loss of population from Great Britain by emigration, which continued through the twenties, was reversed in the thirties: the net gain by migration between 1931 and 1941 was 650,000—more than the net loss of 565,000 in 1921–31.[4]

[1] R. M. Titmuss, *Poverty and Population*, pp. 141–4, 153–5, where examples are also given of the variation in maternal mortality rates by regions. These, being taken from 1936, make the black spots much darker than they were in 1937. See also P.E.P., *Health Services*, p. 323.

[2] R. R. Kuczynski, 'The International Decline of Fertility', in Lancelot Hogben (ed.), *Political Arithmetic: a symposium of population studies* (London, 1938), pp. 47 ff. For the experience of Britain and other countries in the nineteenth century, see also R. C. K. Ensor, *England, 1870–1914* (Oxford, 1934), pp. 103, 269, 498.

[3] *Registrar-General's Statistical Review of England and Wales, 1939*, Tables, II, Civil, pp. 4, 57; *Annual Report of Registrar-General of Scotland, 1939*, p. lxxxiv. Cf. A. M. Carr-Saunders, *Social Structure* (2nd ed.), pp. 211–14.

[4] Royal Commission on Population, *Report* (Cmd. 7695; 1949), p. 9.

Population of Great Britain, 1931 and 1939[1]

	England and Wales	Scotland	Great Britain
1931	39,952,377	4,842,980	44,795,357
1939	41,552,000	5,008,000	46,560,000

Northern Ireland (census of 1937), 1,279,745; (est. pop., 1939), 1,296,000.

Isle of Man: 1931, 49,308; 1939 (National Register), 50,829.

United Kingdom, 1939 (est. pop.), 47,906,000.

In themselves, these figures might not have excited interest. The low birth rate of the early thirties coincided, however, with the efforts of the dictators in Italy and Germany to increase the birth rates of their countries—efforts which in Germany achieved a temporary success. Babies seemed as important as bullets in the new and bitter national rivalries. What was more, a new generation of demographers produced alarming estimates of Britain's future population and wrote books which spread the message amid a public already avid for readable 'non-fiction' books on politics, economics and social questions. The best-known demographers were Lancelot Hogben and his wife Enid Charles, A. M. Carr-Saunders, and R. R. Kuczynski (1876–1947), a distinguished German statistician who settled in England in 1933 and held the first English academic appointment in demography, a readership at London. The London School of Economics was the chief home of the subject.

The new game of estimating the future population was played by using the gross reproduction rate: the number of girl babies being born on the average to a woman during her years of child-bearing.[2] Since the number was that of the potential mothers of the next generations, it put the future population within definite

---

[1] National Register, *Statistics of Population on September 29, 1939, Report and Tables* (1944), pp. ix, 1. The 1931 figures are those of the census. Since no census was taken in 1941, the best figures available are those based on the enumeration of the population on September 29, 1939, for the compilation of the National Register. This, however, excluded persons then in the armed forces or in port; the figures here given include the Registrar General's additions to allow for these exclusions.

Note. Figures of movement of population within Great Britain are given in chapter 8, above.

[2] The net reproduction rate allowed for deaths of women before reaching the child-bearing age; the effective reproduction rate allowed for improvement in existing death rates. Gross and net reproduction rates for several countries, 1870–1936, are given by Kuczynski in L. Hogben, *Political Arithmetic*, pp. 53–67.

limits, which could vary only by emigration or immigration, or by an increase in the size of the family.[1] The latter might follow from earlier marriages—which was the tendency in Great Britain;[2] or from a higher marriage rate. The marriage rate was, however, very stable at about 85 per cent of the persons (of both sexes) of marriageable age. The gross reproduction rate for England and Wales was 2·4 in 1886–90 and had fallen to 1·062 in 1926 and was thereafter below unity, which meant that the population was not replacing itself. The figure for 1933 was 0·845. Scotland's was still 1 in 1931–32, but below unity, 0·901, in 1933–35. The areas of highest fertility in England and Wales in 1931 were Durham, the North and East Ridings of Yorkshire, Monmouthshire (and to a less extent Glamorgan and Brecon), and Montgomeryshire and Anglesey in North Wales.[3]

Using the gross reproduction rate of 1933 as the basis for calculation Enid Charles made two estimates of the future population of Great Britain. The first and more hopeful assumed that fertility and mortality remained at the rates of 1933; the second assumed a further decline of both. In the first the population of England and Wales would begin to decline after 1945, falling from 40,876,000 to 28,522,000 in 2000 and 19,969,000 in 2035; in the second the fall would begin after 1940, and would leave the country with 17,685,000 people in 2000 and no more than 4,426,000 in 2035. If Scotland's population followed the first estimate while England's followed the second, Scotland would have the larger population of the two in 2035 (1935, 4·9 millions; 2035, 4,647,000 (first estimate), 925,000 (second estimate)).[4]

Dr. Charles' warning was not allowed to die away on the desert air. Its tones were grim: '*Whatever changes in mortality ensue, nothing can arrest a continuous decline of the total population, unless something happens to increase fertility above its present level.*'[5] Dr.

---

[1] The size of families had declined in all classes since 1900: see R.C. on Population, *Report*, pp. 25–7.

[2] Proportion of persons born 1906–11 who were married at age 20–4 was 20 per cent, of those born 1914–19 it was 25 per cent (R.C. on Population, *Report*, p. 72).

[3] R. M. Titmuss, *Poverty and Population*, pp. 13–14, using D. V. Glass's figures; from *Political Arithmetic*, p. 161 ff. (see also the findings of Enid Charles and Pearl Moshinsky, ibid., pp. 108–25).

[4] Enid Charles, 'The Effect of Present Trends in Fertility and Mortality upon the Future Population of Great Britain and upon its Age Composition', in *Political Arithmetic*, pp. 72 ff.; tables on pp. 82–4. This paper was first published by the Royal Economic Society in 1935, and also published as Special Memorandum No. 40 of the London and Cambridge Economic Service. Its findings were frequently reproduced; e.g., in A. M. Carr-Saunders, *Social Structure* (2nd ed.), pp. 215–18; R. M. Titmuss, *Poverty and Population*, pp. 8–10.

[5] *Political Arithmetic*, p. 73 (Dr. Charles' italics).

Charles herself wrote a popular tract on the subject, *The Twilight of Parenthood* (later entitled *The Menace of Under-Population*), published in 1936. Other books on population carried on the campaign, particularly the collaborative *Political Arithmetic* (1938) and R. M. Titmuss' *Poverty and Population* of the same year. Moreover, concern over the future population joined and reinforced other inquiries which the aroused social conscience of the thirties was making. Did the public-school boy enjoy advantages beyond his deserts in public and professional life? Was there a waste of talent among working-class children—from whom the population was so largely recruited? R. H. Tawney's *Equality*, which had asked such questions from the socialist side in 1931, was now matched by the studies of the social biologists.[1] Interest in family allowances was also stimulated, and produced its delayed triumph in 1945. The immediate results were confined to the enactment of the Population (Statistics) Act in 1938, by which a long-overdue improvement in England's population statistics was made, and more accurate fertility rates could be calculated. For England and Wales the gross reproduction rate was given by the Registrar-General as ·897 in 1938 and ·892 in 1939.[2]

How far was the scare over population justified, and how far a part of the pessimism of an anguished decade? The birth rate recovered a little during the thirties from its low point in the depression year of 1933, increased greatly in the latter years of the second war, and produced an average of 934,000 births a year in Great Britain in 1946–48, a rate not touched since 1921, at the end of the previous postwar boom in babies. This led the public to scoff at the jeremiahs of the thirties. The experts themselves changed their ground, rejecting the gross reproduction rate as an important index in favour of one based on the size of the family and the age of marriage. This suggested that, though the previous estimates had been too alarmist, the population was not quite reproducing itself even at the birth rate of 1940–48, and allowing for the generally lower age of marriage. The reproduction rate

---

[1] See two studies in *Political Arithmetic*, 'Ability and Opportunity in English Education', by J. L. Gray and Pearl Moshinsky, and 'Opportunity and the Older Universities: a Study of the Oxford and Cambridge Scholarship System', by D. V. Glass and J. L. Gray. With great labour these studies support, but hardly change, the conclusions of K. Lindsay's *Social Progress and Educational Waste* (1926); see above, chapter 4, pp. 206–7. Cf. G. G. Leybourne and K. White, *Education and the Birth Rate: a Social Dilemma* (London, 1940).

[2] See explanation of new data in *Registrar-General's Statistical Review of England and Wales, 1938*, Tables, II, Civil (1944), pp. 108 ff., and ibid., *1938 and 1938*, text (1947), pp. 178–217.

of the female population over the period was ·939.[1] A Royal Commission on Population was appointed in 1944; its report in 1949 was reassuring. It found no sign, despite impressions to the contrary, that the average size of the family was increasing,[2] but it assumed that it would remain at about 2·2 children, the size of the average family of couples married in 1927–38. On this assumption, and expecting also a continuing fall in death rates, it estimated the population of Great Britain in 2047 at 45·5 millions. It gave two other estimates; one, assuming a rise of 6 per cent in the size of the family, put the population in 2047 at 52·7 millions, the other, assuming a decline of 20 per cent in the size of the family, put it at 29·6 millions.[3]

10. ULTRA-MODERN

The declining birth rate was particularly the mark of that England which was the product of the years since the war. A. G. Macdonell left a brilliant description of it in his kindly satire, *England, their England.* It was the country of the long week-end, the house party at Ormerode Towers or some rustic cottage, of sporting cars and country golf clubs, of hunt meets attended by wealthy stockbrokers who drove up with their chauffeurs in Rolls Royces. There were still households such as that described by a butler in which thirty-four servants were kept; the owner had four houses, in London, the Midlands, Scotland, and France, and spent three months in each.[4] There were still people who had racing yachts and could afford to pay £800 for the lease of a service flat in the West End or 466 guineas to go round the world in the *Empress of Britain.*[5]

Of London one of the staff artists of *Vogue* has written: 'The decade before the war was a splendid one for an artist interested in the fashionable world. In it much of the pomp and luxury of the late Victorian Age was revived, with, however, a much greater feeling for elegance and style than in the solid earlier period. There was an eclectic brilliance about it, a merging of Baroque *décor* with Victorian charm that was fascinating.' Special occasions,

---

[1] Colin Clark, 'Age at Marriage and Marital Fertility', *Population Studies*, II, 412–26 (March, 1949).

[2] Royal Commission on Population, *Report* (Cmd. 7695; 1949), pp. 52–6, 220.

[3] Ibid., p. 84. This long report is virtually a handbook on the subject of population as it relates to Great Britain; it includes a technical appendix on 'The Measurement of Reproductivity'. Among the report's many virtues is its use of figures for Great Britain, and not separately for England and Wales and for Scotland.

[4] Ferdynand Zweig, *Labour, Life and Poverty* (London, 1948), p. 46.

[5] A. Hutt, *Condition of the Working Class in Britain*, pp. 237–9.

like the Duke of Kent's wedding in 1934, the Silver Jubilee and the Coronation, added to the gaiety of the London season, and brought many well-to-do foreigners and people of title and fashion to the smart hotels. The royal garden parties, Covent Garden, first nights at the theatre or the ballet, opera at Glyndebourne,[1] the private view at the Royal Academy, the races at Ascot or Goodwood, were occasions for display.[2] A few of the great town houses of the past still entertained in the grand manner. At a reception at Londonderry House the guests were ushered in by powdered footmen and received at the top of the grand staircase by the host and hostess, she wearing a tiara, he his orders and ribbon of the Garter.[3]

There were signs of change after 1936; even the restless younger generation[4] was not untouched by the new social conscience. To talk or write of sex came to be in bad taste; the subject had become dull and old-fashioned. There was a stirring of patriotic feeling and a nostalgic respect for the Victorians whose solid virtues had raised the British Empire to a power and majesty sadly lacking in the age of the dictators. Double beds returned to popularity, Victorian styles to the fashion pages.[5] Divorce was, however, still on the increase. From 1931, when there were 4333 divorces in Great Britain, the number rose unsteadily to 5535 in 1937, 7038 in 1938.[6] The Divorce Act of 1937, a private member's bill introduced by A. P. Herbert, M.P. for Oxford University and well-known as a writer for *Punch*, made desertion and insanity grounds for divorce (after three years of marriage), thus providing an alternative to adultery as proved by the usual 'hotel-room' evidence.

The new England was also to be seen in the new suburbs, particularly those round London. Here lived those whom George Orwell called people of indeterminate social class: the technicians of modern civilisation, the mechanics, airmen, radio experts, film producers, popular journalists, industrial chemists. 'The place to look for the germs of the future England is in the light-industry areas and along the arterial roads.'[7] Slough, Dagenham, Barnet,

---

[1] The Glyndebourne Festival was founded in 1934 by John Christie, who built a Festival Opera House on his estate of Glyndebourne, near Lewes, Sussex.
[2] Francis Marshall, *London West* (London, 1944), pp. 9 ff.
[3] Philip Gibbs, *England Speaks* (London, 1935), pp. 103–5.
[4] Pictured in Nerina Shute, *We Mixed our Drinks* (London, 1945), Hubert Nicholson, *Half my Days and Nights* (1941), and A. G. Macdonell, *England, their England* (London, 1933: reprinted 1946), pp. 82, 249, 267, 275.
[5] N. Shute, pp. 75, 82.   [6] *Statistical Abstract of U.K.*, 1938, p. 27.
[7] George Orwell, *The Lion and the Unicorn* (London, 1941), p. 53.

Letchworth, Hayes were its proving grounds, though their 'little semi-detached houses . . . [with] stucco front, the creosoted gate, the privet hedge, the green front door',[1] were no different from Marion's villa in the prewar Ealing of *Tono-Bungay*. It was Priestley's postwar England, the

> England of . . . filling stations and factories that look like exhibition buildings, of giant cinemas and dance-halls and cafés, bungalows with tiny garages, cocktail bars, Woolworths, motor-coaches, wireless, hiking, factory girls looking like actresses, greyhound racing and dirt tracks, swimming pools, and everything given away for cigarette coupons.[2]

Another symbol was the new super-cinema. A third large chain of cinemas, Odeon, was founded in 1933 by a Birmingham scrap-metal merchant, Oscar Deutsch, with the support of United Artists. Odeon was the largest builder of super-cinemas in the middle thirties, each new theatre being opened with much pomp and local celebration.[3]

The quality and popularity of British films increased during the thirties, partly because of the presence of refugees fleeing from Hitler's persecutions. Alexander Korda, a Hungarian, made in 1933 one of the most popular and profitable of British films of the thirties, *The Private Life of Henry VIII*, in which Charles Laughton triumphed. Korda's later films included *Catherine the Great* (with Elizabeth Bergner), and *The Scarlet Pimpernel* (with Leslie Howard), all made in 1934, and *The Ghost Goes West*, directed by the Frenchman, René Clair, whose films, *Sous les toits de Paris*, *Le Million* and *A nous la liberté* were among the most popular foreign films of the decade. The other coming figure was J. Arthur Rank, but before the war he had only cut his path a small way into the jungle of the film industry.[4]

If the new cinemas represented ultra-modern building, gaudy with chromium and opaque glass, heavy with the weight of poured concrete, it was not for lack of good architects and more imaginative styles. In the thirties many handsome buildings were built in a neo-Georgian style: the Royal Institute of British Architects

---

[1] George Orwell, *Coming Up for Air* (London, 1939), p. 13.
[2] J. B. Priestley, *English Journey*, p. 401.
[3] See above, chapter 4, p. 247. In 1937 Odeon owned 200 cinemas, A.B.C. 431, G-B 345. The number of cinemas in Great Britain was 4448 in 1935, 4734 in 1937, 4967 in 1938 (*Annual Abstract of Statistics, 1935–1946*, p. 72).
[4] Alan Wood, *Mr. Rank*, pp. 57–103, describes the industry on the production and distribution sides during the thirties.

building in Portland Place (1934), the Battersea power station designed by Sir Giles Gilbert Scott (1934), blocks of flats in St. John's Wood and Hampstead and in the provinces, the flats built by the public authorities in London, Leeds and elsewhere, the new Merchant Taylors' School at Moor Park (1933), hospitals and hospital extensions everywhere, among which the Birmingham Hospital Centre (1938) was one of the largest. Of the several town halls, the palm must go to Norwich's, designed by C. H. James and S. R. Pierce, and opened in 1938: its smooth brick surfaces, its slim tower with starkly-simple clock face, provoked inevitable comparisons with the Stockholm city hall. In London Broadcasting House (1932) and the University of London senate house and library, Charles Holden's great design, which was finished just before the war, suggested American influences in their height and massive, block-like structure. Sir Giles Gilbert Scott designed the University Library at Cambridge (1934), and deserted the Gothic style to produce a handsome Romanesque building in brick with massive tower. His annex to the Bodleian at Oxford was heavy, dull and dispiriting by contrast.

At the same time, there was a growing attraction to 'modern architecture' as preached by Gropius and LeCorbusier. In the thirties the influence of the *Architectural Review*, the MARS group (Modern Architectural Research) founded in 1933, and of refugees such as Gropius himself, was on the side of the new style, emphasising clean lines, simplicity, and light, and possessing some of the qualities of abstract painting. Private houses designed by Maxwell Fry, Gropius, and many other architects, and the Highpoint Flats in Highgate (1936) designed by the Tecton Group (a group of young English architects led by a Russian, Berthold Lubetkin) represent the style in domestic architecture. It was applied to some of the new schools on London's outskirts, Boots' factory at Beeston (1932) by Sir Owen Williams, the Pioneer Health Centre at Peckham (1935) also by Williams, to the zoo buildings at Dudley (Tecton) and the pavilion overlooking the shore at Bexhill (1936) —typical ventures of the time. In public buildings it was to be seen in the Shakespeare Memorial Theatre at Stratford-on-Avon (1932) designed by Elizabeth Scott, in the Royal Masonic Hospital (1933), the *Daily Express* building (1932), a composition in plain and dark glass on a steel frame; and perhaps best of all in the new station buildings designed for the London Passenger Transport Board (especially at Chiswick and Sudbury and elsewhere on the

Piccadilly extensions in 1933) by Charles Holden, under the inspiration of Frank Pick.[1]

New life was stirring in the ballet. The Diaghilev ballet had returned to London after the war; but its appeal was to a limited audience. The Camargo Ballet Society was started in 1930 to encourage British ballet and to present ballet productions each year. In 1934 Colonel de Basil's Ballet Russe de Monte Carlo made the first of its annual appearances at Covent Garden. By 1936 ballet was at the height of its popularity. The two chief British companies were Markova's and the Vic-Wells ballet, directed by Ninette de Valois. The latter took part of its name from the Sadlers Wells theatre, which the Old Vic had acquired with the aid of the Carnegie Trust and reopened in January 1931, as a home of popular opera and ballet. The Old Vic, a national theatre in all but name and backing, continued under Lilian Baylis the production of Shakespearean and classical drama for which it had become famous during the war.[2]

11. FAITH AND WORKS

A characteristic of the times was its active social conscience, whether aroused by the problem of the distressed areas or the menace of the dictators. The Spanish civil war was the chief catalyst of political feelings.[3] New activities, amateur in character, added variety to the daily round. Bodies such as the Peace Pledge Union and the National Council for Civil Liberties were both new and typical. In the universities there was political ferment (dating back to the early thirties), most of it boiling up on the left and in pacifist societies; socialist, and especially Marxist ideas had permeated even anti-socialists, it was reported; John Strachey and H. N. Brailsford were the prophets of the young.[4] Among the

[1] The best introduction to modern British architecture is a file of the *Architectural Review*, thoughtful, cosmopolitan, superbly illustrated. There are useful illustrations in J. M. Richards, *Introduction to Modern Architecture* (Penguin Books, 1940) and Nikolaus Pevsner's *Buildings of England* (vols. on London and Middlesex; Penguin Books, 1951–52). For the modern movement see N. Pevsner, *Pioneers of the Modern Movement* (London, 1936; rev. ed., N.Y., 1949). Osbert Lancaster's drawings—part caricature, part documentary—in *Pillar to Post* (London, 1938) for exteriors, *Homes, Sweet Homes* (London, 1939) for interiors, show more of the seamy side of modern building ('Stockbroker's Tudor', 'Pseudish', 'By-pass Variegated', '20th-Century Functional') than pages of text.

[2] R. Graves and A. Hodge, *Long Week-end*, pp. 348–9; Roy Harrod, *J. M. Keynes*, pp. 307, 364, 399–402; *Annual Register* (annual review of drama and music); *D.N.B., Supp., 1931–1940*, s.v. Lilian Baylis (1874–1937).

[3] See chapter 10, pp. 577–80.

[4] *New Statesman*, February 9, 1933, August 22, 1936 (London Diary). John Strachey's *Coming Struggle for Power* (1932) was widely read.

cartoonists David Low, of the *Evening Standard*, was more popular than ever for his savage jibes at the dictators, his satire on the National government and 'Colonel Blimp'. The continuing interest in the Russian experiment, rising in many to a vague admiration which the purges and treason trials of 1935 and 1937 did little to check, was another factor. On the left the 'Russia complex' became more respectable than before when the septuagenarian Webbs published their two-volume *Soviet Communism: A New Civilisation?* in 1935.[1]

The publishers helped in the enlightenment of the people, especially from the Left. 1935 was notable for the birth of the Penguin books, sixpenny paper-bound, pocket-size volumes which at once found a new mass market, first for reprints of novels, detective stories and memoirs but later—after May 1937 when the first Pelicans appeared—for non-fiction books also. Many of the latter were political tracts, such as George Bernard Shaw's *Intelligent Woman's Guide to Socialism*, the Duchess of Atholl's *Searchlight on Spain*, Tawney's *Religion and the Rise of Capitalism*, G. T. Garratt's *Mussolini's Roman Empire*, Geneviève Tabouis' *Blackmail or War*. The founders of this enterprise were three brothers, Allen, Richard and John Lane; Allen Lane had been managing director of John Lane, the Bodley Head. The first Penguins were printed in editions of 20,000 copies; within three years 50,000 had become the minimum initial printing.[2]

Two other publishing ventures were definitely left-wing. *Fact* was a monthly, started in 1937 by Raymond Postgate, Lansbury, Margaret Cole and others; each issue was a complete paper-bound socialist book.[3] The Left Book Club was founded in May 1936, by Victor Gollancz, the publisher; its editorial committee consisted of Gollancz, Harold Laski and John Strachey. Members received a book a month, each book being especially commissioned and socialist in its tendency. The founders expected a few thousand members, but had gathered 12,000 within a month, 50,000 within a year. Four hundred local discussion circles were formed later, and the *Left News* diffused the club's influence still more widely.[4]

Another sign of the times, anxious and hungry for reassurance, was the progress among upper-class people of the religious revival

[1] A second edition (without the question mark in the title) was published in 1937.
[2] *Ten Years of Penguins, 1935–1945* (Penguin Books, 1945). Allen Lane was born in 1902, knighted in 1952.
[3] R. Postgate, *George Lansbury*, p. 307.
[4] R. Graves and A. Hodge, *Long Week-end*, p. 333; *New Statesman*, June 13, 1936.

known as the Oxford Group (after 1938 as Moral Re-Armament). A meeting held at the Albert Hall in July 1936 gave prominence to a movement hitherto known only to those who attended its house-parties or encountered its 'teams' of evangelists.[1]

The scientists were not to be left behind. Not only was the task of popularising the wonders of science continued, but several scientists became actively concerned about politics, chiefly of the left. Lancelot Hogben's transition from marine biology in South Africa to social biology in London was unique only because it was explicit: *Political Arithmetic, Mathematics for the Million* (1936), *Science for the Citizen* (1938) were the happily alliterative results, and his *Retreat from Reason* (1936) a call to the social scientists to live up to the second part of their title.[2]

Other men called forth the spirit of the open road, partly as an escape to freedom and independence and beauty, partly as a means of improving the lives of others. J. B. Priestley's *Good Companions* (1929) owed its success as a novel to everyman's romantic wanderlust, as a film to the charm of Jessie Matthews. A. P. Herbert's *Water Gypsies* (1930) sent everyone vagabonding in imagination on the canals. A curious mind and an old-fashioned love of tramping sent Sir Arnold Wilson, a Conservative M.P., on his walks and talks at home and abroad which produced, in four books published in 1934–39, not the least worthy mirror of the times.

Walking or hiking became a popular pastime: no longer the eccentric habit of the upper classes or the sad necessity of vagrants and hunger-marchers. The Youth Hostels Association (England and Wales) was founded in 1930, followed in 1931 by similar bodies in Scotland and Ireland. The inspiration came partly from the old-established *Jugendherbergen* in Germany, partly from the needs of the numerous but unorganised hikers and cyclists of the postwar years and from a few local associations, particularly in the Merseyside area. The National Council of Social Service convened the conference at which the Y.H.A. was born. Its rapid growth was due to the enthusiasm of its regional groups and the early

---

[1] The best histories of the movement are two American works, W. H. Clark, *The Oxford Group* (New York, 1951), and Allan W. Eister, *Drawing-Room Conversion: a Sociological Account of the Oxford Group Movement* (Durham, North Carolina, 1950). There are four useful articles of appraisal in the *Spectator*, October 11–November 1, 1935, and a critical one by Kingsley Martin in the *New Statesman*, July 11, 1936. An amusing account of the descent of a team on a quiet Worcestershire village is to be found in John Moore's *Brensham Village* (London, 1946; Penguin edition, 1952), part 5.

[2] Cf. J. D. Bernal's *Social Function of Science* (1939).

work-parties, and the devotion of its secretary, E. St. John Catchpool, and its president, G. M. Trevelyan. The first twelve hostels were opened by Easter, 1931—in North Wales, Yorkshire, the Mendips. By the end of 1931 there were 73 hostels and the Y.H.A. (England and Wales) had 6000 members. By 1939 the membership had risen to 83,417; there were 297 hostels with 10,689 beds; the number of ' overnights' in the year was almost 538,000.[1]

Like so much else, the youth hostel movement was helped by the enlightened benevolence of one of the great charitable foundations, the Carnegie United Kingdom Trust, founded by Andrew Carnegie in 1913. Many causes were nobly helped by it: public libraries, village halls, youth organisations, playing fields, adult education, music festivals, little theatres, the National Council of Social Service. The Pilgrim Trust, founded in 1930 by another American, E. S. Harkness, with an endowment of £2 millions, devoted much of its funds and advice to similar objects, and gave special attention to the needs of the unemployed and to the encouragement of medical research, music and the arts. In addition it did much to help other bodies which were working to preserve historic buildings, old churches, manuscripts and art treasures, and the beauty of the countryside.[2]

The most princely English benefactor of the period was Lord Nuffield, the motor manufacturer. In 1936 he gave £2 millions to Oxford University for the development of a post-graduate medical school and the endowment of chairs of medicine. In the same year he gave £2 millions to form a trust which would aid in improving social conditions and employment in the distressed areas. Other gifts, for medical research, for the care of the aged, the blind and the crippled, hospitals and other charities at home and in the Dominions, and for aid to Birmingham and London universities and to three Oxford colleges, brought his benefactions to over £10½ millions before 1940. In 1937 he gave £1 million to found a new post-graduate college at Oxford, Nuffield College, devoted to study of the social sciences by the collaboration of

---

[1] Oliver Coburn, *Youth Hostel Story* (London, 1950)—an excellent, illustrated account.

[2] H. A. Mess, *Voluntary Social Services*, pp. 172–82, is a useful summary of their work. King George's Jubilee Trust (1935), with £1 million collected by public subscription, devoted itself to serving the needs of youth, both directly and through youth organisations (*ibid.*, pp. 183–7). For the Pilgrim Trust see Lord Macmillan, *Man of Law's Tale*, chapter 13. Its original trustees were a remarkable quintet: Baldwin, Lord Macmillan, Sir Josiah Stamp, Sir James Irvine (vice-chancellor of St. Andrew's University) and John Buchan, the novelist and man of affairs. Its first secretary was Thomas Jones.

scholars and practical men of affairs. His gifts to Oxford alone exceeded £4 millions.[1]

12. WRITERS IN ARMS

There were others whose revolt against the times expressed itself in their writings and later, for some of them, in fighting in Spain. The writers of the twenties had emancipated literature from the conventions of the past; but their appeal had been to the intelligentsia. The new, postwar generation of writers which came of age between 1925 and 1930 found itself in a country of depression. To write only for themselves seemed a guilty indulgence; they must strike against bourgeois illusions, such as liberty,[2] they must join forces 'with the millions of workers who have nothing to lose but their chains'. Several of them collaborated in a book of essays which showed how the arts were enchained by the capitalist system; it was entitled *The Mind in Chains: Socialism and the Cultural Revolution* (1937):

> A writer who wishes to produce the best work that he is capable of producing, must first of all become a socialist in his practical life, must go over to the progressive side of the class conflict . . . unless he joins it his writing will become increasingly false, worthless as literature. . . .[3]

For several of them this meant an acceptance of Marxism.

The poets sharing this interest in social ideas included W. H. Auden, Cecil Day-Lewis and Stephen Spender. Though they had already published poems separately, their appearance (with others) in an anthology called *New Signatures* in 1932, and in another, *New Country*, in 1933, proclaimed the existence of a school. Many of their poems were lyrics in the modern manner: tender, bitter-sweet. They lacked the esoteric tone of T. S. Eliot, but at the price of a certain flatness. One theme—the decadence and futility of the times—appeared often, and especially in the masques, or satiric plays, part poetry, part lecture, which were an outgrowth of the new poetry and were performed in the private Group Theatre in London. The best-known of these were the plays written in collaboration by Auden and Christopher Isher-

---

[1] A list of Lord Nuffield's benefactions is in *The Complete Peerage*, vol. xiii, *Peers Created 1901–1938* (London, 1940), pp. 613–14. The Nuffield Foundation was founded in 1943 with £10 millions to advance health, social well-being, the care of the aged.

[2] Christopher Caudwell (C. St. J. Sprigg), *Studies in a Dying Culture* (1938). Sprigg was killed in Spain.

[3] Stephen Spender in *The Mind in Chains*, quoted in Cyril Connolly, *Enemies of Promise*, p. 102.

wood, the novelist, including *The Dog beneath the Skin* and *The Ascent of F6*. The former's opening chorus proclaims:

> Get there if you can and see the land you once were proud to own,
> Though the roads have almost vanished and the expresses never run:
> Smokeless chimneys, damaged bridges, rotting wharves and choked canals,
> Tramlines buckled, smashed trucks lying on their side—across the rails;
> Power-stations locked, deserted, since they drew the boiler fires;
> Pylons fallen or subsiding, trailing dead high-tension wires.

The transition to identification with the working class, and with the 'workers' struggle', was an easy one. In Auden's *Dance of Death* the audience chants:

> One, two, three, four,
> The last war was a bosses' war,
> Five, six, seven, eight,
> Rise and make a workers' state.
> Nine, ten, eleven, twelve,
> Seize the factories and run them yourself.

Such sentiments were fostered in the *Left Review* (1934–38), and less directly in *New Writing*, founded by John Lehmann and his novelist-sister Rosamond, in 1936 as a book-magazine. *New Writing* drew upon British and foreign authors of poetry and prose, and especially on writers of short stories with working-class themes. It encouraged, in fact, a number of writers drawn from the working class, such as George Garrett and B. L. Coombs. And some authors not of that class were ready to earn what they took for its credentials: living in poor quarters, wearing rough clothes, indulging in a cult of toughness which derived in part from Ernest Hemingway and flowered in tracts like Tom Harrisson's *Letter to Oxford* (1933).[1]

The Spanish civil war put all such ideas to the grimmest possible test. It substituted action for ideas, and in so doing changed the ideas. Communism (which few writers had accepted but many sympathised with) gave place to a more general anti-fascism, an intellectual if not a political Popular Front. Pacifism changed to war-mindedness; the National government was attacked not for warmongering but for appeasement; the writers were ready to fight in defence of England in war. Several fought in the international brigade supporting Republican Spain, and some died in

---

[1] See Hubert Nicholson's comments in *Half my Days and Nights*, pp. 177–95.

that cause. Auden, Spender and Day-Lewis were among the many writers who visited Spain during the war and found in it themes for poetry. Day-Lewis' *Overtures to Death* (1938) was representative. In 'The Nabara' he wrote a long, epic poem on the fight of four Basque trawlers against a Nationalist cruiser, *Canaris*—a poem reminiscent of the 'Revenge' but containing like other poems in the collection (for example, 'Newsreel') a warning to his own generation and his elders:

> Freedom is more than word, more than the base coinage
> Of statesmen, the tyrants' dishonoured cheque or the dreamer's mad
> Inflated currency. She is mortal, we know, and made
> In the image of simple men who have no taste for carnage
> But sooner kill and are killed than see that image betrayed.

Another writer who went to Spain and wrote of it was George Orwell; but like everything of this lonely and brilliant man, who burnt himself out and died before his time, it belonged only to himself and not to any school. His *Homage to Catalonia* is concerned with the Anarchists and other minority groups within the Republican movement. Whether writing of his earlier experiences as a police officer in Burma or of middle-class respectability, whether of the drab lives of working people (*The Road to Wigan Pier*) or of socialist ideas, he always went his own way, critical of all pretence, minutely observant, direct and compelling in style.

Of course there were plenty of writers who did not take up arms against the political leaders and the social system. Among the novelists Elizabeth Bowen added to her reputation by her short stories and her longer works, in which the conflicts of character were subtly described. Graham Greene, a Roman Catholic, pictured the tough and seamy side of life in *Brighton Rock* (1938), but saw it as part of the struggle of good and evil for the souls of men. Dorothy Sayers' stories were very popular: detective stories in a high literary vein. Agatha Christie was an older and more prolific author of detective fiction.[1]

---

[1] This account is based on John Lehmann, *New Writing in Europe* (Penguin Books, 1940); George Orwell, *Inside the Whale* (London, 1940), essay of the same title, a masterly survey of the literature of the twenties and thirties; W. Y. Tindall, *Forces in Modern British Literature, 1885–1946* (New York, 1947); R. A. Scott-James, *Fifty Years of English Literature, 1900–1950* (London, 1951). See also R. Graves and A. Hodge, *Long Week-end*, pp. 299, 339, 393; Stephen Spender, *World within World* (London, 1951).

CHAPTER TEN

Great Reversals: 1935—1937

1. JUBILATE

T HOUGH there was little in the affairs of Europe to rejoice the heart in the spring of 1935 there was a feeling of holiday and relaxation in Great Britain. The worst of the depression was over. It was a moment for retrospection, for a joyful commemoration of the quarter-century of King George's reign. Within two years the old king had died and his successor had abdicated. Within the same two years Europe moved from belief in the possibility·of peace to a dull acceptance of the certainty of war.

To celebrate a mere twenty-five years' reign, a silver jubilee, was unprecedented, and some critics saw in it another stunt of the National government to restore its lost popularity. The critics were soon confounded. There was all the pageantry, in London and the country, in town and village, in the Dominions and the outposts of empire, which could do homage to a king who was also the symbol of the Commonwealth's unity: the processions and reviews, the church services, the planting of trees. There was the great procession on Monday, May 6, to St. Paul's Cathedral, where a service of thanksgiving was held. London's streets were decorated, and at night its historic buildings floodlit for the first time.

Not these, but the response of all the people made the jubilee impressive. In London, as a correspondent observed, the most remarkable feature was the demonstrations of enthusiastic loyalty in the back streets. 'For miles on end every street was decorated, every house covered with bunting—across the streets festoons hung so closely that one could hardly see the sky.' The working class was *en fête*, and children feasted at flower-decked tables at every street corner. Citizens in their thousands sent letters of congratulation to the King.[1] King George and Queen Mary—the

---

[1] *New Statesman*, May, 11 1935; for the celebrations see especially the *Illustrated London News* during May, 1935; also R. Graves and A. Hodge, *Long Week-end*, pp. 316–17; Philip Gibbs, *England Speaks*, pp. 4–12; John Gore, *King George V*, p. 429; H. Nicolson, *King George the Fifth*, pp. 524–5.

Queen as much as the King—had raised the monarchy to a place of strong affection in the hearts of the people which it had certainly not held at their accession. The institution of monarchy had never been stronger in Great Britain; the wearer of the crown never more beloved. The public knew little of his long, careful work over official business, how assiduously he 'did his boxes' day after day; still less of his many interventions behind the scenes, when his constitutional right to be informed, to encourage, and to warn had been used to restrain ministers from rash acts and from courses which would bring division among his people. Rather, it was his sharing of common sorrows in peace and war, his strong family affections, his endless appearances to lay corner-stones or open bridges which had brought him close to the people. In times of trouble, when thrones had tottered and decent governments crumbled, the King was unchanging, a reassurance of the solidity and continuity of things. Time had made him the father of his people, the father of the peoples of the empire. His long and critical illness in 1928–29 had begun to call forth these feelings. What gave them their great warmth and universality was his broadcasts.

The King's first broadcast talk (as opposed to public speeches which had been broadcast), a message of two hundred and fifty-one words, was delivered on Christmas Day, 1932, and was heard throughout the empire, and, indeed, across the world. Sir John Reith had proposed a broadcast as early as 1927, but such a thing was not quickly arranged. Its success was tremendous, and to the King most touching.[1] Thereafter it was an annual event which the whole English-speaking world awaited. It brought the King into every home, speaking as a father and grandfather, using the first person singular, not the royal 'We'; his deep rich voice made everyone his friend. 'For you all, and especially for your children, I wish a happy Christmas. . . . God bless you all.' On the evening of May 6, he spoke in great emotion:

At the close of this memorable day I must speak to my people everywhere. Yet how can I express what is in my heart? . . . I can only say to you, my very dear people, that the Queen and I thank you from the depth of our hearts for all the loyalty and—may I say?—the love with which this day and always you have surrounded us. I dedicate myself anew to your service for the years that may still be given to me.[2]

[1] Lord Reith, *Into the Wind*, pp. 168–9.
[2] Texts in *The Times*, December 27, 1934, May 7, 1935, quoted in R. Graves and A. Hodge, p. 316; H. Nicolson, p. 525.

2. THE CHOICES IN FOREIGN POLICY

The change of government which followed the silver jubilee celebrations on June 7 was little more than a re-shuffle. Baldwin and MacDonald exchanged places, Baldwin becoming Prime Minister, MacDonald Lord President of the Council. Simon left the Foreign Office unregretted, and became Home Secretary; Cunliffe-Lister succeeded Lord Londonderry as Air Secretary and soon went to the Lords with the title of Lord Swinton. Hoare became Foreign Secretary, displacing the favourite for the position, Anthony Eden,[1] who entered the Cabinet, at the early age of 37, as Minister without Portfolio with responsibility for League of Nations affairs. Lord Sankey was dropped as Lord Chancellor, despite promises to the contrary, because Lord Hailsham claimed the place; National Labour's part in a National government which was more obviously Conservative than before was sustained by MacDonald, Thomas, and Malcolm MacDonald, who entered the Cabinet, though only 34, and became Colonial Secretary.[2] Churchill was conspicuously absent—an omission approved by Baldwin's friend, Geoffrey Dawson, editor of *The Times*, with whom Baldwin had discussed the changes he proposed.[3] As before, Neville Chamberlain, at the Treasury, was the strongest man in the government.[4]

Another omission which confuted certain tipsters was Lloyd George. At 72, with his *War Memoirs* nearly finished, he was returning to the political fray as an active force. His 'New Deal' to end unemployment was much the same as the programme he had offered in 1929; it was launched in a speech at Bangor on January 17, 1935. The government conciliated public opinion by conducting negotiations with him. He was asked in March to submit his plans to the Cabinet, and attended ten meetings of a sub-committee of the Cabinet between April and June. There was talk of his joining a reconstructed National government. In the end the government decided it could do without him, even in an election year.[5]

[1] Robert Anthony Eden, born 1897, younger son of Sir William Eden, seventh baronet; served in war (brigade major; M.C.); M.P. since 1923; parliamentary private secretary to Austen Chamberlain, 1926–29; parliamentary under-secretary, Foreign Office, 1931–33; Lord Privy Seal, 1934–35; Minister without Portfolio for League of Nations Affairs, 1935; Foreign secretary, 1935–38, 1940–45, 1951–55; Dominions Secretary, 1939–40; War Secretary, 1940; Prime Minister, 1955–57; Knight of the Garter, 1954.

[2] Fenner Brockway, *Jowett*, p. 322.   [3] *History of The Times*, IV, ii, 893.

[4] The memoirs of Sir Samuel Hoare for 1931–40 should be consulted for a defense of the National government's policies: Lord Templewood, *Nine Troubled Years* (London, 1954). They rather confirm than amend the present narrative.

[5] M. Thomson, *Lloyd George*, pp. 415–22; Thomas Jones, *Lloyd George*, pp. 238–239; K. Feiling, *Neville Chamberlain*, pp. 241–2.

It was not a great ministry, usually preferring, like its leader, to wait upon events rather than to master them. Baldwin did not increase his reputation by his last prime ministership. He did not rise to the height of the times. Perhaps his policies were not intended to deceive, but they sometimes seemed so. He turned aside criticism by confessions of failure; he won popularity by his handling of a failure: Edward VIII's abdication.

From start to finish its main problems were those of foreign policy. Germany's rearmament, Hitler's vast and undefined ambitions seemed to lead inexorably to war; Italy under Mussolini resorted to it in her brutal attack on Abyssinia. The danger of a war, coming suddenly and soon, and wiping out hundreds of civilians in their own homes through aerial bombardment and gas attacks, was brought home to the average man by the first air raid precautions circulars which the Home Office distributed in 1935. Articles took up the theme, embellishing it with lurid pictures. Another phenomenon which people were only beginning to be accustomed to was the glorification of war by the dictators and their lackeys, though Mussolini's reversal of the beatitudes was hardly new:

War is to man as maternity is to woman. I do not believe in perpetual peace (1934).[1]

Three methods of maintaining the peace were discussed by all who rejected the method of the pacifist. The first was rearmament and the making of 'agreements freely concluded' with the dictators to limit what could not be prevented. The second was reliance on the collective security provided by the League of Nations, backed up by rearmament; moral condemnation and economic sanctions ought to discourage any aggressor; if not, war must be risked. The third method also relied on the authority of the League, but would strengthen the League by disarmament, partly as an example to the dictators, partly to encourage the pooling of arms and the creation of an international police force, or an international air force.

The third method was that favoured by the Labour party. For one thing, it avoided the need to discuss the risk of war. And war was disliked, not only for itself, and because of a bad conscience over the Treaty of Versailles (a feeling shared by all parties), but also because the National government was distrusted and the machinations of international manufacturers of munitions suspected.

[1] R. W. Seton-Watson, *Britain and the Dictators* (Cambridge, 1938), pp. 176–81.

There was much talk in these years of the evils of the private manufacture and trafficking of arms, some of it stoked by the evidence of the Nye committee in the United States. P. J. Noel-Baker's *Hawkers of Death*, published by the Labour party in 1934, and his two-volume *Private Manufacture of Armaments* (1936), kept the question open in Great Britain, as did *Merchants of Death* published by H. C. Engelbrecht and F. C. Hanighen in 1934 in the United States. A royal commission on the private manufacture of arms was appointed in 1935, but its recommendations for the rigid control of the industry, though leaving it in private hands, received scant attention.[1]

The government's policy was a combination of the first two methods: it supported the League, up to a point; it rearmed, it negotiated outside the League. Later this policy was called 'appeasement' and further damned for its supposed sympathy for Nazism. Its most consistent exponent was *The Times*, under Geoffrey Dawson and his chief assistant, R. M. Barrington-Ward. Convinced that the Treaty of Versailles was unjust, and that Germany had a good case for revision and friendly treatment, *The Times* argued that concessions should be made even to an unfriendly government, carrying the principle so far as to favour greater concessions to the Nazi government than to its more liberal predecessors. 'Agreements freely concluded' were better than an arid insistence on the observance of treaties, even though France's friendship was sacrificed. News was slanted so as to avoid giving Germany offence; moral condemnation was avoided.[2]

When *The Times* came to write its own history fifteen years later, it was stern in its condemnation of its sins, ascribing them to the lack of a foreign editor (after 1928) and to Dawson's preoccupation with imperial questions, his want of sympathy and deep knowledge of foreign countries and people, his 'instinct for politics without policy provided the Conservative party was in power'. His intimate associations with Conservative ministers, particularly Baldwin, Chamberlain, and Lord Halifax, led him to 'connive at Baldwin's subservience to party expediency and his indifference to State security'. Dawson moved in a very limited circle: Eton, All Souls, the *Round Table*, the London clubs, the offices of ministers in parliament or Downing Street. He took the views of this circle to represent 'average British opinion', and followed and en-

[1] Described by Sir Philip Gibbs, a member, in his *Ordeal in England* (London, 1937), pp. 31–87.
[2] *History of The Times*, IV, ii, 881–3, 894, 903, 908.

couraged them—though in former days *The Times* had claimed to lead opinion. *The Times'* idiosyncrasies would hardly have mattered in any other period; in the thirties, when the 'National' government made partisanship disreputable and protest trivial,[1] when power rested in a cosy ring of Tory politicians whose views *The Times* echoed and reinforced, it was a serious thing. For instance, in May 1935, the officials of the War Office and the general staff were working against the Foreign Office which, under its Permanent Under-secretary, Sir Robert Vansittart, was thought to be taking a strong line against Germany and likely to bring on an unwanted war against her; *The Times'* editors knew and supported this intrigue.[2]

In 1935, however, the two dilemmas, peace or war, appeasement or war, had not been reached. Nearly everyone could still put his faith in the League and believe that its authority would prevent war, and do so at little cost and little risk. 'Leagueomania' was almost universal: it 'undermined the sense of national self-reliance without creating in its stead a sense of collective solidarity or collective responsibility'.[3] In 1935 the League was put to the test, but since the test was not carried through to the logical conclusion, it failed. Because the test was incomplete and because few people could bring themselves to face the alternatives, a laodicean faith in the League survived for some time longer.

Quite distinct from these positions, but reinforcing policies of evasion, was the pacifist movement, which in 1935 was at its height. It had many sources. The postwar mood of disillusionment had been revived by the war novels, plays and autobiographies published in the late twenties: Aldington's *Death of a Hero* (1928), Siegfried Sassoon's *Memoirs of a Fox-hunting Man* (1928), Robert Graves' *Goodbye to All That* (1929), R. C. Sherriff's play, *Journey's End* (1929), the American *Farewell to Arms* (1929) by Ernest Hemingway, and the German *All Quiet on the Western Front* (1929) by Erich Maria Remarque, which as a book and a motion picture was a potent influence. In 1933 Vera Brittain's *Testament of Youth* was added. The atrocities of Hitler's Germany, the trumpetings of Mussolini, the talk of air-raids brought many to believe that the evil and uselessness of war must be opposed, if necessary by an individual refusal to serve in a war. A popular writer of the day, Beverley Nichols, capitalised on this feeling in *Cry Havoc* (1933); the Oxford Union's debate in February 1933, expressed it.[4]

[1] Pierre Maillaud, *English Way*, pp. 164–6.
[2] *History of The Times*, IV, ii, 892–3, 903–5, 1023–4.   [3] P. Maillaud, pp. 146–7.
[4] See above, chapter 8, p. 422.

Canon 'Dick' Sheppard of St. Martin-in-the-Fields gave shape to these sentiments in October 1934, when he appealed to men to pledge themselves against war by sending him a postcard saying that they bound themselves by the pledge:

> I renounce War and never again will I support or sanction another, and I will do all in my power to persuade others to do the same.

Out of this was born the Peace Pledge Union, which by the middle of 1936 had 100,000 members and was appealing for a similar number of women members. At the universities peace societies flourished also. And in 1936, 1937, and 1938 George Lansbury made his own contribution in his peace journeys which took him, an old man but game and determined, to call on most of the heads of state to reason with them for peace.[1]

3. MIDSUMMER NIGHTS' DREAMS

The main concern of foreign policy in the spring of 1935 was German rearmament; a secondary issue was Mussolini's warlike intentions against Abyssinia, which though little concealed were little discussed before June. The first response to Hitler's proclamation of conscription and his admission that a German air force was in being was a meeting of British, French, and Italian representatives at Stresa on April 11–14. MacDonald and Simon attended it. The new-found friendship of France, under Laval, and Italy, following the abortive Nazi *coup* in Austria in 1934, had led to a meeting of Laval and Mussolini in Rome in January. From the Stresa conference—from which Mussolini, before it opened, warned his people to expect little—came a pious declaration:

> The three powers, the object of whose policy is the collective maintenance of peace within the framework of the League of Nations, find themselves in complete agreement in opposing, by all practicable means, any unilateral repudiation of treaties which may endanger the peace of Europe, and will act in close and cordial collaboration for this purpose.

No questions were asked about Mussolini's intentions: Abyssinia was not in Europe. He had apparently received an assurance, or an impression, of France's passivity on that score from Laval in January.[2]

---

[1] R. Postgate, *George Lansbury*, pp. 311–20. Lansbury's own account of his journeys in his *My Quest for Peace* (London, 1938).

[2] W. S. Churchill, *Gathering Storm*, pp. 119–20; R. W. Seton-Watson, *Britain and the Dictators*, pp. 232, 236; G. M. Gathorne-Hardy, *Short History of International Affairs*, p. 394.

Following this, Germany's repudiation of the arms clauses of the Treaty of Versailles was debated at the Council of the League on April 15–17. It was condemned: 'Germany has failed in the obligation which lies upon all members of the international community to respect the undertaking which they have contracted.' *The Times* on March 25 protested against spanking Germany: the Treaty of Versailles had been broken; better arrange for the 'formal disappearance' of the clauses 'under the best conditions possible'. This feeling was common inside and outside the government. The *Spectator* followed the same line: now that Germany had equality perhaps she would be satisfied with that and might be ready to talk business about disarmament.[1]

Hitler hastened to produce the olive branch so brazenly solicited —the more so because the treaty of mutual assistance between France and Russia was signed on May 2, and this smarted far more than any words from Stresa or Geneva. His speech of May 21 defended his repudiation of the disarmament clauses of the Treaty of Versailles, but promised to observe the obligations of the Locarno treaty which Germany had freely signed, including the demilitarisation of the Rhineland, 'so long as the other partners on their side are ready to stand by that pact'. He was ready to make non-aggression pacts with Germany's neighbours, but not with Russia. As to armaments, Germany was prepared to limit her forces reciprocally with other countries, would be content with parity with the western powers in the air, and was willing to limit her navy to 35 per cent of the strength of the British navy. The European powers, outside of Great Britain, did not take these reassurances very seriously.

The National government's response was curious. It continued to rearm; but it also made a deal with Hitler. The government had persisted in denying Churchill's statement of November 28, 1934, that German air strength was equal to Britain's, and by 1937 would be twice that of Great Britain. Yet when Simon and Eden visited Hitler in Berlin on March 24 (after Hitler's public admissions of German rearmament), they were told that the German air force was already equal to Britain's, if not even superior to it. The fact was published by the government, and produced alarm which clamoured for reassurance. In a debate on May 2 Churchill reminded the Commons that in 1708, when told that the battle of Almanza had been lost because only 8000 of the 29,000 English

[1] G. M. Gathorne-Hardy, pp. 394–5; *History of The Times*, IV, ii, 891–2; *Spectator*, March 22, 1935.

troops voted for the campaign had been in Spain, the House 'sat in silence for half an hour, no Member caring to speak or wishing to make a comment upon so staggering an announcement'.[1] Yet this far greater miscalculation only produced a public confession which, by its seeming frankness, actually strengthened the government's reputation. It was on May 22 that Baldwin ate his own words of the previous November:

> . . . with regard to the figure I then gave of German aeroplanes, nothing has come to my knowledge since that makes me think that figure was wrong. I believed at that time it was right. Where I was wrong was in my estimate of the future. There I was completely wrong. . . . We were completely misled on that subject. . . .
>
> There is no occasion . . . for panic . . . there has been a great deal of criticism about the Air Ministry, as though they were responsible for possibly an inadequate programme. . . . I only want to repeat that whatever responsibility there may be—and we are perfectly ready to meet criticism—that responsibility is not that of any single Minister; it is the responsibility of the government as a whole, and we are all responsible and we are all to blame.[2]

To remedy the effects of its own miscalculation, the government proposed a further expansion of the air force, which would bring its strength in first-line planes at home to 1500 by 1937, treble the existing home strength and double that which would have been reached by 1937 under the programme of 1934. The Labour opposition voted against this, but its amendment was defeated by 340 votes to 52. Attlee's speech summed up its position on this and several later occasions:

> We stand for collective security through the League of Nations. We reject the use of force as an instrument of policy. We stand for the reduction of armaments and pooled security. . . . Our policy is not one of seeking security through rearmament but through disarmament. Our aim is the reduction of armaments, and then the complete abolition of all national armaments, and the creation of an international police force under the League.[3]

At the same time, the government decided to meet Hitler halfway in his proposal for a limitation of naval rearmament. Negotiations were begun on June 4 and finished on June 18, when the

[1] W. S. Churchill, *Gathering Storm*, p. 110; 301 H.C. Deb., 5 s., 609.

[2] Churchill, p. 111; 302 H.C. Deb., 5 s., 367, 370. G. M. Young (*Baldwin*, p. 183) observes that in 1934 neither MacDonald nor Baldwin was giving effective leadership in the government, and that Baldwin's relations with Lord Londonderry, the air minister, were distant.

[3] W. S. Churchill, *Gathering Storm*, p. 111; 302 H.C. Deb., 5 s., 375; *Annual Register, 1935*, p. 47.

Anglo-German naval agreement was completed. Sir Samuel Hoare (First Lord of the Admiralty before the reorganisation of the government) and Ribbentrop (later Hitler's ambassador to London) were the principal negotiators. By the treaty Germany was permitted to build a fleet up to 35 per cent of the strength of the British navy; in submarines she might build up to 45 per cent of Britain's submarine strength, or up to 100 per cent in exceptional circumstances. Moreover, Germany agreed to abolish her submarines if all other countries agreed to do the same; and in any case not to use them against merchant ships.

The agreement, even in naval terms, could hardly be worth much. Germany's fleet would be modern and concentrated; Britain's was old and dispersed. Germany was already building submarines and the two 'pocket-battleships', the *Scharnhorst* and the *Gneisenau*, of 26,000 tons, and soon laid down the *Bismarck* and the *Tirpitz* of 45,000 tons, larger than any ships of the British, French or United States navies. The only thing to be said for the agreement was that it was 'freely concluded', and that since Germany was building a fleet anyway, it was well to have it limited. 'Opportunism of the best kind', the *Spectator* called it. Against it were some damning arguments. It condoned Germany's violation of the Treaty of Versailles. It encouraged Hitler's liking for bilateral treaties, which undermined the League of Nations and sabotaged collective security by dividing friends and allies. In this case, Hitler succeeded in dividing Great Britain and France. The agreement was made without France receiving any prior notice. Old suspicions in France were revived: Britain would leave France in the lurch. Coldness ensued; with ill results during the Abyssinian crisis.[1]

In this inauspicious setting the results of the great Peace Ballot were proclaimed on June 27. Since late in 1934 volunteers had been conducting a house-to-house canvass of the populace to obtain answers to five questions; preliminary results had already been published. The 'ballot' was conducted by an *ad hoc* body, the National Declaration Committee; Lord Cecil was chairman, and the ballot was closely associated with the League of Nations Union. The questions were tendentious: Should Britain remain a member of the League? 'Are you in favour of an all-round reduction in armaments by international agreement? Are you in favour of an

---

[1] G. M. Gathorne-Hardy, p. 398; W. S. Churchill, *Gathering Storm*, pp. 123–8; *Annual Register, 1935*, pp. 58–9; *History of The Times*, IV, ii, 894; *Spectator*, June 21, 1935.

all-round abolition of national military and naval aircraft by international agreement?' Should the private manufacture and sale of arms be prohibited by international agreement? and finally question 5:

> Do you consider that, if a nation insists on attacking another, the other nations should combine to compel it to stop by
> (a) Economic and non-military measures?
> (b) If necessary, military measures?

The answers were what might have been expected, though they had the force of over 11½ million votes behind them—an unprecedented number for a private referendum. To all the questions the answer was yes: over 11 million voted yes to the first question, around 10 million to the others. To the last question, 5(b), 6,784,368 voted yes, 2,351,981 (20 per cent) no.[1]

The Peace Ballot was the high water mark of postwar pacificism and 'Leagueomania', and the vote on the last question should be read in that light. None the less, the government was impressed. Policy would have to respond to these sentiments. Late in the day the government became a convert to the League. Soon it could put the new policy to the test and discover if it and the public could have peace by wishing for it.

4. PEACE BY WISHING: THE ABYSSINIAN CRISIS

There was nothing sudden about the Abyssinian crisis which provided the test for the new policy. Mussolini began his plans for the conquest of Abyssinia in 1933, as was made clear by Marshal Emilio de Bono, the general to whom he entrusted the preparations, in his memoirs published in 1937. He needed the prestige of military glory to fulfil his boasts and to strengthen his dictatorship. He claimed a share in Europe's 'civilising mission'. Abyssinia, virtually the only independent, non-colonial state in Africa, was an obvious field for such ambitions. It had long been recognised as within Italy's sphere, though the attempt to conquer it had met with disaster at Adowa in 1896. Since then Italy had tried peaceful penetration, had sponsored Abyssinia's admission to the League of Nations in 1923 and had made a treaty of friendship and arbitration with her in 1928. Moreover, there was a good chance that in Abyssinia Mussolini might have his war and win it without its spreading to the point of danger for him.

---

[1] G. M. Gathorne-Hardy, p. 406; Adelaide Livingstone and Marjorie S. Johnston, *The Peace Ballot: The official history* (London, 1935).

The needful incident occured at a border-spot, Walwal, on December 5, 1934. The border was undefined; there was a vast no-man's-land between Italian and Abyssinian territory, from which border tribes made intermittent raids.. A clash occurred, with loss of life, between Italian and Abyssinian forces at Walwal —whether this was within Italian territory was unknown, though more probably it was some sixty miles inside Abyssinia. Italy sent a note of protest; Abyssinia demanded arbitration, and when this was refused submitted the dispute to the League, and on January 3, 1935 made a formal appeal under article 11 of the Covenant (concerning a threat of war). Italy then agreed to arbitration, but meanwhile reinforced her troops in Eritrea. Several more warlike incidents occurred. The preliminaries for arbitration ended in failure, whereupon Abyssinia appealed to the League once more on March 17, under article 15 (which required the Council to inquire into disputes, to attempt to bring the parties together, and to make a report on the case if mediation failed). The appeal was unfortunately timed, as it coincided with Hitler's restoration of conscription in Germany. The Council and the great powers had, therefore, little interest to spare for Abyssinia: a common front against Germany was more important, and was arranged, with the inclusion of Italy, at Stresa, where Abyssinia was not officially mentioned at all. The Council was persuaded, by specious Italian promises of negotiation, to delay action—while Italian preparations for war proceeded apace. From the end of May onwards public concern began to grow in Great Britain; and the government, fearing that Mussolini's intentions would break either the Stresa front or the League, attempted to buy him off. Eden, visiting Rome on June 24–26 to carry reassurances about Britain's own breach of the Stresa front—the naval treaty with Germany—proposed to Mussolini that Abyssinia should cede some territory—part of the Ogaden—to Italy, receiving in return from Great Britain an outlet to the sea at Zeila and a corridor carved out of British Somaliland. The proposal was contemptuously rejected.[1]

By the beginning of September it was clear that a crisis was near. Though negotiations had continued, Mussolini's speeches became more and more bellicose, and new divisions were mobilised. At each turn, public opinion in Great Britain became more solid:

[1] For the development of the crisis see the full account in A. J. Toynbee, *Survey of International Affairs, 1935*, vol. II, and shorter accounts in G. M. Gathorne-Hardy, pp. 395–405; R. W. Seton-Watson, pp. 353–6.

Abyssinia must be protected, the League's authority vindicated against a bully 'drunk with power and pride'.[1] Laval's government, jealous of its new friendship with Italy, distrustful of British actions and altruism, might try to keep negotiations open; Britain must stand by the League. In the press, the Beaverbrook papers were late converts to this idea, and Rothermere and J. L. Garvin stood out against it; but *The Times* and the *Spectator* joined hands with the *New Statesman* in exhorting the government to support the League, as Hoare, the Foreign Secretary, had promised to do in the debate on the adjournment of parliament on August 1. It was a crisis 'in the fate of Europe and the world', declared the *Spectator*; Baldwin had rightly interpreted the sentiments of the country.[2]

This was the context of the remarkable speech which Sir Samuel Hoare delivered before the Assembly of the League at Geneva on September 11. There was still no open war; but equally no prospect of settlement. Hoare's speech gave assurance that Britain would fulfil its obligations under the Covenant.

> The League stands, and my country stands with it, for the collective maintenance of the Covenant in its entirety, and particularly for steady and collective resistance to all acts of unprovoked aggression. The attitude of the British nation in the last few weeks has clearly demonstrated the fact that this is no variable and unreliable sentiment, but a principle of international conduct to which they and their government hold with firm, enduring and universal persistence.

There was a proviso, but it seemed only to strengthen the pledge which was being given.

> If the burden is to be borne, it must be borne collectively. If risks for peace are to be run, they must be run by all. The security of the many cannot be ensured solely by the efforts of a few, however powerful they may be. On behalf of His Majesty's Government in the United Kingdom, I can say that, in spite of these difficulties, that Government will be second to none in its intention to fulfill, within the measure of its capacity, the obligations which the Covenant lays upon it.[3]

The speech aroused great enthusiasm, in the Assembly and in Great Britain. 'Britain's lead to the world', the *Spectator* called it, declaring that if Mussolini persisted in making war, even against the League powers, the choice was between war and the abandonment of the collective system 'whose vindication even by the ordeal

[1] *New Statesman*, July 13, 1935.
[2] *Spectator*, August 23, 1935; *New Statesman* during July and August.
[3] *Survey of International Affairs, 1935*, II, 187, 188; G. M. Gathorne-Hardy, p. 405.

of war would substitute the rule of law for the rule of force in the world'. It noted elsewhere, however, that few people seemed to understand the very real danger of war which existed.[1]

That Hoare was promising less than he seemed to be became clear later. At the time, the spirit of the declaration, reinforced with the weight of public opinion in Great Britain, was what mattered. A few weeks of further negotiations brought no change in Mussolini's plans; but the rainy season in Abyssinia was now over. On October 3 the attack of Italian forces upon Abyssinia began.

The League acted with unwonted speed. On October 7 the Council adopted, with one dissenting vote, that of Baron Aloisi, the Italian representative, the report of a committee which declared that the Italian government had 'resorted to war in disregard of the covenants under article 12 of the Covenant of the League of Nations'.[2]

This action by itself should have automatically put all members of the League at war with Italy and obliged them to begin economic sanctions against her; the contribution of military forces to protect the Covenant against the aggressor was dependent on further recommendations of the Council.

> Should any member of the League resort to war in disregard of its covenants under articles 12, 13, or 15 it shall *ipso facto* be deemed to have committed an act of war against all other members of the League, which hereby undertake immediately to subject it to the severance of all trade and financial relations . . . (article 16).

This was not quite what happened. The Assembly met on October 9, and after two days' debate accepted, with slight opposition, the Council's action. It then set up a committee to co-ordinate the measures to be taken by members under article 16. By October 19 this committee, thanks in great part to the sterling work of Anthony Eden, had adopted certain measures to recommend to the governments of member countries: financial sanctions, refusal to accept imports from Italy, a very limited embargo on exports to Italy (including transport animals, rubber, tin, scrap iron, iron ore and other metals), and the lifting of the embargo which some nations had put on the export of arms to Abyssinia, imposing instead such an embargo against Italy (in fact, the manufacturers and traders of many countries, including Great Britain, had been busily

[1] *Spectator*, September 13, 1935.
[2] *Survey of International Affairs, 1935*, II, 199–207.

T

supplying Italy with war goods all summer while certain governments, including those of Great Britain and France, had bowed to the brazen importunity of Italy by embargoing such exports to Abyssinia[1]). These sanctions, incomplete as they were, were rapidly (though imperfectly) put into effect by the various governments. Satisfaction that the League was doing something, and quickly, and without war, concealed from most people the fact that the work of their spokesmen at Geneva had not imposed sanctions but rather had limited them.[2]

For the moment, however, all was enthusiasm for the bloodless crusade. Italy was execrated. The League and collective security were worshipped. Sanctions would bring the aggressor to heel. These were the circumstances in which, at the beginning of October, the Labour party held high debate, and a little later the National government staged an election.

5. STOCKTAKING IN THE LABOUR PARTY

Since the great desertion of 1931 the Labour party had been trying to collect itself, closing its ranks, and defining its principles and methods. The task was made harder, though also more necessary, by the anxious character of the times. Gradually a second generation of leaders replaced the fallen and the ageing: Clement Attlee, Sir Stafford Cripps, Herbert Morrison, Hugh Dalton, Ernest Bevin, from whose differing ideas and characters the new party was hammered out.[3] George Lansbury, the leader of the party until 1935, was the chief link between the generations. As leader of the party's forlorn hope in the Commons, he was unorthodox but effective; and not the least of his services was the training which he gave his lieutenants, Attlee and Cripps.[4] Arthur Henderson, a sick man, preoccupied with the disarmament conference, remained secretary of the party until 1934 but did not wield the great influence of earlier days. He died in 1935. Labour's success in winning control of the London County Council in 1934 was a sign of its returning strength, and also gave Morrison his head as the Council's leader. The results of the local elections of 1934 were, in fact, a great encouragement throughout the country; Labour controlled 15 of the Metropolitan boroughs, 21 county boroughs and 18 non-county boroughs—twice as many as it had

---

[1] *Survey of International Affairs, 1935*, II, 164–5, 220.
[2] Ibid., 207–31; documents in *Dispute between Ethiopia and Italy: Documents and Proceedings of the League of Nations*, Cmd. 5071 (1936).
[3] See the excellent discussion in F. Williams, *Ernest Bevin*, pp. 173–87.
[4] R. Postgate, *George Lansbury*, pp. 276–9.

controlled in its best previous year, 1929.[1] The respectability of Labour was also increased: in the birthday honours list of June 3, 1935 which, in honour of the King's jubilee, was more comprehensive than usual, the party's chief whip (Charles Edwards), and two trade-union leaders, Walter Citrine, the general secretary of the T.U.C., and Arthur Pugh, were knighted. This reopened an old controversy about the acceptance of honours by Labour men; but a resolution deploring the practice was shelved at the party's conference at Edinburgh in 1936.

In one way the Labour party lost ground in these years: the I.L.P. disaffiliated itself from the party at a special conference at Bradford in July 1932. The immediate point at issue was the Labour party's standing orders which forbade a member to vote in parliament against policies laid down by the party; behind this was a difference of interpretation over the means of achieving socialism. The final vote was 241 to 142. Disaffiliation was the policy of Maxton, Jowett and Brockway; others chose to leave the I.L.P.[2]

The Labour party had lost one gadfly only to find another: the Socialist League. This was founded in 1932 and affiliated with the party. It represented a merging of ex-members of the I.L.P. with an older organisation, the Society for Socialist Inquiry and Propaganda. Ernest Bevin had been chairman of the S.S.I.P., but the ex-I.L.P. members would not accept him and one of their number, E. F. Wise, was chairman of the Socialist League until his death in 1933. One unfortunate result was to confirm Bevin, the strongest trade-union leader of his day, in his distrust of the 'intellectuals' within the party. Cripps was the leading spirit in the League, supported by Sir Charles Trevelyan, William Mellor, H. N. Brailsford, Harold Laski.[3] A parallel but much less contentious organisation, concerned principally with the publication of socialist tracts, was the New Fabian Research Bureau, founded in 1932 with the support of Attlee, Cripps, the Coles, and a younger generation of socialist economists such as E. F. M. Durbin and Hugh Gaitskell. In 1938 the N.F.R.B. amalgamated with the Fabian Society and helped to reinvigorate it.[4]

In the next few years most of the differences of opinion within

[1] G. D. H. Cole, *History of the Labour Party*, pp. 449–50.
[2] Ibid., pp. 275–7; F. Brockway, *Inside the Left*, pp. 237–53; *Life of Jowett*, pp. 295–311.
[3] G. D. H. Cole, *History of the Labour Party*, pp. 282–4; Cole in *New Statesman*, April 21, 1951; E. Estorick, *Stafford Cripps*, pp. 115–16; J. T. Murphy, *New Horizons*, pp. 308–12.
[4] Margaret Cole, *Beatrice Webb* (London, 1945), pp. 184–5.

the Labour party were between the Socialist League and its allies among the constituency parties, representing the left wing, and a right wing consisting of the great body of the trade unionists and the moderates among the parliamentary leaders. The main questions were over the United Front, the application of socialism, and the need for emergency powers. Over the other great issue, the support of military sanctions, the lines were rather differently drawn. A new statement of Labour's policy, *For Socialism and Peace*, was in part the product of these controversies.

The idea of a United Front against fascism and Nazism was first mooted in 1933 by the Communists, acting upon a manifesto from the Communist International. The Communists approached the Labour party, the T.U.C., the Co-operative party, and the I.L.P. and were rebuffed by all except the last. The Labour party and the T.U.C. denounced Communist and Nazi dictatorship with equal fervour in a manifesto, *Democracy versus Dictatorship*, and intensified their efforts to prevent contacts between their members and the Communists. A resolution in favour of the United Front was defeated at the Labour party's annual conference at Hastings in 1933 and the executive upheld in its actions.[1]

The definition of socialist policy was prepared in a series of reports by sub-committees, discussed by the National Council of Labour (representing the party and the T.U.C.), and debated at the annual conferences in 1932, 1933, and 1934. *For Socialism and Peace* was approved at the conference at Southport in 1934; a historic statement, since much of it was put into practice by the Labour government after 1945. Its temper was shown by a resolution carried by Sir Charles Trevelyan at the conference at Leicester in 1932, that the next Labour government, whether possessed of a majority or not, must promulgate 'definite Socialist legislation . . . immediately' and stand or fall 'on the principles in which it has faith'. In *For Socialism and Peace* this was embodied in the section on 'economic reorganisation', which promised 'full and rapid Socialist economic planning, under central direction' and the 'public ownership and control of the primary industries and services as a foundation step, including the banking system, transport, coal and power, water supply, iron and steel, and other key industries' and 'public ownership of the land . . . including the provision of national parks'. A longer list of industries needing drastic reorganisation was given: electricity, gas, agriculture,

---

[1] G. D. H. Cole, *History of the Labour Party*, pp. 285–6, 290, 292–3.

shipping, shipbuilding, engineering, textiles, chemicals, insurance; 'for the most part nothing short of immediate public ownership and control will be effective'. There were promises of housing and slum clearance schemes, a state medical service for domiciliary and institutional care, the immediate raising of the school leaving age to fifteen, and a pledge 'to make adequate maintenance of the unemployed a national charge, and abolish the means test'. Actually, the programme contained little which was not in its predecessors of 1918 and 1928. The Socialist League attempted, at the Southport conference, to stiffen it, and put down seventy-five amendments, all of which were defeated.[1]

Another difference arose over the question whether a future Labour government should take emergency powers to carry through its legislation, on the ground that otherwise it would find itself paralysed either by a financial panic (memories of the 'bankers' ramp' of 1931 were still fresh) or by a counter-revolutionary, fascistic movement. This fear was widespread among advanced socialists—and their demand for emergency powers was equally the text for many Tory fulminations against them. It was explicit in some of the works of Professor Harold Laski. 'If Labour attains an electoral majority and thus dominates the House of Commons, will capitalism meekly abdicate before its onset?'[2] Capitalism, when it ceases to have a margin of success, must choose between its own suppression and the suppression of democratic institutions. Would the 'postulates of democratic government' then continue to be accepted?[3] The Socialist League was obsessed by this fear.[4] Hence its demand that a socialist government should immediately obtain an emergency powers act and establish a temporary dictatorship. The party was not easily convinced of the necessity. *For Socialism and Peace* protested its faith in 'political democracy', and promised only to reform the procedure of the Commons to increase the facilities for discussion and criticism of legislation and to abolish the House of Lords. It did add, however, that 'in the event of the return of a Labour government being accompanied or followed by an emergency situation for which the normal powers of government are not now

[1] G. D. H. Cole, *History of the Labour Party*, pp. 278-99; *For Socialism and Peace* (1934).
[2] H. J. Laski, *Democracy in Crisis* (London, 1933), p. 85.
[3] Laski, *The State in Theory and Practice* (London, 1935), pp. 144, 316.
[4] Sir Stafford Cripps, *Can Socialism Come by Constitutional Methods?* (Socialist League, n.d.), p. 2; L. A. Fenn and others, *Problems of the Socialist Transition* (Forum lectures of the Socialist League, 1934); and *The Labour Party and the Constitution* (Socialist League, 1932).

adequate, the Government would seek for the necessary emergency powers from Parliament'.[1]

In this and other ways the Labour party and the Socialist League seemed almost worlds apart. In contrast to *For Socialism and Peace* the Socialist League's programme, *Foward to Socialism* (1934), was haunted by fascism and anarchy, by the spectacle of a world in arms, by the choice of poverty or plenty. There must be a five-year plan. Key positions must be seized: 'The first positions to be won are Finance and the Land.' A class philosophy is proclaimed:

> Nothing but the united struggle of the workers for the transfer to the community of the means of life now privately owned and controlled will suffice to preserve the workers from the degradation of their standards and their enslavement by a Fascist Capitalist dictatorship.[2]

Peace was, of course, a special interest of the Labour party, as the title of the programme showed. Organise peace through the League of Nations! Remove the causes of war! Away with all secret alliances! Pass a Peace Act to make it impossible for any British government to use force as an instrument of national policy. Disarm drastically; an international police force must replace all national armed forces. Abolish the private manufacture and sale of armaments. Settle all international disputes by pacific means. This was Labour's policy: a Peace Crusade. The cost was hardly mentioned: '. . . economic and financial measures necessary to . . . share in collective action' were spoken of. The only hint of trouble was in a passage on the change which must come in the nature of patriotism: people must 'unflinchingly support our Government in all the risks and consequences of fulfilling its duty to take part in collective action against a peace-breaker'.[3] This was not good enough for the Socialist League, which damned the League of Nations as merely reflecting the 'economic conflicts of the capitalist system'. British workers should resist a war declared by 'this government' by a general strike.[4]

At its annual conference in 1935 Labour reached the parting of the ways. Meeting in Brighton on September 30, at the moment

---

[1] *For Socialism and Peace*, p. 32; G. D. H. Cole, *History of the Labour Party*, pp. 287, 292, 297–8. Two moderate statements of the socialist creed at this time minimise the need for emergency powers: Hugh Dalton, *Practical Socialism for Britain* (London, 1935), pp. 68–9; C. R. Attlee, *Labour Party in Perspective* (London, 1937).

[2] *Forward to Socialism*, in L. A. Fenn, *Problems of the Socialist Transition*, pp. 204, 209.

[3] *For Socialism and Peace*, pp. 4, 13; G. D. H. Cole, *History of the Labour Party*, p. 295.

[4] G. D. H. Cole, p. 300.

when Italy was poised for the attack on Abyssinia but had not begun it, the party had to decide its attitude upon peace and war; for if it supported sanctions it accepted the risk of war. It did not, in fact, come to a clear-cut decision; it did not really do so until 1939. But the debate at Brighton determined the future of the party's leadership; and it reproduced, in dramatic form, that clash of ideas and personalities between three groups within the party out of which the Labour party was remade between 1931 and 1940. The protagonists were Lansbury, Cripps, Bevin, representing respectively the political and moderate side of the party, the intellectual and semi-revolutionary wing, and the solidarity and hard commonsense of the trade unions. The casting was, however, not perfect. Lansbury, in his Christian pacifism, was representative only of a small minority within the party. The political side would have been better represented by Morrison, Bevin's chief rival and cautious adversary.

On the issue of sanctions the T.U.C. had already taken its stand, meeting in the annual congress at Margate on September 2. A resolution had been debated which condemned Italy and promised to support the government in any action it took to uphold the League. In the debate the danger of war was not evaded. The resolution was carried by a large vote.

In the debate in the Dome, Brighton, on October 1—the longest debate in the party's history—Dalton moved the national executive's resolution calling on the government to use 'all the necessary measures provided by the Covenant' to support the League in preventing Italy's 'rapacious attack'. Cripps opposed it, having just resigned from the national executive to do so: the League was nothing but the 'International Burglars' Union', and Labour ought not to 'join without power in the responsibility for capitalist and imperialist war that sanctions may entail'.

The great speech against the resolution was George Lansbury's. This most English of all the parliamentary leaders of these years, a man of strong passions held in check by utter faith in Christ, a pacifist from his innermost convictions, was now a widower of seventy-six, who had not long returned to active life after a fall in which he broke his thigh in December 1933. He was leader of the parliamentary party, but opposed to the party's programme on the issue of sanctions. He was given an extraordinary reception, almost the whole conference rising to sing 'For he's a jolly good fellow'. He now spoke against the official resolution; he was ready to resign his leadership:

. . . One Whose life I revere and Who, I believe, is the greatest Figure in history, has put it on record: 'Those who take the sword shall perish by the sword.' . . . It is said that people like me are irresponsible. I am no more irresponsible a leader than the greatest Trade Union leader in the country. I live my life, as they do, amongst ordinary people. I see them when I am at home every day; I meet them and know all there is to know about them; and they do about me. . . . If mine was the only voice in this Conference, I would say in the name of the faith I hold, the belief I have that God intended us to live peaceably and quietly with one another, if some people do not allow us to do so, I am ready to stand as the early Christians did, and say, 'This is our faith, this is where we stand, and, if necessary, this is where we will die.'[1]

The conference sprang to its feet in heartfelt applause.

Then up rose Ernest Bevin, walked in his slow, heavy way to the front and spoke, as he had at so many conferences, with the weight and warmth and rough directness which held and quelled his audience even when they disliked his words.[2] He was heavier and blunter than was usual even for him; his sneers at Cripps and Lansbury seemed a piece of 'calculated bad temper', beyond what was needed to support the official resolution. He was irked by Lansbury's pacifism, and angered by the devious reasoning of the intellectuals who now supported, now opposed, the League. Above all he hated fascists and Nazis as murderers of working men and women and wreckers of the free trade unions. Lansbury and Cripps had both affronted his stern sense of loyalty: Lansbury, the party leader, by seeming until very recently to support party policy on sanctions, Cripps by going against the executive's policy after sharing in making it. Of Lansbury he said:

. . . I hope this Conference will not be influenced by either sentiment or personal attachment. . . . It is placing the Executive and the Movement in an absolutely wrong position to be taking your conscience round from body to body asking to be told what you ought to do with it.[3]

Bevin's speech roused bitter feeling; but his cause triumphed. The resolution in support of sanctions was carried by 2,168,000 votes to 102,000. Lansbury resigned the leadership of the parliamentary party soon afterwards. Attlee, who had deputised for

---

[1] R. Postgate, *George Lansbury*, pp. 297–304; *Report of the 35th Annual Conference of the Labour Party, 1935*, pp. 153, 158, 176–7.
[2] See Francis Williams' description of him at conferences: *Ernest Bevin*, pp. 178–9.
[3] F. Williams, *Ernest Bevin;* pp. 193–8; *Report of 35th Annual Conference of the Labour Party*, p. 178. Williams gives Bevin's phrase concerning Lansbury as 'trailing your conscience round from body to body'; another version is 'hawking'. See also G. D. H. Cole, *History of the Labour Party*, pp. 306–8.

Lansbury during his illness, succeeded him as acting chairman, and was elected chairman in the new parliament, despite the return of other ex-ministers after the election; Morrison and Arthur Greenwood were his chief rivals for the leadership. Attlee was regarded as one of the intellectuals, and somewhat to the left; but he had shown skill and judgment as a parliamentary spokesman, and had not incurred, as had Morrison, the suspicion of Bevin and the trade-union wing. The change from Lansbury to Attlee did not at the time seem to mark an epoch; seen in retrospect it clearly did so.

6. THE LAST GENERAL ELECTION OF THE PEACE

There had been talk of a general election since September, if not since the reorganisation of the government in June. On October 23, the day after parliament had reassembled, the announcement was made by Baldwin: dissolution on October 25, general election on November 14. The campaign was fairly quiet. As before, broadcast addresses played an important part. Once again, the National government was appealing for support, but its campaign, even more than in 1931, was really that of the Conservatives, with Simon's Liberal Nationals and the National Labour candidates clinging to the Conservatives' coat-tails. The government's manifesto pointed to its record—economic recovery, the boom in housing—and promised more efforts to assist the distressed areas, extension of old age pensions, and the raising of the school-leaving age to fifteen. Its chief concern was with foreign policy, which was both the main issue and the area where disagreement was least obvious. The League of Nations would 'remain, as heretofore, the keystone of British foreign policy'; the government would 'do all in our power to uphold the Covenant and to maintain and increase the efficiency of the League'. In the dispute over Abyssinia 'there will be no wavering in the policy we have hitherto pursued'. This did not remove the necessity of rearmament: gaps in the national defence would be filled, but at the same time the government would work for a general limitation of arms. Rearmament was certainly stressed in many Conservatives' speeches, but it was rather played down as the campaign progressed, and much was made of Baldwin's promise to a meeting of the International Peace Society at the Guildhall on October 31: 'I give you my word that there will be no great armaments.'

Baldwin's campaign left the Liberals and Labour party at a disadvantage. He had stolen their clothes, and they could only

T*

protest that he would never wear them: the Conservatives' conversion to the League and the application of sanctions was recent and insincere; it was they who had wrecked the disarmament conference, and their real intention now was to carry out a programme of rearmament. Another line of attack was directed against the government's record; after four years, unemployment, depression, misery still overshadowed the land. The Liberal party under Samuel conducted a campaign of its own, but only put forward 156 candidates. Lloyd George's campaign centred upon the Council of Action for Peace and Reconstruction which had been founded in July. Its domestic programme was Lloyd George's familiar mixture of public works, agricultural improvement, economic planning, its foreign policy the support of the League and a five years' truce from rearmament and aggression. It did not put up candidates, but asked party candidates to give pledges to support its programme. It was Lloyd George's last attempt to return to power and it was too late.

The Conservatives won the election. They won 387 seats (compared with 454 before the dissolution); with 33 Liberal Nationals and 8 National Labour members the government had a majority (including 3 independent members) of 247 over the opposition. Labour recovered much of the ground lost in 1931, particularly in London, Yorkshire and Scotland; it elected 154 members, compared with 46 in 1931 and 289 in 1929. The return of Morrison, Clynes, Alexander, Dalton and other ex-ministers strengthened the Labour front bench. Once again, the Liberals were the chief victims of the election; their numbers fell from 26 to 17, and Samuel was among the defeated (Sir Archibald Sinclair replaced him as leader). Lloyd George was returned once more by the faithful voters of the Carnarvon Boroughs; his family party numbered four. The I.L.P. returned four members, the Communists one—William Gallacher, whose election for West Fife was the result of a long feud in that mining district against William Adamson, its former Labour member. There were also four independent opposition members.

Thus was the National government confirmed in another term of office, and a House of Commons elected which was destined to serve until 1945. Baldwin had succeeded in an unprecedented fashion in maintaining for his existing government a very large majority—magnified, as earlier majorities had been, by the working of the electoral system, for the government's popular vote was 11½ millions, as compared with the opposition vote of 9,930,300.

The Conservative vote was just under 10½ million. Labour polled 8·3 million votes, a little less than in 1929, 1·6 million more than in 1931. The opposition Liberals polled 1·4 million votes.[1]

It is doubtful if the National label contributed much to the Conservative's success. The result was a vote of confidence in the existing government, already largely Conservative's, and a vote of no confidence in an alternative Labour government. Above all, the result was a measure of Baldwin's high popularity. It was his personal triumph; and followed, by an interval briefer than fate usually allows, by humiliation, unpopularity and, after one short recovery, oblivion. The government's 'National' character was, in fact, almost washed out in the election, for Ramsay MacDonald was defeated by Emanuel Shinwell at Seaham, and Malcolm MacDonald also lost. Seats were eventually found for both, and they remained in the government—Ramsay MacDonald until the Chamberlain government was formed in May 1937; he died in the following November while on a voyage to South America. J. H. Thomas survived the election, but resigned from the ministry, and later from parliament, in June 1936, after some unguarded remarks of his had led to a leak of budget secrets. His passing into an obscure retirement was generally regretted. Baldwin made no changes of importance in the Cabinet after the election. Churchill was still conspicuous by his absence. The advancement of Lord Halifax[2] to be Lord Privy Seal in place of Lord Londonderry was another portent.

A myth grew up later around Baldwin's conduct of the election. It was based on some characteristically ambiguous passages in a speech he made in parliament on November 12, 1936, whose meaning was distorted by incomplete quotation. He was following Churchill, who had accused the government of having lost the 'years which the locust hath eaten' by not beginning rearmament before the general election. Baldwin's reply ('I put before the whole House my own views with an appalling frankness') was that the government had a large majority before the election, but no mandate for rearmament, and that if it had gone to the country on the issue in 1933 or 1934, when the lesson of the East Fulham by-election was still fresh, it would have lost the election and with it the chance to promote rearmament—a damaging enough ad-

---

[1] Election results from *The Times*, November 26, 1935. See also *Annual Register, 1935*, pp. 86–92; G. D. H. Cole, *History of the Labour Party*, pp. 308–12. There is an account of the election in D. E. McHenry, *The Labour Party in Transition* (London, 1938), pp. 183–200.

[2] Lord Irwin had succeeded his father as Viscount Halifax in 1934.

mission in itself, for as Churchill had said, 'The responsibility of ministers for the public safety is absolute and requires no mandate.' As it was, by waiting, 'we got from the country—with a large majority—a mandate for doing a thing that no one, 12 months before, would have believed possible'. The speech, as quoted later (in *Guilty Men* and other books concerned to discredit the Conservatives) was made into a confession that Baldwin, by concealing the need for rearmament though intending to rearm, had won the election of 1935 by deceit.[1] As usual, the best comment on this was David Low's cartoon of Baldwin, the guide who has brought the electorate, on a mule, to the edge of a precipice: 'Be reasonable. If I hadn't told you I wouldn't bring you here, you wouldn't have come.'[2]

What Baldwin and Chamberlain had done was something rather different. They had chosen, as any sensible leaders will do, the best time for themselves for an election. They had been able to divert attention from the government's rather pallid record at home to issues of foreign policy, and they had cashed in on the popular enthusiasm for the League and for sanctions against Italy by supporting it at just the moment before the dangers which it might bring had become evident and controversial. They had held the election in a time of crisis—enough of a crisis to lead people to play for safety by voting for the government and trusting the quiet, honest, old Prime Minister; yet not a crisis too serious for comfort. One result of the victory was to increase the fine which the Conservatives had to pay later when the lease of office fell in.

7. THE RETREAT FROM COLLECTIVE SECURITY: THE HOARE–LAVAL DEAL

The National government's enthusiasm for collective security was soon put to the test. Economic sanctions against Italy, if they were to be effective, must include the cutting off of Italy's imported supplies of things essential for war, particularly oil; and an economic blockade might soon become a naval blockade, with consequent dangers of war. And there was some readiness to contemplate such action. In October the *Spectator* was writing of

[1] R. Bassett, 'Telling the truth to the people: the myth of the Baldwin "confession"', *Cambridge Journal*, II, 84–95 (November, 1948) has established the truth about Baldwin's 'appalling frankness', but in turn exaggerates the importance of rearmament as an issue in the election. See the later correspondence in the *Cambridge Journal*, II, 237, 378, and *The Times* during the election campaign (e.g., leader on 'Election issues', November 12). For Baldwin's and Churchill's speeches, see 317 H.C. Deb., 5 s., 1101, 1105, 1144–5.
[2] Quoted in A. L. Rowse, *End of an Epoch* (London, 1947), p. 110.

'the danger of weak sanctions', and talking of the cutting of Italian communications in the Mediterranean: the sternest action might well be the safest. In the debate in the Commons on October 22 no member talked openly of war: Attlee and other Labour speakers demanded effective sanctions and damned the government's past record of support for the League, especially over Manchuria; Samuel and two other Liberals talked guardedly of military sanctions and the blocking of the Suez canal.[1] Within the Cabinet Neville Chamberlain was in favour of oil sanctions: 'if necessary, we ought to give the lead ourselves'.[2] The government had sent two battle-cruisers, the *Hood* and the *Renown*, to Gibraltar early in September, but the later movement of the Mediterranean fleet from Malta to Alexandria seemed to show a disinclination to risk a battle.

The government was, in fact, in retreat from a policy of effective sanctions from the moment that the first, ineffective sanctions were imposed. Part of the reason was the unwillingness of the French government under Laval to tolerate strong action; but in surrendering to French policy and the vain pursuit of Italian friendship the National government was also surrendering the leadership which it had claimed at Geneva in September. More than this, its actions in the next few months, whether intentionally or not, led the country away from the League and from collective security, away from a possible war in their support while such a war might still have saved them. By June 1936, the nakedness of the government in foreign policy was unconcealed. The League was wrecked, collective security broken, France paralysed, friendship between France and England enfeebled, the aggressors triumphant. And on the other side of the ledger: nothing—save a slow acceleration of rearmament. Strong action against Italy in December, or against Germany in March 1936, might have prevented the Second World War. The British public did not clamour for such action; but its temper in October showed that it would have responded to a strong lead from the government. Instead, it got a course of sedatives and one piece of shock treatment, and became passive, acquiescing in failure and despair.

That the government favoured a settlement between Italy and Abyssinia by negotiation rather than a vindication of the League and collective security by sanctions and force was clear from Sir Samuel Hoare's speech in parliament on October 22, just before the dissolution. There had been, he said, no discussion of military

[1] 305 H. C. Deb. 5s.   [2] K. Feiling, *Neville Chamberlain*, p. 272 (November 29).

sanctions. Much was made of the fact that Britain and her navy must take no isolated action—a point repeated in Baldwin's election broadcast on October 25. Actually, Hoare and Laval had agreed at Geneva on September 10, the day before Hoare delivered his famous speech, in 'ruling out military sanctions, not adopting any measure of naval blockade, never contemplating the closure of the Suez Canal—in a word, ruling out everything that might lead to war'.[1] This earlier 'Hoare–Laval' deal foreshadowed the later one.

Thus it was that during November two forces were pulling in opposite directions. There was a continued demand for effective sanctions, and an undercurrent of distrust about the government's intentions. The *Spectator* found Hoare's speech of October 22 not sufficiently emphatic; in November it urged the government to hold on to the leadership it had previously assumed at Geneva.[2] From the opposite corner the *New Statesman* advocated stiffer sanctions and predicted a 'dirty deal' instead.[3] It was not arguing for war; the premise of all supporters of sanctions was that they would be sufficient to prevent war and to save Abyssinia and the League.

Laval's object in December was to prevent the beginning of oil sanctions and the attendant dangers of war with Italy by presenting terms for a negotiated settlement of the Abyssinian war. He had been able to get the League sub-committee on sanctions to postpone action until December 12; oil sanctions had been formally proposed by the Canadian delegate, Dr. W. A. Riddell, on November 2, and were to have been decided upon on November 29. Meanwhile, in Paris and Rome there were diplomatic and journalistic warnings of Italian retaliation against an embargo of oil exports, including talk of a surprise air attack on the British fleet. Experts of the British and French foreign offices had been at work on proposals for ending the war since mid-October, and pressure was then put on the Abyssinian government through the British ambassador to start peace negotiations. The *Daily Herald* published the peace plan as early as October 30; other papers gave their readers similar scoops on December 5 and 6. Thus things had gone pretty far when Hoare agreed, at Baldwin's urging, to stop in Paris on December 7 on his way to Switzerland for a

[1] A. J. Toynbee, *Survey of International Affairs, 1935*, II, 183–4.
[2] *Spectator*, October 25, November 15, 29, 1935. On December 6 it quoted the *Daily Telegraph* (Conservative): 'can the Italian army win the war before sanctions lose it. Effective petrol sanctions would of course be decisive.'
[3] *New Statesman*, October 26, 1935; cf. November 23, 30.

badly-needed holiday. And in Paris, in talks protracted through-out the next day, December 8, Hoare was persuaded by Laval to agree to the experts' proposals. Dispatches were sent over-night to the Cabinet in London; but to make doubly sure that they could not be rejected Laval allowed the proposals to leak out to the French press, which published them on December 9.

The proposals for ending the Abyssinian war—the Hoare–Laval plan—would have involved Abyssinia in ceding to Italy two-thirds of its territory as the price for the war being brought to an end and the shrunken remainder of the Ethiopian empire being left under the emperor's rule—always provided that Musso-lini agreed to these terms. Some territory was to be ceded to Italy outright; a much larger slice of Abyssinia was to be made into a 'zone of economic expansion and settlement reserved to Italy', which was cession under a different label; in return, Abyssinia would receive a corridor to an outlet on the sea, at Assab. In favour of the proposals—apart from questions of right and wrong —was the argument that by them the emperor, Haile Selassie, would retain half a loaf—or one-third; against them that Musso-lini's legions had not yet overrun a fraction of the territory to be ceded, that their victory in the war was still in doubt, and that the terms seemed to give an unnecessarily large bonus to the aggressor.

Yet the public reaction—in France as much as in Great Britain—confounded the politicians. Stupefaction first: then a universal sense of humiliation and shame.[1] People had believed in the League and trusted that it would defend the territorial integrity of its members. Both the League and Abyssinia were being betrayed by their friends; the bully was rewarded, his helpless victim coerced. But more, the government had just won the election by its support of the League, an appeal which its opponents had branded as insincere. Never was there a better opportunity for saying 'I told you so.' Yet the storm of feeling aroused was quite outside party. *The Times*, normally so devoted to Baldwin, did much to damn the proposals on December 16 by referring to the strip which Abyssinia was to receive as the 'corridor for camels' (it was not clear whether Abyssinia would be permitted even to build a railway along it); it refused in this case to 'endorse an unjust peace'. Letters to *The Times* were of the same tenor; and indeed the press, except for the Beaverbrook and Rothermere papers, was almost unanimous in its condemnation. What was

[1] 'Spectator's Notebook', in *Spectator*, December 20, 1935.

most impressive was the avalanche of letters which M.P.'s received from private citizens.[1]

At first Baldwin decided to ride out the storm. Though the Cabinet was divided, loyalty to a colleague kept it faithful to Hoare's proposals. In the Commons the subject was probed at question time and debated on a Labour motion on December 10. Baldwin replied awkwardly, asking members not to be suspicious and denying what, unbeknownst to him, had already occurred, that messages had been sent from the Foreign Office to Haile Selassie and to Mussolini in support of the proposals. His plea was the old one—trust me; but never spoken more pitiably, and in words which gave a text for David Low's cartoons of him— 'Old Sealed-Lips'—for many a day.

> I have seldom spoken with greater regret, for my lips are not yet unsealed. Were these troubles over I would make a case, and I guarantee that not a man would go into the Lobby against us.[2]

Not for the first time Baldwin's own party was turning away from him. There was talk of an alternative government under Austen Chamberlain. At the last moment, before a debate in parliament arranged for December 19, Baldwin saved himself by sacrificing Hoare, who resigned the foreign secretaryship on December 18. The debate on the 19th, before a crowded house, was dramatic. Hoare, just returned from his unhappy holiday, defended the proposals in a long and able speech, making much of the fact that Britain alone had taken naval and military precautions in support of the League, and could not carry the burden by herself. Baldwin sought strength through weakness and penance:

> I am going to be perfectly frank, I am going to say exactly what I feel, and I am going to describe my own part, which is never an easy matter for a man to do when he does not feel complete satisfaction with it. . . . Never throughout the week had I or anyone of my colleagues any idea in our own minds that we were not being true to every pledge that we had given in the Election. . . . I was not expecting that deeper feeling which was manifested . . . in many parts of the country on what I may call the ground of conscience and of honour. The moment I am confronted with that, I know that something has happened that has appealed to the deepest feelings of our countrymen. . . . It is perfectly obvious now that the proposals are absolutely and com-

---

[1] *Survey of International Affairs, 1935*, II, 67–9, 297; *History of The Times*, IV, ii, 897.
[2] 307 H.C. Deb., 5 s., 856.

pletely dead. This Government is certainly going to make no attempt
to resurrect them.[1]

Even this confession might not have sufficed to save Baldwin.
Attlee, in moving a resolution against the proposals, singled out
two issues:

> the honour of this country and . . . the honour of the Prime Minister.
> If . . . the Prime Minister won an election on one policy and immedi-
> ately after victory was prepared to carry out another, it has an
> extremely ugly look. . . . If you turn and run away from the aggres-
> sor, you kill the League, and you do worse than that, or as bad as
> that: you kill all faith in the word of honour of this country.[2]

Talk of honour is dangerous: Austen Chamberlain admitted the
justice of Attlee's charge when he said, with the illogicality which
feelings of personal and party loyalty can produce, that because
the Prime Minister's honour had been challenged, he would vote
in favour of the government. Baldwin was saved, but his reputation for honesty and good sense had sunk deep into the mud, and
was never quite clean again. He had appeared not only as a fool
but as a knave. His appointment of Anthony Eden as Hoare's
successor as Foreign Secretary began the government's partial
recovery in public esteem.[3]

Though it failed, the Hoare–Laval deal was as effective as if it
had succeeded. It doomed the League and it doomed Abyssinia.
The outburst of public feeling was a purgation. Thereafter, there
was acquiesence in more delay over oil sanctions; in the midst of
which Hitler's next blow, the reoccupation of the Rhineland, came
to push Abyssinia further into the background. Meanwhile the
Italians were succeeding rapidly in their campaign against Haile
Selassie's ill-trained levies, starved of arms and supplies. The
spraying of poison gas from Italian aeroplanes proved to be a quick
means of bringing victory to the forces of civilisation over bar-
barism. On May 2, 1936, the emperor and his family fled from
Addis Ababa to their exile in England. On May 9 Mussolini
proclaimed Italy's annexation of Abyssinia and gave his king the
new title of emperor: 'Italy has her empire at last: a Fascist
empire. . . .'

In Great Britain the general instinct was to forget about an
unhappy affair as quickly as possible, though during May there

---

[1] *Survey of International Affairs, 1935*, II, 319; 307 H.C. Deb., 5 s., 2031–5.
[2] 307 H.C. Deb., 5 s., 2029.
[3] *Survey of International Affairs, 1935*, II, 317; *Annual Register, 1935*, pp. 108–9;
W. S. Churchill, *Gathering Storm*, p. 165.

was much argument about extending sanctions and not condoning successful aggression. Die-hard Tories could now openly denounce sanctions; in June government spokesmen took up the tale. Neville Chamberlain gave the signal in a speech to the 1900 Club on June 10, calling the continuance or intensifying of sanctions 'the very midsummer of madness'. He did this without consulting Eden;[1] the divergence in foreign policy between Chamberlain and the Foreign Office had already begun. There was a last-minute battle by the League of Nations Union and by Liberals and some Labour groups to maintain sanctions; but the government announced that it would abandon them on June 18, the anniversary of the battle of Waterloo.[2] The government lost the day in debate but won in the division lobby: what matter if it had to face Greenwood's fury ('this trembling, vacillating, cowardly government, which is leading people backward instead of forward') and the taunts of Lloyd George in one of his most sarcastic speeches:

> This is a unique occasion. . . . I have never before heard a British Minister . . . come down to the House of Commons and say that Britain was beaten, Britain and her Empire beaten, and that we must abandon an enterprise we had taken in hand. . . . There is no evidence that the Government ever meant business over sanctions . . . [They claimed to be leaders] now they are running away, brandishing their swords—still leading![3]

It's an ill wind that blows nobody any good. One result of the Abyssinian crisis was that Great Britain and Egypt at last put their relations in order. Several attempts to negotiate an Anglo-Egyptian treaty had failed since Britain, in 1922, had declared Egypt's independence, subject to reservations which made this independence worthless to Egyptian nationalists. The war in Abyssinia led to new interventions by Great Britain: the Mediterranean fleet was moved from Malta to Alexandria, British troops in Egypt were reinforced and the Libyan frontier garrisoned by British and Egyptian soldiers. This prompted a united front of Egyptian leaders to propose that negotiations should be reopened, and after some preliminaries conversations were begun on March 2, 1936, the British delegation being led by Sir Miles Lampson, the High Commissioner. A treaty of mutual defence and alliance was

---

[1] K. Feiling, *N. Chamberlain*, p. 296.

[2] *Survey of International Affairs, 1935*, II, 443–80. For the public attitude towards the continuance of sanctions see *Spectator*, May 8, 22, 29, 1936; the *Spectator* first weakened on the subject on May 29.

[3] 313 H.C. Deb., 5 s., 1221–32. The Assembly of the League voted the abandonment of sanctions on July 6, ignoring Haile Selassie's moving plea.

signed on August 26. The British military occupation was ended, but Egypt promised to give British forces all possible help and use of facilities in time of war or international emergency. Britain was granted the right to maintain a stipulated number of troops in the Canal zone for twenty years. The administration of the Sudan was left unchanged. Next year, at an international conference at Montreux, the capitulations were abolished (subject to the survival of the mixed courts for a term of years). In the same year Egypt joined the League of Nations.[1]

8. MAILED FIST AND VELVET GLOVE: RHINELAND CRISIS AND REARMAMENT

Other events besides the fall of Abyssinia made 1936 a year of challenge to old assumptions and beliefs. The familiar postwar world was fast vanishing; the new order was cold and empty, modern and menacing. Hence the nation's mourning for King George V was partly a mourning for its past. The King's reign had been a troubled one, but the troubles were known and hope had still been possible. The King died on January 20 at Sandringham. The public outpouring of grief was increased by the shortness of the interval between the first bulletin and the end, and particularly by the suspense of the last evening, when there was silence on the air, save for the sound of the ticking of a clock, and every quarter of an hour the silken tones of the B.B.C.'s chief announcer, Stuart Hibberd, repeating the words 'the King's life is moving peacefully towards its close' (a phrase drafted by Lord Dawson of Penn, the King's physician). The new King, Edward VIII, was already well-known and well-loved as Prince of Wales, and still thought of as young, an illusion helped by his slim figure and single state, though in fact he was forty-one. Some noted an ill omen: when the old King's body was being drawn on a gun carriage from King's Cross to Westminster Hall a sudden jolt caused a cross to fall off the imperial crown which lay on the coffin.[2]

March brought another jolt to the old order. Hitler had been studiously quiet for a year, since his repudiation of the disarmament clauses of the Treaty of Versailles in March 1935; and in spite of the obvious temptation to make trouble while the relations of Great Britain, France and Italy were greatly strained, he had

[1] Royal Institute of International Affairs, *Great Britain and Egypt, 1914–51* (London, 1952), pp. 33–47.
[2] For the demonstrations of sorrow at the King's death see Philip Gibbs, *Ordeal in England*, pp. 12–15; cf. R. Graves and A. Hodge, *Long Week-end*, pp. 319–22.

refrained from doing so. Even the treaty between France and Russia, ratified in the French chamber on February 27, 1936, did not seem to disturb him. In an interview with a French journalist at the time (published in the *Matin* on February 28) he breathed only friendship and conciliation. Encouraged by this, the French ambassador in Berlin asked for a discussion of the Franco-German *rapprochement* that seemed to be offered; and on March 6 Eden re-opened to the German ambassador in London the proposal of an 'air Locarno'.

Hitler's reply was characteristic. On March 7, 1936, German troops marched into the demilitarised zone in the Rhineland. It was Saturday: Hitler preferred the week-end for a crisis. At the same moment the balm was applied. In a speech to the Reichstag that morning, Hitler justified his action—he alleged that the treaty between France and Russia was incompatible with the Treaty of Locarno and so freed Germany from being bound by it—and offered attractive counter-proposals (coupled with bitter attacks upon Russia). He was willing to establish a bilateral demilitarised zone (which would mean that France would have to abandon its elaborate defences of the Maginot line); he was willing to make twenty-five year non-aggression pacts with the western powers and with those to the east, excluding Russia, and an air pact with the west; he was even willing to bring Germany back into the League provided that the Covenant was separated from the Treaty of Versailles and that Germany's equality was recognised in the matter of colonies. Germany's struggle for equality was now ended: 'We have no territorial demands to make in Europe.'

Whatever the gilding of it, Germany had broken the treaties of Versailles and Locarno; her flouting of the demilitarisation of the Rhineland was automatically, by article 44 of the Treaty of Versailles, 'a hostile act'. The French could with justice have attacked the Rhineland at once. The German general staff had expected this, and had opposed Hitler's action. He had overruled them. His success strengthened his power over his generals, and his belief in his own intuitions.

Why did nothing happen? First, because Hitler had all the advantage of surprise, of the *fait accompli*. Second, because the public, obsessed with the feeling of guilt over the Treaty of Versailles, condoned the breach of the treaty: the Germans were only 'going into their own back-garden'[1]—unlike the Italians, who had wantonly made a war against a foreign country, and for whom

---

[1] Lord Lothian, quoted in W. S. Churchill, *The Gathering Storm*, p. 176.

all the nation's moral indignation was still reserved. Third, because the public admired the plumage and forgot the dying bird: Hitler's offers seemed more important than his act. Fourth, because people did not then believe in war (though they were coming to): war was not in the air.

There was another reason also for inaction. For two weeks before Hitler's *coup* the French had been pressing the British government for a military alliance, and asking what support they might expect if oil sanctions against Italy or German resentment at the Franco-Russian treaty should lead to trouble, or if the rumours of the impending reoccupation of the Rhineland should prove true. The British Cabinet refused to commit itself, Britain's military weakness being one unstated reason.[1] Hence when Hitler acted, Sarraut and Flandin, Prime Minister and Foreign Secretary in the new French government, refrained from ordering a general mobilisation. Had they done so, and war followed, Britain could hardly have failed to join in; Hitler might have been speedily overthrown. But doubtful of Britain (and of France's political unity), the French waited; and the moment passed.[2]

Words took the place of action; words took the sharp edge off the facts. Eden, in parliament on March 9, deplored the blow to the sanctity of treaties, and promised British assistance if France and Belgium were attacked during the discussions then occurring; but found comfort that there was 'no reason to suppose that the present German action implies a threat of hostilities', and that the German memorandum avowed Germany's 'unchangeable longing for a real pacification of Europe'.[3] The *Spectator* saw a danger of imminent war through French demands that withdrawal of the German troops from the Rhineland must precede negotiations; 'the responsibility for saving the world from that disaster lies primarily on British statesmen'. The demilitarisation of the Rhineland was 'a small thing in itself; no one ever supposed that such a mark of inequality could be permanent. Nor is anyone disposed to moralise overmuch about Germany's repeated breaches of the Treaty of Versailles.'[4] *The Times* found it the moment 'not to despair, but to rebuild' (March 9). 'A clear understanding with Germany' it was saying the following July, 'would not solve all the problems of the world, but it would be a strong foundation

---

[1] A. C. Johnson, *Viscount Halifax* (London, 1941), pp. 392–6; G. M. Young, *Baldwin*, p. 222.

[2] L. B. Namier, *Europe in Decay: a study in disintegration, 1936–1940* (London, 1950), pp. 18–25.

[3] 309 H.C. Deb., 5 s., 1812.   [4] *Spectator*, March 13, 1936.

on which to build'; disregarding the fact that an understanding
with Germany (if it could be trusted) meant the abandonment of
central Europe, the abandonment of France, the helplessness of the
British empire.[1]

Thus negotiation replaced action. Eden and Lord Halifax went
to Paris on March 9 (Halifax's influence in foreign policy was in
the ascendant, and it was on the side of compromise). They resisted the French desire to resort to sanctions; instead they proposed that Germany's breach of treaties be submitted to the
League, and that the Council of the League meet in London. To
London Flandin came on March 11. He saw Churchill, and explained that he was going to demand that Great Britain mobilise
her forces at once; the powers of the Little Entente were ready to
do as much. Churchill and his friends did their best to reinforce
him; but Neville Chamberlain told him that public opinion would
not support any kind of sanctions.[2] Baldwin told him as much: 'If
there is even one chance in a hundred that war would follow from
your police operation I have not the right to commit England.'[3]

This was the cue for what followed. The Council of the League
did, it is true, condemn Germany as guilty of a breach of her
obligations on March 19. On the same day the Locarno powers
(France, Belgium and, incongruously, Italy) submitted proposals
to Germany through Ribbentrop, whom Hitler had sent as his
representative to London. Would Germany submit its doubts
about the Franco-Russian treaty to the Hague court? Would it
limit its forces and refrain from making fortifications in the Rhineland pending negotiations over Germany's offers? Nothing happened, beyond more talks between Eden and the plausible Ribbentrop. On March 31 Germany submitted counter-proposals. The
French were dissatisfied, but agreed that Britain should try to get
the proposals elucidated in a questionnaire, which was sent to
Berlin on May 7: what were 'genuine treaties' to Germany? What
parts of the Treaty of Versailles would she observe? Would she
recognise the existing 'political and territorial status of Europe'
except as modified by free negotiation in the future? Would she
extend her offer of non-aggression pacts to Russia, Latvia and
Esthonia? The German government was affronted by such sus-

---

[1] *History of The Times*, IV, ii, 899–903; *The Times*, July 6, 1936.
[2] K. Feiling, *Neville Chamberlain*, p. 279.
[3] W. S. Churchill, *Gathering Storm*, pp. 175–8 (quoting Flandin, p. 177). Cf. Hugh
Dalton in parliament, March 26, 1936, who declared 'bluntly and frankly' that public
opinion, especially in the Labour party, would not tolerate military sanctions, or even
economic sanctions, to put German troops out of the Rhineland (310 H.C. Deb., 5 s.,
1454).

piciousness; it deigned no reply. By the summer there were other distractions: the ending of sanctions against Italy, the beginning of civil war in Spain. Hitler had got safely away with his swag, and without even making new paper agreements. On January 30, 1937, he could announce that 'the period of so-called surprises is now over'.[1]

By the same token, however, a new era had begun: one in which the British people began to face the imminence of war. Churchill has recorded that he was conscious of the new atmosphere when he returned to England from a holiday in January 1936. The Liberal and Labour parties and the people represented by the vote in the Peace Ballot 'were now prepared to contemplate war against Fascist or Nazi tyranny'.[2] This attitude can be illustrated from the Conservative and socialist points of view in the *Spectator* and *New Statesman*. It had three characteristics: there was talk of war; there was always a saving parenthesis; there was always a question left begging—what to do if the advice offered did not work an improvement.

> The British public, sure that the present crisis will pass without war, remains imperturbable as it remained . . . in 1908 and again in 1912 and as it remained in the crisis of July 1914, which did end in war. . . . We cannot too explicitly state our view that without a profound modification in the Nazi regime—and there are moderate as well as revolutionary forces in the Nazi regime—there can be no peace in Europe, but only a terrified waiting for war. (*New Statesman*, March 21, 1936.)

The *Spectator*, over the issue of sanctions, remarked:

> It was once believed that he [the Englishman] would fight, in conjunction with the mass of States, for the principles embodied in the Covenant, which, if they were effectively applied, would make protracted war impossible. That can no longer be assumed.[3]

From this flowed another consequence: Britain reaffirmed its obligations toward France and Belgium under the Treaty of Locarno, and promised, in case of need, to come to their assistance and to take 'all practical measures available' to secure them 'against unprovoked aggression'. For this purpose conversations between

---

[1] The best brief accounts of the Rhineland crisis are in G. M. Gathorne-Hardy, *Short History of International Affairs*, pp. 415–21; R. W. Seton-Watson, *Britain and the Dictators*, pp. 247–70; J. W. Wheeler-Bennett, *Munich*, pp. 218–25, 252–4. A longer account is in the *Survey of International Affairs* for 1936.

[2] W. S. Churchill, *Gathering Storm*, p. 169.

[3] 'Sanctions and After', *Spectator*, June 19, 1936.

the general staffs were begun (on Eden's insistence), though they lasted only three days. These arrangements grew out of the proposals made by the British, French and Belgian governments in London on March 19 which included remonstrances to Germany and agreements on matters to be submitted to the League. They can hardly be described as an Anglo-French military alliance, and were embodied only in letters exchanged between Eden and the French and Belgian ambassadors. Moreover, Belgium's subsequent decision to revert to the status of a neutral (recognised by an Anglo-French declaration of April 24, 1937) reduced France's security by leaving the Franco-Belgian border (which was unfortified) quite unprotected by any joint arrangements for defence. 1914 might come again.[1]

Eden pronounced the funeral oration on the crisis in the debate in parliament on March 26. Britain was a guarantor of Locarno, and would support France and Belgium if they were attacked; he was not going to be the first Foreign Secretary to go back on a British signature. The government's objectives were to avert war, to create the conditions for negotiation, to strengthen collective security. 'I assure the House that it is the appeasement of Europe as a whole that we have constantly before us.'[2]

During the 'loaded pause' (as Churchill has felicitously called it) which followed the reoccupation of the Rhineland Britain began to rearm more vigorously though still without full conviction. The new programme, foreshadowed during the election campaign, was announced, just before Hitler's *coup*, in a White Paper published on March 3, 1936, and owed much to Chamberlain's persistence. The army, which was below the strength of 1914, was to be modernised and four new battalions added, and the Territorial Army was to be reconditioned. In the navy two new battleships and one aircraft carrier would be laid down, existing battleships modernised, and the number of cruisers brought up to seventy (the navy at the time had fifteen battleships and fifty-one cruisers). The first-line strength of the air force for home defence, which under existing programmes was to rise to 1500 planes, would be increased to 1750 planes, and twelve more squadrons would be distributed along the empire's defences. The country's capacity for the production of war goods would be increased by orders and financial

---

[1] *Text of Proposals . . . of Belgium, France, United Kingdom . . . London, March 19, 1936* (Cmd. 5134: 1936), and *Correspondence* [of Eden] *with the Belgian and French Ambassadors . . . London, April 1, 1936* (Cmd. 5149: 1936); L. B. Namier, *Europe in Decay*, pp. 21–2.

[2] 310 H.C. Deb., 5 s., 1435–49.

aid to companies not normally engaged in the manufacture of munitions; in this way companies would be helped to expand their plants and to equip themselves for a quick change-over to war production when necessary.[1]

The Labour opposition resisted this new programme when it was debated on March 9. Labour members were facing an old dilemma: they wanted collective security but advocated disarmament and deplored an arms race; they recognised the dangers in the world, but distrusted the government's foreign policy and criticised its past record. Attlee bid the government work to remove the causes of war through the reform of the world's economic system, and condemned its proposals because they were not designed to support collective security but were rather a 'going back to nationalism and isolation, which cannot give us peace or security but merely leads us on to world war'.[2]

Outside parliament there were efforts to bring the Labour party to a more realistic attitude towards rearmament. Hugh Dalton on the national executive, and Bevin in the National Council of Labour, were active in this cause. Nevertheless, at the party's annual conference at Edinburgh, in October 1936, the issue remained shrouded in a fog of words. The official resolution admitted the need of defence forces 'such as are consistent with our country's responsibility as a member of the League of Nations', but rejected 'a purely competitive armament policy'. The executive was pressed to say whether it meant to continue opposing rearmament; but Dalton would go no further than to declare that Labour could not logically support 'unilateral non-rearmament' while other powers were rearming. The resolution was passed, but it had no meaning; and the parliamentary party, left uninstructed, followed its own inclination by opposing rearmament for several months longer. Such an attitude was a godsend to the government, since it gave it a specious excuse for its evasions and half-measures, despite its large majority and its responsibility for leadership.[3]

One weakness of the government's programme was the arrangements for co-ordinating the demands of the three services. Instead of a Ministry of Supply, which had been proposed as far back as July 1935, there was nothing but a series of committees. Some appointment was, however, promised, and both Churchill and Hoare were considered to be strong candidates for it. Baldwin

---

[1] *Statement relating to defence*, Cmd. 5107 (1936).
[2] 309 H.C. Deb., 5 s., 1853, 2019.
[3] G. D. H. Cole, *History of the Labour Party*, pp. 322–6; F. Williams, *Bevin*, pp. 199–202; *Report of the Annual Conference of the Labour Party, 1936*, pp. 181–4.

wanted to move Neville Chamberlain to the new post, and replace him as Chancellor of the Exchequer by Austen Chamberlain, the party's most influential member outside the Cabinet. Neville Chamberlain refused.[1] The appointment of any other strong man raised awkward problems of party tactics; hence, after a month's dallying, Baldwin decided on a nonentity, and announced to a startled public on March 13, 1936, that the 'Minister for the Co-ordination of Defence'—in itself a significant title—would be Sir Thomas Inskip, the Attorney-General; of whom even the *Annual Register* recorded that his abilities 'had never been regarded as more than mediocre, nor could he lay claim to any great administrative experience'.[2] Other comments were more pungent: Churchill's (if it was his), that 'Baldwin had to find a man of inferior ability to himself and this Herculean task must require time for its accomplishment';[3] and the saying in the lobbies that there had been no appointment like it since Caligula made his horse a consul.[4] Perhaps, for a position which involved chiefly being chairman of a number of committees, the appointment had its merits. It was typical of Baldwin: the soft path, the low tone, the reluctance to decide or to lead.

Criticism of the government's efforts continued, and Baldwin's leadership, never secure for long, was under scrutiny during the summer. The malcontents, if their alarm over the country's defences entitled them to that name, included Churchill, Amery, Austen Chamberlain, Sir Robert Horne, Lord Lloyd, Lord Londonderry, Lord Salisbury, Sir Edward Grigg, Lord Winterton (an Irish peer whose long service in the Commons gave him great prestige). The names recall the Coalition Conservatives of 1922; but if their bearers had any thought of storming the citadel of the Cabinet or displacing the Prime Minister they allowed themselves to be easily satisfied by going as a deputation to Baldwin on July 28 to warn him of the need for greater efforts in rearmament.[5] Their alarm persisted, however, as was shown by Churchill's criticism of the government's delays in the debate on November 12 which produced Baldwin's speech of 'appalling frankness'. All of which was insufficient to disturb the Prime Minister, and Neville Chamberlain's presumptive succession to his office. The indepen-

[1] K. Feiling, *Neville Chamberlain*, pp. 278–9; W. S. Churchill, *Gathering Storm*, p. 179.
[2] *Annual Register, 1936*, p. 16.   [3] *History of The Times*, IV, ii, 902.
[4] 'Cato', *Guilty Men* (London, 1940), p. 76.
[5] K. Feiling, *Neville Chamberlain*, p. 285; W. S. Churchill, *Gathering Storm*, pp. 204–7.

dents lost a distinguished member when Austen Chamberlain died in March 1937.

In these circumstances, the pace of rearmament was not forced. In 1935–36 defence expenditures were £137 millions. For 1936–37 the defence estimates were £158 millions, actual expenditures £186 millions.[1] Chamberlain's Budget for this year estimated total expenditures at £797,897,000 as compared with a budget of £729 millions for 1935; the necessary increase in revenue was found by raising income tax from 4s. 6d. to 4s. 9d. in the £, putting 2d. a pound on tea, and impropriating the Road Fund's £5¼ millions. Germany at the time was estimated to be spending £1000 millions a year on arms. In February 1937 the government asked for powers to borrow (and to use budget surpluses) up to £400 millions for defence expenditures in the next five years; a White Paper issued at the same time mentioned possible expenditures of as much as £1500 millions during the five years. Despite Labour's opposition both to the use of loans for defence when profiteering and waste were rife and to the purposes of the programme the necessary measure was approved.

Two months later came Chamberlain's last Budget, opened on April 20. This time total expenditures were estimated at £862,848,000, and expenditures on defence (apart from what was covered by borrowing) at £198 millions. Income tax was again increased, to 5s. in the £; but to everyone's surprise Chamberlain proposed to find some of the money by a new tax, which he called the National Defence Contribution (N.D.C.), on business profits, graduated according to the growth of profits during recent years, which might, he argued, be ascribed partly to rearmament and to the government's work in promoting recovery. The tax could be calculated either on the firm's capital, or on the basis of average profits during 1933, 1934, 1935. A howl of rage greeted this proposal. Stock exchange values slumped, the City and business organisations were up in arms, and most Conservatives were aghast at what seemed a socialist measure, and an inquisitorial one. Chamberlain, who thought he had 'risked the Premiership' by it, stuck to his guns, and though making concessions defended

---

[1] W. A. Morton, *British Finance, 1930–1940*, p. 286, gives the following figures:

Defence expenditures

Year (ending March 31)	(£ millions)	Per cent of Budget
1932–33	103	12·9
1933–34	107·9	14·9
1934–35	114	15·5
1935–36	137	17·7
1936–37	186·7	22·4

the principle of the N.D.C. In the end, however, he and his successor as Chancellor, Sir John Simon, had to give way, and a straight 5 per cent tax on business profits—which in itself would probably have been intolerable to business before the scare over N.D.C.—was imposed instead.[1]

9. THE MOBILISATION OF THE LEFT: THE SPANISH CIVIL WAR

Meanwhile there had been another change of scene on the international stage; the setting was now Spain. Neither the aggressions of Hitler's Germany and its anti-Jewish atrocities nor Italian barbarities in Abyssinia roused the passions of Liberals and Labour in Great Britain as did that event which might have seemed least likely to do so, the civil war which broke out in Spain in July 1936. The Spanish republic created after King Alfonso's flight in 1931 had had an uneasy history. In the general election of February 1936 the right-wing parties won a small popular majority but were in a minority in the Cortes; the new government was a coalition of liberal republicans, supported by, but not including, the socialists, anarchists and the orthodox and Trotskyite factions of Communists. The parties of the right took alarm at disorder for which both sides were responsible: murders by terrorist gangs, attacks on churches and clergy, strikes, seizures of land. A *coup d'état* planned by army leaders and right-wing politicians, was accelerated by the murder of one of the latter, Calvo Sotelo, on July 13. The first detachments of Moors and foreign legionaires crossed from Morocco to the mainland on July 19, when military revolts occurred in Seville and Cadiz, in Barcelona, and in some of the provinces, including Toledo, Saragossa, Navarre. The leader was General Francisco Franco, who was flown from the Canary Islands to Morocco in a British plane procured at short notice by the right-wing English journalist, Douglas Jerrold.

The attempted *coup* failed. Franco's followers, supported by the land-owning and commercial classes, the church, the monarchists, and part of the army and navy, soon controlled much of northern and western Spain, and set up a nationalist government at Burgos. The constitutional government (the 'loyalists' or republicans), supported by a hastily-raised militia, held Madrid and central and eastern Spain, including Valencia and Barcelona, and the territories

---

[1] K. Feiling, *Neville Chamberlain*, p. 292; *Annual Register*, 1937, pp. 11–15, 35–8, 49–52; E. Davies, *National Capitalism*, pp. 106–12.

of the Basques and the Asturias in the north. The composition of the government underwent several changes. In September, with Largo Caballero, a socialist, as Prime Minister, it included republicans, socialists, Basque nationalists, and two Communists in lesser cabinet posts.

The Spaniards were not, however, allowed to fight it out alone. The civil war was the fascist powers' dress rehearsal for a larger war, and might easily have become that war. The friends of the nationalists represented it as a holy war of order against Communism and irreligion; the friends of the republicans as a struggle for democracy against fascism and dictatorship. Mussolini had promised help to monarchist leaders as far back as March 1934; several hundred German Nazis, storm troopers and technicians, had been in the country, as 'tourists' or commercial travellers, for many months. Italian and German planes—transports, bombers, fighters—began to reach nationalist territory as soon as the revolt began, manned by their own pilots and mechanics. Aid to the republicans began to arrive in September; foreign volunteers, soon formed into the International Brigade, and followed at the end of October by Russian planes, tanks and arms. Germany countered by sending more planes and arms to the nationalists, and also 'volunteers'; Mussolini, with even less pretence of disguise, sent two divisions of the Italian army. By March 1937 there were 80,000 Italians and 30,000 Germans serving the nationalists. There was this difference between the aid which the two sides received: most of the foreigners fighting for the nationalists were present under orders; the republican volunteers came freely, men from Great Britain and the United States and France, anti-fascist refugees from Germany and Italy.

The war began with rapid gains of territory by the nationalists, but soon became a stalemate. Madrid, on the edge of republican territory, was expected to fall to the nationalists in November 1936; in anticipation of which Germany and Italy gave official recognition to the nationalist government on November 18. But Madrid held out, against air raids and bombardment and Franco's 'fifth column', until the end of the war in 1939. In 1937, however, the nationalists began closing in on republican territory; Malaga fell in February, the last of the strongholds of the Asturians and the Basques in the summer—victories for which Mussolini openly sent congratulatory telegrams to his troops.

The first reaction of the British government—and of all shades of British opinion—to the outbreak of the civil war was one of neutrality; and the policy of non-intervention was born. The nationalists were receiving German and Italian help; the republicans appealed to France for supplies. There was danger that the war might spread and become international. In France the Popular Front government under Léon Blum had only recently been formed (on June 4) and was sympathetic to the republicans; but the country was confused and divided by stay-in strikes, Communist violence, and the disorder threatened by fascist organisations such as the *Croix de feu*. Blum himself favoured sending help to the republicans, but his own cabinet was divided and the British government discouraging;[1] hence he proposed, on August 1, 1936, that all countries should adopt a policy of neutrality or non-intervention. Britain, Germany, Italy, Russia and other powers concurred, an agreement was signed at the end of August, and the Non-Intervention Committee, which was to enforce it, held its first meeting in London on September 9. The export of war goods to Spain was suspended—by Great Britain as early as August 19.

From the first the non-intervention policy was unfortunate, and its early popularity soon disappeared as its one-sidedness, to the advantage of the nationalists, became clear, and the savagery with which the war was fought banished all sentiments of neutrality about it. Non-intervention hastened the erosion of peace and collective security in Europe. It evaded the League of Nations; it exalted the dictators both in prestige and in power. Its strategic implications were such that the Conservatives seemed to be surrendering their cherished empire to the policy; for nationalist Spain, in league with Italy (which early in the war came to be in virtual occupation of Majorca), could weaken Britain's advantage in Gibraltar and threaten her life-line through the Mediterranean. Yet what was the alternative? Civil war in France, general war in Europe, divided into two camps all too simply identified as fascist and Communist. In 1936 few people accepted war as inevitable. Non-intervention at least postponed it.[2] As such, it was approved (though not without opposition) by the Labour party at the Edinburgh conference early in October 1936, with the proviso that non-intervention was made effective on both sides.[3] It never was;

[1] J. W. Wheeler-Bennett, *Munich*, p. 260.
[2] Two men as different as Winston Churchill and Professor R. W. Seton-Watson supported non-intervention: *Gathering Storm*, p. 192; *Britain and the Dictators*, p. 284. Cf. *New Statesman*, August 8, 1936.
[3] See the debate, and especially the speeches in opposition of Sir Charles Trevelyan, Christopher Addison, William Dobbie, M.P., P. J. Noel-Baker, and Aneurin Bevan, in *Report of the Annual Conference of the Labour Party, 1936*, pp. 169–81.

but as with earlier policies, once begun it became harder and harder to reverse; it was the dictators' exquisite torture to force their victims to go on throwing good money after bad in a vain effort to prevent the loss of all.

Yet by the end of October the failure of non-intervention was becoming clear. Russia complained of violations to the Non-Intervention Committee on October 7, and on the 23rd announced that she would send help to the republic. The committee's response was a plan for the supervision of the importation of war goods by sea or overland. In parliament the Labour party changed to opposition to non-intervention in a debate on October 29: the policy was not bringing fair play, but an advantage to the nationalists whose victory would be a dangerous precedent, an encouragement to underground aggression and intervention elsewhere. Had the revolt been one against a fascist government by a popular front, 'would anybody have suggested the policy of non-intervention'?[1] The government stuck to its policy; at the end of November it decided, after some deliberation, not to grant belligerent rights to both sides; at the same time it banned the carriage of war goods from foreign to Spanish ports in British ships.

During 1937, the British government struggled valiantly to keep in being the fiction if not the fact of non-intervention by all the powers. At the beginning of January it attempted to safeguard Britain's strategic interests by the unhappily-named 'Gentleman's Agreement' which was signed in Rome on the 2nd by British and Italian representatives, by which both countries disclaimed any intentions of altering the *status quo* in the Mediterranean and promised to discourage unfriendly activities, including propaganda. Nothing was said, however, about 'volunteers', who continued to arrive in large numbers until March, especially from Italy and Germany. The British government decided in January to forbid, under the Foreign Enlistment Act, the recruiting of British subjects for service in Spain (in effect, republican Spain).

On March 8, after lengthy negotiations, the Non-Intervention Committee's scheme of enforcement was adopted and on April 19 it went into effect. Foreign troops were to be withdrawn. The French, Portuguese and Gibraltar borders were to be watched by teams of international observers; merchant ships bound for Spain were to take observers on board; and the Spanish coasts were to be patrolled: in the Mediterranean by the German and Italian

[1] Arthur Greenwood in parliament, October 29, 1936; 316 H.C. Deb., 5 s., 56.

navies, in the Atlantic by the British and French. There were loopholes: the bringing in of men and supplies by air and in naval vessels was not affected; and the Portuguese coast was not patrolled, though Portugal was openly supporting the nationalist government.

The lull which this offered did not endure. Germany and Italy made it clear, by their obstruction in the committee, that they had no intention of withdrawing their troops until Franco's victory was certain. British merchant ships proceeding to Spain continued to suffer from piratical attacks from 'unknown' (i.e. Italian) submarines; one, the *Mary Llewellyn*, attempted to run the nationalist blockade of Bilbao, unprotected by the British navy, and won, from its cargo, the immortal name of 'Potato Jones' for its captain. Questions in parliament brought the assurance of the navy's protection to British merchantmen outside the three-mile limit and several ships thereafter reached Bilbao (which was still in the hands of the republicans).[1] On May 29 the German battleship *Deutschland*, part of the naval patrol, was bombed by republican planes. In retaliation, the helpless town of Almeria, in republican territory, was bombarded by German warships. Germany demanded that in future the ships of other patrolling powers should help any patrol ship under attack. On June 19 it claimed that the cruiser *Leipsig* had been attacked, and asked for support in a counter-demonstration; the British and French governments, sceptical of the facts, refused, whereupon Germany and Italy withdrew their patrols and Portugal stopped the work of the patrols on its land border. Non-intervention was thus in suspended animation (kept alive but unconscious by procrastinating negotiations) during the summer of 1937, and acts of piracy occurred once more, until a new British initiative brought a temporary improvement in September. A conference of Mediterranean powers was held at Nyon; by an agreement made then, and supplemented by a separate agreement with Italy, the naval patrols were restored. Piracy declined.[2]

The more doggedly the government stuck to non-intervention, the more passionate became a large part of the public for intervention on the side of the republicans. The air was full of reports of atrocities: in the dispatches of newspaper correspondents, in

---

[1] 322 H.C. Deb., 5 s., 1402–15 (April 19, 1937).
[2] Brief accounts of the history of non-intervention in G. M. Gathorne-Hardy, *Short History of International Affairs*, pp. 426–39; R. W. Seton-Watson, pp. 384–401; *Annual Register* for 1936 and 1937. A longer account is in the *Survey of International Affairs, 1937*, vol. II.

letters and meetings addressed by volunteers, in books and pamphlets in abundance. In republican territory churches were fired upon and burned, priests and nuns murdered, prisons broken into by mobs and prisoners murdered, citizens shot in the streets or executed by decree of summary courts. The brutality of the nationalists seemed worse because more deliberate; thousands of prisoners—soldiers and civilians—were shot after the capture of each republican town; the capture of every village meant the lining-up of prisoners, who were mown down by machine guns after they had dug their common trench-grave. The policy was one of terror: to end opposition behind the lines once the country had been conquered. *The Times*, neutral in the struggle, condemned the 'irresponsible butchery' on the republican side, but declared that the 'ruthless cruelty' of the nationalists 'has equalled, if indeed it has not surpassed, the worst excesses perpetrated by the other side.'[1] Perhaps the greatest horror excited by the nationalists was over the obliteration by bombing of the Basque town of Guernica on April 26, 1937—a place of 6000 inhabitants, of no military significance.[2]

Such events, and the reports of them, produced a crisis of opinion in Great Britain; it is this which gives the Spanish civil war its tremendous importance in British history in the late thirties. It widened existing divisions, between government and opposition, between right and left (terms hardly used in the political sense in England before this); it brought bitterness and class-consciousness into foreign policy, and so into domestic policies, to an extent unknown before. Division of opinion over the war in newspapers and pamphlets reflected and enlarged the wider cleavage.[3] It led to a changing of sides over peace and war. The left became war-minded: the Spanish civil war mobilised the non-trade-union sections of the Labour movement as Hitler's brutalities had already begun to mobilise the trade unions. The more this happened, the more the government moved away from war; peace with the

---

[1] *The Times*, September 8, 1936.

[2] Duchess of Atholl, *Searchlight on Spain* (Penguin Books, London, 1938), pp. 94–114, 127–34, 256–70, gives a full account of the atrocities, with citation of authorities; cf. R. W. Seton-Watson, pp. 379–82. For the bland denials of nationalist atrocities by nationalist sympathisers see Douglas Jerrold, *Georgian Adventure*, pp. 369–417. For Guernica see Duchess of Atholl, pp. 187–92; *History of The Times*, IV, ii, 907; and G. L. Steer's book, *The Tree of Gernika* (1938).

[3] *The Times* and *Daily Telegraph* were neutral, and their reporters gave frank accounts of both sides. The *Morning Post*, *Daily Mail*, *Daily Sketch* and *Observer* supported the nationalists, the *News Chronicle*, and to a less extent the *Daily Herald*, *Daily Express* and *Daily Mirror*, the republicans (P. Maillaud, *English Way*, p. 136; R. Graves and A. Hodge, *Long Week-end*, p. 336).

U

dictators, at almost any price, seemed to be its policy. Non-intervention and pacifism crossed over from the opposition to the government: 'no war' became the slogan, not of the left, but of the right.[1] This increased the disunity of the country for a time, but helped to bring a united country into the war for its own survival in 1939.

The intrusion of the spirit of class-warfare into politics became more obvious month by month. From this time the government's policies were attacked not only as misguided and dangerous, but as sinister and evil, inspired by a liking of the dictators. That this was unjust is beside the point. That the government's policies were the product of class-bias was alleged by other observers than socialists, for example by Eleanor Rathbone, Independent M.P. of Liberal sympathies, and even before the Spanish war began.[2] Open support of the Spanish nationalists was certainly confined to the upper classes and to Conservatives. The *New Statesman* charac-teristically proclaimed the significance in an article, 'Trenches across Europe', seeing

> . . . the trench-lines drawn, that had divided us unperceived. They mean war, though no herald has declared it. The democracies face the dictatorships—it is a war of ideas. The workers face the owners—it is a war of classes.[3]

Such feelings were largely outside the parties; and the fact is important. The parties did not seem, to the general public, to rise to the challenge which the Spanish civil war threw down. The effect of the war was, therefore, not only to mobilise opinion but to mobilise it outside the parties. It transformed public opinion because it awoke people to political consciousness who had been indifferent to politics before; and this consciousness found ex-pression in new semi-political organisations, in intense activity by amateurs in politics. It was mainly, but by no means exclusively, on the left.

This amateur activity in politics is evident first of all in the books and pamphlets and organisations which the war brought forth. The Duchess of Atholl cites some fifty or more in *Search-*

<hr />

[1] P. Maillaud, *English Way*, pp. 134–6.

[2] M. D. Stocks, *Eleanor Rathbone* (London, 1949), p. 240; correspondence and articles in *New Statesman*, July 11, 18, 25, 1936; R. Graves and A. Hodge, *Long Week-end*, p. 335. Eleanor Rathbone (1872–1946), member of a prominent and civic-minded Liverpool family, M.P., 1929–46, was a lifelong champion of family allowances and a fighter in parliament for the underdog (e.g. for the refugees from fascism, for the right of Indian women to the franchise).

[3] *New Statesman*, August 1, 1936.

light on Spain, published in the middle of 1938; these divide roughly equally between pro-republican and pro-nationalist works, and include some writings by Americans, Frenchmen and Spaniards. Among English authors writing on the nationalist side were Douglas Jerrold and Arnold Lunn (two leading Roman Catholics), Arthur Bryant, a Conservative historian, Sir Henry Page Croft, a Tory protectionist, Francis Yeats-Brown, author of *Bengal Lancer*; Sir Arnold Wilson, Conservative M.P., wrote an introduction to the nationalists' 'official report' on Communist atrocities.[1] The Friends of Nationalist Spain was the principal pro-nationalist organisation.[2] On the other side were several *ad hoc* bodies which were, in effect, 'popular fronts' drawing in members of all parties: the Friends of Spain, the London Committee for Spanish Medical Aid, the National Joint Committee for Spanish Relief, the Basque Children's Committee (which supervised the evacuation of hundreds of Basque refugee children to England; many more went to France), and the Committee of Inquiry into Breaches of International Law relating to Intervention in Spain. In addition, there were the British volunteers in the International Brigade, in whose organisation the Communist Party of Great Britain was active.

It was, however, not only the left wing of the Labour movement and the Communists who were aroused by the war; more significant was the support of the republicans by Liberals and Conservatives.[3] Many members of parliament paid unofficial visits to republican Spain. Among these visits, one deserves notice as revealing the diverse sources of sympathy for the republic: the party consisted of Eleanor Rathbone, the Duchess of Atholl, Ellen Wilkinson, and Dame Rachel Crowdy—the first three were M.P.'s, independent Liberal, Conservative, Labour, Dame Rachel,

---

[1] In addition to the works cited by the Duchess of Atholl there were several others which appeared later. Two give a picture of the harshness of the Communists towards their rivals in the republican forces in Spain: Fenner Brockway, *Inside the Left*, pp. 294–302; Fred Copeman, *Reason in Revolt* (London, 1948).

[2] British business interests tended to favour the nationalists; exports of iron ore and sherry continued from nationalist territory, and the British-owned Rio Tinto Mining Company was permitted to operate under its British staff, though on very disadvantageous financial conditions: J. R. Hubbard, 'How Franco financed his war', *Journal of Modern History*, December 1953.

[3] A letter protesting against the misrepresentation of the war in the press as one fought against a Bolshevist government rather than a Liberal-democratic government was signed by novelists, historians, poets, artists of all parties and of none: included were Norman Angell, Hewlett Johnson (the 'Red' dean of Canterbury), Gilbert Murray, Lady Rhondda, R. H. Tawney, H. G. Wells, Ralph Vaughan Williams, Virginia Woolf. *New Statesman*, August 22, 1936.

a leader of the nursing profession, had been a member of the League of Nations' secretariat.[1]

Similar groupings could be found elsewhere, not so much from zeal about the Spanish war as from alarm at the weakness of Britain's defences and the impotence of the League. Churchill's 'Arms and the Covenant' meeting in the Albert Hall in December 1936, was an impressive 'united front', since the sturdy foe of Labour had as his chairman Walter Citrine, secretary of the T.U.C., and in his audience right-wing Tories, Liberals, and representatives of the trade unions and the League of Nations.[2] Another united front of a sort was that of the 'Next Five Years Group', which included Sir Arthur Salter and Harold Macmillan, Liberals and National Labour men, and such stalwarts of the T.U.C. as Arthur Pugh and John Bromley.[3] Another was the People's Front Propaganda Committee, founded by J. T. Murphy (ex-Communist, ex-member of the Socialist League) and others, and enlisting the support of Eleanor Rathbone, Robert Boothby (Conservative), Richard Acland (Liberal), G. D. H. Cole and John Strachey (Labour); it held several large meetings in London in its campaign for an alternative government.[4]

By contrast, attempts to promote a 'popular front' in a formal sense came to nothing; though informally the Left Book Club came close to being one, and certainly prepared the way, as did the other left-wing activities of these years, for the Labour party's success in 1945. The reason was simple: the initiative for a popular front (or rather, for a more limited 'united front' of working-class parties) came from the Communists and as such was opposed by the Labour party. The policy of the Comintern had favoured the united front since 1933, just as the Soviet government had embarked on an internationalist foreign policy, signified by Russia's entry into the League of Nations and the appointment of Litvinov as commisar for foreign affairs. Earlier attempts to make out of this a united front had failed;[5] in 1935 the Communist party tried a new tack: it applied once more for affiliation with the Labour party. As on earlier occasions, the application was rejected by the national executive, and confirmed at the Labour party's conference at Edinburgh in 1936, when another motion in support of the

---

[1] The Duchess of Atholl, a Scotswoman of great distinction and public service, daughter of Sir James Ramsay of Banff, the historian, was made a Dame of the British Empire in 1918 and was Conservative M.P. for Kinross and West Perth from 1923 to 1938.

[2] W. S. Churchill, *Gathering Storm*, pp. 195–6.

[3] G. D. H. Cole, *History of the Labour party*, p. 339; see above, chapter 8, p. 463.

[4] J. T. Murphy, *New Horizons*, p. 319.   [5] See above, p. 548.

formation of a united front was also rejected. What enthusiasm existed for the united front remained outside the Labour party——in Left Book Club circles, in *Reynolds' News*, the modernised and successful Sunday paper owned by the Co-operative movement.[1]

The next attempt to form a united front was the Unity Campaign, which was launched at a meeting in the Free Trade Hall, Manchester, on January 24, 1937. The initiative on this occasion came from Cripps and the Socialist League; and resulted in long and difficult negotiations in Cripps' chambers in the Middle Temple between the Socialist League, represented by Cripps and William Mellor, the I.L.P. (Brockway and Maxton), and the Communist party (Harry Pollitt and Palme Dutt).[2] A 'Unity Manifesto' was published: it asked for 'Unity in the struggle against Fascism, Reaction and War, and against the National Government', and advocated 'the return of a Labour Government, as the next stage in the advance to working-class power'. The manifesto was not mealy-mouthed; a 'fighting programme of mass struggle' was demanded, 'class-collaboration' condemned, rearmament opposed.[3] The signatures included Cripps, Mellor, Pollitt, Gallacher, Brockway, Maxton, F. W. Jowett, Brailsford, Strachey, and some trade-union leaders.

The Labour party was up in arms at once. The Unity Campaign aroused much enthusiasm, in mass meetings in many of the large cities, in meetings of local branches of trade unions and the Labour party. Unimpressed, the party executive damned such collaboration with the Communists in a circular, 'Party Loyalty'. On January 27 it expelled the Socialist League (which was itself divided over the issue) from the party. The party, it declared, 'calls for a real, and not a sham unity. The real United Front is that of the Socialist, Trade Union, and Co-operative Movements.' The Socialist League countered by dissolving itself in March, leaving members of the Labour party free to support the Unity Campaign as individuals. The executive replied by threatening to expel members who did so (particularly by appearing on Unity Campaign platforms), and followed this by excommunicating a committee of party members which was continuing to support the campaign. At this point the I.L.P. and the Communist party decided to withdraw, and the campaign collapsed. Cripps and

[1] G. D. H. Cole, *History of the Labour Party*, pp. 339–41; A. Hutt, *Postwar History of the British Working Class*, pp. 261–3, 283–6.
[2] F. Brockway, *Inside the Left*, pp. 264–8.
[3] G. D. H. Cole, p. 347; full text in *The Times*, January 18, 1937.

Professor Laski questioned the rightness of these tactics at the party's annual conference at Bournemouth in October 1937; but the executive, defended by Clynes and Morrison, was vindicated by an overwhelming vote. In the ensuing election of members of the executive, however, three supporters of the Unity Campaign, Cripps, Laski and D. N. Pritt, were elected.[1] The movement appeared again later, in the 'Popular Front' campaign of 1938-39. And the Socialist League left the world of Labour with a new weekly, *Tribune*, founded (as a separate venture) by Cripps, Bevan, Mellor, Ellen Wilkinson, G. R. Strauss in 1937.

10. A MESSAGE FROM HIS MAJESTY

Amid these storms the British people passed through a sudden tempest, though one which was quickly over, when Edward VIII abdicated the throne in December 1936, eleven months after his accession. The first bachelor of mature years to ascend the throne since William Rufus, he enjoyed the popularity which for years had been his as the youthful Prince Charming, the Prince of Wales. He had something of the nervous restlessness of the war generation, and a desire to streamline the monarchy and bring it closer to the people. Some of his innovations had caused uneasiness; putting the clocks back to standard time at Sandringham, curtailing the number of court officials and the ceremonial of court functions; his preference for his retreat near Virginia Water, Fort Belvedere or 'The Fort', to Buckingham Palace or Sandringham; his friends, his guests at dinner drawn from circles of London society hitherto rather remote from the court. No one, however, expected the young King to be a replica of the old one; many people sympathised with his love of modernity, and approved, for example, of his inauguration of 'the King's flight', the aeroplane and pilots kept for his travels by air. His first broadcast, on March 1, using the first person singular even more directly (or so it seemed) than his father, struck a new note which, except in official circles, was not unwelcome:

> I am better known to most of you as the Prince of Wales—as a man who, during the War and since, has had the opportunity of getting to know the people of nearly every country of the world, under all conditions and circumstances. And, although I now speak to you as the King, I am still that same man who has had that experience and whose constant effort it will be to continue to promote the well-being of his fellow-men.

[1] G. D. H. Cole, pp. 348-50; A. Hutt, pp. 305-7; F. Brockway, p. 269.

During the summer of 1936 the King was away for several weeks on a cruise in the Mediterranean on a private yacht, the *Nahlin*; one of the party was Mrs. Ernest Simpson, the American wife of a London stockbroker and former wife of an American naval officer. Photographs of the King and his guests inspired *Time* and some American newspapers to comment upon the King's friendship for Mrs. Simpson, which was already talked of in the United States and in London society, but of which, by a remarkable self-censorship, no mention was made in the British press until December.

The King's abdication was set in train in October—by Baldwin, who hitherto had been content to let the matter ride. What followed was the last demonstration of Baldwin's extraordinary power, the power of the old Roman 'dictator', wielded by this least masterful of modern prime ministers—on the rare occasions when he overcame his customary inertia. What he did was the more remarkable since he had appeared, since the spring, to be exhausted—a pitiable leader in parliament, and resting under doctor's orders during the summer to avert a breakdown.[1] He was spurred to action by the announcement early in October that Mrs. Simpson was seeking a divorce from her husband. The news brought on a crisis behind the scenes, though it would not have done so then had Baldwin not intervened. Baldwin asked to see the King, and did so on October 20; they had an informal talk in which Baldwin discoursed on the harm being done by the comments in the overseas press, and asked if the divorce suit could not be withdrawn. It was not, and at Ipswich, on October 27, Mrs. Simpson was awarded a decree *nisi*, leaving her free to marry again after six months. The case received no publicity (beyond the briefest notice of the fact) in the British press.

For almost six weeks the drama which ended in the abdication was enacted out of sight of the public; the news of it only broke like a thunderclap on December 2, when the crisis was almost over. Baldwin learned more of the transatlantic comment from Dawson of *The Times*, and consulted an inner circle of his Cabinet (MacDonald, Chamberlain, Halifax, Simon, Runciman) about the 'King's matter' on November 13. The King's mood was now hardening; at a second meeting with Baldwin on November 16 he said that he intended to marry Mrs. Simpson and was prepared to go. There was, of course, nothing legally preventing the sovereign from marrying the woman of his choice; yet a constitu-

[1] G. M. Young, *Baldwin*, pp. 225–7, 233.

tional crisis would arise if he did so against his Cabinet's advice, and the Cabinet's resignation, which would presumably follow, would bring the King and the monarchy into the furnace of political controversy and, what the King dreaded as much, of publicity in the press. In the negotiations behind the scenes during the next two weeks—weeks during which talk of the matter became general in the lobbies of parliament, and in society—King and Cabinet (when the full Cabinet was finally consulted) were pulling in opposite directions: the Cabinet to keep the King on the throne, but unmarried to Mrs. Simpson; the King to marry Mrs. Simpson (when she was free to marry him) and to remain King if possible, to abdicate if not. The King regarded his possible marriage as a private matter; the Cabinet ministers, expecting in the public the strong disapproval which they felt themselves at the prospect of the King marrying a woman twice divorced, did not. It was afterwards said that ministers were not sorry to see the King go, disliking his unconventional ways, alarmed at his sympathy with the unemployed. In a tour of some of the mining valleys of South Wales on November 19 he was reported to have said 'terrible, terrible, something will be done about this'. The *Daily Mail* took up the cry, and gave *The Times* the occasion for a sermon. There is no evidence, however, that the Cabinet wished to be rid of the King; rather it strove zealously to keep him, but on its own terms.[1]

Secrecy was ended, apparently by accident, on December 2 in a comment in the *Yorkshire Post* upon some remarks by the Bishop of Bradford (A. W. F. Blunt) to a diocesan conference on the King's need of God's grace for his office. The London press joined in on Thursday, December 3. Dawson released his long-prepared salvoes in *The Times*, alluding to a 'marriage incompatible with the Throne' and declaring that the nation could not afford 'the influence of the great office' to be weakened if 'private inclination were to come into open conflict with public duty and be allowed to prevail' (December 3). Newspapers generally were against the King, but the *News Chronicle* and the Beaverbrook and Rothermere papers strongly supported him.

The nation went through an agony of suspense, though it was over in a week. Many women, and many men also, respected the King's feelings and thought that he should be free to marry, like anyone else, the woman of his choice. Large crowds gathered

---

[1] A morganatic marriage was ruled out when the cabinet, after telegraphic consultation with the Dominions' prime ministers, refused to introduce the necessary legislation.

round Buckingham Palace and elsewhere shouting 'Down with Baldwin. We want the King.' Opinion generally, however, was against the King, particularly in the north, as members of parliament discovered on visiting their constituencies over the week-end. The mass of the people knew nothing until the critical week, and nothing precise then; its successive reactions were shock and bewilderment, acceptance of the *fait accompli* of abdication, resentment at the King for not sticking to his job. Deep moral feelings were touched. And in the dominions (for whose association with Great Britain the symbol of the crown was of fundamental importance) the feelings against the King seem to have been stronger than in Great Britain.[1]

There was danger in the protraction of the crisis: danger of political divisions injurious both to the government and the monarchy. Actually the King's decision to abdicate was given to Baldwin on Saturday, December 5, but it was not until the 10th that the necessary arrangements were completed and the fact announced. Baldwin, asked by Attlee in the Commons on December 3 whether 'any constitutional difficulties' had arisen, replied that it was inexpedient that he should be questioned 'at this stage'. A party of 'King's friends' was forming. Winston Churchill spoke out daily, in parliament, at the 'Arms and the Covenant' meeting on December 3, and in a public statement on December 5. He pleaded for time and patience and denounced the government for putting pressure on the King. Again and again he asked that there should be no 'irrevocable decision' before parliament had had a full statement of the issues and the opportunity to express its will. He had little support—a maximum of 90 members of parliament of all parties. Mosley and his blackshirts also supported the King—which was hardly an asset to him. The Labour party was on the side of the government; partly because its supporters tended to oppose the King's choice, partly on the strictly constitutional ground, as important to a future Labour government as to the Conservatives, that the King must accept the advice of his ministers.

On December 10, in a tense and crowded House, Baldwin handed to the Speaker of the Commons a message from His Majesty, signed by his own hand, announcing his intention to abdicate and asking that the necessary steps be immediately taken to give effect to the instrument of abdication he had signed.

[1] There is an excellent, contemporary impression of public opinion in Sir Philip Gibbs, *Ordeal in England*, pp. 94–141.

U*

Baldwin recounted the course of events in a long speech. It was the quintessence of his artistry: apparently an informal account of events, unpremeditated, told with the aid of a few notes jotted on scraps of paper, it was a masterly putting of the case for the government on the advice it had tendered to the King.[1] A Declaration of Abdication bill was introduced, passed through both Houses, and received the royal assent on December 11. Edward VIII then ceased to be King, and was succeeded by his brother, the Duke of York, as George VI. The preamble to the act mentioned that Canada, Australia, New Zealand and South Africa had assented to it.

Baldwin enjoyed a brief moment of adulation. His crumbling popularity had been repaired by a master-stroke. He had shown, as before, that in a crisis he could act with skill and decision, leaving his apparently nimbler opponents wondering just how he had outwitted them. The abdication was really the failure of his hopes; but he made it into a triumph, for himself, for the constitution, for the good sense of the people. 'If it were done, when 'tis done, then 'twere well it were done quickly.' Baldwin had made sure that it was done both quickly and smoothly, leaving the smallest possible wound on the body politic: no slight service to the state.

On the evening of the 11th, now a private citizen (soon to be made Duke of Windsor by his brother, the King) Edward gave a farewell broadcast from Windsor Castle, a speech heard round the world.

At long last I am able to say a few words of my own. I have never wanted to withhold anything, but until now it has not been constitutionally possible for me to speak. . . . I want you to understand that in making up my mind I did not forget the country or the Empire which as Prince of Wales, and lately as King, I have for twenty-five years tried to serve. But you must believe me when I tell you that I have found it impossible to carry the heavy burden of responsibility and to discharge my duties as King as *I* would wish to do without the help and support of the woman I love. . . . I now quit altogether public affairs, and I lay down my burden . . . if at any time in the future I can be found of service to his Majesty in a private station I shall not fail. And now we all have a new King. I wish him, and you, his people, happiness and prosperity with all my heart. God bless you all. God Save the King.

[1] For critical comment on Baldwin's speech (and much else concerning the abdication), see Compton Mackenzie, *Windsor Tapestry* (London, 1938), esp. pp. 508–21.

With these words, almost shouted in the high tones of one under great strain, he ended. He then drove to Portsmouth and embarked for France, and for self-imposed exile, seldom broken in the future, from his native country. He married Mrs. Simpson the following year.[1]

This latest crisis in a year of crises and reversals left singularly little mark upon the public mind. The fabric of the monarchy had been jarred but not broken—not even cracked. Things were very much as they had been; there was still a King on the throne, another George, happily married, with a gracious Queen Elizabeth, a Scotswoman of noble blood, and two handsome daughters. The courage and devotion to duty, the modesty and self-sacrifice of the King and Queen, not only endeared them quickly to their peoples, but restored to the monarchy all the strength and affection which George V had won for it.

Nor, save in one instance, did the abdication leave any mark upon the empire. The dominions assented to what had been done in London, each in its own time and its own way: Australia by resolutions in parliament, New Zealand by Order in Council, Canada by Order in Council confirmed by a bill in parliament in January, South Africa by an abdication act passed by parliament in February.[2]

Only in the Irish Free State, in the midst of the quarrel between De Valera and the National government over the land annuities and Ireland's status, was the pattern different. The opportunity was too good to be missed. The Dail was summoned hastily by telegrams sent to the members on December 10, and met at 3 p.m. on the 11th. Two bills were submitted to it by the government, pushed through by guillotine and completed by the 12th. The Constitution (Amendment No. 27) bill removed the King from the constitution, but permitted the executive council 'to avail, for the purposes of the appointment of diplomatic and consular agents and the conclusion of international agreements of any organ used as a constitutional organ for the like purposes by any of the nations

---

[1] The best accounts of the abdication are in Baldwin's speech in parliament on December 10, in 318 H.C. Deb., 5 s., 2176–87; *History of The Times*, IV, ii, 1027–48; Duke of Windsor, *A King's Story* (London, 1951; New York, 1951). See also Hector Bolitho, *King Edward VIII* (London, 1937); Compton Mackenzie, *Windsor Tapestry*; G. M. Young, *Baldwin*, chap. 24; Frank Owen and R. J. Thompson, *His was the Kingdom* (London, 1937); T. Jones, *Diary with Letters*, pp. 162–4, 280, 284, 286–97, 305-6.

[2] For details see the excellent summary in D. O'Sullivan, *The Irish Free State and its Senate*, pp. 478–80. Cf. K. C. Wheare, *The Statute of Westminster and Dominion Status* (1938), pp. 277–90; W. K. Hancock, *Survey of British Commonwealth Affairs*, I, 387–90, 616–30. See also Compton Mackenzie, *Windsor Tapestry*, pp. 493–503, 528–34.

referred to in Article 1 of this Constitution'. Thus the Irish crown survived as an 'organ'; and the Free State kept a sort of guest-membership of the Commonwealth in its pocket. The Executive Authority (External Relations) bill gave effect, for these limited, diplomatic purposes, to Edward VIII's abdication and the continuing recognition of his unnamed successor. Another link with Great Britain had been snapped. Next year the 'sovereign, democratic state' of Eire would be proclaimed.[1]

Next May the coronation of George VI took place with a brave show of pomp, not seriously marred by the unofficial strike of the London busmen for a 7½-hour day, which hampered London's transport at the time, though the tubes and trams were not affected. On May 28 Baldwin resigned, and shortly retired to the Lords as Earl Baldwin; in effect he left public life. His successor, long foreseen, was Neville Chamberlain, who was to preside over the final act of the tragedy of these years. His role was not an enviable one.

Few reputations have faded as quickly as Baldwin's. When Britain's military unpreparedness was revealed by the ordeal of war, Baldwin, living in retirement, was given much of the blame, partly because of his 'appalling frankness' speech about the general election of 1935, of which the public was reminded by *Guilty Men* in 1940.[2] This was unfair. Certainly he was not a great man, nor a master in the part of leadership in which he was strangely cast. He was also unfortunate. The India Act might have been a monument to him had fate not given it so short a life. He intended to preserve national unity and industrial peace; yet he must be held partly responsible for the general strike of 1926 and for the Trade Disputes Act. If rearmament was too slow, he shared the blame with Chamberlain and with the rest of the government—and with the nation which followed the lead he gave it. *There* is his final defence: that he was tolerated for so long.

[1] D. O'Sullivan, *Irish Free State*, pp. 481–7.
[2] Cf. A. L. Rowse, 'Reflections on Lord Baldwin' [article published in 1941] in *End of an Epoch*.

CHAPTER ELEVEN

Say not the Struggle Naught Availeth : 1937—1940

1. THE LOGIC OF APPEASEMENT

NEVILLE CHAMBERLAIN succeeded to a barren heritage. The rearming of the army and navy, the expansion of the Royal Air Force were only just beginning. The might of Germany, on the other hand, was growing great, and the pause in its aggressiveness which had followed the reoccupation of the Rhineland was unlikely to last much longer. Moreover, the three militarist powers, Germany, Italy and Japan, were now linked together: the Berlin-Rome 'axis' of November 1936 and the German-Japanese Anti-Comintern pact of 1936 were merged into a triangle on November 6, 1937. Following this, Italy left the League of Nations in December, as Germany and Japan had done long since. The peace of the world was crumbling: there was war in China, there was bitter fighting in Spain. Could the ruins be shored up and peace preserved? Chamberlain was determined to make a new attempt.

There were still three possible methods of keeping the peace (apart from the method of the pacifist); collective security through the League, an alliance of the anti-axis powers outside the League, and the appeasement of the dictators. The first was ignored by Chamberlain and not strongly advocated by his critics. In none of the crises of these latter years did the League play a part: no longer did it earn either the blessings of its friends or the curses of its enemies. 'What country in Europe today if threatened by a large Power, can rely on the League of Nations for protection?' asked Neville Chamberlain in March 1938; he answered 'None'.[1]

Alliances or arrangements with the anti-axis powers seemed no more promising. In the United States there was plenty of indignation at Nazi terrorism and Japanese aggression; but the Neutrality

---

[1] In House of Commons, March 7, 1938, quoted in J. W. Wheeler-Bennett, *Munich*, p. 32.

Act of 1935, which was replaced by a permanent measure in 1937, forbade the export of war materials to all belligerents and required countries at war to pay cash for any essential materials from the United States and to carry them away in their own ships. President Roosevelt, in a famous speech in Chicago on October 5, 1937, preached co-operation by the peace-loving nations and damned the dictators; but his hint that the United States should join in a 'quarantine' of the aggressors evoked nothing but alarmed disclaimers from the public. Soviet Russia, a member of the League and an ally of France, was another candidate for British friendship; but Chamberlain distrusted it as a 'half-Asiatic' country, unreliable in its military strength and more concerned to embroil other countries in war than to defend their liberty.[1] In these feelings he was not alone: the great purges of 1937, and particularly the decimation of Russian generals and other officers, convinced the average man of the military weakness which was also the burden of confidential reports from official observers to the government. And, in any case, the old hatred of Bolshevism was far from dead, despite the cooings of Litvinov at Geneva.

There remained France and its system of alliances in the Little Entente. Co-operation with France was, indeed, inescapable; but with Neville Chamberlain, unlike Austen Chamberlain and Henderson, it was never cordial. France, with its fussy hankerings for its own security, had spoiled the peace treaties and perverted the purposes of the League; now the same distrust would block a general pacification. What made it worse, France was no longer a strong military power, and its government, in the hands of Leon Blum and the Popular Front, was as suspect by many British Conservatives as it was by business and conservative circles in France. The stay-in strikes, the civil unrest, and the introduction of the five-day week in the time of the Popular Front all justified a lack of confidence which was not greatly moderated when Blum's government was succeeded by that of Chautemps on June 21, 1937.

How much to be preferred was the policy of appeasement, of seeking the friendship of Germany and of dividing Italy from Germany. 'The appeasement of Europe as a whole' had been Eden's object in March 1936;[2] a 'general scheme of appeasement' was Chamberlain's object two years later,[3] and was not abandoned until March 1939. In one sense it was Chamberlain's own policy,

---

[1] K. Feiling, *N. Chamberlain*, pp. 340, 347, 403.   [2] See above, chapter 10, p. 568.
[3] House of Commons, February 21, 1938, quoted in J. W. Wheeler-Bennett, *Munich*, p. 16.

and a very personal one; but it rested on illusions which were very widely shared. Chamberlain's hatred of war was passionate, his fear of its consequences shrewd. He believed, unlike the indolent but canny Baldwin,[1] that much could be accomplished by personal diplomacy in conference; that there 'must be something in common' between different peoples since 'we are all members of the human race'; that there was a human side to the dictators, which could be appealed to, especially in *tête-à-tête* discussions ('an hour or two *tête-à-tête* with Musso might be extraordinarily valuable in making plans for talks with Germany'[2]). He shared the fatal view of the times that discussion could change the nature of facts and the course of events.[3] To make a general settlement he would go very far, even though at first he was sceptical of the chances of success: 'I don't believe myself that we could purchase peace and a lasting settlement by handing over Tanganyika to the Germans, but if I did, I would not hesitate for a moment.'[4] The trouble was that such a policy, and especially when applied to other lands than Tanganyika, sacrificed Britain's real interests and ignored questions of right and wrong. It also involved negotiations with the Nazi tyrants of Germany whom so many of the British people not merely distrusted as liars but loathed as bestial persecutors of Jews and of Christians.

Yet until after Munich there was no question that appeasement was popular, despite its many critics. It had the greater part of the press behind it: in particular *The Times* (which was often ahead of the game), the *Daily Express* of Lord Beaverbrook and the *Daily Mail* of Lord Rothermere, and the fulminations of J. L. Garvin in the *Observer*. Lloyd George returned from a visit to Hitler at Berchtesgaden in September 1936 enthusiastic for Hitler's work for Germany and for his peaceable intentions[5]—though he was later undeceived. The alternative to appeasement was war—or so the critics were told; and no one advocated that. Certainly not the Labour party; nor Tory imperialist critics such as Churchill, exiled from office because of his views on India and generally distrusted as a 'warmonger'. In retrospect everyone was against appeasement; at the time not so many. One could salve one's conscience by enjoying Low's stinging cartoons and the asininities of Colonel Blimp:[6] the savage taunt against the 'empire on which the sun never sets', the picture of the 'Shiver Sisters Ballet, 1938',

[1] K. Feiling, *N. Chamberlain*, p. 301.   [2] Ibid., pp. 321, 324, 389.
[3] P. Maillaud, *English Way*, p. 141.   [4] K. Feiling, p. 300.
[5] T. Jones, *Lloyd George*, pp. 244–8; *Diary with Letters*, pp. 239–65.
[6] See *Low's Political Parade* (London, 1936) and later collections.

in which Lord Lothian, Geoffrey Dawson, Lady Astor and Garvin danced to Goebbels' baton.[1] One could complain of the 'Cliveden set' without having to produce evidence that the Astors, Lothian, Dawson and their friends really made policy at week-end parties at Cliveden. A more serious complaint was of the uncritical admiration of Nazi Germany by members of the upper class, such as Lord Londonderry.[2] The German Embassy, particularly during Ribbentrop's term as ambassador in 1936–38, was the scene of lavish parties at which many transient converts to a snobbish pro-Germanism were made.

One argument for the policy of appeasement was that the Dominions supported it. They had little chance to do otherwise: their acquiescence was an effect rather than a cause of the policy it served to excuse. Since the war, and particularly since the Chanak episode, their policy had been one of no commitments—and certainly they were not going to be bound by Britain's commitments.[3] Uninstructed as to the course of a personal and secretive diplomacy, soothed by urbane pronouncements by British leaders, they naturally opposed involvement in war and rejoiced that appeasement was keeping the threat of war at a distance.[4] If Czechoslovakia was far away from England, it was a long way farther from Canada or Australia.

Dislike of the policy of appeasement was increased by circumstances partly incidental, partly essential to it—the character and methods of Neville Chamberlain. There was a quality of 'self-sufficient obstinacy' about him;[5] and his rather forbidding features, his dark clothes, his harsh voice, above all his umbrella, made him seem more narrow and smug, and his policies more sinister, than was really the case. He did not, except during the crisis of Munich, court popularity—indeed, his acclaim at that time is a measure of the nation's temporary suspension of judgment in the shock of calamity suddenly looming ahead and as suddenly removed. Rather, he invited opposition by his impatience of criticism, and

[1] *Evening Standard*, January 3, 1938, reproduced in *History of The Times*, IV, ii, 912. For the 'Cliveden set' see particularly T. Jones, *Diary with Letters*, pp. xxxiv-xl and passim; also J. E. Wrench, *Dawson*, esp. p. 366.

[2] See his *Ourselves and Germany* (London, 1938).

[3] The Imperial Conference of May, 1937, endorsed the policy of appeasement: 'nothing would be more damaging to the hopes of international appeasement than the division, real or apparent, of the world into opposing groups': Imperial Conference, 1937, *Summary of Proceedings*, Cmd. 5482, p. 16, quoted in Nicholas Mansergh, *Survey of British Commonwealth Affairs: Problems of External Policy, 1931–1939* (Oxford, 1952), p. 89. Cf. J. E. Wrench, *Dawson*, pp. 367–9, 373–4, 430.

[4] J. W. Wheeler-Bennett, *Munich*, p. 184; *History of The Times*, IV, ii, 938, 1022.

[5] Collin Brooks, *Devil's Decade* (London, 1948), p. 78; cf. P. Maillaud, *English Way*, pp. 139–43.

his tendency to ignore parliament and to evade debate.[1] Within his Cabinet he was master, not only in giving a strong lead to his colleagues as chairman, but in keeping in close touch with their work in the departments. His was a personal government in a very different sense from Baldwin's and in some ways like that of his *bête noire*, Lloyd George. Leading decisions, when not made by Chamberlain alone, were made by an inner cabinet consisting of himself, Lord Halifax, Simon (Chancellor of the Exchequer) and Hoare (Home Secretary). Ministers, even of the inner circle, were kept in the dark about his intentions, or learned of them only through his close friend (though a minor minister) Sir Kingsley Wood.[2]

Nowhere were Chamberlain's activities more intrusive than in foreign policy. He distrusted the officials of the Foreign Office and was ready to circumvent them by his personal diplomacy, intervening not only more than Baldwin, whose indifference to foreign affairs was abnormal, but more than the usual and natural concern of the Prime Minister with foreign affairs would justify.[3] He leaned heavily on the advice of Sir Horace Wilson, a civil servant whose title was Chief Industrial Adviser to the government. Wilson, who had been Permanent Secretary in the Ministry of Labour and was adept in industrial conciliation, was advanced through J. H. Thomas' friendship and won Chamberlain's favour for his services at the Ottawa conference. Very hard-working, rigidly self-controlled, never rushed, quick to master documents, skilful in talking round difficulties, always ready to play for safety and to find the soothing formula which each party will accept in his own sense and both agree to long enough to compromise the issue—no matter how disastrously: he reinforced Chamberlain's weaknesses—his tunnel vision and his faith in talk round a table—and from the best of motives was the worst of advisers in foreign affairs. Yet Chamberlain relied on him heavily, gave him an office adjoining his own, and for three years went a walk with him daily in the park.[4]

The stage was quickly set for the new policies. One of Ribben-

[1] Marion L. Kenney, 'The role of the House of Commons in British foreign policy during the 1937–38 session', in Norton Downs (ed.), *Essays in Honor of Conyers Read* (Chicago, 1953), pp. 170, 175–6.
[2] For examples, see Duff Cooper, *Old Men Forget* (London, 1953), pp. 211, 227, 233.
[3] On this concern, see W. S. Churchill, *Gathering Storm*, pp. 215–16. But Baldwin has been maligned: see T. Jones, *Diary with Letters*, esp. pp. 115, 128.
[4] See the sketch of Sir Horace Wilson in W. J. Brown, *So Far*, pp. 220–22. Chamberlain's personal diplomacy was only another blow at the old professional diplomacy and the Foreign Office; cf. chapter 2, p. 112 above, and Sir Walford Selby, *Diplomatic Twilight, 1930–1940* (London, 1953).

trop's first successes in London had been to procure the recall of
Sir Eric Phipps from the British embassy in Berlin; Phipps, a
veteran diplomatist with no illusions about Nazi Germany, was
transferred to Paris. His successor at Berlin, and a much more
acceptable figure there, was Sir Nevile Henderson, who had been
ambassador in Buenos Aires. Before leaving for Berlin in May
1937, Henderson had a cordial talk with Chamberlain, with whom
he worked very closely thereafter, though as an appeaser he was
often ahead of his master and certainly of the Foreign Office.[1]
'Guarantee us peace and peaceful evolution in Europe, and
Germany will find that she has no more sincere, and, I believe,
more useful friend in the world than Great Britain,' he told the
Anglo-German Fellowship.[2]   Soon this friendship would be proffered in advance of any guarantee.

2. EXIT EDEN; EXIT AUSTRIA

The development of the policy of appeasement soon led to a
rift between Anthony Eden, the Foreign Secretary, and his chief,
backed in the Cabinet by two former holders of his office (Simon
and Hoare) and by Lord Halifax. Eden was the target of criticism
in the German and Italian press and the object of Ribbentrop's
insinuations at London dinner tables. His isolation in the Cabinet
was, in fact, nothing new, and existed as early as Chamberlain's
'very midsummer of madness' speech of June 10, 1936 (opposing
the continuance of sanctions against Italy). Eden's policy was
simple: firmness towards the dictators, co-operation with friendly
countries, and particularly with France. Sanctions had failed;
firmness, at the Nyon conference, had scored a notable if temporary
success—as damaging to him, in Chamberlain's eyes, because it
offended Mussolini and made conciliation difficult, as the failure
of sanctions had been to his reputation with the supporters of the
League. Halifax's ideas were more congenial to Chamberlain:
the reform of the League to facilitate peaceful change, a dislike of
rival blocs, a search for some middle way between appeasement
and war, between collective security and rearmament.[3]   Eden
stuck to his guns: in a speech at Llandudno in October 1937, he
warned against trying to make new friends by abandoning old

[1] L. B. Namier, *Europe in Decay*, pp. 174–5, 184, 190, 210, gives examples. Cf.
F. Gilbert in G. A. Craig and F. Gilbert, *The Diplomats, 1919–1939* (Princeton, 1953),
pp. 537–44, 551–2.
[2] A. C. Johnson, *Lord Halifax*, pp. 418, 426. Henderson's own account of his years
in Berlin is his *Failure of a Mission* (London, 1940).
[3] A. C. Johnson, *Halifax*, pp. 408–10.

ones.[1] Chamberlain's response was to send Halifax to Berlin while Eden attended a conference on the Far East at Brussels.

Japan's undeclared war against China, which had never completely ceased, flared up anew in an 'incident' at Lukouchiao, near Peking, on July 7, 1937. In the fighting which followed, Shanghai was attacked (though the International Settlement was not occupied by the Japanese until 1941), and Nanking and the lower Yangtse valley captured by the end of the year, forcing the government to flee to Chungking. China appealed to the League of Nations in September; the matter was remitted to a committee, on whose advice a conference of the signatories of the Nine-Power treaty was held at Brussels in November, but to no purpose. In December two British gunboats on the Yangtse were fired upon and the United States gunboat *Panay* sunk. Stern notes brought forth apologies and more circumspect behaviour in the future. In September 1938, the League reluctantly passed a resolution in favour of sanctions against Japan, but none of the powers carried it out. The opening of the Burma road, late in 1938, enabled some supplies to reach China from the west (others came overland from Russia). With increasing preoccupations in Europe, Britain could give little thought either to appeasing or to opposing Japan's aggression in China and its threat to Hong Kong. Danger was nearer home.[2]

The first-fruits of the new policy of Chamberlain and Sir Nevile Henderson was an invitation to Lord Halifax, as master of the Middleton Hunt, to visit an international exhibition of hunting arranged by Goering in Berlin. The invitation was unofficial, but despite pretences the visit could not be. Chamberlain thought Halifax should go, though Eden, when he heard of the proposal, disliked it. In due course Halifax went to Berlin, fitted in a visit to the exhibition along with talks with Goering and other ministers and officials, and paid a call on Hitler at Berchtesgaden, his eyrie in the Bavarian mountains, on November 19. The agenda for their talk had been the subject of intelligent speculation in the press beforehand; and since no details of the conversation were published at the time, the reports of it were also speculative, though not far from the mark. A European settlement was the theme: the reform of the League and Germany's return to it, a truce on the colonial question (the return to Germany of her former colonies was much discussed in Britain at the time), and agreement about German

---

[1] A. C. Johnson, *Anthony Eden* (New York, 1939), p. 331.
[2] G. M. Gathorne-Hardy, *Short History of International Affairs*, pp. 328–34.

domination of Central Europe, were means to the end. The meeting did not pass smoothly. Hitler ranted at Halifax; Halifax was polite but unaccommodating. Halifax refused to promise that critics of Germany in parliament and press in England would be silenced. He made it clear that Britain did not oppose changes in Central Europe, provided they were effected peacefully—a qualification which the differing definitions of 'peace' was to render meaningless.[1] The visit accomplished little: it confirmed Hitler's belief in British passivity and Chamberlain's in the possibility of peace by discussion: the visit, Chamberlain wrote, 'was a great success, because it achieved its object, that of creating an atmosphere in which it is possible to discuss with Germany the practical questions involved in a European settlement'.[2]

The trouble was that Chamberlain could not foresee the character of the settlement he was determined to forward. As we now know from the 'Hossbach memorandum' (concerning a meeting of Hitler and his military chiefs on November 5, 1937), Hitler was talking of seizing Austria and Czechoslovakia as the first steps in the winning of *Lebensraum* for Germany. Perhaps they could be taken peaceably; but in any case 'we must place "force with risk" at the head of our programme.'[3] On February 4, 1938, several of the old-style generals were removed and Hitler himself assumed the command of the forces; and Ribbentrop became foreign minister. A month earlier Chamberlain had made a change of the opposite sort which, helping appeasement, helped Hitler. Sir Robert Vansittart, the permanent head of the Foreign Office, a man of conviction and experience, pro-French and anti-German (and something of an autocrat), was promoted to the honorific but powerless post of Chief Diplomatic Adviser to the government; this was done at the new year, when parliament was in recess and debate stilled.

The change was soon followed by a bigger one: the resignation of Eden, another object of Hitler's annoyance. Two incidents, reinforcing the lesson of earlier disagreements and divergent points of view, led to this. The lesser arose from a proposal by President Roosevelt to call a conference of the leading powers to consider ways of returning to more peaceful international relations. Before addressing other governments, the President, on January 4, 1938, sounded out Chamberlain's ideas in a confidential message.

[1] J. W. Wheeler-Bennett, *Munich*, pp. 16–18; A. C. Johnson, *Halifax*, pp. 432–43; A. C. Johnson, *Eden*, pp. 333–6; L. B. Namier, *Europe in Decay*, pp. 208–9.
[2] K. Feiling, p. 332.   [3] J. W. Wheeler-Bennett, *Munich*, pp. 11–14.

Eden was on holiday in the south of France at the time, and Chamberlain replied on his own to this 'bomb', as he called it, suggesting a postponement of the plan and mentioning his own hopes for a friendlier atmosphere, for whose sake he was ready to give *de jure* recognition of Italy's occupation of Abyssinia. The President's initiative would, in fact, put the dictators on the spot— the last thing that Chamberlain wanted; better his own methods of appeasement, even at the price of discouraging the United States' new interest in Europe. Eden was furious when he heard what had happened. At his insistence, after meetings of the foreign affairs committee of the Cabinet, a rather more cordial message was sent to Washington on January 21; but the damage had been done and the President abandoned his proposal. This event was not known to the public at the time of Eden's resignation.[1]

The larger incident was concerned with British policy towards Italy. From the start of his government, Chamberlain had cherished the hope of an understanding with Mussolini which might perhaps draw him away from Hitler; there was a friendly exchange of messages between them in July 1937, and thereafter Chamberlain was in communication with the Italian ambassador in London, Count Grandi, through an agent whom he designated for meeting Grandi, Sir Joseph Ball, head of the research department at the Conservative Central Office. The trouble was that Italian deeds had not improved since the 'gentlemen's agreement' of January 1937: proposals for ending intervention in Spain by the withdrawal of foreign volunteers, made by Great Britain to the Non-Intervention Committee in July, had not resulted in agreement as to the conditions of withdrawal, let alone any withdrawals; and at the same time Italian propaganda against Britain, particularly that broadcast to foreign listeners from the station at Bari, had not been appreciably moderated, as the 'gentlemen's agreement' had promised. Early in February Mussolini made a new offer of negotiations for a general reconciliation. He had noticed the changes in Hitler's government and the pressure which Hitler was renewing against Austria; he was expecting a visit from Hitler in May; he was reluctant to be tied more closely to the Axis. Hence there was a suggestion of 'now or never' about the new overtures and the need for an answer by February 21. Chamberlain was all enthusiasm; Eden scouted

---

[1] J. W. Wheeler-Bennett, *Munich*, pp. 270–1; W. S. Churchill, pp. 225–8; K. Feiling, p. 336. Lord Templewood tones down the episode: *Nine Troubled Years*, pp. 269–74.

their value, insisting that there should be an agreement on the conditions of the withdrawal of Italian volunteers, and the beginning of actual withdrawal, before conversations for a settlement began in Rome. There was no urgency, for him, about the sacrifice of principles and the shirking of responsibilities, as he told an audience in Birmingham on February 12.

The crisis came on Friday, February 18, when Grandi, who had refused to see Eden alone, had a three-hour interview with Eden and Chamberlain, in which the latter, treating Eden almost as an enemy, cut in on Eden's answers to Grandi and fed Grandi with the arguments by which Eden's objections to negotiations could be rebutted. Grandi had been prepared for this interview by Chamberlain's agent, and was congratulated afterwards by Chamberlain, through the same intermediary, on its success.[1] Chamberlain, determined to seize the chance offered him, summoned a meeting of the Cabinet on Saturday afternoon—an unusual time—at which the question of negotiations was discussed. Eden offered to resign; Chamberlain used the threat of his own resignation to get his way, though several ministers supported Eden and were thought likely to resign with him. The Cabinet adjourned until Sunday afternoon (February 20); at the end of its meeting Eden's resignation was announced, at 7.30. A few hours earlier, by an unfortunate coincidence, Hitler had spoken out against him in a speech.[2] Eden's under-secretary, Lord Cranborne (heir of Lord Salisbury), followed him in resigning, but no one else did. Chamberlain was autocratic, and somewhat less than frank, throughout the business. He had sent Mussolini a query about the withdrawal of troops; a telegraphic reply came on Sunday morning, which Chamberlain received through Grandi; but it was not seen by Eden, or sent on to the Foreign Office, until after his resignation.[3]

Eden's resignation caused a sensation. Coming after the dictator's criticism of him, and amid the exultation of the Italian press over the new victories being won for Franco by Italian troops at the time, it seemed to be a new triumph for the aggressor nations and a new humiliation for the democratic powers, lowering

[1] Details of the meeting were given in the memoirs of Count Ciano, Mussolini's foreign minister, in his *L'Europa verso la Catastrofe* (1948), translated as *Ciano's Diplomatic Papers*, ed. Malcolm Muggeridge (London, 1949). See M. L. Kenney, *loc. cit.*, pp. 174–5.

[2] A. C. Johnson, *Eden*, pp. 340–9; K. Feiling, p. 338; G. M. Gathorne-Hardy, pp. 443–5; Duff Cooper, *Old Men Forget*, pp. 210–11.

[3] Lloyd George smoked this out: 332 H.C. Deb., 5 s., pp. 257–9 (February 22, 1938); M. L. Kenney, *loc. cit.*, pp. 175–6.

Britain's prestige still further. Chamberlain had the whip hand over his Cabinet (though critics of his policies remained inside it); the government's most popular, most internationalist member had gone into the wilderness. Churchill has recorded that this event gave him the only sleepless night of these years: 'the dark waters of despair overwhelmed me'.[1] Eden's successor, after a brief interval, was Lord Halifax—a readier supporter of Chamberlain's personal diplomacy, though not a blind one; R. A. Butler was his under-secretary, but Chamberlain answered major questions on foreign policy in the Commons.

Having let its zeal for an agreement with Italy go to such lengths, the government was at some pains to procure one; but it was not till April 16 (after the new crisis caused by Germany's annexation of Austria) that the Anglo-Italian agreement was signed at Rome. It was not worth much: in several annexes and exchanges of notes it reaffirmed the 'gentlemen's agreement', promised that neither country would increase its naval and air bases in the eastern Mediterranean and the Red Sea without notification (which would prevent Britain from fortifying Cyprus), renewed the ban on harmful propaganda, guardedly promised British recognition of Italian sovereignty over Abyssinia, and, concerning Spain, registered Italy's consent to the British proposals for the evacuation of foreign troops, reinforced by a promise that if the evacuation was not complete before the war ended, it would be carried out immediately afterwards. Even so, the agreement was not to go into effect until the 'Spanish question' was settled.[2]

Little difficulty was expected over the fulfilment of this condition. With the aid of more Italian and German 'volunteers' Franco's spring offensive had recaptured Teruel on February 21, and after a ferocious campaign, in which the nationalists used flame-throwers for the first time, reached the Mediterranean on April 15, thus cutting off Barcelona and its territory from the rest of republican Spain. The nationalists proclaimed the end of the war, but in fact it lasted for another year, during which the Germans and Italians continued to use it as a proving ground for their new weapons, and particularly for terroristic aerial bombardments of Barcelona and other open cities outside the war zone. Protests against these tactics from the British and French governments, and from the Pope, were rejected by Franco in

[1] W. S. Churchill, p. 231.
[2] Texts in Cmd. 5726 (1938), and *Annual Register*, *1938*, pp. 403–12.

February. Piratical attacks on British shipping were resumed, and were supplemented by attacks from the air on British ships in republican harbours in January and February, and again in May and June 1938. None the less, the British plan for the withdrawal of volunteers, first put forward in July 1937, was finally agreed to on July 5, 1938. The republican government accepted the scheme; Franco rejected it. Withdrawals did, however, begin; and before the end of the year the Anglo-Italian agreement was brought into force.[1]

In other respects Chamberlain's policy, though long persisted in, was a failure from the start. Close on the heels of Eden's resignation came the brutal annexation of Austria by Germany. The failure of his plans for the *Anschluss* in 1934 had only whetted Hitler's appetite; and a second failure of an attempted *coup* on January 26, 1938, when a leading Nazi was arrested in Vienna, sealed Austria's fate. On February 12 Schuschnigg, the Austrian chancellor, was summoned to Berchtesgaden alone, and at the end of a long day of threats and mental torture submitted to Hitler's ultimatum. The alternative was an immediate invasion, followed by Nazi vengeance. Schuschnigg agreed to take a Nazi, Seyss-Inquart, into his cabinet as minister of the interior, with control of the police, and to legalise Nazi activities in Austria. This was evidently intended as the prelude to the *coup de grâce*—a Nazi revolution, preceded by demonstrations and disorders which the Nazis punctually staged in the next few weeks. At the last moment Schuschnigg decided to strike back, and on Wednesday, March 9 announced that a referendum would be held on the next Sunday on the question whether the people were for a 'free and German Austria'. Such dangerous insubordination must be punished. On Friday evening he was compelled to announce the cancellation of the plebiscite and then to resign in favour of Seyss-Inquart; but by 10 p.m. German mechanised units were already crossing the border, on their way to preserve order. Mechanical breakdowns delayed the victorious advance, and Hitler's entry into Vienna had to wait until Sunday, the 13th. The end of the Austrian republic and the incorporation of Austria into the Reich were then proclaimed.[2]

All went well for Hitler. Mussolini did not move, to Hitler's hysterical relief ('tell Mussolini I will never forget him for this

[1] G. M. Gathorne-Hardy, pp. 454–60; *Annual Register, 1938*, pp. 260–5.
[2] G. M. Gathorne-Hardy, pp. 440, 448–52; W. S. Churchill, *Gathering Storm*, pp. 234–6, 239–42.

. . . never, never, never, whatever happens').[1] Neville Chamberlain, hearing the news of the Nazi invasion when he was actually entertaining Ribbentrop and his wife, the Churchills, and several other guests at lunch at No. 10 Downing Street on Saturday, the 12th,[2] was deeply shocked, the more so when the German reply to an official British protest declared that Austria was no business of Britain's. In parliament on the 14th Chamberlain declared that it was Britain's business: Austria was a fellow-member of the League, and Britain was interested in Central Europe and in whatever concerned the peace of Europe. Hitler's method of action was a shock to all who were working for peace. Churchill was not behindhand in his warning, and pointed to the exposed position which Czechoslovakia was now in. Germany now controlled the communications of south-eastern Europe by road, river and rail; the trade and minerals of many countries lay at her mercy. Europe was 'confronted with a programme of aggression, nicely calculated and timed, unfolding stage by stage. . . .'[3]

3. IRELAND APPEASED?

Chamberlain was not to be so easily deflected from his policy of appeasement, which he next applied to Ireland. In May 1937, De Valera published the text of a new constitution (of which he was apparently the sole author) for Ireland. It was a curious document, and might have been written for some island in the middle of the Atlantic, hundreds of miles from Great Britain (of whose very name it contained no mention). It declared the right of the 'Irish nation' to choose its own form of government and its relations with other nations, claimed as 'national territory' the whole of Ireland, but admitted that 'pending the reintegration of the national territory' the laws of its parliament would apply only to the area of Saorstat Eireann (the Irish Free State). The name of the state was Eire, and it was 'a sovereign independent democratic State'. Its head was a President, elected by popular vote; but the power resided in a prime minister and cabinet, and in a parliament consisting of the Dail and—strange restoration—of a Senate; the Senate was to be elected by the Dail (and by candidates for the Dail who had received at least 500 first-preference votes in the previous election) from panels representing labour, agriculture, industry, public administration and social services, and

[1] W. S. Churchill, p. 241.   [2] Ibid., p. 243.
[3] Ibid., pp. 244–5; J. W. Wheeler-Bennett, *Munich*, pp. 34–5; 333 H.C. Deb., 5 s., 45–52, 95.

cultural and professional interests. As for external relations, the language of the legislation of December 1936 was repeated: 'for the purpose of the exercise of any executive function . . . in connection with its external relations the government may . . . avail or adopt any organ, instrument or method or procedure used or adopted for the like purpose by the members of any group or League of Nations with which Eire is or becomes associated for the purpose of international co-operation in matters of common concern.'[1] Whatever its merits, such a document inevitably made Northern Ireland more determined than ever to perpetuate partition.

The Dail, acting as a constituent assembly, approved the constitution, which was submitted to the electorate at the time of the next general election, held on July 1. The true republicans would have nothing of it, because it did not establish the 'Republic of Ireland', and the people gave it only a grudging approval—less than the two-thirds majority which was required for amending the old constitution.[2] It went into effect on December 29, 1937, when the Irish Free State ceased to exist. The British government accepted the new constitution, publishing a statement on the day of its taking effect that it was prepared to treat it as 'not effecting a fundamental alteration' in the position of the Free State or Eire as a member of the British Commonwealth of Nations; the other Dominions assented to this, and it was given legislative sanction by parliament. So the situation remained until the Republic of Ireland came into being in 1949.

With this encouragement, negotiations were begun for a settlement of the trade war and of other differences. The way had been prepared by a number of informal visits of De Valera, who had called on ministers while passing through London on his journeys to the League of Nations or to his oculist. He now came to London on January 17, 1938 at the head of an Irish delegation to meet Chamberlain and a British delegation; the minister most responsible for the success of the long negotiations was, however, Malcolm MacDonald, the Dominions Secretary. De Valera made a strong bid for the ending of partition, or at least for the British government's benevolent neutrality in the matter. Lord Craigavon

[1] Text from *New York Times*, May 2, 1937; lengthy excerpts in J. Ireland, *Ireland, Past and Present*, pp. 769–81. Cf. N. Mansergh, *Survey of British Commonwealth Affairs*, pp. 289–304.
[2] D. O'Sullivan, *Irish Free State and its Senate*, pp. 414–18, 490–503.

For the new constitution	685,105	39 per cent of electorate
Against	526,945	30 per cent of electorate
Total of voters on register	1,775,055	(31 per cent did not vote).

roused himself at once, called an election in Northern Ireland on February 9 on the issue of 'No surrender', and in due course received an increased majority from his obedient voters. De Valera yielded to the British government's refusal to oblige him, and agreement on other points was reached fairly quickly; no doubt the government's generosity was stimulated by its initial victory over partition.

Actually, three 'Agreements' were signed on April 25, beginning with a preamble expressing the friendship and good understanding between the government of the United Kingdom and the 'Government of Eire'. In place of land annuities and other payments due to her, Britain accepted a single, lump sum of £10 millions, thus forswearing claims to a total sum of about £100 millions (of Ireland's old claims on Great Britain nothing was said); the annual payment from Ireland of £250,000 for damages during the war, which the Dail had agreed to in 1925, was to continue. The trade war was ended and a trade agreement made providing for freedom of trade, subject to certain quotas and preferential duties applying to the Commonwealth countries. And, most remarkable of all, Great Britain agreed to abandon the treaty ports.[1]

Chamberlain defended the agreements in parliament on May 5 in asking for their confirmation, mainly on the ground that generosity and an act of faith would bring about a friendly Ireland. Churchill would have none of it. He scorned the talk of good will and the official use of the name Eire: 'It is usual to say "Paris", not "Paree".' He prophesied, truly enough, a neutral Ireland in war, and pointed out that there was no guarantee even of that. If the ports were denied to British use, the defence of the approaches to the Irish Sea from the north and to the English Channel from the south would be made extremely difficult. 'A more feckless act can hardly be imagined,' he wrote later; the only justification given was that the holding of ports which were dependent for necessities upon a hostile population behind them was not worth while. No other parliament, Churchill declared, would have accepted such an agreement so easily. But Chamberlain's obediently did so.[2]

[1] Text in Cmd. 5728 (1938). See also *Annual Register, 1938*, pp. 32, 118–19; J. Ireland, *Ireland*, pp. 788–801; D. O'Sullivan, *Irish Free State and its Senate*, pp. 574–80; N. Mansergh, *Survey of British Commonwealth Affairs*, pp. 306–20.
[2] W. S. Churchill, *Gathering Storm*, pp. 248–9; K. Feiling, *N. Chamberlain*, p. 310; 335 H.C. Deb., 5 s., 1071–1105.

4. THE FATAL QUADRILATERAL: CZECHOSLOVAKIA, GERMANY, FRANCE, GREAT BRITAIN

The *Anschluss*, shocking as it was, did not cause Chamberlain to abandon the policy of appeasement. He was at once asked to give some pledge of support for Czechoslovakia, should her independence be threatened. He refused. He received a proposal from the Russian government for a four-power conference to discuss means of preventing further aggression. He rejected it. The body representing the Labour party and the T.U.C., the National Council of Labour, proposed that the peace-loving countries, particularly Britain, France, and Russia, unite in a common stand against an aggressor. He replied that this would only divide Europe into two opposing camps, and so far from contributing to peace, 'would inevitably plunge us into war' (House of Commons, April 4). In defining to the Commons on March 24 the circumstances under which Britain would fight he included: aggression against France and Belgium in violation of the Locarno agreement, threats to Britain's liberty and independence, and last of all a possible decision to help the victim of aggression when, in Britain's judgment, it would be proper under the Covenant of the League to do so. The last case, he added, might cover Czechoslovakia; but he would not promise in advance that Britain would assist France if France was called upon to help Czechoslovakia, since that would take the decision out of the government's hands.[1]

Why all the pother about Czechoslovakia—all the more since Goering had told the Czechoslovakian minister in Berlin at the time of the *Anschluss* that Czechoslovakia had 'nothing to fear from the Reich', and had given his word of honour?[2] Czechoslovakia was the strongest and best-governed of the new states which had come into being after 1918. It occupied a strategic position in central Europe and had protected its frontiers with elaborate fortifications comparable to the Maginot line. Its diplomacy, under Benes, its foreign minister and now its president, had won for it treaties of mutual assistance with France in 1925 and Russia in 1935. With Germany it had an arbitration convention dating from 1925 and explicitly continued by Hitler, but it

---

[1] J. W. Wheeler-Bennett, *Munich*, pp. 36–9 (on which this whole account mainly rests); 333 H.C. Deb., 5 s., 1399–1413 (March 24, 1938), 334 *ibid.*, 61 (April 4). See also Jules Menken, 'How World War II Came', in Geoffrey Dennis (ed.), *The World at War* (London: Caxton Publishing Co.; 1951), I, 122 ff.—an excellent, fully-documented account of the events of 1938–39 and their background which is far too little known.

[2] J. W. Wheeler-Bennett, *Munich*, pp. 25–7.

had refused all offers of a non-aggression pact from Hitler.[1] It was a state of many peoples and some internal disharmony: 7·5 million Czechs, 3·2 million Germans, 2·3 million Slovaks, and smaller numbers of Magyars, Ruthenians, Poles.[2] The Sudeten Germans were descendants of people who had been outside Germany, and within the Austro-Hungarian empire, for centuries; if they had grievances as a minority, they were neither new nor irremediable. In fact, their grievances were only a talking-point for Hitler and, unfortunately, for Chamberlain. Hitler did not care about reuniting the Sudeten Germans with the Reich; his real aim was to crush Czechoslovakia and gain control of her resources and her strategic position; as an independent country she was especially dangerous to him because of her links with France and Russia.

By the same token, any move by Germany against Czechoslovakia would involve France—and perhaps therefore Great Britain. This was only too clear to Chamberlain. To preserve peace he must, if he could not restrain Germany, restrain France and Czechoslovakia, and ignore Russia. The matter became urgent at the end of April, when Hitler sent instructions to Henlein, leader of the pro-Nazi Sudeten German party, to stand ready to stir up trouble on orders from the German minister at Prague. The demands of the party, as Henlein proclaimed them, were full autonomy for the German areas, and a revision of Czechoslovakia's foreign policy. Daladier, the new French Prime Minister, and his Foreign Secretary, Bonnet, came to London on April 28 for talks with Chamberlain and Halifax. Daladier was ready to fight, if Czechoslovakia was attacked, and urged that Britain and France should warn Hitler that they would take joint action. Chamberlain refused, and nearly broke off the talks; he would only agree that the Czechoslovakian government might be told that if, despite the negotiations with Germany which it must be made to undertake, the country was attacked and France intervened, Britain could not guarantee to remain aloof. On this slender basis Anglo-French military staff talks continued.[3] To complete the work of eroding French and Czech determination, Chamberlain made it clear to some Canadian and American journalists, whom he spoke to 'off the record' at Lady Astor's on May 10,

<hr>

[1] J. W. Wheeler-Bennett, *Munich*, p. 28; W. S. Churchill, pp. 258–9.

[2] G. M. Gathorne-Hardy, p. 461.

[3] J. W. Wheeler-Bennett, pp. 44–9; K. Feiling, p. 353. Pressure on Czechoslovakia from the British Foreign Office began as early as April 12: L. B. Namier, *Europe in Decay*, p. 185.

that Britain and France would not fight for Czechoslovakia in its present boundaries, and that he looked forward to a peaceful solution, followed by a four-power pact to preserve the peace of Europe; the fourth power to be Italy, not Russia. His remarks were reported in the Canadian and American press. Though Chamberlain, with his usual impatient rudeness, tried to belittle the reports in answer to questions in parliament, they did their work.[1]

Yet what Chamberlain feared almost occurred. On May 19 reports of German troop movements, followed by a border incident in which two Sudeten Germans were shot, aroused fears of a *putsch* in Czechoslovakia. Henlein broke off the negotiations which had begun. The Czechoslovakian government ordered a partial mobilisation of the forces. Russia was ready to act; so was France. And Halifax, whose intervention was perhaps responsible for this last piece of firmness on Britain's part, told the German ambassador in London that if Czechoslovakia was attacked and France went to war the result would be a general conflagration which might well involve Britain. He followed this up by a strong message to Berlin. Britain and France acted together against the threat of another week-end *coup*. It was for the last time, and that even though (and perhaps because) it was successful. Hitler was dismayed, the German general staff more so. Hitler backed down. So much the worse for the Czechs. Next time he must succeed, and must crush them; more, he must have revenge. He gave orders on May 28 that the Sudeten-German question must be settled, once and for all, that year, and by October 1—a timetable from which he never deviated.[2]

Chamberlain, also, must not be caught napping again. Before another crisis occurred, he must soften up the Czechs, immobilise France and restrain Germany; and since Hitler was likely to be the most reckless, his main efforts must be directed against his friends rather than against Hitler. Not that it was very difficult to keep France in a state of twilight sleep: cabinet and country were divided and irresolute, and the slippery Bonnet pursued a course of defeatism which assisted Chamberlain's efforts. His first step was to send a British representative—or rather a mission— to Czechoslovakia to mediate between the government and the Sudeten Germans by assisting in negotiations and giving advice.

[1] J. W. Wheeler-Bennett, pp. 52–3; 337 H.C. Deb., 5 s., 854–8, 957, 1540 (June 20, 21, 27, 1938).
[2] J. W. Wheeler-Bennett, pp. 55–9; W. S. Churchill, pp. 256–7; A. C. Johnson, *Halifax*, pp. 465–6.

The Czechoslovakian government accepted the mission reluctantly; the French refused any part in it. Chamberlain entrusted the task to that icy elder statesman, Lord Runciman. Runciman got to work in Prague on August 4, but could accomplish little: Henlein was not free to negotiate, and the Czechs saw little reason to yield much. New German troop manoeuvres in mid-August suggested that a blow would soon be struck; Chamberlain, after consulting his inner cabinet, sent warnings to Berlin and instructed Sir Nevile Henderson to begin arranging for a personal contact between himself and Hitler (August 24). At the same time the Czechoslovakian government was urged to make further concessions. It was then Benes' turn to take the wind out of his opponent's sails by offering, on September 4, to concede all the demands of the Sudeten Germans (principally local autonomy) except the revision of Czechoslovakian foreign policy. Hitler might be cheated of his war and the crushing of Czechoslovakia after all; everything turned, it was thought, on the speech which he was to make at the Nazi party rally at Nuremberg on September 12.[1]

Though war seemed to be coming nearer as August ended there were several voices raised to send it away. The *New Statesman*, on August 27, declared that the strategical value of the Bohemian frontier should not be 'made the occasion for world war'.[2] *The Times*, in a famous intervention which owed a good deal of its devastating shock to a last-minute alteration of his leader-writer's text by Dawson, recommended the Czechoslovakian government on September 7 to consider 'whether they should exclude altogether the project, which has found favour in some quarters, of making Czechoslovakia a more homogeneous State by the secession of that fringe of alien populations who are contiguous to the nation with which they are united by race'.[3] This suggestion—that Czechoslovakia should cede to Germany the Sudeten German districts and thus abandon its strategic and well-fortified frontiers—went far beyond anything hitherto urged officially upon Benes. Because of *The Times'* reputation, and its close connections with the government, it had to be countered at once; and Halifax issued a statement from the Foreign Office reaffirming that in the event of a general conflict in which France was menaced Britain could not stand aside. Its effect was promptly undone by whispers started by Bonnet in Paris and by a weaker

---

[1] J. W. Wheeler-Bennett, pp. 70–91; F. T. A. Ashton-Gwatkin, 'The Personal Story of the Runciman Mission', *Listener*, October 21, 1948.
[2] J. W. Wheeler-Bennett, p. 95.   [3] *History of The Times*, IV, ii, 929–30.

statement made by Chamberlain to the British press on September
11 and by Halifax to Sir Eric Phipps in Paris on the 12th.[1] Yet
Hitler's speech on the 12th, venomous though it was against the
Czechs, and punctuated by the barbaric, mechanical roars of
'Sieg Heil' from his massed followers, did not declare war (he
had not reached that point in his timetable) and left things more
confused than ever. Henlein fled from Czechoslovakia, 'incidents'
and press reports of incidents multiplied on the next two days;
on September 15 Runciman left Prague. Germany seemed to be
on the verge of attacking Czechoslovakia and plunging all Europe
into war.[2]

September 13 was the fatal day, its decisions the first link of the
chain which led to the settlement at Munich a fortnight later. The
French cabinet met to decide whether it would back up Czechoslovakia by war, if she was attacked. On the decision hung not
only Czechoslovakia's fate but France's, and Europe's. A
majority was for war, but Bonnet and the appeasers outweighed
them. No mobilisation was ordered. Daladier passed the responsibility to Chamberlain and urged him to seek some settlement for
Czechoslovakia by conference. But already Chamberlain had acted,
and entirely alone; he had sent a telegram to Hitler (September
13) asking if he might come to see him 'in view of the increasing
critical situation . . . with a view to trying to find peaceful solution'. He was ready to come by air the next day.[3] The plan he
had begun to lay in August was to be put into effect.

Chamberlain was determined to preserve peace, at almost any
price to himself, and to the Czechs; even so, he almost failed at the
last moment. The French were ready to follow him. The reasons
were not disreputable. France was at the time weak in air power,
Germany strong in it, Russia weak; these impressions, reported
by military attachés on many occasions, were reinforced by the
accounts given in Paris and London in September by Colonel
Charles A. Lindbergh, the American aviator, of what he had seen
in his recent visit to Russia and Germany. Geography alone prevented France (or Britain) from assisting Czechoslovakia directly;
and Russian land forces could reach her only by crossing Poland
or Rumania, the former of which, at least, was likely to oppose
them. The Dominions would offer no encouragement for a war
over Czechoslovakia. Against these arguments for caution were

[1] J. W. Wheeler-Bennett, pp. 96–8; A. C. Johnson, *Halifax*, pp. 476–7; W. S.
Churchill, p. 267.
[2] J. W. Wheeler-Bennett, pp. 93–5.   [3] K. Feiling, p. 363.

those supporting a declaration of war against Germany, if Czecho-slovakia was attacked, on the ground that Germany was unready for a war on two fronts and Czechoslovakia was strongly armed, well fortified, and so placed as to expose Germany to counter-attack. True, Czechoslovakia might be ravaged by the war; but she could be restored. On the other hand, Russia might be on the side of France and Britain. Yet Russia was ignored throughout the crisis, with results which made war more certain, and more perilous, a year later. Why? Chamberlain's distrust of Russia was of long standing. He therefore discounted Russian pledges of assistance as much as Churchill trusted them. On September 21, Litvinov told the Assembly of the League at Geneva that Russia would fulfil her obligations to Czechoslovakia under her pact with her, if France would do the same; he repeated this two days later. Churchill was convinced, as much by earlier conversations with Maisky, the Russian ambassador in London, as by Litvinov's speeches, that Russia would have fought in 1938.[1] Yet Russia was ignored; and partly for the reason that if any deal was to be made with Hitler this would be one of Hitler's chief conditions.[2]

5. WAR AVERTED: BERCHTESGADEN, GODESBERG, MUNICH

Hitler was amazed to receive Chamberlain's telegram: 'Ich bin vom Himmel gefallen.' He invited Chamberlain to see him at Berchtesgaden. Next morning Chamberlain told the Cabinet what he had done, and on September 15 he set off. He was accompanied only by Sir Horace Wilson, and William Strang, head of the Central European department of the Foreign Office. This was personal diplomacy with a vengeance and might be thought to be a humiliation for Great Britain. Yet the picture of this elderly man, making his first flight on a desperate mission of peace, caught the public imagination and lifted the fear of war; there was admira-tion that such a man, the very embodiment of the civilian and the solid man of business, with his sombre clothes and his umbrella, was braving the dictator in his lair. But if Hitler was amazed, the

[1] Max Beloff, *Foreign Policy of Soviet Russia, 1929–1941*, vol. II (Oxford, 1949), pp. 143–55, 160, 166, demonstrates that Russia, notwithstanding Litvinov's speeches, showed no signs of preparing to take military action during the crisis, though ready to denounce Chamberlain's diplomacy.

[2] J. W. Wheeler-Bennett, pp. 105–6, 127, 143; W. S. Churchill, pp. 263–5, 273–4; Agnes Headlam-Morley, 'Was Neville Chamberlain's Policy Wrong?' *Listener*, October 14, 1948; J. F. Kennedy, *Why England Slept* (New York, 1940), pp. 187, 192.

The evidence on the British negotiations with Czechoslovakia before Munich in *Documents on British Foreign Policy*, Third series, I, is summarised in L. B. Namier, *Europe in Decay*, pp. 171 ff., 'The Road to Munich'.

Czechs were aghast: they had things under control, and now feared betrayal from their friends.

The three-hour talk of Chamberlain and Hitler in the vast room overlooking the mountains at Berchtesgaden on September 15, when the two men, *tête-à-tête* except for Hitler's interpreter, conversed together, determined almost all that followed, for it convinced Chamberlain that Hitler would fight to get his way, and Hitler that Chamberlain would not fight to prevent it. Hitler was consequently unready to bargain, and Chamberlain, annoyed, asked why he had allowed him to come all that way for nothing. Hitler replied that if Chamberlain would agree that the problem of the Sudeten Germans should be settled on the principle of self-determination (fatal formula), the ways and means could then be discussed. Chamberlain said he must consult his Cabinet; and next day was back in London.[1]

The Cabinet, at its meeting on the 16th and on the following days, had before it not only Chamberlain's report of his visit to Hitler, but also Runciman's report of his mission. Runciman recommended even more sweeping concessions at Czechoslovakia's expense than had been considered hitherto: the immediate transfer to Germany, without a plebiscite, of all frontier districts where the Germans were an important majority and the remodelling of Czech foreign policy. Chamberlain went further still, and argued for the immediate transfer of all districts where the Germans constituted more than 50 per cent of the population. This proposal of forcible incorporation of large Czech minorities within Germany roused some members of the Cabinet to opposition, particularly Duff Cooper and Malcolm MacDonald; Simon and Hoare supported it. On the 18th Daladier and Bonnet came to London, and were persuaded by Chamberlain to accept the ruin of Czechoslovakia—its strategic frontiers would be lost to it—and with it the abdication of France as a major power. The 'whole system of security built up in the postwar treaties' was sacrificed in a few hours.[2] Daladier demanded that Czechoslovakia's new frontiers should be guaranteed by Britain and France; Chamberlain made even this guarantee worthless by insisting it should be general, and include Germany. Thus was found, as Chamberlain told the Commons on September 28, 'a solution which would not bring about a European War, and, therefore, a solution which would not

---

[1] J. W. Wheeler-Bennett, pp. 105–11; K. Feiling, pp. 365–8.
[2] A. C. Johnson, *Halifax*, p. 481.

automatically compel France to take action in accordance with her obligations'.[1]

But how to get Czechoslovakia to agree to her self-immolation? The 'Anglo-French Plan' (the immediate cession to Germany of all districts with a German population of more than 50 per cent) was at once transmitted to the Czechoslovakian government. Bonnet gave them to the Czechoslovakian ambassador in Paris with a 'terse and sardonic "acceptez"', over-ruling all protests. In Prague, the proposals were delivered on September 19 with the request to Benes for an immediate reply, since Chamberlain hoped to see Hitler again on the 21st. Territory must be surrendered, the Russian treaty abandoned. The alternative was presumably war—war begun by Germany, and in which France and Britain, far from intervening on Czechoslovakia's behalf, would hold her responsible before the world. For by meeting—even anticipating—Hitler's demands they had made them their own, and Czechoslovakia the enemy.[2] Yet even this pressure did not daunt Benes: he refused the proposals, and instead offered to submit any differences to arbitration under the German-Czech treaty of 1925. He was told to think again: at 2 a.m. on September 21 the British and French ministers called on him to tell him to withdraw his reply and 'consider an alternative that takes account of realities'; if there was war, Britain and France would stand aside. That evening Benes gave in, even though Litvinov, at Geneva, reiterated Russia's pledge of support.[3]

Now, however, Chamberlain had got ahead of Hitler's timetable· Hitler had never imagined that Britain and France would accept— or rather propose—such demands and obtain, at pistol point, the submission of Czechoslovakia to them. He would miss his war, which he was now counting on having without danger of French or British intervention. His military preparations (Operation Green) had continued unchecked, and new 'atrocities' were being reported from the Sudeten districts. When Chamberlain returned joyfully to Germany, for a second meeting with Hitler at Godesberg (on the Rhine, near Bonn) on September 22, he was told that his proposals were no longer of any use: the procedure was too slow. Hitler demanded the immediate occupation by German troops of the German-speaking areas. Chamberlain was profoundly shocked, and an angry debate followed, lasting some three

[1] J. W. Wheeler-Bennett, pp. 112–16; 339 H.C. Deb., 5 s., 16.
[2] J. W. Wheeler-Bennett, pp. 116–20.   [3] Ibid., pp. 120–7; W. S. Churchill, p. 272.

hours. The deadlock was complete, and Chamberlain crossed the river to his hotel. Next morning he made another effort; he wrote a note to Hitler, saying that he could put forward no plan unless it would be accepted by British and French opinion, and world opinion, 'as carrying out the principles already agreed upon in an orderly fashion, and free from the threat of force'. Not the deed but the method mattered; anything to keep hold of the idea of 'negotiation'. Hitler's reply did not come until after lunch, and was a mere tirade against the Czechs. Chamberlain asked for a memorandum of the German demands, for transmission to Prague. After another delay he was invited to see Hitler again at 10.30 that evening (Friday, September 23). He was given a paper demanding the evacuation by the Czech authorities of stipulated German-speaking areas between September 26 and September 28. This was an ultimatum, he protested; no, he was told, it was entitled a memorandum. He could restrain himself no longer. As he told the Commons on the 28th:

> I dwelt with all the emphasis at my command on the risks which would be incurred by insisting on such terms, and on the terrible consequences of a war, if war ensued. . . . I bitterly reproached the Chancellor for his failure to respond in any way to the efforts which I had made to secure peace.

Hitler seemed to soften: he agreed to extend the time-limit to October 1 (the day on which Operation Green was supposed to begin, in any case), made a few small alterations in the memorandum, and sent Chamberlain home happy in assurances that he had no more territorial demands to make and that Chamberlain was the first man to whom he had made any concession.[1]

Surely Chamberlain would not accept the Godesberg Memorandum and get the Czechs to swallow it also? In the Cabinet, when it met on the 24th, there was strong opposition; and next morning Halifax told Chamberlain it must be rejected. The Cabinet, meeting again on Sunday morning, September 25, agreed, and Chamberlain assented. The French cabinet found courage also, and unanimously rejected the memorandum. Daladier ordered a partial mobilisation of the forces on the 24th. The Czechoslovakian government rejected the memorandum 'absolutely and unconditionally' on the 25th, as a 'de facto ultimatum of the sort usually presented to a vanquished nation and not a

---

[1] J. W. Wheeler-Bennett, pp. 130–8; K. Feiling, pp. 369–70; the texts of the Anglo-French proposals of September 19 and the Godesberg Memorandum are in Wheeler-Bennett, pp. 456–7, 461–2. 339 H.C. Deb., 5 s., 21.

proposition to a sovereign state'. Deadlock was complete and war was imminent.[1]

There had, in fact, been a hardening of public opinion since September 19 against Chamberlain's readiness to sacrifice Czechoslovakia in the cause of peace. The public was bewildered by the crisis and was not kept well-informed either by the press, or the B.B.C., thanks to Chamberlain's secretive diplomacy. But what was known was not liked, though hostility to Chamberlain's policy was much stronger among the men than the women, with whom the passion for peace blotted out other feelings.[2] Parliament was not in session, and when it met could only accept a *fait accompli*; but the opinions of the Opposition were not completely silenced.

The Labour movement came out wordily but undeniably for war rather than surrender. The T.U.C., meeting in Blackpool on September 5–9, adopted a manifesto issued on September 7 by the National Council of Labour, entitled *Labour and the International Situation: On the Brink of War*. It traversed the government's foreign policy over the last seven years, denounced its policy towards Spain, and warned that in the new threat to Czechoslovakia the fate of the world was involved. It condemned Germany's demands and British support of them.

> The time has come for a positive and unmistakable lead for collective defence against aggression and to safeguard peace. The British Government must leave no doubt in the mind of the German Government that they will unite with the French and Soviet Governments to resist any attack upon Czechoslovakia.[3]

Later in the crisis the National Council sent deputations to Chamberlain 'and Halifax, and organised scores of meetings of protest up and down the country.[4] By Sunday, the 25th, the press was also supporting a strong stand against Hitler's demands: Garvin in the *Observer*, on Monday *The Times* and the *Daily Telegraph*, when the Godesberg memorandum was published: the *Telegraph* called it an attempt to exact 'an abject and humiliating capitulation'. *The Times'* partial change of front was not soon enough to save it from resignations by some members of its staff, disgusted at its previous line.[5]

[1] J. W. Wheeler-Bennett, pp. 139–43.

[2] Charles Madge and Tom Harrisson, *Britain by Mass-Observation* (Penguin Books: 1939), pp. 70–8; the first half of this book is a useful survey of public opinion during the Munich crisis, with some reference to the role of the press (a subject still not sufficiently investigated).

[3] G. D. H. Cole, *History of the Labour Party*, p. 335.

[4] *Annual Register, 1938*, pp. 66, 69–71.

[5] J. W. Wheeler-Bennett, p. 140; *History of The Times*, IV, ii, 941, 945.

Once more, however, Chamberlain began sapping the resolve of the French and the Czechs. Once more Daladier and Bonnet came to No. 10 Downing Street, on Sunday evening, the 25th. France would come to the assistance of Czechoslovakia, they said. Chamberlain, Simon, and Hoare belittled French arms and air power, and warned that in a war Czechoslovakia would be overwhelmed in a few days. Chamberlain was asked if he was suggesting that France should remain aloof, and coldly replied that that was a matter for the government of France to decide.[1] At the resumed meeting next morning, the 26th, he said he was sending a final appeal to Hitler. He repeated earlier assurances that if France was in danger (from fulfilling her treaty obligations) Britain would come to her assistance. This grudging assurance was made public in stronger terms, thanks to Lord Halifax, in a Foreign Office statement made on the evening of the 26th and published next day: if Czechoslovakia was attacked, France would be bound to come to her assistance 'and Great Britain and Russia will certainly stand by France'. Despite this, no plans were made for joint action or for gaining the co-operation of Russia; and Bonnet did his best to undo the effects of the Foreign Office statement next day.[2]

Chamberlain was still hoping for some way of escape. The faithful Sir Horace Wilson was despatched to Berlin on the 26th to give Hitler a new proposal before he made his speech at the Sportpalast at 8 o'clock that evening. Hitler brushed it aside, as he did a further message from Sir Horace and Sir Nevile Henderson on the 27th: Great Britain would see that Hitler's demands on Czechoslovakia were carried out provided the terms of transfer were settled by discussion and not by force. At the same time, on the night of the 27th, Chamberlain sent two messages to Benes: one warning him that Czechoslovakia would be invaded the next day, and that no country could save it from destruction, even if a world war followed, but that the British government could not assume the responsibility of giving advice to him on the matter, the other advising him, in effect, to accept the Godesberg Memorandum: the military occupation by Germany of Czechoslovakian territory under a modified timetable which the British government would supervise. By this time, however, almost all hopes for

[1] J. W. Wheeler-Bennett, pp. 143–4; E. L. Woodward and Rohan Butler (eds.) *Documents on British Foreign Policy. 1919–1939*, 3rd series, II (London, 1949) pp. 520–34, 536–42.
[2] J. W. Wheeler-Bennett, pp. 145–7; W. S. Churchill, pp. 277–8; A. C. Johnson, *Halifax*, pp. 484–5.

peace had faded. Hitler's speech on the 26th, with its foul abuse of Benes, its threat to occupy all the Sudeten territory by October 1 if it had not been yielded up by then, left no ray of hope, notwithstanding the parrot assurance that he had no further territorial claims in Europe.[1]

By Tuesday night, September 27, almost everyone in Great Britain expected that the country would be at war next day, or at least by the week-end. The Air Raid Precautions personnel had been mobilised on the 25th, cellars and basements had been requisitioned for air raid shelters, school children and hospital patients had been evacuated from London on the 26th, and gas masks had been distributed. In the London parks miserable-looking slit trenches were being dug. On the evening of the 27th, after Sir Horace Wilson's return from Berlin, the inner cabinet decided to declare a state of emergency by Order in Council and to mobilise the fleet and the Auxiliary Air Force; the fleet was mobilised and the news announced (thanks to Duff Cooper) next day.[2] The climax of despair came with Chamberlain's broadcast at 8.30 p.m. on the 27th; his flat, tired voice was the epitome of failure. He loathed war, he had done his utmost for peace; only details prevented a settlement already agreed to in principle.

> How horrible, fantastic, incredible, it is that we should be digging trenches and trying on gas-masks here because of a quarrel in a far-away country between people of whom we know nothing. . . .[3]

The test was not to be made just then. Before he went to bed, Chamberlain received a reply from Hitler to his message sent by Sir Horace: Would not he continue to use his good offices and bring the Czechs to reason? He at once drafted a reply, in his own hand, without consulting anyone but Sir Horace:

> After reading your letter I feel certain that you can get all essentials without war, and without delay. I am ready to come to Berlin myself at once to discuss arrangements for transfer with you and representatives of the Czech government, together with representatives of France and Italy if you desire. I feel convinced that we could reach agreement in a week. . . .[4]

This was the nadir of diplomacy—a personal deal between two men at the expense of a third party: I can give you all you want, without war and without delay. Moreover, it would be cosily

---

[1] J. W. Wheeler-Bennett, pp. 148–55.
[2] Ibid., pp. 151, 158–9; W. S. Churchill, p. 279; Sir Robert Bruce Lockhart, 'September crisis—and after', *Listener*, October 28, 1948.
[3] *The Times*, September 28, 1938.   [4] K. Feiling, p. 372.

arranged by the 'Four Powers': no bother about Russia's presence now. Chamberlain sent a telegram to Mussolini and telephoned Daladier and Bonnet; they were delighted at the news. Bonnet had, in fact, anticipated Chamberlain in a message which reached Hitler first and outdid Chamberlain's in generosity.[1] Everything was really settled before Chamberlain addressed the House of Commons on the afternoon of the 28th: the dramatic interruption of his speech was all but a put-up job.

Hitler had saved Chamberlain from war; but even more, Chamberlain had saved Hitler as well as 'peace'. Hitler's change of mind no doubt had many reasons: if he could gain by negotiation all that he could gain by war without its risks, even he could court prudence.[2] He was confronted with a memorial of protest and of warning from several of his generals, pointing out Germany's military unreadiness for war. At the same time—though this he could not know—General Halder and several other generals were hesitantly preparing a plot to overthrow him, declare a military government, and save the country from the ruin they foresaw. They were forestalled by the announcement of the conference to be held at Munich.[3]

None of this was known when Chamberlain rose to address the Commons on the 28th. Parliament had been hastily summoned, and was meeting for the first time since July. The House was crowded and the galleries full, those present including the ambassadors of Russia, Germany, and Czechoslovakia (Jan Masaryk). Chamberlain's speech was a long and gloomy recital of his efforts for peace during the crisis; it supplemented a White Paper issued that morning, but neither gave a complete account of events. At 4.15 p.m. Chamberlain had been speaking for 80 minutes and was apparently near a conclusion of despair when Halifax was seen to leave the peers' gallery in response to a message. A note was then handed to Simon on the front bench; with some difficulty he got Chamberlain's attention and handed it to him. Chamberlain read it and joyfully announced: 'That is not all. I have something further to say to the House yet. I have now been informed by Herr Hitler that he invites me to meet him at Munich tomorrow morning.' Mussolini had accepted and doubtless Daladier would do so. 'I need not say what my answer will be.' [An hon. member: 'Thank God for the Prime Minister!'][4]

[1] J. W. Wheeler-Bennett, pp. 164–7; W. S. Churchill, pp. 283–4.
[2] J. W. Wheeler-Bennett, pp. 161–3.
[3] J. W. Wheeler-Bennett, pp. 161–3.
[4] J. W. Wheeler-Bennett, pp. 168–70; 339 H.C. Deb., 5 s., 5–26.

At once pandemonium broke forth. Everyone was on his feet, cheering, tossing his order papers in the air, some members in tears. It was an unprecedented and most unparliamentary outburst of mass-hysteria and relief, in which only a few did not join. Masaryk, in the gallery, was dumbfounded: his country's fate to be settled by the four powers without its being heard at all. He went round at once to see Halifax and Chamberlain in the Foreign Office. 'If you have sacrificed my nation to preserve the peace of the world, I will be the first to applaud you,' he told them; 'but if not, gentlemen, God help your souls.'[1] Not only the matter but the manner of Chamberlain's diplomacy was to prove disastrous: it has been wisely said that by receiving the message in the middle of his speech he 'prolonged by this dramatic effect an era of mental confusion and self-delusion'.[2]

Next morning Chamberlain flew to Munich, accompanied by the faithful Sir Horace and three Foreign Office officials. He was in high spirits, and in no mood to be cheated out of a settlement this time. At Heston airport he had repeated to reporters a refrain of his childhood: 'If at first you don't succeed, try, try, try again.' He did not consult with Daladier before the conference, though Hitler and Mussolini met and talked in advance. Daladier came with a clear idea of those strategic frontiers of Czechoslovakia which must be preserved if France was not to be endangered; but he gave in before the swaggering self-assurance of the dictators and the ready acquiescences of Chamberlain. The Munich conference was an anti-climax. It accepted the Godesberg Memorandum, as modified by a German draft given first to Mussolini and edited by Sir Horace Wilson. Agreement was reached at 2.30 a.m. on September 30. Czechoslovakia was betrayed and handed over, gagged and bound, to Hitler's mercies; the Czech representatives were called into the conference room after the dictators had left and told to accept the terms; no comments were expected or allowed. Benes, deserted by all save the Russians, and doubtful of some of his own people, agreed, and soon afterwards resigned his post and went into exile. Hitler had got all he wanted, and without firing a shot: Czechoslovakia ruined, Britain and France humbled before himself and in the eyes of the world, Poland exposed to attack, Russia isolated, Hitler himself raised to a pinnacle of power and success among his own people.[3]

At Munich Chamberlain and Daladier gave Hitler what even

[1] J. W. Wheeler-Bennett, *Munich*, pp. 170–1.
[2] P. Maillaud, *English Way*, p. 168.   [3] J. W. Wheeler-Bennett, pp. 171–5.

*x

they had refused after Godesberg.[1] The only difference between the Munich agreement and the Godesberg Memorandum was that the former was technically an agreement, preserving the precious principle of peace by negotiation, and provided for the occupation of the Sudeten territory which Czechoslovakia was to surrender in four stages, beginning on October 1 and ending on the 7th, instead of all at once a few days earlier. An international commission, on which Czechoslovakia was to be represented, was to delimit further areas for German occupation with or without plebiscites, and might in 'exceptional cases' make minor adjustments in the 'ethnographical determination of zones'. Britain and France, and, more remotely, Germany and Italy were to guarantee the new Czech frontiers. There was not much left to guarantee: Czechoslovakia lost her defences (the Germans, occupying the frontier fortifications unopposed, were amazed at their strength, which taught them much about the Maginot line), and most of her industrial resources; her rail communications were cut; her treaties with France and Russia forfeited. She still had a quarter of a million Germans within her shrunken borders; and 800,000 Czechs, a new oppressed minority, and any anti-Nazis among the 2·8 million Germans in the ceded territories, had to face inquisition, torture and murder at the hands of Nazi storm troopers and the Gestapo.

Chamberlain was well pleased with his work, for he brought back not only the Munich agreement, but something else. During the night of the conference he had asked Hitler if he would care for another talk, and they had gone to his flat. Chamberlain pulled out of his pocket a typed declaration in two copies: in it Chamberlain and Hitler announced their resolve to follow the method of consultation in any future questions arising between them, and avowed that the Munich agreement was 'symbolic of the desire of our two peoples never to go to war with one another again'. Hitler accepted it with enthusiasm, and the two men signed it on the spot.[2] 'I've got it', Chamberlain told his colleagues on returning to the hotel later; and he waved this same document at reporters and members of his Cabinet on his arrival back at Heston. It was something of solid worth; an agreement by Hitler renouncing warlike intentions against Great Britain; a promise to be trusted because, as he explained to a friend, unlike other promises

[1] J. W. Wheeler-Bennett, pp. 176–7, 192–9; text of the agreement, *ibid.*, pp. 465–7, and in *Annual Register, 1938*, pp. 412–13.
[2] K. Feiling, pp. 376–7.

which had been broken, 'this time it is different; this time he has made the promises to me'. To the crowd in Downing Street, shouting 'Good old Neville' on his return on October 1 he said, from his first-floor window:

> My good friends: this is the second time in our history that there has come back from Germany to Downing Street peace with honour. I believe it is peace for our time.[1]

6. WINTER, 1938–39: IS IT PEACE?

Before blaming Chamberlain for the evils of the Munich settlement we must remind ourselves that he was not alone in his enthusiasm for it. He was deluged with letters of praise from people at home and abroad, high and low, from the King, from General Smuts, from the kitchen-maid of the Chamberlain family.[2] *The Times* declared that 'no conqueror returning from a victory on the battlefield had come adorned with nobler laurels'. A popular journalist (Godfrey Winn) had written before the Munich conference: 'Praise be to God and to Mr. Chamberlain. I find no sacrilege, no bathos, in coupling those two names.'[3] Most of the press was nearly as enthusiastic; and the vehement defence of the Munich settlement continued until the end of the year, though more and more the subject became one causing bitter divisions, in society as in politics, in bar-rooms and in clubs. The chief defenders in the government, beside Chamberlain, were Simon, Hoare, Inskip, and Lord Maugham (who succeeded Lord Hailsham as Lord Chancellor in March 1938).[4]

Criticism, however, was not lacking from the first. Talk of peace for our time seemed to be belied by the recruiting posters, the balloon-barrage, the distribution of gas masks, the A.R.P. activities which continued after Munich.[5] Books about Czechoslovakia and the European situation, such as Douglas Reed's *Disgrace Abounding* and a Penguin Special, *Europe and the*

---

[1] J. W. Wheeler-Bennett, pp. 179–82; text of declaration, *ibid.*, p. 478. A study of the Munich settlement based on the first two volumes of *Documents on British Foreign Policy*, Third series, and other recent material, is B. E. Schmitt, 'Munich', *Journal of Modern History*, 25 (1953); 166–80; also *Survey of International Affairs, 1938*, II (Oxford, 1951). Opposition within the cabinet, Chamberlain's obstinate autocracy, the defeatist counsels of Sir H. Wilson and Sir Nevile Henderson, are shown in Duff Cooper, *Old Men Forget*, pp. 225–42.

[2] K. Feiling, pp. 378–81.

[3] J. W. Wheeler-Bennett, p. 180; C. Madge and T. Harrisson, *Britain by Mass-Observation*, pp. 82–5.

[4] J. W. Wheeler-Bennett, pp. 294–7, 299–300.

[5] See the lines from *Punch* (October 12, 1938), quoted in G. M. Gathorne-Hardy, p. 477.

Czechs, which enjoyed a very large sale, stirred—or rather echoed —second thoughts about Munich.[1] The sacrifice of Czechoslovakia was a sin not expiated until Britain had gone through her own lonely ordeal in 1940–41.[2] Before parliament met again, on October 3, Duff Cooper, the First Lord of the Admiralty, had resigned in protest, and there were signs of revolt among some of the 'young Turks' of the Conservative party. Professor R. W. Seton-Watson had circulated a memorandum among members of parliament describing some of the pressures to which the Czechoslovakian government had been exposed from its friends, and this, though rather too vigorously contradicted by Hoare, had had its effect.[3]

The Commons debated the Munich agreement for four days (October 3–6). Chamberlain reiterated his belief that his action had avoided war, and that he had been right in taking it; his purpose since taking office had been 'to work for the pacification of Europe', even though 'the path which leads to appeasement is long and bristles with obstacles' (October 3). Simon asked critics if they would, if they could, undo what had been done, and 'fling the world into the cauldron of immediate war'. Few took up this challenge. Attlee condemned the settlement as one of Britain's greatest diplomatic defeats and a bitter humiliation; a gallant and democratic people had been 'betrayed and handed over to a ruthless despotism'; brute force had triumphed, and Hitler had won dominance over Europe without firing a shot.[4] Churchill foretold doom. 'We have sustained a total and unmitigated defeat', the fruits of five years of 'uninterrupted retreat of British power'. He concluded:

And do not suppose that this is the end. This is only the beginning of the reckoning. This is only the first sip, the first foretaste of a bitter cup which will be proffered to us year by year unless by a supreme recovery of moral health and martial vigour, we arise again and take our stand for freedom as in the olden time.[5]

Duff Cooper gave an explanation of his resignation. If war had come over Czechoslovakia it would have been, as in 1914, to prevent one country from dominating the continent 'by brutal force'. 'For that principle we must ever be prepared to fight, for

---

[1] G. M. Gathorne-Hardy, p. 476; *Britain by Mass-Observation,* p. 86.
[2] Eleanor Rathbone, quoted in Mrs. Stocks' life of her, p. 267; cf. M. A. Hamilton, *Remembering my good friends,* p. 304.
[3] J. W. Wheeler-Bennett, p. 182.   [4] 339 H.C. Deb., 5 s., 48, 51, 350.
[5] 339 H.C. Deb., 5 s., 359–73.

on the day when we are not prepared to fight for it we forfeit our Empire, our liberties and our independence.'[1]

Despite these criticisms, there was no doubt that the government would be sustained in parliament, as it was supported by a majority of the people outside. Opposition came from the Liberals and the Labour party, and from some thirty Conservatives: Eden, Cranborne and their followers, and Churchill, Amery, Robert Boothby, Duncan Sandys, Harold Macmillan, Brendan Bracken, Lord Lloyd, Lord Cecil. In the Commons such critics abstained from voting, and the government carried the motion of approval by 366 votes to 144. In November the Duchess of Atholl resigned her seat in protest against the government's foreign policy, and ran for re-election as an Independent, but was defeated.

Yet it was soon clear that whatever else had been saved by the Munich agreement, Czechoslovakia had been abandoned even more shamefully than had at first appeared. The so-called international commission which was to delimit the fifth and last zone which the Germans were to occupy, and to supervise other arrangements, consisted of two German generals, the British, French and Italian ambassadors in Berlin, and a Czech representative. To decide which districts should, on an ethnographical basis, be included in this fifth zone, the Germans insisted that the census of 1910 be used, thus greatly and unjustifiably increasing their 'take': the Czech representative appealed for help to the British and French ambassadors and was coldly ignored. The Germans took what they wanted without let or hindrance. Poland and Hungary presented claims to Czechoslovakian territory also, and these were settled, not by a four-power conference which the Munich agreement had promised, but by an 'award', in the case of Hungarian claims, made by Ribbentrop and Ciano, the Italian foreign minister, at Vienna on November 2. The British government accepted this exclusion placidly, and the 'guarantee' which had been given for Czechoslovakia's new frontiers was allowed to fade away, until on March 2, 1939, in response to a query about it, the German government insolently stated that even to raise the question was an unwarranted and undesirable interference in Germany's sphere of influence.[2] All Czechoslovakia got from Great Britain was a loan of £30 millions, which provoked rude comparisons with a certain thirty pieces of silver, and the balance

[1] 339 H.C. Deb., 5 s., 32–40. See also J. W. Wheeler-Bennett, pp. 183–9; W. S. Churchill, pp. 286, 291–4; *Annual Register, 1938*, pp. 75–9; Harold Nicolson, 'The Commons and the 1938 Crisis', *Listener*, November 25, 1948.
[2] J. W. Wheeler-Bennett, pp. 192–4, 313–18; A. C. Johnson, *Halifax*, pp. 507–8.

of which, remaining in London after Germany extinguished what little survived of Czechoslovakia in March 1939, was, amid the stupefied disgust of the public, handed over to the German government.[1]

What was left, then, of Chamberlain's gifts from Munich? The democratic powers had lost, to Hitler, the strategic position of Czechoslovakia, her fortified frontiers, her 21 regular divisions and 15 or 16 second-line divisions;[2] they had lost a just cause, they had lost their good name, they had lost the support of the smaller powers, they had exchanged, in the event, the possible assistance of Russia for a cold and fatal neutrality on her part. As it became clearer that in spite of all this they would still, in all likelihood, have to fight, only two points of justification remained: when war came, the country entered it with greater unity than it would have done in 1938 and with much greater support from the Dominions; and it entered it with greater strength, because the breathing spell which it won was decisive for Britain's rearmament. The last argument was inconsistent with the earlier claim that Chamberlain had brought back 'peace for our time'.[3]

Appeasement had, however, nearly six months to run, though from the first circumstances were inauspicious. As early as October 9 Hitler, speaking at Saarbrucken, announced that he was strengthening Germany's western fortifications and hurled denunciations at all and sundry, including Churchill, Eden and Duff Cooper who, in a democratic system of government, might at any time replace the pacific Chamberlain. He also warned the English people to drop certain airs 'inherited from the Versailles epoch', and expressed in inquiries concerning the fate of Germans within the Reich which 'are not in place'. 'We cannot tolerate any longer the tutelage of governesses.'[4] This was followed by the pogrom against the Jews in Germany, carefully prepared and set in motion in revenge for the murder of a German diplomatic official in Paris by a Polish Jew on November 7: Jewish shops and synagogues were burned, thousands of Jews murdered by Nazi toughs while the police turned a blind eye, the Jewish community subjected to a collective fine of £80 millions and forced to pay for the repair of the damage their enemies had done, after which they were excluded from all economic activities. None the less, the defenders

[1] J. W. Wheeler-Bennett, pp. 186, 358–9; Cato, *Guilty Men*, p. 56.
[2] W. S. Churchill, p. 301.
[3] See Wheeler-Bennett's summing-up: *Munich*, pp. 433–7.
[4] W. S. Churchill, pp. 294–5.

of Munich were unabashed; critics of it were told earlier by
Chamberlain that they were like birds fouling their own nests
(November 1).[1]

Chamberlain had, however, his second string: friendly relations
with Mussolini, which might draw him away from Hitler. The
first step was to declare the Anglo-Italian agreement of April
16, 1938, to be in effect even though the condition precedent, that
the Spanish question should be settled first, had not been ful-
filled. This was done on November 2, accompanied by Halifax's
frank admission that the agreement never had had the value im-
puted to it, of encouraging Mussolini to withdraw his troops from
Spain, since he had always made it clear that he was not prepared
to see Franco defeated. Further gestures were made difficult by
renewed Italian bellicosity towards France, beginning in the shouts
of 'Tunis! Corsica! Nice!' in the Fascist Chamber in November 30
and followed by Mussolini's denunciation of his agreement of
January 1935 with Laval. Chamberlain took occasion, on December 12, to remark that Britain was not obligated by any treaty to
support France against an Italian attack; this statement he quickly
qualified by saying that Anglo-French relations were so close 'as
to pass beyond mere legal obligation'. The main effect of all this
was to solidify French patriotism in support of France's territories
and the Daladier government. In these unfavourable circumstances
Chamberlain and Halifax journeyed to Rome in January 1939; but
apart from conversing with Mussolini and Ciano and toasting
King Victor Emmanuel as Emperor of Ethiopia at a state banquet
they accomplished nothing—except to add to Mussolini's dangerous
contempt for Britain. On May 22 Germany and Italy converted
their axis into a military alliance (the 'Pact of Steel').[2]

By then the Spanish civil war had ceased to be an irritation to
government or opposition. Franco's campaign against Catalonia,
begun at Christmas, 1938, led the republicans to abandon Barcelona on January 25. The war continued elsewhere; but Chamberlain showed almost indecent haste in granting recognition to
Franco's government as the government of Spain on February 27,
1939. Labour's disgust at this action was increased by the fact
that it was suddenly sprung upon parliament four days after
Chamberlain, by an evasive reply to a parliamentary question, had
implied that no change was contemplated—when in fact he had
already made the decision and had urged the French government

---

[1] J. W. Wheeler-Bennett, pp. 295–9.
[2] Ibid., pp. 307–13; A. C. Johnson, *Halifax*, pp. 494–503.

to follow suit.[1] Yet it was not till March 30 that all resistance to the nationalists ceased in Madrid and the civil war came—but for its grim aftermath of executions and imprisonments—to its end.

In one other part of the world, in Palestine, the government attempted to reconcile the irreconcilable and to end bitter disagreements which were international in their effects. After the disorders of 1929 there had been an uneasy peace in Palestine. In 1933, however, the Arabs again became apprehensive about the future because of the heavy increase in the number of Jewish immigrants —mainly refugees from the Nazi terror—and in October declared a general strike, which was followed by rioting in the principal cities. Order was restored, but the anxieties of the Arabs continued. They feared that unrestricted Jewish immigration and Jewish purchases of land would eventually bring them under the domination of the Jewish population. From April to October 1936, Palestine was racked by disorders stirred up by the Arabs in a campaign to overthrow the mandatory power, Great Britain: a general strike of unprecedented duration, murders, ambushes, attacks on trains and convoys of motor vehicles, the blowing up of railway tracks—these and other acts of violence by the Arabs provoked Jewish reprisals and the organisation of Jewish military bodies, the Hagana and the terrorist Irgun Zvei Leumi. The government's reply to these happenings was to appoint a royal commission, presided over by Lord Peel. Its report, published in July 1937 (Cmd. 5479), recommended the partition of Palestine into three, an Arab state, a Jewish state, and a mandated one consisting of Jerusalem and Bethlehem and a corridor to the sea at Jaffa. The proposal had a poor reception both in Great Britain and in the world at large; the government bought more time by appointing a Partition Commission, under Sir John Woodhead, which reported that any scheme of partition was impossible.

By this time the government had a minor war on its hands in Palestine. In the autumn of 1937 it began to apply policies reminiscent of those used with such unfortunate effect in Ireland in 1920–21. By April 1938, the Arabs were in open rebellion, and town and country were torn by the activities of armed gangs of men: murders, ambushes, sabotage. The military forces were compelled to carry out 'a virtual military reoccupation' of the country; casualties in 1938 among all groups totalled 3717, including 1785 persons killed. The German government, with

[1] E. Windrich, *British Labour's Foreign Policy*, pp. 155–7.

leering hypocrisy, denounced the military brutalities of this British campaign.

Something must be done to restore peace, even though the government was hopelessly impaled on the horns of a dilemma. Arab goodwill was much to be desired. Yet to appease the Arabs by suspending Jewish immigration was not only to outrage the Jewish people throughout the world, but to doom to death those who still hoped to find a refuge from the horrors of Nazi persecution. One last expedient remained: a Round Table Conference of Jews and Arabs—including representatives from both sides from countries outside Palestine—which was held in London in February and March 1939. No agreement could be reached. The government was therefore forced to announce an award of its own. The White Paper of May 17, 1939 (*Palestine: Statement of Policy*: Cmd. 6019) laid down that Jewish immigration should continue for five years more, at the rate of 10,000 persons per year, or, allowing for 25,000 extra immigrants, 75,000 persons in all, bringing the Jewish population up to one-third of the total population. Thereafter immigration would cease, except with the consent of the Arabs. At that point an independent Palestinian state would be established, with a constitution framed by representatives of the people of Palestine and the British government. This attempt to satisfy both sides inevitably satisfied neither. Palestine remained unappeased; even the outbreak of the world war in September did not end the violence and murder which mocked the name of the Holy Land.[1]

7. REARMAMENT: ARGUMENT AND ACHIEVEMENT

In the months following the Munich settlement as much energy was devoted to rearmament as to appeasement, inconsistent though they were. Britain had begun to enlarge the air force, in a very modest way, in 1934; rearmament became an official policy in 1935, and policy was translated into practice in 1936.[2] The pace, however, remained leisurely until after Munich: Treasury control exercised its normal restraints; rearmament must not lead to the 'sacrifice' of British commerce or prejudice policies of conciliation; the public was not ready for large programmes. Rearmament was

---

[1] This account rests on the Royal Institute of International Affairs paper, *Great Britain and Palestine, 1915–1945* (London, 1946), which has a full bibliography. But see the comments in L. B. Namier, *Conflicts* (London, 1942), pp. 110–19, 147.
[2] See above, chapter 8, pp. 476–8, chapter 10, pp. 540, 568–71.

still thought of as a deterrent to aggressors, not as a preparation for war.[1]

Between the beginning of 1936 and the end of 1938 the main progress made was in the enlargement and re-equipment of the R.A.F. New types of aircraft began to appear: their prototypes were first seen by the public in 1936, and represented the fruits of Lord Londonderry's term at the Air Ministry: the Wellington, Hampden and Blenheim bombers, the Spitfire and Hurricane fighters, on which Britain's survival in 1940 largely rested. The Spitfire was the last and most beautiful of the designs of R. J. Mitchell: an attempt to translate the flight of birds into the lines of an aeroplane which his tragically short life only just permitted him to realise.[2] Under Lord Swinton the Air Ministry became very busy. A new programme, Scheme F, approved by the Cabinet in February 1936, provided for the construction of 8000 planes in three years as compared with 3800 which the previous programmes would have produced in two years: this allowed for a much greater reserve of planes. The strength of the R.A.F. was expanded,[3] and the Royal Air Force Volunteer Reserve was inaugurated.[4]

Even these developments were necessarily slow in producing results; a new and warlike temper was needed, and appeared after the *Anschluss*—six months before the new spirit, born of Munich, began to transform the rearmament of the two older services. After a tug-of-war between Swinton and Simon, the Chancellor of the Exchequer, financial restraints were practically given up, and industrial capacity became the chief limitation. The new programme, Scheme L, approved on April 27, 1938, provided for 12,000 new planes in two years (the figure was raised to 17,500 just before the war began). This involved close planning of production with the aircraft companies. The production staff of the Air Ministry was strengthened by the appointment of Air-Marshal Sir Wilfrid Freeman as Air Member for Development and Production, and Ernest Lemon (of the L.M.S. Railway) as Director-General of Production. The expansion of aircraft factories and the construction of shadow factories were pushed forward; sub-con-

---

[1] K. Feiling, *N. Chamberlain*, p. 314; M. M. Postan, *British War Production* (History of the Second World War: United Kingdom Civil Series; London, 1952), pp. 10–11.

[2] See *D.N.B.*, *Supplement, 1931–1940*, s.v. R. J. Mitchell (1895–1937).

[3] Strength of the R.A.F.: 1935, 32,145; 1936, 45,804; 1937, 56,163 (years to March 31): *Statistical Abstract of U.K.*, *1938*, p. 170.

[4] Norman Macmillan, *The Royal Air Force in the World War*, I (London, 1942), pp. 21–32.

tracting was developed; the potential of the aircraft industry was so increased that in 1939 deliveries exceeded expectations. In April, the first mission for the purchase of planes went to the United States: 400 planes were ordered as a result, to the benefit of the American aircraft industry's war potential. When war came, the R.A.F., with the industrial strength on which it depended, was better prepared than the army or navy. This was not enough, however, to save the government from severe criticism in a debate on air strength on May 12, 1938; as a result of which Lord Swinton was replaced by the brisk and more genial figure of Sir Kingsley Wood, the Minister of Health (succeeded in turn by Walter Elliot).[1]

Progress was much slower in the other services. The navy, which had less lost ground to recover, began a modest programme of expansion in 1935, designed to supplement its 'one-power standard' (the power being Japan) by new vessels, chiefly cruisers and destroyers, to provide protection against German depredations on commerce during a war in Europe. This was slightly accelerated in 1936.[2] The army had been the most neglected of the services. The regular army consisted of five divisions, of which one (divided into two in 1938) was mobile; but only two were fully equipped by October 1938. Mechanisation was more of a theory than a practice: it was not until 1938 that the army possessed its peacetime complement of wheeled vehicles and half the needed number of tracked vehicles.[3] Its greatest limitation was, however, in the idea of its use: it served a doctrine of limited liability, under which it was expected to provide for home defence and for imperial garrisons, but not to produce an expeditionary force nor support commitments on the continent of Europe. This, among other things, meant that the chief effort in its re-equipment was devoted to its tasks in anti-aircraft defence. There was, none the less, an important expansion of the arms industry after 1936 under a new official, the Director-General of Munitions Production, Engineer Vice-Admiral Sir Harold Brown: new Royal Ordnance Factories and private arms factories were built, and in 1937 the stockpiling of strategic materials was begun. Moreover the enlargement and re-equipment of the Territorial Army increased the efficiency of the regular army also.[4]

[1] M. M. Postan, *British War Production*, pp. 14–21, 68; W. S. Churchill, *Gathering Storm*, p. 208.
[2] For details, see M. M. Postan, pp. 2–4, 23–8, 469.   [3] M. M. Postan, p. 6.
[4] Ibid., pp. 6–8, 28–30, 36–47.   The strength of the Territorial Army was 131,617 in 1935, 156,765 in 1937, 186,421 in 1938 (years to October 1): *Statistical Abstract of U.K., 1938*, p. 170.

Such measures of rearmament, large and indeed unprecedented in their cost in peacetime, were much less than those of Germany. In 1938 Germany was spending £1710 millions, or a quarter of her national income, on armaments, Great Britain £358 millions, 7 per cent of her national income.[1] The increase in expenditure on armaments in Great Britain, great as it was (250 per cent more than the figure for 1934), was less than Germany's (470 per cent); by 1938 Britain's expenditure exceeded that of France, a reversal of the situation in 1934.

British and German Expenditure on Armaments[2]

	1934 (£ millions)	1938 (at 1934 prices)	Increase (per cent)
Great Britain	99·1	350·0	250
Germany	280·0	1600·0	470

Estimated Annual Expenditure on Rearmament in Great Britain, 1934–39 (£ millions)[3]

	Total	Factory construction (Royal Ordnance Factories and others)	Army	Navy	R.A.F.
1934	37·2	—	6·9	20·9	9·4
1935	42·6	—	8·5	24·2	9·9
1936	60·7	—	12·5	29·6	18·6
1937	104·2	1·5	21·4	42·0	39·3
1938	182·2	8·7	44·3	63·2	66·0
1939	273·1	12·7	67·6	82·9	109·9

Such expenditures put a heavy strain on the budget. For 1938 total expenditure was estimated at £944 millions, compared with £862·8 millions in 1937; of this the defence services accounted for £253 millions (plus £90 millions to be provided by borrowing). The standard rate of income tax was raised from 5s. to 5s. 6d. in the £. In the last peacetime budget, that of 1939, expenditure

[1] A. J. Brown, *Applied Economics: Aspects of the World Economy in War and Peace* (London, 1947), p. 23.
[2] Ibid., p. 41 (based on League of Nations, *Armaments Year Book*).
[3] M. M. Postan, p. 12. These figures do not include the pay and maintenance of the armed forces.

was estimated at £942 millions, of which defence demanded £250 millions (plus £380 millions to be found by borrowing). The limit on borrowing for defence was raised from £400 millions to £800 millions. On this occasion surtax rates and death duty on the larger estates were increased. Actual expenditures were, of course, higher than the estimates.[1]

The war-scare over Czechoslovakia revealed to the public some—though not necessarily the most serious—of the deficiencies in the country's defences. Most serious seemed to be the anti-aircraft defences: the cupboard was almost bare, and could hardly provide for London, let alone any other city: only 44 of the larger (3·7 inch) A.A. guns ordered were available; and there were only 60 fire pumps in London.[2] Nor did the spirit of urgency produced by the crisis pass with Chamberlain's return from Munich: indeed the unanimity with which increased efforts in rearmament were called for was a measure of the confidence which friend and foe put in 'peace for our time'. In the year of peace which remained many deficiencies were made good, though not so much as a result of new plans as of the carrying forward, more or less to schedule, of those already made. The R.A.F.'s programmes were now being achieved in full measure. The navy's main addition was in the construction of trawlers and escort vessels for protection against mines and submarines. A list of reserved occupations promised the proper husbanding of man-power in January 1939. Financial restraints on defence measures thawed rapidly. And in April 1939, Chamberlain even agreed to the creation of a Ministry of Supply, though without responsibility for the requirements of the Admiralty and R.A.F. It began to function in July, though Chamberlain's choice of minister, Leslie Burgin (a National Liberal who had been Minister of Transport) did not inspire enthusiasm.[3] All these developments expressed a change of spirit: rearmament in preparation for war, and no longer as a safeguard for peace. Yet it still fell short of the full mobilisation of the country's resources. It was based on the supposition that resources could be built up over two years: by the summer of 1940 Britain would be ready for war; before then she must begin no premature military action.[4]

One great change there was: in the conception of the army's function. The idea of 'limited liability' was dropped early in 1939,

---

[1] *Annual Register, 1938*, pp. 29–30; *1939*, p. 39.
[2] Details in M. M. Postan, p. 55; on the fire pumps see K. Feiling, *N. Chamberlain*, p. 456.
[3] M. M. Postan, pp. 58, 78, 81–2, 96.   [4] Ibid., pp. 53–4 (an important evaluation).

thanks to Leslie Hore-Belisha (the War Secretary) and Halifax. The defence of Britain was understood to involve the defence of France. Anglo-French military conversations were resumed on a serious level.[1] A British expeditionary force was to be prepared, consisting of 19 infantry and 2 cavalry divisions; in the event 4 divisions were ready by September 1939, and 6 by January 1940.[2] The army was to be raised to 32 divisions (the six regular divisions and 26 Territorial divisions) by bringing the Territorial Army to full strength and doubling its size; these decisions were made on March 29 and April 21, 1939. The final measure was the introduction, for the first time during peace, of conscription.[3]

How far did the progress of rearmament after Munich justify the settlement on the ground, of which its apologists came to make so much, that the time gained was greatly, even indispensably, to Britain's advantage? Stocks of rifles, guns, tanks were increased: in October 1938, only two army divisions were fully equipped; by September 1939 there was equipment for five.[4] Industrial mobilisation had a year more in which to pick up momentum. The provision of anti-aircraft guns increased fourfold, to about two-fifths of the estimated 'ideal' requirements.[5] The chain of 20 radar stations, first proposed by Robert Watson-Watt in 1935, was completed: even during the Munich crisis it had been in operation in the Thames estuary.[6] And the number of modern planes, of the necessary speed and fire power, which Britain possessed had increased. In September 1938, the R.A.F. had five squadrons of Hurricanes and one of Spitfires; a year later it had 26 squadrons equipped with one or the other.[7] The expansion of Germany's air force was nearly complete in 1938, Britain's was beginning; the disparity between the two was therefore reduced in the year which followed as far as quality of planes was concerned, though it was increased in the comparative size of the two forces. It was Britain's monthly output of planes which was the hopeful sign: in 1938 it was over 200 a month, in 1939 over 600.[8] It was in the strengthening of her air power that the breathing spell afforded by Munich was of supreme value to Great Britain.

---

[1] M. M. Postan, pp. 70–1.   [2] J. W. Wheeler-Bennett, *Munich*, p. 325.
[3] M. M. Postan, p. 72.
[4] Ibid., pp. 103, 109. For a summing-up of gains and losses from Munich, see Jules Menken, *loc. cit.*, pp. 139–41.
[5] See table in M. M. Postan, p. 106.
[6] M. M. Postan, pp. 106–7.   [7] Ibid., p. 108.
[8] See table, M. M. Postan, p. 484: monthly output of Hurricanes rose from 26 to 44, of Spitfires from 13 to 32. between October, 1938, and September, 1939 (*ibid.*, p. 106).

British and German Air Strength, 1938–39[1]

	German		Britain (home strength) (a)	
	1938	1939	1938	1939
First-line aircraft	2847	3609	1854	1978
Totals of new aircraft production in year	5235	8295	2827	7940

(a) France had 1735 first-line aircraft in 1939.

So far so good. What was lost, by not fighting in September 1938, were the 36 Czech divisions, and the fact that at that time Germany had only 13 divisions on her western front. A year later Germany could dispose most of her forces in the west after the fall of Poland and by that time had greatly strengthened her fortifications in the west (the Siegfried Line). In 1938 Germany had between 21 and 51 fully-equipped divisions, by 1939, 106; yet in that year French strength had not increased and that of the British army not very much. Churchill claimed that in 1938 France still possessed military superiority over Germany; by 1939 the reverse was true. In 1938 Britain was weaker in the air than in 1939; but Germany could not then have won easily the bases in France and the Low Countries from which to raid England on a large scale.[2] Whether the gains of the Munich year are held to outweigh the losses will depend on one's judgment of the value of a year in increasing Britain's air power and industrial potential for war— an increase which came, not so much from what was done in the year, as from the greater length of time in which programmes of production already begun could gain momentum.

In one other sphere there was a gain. After Munich, Britain's civil defences were put in order. The work of A.R.P. (Air Raid Precautions) had begun in 1935, under the Home Office: doctors, air-raid wardens, policemen had been given training, volunteer workers recruited, handbooks prepared. Late in 1937 the Air Raid Precautions bill was enacted, imposing A.R.P. duties on the local authorities at the charge, up to 90 per cent of the cost, of the national government. In late October 1938, Sir John Anderson, the distinguished civil servant, was made Lord Privy Seal with responsibility for civil defence, and new plans were made and put

[1] M. M. Postan, pp. 107–8. Cf. W. S. Churchill, p. 303.
[2] W. S. Churchill, pp. 301–4; M. M. Postan, p. 108.

into action. Emergency fire services and transport services were prepared, and 400,000 small steel shelters (Anderson shelters) ordered for use in private houses and gardens (plans for deep air raid shelters were rejected). In January 1939, the government's *Guide to National Service* was distributed to every household in the kingdom, and everyone was urged to volunteer for service of some sort. Plans for evacuation of people from the cities, especially children and hospital patients, were completed—a task falling chiefly to Walter Elliot and the Ministry of Health. The calls which war was likely to make upon all, civilians and soldiers alike, were clear, even exaggeratedly so, as 1939 opened.[1]

Under the pressure of events Labour slowly and doubtfully abandoned its opposition to rearmament. Belief in pacifism, disarmament, collective security had been gradually undermined, partly by the events in Spain, Austria, Czechoslovakia, partly by the efforts of such leaders as Dalton and Bevin, respectively chairman of the Labour party and of the T.U.C. in 1937.[2] The Parliamentary Labour Party abandoned direct opposition to the estimates of the service departments—and hence to rearmament— in July 1937, when it decided by a vote of 45 to 39 to abstain in such votes in future; even this change, however, was resisted by Attlee, Morrison, Greenwood, so great was their distrust of Chamberlain's policies. The next statement of the National Council of Labour on foreign policy, *International Policy and Defence*, issued in July 1937, still talked of restoring the League, of disarmament and the avoidance of an arms race; but it added that the country must be strong enough to defend itself and fulfil its part in collective security, and that until conditions improved a future Labour government would not reverse the policy of rearmament. This report was adopted by overwhelming majorities by the T.U.C. in September and by the Labour party conference at Bournemouth in October 1937: both actions were taken to imply support for rearmament. A circular of the National Council of Labour in March 1939, was more specific: 'rearmament is necessary, and indeed unavoidable in the interests of self-defence alone'.[3] Labour had shown on the eve of Munich that it would accept, even welcome, a strong policy; and in this, despite its opposition to conscription, it remained firm.[4]

[1] *Annual Register*, 1937, pp. 89–91; 1939, pp. 4–6, 38; J. W. Wheeler-Bennett, p. 324.
[2] See above, chapter 10, pp. 540, 550–2, 569–71, for Labour policies in 1935–37.
[3] G. D. H. Cole, *History of the Labour Party*, p. 363.
[4] Ibid., pp. 331–5; F. Williams, *Bevin*, p. 203; J. W. Wheeler-Bennett, p. 265. Cf. A. L. Rowse, *End of an Epoch*, pp. 8, 87, 110.

8. POLITICS GONE SOUR

Feelings of relief, after Chamberlain's return from Munich, had been intense and brief: the reaction was correspondingly protracted and enfeebling, as it became clear that the agreements which had been made were as much use as a sieve for carrying water. In the six months which followed there were two sorts of response to the nation's predicament. One was an almost frantic energy, particularly by the amateurs in politics: meetings, resolutions, campaigns, a new attempt to form a 'people's front' against the government. The other was a feeling of desperation: nothing could be done to arrest the drift to war or to make the country sufficiently strong to be able to face war with confidence; alternatively, war might be evaded, but at the price of honour, freedom, survival. From this grew distrust—distrust not only of the government but of parliament, of the fundamental soundness of society and of the constitution.

A new sort of political literature was the product of this distrust, a battle of the books waged by pseudonymous authors, some evoking the glory of ancient Rome. 'Simon Haxey', author of *Tory M.P.* (1939), set the fashion. He anatomised the character of the Conservatives in the House of Commons in a manner reminiscent of Professor L. B. Namier's investigation of the structure of politics in George III's time: their wealth, their company directorships, their business connections with munition-makers, with gold and diamond mines, with the exploiters of colonies, with brewers and bankers were exposed, with much naming of names and counting of companies. The reader learned of the modern cousinhood, the surviving strength of the aristocracy in the Commons; he learned how many Conservative M.P.'s hailed from Eton or Harrow, from Oxford or Cambridge, from the commissioned ranks of the army and navy. Such associations, it was implied, influenced points of view, votes, policy. Some members had avowed sympathy and support for Hitler and the Nazis, for Mussolini, for Mosley's fascists at home; 27 of them were members of the Anglo-German Fellowship; others belonged to a similar but more exclusive organisation, The Link, and were dangerously intimate with Ribbentrop and other members of the flashy German colony. Later books of this *genre* attempted to corrode the respect and credit of the Conservatives by quoting damning excerpts from their speeches: 'Cato's' *Guilty Men* (1940) did this for the leaders, 'Gracchus'' *Your M.P.* (1944) for the rank and file. Thus were Conservative charges that Labour had opposed rearmament turned aside, and the Conservatives' record shouted from the housetops—sympathy for Nazism, dislike of Russia, distrust of the League, rearmament on the principle of business-as-usual. Such books contained more malice than truth, but enough truth to help decide the votes of many people in 1945.

Other authors, writing under their own names, expressed the same scepticism less directly. Ernest Davies' *'National' Capitalism* (1939) explained its message in its subtitle, 'The Government's Record as Protector of Private Monopoly'. National Capitalism in Britain, National Socialism in Germany, both put private property before public welfare. H. R. G. Greaves' *The British Constitution* (1938) described the real constitution as one in which a very small part of the population controlled all the levers of power. The monarchy, the House of Commons, the Lords, the officer class in the army and navy, the judges on the bench, the bishops of the church were examined in this light: birth, business wealth, landed property led to power and office, particularly when reinforced by education at one of the better public schools; few rose far outside the charmed circle.[1]

A longer view will show the Conservatives' record of legislation in the Baldwin-MacDonald-Chamberlain era to have been less sinister than its opponents would admit. In the last three years of peace, however, little was done that did not bear upon rearmament and civil defence. The Matrimonial Causes Act (1937), the Coal Act (1938) deserved the attention given to them. The Ministers of the Crown Act, 1937, is of constitutional importance: it not only equalised and raised ministers' salaries and gave a salary to the leader of the Opposition but gave statutory recognition to the Cabinet and to the office of Prime Minister for the first time in their two centuries of existence. The salary of M.P.'s was raised in the same year from £400 to £600. In November 1938, Sir Samuel Hoare, as Home Secretary, introduced a Criminal Justice bill with the object of bringing greater humanity into the prison; it also proposed the abolition of flogging as a punishment (despite the judges' opposition). The bill had not been passed before the outbreak of war, and was abandoned in November 1939.

Distrust of government and parliament sprang from other causes: from dislike of the manner of the Prime Minister quite as much as of the matter of his foreign policy. His self-righteousness,

[1] See also Greaves' *Reactionary England* (1936), and Lewis Clive, *The People's Army* (1938).

his treatment of all criticism as a personal affront to himself, irked many of his supporters almost as much as it did Liberal and Labour members. Many people credited him with ideas of dictatorship, which his friends were hard put to it to deny; as when in parliament on August 2, 1939, he resisted the plea of the Opposition, supported by many members of his own party, that parliament should adjourn for three weeks rather than until October 3 and turned the question into a vote of confidence.[1] Yet he was frequently opposed by his own back-benchers, both young and old, some forty in all; and not only on foreign policy but on the niggardly and unimaginative measures taken for the distressed areas. The rebels found that the party whip was no mere figure of speech; and if they were not silenced by accepting a position as P.P.S. (Parliamentary Private Secretary) to some minister they might find sanctions invoked against them in their constituencies— the threat of the local party association to withdraw its support.[2]

Another problem faced Chamberlain: to strengthen his government to meet the criticisms of it in a time of danger. It was not truly National; many of its members were undistinguished. He did, to his credit, refuse to capitalise on his popularity immediately after the Munich settlement by holding a general election. In this he followed Halifax's advice, but he rejected the remainder of Halifax's counsel, that the government be reconstructed, including such men as Eden and Churchill, and some Liberal and Labour members. A fruitless approach to Lord Samuel was the only result. A few Cabinet offices were reshuffled at the turn of the year.[3]

Against a government so impregnable and imperturbable a new public campaign of opposition was born early in 1938. It was the successor of the United Front campaign of 1937, which official Labour's opposition had ended; but it was more inclusive, and instead of being based on a working-class solidarity which would bring Labour and Communists together it abandoned the idea of the class struggle in favour of a united movement of people of all sorts, Labour, Liberals, independents, who would join in opposing

[1] 350 H.C. Deb., 5 s., 2425 ff.
[2] See the life of one of the young Conservative critics in parliament by his sister: Barbara Cartland, *Ronald Cartland* (London, 1942), pp. 75, 83–5, 130–9. Cf. J. R. J. Macnamara [another young Conservative M.P.], *The Whistle Blows* (London, 1938), pp. 145–50. For the controversy over Duncan Sandys, M.P., and the possible application of the Official Secrets Act to members of parliament who divulged official information in the course of questions or debate, see *Annual Register, 1938* and *1939* and 337, 338 H.C. Deb., 5 s. (June 27, 29, 30, July 11, 1938).
[3] K. Feiling, pp. 384–7.

the National government. It reflected the frustration of many people with a parliament elected in 1935, in greatly different circumstances, and under no compulsion to appeal to the country before 1940. The campaign aimed at turning the government out of office, uniting all its opponents, all who hated fascism and Nazism. It had support from *Reynolds' News* and the *News Chronicle*, from parts of the Co-operative movement, and from as many as 120 local Labour parties. In so far as it had a name—since it was largely local, informal, spontaneous, a matter of meetings and demonstrations—it was the Popular Front. It reached its height in the autumn of 1938, when the government did badly in several by-elections and lost one, Bridgwater, to an independent (Vernon Bartlett, the journalist) who ran with Liberal and Labour support.

The Labour party executive, a veritable Mrs. Grundy, set its face against the Popular Front, lecturing (and on occasion disaffiliating) local Labour parties which supported it for their impropriety. The thing to do was to convert voters to Labour, so that the party might win the next election, whenever that might be, rather than to flirt with the Liberals and to shelve socialist principles. In January 1939, Sir Stafford Cripps, a member of the national executive, submitted a memorandum to his colleagues advocating a Popular Front campaign supporting a 'positive policy of peace by collective action' with France, Russia, the United States and other democratic countries (in this and his subsequent National Petition Cripps evaded the issue of rearmament). The executive rejected the memorandum; whereupon Cripps circulated it as his own proposal to local Labour parties and other bodies. Recalled by the executive, Cripps refused to retract the memorandum or reaffirm his loyalty to the party, and was expelled from the party. Later other members of the party who continued to support Cripps' campaign—notably Sir Charles Trevelyan, Aneurin Bevan and G. R. Strauss—were expelled also. The annual conference of the party, held at Southport in May 1939, upheld the executive's action. The Labour party marched off to war temporarily parted from some of its own left wing.[1]

9. THE GREAT SWING IN FOREIGN POLICY

It was not the scepticism and opposition of critics from right and left, nor the sense of shame and danger, which ended the policy of

[1] G. D. H. Cole, *History of the Labour Party*, pp. 352–60; E. Estorick, *Stafford Cripps* (New York, 1949), pp. 162–9; J. T. Murphy, *New Horizons*, pp. 326–33.

appeasement. It endured through the winter of 1938–39, its life prolonged by injections of false optimism from the Prime Minister's office, over the protests of Lord Halifax. On March 10 Chamberlain told the press correspondents in the House of Commons that 'Europe was settling down to a period of tranquility', and on the same day Hoare, speaking at Chelsea, denounced the 'jitterbugs' who were predicting war and offered instead the vision of a new age in which the three dictators (Hitler, Mussolini and Franco) and the British and French prime ministers, working together, would bring not merely peace but standards of living raised to heights never possible before. *Punch*, in an unfortunate cartoon entitled 'The Ides of March', depicted the nightmare of war escaping out of the window as John Bull, wearing an A.R.P. helmet, woke from his night's rest. It was published on March 15.[1]

On that very day Hitler struck, and Czechoslovakia, desperately wounded since Munich, received its death-blow. Profiting from the internal divisions of the state, Hitler encouraged Slovakia and Ruthenia to proclaim their independence (under German tutelage) and summoned President Hácha to Berlin. There the President, a sick man, was bullied and cajoled by Goering and Ribbentrop, between 1 and 4.30 in the morning of March 15, into signing a treaty putting his country under German protection. German troops at once moved in, Prague was occupied by 9 that morning. 'Bohemia-Moravia' was declared to be a German Protectorate. The Gestapo and its apparatus of delation and death quickly followed.[2]

In Britain the news was received with feelings of horror and disgust. There was an awakening, as from a drugged sleep, a determination that the country must unite and now, if not too late, bring Hitler's aggressions to an end. He had now annexed non-German peoples to the Reich. Even *The Times* denounced the seizure of Bohemia as something for which no 'moral case' existed. Yet in parliament Chamberlain seemed little disturbed, and made light of angry questions both from the Opposition and from government supporters; Simon held to the Munich line, and refused to admit that Britain's previous guarantee to Czechoslovakia could apply to something which had become non-existent. The tide of feeling threatened Chamberlain's position until he was saved by Halifax, who first tried once again to persuade

[1] J. W. Wheeler-Bennett, pp. 328–30, 349–50; K. Feiling, pp. 396–7.
[2] J. W. Wheeler-Bennett, pp. 331–46.

him to broaden the government and then convinced him that he must speak out strongly against Hitler in a speech he was to make in Birmingham on March 17. Chamberlain wrote a new speech.[1]

Chamberlain's speech inaugurated a new course in British policy, though in a strange, sullen fashion. He defended what he had done at Munich, and denounced Hitler's breach of faith as a personal affront to himself, in the tone (it has been said) of a tradesman rebuking a customer for failing to pay his bill.[2] 'Surely as a joint signatory of the Munich Agreement I was entitled, if Herr Hitler thought it ought to be undone, to that consultation which is provided for in the Munich Declaration. Instead of that, he has taken the law into his own hands.' Where was the process going to stop? 'Is this the last attack upon a small State, or is it to be followed by another?' There was hardly anything he would not sacrifice for peace, but one thing he must except, 'the liberty we have enjoyed for hundreds of years and which we will never surrender'. If Hitler was attempting to 'dominate the world by force', then he must realise that 'this nation' would 'take part to the uttermost of its power in resisting such a challenge'.[3]

Yet the swing-round in foreign policy began slowly. The visit of two ministers to Germany for trade talks was cancelled, to Goering's indignation, and Sir Nevile Henderson was recalled for consultations (though not, as Halifax wished, withdrawn from Berlin permanently). The next country to be absorbed by Germany seemed likely to be Rumania, which was under pressure to grant trade concessions in oil and grain to Germany which would be ruinous to itself, and was preparing to resist. What to do? The Russian government proposed on March 18 a conference of the British, French, Russian, Polish, Rumanian and Turkish governments to concert means of resisting aggression against any one of their countries. The Munichers, led by Simon, resisted such sweeping commitments. Chamberlain rejected the Russian initiative as premature, and thereby doomed the hope—the anxious hope, as it soon became—of an Anglo-Russian agreement.[4] Instead he proposed on March 21 that Britain, France, Russia and Poland should issue a declaration that they would act together if there were signs of new aggressions by Germany. This plan was

[1] J. W. Wheeler-Bennett, pp. 349–56; A. C. Johnson, *Halifax*, pp. 510–14; *History of The Times*, IV, ii, 961.
[2] M. A. Hamilton, *Remembering my good friends*, p. 305.
[3] J. W. Wheeler-Bennett, pp. 356–58; W. S. Churchill, pp. 308–10.
[4] J. W. Wheeler-Bennett, pp. 364–8; A. C. Johnson, *Halifax*, pp. 515–16.

blocked immediately by Poland, whose suspicion of Russia was not diminished by her own danger.[1]

Simultaneously Poland was placed under the spotlight of German aggrandisement. On March 21 the Polish ambassador in Berlin received from Ribbentrop a series of demands on his country: the Free City of Dantzig must be ceded to Germany and the Polish Corridor amended; in return, Germany would give Poland a new guarantee of its frontiers. Rumours of troop movements suggested that a *coup* was imminent. On March 22 Memel was ceded by Lithuania to Germany, on the threat of its immediate occupation. Poland then appealed for help. At this point Chamberlain swung around full circle. On March 31 he announced to the House of Commons that in the event of any action which threatened Poland's independence 'His Majesty's Government would feel themselves bound at once to lend the Polish government all support in their power'. France, he added, joined in this guarantee (it had a military alliance with Poland, dating from 1921). On April 6 it was replaced by a reciprocal agreement between Britain and Poland.[2]

This was an extraordinary revolution in British policy. At Birmingham Chamberlain had spurned new and unspecified commitments; now, two weeks later, he accepted a commitment which was of unlimited extent. Having refused any help to Czechoslovakia, he now offered all possible help to Poland, a more distant country. Such a plunge can be ascribed to the indignation of an obstinate man who, balked of his hopes, throws caution to the winds. Chamberlain, however, intended it as a deterrent to Hitler. He, unlike most people, still regarded war as not inevitable, and was determined not to permit it to come through the vagueness which had cloaked Britain's intentions in 1914.[3]

Yet what incredible rashness it was! To guarantee Poland without agreement with Russia, her neighbour, and unfortunately a hated neighbour. Lloyd George put his finger on the futility of the policy in the debate in parliament on April 3. 'If war occurred tomorrow, you could not send a single battalion to Poland. . . . I cannot understand why before committing ourselves to this tremendous enterprise, we did not secure beforehand the adhesion of

---

[1] J. W. Wheeler-Bennett, pp. 368–9; L. B. Namier, *Diplomatic Prelude, 1938-1939* (London, 1948), pp. 83, 92–6: the whole book gives a very close account o British diplomacy from Munich to the outbreak of war.

[2] J. W. Wheeler-Bennett, pp. 370–4.

[3] Ibid., pp. 375–7; L. B. Namier, *Europe in Decay*, p. 241; K. Feiling, pp 402–4.

Russia. . . . We have undertaken a frightful gamble. . . .'[1] More-over, once begun the policy had no end. In default of an alliance with Russia, Britain could only move helplessly to shore up other threatened countries with guarantees. In violation of Good Friday, Mussolini ordered the invasion of Albania by his troops on April 7 and forthwith annexed it to Italy. Britain countered by offering, with France, guarantees of their independence to Rumania and Greece, followed in May by an Anglo-Turkish declaration that the two countries would take joint action against any aggression in the Mediterranean. 'A guarantee a day keeps Hitler away', it was said. Other countries were doubtful of their efficacy: the Netherlands, Switzerland, Denmark, rejected similar guarantees, though Denmark, like Esthonia and Latvia, signed a non-aggression pact with Germany.

To reassure the doubters Chamberlain made another startling announcement on April 26: that the government would bring in a measure for the introduction of military conscription. True, the proposal involved no more than calling up all men aged 20 and 21 for six months' military training and could have no effect in increasing Britain's armed strength for some time; but to impose conscription on the British people in peacetime was a tremendous break with the past. It owed much to the pressure of Hore-Belisha at the War Office, and to Conservative party opinion. It was bitterly opposed by most of the Liberals and by the Labour party. Attlee denounced it as useless and divisive, destructive of freedom and carrying with it the threat of industrial conscription. It did not apply to Northern Ireland: despite the fury of Lord Craigavon the government yielded to the warnings of De Valera and an all-party protest in the Dail against the dangers which would follow the imposition of conscription upon the large Irish Nationalist minority in the six counties.[2]

Hitler was unimpressed. In any case, he was resolved to crush Poland—using German claims to Dantzig as an excuse for aggression—to gain *Lebensraum* and food supplies for Germany in the east. He was prepared for war, and expected it, though preferably not simultaneously against Poland and against France and Britain, as he told his military leaders on May 23. He had given orders on April 3 for the plans for the campaign against Poland (Operation White) to be put into effect: the attack was to come at the first suitable opportunity.[3] In his address to the Reichstag on April 28

[1] L. B. Namier, *Diplomatic Prelude*, pp. 109–10; 345 H.C. Deb., 5 s., 2505–11.
[2] D. O'Sullivan, *Irish Free State and its Senate*, pp. 585–7.
[3] J. W. Wheeler-Bennett, pp. 379, 385–7; L. B. Namier, *Diplomatic Prelude*, pp. 213–17.

he demanded the return of Dantzig and denounced the German-Polish non-aggression treaty of 1934 (though offering a new one for twenty-five years). He also denounced the Anglo-German naval treaty. He poured scorn on President Roosevelt's proposal to himself and Mussolini on April 14 that they pledge themselves not to attack any one of a list of thirty countries for ten years: instead he offered such countries non-aggression treaties of his own brand. At the same time he bound Mussolini more closely to himself, and hurried him and Ciano (both furious at his one-sided action in despatching Czechoslovakia in March) into a military alliance, the 'Pact of Steel', which was announced on May 6 and signed on May 22.[1]

10. THE SUMMER'S DALLIANCE

Few doubted after the Ides of March that there was going to be war, and that soon. The spring and summer were a time of waiting. Some people were tense, others banished thought with a forced and hectic gaiety, having a last fling on a holiday abroad or in some still unfenced seaside spot; almost all were resigned. A campaign was carried on by several newspapers in the spring and early summer for the reconstruction of the government on truly national lines, including Churchill among its members. Several Conservatives supported it, and Sir Stafford Cripps was active in the same cause. It reached its height in June when several leading Liberals, including Lady Violet Bonham-Carter (Asquith's daughter), wrote a letter to *The Times* arguing that national unity could best be shown by the formation of such a government rather than by rebuking Sir Archibald Sinclair for spreading disunity by daring to criticise Chamberlain's foreign policy. *The Times* refused to publish the letter (which duly appeared in the *Telegraph*) and then got itself into more hot water by refusing to print another letter from the veteran Liberal journalist, A. G. Gardiner, criticising this censorship of opinion. Poor old Thunderer! But the government remained unaltered.[2]

The summer was occupied with a curious, three-sided diplomatic dalliance. Great Britain was languidly wooing Soviet Russia who, bored and distrustful of her British suitor, looked with spasmodic favour on his German rival, who in turn showed suspicion, interest and finally an embarrassing ardour. There was death in the air;

[1] L. B. Namier, *Europe in Decay*, p.129 ff.
[2] W. S. Churchill, pp. 320–1; *History of The Times*, IV, ii, 969–72.

in trying to avert it the British government (and the French) walked slowly, as in a trance, towards it.

After his rejection of Russia's proposals of March 18 for a conference, Chamberlain ignored the Russian government until April 14 when (thanks in part to parliamentary criticism) he suddenly turned to it and proposed that it should make a declaration that if Britain and France were 'involved in hostilities' as a result of the guarantees they had given to Poland and Rumania the Russian government would also lend its support. To this proposal the Russians replied with the suggestion of a pact of mutual assistance between Britain, France and Russia, coupled with a military convention and a guarantee to all the border states from the Baltic to the Black Sea. The smaller powers objected, fearing the protection of Russia as much as the menace of German aggression. The pressure put on Czechoslovakia was not repeated. Instead, the Russian proposal was rejected on May 1 in favour of the earlier suggestion of a unilateral guarantee. The Russian reply was immediate. Litvinov, the advocate of collective security and co-operation with the western powers, was dismissed as commissar for foreign affairs on May 3 and replaced by Molotov. At about the same time, when Hitler began to make a cautious approach toward friendly relations with Russia by means of negotiations for a trade agreement, Molotov let it be known that Stalin desired closer political relations with Germany.

None the less, the British and French governments on May 27 opened discussions with Russia for a pact of mutual assistance and a military convention through their ambassadors in Moscow. Negotiations proceeded slowly. The Russians still distrusted the western powers, and feared that an agreement with them might precipitate rather than avert a war with Germany. The British and French governments, though the initiative in negotiations came from them, seemed more concerned to play for time, believing that an agreement, or even the possibility of one, was enough to deter Hitler and that military arrangements were not an urgent need. It was typical of the British attitude towards the negotiations that they were left in the hands of officials. Halifax was invited by Molotov to come to Moscow, but refused (perhaps from fear of failure) and sent instead William Strang, head of the Central Department of the Foreign Office; and Chamberlain, who had flown to see Hitler thrice, brushed aside suggestions that he should make personal contact with Stalin. In the negotiations, both sides raised difficulties: about the list of countries to be guaranteed against aggression, about the definition of 'indirect aggression', about the means for invoking the pact. On most points the British and French gave way; and finally they agreed on July 27 to Molotov's demand that negotiations by military missions for a military agreement should begin before the political agreement had been concluded. Yet the sense of urgency was still lacking. The military mission, which was to meet one headed by Marshal Voroshilov, the commander-in-chief of the Russian army, contained an admiral, a general and an air marshal who were all of second rank; and the French mission was no stronger. The British mission did not leave London until August 5, and after a leisurely cruise in the Baltic reached Moscow on August 11.

From August 12 onwards two parallel sets of negotiations were carried on in Moscow. The military conversations with the British and French made slow progress; the major stumbling block, introduced by the Russians, being the question of the passage of Russian troops across Polish and Rumanian territory in the event of a German attack upon Britain and France. Meanwhile, on August 12, the Russian government at last responded to German suggestions (dating back to mid-July) by a message that it was ready for political talks. Hitler's decision to seek an understanding with Russia—a complete reversal of his previous frenzy against Russia and Communism, and bound up with his determination to force a decision with Poland—was made about August 4. The Russians were ready, but not too ready, to reciprocate. Too early a breach with Britain and France would put them at Hitler's mercy; too early an agreement with Hitler might lead the western powers to give Hitler another bloodless conquest and reopen the possibility of a coalition against Russia. For Russia's safety, both sets of negotiations must be kept going until as near as possible to the time when Hitler must, if at all, start his attack on Poland: the classic time for beginning war, around September 1, between the gathering of the harvest and the coming of autumn rains.

On August 19 a Russo-German commercial agreement was signed: a curtain-raiser for the real play. On the day before, Hitler sent a message to Stalin urging that Ribbentrop be invited to come to Moscow for political negotiations. The Russians delayed their reply, but eventually agreed to receive Ribbentrop on August 26. This left Hitler too slight a margin for his plans against Poland; a further telegram from him eventually, on the 21st, brought Russian consent that Ribbentrop might come on the 23rd. He arrived by air that afternoon, and the negotiations were concluded with indecent speed, Hitler having given Ribbentrop instructions which conceded all that the Russians could demand. The Russo-German treaty of August 23 was in two parts: a mutual non-aggression pact to run for ten years, neither country to join a third party in war against the other; a secret protocol in which Germany recognised Finland, Latvia and Esthonia as being in Russia's sphere of interest, declared her lack of interest in Bessarabia (Rumanian territory) and agreed on a demarcation line between the Russian and German spheres in Poland, should Poland be partitioned. On the 25th the talks between the Russians and the British and French military missions came to an end.[1]

The news of the Russo-German treaty was received with horror around the world. Britain and France had gambled on winning Russian support for their guarantees and had lost. True, what was lost in Russian support was gained in national unity and resolution; Russia would have been an embarrassing ally, to most Conservatives, but could now be ignored. For her part, Russia had won freedom from German attack, at least for the time being. Germany had secured Russian neutrality and could now safely attack Poland —even if Britain and France should still stand by their guarantees in this new and hopeless situation. It was Hitler's grand slam. It might mean another Munich. In Britain almost everyone decided that it did and should mean war—immediate and terrible war.

11. SHALL I, SHALL I NOT?

The *casus belli* was not lacking, and had been obvious since the spring: Hitler's demands for the incorporation of Dantzig—a free city placed after the war under the authority of the League of Nations—into the Reich and for extra-territorial rights of way across the Polish corridor; ultimately for the extinction of Poland, as Czechoslovakia had been extinguished. Dantzig had long been under the control of the Nazis, marshalled by a Gauleiter, Forster. It was not difficult to arrange for incidents involving, for instance, Nazi storm troopers and Polish customs officers; there were, in

[1] Anglo-Russian negotiations are the subject of *Documents on British Foreign Policy, 1919–1939*, vol. VI, which cover the period June 8–August 14, 1939: see A. J. P. Taylor, 'Moscow Mission in 1939', *Manchester Guardian Weekly*, November 5 and 12, 1953. German-Russian relations are recounted in German documents captured in the Second World War and published by the U.S. State Department, *Nazi-Soviet Relations, 1939–1941*: see L. B. Namier, *Europe in Decay*, pp. 259 ff. Full accounts of the negotiations of June-August are given in L. B. Namier, *Diplomatic Prelude*; J. W. Wheeler-Bennett, *Munich*, pp. 388–411, 480–2; Jules Menken, *loc. cit.*, pp. 182–220; see also W. S. Churchill, *Gathering Storm*, chapters 20, 21.

fact, some incidents in May which led to fears of a *coup*, but if Hitler had such intentions at the time he drew back. The Polish government showed both firmness and moderation; it was ready to negotiate with Hitler, but not on his terms. Colonel Beck, its foreign minister, had great experience in keeping Polish policy steady on a tight-rope, yielding nothing either to Germany or Russia; he hardly needed Halifax's warnings to maintain correct behaviour and furnish no pretexts for a staged attack by Germany. And both Chamberlain, on July 10, and Sir Nevile Henderson on July 14, warned Hitler that an attack on Dantzig would mean war in which Great Britain would join.[1]

Early in August the incidents began once again, accompanied by the usual campaign of hate in the German press. On August 22, feeling sure of Russian complaisance, Hitler gave his leaders the secret orders for war: an attack on Poland. Zero hour was 4.40 a.m. on August 26. On the same day, August 22, the British Cabinet met (and the French also). The Cabinet had before it news that a Russo-German non-aggression pact was imminent and that menacing movements of German troops were being made. It decided, none the less, to stand firm in its obligations to Poland, and told the world so in a communiqué. Parliament was summoned for August 24, to enact an Emergency Powers (Defence) bill; reserves in the army, navy and air force were called up and the A.R.P. services alerted. That evening Chamberlain sent Hitler a personal letter; but it was not quite the sort of letter which he had written nearly a year before, on September 27, 1938. It had two parts. One warned Hitler that 'no greater mistake could be made' than to think that British intervention on behalf of Poland need not be reckoned with; the government's obligation to Poland was one 'they are determined to fulfil'. The government was resolved that there should be 'no such tragic misunderstanding' of Britain's intentions as there perhaps was in 1914. The other part deplored the calamity of a war over questions between Germany and Poland which could be settled without the use of force; it urged a truce to 'press polemics', followed by direct negotiations, perhaps with the aid of a neutral intermediary. 'At this moment I confess I can see no other way to avoid a catastrophe that will involve Europe in war.'[2]

---

[1] L. B. Namier, *Diplomatic Prelude*, pp. 218–27, 237–9. On the events of August see also Jules Menken, *loc. cit.*, pp. 220–80.

[2] L. B. Namier, *Diplomatic Prelude*, p. 304. The text given in W. S. Churchill, *Gathering Storm*, p. 353, is not complete; it is given in full in *Correspondence between H.M. Government . . . and the German Government* (Cmd. 6102; 1939), pp. 1–2.

Hitler wavered.[1] He received Sir Nevile Henderson at Berchtesgaden on August 23, but in two interviews he was uncompromising
—furious that Britain showed no sign of backing down, contrary
to what Ribbentrop had promised him. Then on August 25 he
summoned Henderson to see him (in Berlin) at 1.30 p.m., and
gave him a 'large comprehensive offer' to settle all difficulties
with Great Britain. He pledged himself for the continued existence of the British Empire, and promised the power of the Reich
in its defence if it was threatened anywhere in the world. Regarding Poland, however, he offered nothing: he was determined to
settle the problems of Dantzig and the Corridor; Polish provoca-
tions might lead to war at any moment. Henderson was urged to
fly to London with the offer (a similar but less sugary one was made
to France). The same offer was sent informally at the same time
by a curious, unofficial agent, Birger Dahlerus, a Swedish engineer
who had contacts with Goering and with British businessmen and
had already been dabbling in the diplomacy of appeasement. In
this final week Dahlerus made no less than three round-trip
flights between Berlin and London: a mystery man bearing messages from Goering which Halifax received but treated circum-
spectly.[2] Such activities led to fleeting hopes of preserving peace,
and jarred but did not destroy Chamberlain's resolute stand. Hitler
was ready to appease Britain once more, and separate her from
France and Poland; but he must have his little war also, and was
too impatient to let appeasement take shape.

There was much to madden Hitler. Parliament met on August
24, passed the Emergency Powers bill (a new Defence of the
Realm Act, it might be called, reminiscent of 1914's DORA), and
made it clear, in Chamberlain's speech as much as in those of
Greenwood, Eden, and Sinclair, that the country stood united and
ready to fight, not so much for Poland as for the freedom and
security of the peoples of the world. A broadcast by Halifax that
night was no less firm. The National Council of Labour, meeting
on the same day, confirmed Labour's support of the government
in resisting aggression and defending Poland's independence. A
more dramatic demonstration of the nation's will was, however,

[1] Until the end of August, Hitler had had reasons for doubting Britain's determination to fight over Poland. There had been friendly, though unofficial trade talks in
London in July between a German representative, Wohlthat, and R. S. Hudson,
secretary of the department of overseas trade; and Sir Horace Wilson had encouraged
German illusions of Britain's lack of resolution in talks with Dirksen, the German
ambassador in London: L. B. Namier, *Europe in Decay*, pp. 222–5.
[2] See Namier's account, 'An Interloper in Diplomacy', in *Diplomatic Prelude*,
pp. 417–33.

the signing on August 25 at 5.30 p.m. in London, of an Anglo-Polish treaty of alliance, reaffirming the agreement previously made on April 6. Hitler received the news of this not long after he had learned that Italy, despite the 'Pact of Steel', would not go to war in support of Germany: Mussolini was not ready. At about 6.30 p.m. Hitler cancelled the orders for Operation White to begin against Poland next morning.

Peace appeals to Hitler multiplied, from President Roosevelt, from the Pope, from King Leopold III of Belgium. Daladier's reply to Hitler's message of the 25th was conciliatory yet firm: the decision of peace or war was in Hitler's hands. The British Cabinet received Hitler's message from Henderson on Saturday the 26th, and on that day and on Sunday hammered out its reply: it hoped for a settlement safeguarding 'Poland's essential interests', which would open the way for negotiation for a 'wider and more complete understanding' between Britain and Germany; but the alternative was war. Henderson delivered this reply to Hitler at 10.30 p.m. on August 28. The Polish government was urged to agree to negotiate with Hitler—but not in the harsh terms of the advice given to Czechoslovakia. Colonel Beck agreed; but at the same time the Polish government, which had already mobilised much of its forces, gave orders on the 30th for complete mobilisation to begin on the 31st. A new crop of incidents involving alleged Polish brutalities towards Germans was ominously reported in the German press on the 29th.

At 7.15 p.m. on August 29 Henderson received the German reply to the British message from Hitler and Ribbentrop. Germany was ready to negotiate with Poland, but only if an emissary arrived in Berlin with full powers next day and was ready to accept whatever Germany proposed. Henderson protested that this was an ultimatum, which was angrily denied. Beck was informed, agreed to negotiate on equal terms, but was in no hurry to send a representative to Berlin: Poland would fight rather than submit to the humiliation of the sort of negotiation offered.

At midnight on August 30–31 Henderson again saw Ribbentrop, who read off to him at high speed Germany's offer to Poland: terms only momentarily plausible and strongly reminiscent of the Godesberg Memorandum. Next morning (August 31) Henderson received a copy of them (through Dahlerus) and tried to persuade Lipski, the Polish ambassador, to think well of them. When, however, Lipski received his instructions from Beck at 12.40 p.m., they did not give him full powers to negotiate; he was merely to transmit any German proposals to his government. The German government intercepted the message (sent by wireless) and Goering—at the moment the main agent in any 'appeasement'—was furious at its tone. It made little difference: the orders for the attack on Poland, to begin at 4.45 a.m. next day (September 1), had been given (not, of course, to the public) almost at the same time, 12.40 p.m. on August 31, before the German government knew of the contents of Lipski's instructions. Appeasement was snuffed out—by Hitler's impatience,[1] by the firmness of Poland and the steadiness of Britain and France. At 9 that evening the German government broadcast its reply to the offer of negotiations (subsequently given to Henderson and the French ambassador); it included the German proposals to Poland (never officially given to her), but complained of Poland's mobilisation and her refusal to send a plenipotentiary, and warned that the situation was such that an explosion might occur at any moment. It was a clumsy attempt to put on Poland the blame for war and for the failure of negotiations which Germany had snapped off before they had begun. The Second World War began punctually in the small hours of September 1, when German forces invaded Poland.[2]

On September 3 Britain and France declared war on Germany. Last minute waverings, as of an irresolute diver on the high diving board, explain the delay. Henderson was instructed on the evening of September 1 (after a Cabinet meeting that afternoon) to present a note to the German government declaring that Britain would stand by her obligations to Poland unless German aggression was stopped and German forces withdrawn; he delivered the note to Ribbentrop at 9.30 p.m. The French government sent a similar note, and it also ordered a general mobilisation. In England the evacuation of school children and mothers with small children from London and other danger zones was begun on September 1. Parliament, meeting that night, was told by Chamberlain that the ambassador was instructed to ask for his passports if the note elicited no satisfactory reply. If Germany insisted on using force, it must know 'that we were resolved to oppose them by force'.

Then nothing happened all next day, Saturday, September 2, while the nation waited, tense and uneasy. The delay was caused by a proposal for mediation made by Mussolini on August 31;

[1] And perhaps his fury over the grossly-exaggerated Polish 'atrocities' reported to him by the German news agencies: see F. A. Voigt's review of Fritz Hesse, *Das Spiel um Deutschland* (Munich, 1953), *Manchester Guardian Weekly*, September 17, 1953.
[2] This account rests on Namier's very full narrative in *Diplomatic Prelude*, pp. 211–281, and on J. W. Wheeler-Bennett, *Munich*, pp. 416–25.

he would invite Hitler to a conference if Britain and France would first agree. Consultations between the British, French and Italian governments followed. The British Cabinet accepted the idea on the evening of the 2nd, but only on the condition, which Mussolini rightly characterised as impossible for Hitler to accept, that all German forces be withdrawn from Poland first. In the French cabinet Daladier stood firm, but Bonnet pursued this last will o' the wisp of appeasement with a pertinacity lacking in Halifax and Chamberlain. When parliament met again, in the evening of the 2nd, members were angered to hear from Chamberlain only that the government would take action against Germany unless it heard that German forces had been withdrawn from Poland; it was still waiting for a reply to its note (which contained no time-limit) of the 1st. Arthur Greenwood, deputy leader of the Labour party in Attlee's absence through illness, rose to speak. 'Speak for England!' called out Amery, the stout imperialist Conservative and critic of the government. And Greenwood did so. He was 'gravely disturbed' at the delay; Germany had been at war against Poland for thirty-eight hours, and still nothing had happened— the treaty obligations toward Poland had not automatically been put into effect. 'I wonder how long we are prepared to vacillate at a time when Britain and all that Britain stands for, and human civilisation, are in peril.' Chamberlain strongly denied that there was any weakening on the part of the government, and referred to the need of synchronising action with the French.

This faltering approach to war ended on Sunday, September 3. The Cabinet met again that night, and Halifax telephoned to Bonnet that a declaration of war would have to be brought to parliament next day. At 5 a.m. Henderson was ordered to present an ultimatum to the German government: if no satisfactory reply to the note of September 1 was received by 11 a.m., British summer time, a state of war would exist between Britain and Germany from that hour. Henderson delivered the ultimatum at 9 a.m. Hitler, Goering and Goebbels received the news with stunned surprise; but their reply, delivered too late, was no more than an absurd and lengthy self-justification of Germany's actions. At 11.15 that Sunday morning Chamberlain broadcast to the people of Britain that they were at war. It was no clarion call: a tired, old man telling of the bitter blow to *his* hopes of peace; 'I cannot believe that there is anything more, or anything different, that I could have done. . . .' The country went to war with a clear conscience. '. . . It is evil things that we shall be fighting against,

Y*

brute force, bad faith, injustice, oppression and persecution. And against them I am certain that the right will prevail.' To parliament at noon, after telling of the expiry of the ultimatum, he bared his soul:

> . . . everything that I have worked for, everything that I have hoped for, everything that I have believed in during my public life, has crashed in ruins.

His world was indeed being reduced to ruins; but for the people of Britain a new life would in time begin. The French government, thanks to Bonnet's delays, lagged behind Britain by a few hours. Its ultimatum to Germany expired at 5 p.m. that day, and the French people were also at war.[1] The countries of the British Empire declared war within the next few days—South Africa only after a political crisis and a change of government. Eire declared herself neutral.

12. THE FALL OF CHAMBERLAIN

Before Chamberlain had finished his broadcast on September 3 the wailing of air-raid sirens broke in upon it in London. It was a false alarm; there was little real war on land or in the air for the British people for another seven months. The twilight peace had been replaced, apparently, by the twilight war (Chamberlain's private phrase: others called it the 'phony war'). True, the Cunard steamer *Athenia*, Canada-bound, was sunk by a U-boat on September 3 when about 200 miles out in the Atlantic. One hundred and twenty persons were drowned: survivors related that passengers awaited death singing the then-popular song 'Roll out the barrel', which shocked some moralists but reassured others of the courage of ordinary people. The sinking of the aircraft carrier *Courageous* on September 19 with the loss of more than half its crew, and of the battleship *Royal Oak* on October 14 while at anchor in Scapa Flow (whose defences, strangely incomplete, were daringly penetrated by a U-boat), were further reminders of the grim business of war.

Chamberlain at once reorganised his Cabinet, on September 3. Churchill at last was brought in, and given the same post he had had held in 1914, First Lord of the Admiralty. His presence reassured the public; and his magnanimity assured Chamberlain

---

[1] L. B. Namier, *Diplomatic Prelude*, pp. 382–402; K. Feiling, *N. Chamberlain*, pp. 415–17; H.C. Deb., 5 s., 126–38, 280–6, 291–5 (September 1–3, 1939); *The Times*, September 4, 1939.

of a colleague who in loyalty and weightiness of advice in every field was second to none. Eden was also brought in, as Dominions Secretary, replacing Inskip, who became Lord Chancellor (as Lord Caldecote). The Labour and Liberal leaders refused, however, to serve under Chamberlain, so that the government remained much less than national. A large War Cabinet of nine was set up; Chamberlain, Simon, Halifax, Hoare, Lord Chatfield, the three service ministers, Churchill, Hore-Belisha, Kingsley Wood, and Lord Hankey, who had retired in 1938 after 22 years' service as secretary of the Cabinet. Originally, Churchill was to have been Minister of Defence, but Chamberlain yielded to pressure and brought Hore-Belisha and Wood into the War Cabinet also; hence its size.[1] Churchill complained of its age: six of them had an average age of over 64, 'only one year short of the Old Age Pension!'[2]

The chief events of the twilight war may be quickly described. The war in Poland was over in three weeks, Russian forces joining those of Germany for the kill. From November 30 until the following March Russia was at war with Finland, which had refused her neighbour certain bases peremptorily demanded; this hard-fought war was not allowed to spread, despite plans for aid for Finland from Britain and France. On the 'western front' of the First World War the French army and the British Expeditionary Force took up positions on the Maginot line and north of it, but neither attacked nor were challenged by the German forces which, at first, had little strength behind their Siegfried line.

At home there was a gradual transition from normal civilian life. The blackout was enforced at night. The evacuation of school-children, mothers and young children from London and other large cities was carried out between September 1 and 3; but the appearance of safety and the difficulties which billeting entailed for guests and hosts led to the unofficial return of many evacuees (88 per cent of the mothers, 44 per cent of the school-children) by January.[3] Military conscription was extended to all men between the ages of 18 and 41 in September. Rationing of food began in January. The first war budget, in September, raised the income tax from 5s. 6d. to 7s. 6d. in the £ and introduced an excess profits tax

---

[1] A. C. Johnson, *Halifax*, p. 550.

[2] W. S. Churchill, *Gathering Storm*, pp. 361–3, 374; K. Feiling, *N. Chamberlain*, pp. 420–1.

[3] Particulars of evacuation in R. M. Titmuss, *Problems of Social Policy* (History of the Second World War: United Kingdom Civil Series; London, 1950), pp. 101–9 and appendices 2–5; also Richard Padley and Margaret Cole, *Evacuation Survey* (London, 1940).

of 60 per cent. The regular budget next year (April 23) provided for expenditures of £2667 millions, of which £2000 millions was for war purposes.

The quiet of the opening phase of the war was shattered on April 9, just five days after Chamberlain, in a confident speech at a Conservative meeting (on April 4), had declared that Hitler, by not attacking Britain and France up till then, had 'missed the bus'. His confidence in victory, ten times greater than when the war began, sprang from the great increase in the country's fighting strength which the seven months had brought.

On April 9 German forces invaded Denmark, despite Hitler's recent non-aggression pact, and compelled it to submit to military occupation. On the same day forces were landed from the sea and air at several points in Norway—Oslo, Stavanger, Bergen, Trondheim, Narvik. The Germans had been maturing their plans against Norway since October. Britain had had similar plans, partly in connection with a project for sending help to the Finns; instead, it was decided on March 28 to mine Norwegian waters which formed a neutral corridor for German iron-ore ships from Narvik.

Counter-strokes against the German forces in Norway were immediately prepared: particularly a large-scale naval attack and landings at Trondheim. Caution counselled more limited measures. Troops were landed at Namsos and Andalsnes on April 14 and 17, but could not be properly supported against German air power, and were evacuated on May 1 and 3. A large force sent to capture Narvik was kept idle for a month at Harstad, on the Island of Hinnoy, until the snows melted, and though it eventually captured Narvik on May 28 it was withdrawn on June 8.[1]

The news of the evacuation of the troops from Andalsnes and Namsos was a stunning blow to public confidence, the more so after Churchill and Chamberlain had spoken in optimistic terms in mid-April. The government yielded to demands for a debate on the failure of the expedition, which was held on May 7 and 8. There have been few debates of greater importance in parliament's history.

Chamberlain opened the debate with a matter-of-fact defence of the conduct of the operations and the character of the War Cabinet. He was interrupted with taunts about 'missing the bus', and digressed to explain the context of the phrase. It was soon

[1] W. S. Churchill, *Gathering Storm*, pp. 478–592; T. K. Derry, *The Campaign in Norway* (History of the Second World War; United Kingdom Military Series: London, 1952).

clear that wider issues than the Norwegian campaign were involved. Attlee criticised the War Cabinet as not being efficient for the conducting of the war; more than that, its members were the same men who had had 'an almost uninterrupted career of failure' (this attack on Simon and Hoare was repeated later in the debate). 'Everywhere the story is "Too late".' To win the war there must be different people at the helm; and members should put loyalty to the country above loyalty to the chief whip. Others, particularly younger Conservatives who were in the armed services, followed with charges of troops rushed into battle untrained, of equipment inadequate or lacking, of failure to anticipate German plans. Admiral Sir Roger Keyes entered the House in full uniform to denounce the government for not ordering a big naval attack on Trondheim. Amery, who had shared so many of Churchill's beliefs but unlike him was still outside the government, made the most powerful speech of the day. 'We cannot go on as we are. There must be a change'—in the governmental machine but even more of men. He quoted Cromwell's words to the Long Parliament:

You have sat too long here for any good you have been doing. Depart, I say, and let us have done with you. In the name of God, go.

Next day, May 8, the debate waxed hotter, with many interruptions. Labour, with some trepidation, decided to move a vote of censure—an action which was more likely to rally support to the government out of party loyalty than to reveal the deep distrust of it inside and outside parliament. Of distrust there was plenty; indeed the fall of the government would not have occurred but for a revolt among Conservative back-benchers, men who had been growing restive since Munich and some of whom (Amery and Boothby and Duff Cooper among them) had banded together several months earlier. Yet this distrust would hardly have been decisive but for an ill-judged intervention of Chamberlain, curiously insensitive to the general feeling of the moment, on May 8. He accepted Herbert Morrison's speech, moving the vote of censure, as a challenge:

No government can prosecute a war efficiently unless it has public and Parliamentary support. I accept the challenge. I welcome it indeed. At least we shall see who is with us and who is against us, and I call upon my friends to support us in the Lobby tonight.

This reduction of the weightiest criticism of the whole conduct of the war to the level of a personal question, in which his friends must rally to his side, was much resented, as several later speeches showed. Soon afterwards Lloyd George made his last decisive intervention in the debates of the House which he had first entered fifty years before: the great leader in the first war summoning forth his equal in the second.

> The Prime Minister is not in a position to make his personality . . . inseparable from the interests of the country. . . . It is not a question of who are the Prime Minister's friends. It is a far bigger issue. . . . He has appealed for sacrifice. The nation is prepared for every sacrifice so long as it has leadership. . . . I say solemnly that the Prime Minister should give an example of sacrifice, because there is nothing which can contribute more to victory in this war than that he should sacrifice the seals of office.

After this, not all Churchill's eloquence and skill, gallantly expended in its defence, could save the government. It won its vote indeed; but some 40 Conservatives voted against it and 80 or more abstained, so that its majority fell to 81: 281 to 200.[1]

Chamberlain at once considered resigning, so that a national government, including Labour and Liberals, might be formed. Next day he decided to see if he could form such a government himself, and sent for Attlee and Greenwood to meet Lord Halifax, Churchill and himself at No. 10 Downing Street. Would Labour join? They must consult the national executive of the party, but they were not hopeful. The executive refused to support a national government if Chamberlain was at the head of it. Next day, May 10, came the news of the German invasion of the Low Countries in the early hours: the war in the west was beginning with a thunderclap, piling military crisis on top of the political. Chamberlain thought he must hang on; his friend Sir Kingsley Wood convinced him that he must not, in view of the Labour leaders' reply. Churchill was summoned again to No. 10, where he found Halifax, Chamberlain's choice as successor, with him. Chamberlain said that he must resign, since he could not form a national government. Whom should he advise the King to send for? After a pause, Halifax answered, to decline the unspoken offer: he was a peer, and in such a war as this he could not lead a government from outside the House of Commons. Clearly the lot must fall upon Churchill, by popular choice and by Labour's decision as much as by lack of any convincing alternative.[2]

At six that evening (Friday, May 10) Churchill was summoned

[1] 360 H.C. Deb., 5 s., 1073–1196, 1251–1362; W. S. Churchill, pp. 593–5; *Annual Register*, 1940, pp. 37–8.

[2] W. S. Churchill, pp. 595–8; A. C. Johnson, *Halifax*, p. 557.

to Buckingham Palace. He accepted the King's commission to form a government, and promised to give him the names of at least five ministers, to form a War Cabinet, before midnight. He saw Attlee and Greenwood at once; they agreed to serve. The Labour party was holding its annual conference at Bournemouth on the following Monday, the 13th; thither Attlee went to appeal for the party's mandate, handsomely given, in support of what he and his colleagues, with the national executive's advice, had already done.[1]

Churchill's government included a War Cabinet of five: himself as Prime Minister and Minister of Defence, Chamberlain, Halifax, Attlee, Greenwood. Attlee was Lord Privy Seal and Deputy Leader of the House of Commons—in effect already deputy prime minister. Other ministers from the Labour party included Dalton, Morrison, Alexander, and also Ernest Bevin, whose appointment as Minister of Labour and National Service was the most dramatic and perhaps the most brilliantly successful of all Churchill's choices. Sir Archibald Sinclair, the Liberal leader, was Air Secretary. Among the Conservatives who returned to office were Amery, Eden, Duff Cooper, Lord Lloyd, Lord Cranborne. Simon became Lord Chancellor; Hoare received no office. Offers were made (despite Chamberlain's reluctance) to Lloyd George, but from age he evaded and declined them. To Chamberlain the new Prime Minister was loyal and generous, retaining him as Lord President of the Council, and offering him, until Labour objections made it impractical, the leadership of the House, and refusing later suggestions that he resign in response to parliamentary criticism. Chamberlain was not behind him in loyalty—and indeed without this Churchill might have lacked the support (as he lacked the affection) of a majority of the Conservatives. Thanks to Chamberlain, neither the Conservative party nor the country was divided by the change of government; rather, the unity of both was reinforced, in contrast to the fatal division among the Liberals which Asquith had accepted when Lloyd George took office in 1916. This was magnanimity in defeat, and a true service to his country. A breakdown in his health forced Chamberlain to resign on September 30, a few weeks before he died, on November 9.[2] It was only after this, on October 9, that Churchill was elected leader of the Conservative party.

[1] Both Churchill and Feiling are in error in stating that the Labour party conference was in session during May 9–10.
[2] W. S. Churchill, pp. 599–600; K. Feiling, pp. 451–7.

The end of Chamberlain's government was the end of an era. The National government, with its nine years of Conservative rule prolonging the dominance of the Conservatives during the twenties, had reached its term; the indecisions, the weaknesses of leadership—Baldwin's indolent optimism, Chamberlain's misdirected zeal—the disunity within the nation, all had run their course to this fatal moment. Churchill's government promised two things: national unity and the utmost vigour in fighting the war for survival; and, more at first by implication than by avowal, a new society with much more equality in it than the old. For the Labour party this made May 10, 1940, a day of fulfilment and of promise: for the first time in its history of forty years it was accepted as the full equal of the other parties in the counsels of the nation.

13. ALONE

It was a solemn moment. German forces on May 10 were invading the Netherlands and Belgium, German aeroplanes were dropping parachute troops on Dutch airfields and dive-bombing concentrations of troops even before Churchill began to form his government. As he told the House of Commons on May 13, he could offer nothing but 'blood, toil, tears, and sweat'; his policy, to wage war 'with all our might', the aim, victory, 'however long and hard the road'.

While the fighting continued in Belgium, the Germans struck their unexpected master-blow by forcing their way through the Ardennes and reaching that part of the French frontier which was north of the Maginot line and weakly held. Sedan fell on May 14, and a gap 50 miles wide in the Allied defences was speedily opened. Early on the morning of the 15th Reynaud, the French Prime Minister, telephoned Churchill saying 'we are beaten; we have lost the battle'. Churchill, who flew to Paris that afternoon, found nothing but pessimism and defeat: the French had no strategic reserves, and were reduced to utter inferiority in the air, in spite of the aid of several of Britain's ill-spared fighter squadrons. The changes which Reynaud made at the time, bringing Pétain into the cabinet as vice-president of the council on the 18th and summoning General Weygand to replace Gamelin as commander-in-chief on the 19th, were not of good omen.

The German advance continued with unprecedented speed. By May 20 they had reached the channel, and had divided the British and French forces in Belgium and the north of France from the larger, but still mostly unengaged forces to the south. On May 28

Belgian resistance ended when King Leopold decided to surrender to the Germans. The British and French forces, caught in a narrowing pocket between the coast (from Calais to Ostend) and Ypres, could only with difficulty keep clear a corridor to the sea and prepare for an evacuation that was the only alternative to surrender or useless annihilation.[1]

The end was not long delayed. The British Expeditionary Force was evacuated from Dunkirk between May 26 and June 4: 338,226 men were ferried across the Channel, including 26,000 French troops, though the original hope had not been higher than to rescue some 45,000 men in all. It was an epic of courage and improvisation in which 693 British ships took part, of which 372 were yachts, motor-boats, tugs, pleasure-steamers and 'other small craft', the rest larger vessels of the navy and the merchant fleet.[2] French resistance in the west was hampered by the speed of the German movements and the clogging of the roads by refugees. Paris was occupied on June 14; the defenders of the Maginot line, unscathed but surrounded from the rear, surrendered on the 17th. A new government under Marshal Pétain took over and sued for an armistice on June 17; it began on June 25.[3]

Now there remained, alone, Britain and the Commonwealth, together with those patriots who had escaped when the Nazis occupied their countries. The British people must fight for their own survival and for the 'survival of Christian civilisation' to which, in Churchill's words, they were committed. In the summer of 1940, as they awaited the battle of Britain, they found themselves again, after twenty years of indecision. They turned away from past regrets and faced the future unafraid.

[1] W. S. Churchill, *Their Finest Hour* (London, 1949), pp. 25–86; J. F. C. Fuller, *The Second World War, 1939–45* (London, 1948), pp. 62–76. L. F. Ellis, *The War in France and Flanders, 1939–40* (History of the Second World War; United Kingdom Military Series: London, 1954).

[2] W. S. Churchill, *Their Finest Hour*, pp. 88–102; John Masefield, *The Nine Days Wonder* (London, 1941).

[3] W. S. Churchill, *Their Finest Hour*, pp. 127–212; L. B. Namier, *Europe in Decay* pp. 35 ff.

Bibliographical Note

THE beginnings of a bibliography of the history of the inter-war years in Great Britain will be found in the references given in the footnotes throughout this book. The purpose of this note is simply to give some general references to books which will lead the reader further into the various subjects.

There are very few general histories of the period. The most useful are J. A. Spender, *Great Britain: Empire and Commonwealth, 1886–1935* (London, 1936); G. D. H. Cole and R. Postgate, *The Common People, 1747–1938* (London, 1938; revised and enlarged edition, 1946, also published in New York as *The British People, 1746–1946*); D. C. Somervell, *Reign of King George the Fifth* (London, New York, 1935) and his *British Politics since 1900* (London, New York, 1950); Keith Hutchison, *Decline and Fall of British Capitalism* (New York, 1950; London, 1951). K. B. Smellie, *Hundred Years of English Government* (London, 1937; revised edition, 1950) contains a good historical survey as well as an excellent account of the development of government. G. D. H. Cole, *History of the Labour Party from 1914* (London, 1948), covers a wide ground and has no counterpart for the other parties. *The History of The Times*, vol. IV, *1912–1948* (2 parts; London, 1952) contains much important, general information. For the year's events the *Annual Register* is an invaluable guide; for a wealth of statistical information the annual volumes of the *Statistical Abstract for the United Kingdom*; and for much else *Whitaker's Almanack* and the (often tantalisingly reticent) entries in *Who's Who*.

For affairs of state the *Parliamentary Debates* must be consulted. The reports of royal commissions and of some departments, and white papers on foreign policy and other matters, are Command Papers, and can be found in the *Parliamentary Papers* for each year; non-command papers must be obtained separately (see the Stationery Office's *Consolidated List of Government Publications* for each year). There is a useful list and epitome of these materials in P. and G. Ford, *A Breviate of Parliamentary Papers, 1917–1939* (Oxford, 1951). Texts of current statutes will be found in the

Complete Statutes of England: in Continuation of Halsbury's Laws of England (1930–), and in *Public General Acts* (annual); see also the annual volumes of *Statutory Rules and Orders.*

Biographies and memoirs provide much important information. Some of the more valuable are: J. A. Spender and Cyril Asquith, *Life of Lord Oxford and Asquith* (2 vols., London, 1932) ; Thomas Jones, *Lloyd George* (London, Cambridge, Mass., 1951) ; Malcolm Thomson, *David Lloyd George* (London, 1948); Keith Feiling, *Life of Neville Chamberlain* (London, 1946); Stanley Salvidge, *Salvidge of Liverpool* (London, 1934) ; Sir Charles Petrie, *Life and Letters of Austen Chamberlain* (2 vols., London, 1939–40); L. S. Amery, *My Political Life,* II, *War and Peace, 1914–1929* (London, 1953) ; Philip Snowden, *Autobiography* (2 vols., London, 1934); M. A. Hamilton, *Arthur Henderson* (London, 1938); Fenner Brockway, *Inside the Left* (London, 1942) for the I.L.P. ; Raymond Postgate, *Life of George Lansbury* (London, 1951); Francis Williams, *Ernest Bevin* (London, 1952); J. T. Murphy, *New Horizons* (London, 1942) for early Communist activities; Robert Boothby, *I Fight to Live* (London, 1947); Mary D. Stocks, *Eleanor Rathbone* (London, 1949). M. A. Hamilton's *Remembering My Good Friends* (London, 1944) contains excellent character sketches of Labour leaders and valuable impressions of the times. Gilbert McAllister's *James Maxton* (London, 1935) is the best introduction to the Clydesiders. For further information on books dealing with the Labour movement see my bibliographical articles in the *Journal of Modern History,* 17 (1945), 23 (1951). G. M. Young's *Stanley Baldwin* (London, 1952) is brief and unsatisfactory. R. F. Harrod, *Life of John Maynard Keynes* (London, 1951) is of much value. Duff Cooper's *Old Men Forget* (London, 1953) throws much light on Chamberlain's cabinet, down to the Munich settlement. Of the greatest importance is Harold Nicolson, *King George the Fifth: his life and reign* (London, 1952; New York, 1953). The supplements to the *Dictionary of National Biography* for 1922–30 and 1931–40 contain several notable lives.

For the history of foreign policy there are the annual volumes of the *Survey of International Affairs* (1925–), published by the Royal Institute of International Affairs and edited by Arnold Toynbee. Good brief accounts are G. M. Gathorne-Hardy, *Short History of International Affairs* (3rd ed., *1920 to 1939,* London, 1942); W. N. Medlicott, *British Foreign Policy since Versailles,*

1919–1939 (London, 1940). For particular phases see R. B. Mowat, *History of European Diplomacy, 1914–1925* (London, 1927); R. W. Seton-Watson, *Britain and the Dictators* (London, New York, 1938); J. W. Wheeler-Bennett, *Munich: Prologue to Tragedy* (London, New York, 1948); L. B. Namier's *Diplomatic Prelude, 1938–1939* (London, 1947) and *Europe in Decay . . . 1936–1940* (London, 1950). Winston Churchill's *Second World War*, vol. I, *The Gathering Storm* (London, New York, 1948; new edition, 1949) is of great value. For the bearing of the Dominions on foreign policy see Nicholas Mansergh, *Survey of British Commonwealth Affairs: Problems of External Policy, 1931–1939* (Royal Institute of International Affairs: Oxford, 1952).

Foreign Office papers have been edited by E. L. Woodward and Rohan Butler, *Documents on British Foreign Policy, 1919–1939*, in three series: I, 1919 onwards (1947–), II, 1929 onwards (1946–), III, 1938–39 (1949–55). The U.S. Department of State is publishing *Documents on German Foreign Policy, 1918–1945* from the German Foreign Office archives (Washington, 1949–), and has published *Nazi-Soviet Relations, 1939–41* (Washington, 1948) from the same source. Documents from the Nuremberg Trials have been published: *The Trial of the Major War Criminals* (42 vols., 1947–49). The Soviet government has published *Documents and Materials Relating to the Eve of the Second World War* (2 vols., 1949).

Constitutional history is treated in D. L. Keir, *Constitutional History of Modern Britain, 1485–1937* (3rd ed., London, 1948), in the works of K. B. Smellie, A. B. Keith, Herman Finer, W. A. Robson and in W. Ivor Jennings' *Cabinet Government* (Cambridge, 1936) and *Parliament* (Cambridge, 1940). See also Michael Stewart, *British Approach to Politics* (London, 1938); and for the analysis of election results D. E. Butler, *Electoral System in Britain, 1918–1951* (Oxford, 1953). For the development of the social services see R. C. Davison, *The Unemployed, old policies and new* (London, 1929) and *British Unemployment Policy since 1930* (London, 1938), H. F. Hohman, *Development of Social Insurance and Minimum Wage Legislation in Great Britain* (Boston, 1933), W. H. Wickwar's *Social Services* (London, 1936, rev. ed., 1949) and *Public Services* (London, 1938), P.E.P., reports on *British Health Services* (1937) and *British Social Services* (1937), and the works of Sir Arnold Wilson and Hermann Levy.

For the economic history of these years W. A. Lewis, *Economic Survey, 1919–1939* (London, 1949) is a valuable introduction. Other useful works are F. C. Benham, *Great Britain under Protection* (New York, 1941); A. E. Kahn, *Great Britain in the World Economy* (New York, 1946); G. P. Jones and A. G. Pool, *Hundred Years of Economic Development in Great Britain* (London, 1940): *Britain in Depression* (London, 1935) and *Britain in Recovery* (London, 1938); M. Compton and E. H. Bott, *British Industry: its changing structure* . . . (London, 1940); G. D. H. Cole, *British Trade and Industry, past and future* (London, 1932); G. C. Allen, *British Industries and their Organization* (London, 1933; new edition, 1951); A. Plummer, *New British Industries in the Twentieth Century* (London, 1937); J. H. Richardson, *British Economic Foreign Policy* (London, 1936). A. L. Bowley, *Studies in National Income, 1924–1938* (Cambridge, 1942); Colin Clark's *National Income, 1924–1931* (London, 1932), *National Income and Outlay* (London, 1937), *Conditions of Economic Progress* (London, 1940, second ed., 1951) may also be referred to. For financial matters see E. Victor Morgan, *Studies in British Financial Policy, 1914–25* (London, 1952), and W. A. Morton, *British Finance, 1930–40* (Madison, 1943). Books on individual industries are noticed in chapter 5; particularly useful is Stephen Miall, *History of the British Chemical Industry* (London, 1931). On agriculture C. S. Orwin, *History of English Farming* (London, 1949), E. J. Russell, *The Farm and the Nation* (London, 1933), Viscount Astor and B. S. Rowntree, *British Agriculture* (London, 1938) furnish sound introductions. For economic geography see L. Dudley Stamp and S. H. Beaver, *The British Isles: a Geographic and Economic Survey* (2nd ed., London, 1937), and Wilfred Smith, *Economic Geography of Great Britain* (London, 1949).

The best introduction to the social history of the times is, despite its flippant tone, Robert Graves and Alan Hodge, *The Long Week-end: A Social History of Great Britain, 1918–1939* (London, 1940). For guidance to and through the necessary statistical information A. M. Carr-Saunders and D. Caradog Jones, *A Survey of the Social Structure of England and Wales* (Oxford, 1927; second ed., 1937) is indispensable. For the 'condition of the people' see A. Hutt's *Postwar History of the British Working Class* (London, 1937, New York, 1938) and his *Condition of the Working Class in Britain* (London, 1933); also G. D. H. and M. I. Cole, *Condition of Britain* (London, 1937). For the unemployed the best works are *Men without Work* (Cambridge, 1938) and George Orwell, *The Road to Wigan Pier* (London, 1937). B. Seebohm Rowntree's *Poverty and Progress* (London, 1941), Herbert Tout, *Standard of Living in Bristol* (Bristol, 1938), D. Caradog Jones, *Social Survey of Merseyside* (3 vols., London, 1934), and the *New Survey of London Life and Labour* (9 vols., London, 1930–35) are among the best of the social surveys. Asa Briggs' *History of Birmingham*, vol. II, *Borough and City, 1865–1938* (Oxford, 1952), is a model for other badly-needed studies of the modern history of British cities. J. B. Priestley, *English Journey* (London, 1934) is an excellent report of the times. John Hilton's *Rich Man, Poor Man* (London, 1944) is a small but extraordinarily suggestive work. On matters of health and mortality see R. M. Titmuss, *Poverty and Population* (1938), *Birth, Poverty and Wealth* (1943); on housing, Marian Bowley, *Housing and the State, 1919–1944* (London, 1945); on education the histories of H. C. Barnard (1947), S. J. Curtis (1948; also his *Education in Britain Since 1900* [1952]), John Graves, *Policy and Progress in Secondary Education, 1902–1942* (1943), J. Dover Wilson (ed.), *Schools of England* (1928). The *Year Book of Education* (1932–   ) is useful. For entertainment and enlightenment Bruce Truscot, *Red Brick University* (London, 1943) should not be missed. For transport, C. E. R. Sherrington's *Hundred Years of Inland Transport* (London, 1934) is a valuable introduction. Religion is treated in Roger Lloyd, *Church of England in the Twentieth Century, II* (London 1950), G. S. Spinks (ed.), *Religion in Britain since 1900* (London, 1952), the lives of Archbishop Temple by F. A. Iremonger (1948), Archbishop Davidson by G. K. A. Bell (2 vols., Oxford, 1936) and Archbishop Lang by J. G. Lockhart (1949); see also Bishop Hensley Henson's *Retrospect of an Unimportant Life* (2 vols., Oxford, 1942–43) and Archbishop Garbett's *In an Age of Revolution* (1952). For the history of science J. G. Crowther, *British Scientists of the Twentieth Century* (London, 1952) provides an introduction. For the changing world of society and literature Sir Osbert Sitwell's *Laughter in the Next Room* (1949) contains reminiscence which is both readable and stimulating.

References to books on particular subjects of social history will be found in chapters 4 and 9.

For Scotland the best introduction is J. A. Bowie, *Future of Scotland* (Edinburgh, 1939).

For Anglo-Irish history the most useful general accounts are W. A. Phillips, *Revolution in Ireland, 1906–1923* (2nd ed., London, 1926), strongly pro-Union; P. Beasley (Beaslai), *Life of Michael Collins* (2 vols., London, 1926), strongly pro-Collins; Dorothy Macardle, *Irish Republic* (London, 1937), strong for the irreconcilable Republicans; T. Ireland, *Ireland, Past and Present* (New York, 1942); D. O'Sullivan, *Irish Free State and its Senate* (London, 1940); W. K. Hancock, *Survey of British Commonwealth Affairs*, vol. I (Oxford, 1937); C. J. C. Street ('I.O.'), *Administration of Ireland, 1920* (London, 1921), and *Ireland in 1921* (London, 1922).

Certain works which appeared while this book was in press should be noticed: Thomas Jones, *Diary with Letters, 1931–1950* (Oxford, 1954); Lord Templewood, *Nine Troubled Years* (London, 1954); Frank Owen, *Tempestuous Journey: Lloyd George, his Life and Times* (London, 1954); W. H. B. Court, *Concise Economic History of Britain from 1750 to Recent Times* (Cambridge, 1954); R. T. McKenzie, *British Political Parties* (London, 1955); G. Le May (Editor), *British Government, 1914–1953, Select Documents*.

List of Cabinets[1]

Lloyd George's Coalition: January, 1919–October, 1922

Prime Minister: David Lloyd George.
Lord Privy Seal and Leader of the House of Commons: Andrew Bonar Law.
Lord President of the Council: Lord Curzon.
Chancellor of the Exchequer: Austen Chamberlain.
Minister without Portfolio: G. N. Barnes.
Minister without Portfolio: Sir Eric Geddes.
Lord Chancellor: Lord Birkenhead.
Secretary of State for Home Affairs: Edward Shortt.
Secretary of State for Foreign Affairs: A. J. Balfour.
Secretary of State for War and Air: W. S. Churchill.
Secretary of State for Colonies: Lord Milner.
Secretary of State for India: E. S. Montagu.
First Lord of the Admiralty: Walter Long.
President of Board of Trade: Sir Albert Stanley.
President of Local Government Board: Christopher Addison.
President of Board of Agriculture: R. E. Prothero.
President of Board of Education: H. A. L. Fisher.
Minister of Labour: Sir R. S. Horne.
Secretary for Scotland: Robert Munro.
Chief Secretary for Ireland: J. I. Macpherson.

Sir Auckland Geddes succeeded Stanley at the Board of Trade in May 1919; Lord Lee of Fareham succeeded Prothero at the Board of Agriculture in August 1919. In October 1919, Curzon and Balfour changed places, Sir Eric Geddes became Minister of Transport and Dr. Addison Minister of Health (on the disappearance of the Local Government Board). Horne succeeded Sir Auckland Geddes at the Board of Trade in March 1920, and was succeeded as Minister of Labour by T. J. Macnamara. Sir Hamar Greenwood succeeded Macpherson at the Irish Office in April 1920. In January 1921, Churchill succeeded Milner at the Colonial Office and was succeeded by Sir L. Worthington-Evans at the

---

[1] Based on lists in *Annual Register*.

War Office; Lord Lee of Fareham succeeded Long at the Admiralty and was replaced by Sir A. Griffith-Boscawen at the Ministry of Agriculture. Bonar Law retired in March 1921, and was succeeded by Austen Chamberlain, who was succeeded at the Exchequer by Horne; Stanley Baldwin became President of the Board of Trade. Sir Alfred Mond succeeded Addison as Minister of Health in April 1921. Viscount Peel succeeded Montagu at the India Office in March 1922.

Bonar Law's Cabinet: October 1922–May 1923

Prime Minister: A. Bonar Law.
Lord President: Lord Salisbury.
Lord Chancellor: Lord Cave.
Chancellor of the Exchequer: Stanley Baldwin.
Home Office: W. C. Bridgeman.
Foreign Office: Lord Curzon.
Colonies: Duke of Devonshire.
War: Lord Derby.
India: Lord Peel.
Scotland: Lord Novar.
Admiralty: L. S. Amery.
Board of Trade: Sir P. Lloyd-Greame.
Education: E. F. L. Wood.
Health: Sir A. Griffith-Boscawen.
Agriculture: Sir Robert Saunders.
Labour: Sir Montague Barlow.
    Neville Chamberlain succeeded Griffith-Boscawen in February, 1923.

Baldwin's First Cabinet: May 1923–January 1924

Prime Minister: Stanley Baldwin.
Lord Privy Seal: Lord Robert Cecil.
Chancellor of the Exchequer: Neville Chamberlain (from August 28).
Air: Sir Samuel Hoare.
Health: Neville Chamberlain (until August 27);
        Sir William Joynson-Hicks.
Postmaster-General: Sir L. Worthington-Evans.
    Other positions were filled by the ministers who had held them under Bonar Law.

MacDonald's First Labour Cabinet: January–November, 1924

Prime Minister and Foreign Secretary: J. Ramsay MacDonald.
Lord Chancellor: Lord Haldane.
Lord Privy Seal: J. R. Clynes.
Lord President: Lord Parmoor.
Chancellor of the Exchequer: Philip Snowden.
Home Office: Arthur Henderson.
Colonies: J. H. Thomas.
War: Stephen Walsh.
India: Lord Olivier.
Air: Lord Thomson.
Scotland: William Adamson.
Board of Trade: Sidney Webb.
Education: C. P. Trevelyan.
Admiralty: Lord Chelmsford.
Health: John Wheatley.
Agriculture: Noel Buxton.
Labour: Thomas Shaw.
Postmaster-General: Vernon Hartshorn.
First Commissioner of Works: F. W. Jowett.
Chancellor of the Duchy of Lancaster: Josiah Wedgwood.

Baldwin's Second Cabinet: November 1924–June 1929

Prime Minister: Stanley Baldwin.
Lord President: Lord Curzon.
Lord Privy Seal: Lord Salisbury.
Lord Chancellor: Lord Cave.
Chancellor of the Exchequer: W. S. Churchill.
Home Office: Sir William Joynson-Hicks.
Foreign Office: Austen Chamberlain.
Colonies: Leopold Amery.
War: Sir L. Worthington-Evans.
India: Lord Birkenhead.
Air: Sir Samuel Hoare.
Scotland: Sir John Gilmour.
Board of Trade: Sir P. Cunliffe-Lister (Lloyd-Greame).
Education: Lord Eustace Percy.
Admiralty: W. C. Bridgeman.
Health: Neville Chamberlain.
Agriculture: E. F. L. Wood.
Labour: Sir Arthur Steel-Maitland.

Attorney-General: Sir Douglas Hogg.

First Commissioner of Works: Lord Peel.

Chancellor of the Duchy of Lancaster: Lord Cecil.

Lord Balfour succeeded Lord Curzon in April 1925; Walter Guinness succeeded Wood in November 1925. Lord Cushendun succeeded Lord Cecil in October 1927. Lord Hailsham (Sir Douglas Hogg) succeeded Lord Cave in March 1928, and was succeeded as Attorney General by Sir Thomas Inskip. Lord Peel succeeded Lord Birkenhead in October 1928, and was succeeded at the Office of Works by Lord Londonderry.

MacDonald's Second Labour Cabinet: June 1929–August 1931

Prime Minister: J. Ramsay MacDonald.

Lord President: Lord Parmoor.

Lord Chancellor: Lord Sankey.

Lord Privy Seal: J. H. Thomas.

Chancellor of the Exchequer: Philip Snowden.

Home Office: J. R. Clynes.

Foreign Office: Arthur Henderson.

Dominions and Colonies: Lord Passfield.

War: Thomas Shaw.

India: Wedgwood Benn.

Air: Lord Thomson.

Scotland: William Adamson.

Board of Trade: William Graham.

Education: Sir Charles Trevelyan.

Admiralty: A. V. Alexander.

Health: Arthur Greenwood.

Agriculture: Noel Buxton.

Labour: Margaret Bondfield.

Works: George Lansbury.

Vernon Hartshorn succeeded Thomas as Lord Privy Seal in June 1930; Thomas went to the Colonial Office (separated from Dominions); Christopher Addison succeeded Noel Buxton at Agriculture. In October 1930, Lord Amulree succeeded Lord Thomson at the Air Ministry. In March 1931, Thomas Johnston succeeded Vernon Hartshorn, and H. B. Lees-Smith succeeded Trevelyan; Herbert Morrison, Minister of Transport, joined the Cabinet.

MacDonald's First National Government, August–November 1931

Prime Minister: J. Ramsay MacDonald.
Lord President: Stanley Baldwin.
Lord Chancellor: Lord Sankey.
Chancellor of the Exchequer: Philip Snowden.
Home Office: Sir Herbert Samuel.
Foreign Office: Lord Reading.
Dominions: J. H. Thomas.
India: Sir Samuel Hoare.
Board of Trade: Sir P. Cunliffe-Lister.
Health: Neville Chamberlain.

MacDonald's Second National Government, November 1931–June 1935

Prime Minister: J. Ramsay MacDonald.
Lord President: Stanley Baldwin.
Lord Chancellor: Lord Sankey.
Lord Privy Seal: Lord Snowden.
Chancellor of the Exchequer: Neville Chamberlain.
Home Office: Sir Herbert Samuel.
Foreign Office: Sir John Simon.
Colonies: Sir P. Cunliffe-Lister.
Dominions: J. H. Thomas.
War: Lord Hailsham.
India: Sir Samuel Hoare.
Air: Lord Londonderry.
Scotland: Sir Archibald Sinclair.
Board of Trade: Walter Runciman.
Education: Sir Donald Maclean.
Admiralty: Sir Bolton Eyres-Monsell.
Health: Sir E. Hilton Young.
Agriculture: Sir John Gilmour.
Labour: Sir Henry Betterton.
Works: W. Ormsby-Gore.

Lord Irwin succeeded Maclean in July 1932. Snowden, Samuel, Sinclair resigned in September 1932, and were replaced by Baldwin (combining the offices of Lord Privy Seal and Lord President), Sir John Gilmour and Sir Godfrey Collins; Walter Elliot succeeded Gilmour at the Ministry of Agriculture. Sir Kingsley Wood (Postmaster-General) entered the Cabinet in 1932. Oliver

Stanley succeeded Betterton at the Ministry of Labour in June 1934.

Baldwin's National Government, June 1935–May 1937

Prime Minister: Stanley Baldwin.
Lord President: Ramsay MacDonald.
Lord Chancellor: Lord Hailsham.
Lord Privy Seal: Lord Londonderry.
Chancellor of the Exchequer: Neville Chamberlain.
Home Office: Sir John Simon.
Foreign Office: Sir Samuel Hoare.
Colonies: Malcolm MacDonald.
Dominions: J. H. Thomas.
War: Lord Halifax.
India: Lord Zetland.
Air: Sir P. Cunliffe-Lister (Lord Swinton).
Scotland: Sir Godfrey Collins.
Board of Trade: Walter Runciman.
Education: Oliver Stanley.
Admiralty: Sir B. Eyres-Monsell (Lord Monsell).
Health: Sir Kingsley Wood.
Agriculture: Walter Elliot.
Labour: Ernest Brown.
Works: W. Ormsby-Gore.
Minister without Portfolio for League of Nations Affairs: Anthony Eden.
Minister without Portfolio: Lord Eustace Percy.

In November 1935, Lord Halifax succeeded Lord Londonderry, and J. H. Thomas and Malcolm MacDonald changed places; A. Duff Cooper succeeded Lord Halifax at the War Office. In December 1935, Eden succeeded Hoare at the Foreign Office. In March 1936, Sir Thomas Inskip joined the Cabinet as Minister for the Co-ordination of Defence, and Lord Eustace Percy resigned. In May 1936, Thomas resigned from the Colonial Office, and was succeeded by Ormsby-Gore, who in turn was replaced at the Office of Works by Lord Stanhope. In June 1936, Sir Samuel Hoare succeeded Lord Monsell at the Admiralty. In October 1936, Walter Elliot succeeded Collins at the Scottish Office and was succeeded at the Ministry of Agriculture by W. S. Morrison; Leslie Hore-Belisha, Minister of Transport, joined the Cabinet.

Neville Chamberlain's Cabinet, May 1937–September 1939

Prime Minister: Neville Chamberlain.
Lord President: Lord Halifax.
Lord Chancellor: Lord Hailsham.
Lord Privy Seal: Lord De La Warr.
Chancellor of the Exchequer: Sir John Simon.
Home Office: Sir Samuel Hoare.
Foreign Office: Anthony Eden.
Colonies: W. Ormsby-Gore.
Dominions: Malcolm MacDonald.
War: Leslie Hore-Belisha.
India: Lord Zetland.
Air: Lord Swinton.
Scotland: Walter Elliot.
Board of Trade: Oliver Stanley.
Education: Lord Stanhope.
Admiralty: A. Duff Cooper.
Health: Sir Kingsley Wood.
Agriculture: W. S. Morrison.
Labour: Ernest Brown.
Co-ordination of Defence: Sir Thomas Inskip.
Transport: Leslie Burgin.

Lord Halifax succeeded Eden at the Foreign Office in February 1938 and was succeeded as Lord President by Lord Hailsham (succeeded in October 1938, by Lord Runciman); Lord Maugham succeeded Hailsham as Lord Chancellor; Lord Winterton, Chancellor of the Duchy of Lancaster, entered the Cabinet (March). In May 1938, Malcolm MacDonald succeeded Ormsby-Gore at the Colonial Office, and was succeeded by Lord Stanley at the Dominions Office (in October 1938, MacDonald combined the Colonies and Dominions posts, but in January 1939 parted with the Dominions in favour of Inskip); Sir Kingsley Wood succeeded Lord Swinton at the Air Ministry and was succeeded at the Ministry of Health by Walter Elliot; D. J. Colville succeeded Elliot at the Scottish Office. In October 1938, Lord Stanhope succeeded Duff Cooper at the Admiralty, and Sir John Anderson succeeded Lord De La Warr as Lord Privy Seal; Lord De La Warr succeeded Lord Stanhope at the Board of Education. In January 1939, W. S. Morrison succeeded Lord Winterton as Chancellor of the Duchy of Lancaster, and was succeeded at the Ministry of Agriculture by Sir R. H. Dorman-Smith; Admiral Lord Chatfield replaced Inskip as Minister for the Co-ordination of Defence. Euan Wallace succeeded Burgin as Minister of Transport in April 1939; Burgin became Minister without Portfolio (Minister of Supply in July).

Neville Chamberlain's War Cabinet: September 1939–May 1940

Prime Minister: Neville Chamberlain.
Chancellor of the Exchequer: Sir John Simon.
Foreign Secretary: Lord Halifax.
Minister for Co-ordination of Defence: Lord Chatfield.
Admiralty: W. S. Churchill.
War: Leslie Hore-Belisha.
Air: Sir Kingsley Wood.
Lord Privy Seal: Sir Samuel Hoare.
Minister without Portfolio: Lord Hankey.

Ministers outside the War Cabinet included Lord Stanhope (Lord President), Sir Thomas Inskip (Lord Chancellor as Lord Caldecote), Sir John Anderson (Home Secretary), Anthony Eden (Dominions Secretary); other ministers remained unchanged from the peacetime ministry.

In January 1940, Hore-Belisha was succeeded by Oliver Stanley; in April 1940, Hoare and Kingsley Wood changed places.

Winston Churchill's War Cabinet: May 1940

Prime Minister and Minister of Defence: W. S. Churchill.
Lord President: Neville Chamberlain.
Lord Privy Seal: C. R. Attlee.
Foreign Secretary: Lord Halifax.
Minister without Portfolio: Arthur Greenwood.
    Outside the War Cabinet:
Minister of Aircraft Production: Lord Beaverbrook.
Chancellor of the Exchequer: Sir Kingsley Wood.
Minister of Labour and National Service: Ernest Bevin.
Admiralty: A. V. Alexander.
Agriculture: R. S. Hudson.
Air: Sir Archibald Sinclair.
Colonies: Lord Lloyd.
Dominions: Lord Caldecote.
Duchy of Lancaster: Lord Hankey.
Economic Warfare: Hugh Dalton.
Education: H. Ramsbotham (from April 1940).

Food: Lord Woolton (from April 1940).
Health: Malcolm MacDonald.
Home Office: Sir John Anderson.
India: L. S. Amery.
Information: A. Duff Cooper.
Lord Chancellor: Lord Simon.
Scotland: Ernest Brown.
Supply: Herbert Morrison.
Board of Trade: Sir Andrew Duncan (from January 1940).
Transport: Sir John Reith.
War: Anthony Eden.

z

Index

Aberavon, 191, 318
Abyssinia, 538, 542–6, 553, 557–62, 623
Acland, Sir Richard, 580
Adamson, William, 7, 83, 392, 554
Addison, Christopher (Viscount Addison), 13, 44, 365, 392, 574
Adult education, 207–8
Advertising, 241
Agricultural Economics Research Institute, 254
Agricultural workers and wages, 45, 124, 175, 251–2, 255, 491, 495, 501
Agriculture, 250–4, 256, 273, 349, 438–440; mechanisation, 254; marketing schemes, 365, 437–9; import quotas, 438–9
Air Ministry, 15, 626
Air raid precautions (A.R.P.), 535, 615, 619, 629–32
Air services, 238–40, 448–50
Air strength; rearmament; see Royal Air Force
Airships, 239, 361, 449
Albania, 159, 640
Alcock, Sir John, 239
Aldington, Richard, 9, 537
Alexander, A. V. (Viscount Alexander of Hillsborough), 146, 172, 392, 554, 655
Allen, Clifford (Lord Allen of Hurtwood) 151–2, 286–7
Aloisi, Baron, 545
Aluminium, 469
Amalgamated Engineering Union, 19, 288
Amery, Leopold, 134, 143, 195, 309, 391, 414, 570, 621, 649, 653, 655
Amritsar, 111
Amulree, Lord, 392, 401, 501
Anderson, Sir John (Lord Waverley), 295, 631
Angell, Sir Norman, 579
Anglesey, 507, 519
Anthropology, 221
Archangel, 55–6
Archbishop of Canterbury; Randall Davidson, 82, 223, 320; Cosmo Gordon Lang, 223, 410; William Temple (q.v.), 223
Architecture, 218–19, 524
Arcos raid, 337–8
Argentina, 436–8

Armaments, private manufacture of, 536, 542
Armistice celebrations, 1918, 2
'Arms and the Covenant', 580, 585
Army: rearmament, 627, 629–30
Art, interest in, 218
Ashfield, Lord, 450–1
Asquith, Herbert Henry (Earl of Oxford and Asquith), 3, 8, 82, 133, 167–9, 171, 176, 179, 186, 190, 319, 347–8
Asquith, Margot, 3
Associated British Cinemas, 247, 523
Astbury, Mr. Justice, 323
Astor, J. J., 125, 244
Astor, Lady, 6, 156, 462, 592, 605
Astor, Viscount, 6, 254
Astronomy, 221
Athenæum, 246
Athenia, 650
Atholl, Duchess of, 526, 577–80, 621
Atlantic, flying the, 239, 449
Atomic physics, 220
Attlee, Clement, 146, 152, 172, 360, 411, 415, 428, 540, 546, 547, 550; leader of Labour party, 553, 557, 561, 569, 585, 620, 632, 640, 653–5
Auden, W. H., 529–31
Australia, 49, 109, 197, 226, 239, 438, 515, 586–7
Austria, 52, 380, 477, 596, 600–1
Automobiles, see Motor cars
Auxiliary Division, R.I.C., 65, 67, 71, 77

Bailey, Sir Abe, 324
Balance of payments, 264, 434–5
Balcon, Sir Michael, 247
Baldwin, Stanley (Earl Baldwin), 7, 119, 132, 142, 186, 190, 194, 218, 528; character, 139, 163, 195–7, 289, 330, 535, 583, 586, 591, 593; part in revolt against Coalition, 136, 138, 141–2; becomes Prime Minister (1923), 160, 162–5, 170; U.S. debt settlement, 161; election of 1923, 165–8; leadership challenged, 177, 347, 366–71, 560, 570; as broadcaster, 187; second Prime Ministership (1924–9), 194–200, 289–290, 336–8, 342, 346–7, 350–1, 353; coal strike, general strike, 1926, 292, 300–10, 317–18, 320–8, 330, 331–5;

Baldwin, Stanley–*cont.*
  attitude to second Labour government, 355, 361; in 1931 crisis, 386–7, 389, 391–5, 396–9; 1931 election, 407, 409; in National government, 413, 415, 417; Indian policy, 426, 428; and re-armament, 476, 540, 570; third Prime Ministership, 479, 534, 536, 566, 588; 1935 election, 553–6, 558, 561; Hoare-Laval plan, 558, 560; Edward VIII's abdication, 583–6; and foreign policy, 593 (note)
Balfour, Sir Arthur (Lord Riverdale), 31, 260, 359
Balfour, Arthur James (Earl of Balfour), 8, 12, 48, 115–16, 118, 135, 138–9, 142, 144, 161, 162, 177, 196, 323, 346, 426
Ball, Sir Joseph, 597–8
Ballet, 525
Banbury, Sir Frederick (Lord Banbury), 155
Bank of England; and 1931 crisis, 381–3, 385, 386, 390–2, 403
Bank rate, 26, 267, 268, 382, 404, 456
Bankers' Industrial Development Cor-poration, 269, 443, 445, 457
'Bankers' ramp', 383–5, 388, 391–2, 410, 549
Banking, 26, 262
Barlow, Sir Montague, 463
Barnes, Rt. Rev. E. W., 222
Barnes, G. N., 4, 13, 48
Barrington-Ward, R. M., 536
Barrow-in-Furness, 126, 315
Barthou, Louis, 477
Bartlett, Vernon, 636
Barton, Robert, 87, 89, 93
Batsford, publishers, 257
Baylis, Lilian, 525
Beatty, Lord, 405
Beaverbrook, Lord, 136, 137, 140, 144, 177, 245, 247, 367–71, 544, 559, 584, 591
Beck, Joseph, 645, 647
Beckett, John, 378
Becontree, 230, 237
Beecham, Sir Thomas, 219
Beer, consumption, 250, 501
Beets, sugar, 253, 439
Belfast, 73, 74–5, 81, 84, 101, 239
Belgium, 157, 179, 198–9, 266, 267, 565–568, 647, 656–7
Bell, Alan, 67
Bell, Clive, 218
Benes, Edouard, 198, 604, 607, 611, 614, 617
Benn (publisher), 221
Bennett, Arnold, 215, 317
Bennett, R. B., 368
Bensusan, S. L., 257
Berne, International Socialist Conference (1919), 150

Berry brothers, 245
Betting, 249; *see also* Pools
Bevan, Aneurin, 361, 574, 582, 636
Beveridge, W. H. (Lord Beveridge), 21, 211, 294, 495
Bevin, Ernest, 19, 38, 41, 285, 359, 456–7, 546–7, on Macmillan Com-mittee, 260, 267, 372; general strike, 289, 301, 303–4, 313, 326, 336; 1931 crisis, 388, 390; attacks Lansbury, 551–2; on rearmament, 569, 632; Minister of Labour, 655
Biology, 220
Birkenhead, Earl of (F. E. Smith), 12, 376; Irish policy, 65, 84, 90, 93; supports coalition, 118, 133, 135–6, 138–9, 141, 144; rejoins Conservative leadership, 167, 177, 195; general strike, 300, 305–9, 319, 322, 325; re-tires, 347
Birmingham, 207, 222, 227, 233, 242, 272, 318, 507, 508, 514, 524, 528; housing estates, 229–30, 511
Birth rates, 517–18
Black and Tans, 64–72, 76–8, 83
Black Friday, 122–3
Blanesburgh, Lord, 339
Bloomsbury, 215, 217
Blum, Léon, 574, 590
Blunt, A. W. F., Bishop of Bradford, 584
Blythe, Ernest, 108
'Bolshevism', 5, 56, 132, 135, 153, 187–190, 337, 410, 579, 590
Bonar Law, Andrew, 48, 61, 65, 76, 166; friendship with Lloyd George, 3, 11, 134; character, 11, 156; break-up of Coalition, 135–6, 140–2; Prime Minis-ter, 143, 145, 157, 162–3
Bondfield, Margaret, 151, 172, 289, 340, 354, 362, 392
Bonham-Carter, Lady Violet, 641
Bonnet, Georges, 605–8, 610, 614, 616, 649
Bono, Emilio de, 542
Boothby, Sir Robert, 10, 347, 580, 621, 653
Bottomley, Horatio, 148
Bowen, Elizabeth, 531
Bowley, Sir A. L., 125
Bracken, Brendan (Viscount Bracken), 621
Bradbury, Lord, 200, 260
Brailsford, H. N., 152, 286–7, 525, 547, 581
Bramley, Fred, 288–9
Brand, R. H. (Lord Brand), 260
Brassert, Henry, 443, 444
Breen, Dan, 63
Briand, Aristide, 113, 198, 343, 345, 372
Bridgeman, W. C. (Lord Bridgeman), 309, 346, 370
Bristol, 4, 124, 127, 245, 315, 328, 492, 496, 502, 507; University, 211; housing estates, 230, 511

British Broadcasting Corporation(B.B.C.) 219, 242–4, 320, 322, 448, 524
British Empire, 48, 109–12, 115, 118, 226, 650; air routes, 239–40; broadcasting service, 244; trade, 265–6, 417–18, 436–7; constitution, 346, 426; Edward VIII's abdication, 584, 586–7; and appeasement, 592, 608, 622
British Empire Exhibition, 177–8
British Gazette, 316–23, 327–8
British Iron and Steel Federation, 442–3
British Overseas Airways Corporation, 449
British Socialist Party, 151
British Union of Fascists, 473–4, 585, 633
Brittain, Vera, 537
Broadcasting; political speeches, 187; church services, 224; development, 241–4; King George V, 533
Brockway, Fenner, 152, 175, 363, 378, 547, 579, 581
Bromley, John, 288, 331, 580
Brown, Sir Harold, 627
Brown, W. J., 361, 363
Bruening, Heinrich, 373, 423
Bruga, Cathal, 58, 59, 60, 87, 89, 95, 104
Bryanston School, 204
Bryant, Sir Arthur, 579
Brynmawr, 126, 481, 489
Buchan, John(Lord Tweedsmuir), 10, 528
Buchanan, George, 147, 155, 184
Buckinghamshire, 225, 228
Buckland, Lord, 245
Buckley, Donal, 429
Budgets (1920), 26; (1921), 129; (1922), 131; (1924), 176; (1925), 199–200, 339; (1926–9), 339, 340; (1930), 367–8; (1931, April), 379; (Sept.), 402; (1932), 455; (1933), 455–6; (1934), 456; (1935), 456; (1936), 458, 571; (1937), 571; (1938), 628; (1939), 629; (Sept.), 651; (1940), 652
Building societies, 460
Building trades, 126, 176, 311, 453, 459–61
Burden, Rev. G. S., 489
Burgin, Leslie, 629
Burnham, Lord, 210, 245
Burnham Scales, 210
Bus services, 232–5
Butler, R. A., 599
Butlin's camps, 502
Buxton, Noel (Lord Noel-Buxton), 146

Cabinet secretariat, 14
Cambridge University, 210–11, 524
Campbell, J. R., 184–6 ('Campbell case'), 297
Camrose, Lord, 245
Canada, 91, 94, 109, 116, 118, 226, 266, 358, 369, 558, 586–7

Canford School, 204
Cannes conference (1922), 113
Capital issues, 264, 269–70, 435, 457
Capital levy, 19
Cardiff, 127, 134, 189, 219, 315, 328, 484, 488, 500, 514
Carlisle, 29, 506
Carlton Club meeting (1922), 139, 142
Carnarvon, Lord, 222
Carnegie Trust, 525, 528
Carpenter, Edward, 214
Carr-Saunders, Sir A. M., 518
Carshalton, 227
Carson, Sir Edward (Lord Carson), 57, 58, 65, 74, 77, 80, 107, 133
Carter, Howard, 222
Cartland, Ronald, 635
Catchpool, E. St. J., 528
Cave, Viscount, 125
Cavendish-Bentinck, Lord Henry, 82
Cecil, Lord Hugh (Lord Quickswood), 137
Cecil, Lord Robert (Viscount Cecil), 48, 82, 159, 180, 345, 419, 541, 621
Central Electricity Board, 243, 342–3, 442
Chamberlain, Sir Austen; in Coalition, 8, 12; Irish policy, 84, 90; supports coalition, 118, 135–42, 144; rejoins Conservative leadership, 164, 167, 176–7; Foreign Secretary, 193, 197–9, 338, 343–4, 351, 376; 1931 election, 410, 414; elder statesman, 560–1, 570–1
Chamberlain, Neville, 360; character, 414, 592, 634–5; in office (1922–3), 144, 168–9, 177; Housing Act (1923), 164–5; Minister of Health (1924–9), 195, 196, 338–41, 516; general strike, 300, 309, 323, 325; party leadership, 347, 368–70, 655; 1931 crisis, 381, 383, 386, 388–9, 392–3, 397–9, 406, 408–9; tariff, 415–19; Chancellor of Exchequer (1931–7), 455–6, 471, 534, 536, 556, 571, 583; sanctions, 557, 562, 566; rearmament, 568, 570, 626–631; Prime Minister, 558, 593, 603, 634–5; shapes foreign policy, appeasement, 589–94, 595–6, 601, 620, 637 (Italy, 597–9, 623); Czechoslovakia, Munich, 604–19, 620, 622–3; new foreign policy (1939), 637–40, 642; warns Hitler of war, 645; coming of war, 646, 649–50; wartime government, 651–4; death, 655
Chanak, 116–19, 138, 157
Channel Islands, 239–40, 449
Charities, 496–8, 528
Charles, Enid, 518–20
Chatfield, Lord, 651
Chelmsford, Bishop of, 71
Chelmsford, Viscount, 111, 172

Chemicals industry, 274–5
Chepstow shipyard, 29
Chequers, 138, 179, 397
Cheshire, 226, 274
Chesterton, G. K., 223
Chiang Kai-shek, 344
Chicago, 515, 590
Childers, Erskine, 72, 87, 89, 97, 98, 105
Children's health, height and weight, 495, 506, 513
China, 183, 337, 344, 422, 595; Manchurian crisis, 419–22
Chingford, 227
Christie, Agatha, 531
Christie, John, 522
Church of England, 222–5, 320, 333; Church Assembly, 224
Churches, 209–10, 222–5, 320, 333
Churchill, Sir Winston Spencer; in Coalition, 10, 12, 16, 22, 56; Irish policy, 64–5, 83, 90–3, 101, 103, 108; Chanak, 118–19; supports Coalition, 135–6, 138–9, 145, 168; rejoins Conservatives, 177, 190, 347; Chancellor of Exchequer, 195, 196, 199–200, 266, 338–40, 345, 367, 379; general strike, 309–10, 319–20, 322, 333–4, 337; leadership of Conservatives, 353, 364, 368–9, 376; Indian policy, 370–1, 378, 427; in lonely opposition, 371, 391, 400, 406, 414, 534, 566–7, 569–70, 591, 599, 601, 603, 635, 641; rearmament, 424, 475, 539, 555–6, 580; Spanish civil war, 574; on Munich crisis, 609, 620–2; Edward VIII's abdication, 585; in Chamberlain's government, 650–4; becomes Prime Minister, 654–7
Ciano, Count, 598, 621, 623, 641
Cinemas, 247, 250, 501, 523
Cinematograph Films Act, 247
Cippenham depot, 29
Citrine, Sir Walter (Lord Citrine), 289, 305–7, 359, 388, 547, 580
Civil service, 15–16, 37, 125, 336, 365, 501
Clair, René, 523
Clarendon, Lord, 243
Clark, Colin, 359
Class, 490; class-war, 578
Clemenceau, Georges, 48, 54, 61
Cliveden, 592
Clyde Workers' Committee, 17, 24
'Clydeside brigade', 147–8, 154–6, 170, 287, 412
Clynes, J. R., 7, 17, 41, 128, 146, 148, 170, 171, 173, 288, 289, 319, 336, 353, 392, 554, 582
Coal Mines Reorganisation Commission, 364, 447–8
Coal mining industry, 26, 158; nationalisation proposed, 16, 19; Sankey Commission, 31–5; legislation (1919–20),

35; (1926), 332; (1930), 364, 446; (1938), 448; 'Mines for the Nation,' 35; strikes (1919–20), 34, 42; (1921), 120–4; (1926), 299–302, 324–7, 331–335; (1936), 473; wages, 120, 123–4, 290–3, 301–2, 334, 447, 491; exports, 266, 271, 290–1, 335, 437; employment, 273–4; conditions in the 20's, 276–7; Red Friday, 291–3; Samuel Report, 291, 294, 297–8; conditions in the 30's, 446–8; Coal Act (1938), 448; royalties nationalised, 448, 634; Scotland, 468
Coalition government (1918–22); coupon election, 2–3, 6; leaders, 10–13; and Ireland, 62, 72–4; disintegration, 132–7; fall, 137–42
Coatbridge, 443, 510
Cobham, Sir Alan, 239–40
Cohalan, Judge Daniel F., 61
Cole, G. D. H., 20, 359, 547, 580
Cole, Margaret (Mrs. G. D. H.), 526, 547
Coleg, Harlech, 489
Collectivism, tendencies toward, 16–17, 43, 127, 164, 243, 338–9, 341–3, 446–450, 466
Collins, Michael, 58–9, 60, 62, 63, 80, 89–93, 96–105, 107
Colonial empire, British, 109–10
Colvilles, 442–4, 445
Committee on Finance and Industry (Macmillan Committee), 260, 262, 267, 269, 372, 380, 385, 403, 456, 457
Committee on Industry and Trade (Balfour Committee), 260, 275
Commons, see House of Commons
Commonwealth of Nations, British; see also Dominion status; British Empire; 109, 118
Communist International, 151, 188, 548, 580
Communist Party; founded, 20; Labour Party rejects it, 20, 153, 285; relations with I.L.P., 151, 548, 580–1; in parliament, 145, 190, 351, 412, 554; Campbell case, 184–5; Zinoviev letter, 188, 193–4; leaders arrested, 296, 318; Spanish civil war, 579
Conscientious objectors, 6
Conscription (1939), 640, 651
Conservative party; coupon election, 3, 6–7; restive under Coalition, 133–7; revolt, 138–9; Carlton Club meeting, 139, 142; divisions and leadership (1922–4), 144, 164, 166–7, 177; (1927), 346–7; (1930–1), 366–71; (1935), 560, 570; 1924 election, 190; attitude towards Labour government, (1929–31), 358, 361, 362, 364–6, 368; in 1931 crisis, 386 ff., 399, 406; in 1931 election, 406–12; 1935 election, 553–4; attacks upon, in books (1939–1944), 633–4; internal criticism, 635

Constantinople, 54–5, 117-19
Consumption and consumer industries, 451–4
Conversion, war loan, 456
Cook, A. J., 285, 288, 296, 299, 306, 309, 324–5, 331, 333, 361
Coolidge, President Calvin, 160
Coombs, B. L., 530
Co-operative movement, 35, 314, 454, 548, 581, 636
Cope, Sir A. W., 85, 89
Corby, 444
Corfu, 159–60
Cork, 66, 67, 68, 77, 98, 104
Corn Production Acts, 251–2
Cosgrave, W. T., 75, 97, 105, 107–8, 428
Cost of living, 27, 205, 261, 268, 434, 440, 452, 458, 492–3
Cotton industry, 26, 40, 266, 271, 273–4, 281–3
Council of Ireland, 73
Countryman, 256
Country towns, 257–8
County Donegal Railways Joint Committee, 236
Coupon election, 2–8
Courtauld, Samuel, 218, 454
Coward, Noel, 214
Craig, Sir James (Lord Craigavon), 74, 80, 85–7, 92–3, 101, 107–8, 602, 640
Cramp, C. T., 330
Cranborne, Lord, 598, 621, 655
Crawford and Balcarres, Earl of, 242–243
Credit Anstalt, 380
Creech, Jones, A., 286
Criminal Justice bill (1938), 634
Cripps, Sir Stafford, 401, 411, 546, 547, 551–2, 581–2, 636, 641
Croft, Sir Henry Page, 579
Crook, 481, 483, 489
Crossword puzzles, 196, 202
Crowdy, Dame Rachel, 579
Crowe, Sir Eyre, 192
Crozier, Brigadier General F. P., 65, 66, 70, 72, 82
Cumberland, 274, 463–5
Cunard-White Star merger, 446
Cunliffe Committee, 199
Cunliffe-Lister, Philip, see Swinton, Viscount
Curtis, Lionel, 14, 82, 90, 109, 111
Curzon, Marquess of, 12, 117–19, 133, 137, 138–9, 141, 143, 156–60, 162–3, 178, 181, 195, 245, 473
Czechoslovakia, 52, 54, 56, 198–9, 596, 637; Munich crisis, 604–18, 621–2

D'Abernon, Lord, 198
Dagenham, 227, 230, 522

Dahlerus, Birger, 646–7
Dail Eireann, 58, 59, 62, 64, 75, 80, 81, 85, 87, 95–7, 100, 105
Daily Express, 245, 524, 591
Daily Herald, 20, 40, 245, 320, 331, 384, 558
Daily Mail, 4, 51, 81, 130, 168, 192–4, 239, 241, 244–5, 308, 327, 386–7, 389, 585, 591
Daily Telegraph, 245, 558
Daladier, Edouard, 605, 608, 610, 612, 614, 615–17, 623, 647, 649
Dalton, Hugh, 374, 392–3, 546, 550, 551, 554, 566, 569, 632, 655
Dancing, 215, 501
Dantzig, 50, 52, 639, 641, 644–6
Dardanelles, 55, 117–18
Davidson, J. C. C. (Viscount Davidson), 368, 465
Davidson, Rt. Rev. Randall, Archbishop of Canterbury, 223
Davies, Ernest, 634
Dawes, General Charles, 178, 375
Dawes report, 160, 178–9, 374
Dawson, Christopher, 223
Dawson, Geoffrey, 244, 395, 534, 536, 583, 584, 592, 607
Dawson of Penn, Lord, 563
Death duties, 367, 494
Death rates, 513–16
Decontrol (1920–1), 28–29, 119–20
Delius, Frederick, 219
Demobilisation (1919), 22
Denmark, 266, 436–8, 516, 640
Derating, 340–1, 347
Derby, Lord (17th Earl), 85, 135, 143, 347
Detective stories, 196, 216, 531
Deutsch, Oscar, 523
De Valera, Eamon, 58, 59–60, 61, 80, 85–9, 91, 95–7, 98, 100, 103, 106, 428–31, 587, 601–3, 640
Disarmament, 115, 180–1, 344–5, 373, 475, 478, 535, 540, 542; Disarmament Conference (1932–4), 423–5, 475
Discovery, 221
Distressed Areas, 463–8, 481 ff., 528, 635
Distribution of the national income, 205, 491–4, 499
Divorce, 214, 522, 634
Dobbie, William, 574
Dockers, 28, 38, 41, 311
Dolfuss, Engelbert, 477
Domestic servants, 24, 45, 204, 488, 495
Dominion status, 82, 87–8, 91, 94, 96, 118, 346, 426
Dominions, 197; at Paris peace conference, 48–9; at Washington conference, 115; Edward VIII's abdication, 584, 586–7; and appeasement, 592, 608, 622
Doncaster, 317–18

Dorman Long, 443
Dove, John, 82
Dowlais, 443
Drinking, 250
Dublin, 58, 62, 63, 64, 66, 67, 70, 76, 79, 99, 103–4, 106
Duckham, Sir Arthur, 31, 34–5
Duff Cooper, A. (Lord Norwich), 370, 610, 615, 620–1, 622, 653, 655
Duffy, George Gavan, 89, 97
Duggan, E. J., 62, 89, 97, 98
Duncan, Sir Andrew, 442
Dundee, 16, 127, 145, 469
Dunedin, Lord, 134
Dunkirk, 657
Durbin, E. F. M., 547
Durham, County, 274, 277, 301, 463–7, 471, 481 ff., 507, 514, 516, 519
Dutt, Palme, 581
Dyer, General R. E. H., 111
Dyestuffs industry, 131–2

Ebbw Vale, 444–5, 466
Eckersley, P. P., 241
Economic Advisory Council, 359
Economic conditions; boom of 1919, 25–26; slump (1921), 125–6, 280; in the 20's, 259 ff.; depression and recovery, 432–5, 441 ff., 451 ff., 461
Economic theory, 372, 404, 456, 461–2
Economies (1931), 402, 406, 455–6, 459, 498
Economist, 246, 262, 270, 382, 406, 411
Eddington, Sir Arthur, 221
Ede, Chuter, 443
Eden, Sir Anthony, 424, 534, 539, 621, 622, 635, 646, 651, 655; Abyssinian war, sanctions, 543, 545; Foreign Secretary, 561, 562, 564, 594–5; Rhineland crisis, 565–6, 568; resignation, 596–8
Edinburgh, 232, 238, 249, 318, 470, 500, 510
Education, 130–1, 175, 206–11, 257, 341, 365, 498
Edward VIII, King (Prince of Wales; Duke of Windsor), 109, 488, 563, 582; abdication, 583–7
Edwards, Sir Charles, 547
Egypt, 110, 376, 397, 562
Einstein, Albert, 220
Eire, see Ireland
Electoral reform (1930), 366; see also Franchise; Representation
Electrical industry, 266, 272, 454
Electricity; nationalisation proposed, 16, 19, 176; Electricity Commissioners, 29, 130; Central Electricity Board, 243, 342–3, 455; rural supply, 255–6; growth of the industry, 453, 455; hydro-electric power in Scotland, 469; electrification of railways, 237

Eliot, T. S., 214, 217, 529
Ellerman, Sir John, 494
Elliot, Walter, 438, 627, 632
Ellis, Havelock, 214
Emergency Powers Act (1920), 42, 121, 295, 304, 318, 332; (Defence, 1939), 645–6
Emigration, 226, 517
'Empire Free Trade', 367–71
Encyclopædia Britannica, 221
Engineering industry, 26, 126, 165, 279, 454
Epstein, Sir Jacob, 218
Esthonia, 566, 640, 644
Evacuation of mothers and children (1939), 648, 651
Evening Standard, 245, 526
Exchange Equalisation Fund, 436, 440
Export trade, 261–4, 266, 268, 270–1, 272, 278–9, 281–2, 358, 432

Fabian Society, 18, 547
Fact, 526
Family allowances, 45, 46, 128, 286, 298, 495, 503, 520, 578
Family, size of, 519, 521
Farms and farming, 203, 250–4, 255, 256; see also Agricultural workers
Fascists, British, 294, 473–5
Fashions, dress, 202, 212–13
Feetham, Mr. Justice, 107
Financing of industry, 260, 262, 267, 269
Finland, 644, 651–2
Firth, Sir William, 445
Fisher, H. A. L., 13, 207–8, 210, 243
Fisher, J. R., 107
Fishing industry, 438
Fitzalan, Viscount (Lord Edmund Talbot), 85
Fitzgerald, Desmond, 95
Flandin, Étienne, 565, 566
Floodlighting, 532
Fontainebleau memorandum, 50, 53
Food; home-grown, 251, 253, 439; consumption, 452, 505
Food ministry, 29, 40
Foot, Isaac, 419
Football pools, 248–9, 500
Forbes, Henry, 236
Forde, Liam, 99
Foreign policy, British; see also France; Paris peace conference, 46–51; in 1919–20, 52–6; 1921–2, 112–16; 1922–3, 156–60; Labour government's (1924), 178–83; A. Chamberlain's, 197–9, 343 ff.; A. Henderson's, 372–6; Manchuria, 419–22; attitude towards Germany (1932–5), 423, 536; changing opinions (1935–7), 535–7, 561, 567, 577–8, 589–91; naval treaty with Germany, 540–1; Abyssinian war, sanctions, 538, 542–6, 557–62,

567; Rhineland crisis (1936), 564–8; alliance with France, 568; 'appeasement', 568, 590–4, 604 ff., 620, 637; Spanish civil war, 573–7, 599–600, 623; distrust of Russia (1937–9), 590, 622, 638; agreement with Italy, 575, 597–9, 623; Czechoslovakia: Munich settlement, 604–18, 621–2; new policies, Poland (1939), 637–40, 645–9; Anglo-Russian negotiations, 641–4; coming of war, 645–9

Forestry Commission, 15

Forster, E. M., 112, 215

Four Courts, Dublin, 99, 103

France, 263, 266, 267, 383–4, 538; at Paris peace conference, 47–52; projected treaty with Britain and U.S., 50, 53, 113; and Turkey, 54–5, 117–19; reparations, European security, 112–115, 197–9, 374–5, 380; Anglo-French entente, 115, 118, 156–8, 178–81, 344–5, 541, 557, 568, 590, 605–6, 610, 614, 623; Ruhr occupation, 157–159, 179–80; Locarno Pact, 198–9, 539, 566–8, 604; disarmament, 344, 372, 375, 423–5, 478; Stavisky riots, 477; treaty with Russia, 477, 539, 564, 566; sanctions, Hoare-Laval plan, 544, 557–559; remilitarisation of Rhineland, 564–8; military alliance with Britain (1936), 565, 568, 605, 614, 630; Spanish civil war, 574–6; policy towards Czechoslovakia; Munich, 605–608, 610–18; diplomacy (1939), 638–639, 642–4, 646–50; defeat, 656–7

Franchise, extension of (1918), 5; (1928), 343

Franco, General, 572, 576, 598–9, 623, 637

Francs case, 192, 193

Fraser, Sir Malcolm, 138

Freeman, Sir Wilfred, 626

French, Lord, 64, 66, 68

Freud, Sigmund, 214

Fry, Maxwell, 524

Fry, Roger, 217

Fulham, East, by-election, 422, 555

Fusion movement (1920), 132–6

Fyfe, Hamilton, 303, 315, 331

Gainford, Lord, 243, 322

Gaitskell, Hugh, 547

Gallacher, William, 24–5, 554, 581

Galsworthy, John, 215

Gandhi, Mahatma, 111, 378, 427

'Garden suburb', 14, 133

Gardiner, A. G., 641

Garrett, George, 530

Garvin, J. L., 16, 135, 300, 387, 396, 544, 591, 592, 613

Gaumont-British, 247, 523

Geddes, Sir Auckland (Lord Geddes), 4

Geddes, Sir Eric, 4, 13, 29; Geddes axe, 130, 208, 382

General and Municipal Workers' Union, 19

General Council; see Trades Union Congress

General elections: Coupon (1918), 2–8; (1922), 145; (1923), 167–8; (1924), 187–90; (1929), 350–2; (1931), 409–412; (1935), 553–5

General strike; threats of, 24, 39–40, 42, 121–3; (1926), 243, 284–5, 291–330; bibliography, 331

Geneva Conference (1927), 344–5

Genoa Conference, 114

George V, King, 61, 81, 84–5, 88, 142, 162, 167, 173, 177, 187, 211, 248, 304; and general strike, 317, 323, 328, 335; in 1931 crisis, 386, 389, 391–3, 394–5, 398, 408; silver jubilee, 532–3; broadcasts, 533; death, 563

George VI, King, 586–7, 588

Germany, 266, 267, 436, 441; peace conference, 4, 46, 48–51; colonies, 48–9, 52; disarmament, 49, 52, 373, 423, 475; and Treaty of Versailles, 52, 423–5, 539, 564–6; fleet scuttled, 52; postwar policy towards, 53; reparations, 112–13, 157–9, 178–9, 357, 372, 374, 380; Genoa conference, 114; occupation of Ruhr, 157–9, 160, 179–180; Locarno Pact, 198–9; enters League of Nations, 198–9, 343; leaves it, 425; financial crisis (1931), 380–1; Hitler comes to power, 424; purge, 477; rearmament, 475–8, 538–41, 543, 571, 628–31; naval treaty with Britain, 541; reoccupies Rhineland, 564–8; opposes Russia (1936–9), 564, 566; Spanish civil war, 573–6; 'Axis', 589, 623, 641; and Austria, 596, 600–601; Czechoslovakia, 596, 604–18, 621, 637; pressure on Poland, 639–41, 643–8; negotiations with Russia, 642–4; begins war, 648–9; in the war, 651–2, 656–7

Gibbon, Lewis Grassic, 468

Gibbs, Sir Philip, 121, 536

Gilbert, S. P., 179

Gill, Eric, 218

Glasgow, 17, 24, 62, 126, 127, 147, 151, 164, 187, 232, 249, 317–18, 467, 472, 481, 488, 511, 515

Glyndebourne, 522

Goebbels, Joseph, 649

Goering, Hermann, 595, 604, 637, 638, 646, 648–9

Gold standard, 199–200, 267, 268, 384–5, 390; abandoned, 403–4, 436

Goldring, Douglas, 71

Gollancz, Victor, 526

Goodhart, A. L., 323

z*

Government, enlargement of, since 1914, 13, 15–16
Graham, William, 172, 381, 391–2
Grandi, Count, 597–8
Grant, Sir Alexander, 183–4
Graves, Robert, 537
Great Northern Railway (Ireland), 236
Great Western Railway, 30, 236–7, 327, 451
Greaves, H. R. G., 634
Greece, 55, 116–17, 119, 159, 640
Greene, Graham, 531
Greenwood, Arthur, 83, 146, 172, 365, 390, 392, 508, 553, 562, 575, 632, 646, 649, 654–5
Greenwood, Sir Hamar (Viscount Greenwood), 64, 67, 70, 77, 90, 134
Gregory, Holman, 362, 471
Gregory, J. D., 189, 192, 193
Gregory, T. E., 260, 385
Gresley, Sir H. N., 236, 238
Gretton, Col. J., 370
Grey, Viscount, 348
Greyhound racing, 249
Grierson, John, 247
Grieve, C. M., 468
Griffith, Arthur, 57, 58, 60–1, 62, 80, 86, 87, 89–93, 95–7, 100, 104–5
Griffith-Boscawen, Sir Arthur, 134, 165
Grigg, Sir Edward (Lord Altrincham), 84, 137, 570
Grigg, Sir James, 131, 200
Gropius, 524
Guernica, 577
Guildford Cathedral, 224
Guilty Men, 556, 570, 588, 633
Gunn, Neil, 468

Hácha, President, 637
Hackwood Park, 13, 245
Hadow report, 208–9, 498
Hague Conference (1929), 374
Haile Selassie, Emperor of Abyssinia, 559–62
Hailsham, Viscount, see Hogg, Sir Douglas
Haldane, J. B. S., 220, 222
Haldane, Viscount, 15, 172, 192, 319
Halder, General, 616
Half Circle Club, 173
Halifax, Earl of (E. F. L. Wood, Lord Irwin), 133, 143, 347, 377, 419, 426–7, 536, 555, 583, 593, 635; influence on foreign policy, 566, 594; visits Hitler, 595–6; Foreign Secretary, 599, 623, 630, 637, 638, 642, 645–6, 649; in Czechoslovakian crisis, 605–8, 612–17; in wartime governments, 651, 654–5
Hambling committee, 240
Hamilton, Mrs. Mary Agnes, 9, 152, 243, 397
Handsworth, 126

Hankey, Maurice (Lord Hankey), 14, 651
Hannington, Wal, 126, 472
Hardinge, Lord, 118
Harington, General Sir Charles, 118–19
Harkness, E. S., 528
Harrisson, Tom, 530
Hartlepool, 126
Hartshorn, Vernon, 35, 360
Harvey, Sir Ernest, 382, 391–2
Harvey, George, 161
Hastings, Sir Patrick, 155, 184–5
Hatry, Clarence, 269, 357
Hayes (Middlesex), 227, 523
Health, the nation's, 495, 506, 512 ff.
Health, Ministry of, 15, 44, 129
Healy, T. M., 106
Hebburn, 481, 507
Hemingway, Ernest, 530, 537
Henderson, Arthur; Labour party (1918–1922), 7, 17–18, 20, 41, 83, 145, 148; in Labour government (1924), 170–2, 180–1, 185, 285; general strike, 303, 306, 310, 319; Labour government (1929–31), 353–4, 360; Foreign Secretary, 373–4, 376; 1931 crisis, 381, 388, 390, 392–3, 397, 400, 402, 411; Disarmament Conference, 423–4, 546
Henderson, Sir Hubert, 359
Henderson, Sir Nevile, 594, 595, 607, 614, 619, 638, 645–9
Hendon, 227
Henlein, Konrad, 605–8
Herbert, Sir A. P., 522, 527
Herriot, Edouard, 179–81
Hewart, Sir Gordon (Lord Hewart), 90
Hibberd, Stuart, 563
Highlands, Scotland, 469
Hillman, Edward, 448
Hilton, John, 499
Hilton Young, Sir E. (Lord Kennet), 508
Hire purchase, 499
Hitchcock, Alfred, 248
Hitler, Adolf, 159, 380, 424–5, 473, 477, 539, 598, 600, 622; Rhineland crisis, 564–8; visit from Halifax, 595–6; Czechoslovakia, 605–18, 637; prepares for war on Poland, 640, 643, 645–9
Hoare, Sir Samuel (Lord Templewood), 143, 195; 1931 crisis, 388, 393, 414; India Act, 428; Foreign Secretary (1935), 534, 541; Geneva speech, 544–5; Hoare-Laval plan, 557–60, 569; Chamberlain's inner cabinet, 593–4, 610, 614, 619–20, 634, 637; in wartime government (1939–40), 651, 653, 655
Hobhouse, L. T., 221
Hobson, J. A., 286
Hodges, Frank, 31–2, 122–3, 288
Hodson, H. V., 359
Hogben, Lancelot, 518, 527

Hogg, Sir Douglas (Lord Hailsham), 143, 309, 323, 347, 406, 414, 534, 619
Holden, Charles, 219, 524–5
Holidays, holiday trades, hotels, 452, 501–2; holiday camps, 501
Hollywood, 246
Home market, 451–5
Honours, sale of, 134
Hoover, President Herbert, 375, 380
Hore-Belisha, Leslie (Lord Hore-Belisha) 630, 640, 651
Horne, Sir Robert (Viscount Horne), 36, 45, 136, 138, 144, 185, 195, 470, 570
Horse-drawn vehicles, 231; horses on farms, 254
Horse-racing, 249
Hosier, A. J., 254
Hospitals, 496, 497, 524
Hossbach memorandum, 596
House of Commons; composition (1919), 7–8
Housing; Acts; (1919), 43–4, 509; (1923), 164–5, 509; (1924), 176, 508, 509; (1930), 365, 508; (1933), 508; (1935), 507, 508; housing boom in 30's, 458–61, 509–10; numbers of houses built, 458–9, 509–10; housing conditions, 506–10
Housing estates, 228–31, 233, 511–12
Hudson, R. S., 646
Hughes, Charles Evans, 115, 160
Hughes, W. M., 49
Hull, 318; University College, 210
Hungary, 621
Hunter, Ernest, 152
Huxley, Aldous, 214, 216, 220
Huxley, Julian, 220

Illegitimacy, 515
Imperial Airways, 240, 448–9
Imperial Chemical Industries, 274–5
Imperial Conference, (1921), 115; (1923), 165; (1926), 246, 345–6; (1930), 369, 374, 426; (1932), Ottawa, Imperial Economic Conference, 417–18; (1937), 592
Imperial Defence, Committee of, 14
Imperial preference, 131, 266, 369, 371, 416-·18, 436–7
Import duties; Act, (1932), 415–16; Advisory Committee, 416–17, 441–2
Import trade, 261–4, 265, 267, 432, 437
imThurn, Conrad Donald, 194
Inchcape, Lord, 131, 149
Incitement to Disaffection Act (1934), 475
Independent Labour Party (I.L.P.), 18, 147–8, 150–2, 170, 175, 286–7, 350–1, 362–3, 412, 547, 548, 581
India, 54, 110–12, 117, 239–40, 282, 347, 360, 370–1; Simon Report, 377–8; Round Table Conferences, 378, 427;

Government of India Act (1935), 426–8
Industrial courts, 37–8, 292
Industrial insurance, 500
Industries; new, 272–5, 453–5; staple, 271, 273–83, 441 ff.; service, 452–4
Infant mortality, 514–16
Inflation (1919–20), 27
Influenza epidemic (1919), 22
Inskip, Sir Thomas (Lord Caldecote), 144, 225, 419, 570, 619, 651
Inverforth, Lord (Andrew Weir), 29
Invergordon mutiny, 403–6
Investments, British overseas, 264–5, 268
Iraq, 49, 55, 157
Ireland; British Labour's sympathy for (1920), 42, 70, 72, 83; Dail proclaims independence (1919), 58; · the war against Great Britain, 63–72, 76–81, (bibliographical note, 72); casualties, 64, 69, 80; 'bloody Sunday', 67, 69, 70, 77; partition, 72–3, 602–3; Republican government, 75; martial law, 76, 78, 79; election (1921), 80; (1922), 99–100; truce (1921), 84–6; treaty negotiations, 89–93; the treaty, 93–4, 100, 108, 429; ratification, 95–7; British troops evacuated, 98, 106; boundary, 92, 94, 101, 107–8; civil war, 98–9, 103–6; border war, 101; Irish Free State inaugurated, 106 (constitution, 100–1); financial obligations and land annuities, 94, 96, 108, 429–31, 603; deportation of Irishmen from England, 155; constitutional changes (1932–6), 428–30, 587–8; trade war, 431, 603; new constitution, Eire (1937), 601; agreements with Britain (1938), 603; neutrality (1939), 650; Republic of Ireland, 430, 602
Irish Free State, see Ireland
Irish Nationalist Party, 57, 58
Irish Republican Army, 62, 65–71, 75, 76–8, 80, 86, 88, 98–9, 102–6, 429
Irish Volunteers, 57; see Irish Republican Army
Iron, see steel
Ironmoulders, 40
Irvine, Sir James, 528
Irwin, Lord, see Halifax, Lord
Isherwood, Christopher, 529
Isle of Man, 449, 518
Italy, 54, 115, 119, 159–60, 179, 198–9, 263, 266, 344, 375, 423–4, 477, 538, 566, 640, 649; at Paris peace conference, 48–51; Abyssinian war sanctions, 542–6, 557–62, 564, 597, 599; Spanish civil war, 573–6, 597–9; agreements with Britain (1937–8), 575, 597, 599–600, 623; 'Axis', 589, 597, 623; Munich crisis, 615–17, 621

Jackson, Holbrook, 218
James, C. H., 524
Japan, 48–9, 115–16, 179, 262, 282, 344–345, 375, 400, 478, 589, 595; and Manchuria, 419–22
Jarrow, 26, 126, 443, 445, 466, 481, 489, 516
Jarvis, Sir John, 443
Jeans, Sir James, 221
Jebb, Eglantyne, 497
Jenkinson, Rev. Charles, 511
Jerrold, Douglas, 572, 577, 579
Joad, C. E. M., 222
Johnson, Amy, 239
Johnson, Hewlett, 579
Johnston, Thomas, 147, 174, 358–9, 390, 392
Jolly George, 41, 56
Jones, Kennedy, 51
Jones, Jack, 184
Jones, Thomas, 11, 90, 92, 322, 489, 528
Jowett, F. W., 83, 146, 152–3, 155, 172–3, 286–7, 354, 363, 547, 581
Jowitt, W. A. (Lord Jowitt), 354, 419
Joyce, James, 217
Joynson-Hicks, Sir William (Lord Brentford), 137, 144, 193, 195, 225, 309, 316, 338, 347
Jute, 469

Kegan Paul & Company, 222
Kellogg-Briand Pact, 345, 372, 374, 400, 419
Kemal, Mustapha, 54–5, 116–18
Kemsley, Lord, 245
Kenya, 110
Kerr, Philip, *see* Lothian, Marquess of
Keyes, Sir Roger, 653
Keynes, J. M. (Lord Keynes), 4, 7, 10, 200, 217, 260, 262, 267, 349, 359, 372, 456, 457, 525; Keynsian economics, 372, 461–2
Kilmichael, 67–8
King George's Jubilee Trust, 528
Kingsbury, 227
Kirkwood, David (Baron Kirkwood), 24, 147, 154, 156, 363, 446
Knox, Msgr. Ronald, 223
Korda, Sir Alexander, 523
Kuczynski, R. R., 518

Labour, Ministry of, 15, 37, 130
Labour party; coupon election, 3, 5–7; new constitution, 18; *Labour and the New Social Order*, 18–19; relations with T.U.C., 20, 35, 548; headquarters, 20; annual conferences: Nottingham (1918), 18; Southport (1919), 41; Edinburgh (1922), 152; London (1923), 153; London (1924), 185; Liverpool (1925), 285; Birmingham (1928), 530; Llandudno (1929), 360–1; Leicester (1932), 548; Hastings (1933), 548; Southport (1934), 548–9; Brighton (1935), 550–2; Edinburgh (1936), 547, 569, 574, 580; Bournemouth (1937), 582, 632; Southport (1939), 636; Bournemouth (1940), 655; interest in Russia, 41, 150–1, 287; League of Nations, 48, 180, 550; sympathy for Ireland, 42, 70–2, 77, 83; in 1922 parliament, 145–147, 150–6, 158, 162; MacDonald as leader, 148, 155; in 1923 election, 167–8; Labour government, (1924), 170–86, 207, 209, 252, 260; foreign policy, 178–83; 1924 election, 190; tendencies in the 20's, 285–6, 343; general strike, 317–18, 332, 336; Labour government (1929–31), 209, 353 ff.; Labour and the Communist party, 20, 153, 185, 285, 548, 580–1; political levy, 336–7; *Labour and the Nation* (1928), 350, 373; 1929 election, 350–1; crisis of 1931, 382–92, 394, 396, 400–1; in 1931 election, 409–12, 415; and rearmament, 476, 540, 550, 569, 571, 632; change of leadership (1935), 546, 551–3; in local government, 546; honours, 547; Socialist League, 547–8; *For Socialism and Peace*, 548–50; United Front, 548; Popular Front, 636; emergency powers, 549; sanctions under League of Nations, 550–2, 557; 1935 election, 553–5; Rhineland crisis (1936), 566; attitude to Spanish civil war, 574–5, 577, 623; attitude towards a popular front, 580–2; Edward VIII's abdication, 585; Czechoslovakia, Munich, 604, 613, 621; opposes conscription, 640; supports war on Germany, 646, 649; censures Chamberlain's government (1940), 653; joins Churchill government, 654–5, 656
Labour Research Department, 20, 40, 331
Lampson, Sir Miles (Lord Killearn), 562
Lancashire, 26, 40, 177, 225, 274, 281–3, 463, 481
Land Utilisation bill, 365
Land Utilisation Survey, 254
Land values tax, 368, 379, 419
Landed estates, 203
Lane, Sir Allen, 526
Lang, Rt. Rev. Cosmo Gordon, Archbishop of Canterbury, 223
Lansbury, George, *Daily Herald*, 20; Poplar Guardians, 129; 1922–4 parliaments, 146, 174, 182, 184; in 1929 government, 354, 358–9; in 1931 crisis, 390, 392–3, 411; leader of Labour party, 415, 546; *Fact*, 526; journeys for peace, 538; resigns leadership, Brighton conference, 551–2

Laski, Harold J., 171, 392, 526, 547, 549, 582
Latvia, 566, 640, 644
Lausanne, Conference of, (1922–3), 156–157; (1932), 422
Laval, Pierre, 477–8, 538, 544; Hoare-Laval plan, 557, 558–61
Lawrence, D. H., 216
Lawrence, Sir Herbert, 294
Lawrence, T. E., 215
Layton, Sir Walter (Lord Layton), 262, 333, 408
League of Nations, 61, 157; at Paris peace conference, 48; in treaty of Versailles, 52; mandates, 48, 109; and Labour government, (1924), 180–1; disarmament, 343–4, 373, 423–5, 539; Corfu, 159–60; Locarno, Germany, 197–9; Manchurian crisis, 400, 419–422; Abyssinian war, sanctions, 543–6, 553, 557–62, 567; Rhineland crisis, (1936), 566; ignored after 1936, 589, 594, 595, 604, 609, 611; Peace Ballot, 537, 541–2
Lee, Jennie, 361, 363
Lee, Kenneth, 294
Lee of Fareham, Lord, 138
Leeds, 17, 20, 26, 317, 507, 509, 511
Lees-Smith, H. B., 392
Left Book Club, 481, 483, 526, 580
Lehmann, John and Rosamond, 530
Leicester, 5, 127, 168, 483; University College, 210
Lemon, Sir Ernest, 626
Letchworth Garden City, 228, 523
Lever Brothers, 274
Lewis, Cecil Day, 529–31
Liberal Industrial Inquiry, 262, 349
Liberal National party (Simon), 407, 409, 411, 414, 419, 553–4
Liberal party, 336, 476; divisions, 2, 3, 8, 347–8, 362, 372; in coupon election, 3, 7–8; after the war, 17; attitude toward Coalition, 133, 135–6; recruits to Labour party, 146; 1923 election, 168–9; relations with Labour government, (1924), 169, 171, 176, 185–6; 1924 election, 190; 1929 election, 262, 348–51; attitude to Labour government (1929–31), 356, 358, 361–2, 363–4, 366, 368; in 1931 crisis, 386 ff., 399, 401; in 1931 election, 407–12; and National government, 415–16, 418; 1935 election, 554; in 1939–40, 641, 655
Licensing (liquor), 29
Lincoln and Lincolnshire, 60, 62, 224, 233, 315, 442, 444–5
Lindbergh, Charles A., 239, 608
Lindsay, A. D. (Lord Lindsay of Birker; Master of Balliol), 489
Lindsay, Kenneth, 206–7, 520
Linlithgow, Lord, 428

Lipski, Joseph, 647–8
Listener, The, 221
Literature, 201, 215–17, 529–31
Lithgow, Sir James, 445
Lithuania, 639
Little Entente, 54
Litvinov, Maxim, 192, 580, 590, 609, 611, 642
Liverpool, 39, 77, 80, 127, 204, 207, 227, 232, 250, 500; cathedral, 224; housing, 230, 507–9; general strike, 295, 315, 318; unemployed, 483, 488; health, 506, 515
Lloyd, Geoffrey, 474
Lloyd, Lord, 376, 427, 570, 621, 655
Lloyd George, David (Earl Lloyd-George), 2, 161, 182, 208, 244, 598, 655; coupon election, 2–3; character, 10; friendship with Bonar Law, 11; with Churchill, 12, 353, 369; methods of administration, 13; foils Labour (1919), 30–37; strikes of 1919–21, 39–42, 122; intervention in Russia (1920), 41–2, 55–60; Paris peace conference, 46–51; postwar diplomacy, 52–6, 112–15; Irish policy, 65–6, 71, 76–7, 84–93, 107; Chanak, 116–19; preserving the Coalition, 133–8; Lloyd George fund, 134, 348; resigns Prime Ministership, 142; 1923 election, 167–8; creation of peers, 134, 204; agricultural policy, 251; Liberal Industrial Inquiry, 262; general strike, 319; plans for national development and combating unemployment, 342, 348–9, 457, 465, 534; Liberal leadership (1926), 347–8; 1929 election, 350–2; attitude toward Labour government (1929–31), 353, 355, 358, 361–2, 364, 366; in 1931 crisis, 386, 389, 391, 400–1; in 1931 election, 408, 410, 412, 415; National government, possibility of joining in 1935, 534; in 1935 election, 554; on sanctions, 562; Polish guarantee, 639; visits Hitler, 591; attacks Chamberlain (1940), 654
Lloyd George, Gwilym, 401, 412
Lloyd George, Megan, 412
Lloyd-Greame, Philip, see Swinton, Viscount
Local government and local authorities, 44, 127; Act of 1929, 340–2
Locarno Pact, 198–9, 539, 564, 566–8, 604
London; police strike, 39; unemployed demonstrations, 127; servants, 204; schools, 206, 208; growth of London area, 225–8, 274; traffic, 227, 231–2, 349, 450; housing estates, 229–31, 512; flats, 460, 512; over-crowding, 507–9; buses, 233; cinemas, 250; general strike, 311, 312, 315, 317, 327; poverty, 481, 483, 484, 502, 506; health, 514–15; society, 521–2

London and North Eastern Railway, 30, 218, 236–8, 451
London conferences; (1924), 179–80; Naval conference (1930), 375; World Economic Conference, (1933), 440
London, Midland and Scottish Railway, 30, 234, 236–7
London Passenger Transport Board, 365, 450–1, 524
London, Treaty of (1915), 54
London University, 210–11, 221, 254, 260, 518, 524, 528
Londonderry, 7th Marquess of, 322, 347, 414, 479, 522, 534, 540, 555, 570, 592, 626
Long, Walter (Viscount Long), 13, 65, 135
Lords, House of, 346, 362, 365–6, 466, 549
Lossiemouth, 170–1, 183, 382
Lost generation, the, 9, 201, 216, 255
Lothian, Marquess of (Philip Kerr), 14, 109, 262, 361, 419, 462, 489, 564, 592
Low, David, 396, 526, 556, 560, 591
Lubetkin, Berthold, 524
Ludendorff, General, 159
Lugard, Sir F. J. D. (Lord Lugard), 109
Lunn, Sir Arnold, 579
Lutyens, Sir Edwin, 219
Lytton Report, 420–2

MacCurtain, Thomas, 68
MacDonald, James Ramsay; in 1918, 5, 17, 252; character, 148–9, 183, 186, 191, 397–8; leader of Labour party (1922), 142, 148, 150, 155; in I.L.P., 151–2; Prime Minister (1924), 170–186; Foreign Secretary (1924), 178–182; motor car, 183–5; Zinoviev letter, 189–93; Labour party policies in 1925, 285–7; general strike, 303–4, 306, 319–20, 321, 328, 332; Prime Minister (1929–31), 353 ff. (foreign policy, 373, 375); in 1931 crisis, 382–99, 401, 408; National government (1931–37), 414, 416, 418–19, 440, 540; disarmament, 424; rearmament, 479; India Act, 426–8; retires as Prime Minister, 479, 534, 583; 1935 election, 555; death, 555
MacDonald, Malcolm, 401, 534, 555, 602, 610
Macdonell, A. G., 521
McDougall, William, 221
McGovern, J., 363
McGowan, Sir Harry (Lord McGowan), 275
McKenna, Reginald, 130, 131, 164, 200, 260, 372
McKenna duties, 131, 176, 266, 368
Mackenzie, Sir Compton, 223, 470
Maclean, Sir Donald, 8, 340, 386, 388, 416, 449

McManus, Arthur, 188
Macmillan, Harold, 260, 347, 463, 580, 621
Macmillan, Hugh P. (Lord Macmillan), 211, 260, 292, 528; Macmillan committee, see Committee on Finance and Industry
McNeill, Eoin, 107–8
MacNeill, James, 429
Macready, Sir Nevil, 39, 64, 67, 71, 72, 75, 76, 79, 86, 101, 103, 106, 119
MacSwiney, Terence, 76, 97
Maes-yr-Haf, 489
Maisky, Ivan, 609
Major, Rev. H. D. A., 222
Malinowski, Bronislaw, 221
Malnutrition, 504, 516
Manchester, 1, 22, 63, 139, 177, 223, 227, 239, 242, 249, 481, 514; housing, 508, 509, 511; University, 210, 220
Manchester Guardian, 172, 244, 411
Manchurian crisis (1931–2), 419–22
Mandates and mandated territories, 48–9
Marconi Company, 241–2
Marketing schemes, 365, 437–9
Markova, 525
Marlowe, Thomas, 193
Martin, Hugh, 69, 71, 72, 75
Masaryk, Jan, 616–17
Massingham, H. W., 246
Masterman, C. F. G., 135, 171, 262
Maternal mortality, 516
Maternity centres, 496
Mather and Platt, 454
Matthews, Jessie, 527
Maufe, Sir Edward, 224
Maugham, Lord, 619
Maurice debate, 3
Maxton, James, 147, 154–5, 184, 287, 358, 360, 362–3, 412, 547, 581
Maxwell, John, 247
May, Sir George (Lord May), 379, 417
May Report, 379, 381–2, 386
Maybury, Sir Henry, 227, 449
Means test, 470, 483–484
Medical Research Council, 15
Mellon, Andrew, 161
Mellor, William, 547, 581, 582
Merchant Taylors' School, 524
Mersey road tunnel, 232
Merthyr Tydfil, 225, 245, 464, 514
Methodist churches, 223
Metropolitan Railway, 237
Middlesbrough, 315, 318
Middlesex, 225
Midland Bank, 26
Midleton, Earl of, 86
Milk Marketing Board, 438–9
Milk, production and consumption, 253, 439
Milling (flour), 454
Millionaires, 206, 494, 500

Milner, Lord, 13, 244
Miners' Federation, 31, 35, 42, 120–3, 288, 290, 298–9, 301–3, 305–8, 310, 324–7, 330
Miners' Industrial Union, 334
Mines, see Coalmining industry
Mines Department, 35, 130
Mining Association, 297, 298, 300–2, 331–4
Ministers of the Crown Act (1937), 634
Ministers, re-election of, 15
Mitchell, R. J., 626
Mitford, Unity, 473
Molotov, Vyacheslav, 642–3
Mond, Sir Alfred (Lord Melchett), 154, 175, 200, 274–5
Money, Sir Leo Chiozza, 32
Montagu, E. S., 13, 111, 117, 137
Montague, C. E., 215
Monteagle, Lord, 82
Montreux; convention (1936), 157; conference (1937), 563
Morden, 227, 230, 237
Morel, E. D., 145, 171, 173, 174, 182, 193
Morley, Lord, 149
Morning Post, 108, 245, 320
Morris, W. R. (Lord Nuffield), 371, 490, 528
Morrison, Herbert, 354, 365, 392, 395, 450, 546, 551, 553, 554, 582, 632, 653, 655
Mosley, Sir Oswald, 216, 358–61, 363, 371, 412, 473–4, 585
Mosul, 157
Motion pictures, 246–7, 523
Motor cars and motor industry, 231, 266, 272, 275, 437, 454
Motor coaches, 234, 448
Mottram, R. H., 215
Mudania, 118–19
Muir, Ramsay, 262, 336
Mulcahy, Richard, 62, 97, 105
Mumford, Lewis, 231
Munich crisis: public opinion, 613, 615, 617, 619–21; value to Britain of time gained, 629–31
Munitions, Ministry of, 29
Murphy, J. T., 297, 580
Murray, Sir Evelyn, 243
Murray, Gilbert, 180, 579
Murray, Lord, of Elibank, 8
Music, 219
Mussolini, Benito, 119, 159–60, 198, 373, 424, 535, 538, 542–5, 559–61, 573, 597, 600, 616–17, 623, 641, 648–9

Nation, 246
National Council of Labour, 20, 548, 569, 604, 613, 632, 646
National Council of Social Service, 466, 488, 489, 497, 527, 528

National Defence Contribution (N.D.C.), 571–2
National government; formation of, 386, 391, 393, 394–7, 400; 1931 elections 406–12; history, 413 ff., 656; Liberals leave, 418; Baldwin becomes Prime Minister, 534; 1935 election, 553–6; possible reconstruction, 635, 641
National Health Insurance, 339, 495
National income, 205–6, 491
National Industrial Conference (1919), 21, 31, 36, 45, 125
National Joint Council, see National Council of Labour
National Labour party, 401, 409, 411, 534, 553–5
National Library of Scotland, 184
National Minority Movement, 284, 288
National Provincial Bank, 26, 247
National Sailors' and Firemans' Union, 312, 323
National Shipbuilders' Security, 445
National Unemployed Workers' Movement, 126, 472–3, 488
National Union of Railwaymen, 40, 42, 121–3, 311, 328–9, 330, 401
Nationalisation, 28, 243, 286, 342, 448–450, 548; talk of (1919), 16, 19, 30–35
Naval disarmament, 115, 175, 344–5, 374–5; rearmament, 627, 629
Nazi party, 373, 380, 424, 474, 477
Netherlands, 266, 515, 516, 640, 656
Nevinson, H. W., 70, 72, 191
New Fabian Research Bureau, 547
New Party, 361, 372, 412
New Statesman, 43, 48, 246, 544, 558, 567, 578, 607
New Writing, 530
New Zealand, 49, 109, 118, 197, 226, 438–9, 515, 586–7
Newbattle Abbey, 489
Newbold, J. T. Walton, 145
Newcastle-on-Tyne, 232, 238, 245, 314, 318
Newman, Sir George, 516
News Chronicle, 245, 262, 584, 636
Newspapers, 244–6, 249
Newton, Chambers, 454
'Next Five Years Group', 463, 580
Nichols, Beverley, 537
Niemeyer, Sir Otto, 200
Nigeria, 109
Noble, Emma, 489
Noel-Baker, P. J., 536, 574
Non-ferrous metals, 275
Non-intervention in Spain, 574–6, 597–600
Norfolk, 252
Norman, Montagu (Lord Norman), 161, 267, 383, 403, 456
Northcliffe, Viscount (Alfred Harmsworth), 2, 51, 81, 244

Northern Ireland, 244; Government of Ireland Act (1920), 72–4, 80; riots (1920–1), 74–5, 81; King opens parliament (1921), 84–5; attitude towards treaty negotiations (1921), 87, 91–2; in treaty, 94, 96; border war, 101–2; character of the regime, 102; boundary (1925), 107–8; unemployment, 126, 463; population, 518; attitude to 1938 agreement, 602–3; no conscription, 640

Northumberland, 274, 277, 463–7, 514

Northumberland, Duke of, 134

Norwegian campaign (1940), 652

Norwich, 524

Nottingham; University College, 211

Nuffield, Lord, see Morris, W. R.; Nuffield Foundation, 529; Nuffield College, 528

Nursery schools, 208, 496

Nyon agreement, 576

O'Brien, Art, 85

O'Connell, J. J., 103

O'Connor, Batt, 63

O'Connor, Rory, 99, 102–3, 105

Odeon cinemas, 523

Odhams Press, 245

Official Secrets Act, 635

O'Flanagan, Father, 77

O'Higgins, Kevin, 97, 98, 105, 108, 429

Old age pensions, 175, 339

Old Vic, 525

Oliver, F. S., 196

Olympia meeting (1934), 474

Onslow, Lord, 340

Optional Clause, 373–4

Organisation for the Maintenance of Supplies, 294–5, 312, 316

Ormsby-Gore, William (Lord Harlech), 144

Orr, Sir John Boyd (Lord Boyd-Orr), 504–6

Orwell, George, 486, 522, 531

Orwin, C. S., 254

Ostrer, Isidore, 247

Ottawa agreements (1932), 417–18, 436–7

Overcrowding, 507–10

Owen, Goronwy, 412

Oxford, 507, 514

Oxford Group, 527

Oxford University, 210–11, 213, 254, 489, 522, 524, 528–9; Oxford Union resolution, (Feb. 9, 1933), 422, 537

Oxfordshire, 255

Pacifism, 537–8

Page, F. Handley, 239

Palestine, 49, 54–5, 376, 624–5

Pall Mall Gazette, 245

Palmers' shipyard, see Jarrow

Paris peace conference (1919), 46–51, 58, 61

Parmoor, Lord, 172, 174, 180–1, 392, 401

Parsons steam turbines, 280

Peace Ballot, 541–2, 567

Peace Pledge Union, 525, 538

Peace Society, 422

Peacock, Sir E. R., 382

Peel, Lord, 624

Peerages; new creations, 204

Penguin Books, 526, 577, 619

Pensions, Ministry of, 15

People's Front Propaganda Committee, 580

Pétain, Marshal, 656–7

Petter, Sir Ernest, 370

Pettigo, 101

Phipps, Sir Eric, 594, 608

Physical Training Act (1937), 505–6

Physics, 219–20

Pick, Frank, 450, 525

Pierce, S. R., 524

Pilgrim Trust, 260, 528

Planning, 349, 462–3

Plastics, 272

Plender, Lord, 379

Plunkett, Sir Horace, 82

Poincaré, Raymond, 113–14, 117–19, 156–60, 178–9

Poland, 41–2, 50, 51, 56, 198–9, 424, 436, 621; diplomacy and war (1939), 638–41, 643, 646–8, 651

Pole, Sir Felix, 236

Police, 38–9, 126, 314–18, 327, 472, 474–5

Political and Economic Planning (P.E.P.) 462

Political levy, trade unions', 289, 336–7, 365

Pollitt, Harry, 288, 297, 581

Ponsonby, Arthur (Lord Ponsonby), 146, 181–2

Pontypool Educational Settlement, 489

Pools, football, 248–9, 500

Poor Law and poor relief, 46, 127, 128, 129, 335, 470–1; suspension of Guardians, 340; abolition of the Poor Law (1929), 341, 496

Poplar, 129, 175, 317, 327, 340

Popular Front (1938), 636

Population, 225–6, 256, 518; geographical shifts in, 464, 467, 469; estimates of future population, 518–21

Portal, Sir Wyndham (Viscount Portal of Laverstoke), 465

Post Office and broadcasting, 241–3

Postgate, Raymond, 526

'Potato Jones', 576

Poverty, 492, 496, 499, 502–4, 506

Prayer Book, revised, 225

Priestley, J. B., 480, 523, 527

Prime Minister, office of, 14, 634
Prince of Wales, *see* Edward VIII
Pritt, D. N., 582
Production, increase in, 265, 432–3
Productivity, 453
Protection (tariff), *see also* Import duties; 131–2, 133, 165–7, 177, 252, 266, 347, 360, 366–72, 399, 406–10, 415–17, 436–7, 441
Protocol for the Pacific Settlement of International Disputes, 181, 197, 345
Psychology, 214, 221
Public Assistance Committees, *see also* Poor Law; 470–2, 483
Public houses, 29, 229, 250
Public Order Act (1936), 475
Public schools, 204, 520
Public works, *see* Relief works
Pugh, Sir Arthur, 289, 303, 305, 307, 309, 325–6, 330, 547, 580
Purcell, A. A., 151, 182, 288, 303, 313

Quakers, 489–90
Queen Mary, 532–3
Queen Mary, 446, 457

Racecourse Betting Control Board, 249
Railways, 28, 42, 341, 350, 358, 457, 524; and nationalisation, 16, 19, 29–30; grouping (1921), 30, 238; strike (1919), 39–40; damage on Irish railways (1922), 106; road competition, 234–5; progress (1923–39), 236–8, 451; in general strike, 311–13, 327–9
Rakovsky, M., 181–2, 189, 191–3, 197
Rank (millers), 454, 494
Rank, J. Arthur, 523
Rapallo, treaty of, 114
Rathbone, Eleanor, 578, 579, 580
Rationing; ends, 28; begins, 651
Rayon, 202, 212, 266, 272, 275, 454
Reading, Marquess of, 322, 336, 389, 393
Reading University, 210
Rearmament, British; East Fulham election, 422; begins, 458, 476–8, 535, 540, 568–71; progress (1938–9), 625–32; Labour opposition, 476, 540, 569, 571, 632; in 1935 election, 553–6
Reconstruction, Ministry of, 15, 22, 28, 37, 43, 340
'Red Friday', 290–3
Redmayne, Sir Richard, 33, 34
Reed, Douglas, 619
Reid Committee, 276–7
Reith, Sir J. C. W. (Lord Reith), 242–3, 320, 448, 538
Relativity, 220
Remarque, Erich Maria, 537

Relief work (public works), 128, 175, 349, 358–9, 434, 457, 462, 466
Rents Restriction Acts, 164–5
Reparations, 49, 51, 112–13, 115, 157–9, 160, 178–9, 372–4, 422
Representation of the People Acts; (1918), 5; (1928), 343; Bill of 1930, 366
Reynaud, Paul, 656
Reynolds' News, 581, 636
Rhineland, 49–50, 52, 160, 198–9, 539; evacuation (1930), 372, 374; re-militarisation (1936), 564–7
Rhondda, 225, 483, 489, 514
Rhondda, Lady, 246, 579
Ribbentrop, Joachim, 541, 566, 592, 594, 596, 601, 621, 633, 637, 643–4, 647–8
Richard Thomas and Company, 442, 444–5, 466
Richardson, W. P., 324, 333
Riddell, Dr. W. A., 558
Rio Tinto Mining Company, 579
Roads, new, 232, 341–2, 349, 358, 457
Road Fund, 232, 339, 402, 571
Road Traffic Acts (1930, 1933), 235
Road transport, 40, 235, 295, 312, 314–15
Robertson-Scott, J. W., 255, 257
Robinson, Sir J. B., 134
Roman Catholic church, 223, 224
Roosevelt, President F. D., 436, 440, 590, 596–7, 641, 647
Rose, Sir Arthur, 465
Rothermere, Viscount (Harold Harmsworth), 2, 177, 244–6, 367–71, 474, 544, 559, 584, 591
Round Table, 43, 48, 72, 82, 109, 536
Rowlatt, Sir Sidney, 111, 249
Rowntree, B. Seebohm, 125, 254, 262, 333, 361, 502–4, 506
Royal Air Force, 238–40; rearmament, 476–8, 539–40, 626–8, 629–31
Royal Irish Constabulary, 64–5, 66, 68, 78
Royal Oak, 650
Royalties, coalmining, 32, 35, 448
Royden, Sir Thomas (Lord Royden), 31
Rugby, 208
Ruhr, 112–13, 157–9, 198
Rumania, 638, 640, 643–4
Rumbold, Sir Horace, 119, 157
Runciman, Walter (Viscount Runciman), 348, 411, 414, 415, 466, 583; mission to Czechoslovakia, 607–8, 610
Russell, Bertrand (Lord Russell), 222
Russia, 54, 117, 157, 199, 373, 436; Russian Revolution, 17; British intervention (1919–20), 41–2, 55–6; at Genoa Conference, 114; trade agreement with Britain, 114; ended, 337–8; Labour party's interest in (1920), 150–1; Anglo-Russian treaties (1924), 181–3, 185–6, 188, 197; Zinoviev letter, 188–94; T.U.C. and Russia,

Russia–*cont.*
   287–8, 313; help for British miners, 335; Arcos raid, 337–8; relations with Britain resumed, 374; popularity in 30's, 462, 526; treaty with France, 477, 539, 564, 566; rejoins League of Nations, 477; Spanish civil war, 573, 575; British attitude towards (1937–1939), 590, 604–6, 622, 638; in Munich crisis, 609, 611, 616, 617; Anglo-Russian negotiations (1939), 641–4; negotiations with Germany, 642–4, 651
Rutherford, Sir Ernest (Lord Rutherford), 219–20

Saar, 50, 52, 477
Safeguarding of industries, 132, 166, 266, 368, 371
St. Paul's Cathedral, 224
Saklatvala, S., 145, 190
Salisbury, 4th Marquess of, 570
Salter, Sir Arthur (Lord Salter), 463, 580
Salvidge, Stanley, 11, 135–6, 139, 140–1, 177
Samuel, Sir Herbert (Lord Samuel), 262, 554, 557, 635; Samuel Commission (coal), 291, 294, 297–8, 302, 307, 332, 334; intervenes in general strike, 324, 326, 331; Liberal party organisation, 348; 1931 crisis, 386, 388–9, 391–5, 398–9; 1931 election, 407–9, 414; opposes tariff, 415–16; leaves National government, 418–19
San Remo, 55
Sandys, Duncan, 621, 635
Sankey, Sir John (Lord Sankey), 31–4, 172, 354, 392–3, 401, 414, 419, 534
Sassoon, Siegfried, 537
Savings, 499–500
Sayers, Dorothy, 531
Scanlon, John, 285
Schools, 204, 206–10, 234, 257, 498
School Certificate, 210
School leaving age, 208–10, 365, 498
Schuschnigg, Kurt von, 600
Schuster, Sir Felix, 198
Scientific and Industrial Research, Department of, 15
Scotland; condition of, 468–70; universities, 207, 210; National Library, 184; churches, 223; roads, 232; sport, 248–249, 501; population, 225–6, 467, 518, 519; farming, 251, 256; local government, 341; industry, unemployment, 442, 444–6, 464–6, 467, 468–9, 481; housing, 458–9, 510; Highlands, 469; Gaelic speakers, 470; Nationalist movement, 470; health, 512; death rates, 514–16; birth rate, 517, 519
Scott, C. P., 244, 355
Scott, Elizabeth, 524

Scott, Sir Giles Gilbert, 224, 524
Scott, Peter, 490
Scrymgeour, E., 145
Scurr, John, 184, 210
Seligman, C. G., 221
Selwyn, E. G., 222
Seton-Watson, Professor R. W., 574, 620
Severn barrage, 176
Sèvres, Treaty of, 55, 117, 156
Sex, 213–14, 221, 522
Seyss-Inquart, Arthur, 600
Shanghai, 344, 420–1, 595
Shaw, George Bernard, 215, 462, 526
Shaw, Lord, of Dumfermline, 38
Shaw, Tom, 392
Sheffield, 127, 227, 278, 472, 509
Sheppard, Rev. H. R. L., 224, 538
Sherriff, R. C., 537
Shinwell, Emanuel, 24–5, 147, 148, 172, 401, 555
Shipbuilding, 26, 126, 165, 266, 273–4, 279–80, 445–6
Shipping industry, 26, 28–9, 264, 281, 446, 469
Shrewsbury, 229–30
Shropshire, 204
Siegfried, André, 380
Silesia, Upper, 51
Simon, Sir Ernest (Lord Simon of Wythenshawe), 508, 511
Simon, Sir John (Viscount Simon), 82, 262; criticises Irish policy, 82; Campbell case, 184; general strike, 322; leaves Liberal party and forms Liberal National party, 362, 365–6, 372, 407, 419, 553; Simon Commission (India), 360, 377–8, 428; Foreign Secretary, 414, 420–5, 478, 479, 534, 539; Chancellor of Exchequer, 572, 626; in inner cabinet, 583, 593–4; supports Munich policy, 610, 614, 619–20, 637–8; in wartime governments, 651, 655
Simons, Dr., 112
Simpson, Mrs. (Duchess of Windsor), 583–4, 587
Sinclair, Sir Archibald (Lord Thurso), 362, 416, 419, 554, 641, 646, 655
Singapore naval base, 175, 374
Sinn Fein party, 57–8, 60, 64, 76, 77, 100
Sitwell, Sir Osbert, 216, 217, 322
Slough, 29, 235, 522
Slums, 507, 508–10
Smillie, Robert, 31–2, 174
Smith, Sir Allen, 36
Smith, Sir Charles Kingsford, 239
Smith, Herbert, 31–2, 288, 299, 303, 324–5, 333
Smith, Ross and Keith, 239
Smuts, General J. C., 48, 84, 85–6, 87, 109, 619
Smyrna, 54–5, 117

Smyth, Colonel G. F., 67
Snowden, Ethel (Mrs., later Viscountess Snowden), 151, 243
Snowden, Philip (Viscount Snowden); 1918 election, 5, 17; 1922 parliament, 146; I.L.P., 150, 152, 287; capital levy, 154; Labour government (1924), 170, 171–6, 184, 189; Labour party policy (1925), 285; general strike, 322; Trade Disputes bill, 336; Labour government (1929), 353–5, 359–60, 367–8, 379; Hague conference, 374, 376; 1931 crisis, 381–96, 399; in National government, 401–3; 1931 election, 407–10, 414; opposes tariff, 415–16; leaves government, 418–19
Social services, see Welfare
Socialism, see Collectivism; Labour party
Socialism in Our Time, 286–7
Socialist Labour party, 151
Socialist League, 547–50, 581–2
Sociology, 221
South Africa, Union of, 49, 109, 226, 586–7, 650
South Wales, 121, 124, 225, 233, 274, 278, 301, 437, 443, 445, 463–8, 472, 481 ff., 514, 584
Southern Railway, 30, 236–7
Southwood, Lord (J. S. Elias), 245
Spanish civil war, 525, 529–31, 572–7, 597, 599–600, 623–4; popular interest in, 579–80; British press, attitude of, 577
Special Areas, see Distressed Areas
Spectator, 16, 43, 246, 346, 406, 420–2, 423, 539, 541, 544, 557, 558, 562, 565, 567
Spencer, G. A., 334
Spender, J. A., 245, 322
Spender, Stephen, 529–31
Sport, 248, 452
Sprigg, C. St. J., 529
Squire, J. C., 216
Stack, Austin, 87, 89, 95
Stack, Sir Lee, 110
Stalin, Josef, 642–3
Stamfordham, Lord, 81, 84, 162–3, 174, 317, 395
Stamp, Sir Josiah (Lord Stamp), 178, 236, 260, 359, 493, 528
Stamp, L. Dudley, 254
Standard of living, 205, 452, 458, 492–3, 502 ff.
Stanley, Oliver, 347
Stapledon, Sir R. G., 253–4
State scholarships, 207
Steed, Wickham, 81, 84, 141, 193, 244
Steel industry, 26, 28, 125, 126, 266, 270, 271, 273–4, 278, 441–5
Steel-Maitland, Sir Arthur, 305, 306, 308–9, 324–6, 333
Stephen, Campbell, 147, 155, 363
Stewart, Sir Malcolm, 463, 466

Stewart and Lloyds, 444
Stimson, H. L., 420–1
Stockton-on-Tees, 126, 274, 481, 505
Stopes, Dr. Marie, 214
Stowe School, 204
Strachey, J. St. Loe, 246, 361
Strachey, John, 361, 363, 525, 526, 580, 581
Strachey, Lytton, 215, 217
Strang, Sir William, 609, 642
Strauss, G. R., 582, 636
Street, A. G., 257
Stresa Conference (1935), 538, 543
Stresemann, Gustav, 159, 179–80, 198, 373
Strikes; days lost in strikes (1918–24), 124; (1925–38), 331; Glasgow (1919), 24; Coal (1919–20), 31, 34, 120–3; (1926), 299–302, 324–7, 331–5; police, 39; railway (1919), 39–40; cotton; ironmoulders (1919), 40; threat of, over intervention in Russia (1920), 41; engineers (1923), 124; farm workers (1923), 252; general strike, 291–330, Harworth colliery (1936), 473; London busmen (1937), 588
Suburbs, 228, 522, 525
Sudan, 110, 376, 563
Sudeten Germans, 605–8, 610–18, 621
Sunderland, 507, 514, 516
Supertax payers, 205, 493–4
Supply, Ministry of, 569, 629
Surrey, 225, 443, 515
Swales, A. B., 288–9, 305, 307
Swansea, 315, 318; University College, 210
Swanwick, Mrs. H. M., 180
Sweden, 263, 436, 515, 516
Swinton, Viscount (Philip Lloyd-Greame, later Cunliffe-Lister), 134, 143, 309, 393, 414, 534, 626–7
Syria, 49, 54–5, 117

Tariff, see also Protection, Import Duties, 415–17, 436–7, 441–2
Tawney, R. H., 21, 32, 209, 350, 359, 520, 526, 579
Taylor, Vice-Admiral E. A., 370
Telephones, number of, 349
Television, 244
Temple, Rt. Rev. William, Archbishop, 223, 224, 333, 483
Tewkesbury, 258
Textile industry, 28, 165, 271, 273, 281–283, 491
Thomas, Sir Ben Bowen, 489
Thomas, G. Holt, 239
Thomas, J. H.; railway strike (1919), 40; threatened strike against Russian policy (1920), 41; coal strike (1920), 42–3; (1921), 123; 1922 parliament, 146; Labour government (1924), 169,

Thomas, J. H.–*cont.*
170–3, 186; general strike, 288–9, 296, 303, 305–7, 310, 319, 322, 324–5; attacks unemployment in second Labour government, 353–4, 358–60, 593; on imperial preference (1930), 369; 1931 crisis, 381, 392–3, 396, 401; in National government, 414, 419; at Ottawa conference, 417; Irish policy (1932–6), 430–1; resignation, 555
Thomson, C. B. (Lord Thomson), 83, 361
Thomson, Sir J. J., 220
Thorne, Will, 19
Tillett, Ben, 288
Tilling, Thomas, Ltd., 234
Time and Tide, 246
Times, The, 2, 4, 51, 65, 77, 81–2, 84, 136, 187–9, 218, 244, 319, 387, 390, 465, 559, 577, 584, 641; and 'appeasement', 536–7, 539, 565, 591, 607, 613, 637
Tobacco, consumption of, 501
Tomsky, M., 288
Tory M.P., 633
Tote, 249
Tow Law, 482, 489
Trade; decline of (1921), 125; in the 20's, 262–6; in the 30's, 434–6, 440; terms of trade, 263, 435–6; trade agreements, 436
Trade Boards, 124, 501
Trade Disputes and Trade Union Act (1927), 323, 335–7, 365
Trade unions, *see also* Trades Union Congress; membership, 19, 337
Trades Union Congress, 41, 126, 151, 192, 287–9, 372, 548; Congresses: Glasgow (1919), 35; Hull (1924), 288; Scarborough (1925), 288; Bournemouth (1926), 330; Margate (1935), 551; (1937), 632; Blackpool (1938), 613 (Munich crisis); interest in Russia, 287–8; General Council, 19–20, 288–9, 291–2; and general strike, 296, 300–10, 313–14, 317, 319–20, 324–8, 329–31, 334; in 1931 crisis, 388, 390, 397, 410
Trading estates, 466–7
Traffic problems, 231–2
Tralee, 69
Trams, 232–3
Transport, *see* Roads; Railways; Air Services; Motor cars; Bus services
Transport and General Workers' Union, 19, 20, 42
Transport House, 20
Transport, Ministry of, 15, 29–30, 130, 232
Transport Workers' Federation, 121
Trevelyan, Sir Charles, 146, 175, 208, 365, 547, 548, 574, 636
Trevelyan, G. M., 146, 528
Tribune, 582

Trinity College, Dublin, 80, 97, 100
Triple Alliance (miners, railwaymen, dockers), 17, 42, 121–3
Trolley-buses, 233
Trusts, 27
Tuberculosis, death rate, 514
Tudor, Major General Henry, 65
Turkey, 49, 54–5, 116–19, 137, 156–7, 638, 640
Turner, Sir Ben, 151, 330
Tut-ankh-Amen, 222
Tyneside, *see* Durham, Northumberland
Typography, 218

Ullswater, Lord, 366
Ulster, *see also* Northern Ireland, 57, 58, 65
Ulster Unionist Council, 74, 80
Underground Railways, London, 219, 230, 233, 237, 450–1, 524
Unemployed, the, 482 ff.; demonstrations, 126–7; hunger marches, 127, 472–3; the long unemployed, 483; means test, 483–4, 495 (*see also* Unemployment Insurance); youths unemployed, 484, 485, 487; clubs, settlements, 488–9; poverty, ill health, 503–4, 514, 517
Unemployment Assistance Board, 471–2, 483
Unemployment; figures, 126, 165, 273–275, 357, 379, 432–3, 464–5, 469; measures to relieve unemployment, 358–9, 361, 483; (*see also* Relief works)
Unemployment Insurance and assistance; *see also* Relief works; Acts: (1920), 45–6; (1921–2), 127–8; (1924), 175; (1927), 339–40; (1930), 362; (1931), 363; (1934), 471, 495; borrowing for, 362, 379, 402; economies in (1931), 382, 387–92, 402, 410, 456, 470; Royal Commission on Unemployment Insurance (Holman Gregory), 362, 379, 383, 471
Union for Democratic Control, 48, 145, 180
Unionists (Ireland), 58, 65, 73–4, 76, 86, 100
United Empire Party, 367
United Front, 548
United States, 160, 179, 200, 241–2, 246–8, 262, 268, 272, 357, 436, 453; Paris peace conference, 48–51; non-ratification of Treaty of Versailles, 52; projected treaty with France and Britain (1919), 51, 53; interest in Ireland, 60, 72, 73, 81, 99; Washington conference (1922), 115–16; war debts, 159, 161–2, 380, 423; disarmament (1927), 344–5; (1930), 373–5; (1932), 423; and 1931 financial crisis, 382–4, 391–2; Manchurian crisis, 420–2; World Economic Con_

ference (1933), 436, 440; neutrality (1935), 589–90; Roosevelt's peace initiatives, 596–7, 641, 647
'United States of Europe', 372
United Steel Companies, Ltd., 270, 442, 444
Unity Campaign (1937), 581–2
Universities, 207, 210–11
University Grants Committee, 211
University representation, 366
Upminster, 230, 237

Valois, Ninette de, 525
Vansittart, Sir Robert (Lord Vansittart), 537, 596
Vaughan Williams, Ralph, 219, 579
Venizelos, Eleutherios, 55, 116
Versailles, Treaty of, 52, 423, 478, 536, 539, 541, 564–6, 622
Village life, 224, 234, 255–7, 527

Wages, 27, 125, 200, 205, 261, 268, 452, 491–3
Wales, see also South Wales. Welsh statistics are usually combined with those of England, 207, 244, 248, 516; University, 210; Church of, 223; population, 225–6, 519; agriculture, 253–4; Welsh language, 468
Walker, Sir Herbert, 236
Wallace, Edgar, 216
Wallace, Euan, 465
Wallhead, R. C., 151, 174, 182, 363
Walter, John, 244
Walters, Sir John Tudor, 228
Walwal, 543
War debts, 159, 161–2, 423
War, Second World; begins, 648–9, 651; Norwegian campaign, 652; invasion of Low Countries, 654, 656; fall of France, 656–7; evacuation of B.E.F., 657
Washington conference (1922), 115–16
Water, piped, in villages, 255
Waterhouse, Sir Ronald, 11, 162
Waterloo Bridge, 227–8
Watling, 230–1
Watson-Watt, Sir Robert, 630
Watson, Professor J. A. S., 255
Waugh, Evelyn, 203, 214
Webb, Beatrice (Mrs. Sidney Webb), 172, 174, 246, 462, 526
Webb, Sidney (Lord Passfield); Labour and the New Social Order, 18; Sankey Commission, 32; 1922 parliament, 146, 155; 'inevitability of gradualness', 153; Labour government (1924), 170; (1929), 354, 360; 1931 crisis, 392–3, 395, 397; interest in Russia, 462, 526
Wedgwood, Sir Ralph, 236

Wedgwood (China), 454
Wedgwood Benn, W. (Lord Stansgate), 354, 392
Weir, L. Macneill, 147, 393, 395
Weir, Lord, 342
Welfare, provisions for, 43, 45, 338–9, 471, 492, 495 ff.; cost, 496–7
Wells, H. G., 215, 222, 579
Welwyn Garden City, 228, 511
Wembley, 177, 227, 248, 249
West Ham, 340, 514
Westminster Bank, 26
Westminster Gazette, 245
Westminster, Statute of, 346, 426, 428
Wheat production, 250–1, 253, 370, 439
Wheatley, John, 147, 155, 156, 172–3, 175–6, 354, 358, 363
Whitehead, A. N., 220
Whitley, J. H., 37, 243
Whitley Councils, 36, 37
Whitten-Brown, Sir Arthur, 239
Widows' pensions, 339
Wigan, 481, 490, 514
Wigram, Sir Clive (Lord Wigram), 386, 395
Wilkinson, Ellen, 315, 321, 443, 579, 582
Williams, Sir Evan, 333
Williams, Sir Owen, 524
Wilson, Sir Arnold, 495, 500, 527, 579
Wilson, Havelock, 312
Wilson, General Sir Henry, 65–6, 74, 76–7, 83, 85, 102
Wilson, Sir Horace, 305, 325, 418, 593, 609, 614–15, 617, 619, 646
Wilson, Sir Leslie, 138
Wilson, President Woodrow, 1, 48–52, 61
Wimborne, Lord and Lady, 322, 325
Winn, Godfrey, 619
Winterton, Lord, 570
Wise, E. F., 286, 363, 547
Wodehouse, P. G., 216
Women; enfranchisement, 6, 343; Sex Disqualification Removal Act (1918), 6; in industry, 23; in universities, 210–11; dress, 202, 212; manners, 212–14
Women's Institutes, 256
Wood, E. F. L., see Halifax, Earl of
Wood, Sir Henry, 219
Wood, Sir Kingsley, 184–5, 314, 318, 593, 627, 651, 654
Woodhead, Sir John, 624
Woolf, C. M., 247
Woolf, Virginia, 217, 579
Woollen industry, 273–4, 283
Wootton, Barbara, 463
Workers' Educational Association, 208, 224
World Economic Conference (1923), 440
Worthington-Evans, Sir Laming, 90, 136, 144

Wythenshawe, 511

Yeats, W. B., 215
Yeats-Brown, Francis, 579
York, 502–4, 506–7
Yorkshire, 34, 121, 124, 226, 274, 277, 291, 519

Young Plan, 372, 374, 380
Younger, Sir George (Lord Younger), 3, 136, 138, 142
Youth hostels, 257, 527–8

Zinoviev letter, 188–94